WITH BIRTH CH

(in alphabetical order by f

MW01026679

Demetra George, Asteroid Centerea. D.A. rnilosophy; M.A. Classics, received the 2002 Regulus Award for Theory and Understanding. A practitioner of astrology for over 30 years specializing in archetypal mythology, she is the author of: *Astrology For Yourself* (with Douglas Bloch); *Asteroid Goddesses; Mysteries of the Dark Moon,* and *Finding Our Way Through the Dark.* Currently, she translates Greek Hermetic astrological texts, teaches Hellenistic astrology, and is on the faculty of Kepler College and the University of Oregon, lecturing on the history of astrology in ancient and medieval civilizations. Contact info.: POB 5431, Eugene OR 97405, tel. (541) 345-5680, dgeorge@orednet.org.

Evelyn Roberts, Archetypal. D.F., Astrol. S. A student of astrology most of her life (who predicts this will never end), and a practicioner for over 11 years, Evelyn's formal training was in London at the Faculty of Astrological Studies and Liz Greene's Centre for Psychological Astrology. She holds the FAS Diploma and the CPA Certification. These diverse yet complementary approaches, coupled with her own spiritual beliefs, have helped shape her personal style of chart analysis. In her practice, her goal is to use astrology as a tool for deepening self-knowledge, and love and acceptance of the self, enabling the individual to have a more authentic relationship to the rest of life. Besides her consultancy practice she teaches classes at all levels. Contact info.: tel. (805) 688-6789, astroeve@earthlink.net, www.evelynroberts.com.

Gary Christen, Uranian and New Wave. B.A. in Astrology, Livingston College, Rutgers University, Level 4 NCGR, PMAFA. An astrologer for over 36 years, he started his career working for the New York Astrology Center in 1968. A protégé of Hans Niggemann, he is regarded as one of today's foremost experts in Uranian astrology. He teaches and lectures nationally and internationally. He has been continually employed in the astrological field doing projects ranging from designing astrological software, writing and producing periodicals, magazines and books to salaried work as a corporate astrologer for an international steel company. A co-founder of Astro-Graphics Services in 1979 (now Astrolabe), he is currently President and CEO of Astrolabe, Inc. Contact info: PO Box 1750, Brewster, MA 02631, (508) 896-5081, gc1@alabe.com.

Hadley Fitzgerald, Psychological. B. A. English, M.A. Psychology, M.F.T. An astrological consultant for more than 35 years and a psychotherapist for 23 of those, Hadley Fitzgerald uses the birthchart as a map to help clients discover: the soul's best intentions for this incarnation; the ways to resonate consciously with those intentions; and methods for dealing with the challenges to both earthly progress and spiritual evolution. The question: "What does your soul want of you?" is at the heart of her training and her work. She has degrees from UCLA and

Phillips Graduate Institute and is currently at work on a book entitled *Traveling Eternity Road.* Contact info: POB 55576, Sherman Oaks, CA 91413, tel. (818) 783-3891, FitzHere2@aol.com, www.EternityRoad.com.

John Marchesella, Modern Western. A professional astrologer in New York City, John is certified by the National Council for Geocosmic Research, Chairman of Faculty for the New York Chapter, and a frequent lecturer and contributor to astrological publications. John is also a certified psychotherapist and bereavement counselor. His approach to astrology, both natal and predictive, is with the adage, "To every season under heaven, there is a purpose." The horoscope describes the meaning of a moment, thereby illuminating its purpose. Contact info.: www.astrojohn.com; astrojohn@earthlink.net.

Ken Bowser, Western Sidereal. Ken Bowser has studied astrology since 1970, first as a tropicalist and fairly early on as a siderealist. He has a B.A. in history and has studied Akkadian at the University of California and the University of Minnesota. He became a personal service astrologer for *American Astrology* magazine in 1979 and began to write articles in that magazine and others in 1980. He was twice a long-term columnist for *American Astrology* and has made his living solely from writing and astrological interpretations since 1991. Contact info: k.b.bowser@worldnet.att.net, tel. (612) 331-1475.

Kim Rogers-Gallagher, Light-Hearted. After years of examining potential nesting locations, Kim Rogers-Gallagher has settled happily in Florida (where she's working on her Professional Tanning Certificate), with her much-loved furry family: a very large, very spoiled dog, and several cats, ferrets, and parakeets. Kim writes for magazines and online venues (please search "Google" for specifics) and serves on the board of ISAR. She lectures internationally and has authored several books, including *Astrology for the Light Side of the Brain.* She also claims full responsibility for "The Cosmic Café," a creative column available at StarIQ.com and astrocom.com. Contact info.: KRGPhoenix@hotmail.com, tel. (941) 794-5821.

Robert Hand, Medieval. B.A. History, Brandeis University. Patron, Faculty of Astrological Studies. An astrologer for over 43 years, his books include *Planets in Composite, Planets in Transit, Planets in Youth, Horoscope Symbols, Essays on Astrology,* and tracts on ancient and medieval astrology. In 1979 he co-founded Astro-Graphics Services, Inc. (now Astrolabe, Inc) and Astrolabe Software. He uses a synthesis of heliocentric, sidereal, Uranian/cosmobiological, in mundo and more usual techniques. He is completing an M.A. from Catholic University in medieval history. In addition he publishes books on traditional astrology under the name ARHAT. He lives with his wife Elyse in Reston, VA. Contact info: 11901 Escalante Court, Reston, VA 20191, www.robhand.com, tel. (703) 758-7150.

Robert H. Schmidt, Hellenistic. Robert is a co-founder and current director of Project Hindsight, for which he has translated many of the original astrological source texts from the Hellenistic period into English. Believing that "great ideas have great beginnings," he has nearly completed his reconstruction of "The System of Hermes" as a practical predictive system supported by a comprehensive theoretical framework. In addition to historical investigations, Robert conducts research into the problem of astrology from many other angles: scientific, epistemological, and philosophical. Contact info: 532 Washington St., Cumberland MD 21502, tel. (301) 724-4463, fax: (301) 724-3003, rhschmidt@charter.net, www.projecthindsight.com.

Ronnie Gale Dreyer, Vedic. B.A. English/Theatre; C.A. NCGR. An internationally known consultant, lecturer and teacher, Ronnie was a pioneer in bringing Vedic astrology to Western audiences. She authored *Healing Signs, Vedic Astrology, Your Sun and Moon Guide to Love and Life, Venus,* and numerous columns, articles and reviews in publications and websites. Ronnie conducts Vedic astrology courses and lectures for groups and conferences worldwide, and is on the faculty of the American College of Vedic Astrology (ACVA) and Sri Jagannath Center (SJC). She studied Jyotish (Vedic astrology) in Benares, India, was AFAN's Corresponding Secretary (1992-1998) and Presiding Officer (1999-2003), and edits NCGR's Memberletter. In 2002, she received the Marion D. March Regulus Award for Community Service. Contact info.: POB 8034, FDR Station, New York NY 10150, tel. (212) 799-9187, RGDreyer@aol.com, www.ronniedreyer.com.

Steven Forrest, Evolutionary. A full-time counseling astrologer since 1976, Steven's first book, *The Inner Sky,* was published to critical acclaim in 1984. His books include: *The Changing Sky; Skymates* (with his wife, Jodie Forrest)*; The Night Speaks; The Book of Pluto*; a novel, *Stalking Anubis;* and *Measuring the Night Vols. I* and *II* (with Jeffrey Wolf Green). Many of Steven's books are translated into several foreign languages. He wrote the text for Matrix Software's "Sky Within" and "SkyLog" astrology reports. He and Jodie co-wrote the text for AIR Software's "The Sky We Share" and "The Single Sky," soon to be released in a slightly different format by Matrix. An active lecturer on the astrological circuit, Steven has taught in-depth evolutionary astrology to over 150 students through his Apprenticeship Program. He is Chair of the Kepler College Advisory Council and serves on the ISAR Ethics Committee. Contact info.: POB 2345, Chapel Hill NC 27515, tel. (919) 929-4287, fax (919) 929-7092, www.stevenforrest.com.

Wendy Z. Ashley, Mythological. B.A.s: Anthropology, Observational Astronomy, Cross Cultural Studies of Women. Private study in mythology, dream interpretation and symbol with Dr. Charles Ponce and Dr. Joseph Campbell. An internationally known teacher and consultant to private clients, she's published *Sticks and Stones: Paleolithic Astrology and Naked-Eye Astronomy*, numerous articles, and contributed to *Communicating the Horoscope*, ed. Noel Tyl. She's completing *Goddess in the Sky: Stars and Mythology in the Lives of Women*. She lives on the coast of Maine, where she can see the stars clearly. Contact info.: 53 Luther St., Peaks Island, ME 04108, starmyth@maine.rr.com.

Rafael Nasser. B.S. in Economics, Wharton School of Business, University of Pennsylvania. By the time I was five I lived in three different European countries and at age eleven, when my family relocated to the United States, I could speak five languages. My youthful peregrinations prevailed upon me to adopt a chameleon like personality that reflected the cultural context in which I found myself. My sense of identity vacillated like a weathervane. About fifteen years ago I discovered astrology and came to realize—to my utter amazement—that below my shape-shifting self existed a deeper, integrated structure that could be coherently discerned by people who interpreted weird looking scratchmarks placed around a twelve-spoked wheel. I was wonderstruck. This book was inspired by my earnest desire to demythologize and demystify astrology in order to deepen our understanding of this ancient science, discover the nature of our profound relationship to the the kosmos, and perhaps shine a ray of light on the mystery of our being.

UNDER ONE SKY

Rafael Nasser

Featuring birthchart analyses of Joyce by:

Demetra George
Evelyn Roberts
Gary Christen
Hadley Fitzgerald
John Marchesella
Ken Bowser
Kim Rogers-Gallagher
Robert Hand
Robert Schmidt
Ronnie Galc Dreyer
Steven Forrest
Wendy Z. Ashley

Edited by Jodie Forrest

Published by Seven Paws Press

POB 2345, Chapel Hill NC 27515 USA
Tel. 919.929.4287; fax 919.929.7092
info@sevenpawspress.com
www.sevenpawspress.com

Printed in the United States of America

First Edition
First Printing, March 2004

ISBN 0-9649113-7-X
Library of Congress Catalog Card Number 2003116900

For information and orders of additional copies, please contact Seven Paws Press at the above address.

Cover art by Tobin Dorn

ACKNOWLEDGMENTS

FROM RAFAEL NASSER:

Kind words of encouragement and guiding words of wisdom are the invisible props that shore up this book. I'd like to honor and thank everyone whose hand touched this project in some significant way, directly or indirectly.

Friends: Jon, Sharon and Inge Abrams, Don and Lloyd Abrams, Rachel Cahn, Joe Carasso, Sara Carlson, Eli Catalan, Ajahni Ishmael Cato, Rita Chabot, Rebecca Clark, Shrimatie Devi, Patrick Dillon, Tobin Dorn, Robert Gehorsam, Jeanette Girosky, Jonathan Hall, Jim Haughton, Karen Hawkwood, David Ingber, Kabiro, Karinna Kittles, Robert T. Lafargue, M.D., Lawrence Lyons, Julka Marchevkova, Inge Maassen, Ken Neill, Vinessa Nevala, Nancy Packes, Wade Plunkett, Swami Prajñanananda Giri, Mitchell Jay Rabin, Audrey Ryan, Paul Sharkey, Uzi Silber, Peter Szonk, Mike Telkamp, John Williams, and Michael Winn.
Family: My parents Albert and Beatrice, Michael Stolowitzky, Nancy Nasser, James Nasser, Alicia, Maurice, Joëlle, Joseph and Arielle Dabbah, my namesake Rafael M. Nasser and Alexandra Autogue, Ralph and Yasmeen Bernstein, Ezra and Selma Nasser, Michal Honig-Szwarc, Perah Dwek, Sylvie Dabbah, Marsha Lee and the Toussies, in particular Ralph and Isaac.
And finally: The enchanting starry sky that pours shimmering light on us all to whom this is dedicated.

FROM JODIE FORREST:

I'd like to thank:
* my clients and students, from whom I have learned and continue to learn so much.
* the twelve astrologers who participated in this project; Joyce, who allowed her chart to be analyzed; and Rafael Nasser—the book that you hold in your hands is his brainstorm.
* Paul Cory, who saved my cyber-neck countless times.
* Laura Haywood-Cory, editorial assistant extraordinaire, who asserts her views in a confident manner.
* my husband, Steven Forrest. Always.

UNDER ONE SKY

TABLE OF CONTENTS

EDITOR'S NOTE

It is a privilege for Seven Paws Press to publish this important book with its twelve "blind" analyses of the birthchart of the woman called "Joyce" in the text. I would like to describe the attitude with which I approached the task of editing. My goal was to preserve not only the intent of each astrologer's analysis, but also his or her original voice. Given the unusual nature of this work, the risk of distorting each writer's individual intent by an unconscious editorial slant far outweighed more literary considerations. To that end, I focused on spelling, grammar, punctuation, and a glossary of terms that might be unfamiliar to astrological beginners.

I also edited the Preface, Prologue and Epilogue by Rafael Nasser, whose brainchild this book is, with the same intentions and the same very light hand.

With those exceptions, what you will read in these pages is what first Rafael Nasser and then Seven Paws Press received from each astrologer and from Joyce herself.

I would also like to take this opportunity to assure readers that most of the astrologers did not read Joyce's autobiography, published in this book, until after the book had been printed. Two of the astrologers were curious enough about Joyce to ask to see her autobiography as soon as possible, so I sent them a copy of it *after* the galleys had been finalized and sent back to the printer.

JODIE FORREST
Editor-in-Chief, Seven Paws Press
Chapel Hill, NC

PREFACE

I heard the voice murmur the words for the first time when transiting Uranus was merely a few minutes of arc away from conjoining my Midheaven. The message sounded so harebrained I ignored it, merely dismissing the directive as the raving of my hyperactive imagination. That was a mistake. The gods disdain the cold shoulder. What began as a subdued undertone gradually intensified into a haunting refrain that reverberated over my entire being. I foolishly continued to turn a deaf "inner ear," and the voice countered my brazenness by intensifying its volume with increased frequency until every streaming bit of consciousness, no matter where it originated and regardless of its destination, morphed into the now familiar chorus. When I finally yielded and cried out *"Yes, I'll do it!"* the message stopped instantly. I never heard the words again, but by then there was no turning back because I had become the voice of Uranus.

Let me recount the story of my mercurial relationship with astrology to provide you with a context for what I'm about to say. I discovered astrology in my early twenties, and from the outset my relationship with the sacred art was a precarious one. No self-respecting young man shedding adolescence wants to hear the words "You were born under the sign of the Virgin" from an attractive woman. But the fates decreed me a Virgo, and her brief but biting description of the sign was a clear mirror held up to my face. *How can this be? She must be making this up around what she already knows about me!* I was convinced she was describing me—not my sign—and resolved to confirm my suspicion by reading a description of Virgo in a randomly chosen astrology book.

I went to the bookstore and waited for the New Age section to clear before grabbing a book I had been eyeing. I scurried off to another aisle. Behind the safe cover of the philosophy volumes I opened it up. I read about Virgo's natural skepticism and inclination to refute irrational and superstitious beliefs through the application of systematic reasoning and logic. My face broke into a grin as I registered the irony of the situation. In my determination to apply my powers of critical reasoning to disprove what I believed was the irrational belief in astrology, I was inadvertently confirming its accuracy. I graciously admitted my loss, but not defeat. *Check.* Admittedly, I had taken a step closer but I was not yet ready to embrace it.

1

I decided that the only way to unriddle the issue was to get an astrological reading. I would approach the experience with an open mind, albeit guarded by my fierce powers of critical judgment which the experience at the bookstore had sharpened. I opted for a blind reading, believing that my presence would unduly bias any interpretation. Only an anonymous reading would positively convince me. I found an astrologer who did blind readings who lived far away and sent that stranger my birth data along with a check, nothing else. A few weeks later I received a ninety minute taped natal interpretation that thawed my doubts like frost at daybreak on a summer day. *Check mate.* I was dumbfounded and confused about *why* astrology worked, but one thing was clear. *I had to learn how to do this!* And so I did.

I live in New York City where you can find anything and everything. As years passed I read many books, attended countless conferences and studied diverse astrological traditions. But almost from the very beginning I felt that something was amiss. For example, I would attend two lectures at the same conference and hear astrology described in mutually exclusive ways. My frustration grew as I realized that there is no such thing as astrology *per se.* There is no monolithic, authoritative doctrine subsumed under one rigorous framework. Different astrological traditions have different symbol sets that astrologers filter through their subjective values and world views. Astrological systems, it seemed to me, were less like branches on a sturdy oak tree than wild flowers in a field, each flaunting its distinctive colors and emanating its own particular scent. My Virgoan sense of critical judgment reasserted itself, and the frost of doubt began to encrust astrology once more. This time, however, it wasn't the validity of astrology that was in question but its *essential nature* and its *natural limits.*

I was encountering too many overly self-assured experts making extravagant claims about the power of astrology. I felt that some of those hyperbolic claims distorted astrology by extending the symbols beyond their natural bounds. Increasingly, I heard astrologers vaunt their particular system as *The System.* At the other end of the spectrum, I was encountering reflexively open-minded astrologers who indiscriminately accepted far-flung astrological claims notwithstanding their irreconcilable underpinnings. At some point, I don't recall exactly when, I awoke to the realization that astrologers (myself included) are generally confused about what *astrology really is,* and can't explain rationally how or why it works. Irrespective of the system they practice, astrologers tend to sweep thorny questions about the nature of astrology under a thick carpet of esoteric jargon, shrugs and blank stares. Astrologers of different stripes feel the same visceral discomfort in discussing the foundation on which their art stands. Opposite ends of an axis are united by virtue of the shadow they share, and I realized that the iron-mindedness of the absolutists and the indiscriminate all-embracing political correctness of the relativists cast the same umbrage. Both are in the dark about the essential nature of astrology: *everyone knew how to do it; no one knew what it was.* I had stumbled upon the collective shadow of astrology. It was soon thereafter that I began to hear the voice.

The imposing words of Uranus were clear and distinct: *"Gather astrologers from different traditions, and they will interpret the same anonymous birthchart. Collect the readings into a book and don't worry—I assure you that it will work out."* When I finally accepted my mission I knew intuitively that things would work out, although practically I had no clue where to start. I had never worked on a book before, and I couldn't envision any astrological superstars staking their reputation by doing a blind reading for an unknown astrological enthusiast like myself. But Uranus was right, and gradually the book you hold in your hands materialized. I named it *Under One Sky* in deference to the god of the starry night sky, Uranus, who astrologically symbolizes the urge to shine liberating light on airless darkness, and who seems content with the way things have turned out.

RAFAEL NASSER
New York City
January, 2004

PROLOGUE

What happens when astrologers interpret the same birth chart using dissimilar symbol sets? Or the same symbols are interpreted by astrologers anchored to different world views? What are the natural limits of astrology? How far can the symbols stretch before they snap? The answer to these and many other questions lie buried within the pages of this book.

The image of the white bearded Magus bedecked in majestic purple robes embroidered with golden stars, sitting beside an astrolabe, poring over dusty tomes as he painstakingly calculates the position of the planets has been replaced by the picture of the modern astrologer a mouse click away from powerful charting tools that would have bedazzled the old wizard. Technology has changed the face of astrology. The technical aspect of astrology, which daunted even the sharpest minds in the ancient world, has now become a trivial part of the practice. The computer has significantly lowered the price of admission into the world of astrology, and in recent years countless souls have poured in through the gates. The inflow of interest, however, has done more than merely revivify the archaic science. It has transformed it.

In pre-modern times *Tradition* held pride of place in the pantheon of values, and under the aegis of this ideal the basic lore of astrology was sustained over long periods of time. To the extent that astrology underwent any alterations as succeeding civilizations co-opted the practice, no effort was spared to preserve the form of the ancient teachings. Modernity, however, has turned the traditional ethos on its head. Today, common wisdom holds that knowledge is the fruit of a forward-looking process, and *novelty* and *change* are encouraged as High Virtues that lead up the path of Progress. The spirit of modernity has ingressed into astrology, and *Innovation* and *Diversity*—two of the gods worshipped in the modern age—are now guiding the ancient art form into the future. It's not just the number of astrologers that is mushrooming. New-sprung symbols are continually streaming into the modern astrologer's toolbox, and interpretative techniques cross-pollinate seamlessly between systems. Astrology is no longer the fixed tradition it once was; it has become a mutable art form.

Astrology is experiencing a springtime buzz but paradoxically, although it has never been simpler to generate complicated birth charts, it has never been harder to interpret them due to the overwhelming number of symbols and

complexity both describe the condition of contemporary astrology. This conundrum is challenging modern astrologers to develop a deeper, more profound understanding of their science—one that can match the higher degree of complexity it now embodies. The taller the tree grows, the deeper its roots must sink . . . or else.

The pervading influence of astrology in the modern world is undeniable—the average person is more likely to know his Sun sign than his blood type—but equally undeniable is the fog of confusion that surrounds it. The stage is set for an evolutionary leap in our understanding of astrology, or a dissociative breakdown. That, I believe, is the choice astrology faces as it stands at the crossroads that leads either to the Palace of Wisdom or the Tower of Babel. *Under One Sky* is a determined step on the road of astrology's quest for higher-order integration. The basic premise of the book is that a *blind reading*—an astrological interpretation which denies the astrologer any contact with the subject—is the most accurate standard by which the efficacy of astrology can be measured. A blind reading is, in my opinion, the most reliable way to survey the bounds of astrology. Squeezing a narrative out of a handful of abstract symbols pits astrological theory against the hard actuality of human life. The sobering process of navigating a birth chart solely by the light of the symbols is both a humbling and rewarding experience that leads to enhanced clarity and wisdom. The blind reading of a birth chart is the ultimate astrological challenge. But I reasoned that two blind readings, done for the same birth chart by different astrologers using distinct symbol sets, would create an analytical angle that sheds even more light on the nature of astrology. The dual interpretations could be compared and contrasted not only to the life story of the subject but also to each other. The next logical stepping stone I skipped over was that three is better than two and so on. I finally settled on the number twelve. I felt that twelve blind readings of the same birth chart performed by astrologers from different traditions would create an astrological mosaic from which would emerge, when viewed in its entirety, radical insights about the nature of astrology. So I invited twelve astrological masters to pick up the gauntlet and interpret the birth chart of a woman named *Joyce*. To my great surprise, almost everyone I contacted enthusiastically accepted the challenge.

All the participants painted an astrological portrait of Joyce derived exclusively from her birth data, using only their symbol-palette. Their collection of readings can be envisioned as a gallery of Joyce portraits painted by twelve masters specializing in different styles and techniques. In this gallery also hangs

Joyce's self-portrait, her autobiography, against which the twelve interpretations can be contrasted. The astrologers and their respective systems include (in alphabetical order by their first names): *Demetra George*, Asteroid Centered; *Evelyn Roberts*, Archetypal; *Gary Christen*, Uranian; *Hadley Fitzgerald*, Psychological; *John Marchesella*, Modern Western; *Ken Bowser*, Western Sidereal; *Kim Rogers-Gallagher*, Light Hearted; *Rob Hand*, Medieval; *Robert Schmidt*, Hellenistic; *Ronnie Gale Dreyer*, Vedic; *Steven Forrest*, Evolutionary; *Wendy Z. Ashley*, Mythological.

You may be wondering, *Why these twelve?* When I first decided to embark on this project, I was confronted with a big problem. There are many gifted astrologers, and I knew it would be impossible to include even a fraction of them in the book. How should I narrow the list of participants from the vast sea of enticing possibilities? Moreover, I was concerned about biasing the selection process. After much reflection I yielded to my Virgoan nature and devised a system. I asked a few astrologer friends to draw up a list of people they would want to see featured in the book. I cross-referenced the lists, tallied up the results and contacted those astrologers whose names appeared most frequently. I continued with this method by asking the same question of astrologers who climbed on board. The lists grew fast and the empty slots filled in quickly. Many noteworthy names came up that I regret not having been able to include in the book. The main point I wish to stress, however, is that the list of astrologers essentially created itself.

How about Joyce? How did she materialize into the project? I wanted a subject who was nearing or past the second Saturn return (about 58 years old). Either gender would do. I cast about ineffectively for the better part of six months until I eventually stumbled upon an extraordinary person who courageously—after several months of careful deliberation—agreed to play the role of Mystery Guest and write her autobiography for the book.

The accuracy of Joyce's official birth data (January 16, 1943, 4:18 PM, Pryor, Oklahoma) was a crucial issue. I was acutely aware that an incorrect birth time would invalidate any interpretations derived from it. My concern was allayed by two sobering facts. First, Joyce's original birth certificate, which she still has in her possession, was recorded by her doctor's own hand. Second, I asked the astrologer Doris Hebel to rectify Joyce's birth chart, and she concluded that the Midheaven calculated for Joyce using her official birth time (7 degrees 57 minutes of Pisces) aligned very closely with her rectified Midheaven (7 degrees 30 minutes of Pisces). The 27 minutes of arc separating

7

the two Midheavens translates into a time span of approximately two minutes. Doris's rectification confirmed the accuracy of the official birth time to an uncommon degree of exactitude. Her conclusion green-lighted my decision to enlist Joyce. The astrologers, by the way, were permitted to choose between the official birth time of 4:18 PM and the rectified birth time, 4:16 PM.

A few words about the safeguards I took to ensure the integrity of the project. Signing Joyce on was an act of faith for me because I knew almost nothing about her personal history when I asked her to become involved. And that's the way I wanted to keep it. Until the very end I chose to remain in the dark about the details of her life, just like everyone else. I felt it was essential for me to keep Joyce's story hermetically sealed from everyone, including me. Consequently, I can in good conscience say that I was never in a position to convey—intentionally or unintentionally, consciously or unconsciously—any information that might have unduly influenced anyone's impression of Joyce.

Putting up a wall around Joyce was especially important since I was in constant communication with the twelve astrologers, in particular John Marchesella and Steven Forrest, two participants who also happen to be my primary astrology teachers and friends. All three of us understood that any discussion about Joyce was strictly off limits. As an added safeguard, I asked all the participants to sign a clause in their contract precluding them from discussing their work with anyone, other than myself.

There was another crucial issue I had to wrestle with to ensure the integrity of the material. This book was my first excursion into the publishing world, and before setting off on that leg of the journey I sought counsel from battle-hardened authors. These veterans told me the same basic story over and over. I was warned about the danger of the trigger-happy editor blasting away at the text. To make matters worse, I realized that an editor would be in a position to bias the editing process through his or her foreknowledge of Joyce's story. The *editor problem* felt like an unyielding boulder blocking the way forward. Self-publishing seemed like the only sensible option, until I learned about the hardships and steep incline of that path. *Another dilemma.* Under the weight of this predicament, the momentum that had vigorously propelled this project diminished and died out. I felt helpless. I needed a miracle: a publisher willing to sign the deal without first reading Joyce's biography, and willing to grant me veto power over editorial process. The situation looked bleak. *But there had to be a simple solution to this problem.* I appealed to Uranus for guidance.

One cold winter evening, I recall discussing my troubles with Steven and Jodie Forrest over the telephone. I explained to them my concerns and shared with them at length the depth of my frustration. I knew the Forrests owned a small astrological publishing house, Seven Paws Press. I was speaking with them mostly because I knew they could give me advice about the realities of self-publishing, which was increasingly appearing to be my least bad option. I hadn't considered the possibility of publishing with them because Steven was one of the astrologers featured in the book, and I assumed that created a knot that couldn't be unsnarled. When I finished talking a moment of pregnant silence ensued followed by Steven's voice, "If we published the book, we would insist on not seeing Joyce's bio until after Jodie edited the readings." I instantly realized that the miracle I was looking for was staring me in the face. I replied, "It may be a little unconventional, but if you agree to do that and to have Jodie do all the editing, I would love for Seven Paws Press to publish *Under One Sky*."

The unusual degree of control Seven Paws Press was prepared to give me over the editorial process is the primary reason I decided to entrust this project to them. Jodie Forrest is an experienced editor, a published author and an accomplished astrologer, and I knew she would work diligently to preserve the voice of the contributors by keeping a light touch. Only form—never content—was ever subject to editorial scrutiny. Meaning was not edited into the text. Jodie used the same conservative approach with Joyce's material.

The bottom line: I made every reasonable effort to keep Joyce's life story shielded from the twelve astrologers, the editor and myself in order to preserve the integrity of everyone's work. To my knowledge there were no leaks.

You are about to set off on an adventure that unfolds like a detective story. The first part of *Under One Sky* introduces the twelve astrologers, their background, personal values and beliefs. The second part is an intimate account of Joyce's life that she wrote herself. In the third part, each astrologer slides open the top lid of his or her toolbox to reveal the *strategy* he or she devised to organize the basic outlines of Joyce's reading out of a scattering of symbols. That section is followed by their interpretations of her birth chart. I will conclude the book with a brief account of how this project transformed my understanding of astrology.

One final note before you begin. The journey into the heart of Joyce's birthchart is also a pilgrimage into the mystery of human existence. To the extent that this book illuminates your understanding of astrology and elevates your level of self-knowledge, it will have served its highest purpose. In an essay entitled "Circles," Ralph Emerson writes: "Our life is an apprenticeship to the truth, that around every circle another can be drawn; that there is no end in nature, but every end is a beginning; that there is always another dawn risen on mid-noon, and under every deep a lower deep opens." It is my sincere hope that *Under One Sky* inspires you to draw another circle around astrology and around yourself.

PART ONE:
THE ASTROLOGERS' FORUM

1. GIVE A BRIEF BIOGRAPHY OF YOURSELF BEFORE YOU BECAME INVOLVED IN
ASTROLOGY, AND OF WHAT YOU HAVE DONE SINCE.

Demetra George: I became involved with astrology in the summer of 1971, a
few years out of college where I had studied mathematics and philosophy. In
1973 I was introduced to the asteroids and began using them immediately.
Thirteen years later, the results of my research were published in my first book,
Asteroid Goddesses (1986). *Astrology For Yourself* (1987, with Douglas Bloch),
Mysteries of the Dark Moon (1992), and *Finding Our Way Through the Dark*
(1994) followed. The work of this first period was characterized by a synthesis
of archetypal mythology with contemporary psychological astrology. I taught
locally, nationally, and internationally in both the astrological and women's
spirituality communities, and led pilgrimages to the archaeological sites of
ancient Greece.

The second period of my work began in 1997 with a return to graduate
school where I obtained an M.A. in Classics from the University of Oregon,
learning to read ancient Greek and Latin. My thesis consisted of an original
translation of a twelfth century Byzantine Emperor's Christian defense of
astrology. I currently teach the history of ancient and medieval astrology,
beginning Greek, and an introduction to Hellenistic astrology at Kepler College
and at the Astrological Institute of Arizona, both schools which have been either
authorized or accredited to offer higher academic degrees in astrology. The
future holds promise of the translation of Hermetic manuscripts and the
education of new students in the rich intellectual history of the astrological
tradition.

Evelyn Roberts: I was born in Scotland and grew up in Europe. I originally
studied art and art history, developing a lifelong passion for the Renaissance
period. This started me traveling; at age sixteen I hitchhiked to Italy to see the
Great Masters. Later I spent several years traveling, stopping in the Greek
islands for three months, Israel for six, Mexico for five. I finally ground to a halt
in southern California in 1975 via a complex and circuitous journey.

I developed roots with the birth of my children, and have maintained a home in the vicinity of Santa Barbara since 1976. I've been a single parent since my children were 3 and 5 years old; they are now 24 and 26. I spent years supporting my family as a waitress and managing a wine tasting room. In the mid-eighties I took a massage class for fun that developed into a lucrative and rewarding career, something I enjoy to this day; I still maintain a small clientèle. Astrology had been a big part of my life for as long as I can remember. I was largely self-taught, and have been gathering groups of like-minded people together and doing charts since the early '90s. My other obsession, besides exploring the world, is yoga.

When my youngest child was eighteen, *I* left home; luckily I had raised independent souls. With Pluto crossing my Sagittarius Ascendant my whole life changed. I planned to travel the world with my partner. Before this happened I discovered I had malignant melanoma (happily completely cured), my relationship dissolved, I sold my massage business, rented my home out and sold most of my possessions, with the exception of my books.

I headed for South America and spent five amazing months traveling and trekking through Peru and Bolivia. Whilst in the jungles of Bolivia, I realized it was time to change direction. I headed back to the U.S., holed up in Santa Fe, and pondered my future. I literally woke up one morning knowing it was time to put my all into astrology, and for me that meant an apprenticeship.

Liz Greene's work had always inspired me, so I gravitated towards her school, The Centre for Psychological Astrology. I took a giant step and moved to London with ninety pounds of astrology books and a massage table. I have unfailing respect for the tradition and history of astrology, and simultaneously attended the Faculty for Astrological Studies where I built a foundation on these principles. The challenge for this right-brained being was tackling astronomy, math, history, techniques and all the facts and figures involved. Acquiring the Diploma from the FAS was a great achievement in my life; my Saturn in the tenth was very happy! Sue Tompkins, Ron Gwynn and Mike Harding were some of the wonderful teachers at the Faculty. The CPA provided the creative model to build on that foundation. I was blessed because Charles Harvey was still living and a tutor; he was inspirational, wise and unfailingly kind. It was also a gift to have Liz Greene, Darby Costello, Lynn Bell, Melanie Reinhart, Karen Hamaker-Zondag and Juliet Sharman-Burke as mentors for two years. It was a powerful experience from more than the astrological perspective, CPA students are required be in therapy during part of their attendance; it is an intense experience opening up psychologically whilst exploring astrology. These dynamic teachers are diverse in their systems and ideas; this teaches openness and stretches one's thinking. The combination of the FAS and the CPA was ideal, a solid core of tradition and science coupled with psychological depth and creative vision. And I've never worked so hard in my life.

I was then drawn back to California. It is hard for me to live permanently on a different continent than my children. It would also be a challenge to find a more serene, beautiful place to live where I can practice astrology full-time. I returned to a nearly idyllic life seeing clients, teaching classes, and hosting seminars for visiting astrologers.

Since writing the above, I've had another adventure. Under a Neptune transit, I literally sailed away. In April 2003, I crewed on a sailboat from Malta to the U.K. via Majorca, Gibraltar, Portugal and Guernsey. It was an incredible experience. What is most amazing is that the yacht is named *Aquarius*, the very sign of my Sun being transited by Neptune. My next plan is to head for Bali, probably in May 2004. I have visions of setting up home there for few months and practicing both astrology and yoga. Thanks to modern technology, my laptop always goes with me, and it's getting easier to stay in touch with the rest of the world no matter where you are. My plan is to have it all, to travel between extended periods in the U.S., and to practice astrology wherever I am.

Gary Christen: I was 17 when I became involved with professional astrologers. Prior to that time I was attending the School of Visual Arts in NYC, majoring in film. I wanted to become a director of film. Serious astrology short-circuited that ambition. I had always dabbled in Sun sign stuff, but it was a teacher at SVA that got me interested. One of my classes was a weekly eight-hour workshop in experimental film. The teacher quickly got sick of viewing student films for such a long stretch and created different excuses each week to shorten the class. One week he had us break at noon to celebrate Saturn entering Taurus. Being a Taurus and curious I asked the teacher what the significance of this event was. Knowing that I was a Taurus, he said, "I'm an Aries and I'm sick of the limitations and responsibility of Saturn. You're a lazy, good-for-nothing Taurus and you need two years of work and responsibility."

That freaked me out. I went right down to the New York Astrology Center on East Sixth Street, walked in and demanded to know exactly what my teacher meant by "two years of work and responsibility." Well they sold me forty dollars worth of books and sent me on my way. Forty dollars was a lot of money in

1968. I got home, mad as hell, and started to try to figure out how to evade this Saturn thing.

I taught myself how to cast a chart and did my friends. Understand that I was trying to debunk astrology, to sniff at it and pronounce it wrong. Unfortunately, the more I looked at the charts of my friends, the more I saw my friends in them. I became hooked and dropped out of SVA to study astrology.

Hadley Fitzgerald: I left college in 1963 to pursue a career in the theatre. After moving around in that world for two very intense years, I returned to UCLA in 1965 as an English major with plans to teach, then ultimately become a Shakespearean scholar. When I graduated in March 1968 I was 24 years old, working full-time, politically active, newly married with two stepchildren, and exhausted. I took five months off to ghostwrite a book for one of my employers.

At a dinner party on May 11, 1968, I asked a new friend some casually earnest questions about her recent stay in Hong Kong. She responded cordially, and I offhandedly asked what she'd liked best about being there. She said she'd had quite a few interesting experiences, but "the most fascinating" was having her horoscope done by an American astrologer who lived there. I felt mildly dizzy, my knees were suddenly weak, and I managed to say, "Oh."

In the next instant, what I can only describe as "The Voice" inside my head announced with absolute certainty: "Oh, *that's* the work I'm supposed to do." There was no challenge to this statement, no curiosity about its source, no internal debate. I didn't know what an astrologer was or did, but I had been taken over by the uncomplicated certainty that I had to be one.

In my office some years later I had a "vision" that the psychotherapy of the future would, quite naturally, involve astrology as a primary tool/adjunct. So, in order to discover how to bring the two fields together, I returned to school in 1975, got my master's degree, and became a licensed therapist in 1981. That decision cost me everything "familiar" in my world, but led me to understand what Neruda wrote about the arrival of poetry in his life: ". . . I, infinitesimal being . . . felt myself a pure part of the abyss, I wheeled with the stars, my heart broke loose on the wind."

John Marchesella: Since I got into astrology at the ripe old age of 20, there's not much to say about life before astrology. I was a well-disciplined, serious kid, a little precocious, and I read my daily horoscope from the time I was 8 years old, shall we say, religiously. In college, I began as a film major, and that's where

I met my first astrologer. It was the '70s and I was lucky; and I was lucky that it was the '70s when astrology classes were easily found. Hand, Greene and Arroyo were changing the face of astrological publishing. And everyone was so curious about themselves that starting a practice was a breeze!

By the early '80s, my astrological clients were telling me that I should be a shrink, so I went back to school for training in psychology and counseling with a Jungian bent. I also worked extensively as a bereavement counselor. After graduation, I worked for five years as a psychotherapist in private practice (with and without the use of the horoscope), until I realized I enjoyed astrology much more, and that I could be more effective with it. So I went back to the full-time astrology practice.

I thought astrology would make me a more effective therapist, but in hindsight, I see that the study of psychology and counseling made me a much better astrologer. Along with my practice, I teach group classes and supervise upcoming astrologers. I also think participation in the astrology community is imperative as a way of giving back to astrology as well as to being a good astrologer, so volunteer work takes up a good deal of my time.

Ken Bowser: I took up astrology in 1970 at age 24. At the time I was working part-time and attending school part time as well. I had been married for a year and a half and had a 6 month old son. My exposure to astrology up to that time had been extremely modest. My mother bought *American Astrology* and *Horoscope* and I read through them from time to time.

My wife and I met another couple in 1970 who had some knowledge of astrology. The wife did my horoscope and I thought that while her interpretation wasn't first rate, I could see myself in it. I asked how she had done it. She recommended some books which I promptly bought, and found that I had a head for the material. Astrology quickly displaced my other diversions and passed from a hobby to the main interest in my life over a period of about three years.

I'm an avid reader, with about five thousand books in my house and have spent a lot of time in libraries and classrooms. I have only a B.A. in history but have a longtime interest in scholarship. I have two adult children, am divorced, and have lived with my girlfriend for many years. While it is secondary in my life, I have been quite interested in fast cars since high school and have owned a few.

15

Kim Rogers-Gallagher: Before I found astrology, I was a Jill of all trades. I waitressed, tended bar, did floral design and worked as a receptionist at a YMCA. My degree is in English/Journalism, but after I'd obtained it, I realized there was absolutely no way I could ever stand having a nine to five job. I love working odd hours—nights, in particular. (In fact, my most creative hours are from 4:00 p.m. to midnight.) I *didn't* realize that it was a heavy pack of Sagittarius and Aquarius energies, along with Uranus in the sixth house, that were behind that fact.

Robert Hand: I began studying astrology at the age of 17 during my first year of college. My father had been studying it for some time as an adjunct to his efforts in forecasting the stock market. Therefore, my first exposure to astrology was stock market astrology. But my father was not in the usual sense my teacher. He and I worked together more or less as equals except for the fact that he had been studying it a few years longer.

After he died in 1963 I continued studying it on my own, although there was a period of a few years, when I was a teacher in a secondary school and later for a time a graduate student, when I did not do a great deal with it. In 1971 I began working again with astrology very extensively and in the spring of 1972 I became a full time professional astrologer. Subsequently I practiced in New York and Boston. While in Boston I began to write texts for computer programs marketed by Para Research in Gloucester, MA. Some of these became the base for my first three books, *Planets in Composite*, *Planets in Transit*, and *Planets in Youth*. Later in the '70s I wrote *Horoscope Symbols*, and *Essays on Astrology*.

Having been interested in astrological research for some time, in the late '70s I began to get into computers. In 1978 I obtained an early microcomputer and began programming it to do astrology. I was among the first to do so with microcomputers. In the early '80s this led to my founding a company called Astro-Graphics Services, along with several partners. This later became Astrolabe, a company which creates and markets software for astrologers. This pretty well took up the '80s for me.

In 1992 at the United Astrology Congress, a group of us got together to discuss the history of astrology and what could be done to facilitate the translation of ancient and medieval astrology texts into English to make them accessible to modern students. This movement first took the name ARHAT, or Association for the Retrieval of Historical Astrological Texts. In the next year Robert Zoller, one of the first major translators of Latin texts, Robert Schmidt of the Golden Hind Press, and myself started Project Hindsight as a way of supporting the translation of these old texts. (There was an earlier Project Hindsight, started by Robert Schmidt, working in the area of the history of mathematics. Otherwise the two projects had nothing in common.) After a couple years of collaboration Robert Zoller left the Project and then in 1997 so did I.

I have continued my involvement in the work, however, again under the name ARHAT which now stands for *Archive* for Retrieval of Historical Astrological Texts. And for the last couple of years, under the name Arhat Media Inc., this has been a Virginia corporation run by myself and my wife, Elyse Karin. In 1997 Astrolabe and I had an amicable parting of the ways as the result of the fact that I had become much more interested in traditional astrology than in computer programming. Astrology more than computers has always been my first love. And since 1993 I have written several shorter works on traditional astrology, several translations from Latin, and two as yet incomplete longer works. ARHAT has also published works and translations by other authors. All of this brings us pretty much up to the present time.

Robert Schmidt: My earliest interests were mathematics and science, particularly mathematical physics, and in my high school years I fully intended to pursue these studies at MIT. However, by a fortunate accident, I found out about St John's College in Annapolis, MD, the original "Great Books" school and decided to go there instead.

At St John's I learned the importance of studying original sources in the original languages. There my interest gradually shifted to the foundations of mathematics and science, and more broadly, the Western philosophical tradition. Heeding the advice of a professor at St John's who believed that graduate school could have a corrupting influence on someone seriously interested in philosophy, after St John's I held a series of "blue-collar" jobs that left me free to pursue my studies at night. I was particularly attracted to problems that no longer seriously interested modern scholars, such as the content of certain lost books of the Greek mathematicians, which I tried to reconstruct on the basis of the surviving fragmentary evidence. I also translated and published a number of ignored but important treatises from the history of mathematics.

In 1989, another fortuitous accident led me to the first Neo-Astrology Conference, sponsored by Michael Erlewine of Matrix Software, which plunged me—though not exactly kicking and screaming—into the astrological community. For a few years I worked on problems connected with the scientific and philosophical foundations of astrology, but I gradually realized that it was first of all necessary to understand what the Western astrological tradition had been originally, and how it had been transmitted to modern times, before coming to grips with the scientific and philosophical issues. Consequently, true to my St John's background, I started reading and translating the original Hellenistic sources surviving in Greek.

Since 1993, my translations have been made available to the astrological community under the name Project Hindsight. After a number of years I began to discern the structure of the Hellenistic system and its theoretical basis. I now believe I have faithfully reconstructed the original Hellenistic astrology. As research director of the PHASER Foundation, I am presently beginning to return to my scientific and philosophical investigation of the foundations of astrology.

Ronnie Gale Dreyer: I became interested in astrology when I was 19 and in college where I majored in English and Theater Arts. My career goal at the time was to become a professional actress and director. After graduation I went to Europe for what was supposed to be a few months but instead turned into a three-year journey through Europe and Asia. During that time I studied Western astrology in Amsterdam, Holland where I lived for nine months, and then traveled overland to India where I studied Hindu astrology.

After returning to America in 1977, I felt very out of place and decided to move to Amsterdam permanently. In 1978, I was offered a job teaching a beginning astrology class at a metaphysical center, and for the next nine years I worked as an astrology teacher and consultant.

In September 1987, I signed a contract with Aquarian Press in England to write my first book—*Indian Astrology: A Western Approach to the Ancient Hindu Art.* The following week I returned to the United States after having lived in Amsterdam for almost ten years. The book was published in 1990, and *Venus: The Evolution of the Goddess and her Planet* was published in 1993 by the Aquarian Press as well.

In 1992 I became secretary of AFAN (Association for Astrological Networking) and became more visible and active in the astrological community, lecturing at numerous conferences and astrology groups. I began teaching Vedic astrology, a subject that has gained popularity in the West over the past decade.

I revised my first book that Samuel Weiser Inc. published in 1997 as *Vedic Astrology: A Guide to the Fundamentals of Jyotish*. I also wrote a series of Sun sign books, columns, chapter anthologies, and computerized reports. In 2000, Doubleday published my book *Healing Signs: The Astrological Guide to Wholeness and Well-Being*.

At present, I practice astrology full time as a consultant, author, lecturer and teacher. I teach ongoing Vedic astrology classes and workshops, and have lectured throughout the world at conferences in the United States, Australia, Canada, England, Ireland, and Scotland. After serving as AFAN secretary for six years, I was appointed its Presiding Officer in 2000. At UAC 1998, I was presented with its Jim Lewis Community Service award.

I also now use my editing and writing skills as editor of the NCGR member newsletter and have learned desktop publishing to lay it out as well. My life has ben enriched through the study of astrology due to all the wonderful people that I have met including clients, colleagues, students, and most of all friends.

Steven Forrest: There literally wasn't much in the way of "a time before I got involved with astrology." My first memory was wanting a telescope so I could look at the heavens. My parents got me a little spy glass for Christmas that year. I remember being terribly disappointed—I had the Mount Palomar Observatory in mind! I must have been six years old. I began my study of the heavens through amateur astronomy, not astrology, when I was about twelve.

Due to a "chance meeting" with a young German woman in the mountains of upstate New York, I almost immediately began to learn palmistry at the same time too. On your hand, there's a "mound of Venus" and a "Jupiter finger"—once you begin to learn palmistry, you've begun to organize your mind in an astrological way. Both systems stem from the same roots in ancient psychology. By the time I was 18 or so, all those "lines in my palm" had come together. I got my first halfway serious astrology book (*Write Your Own Horoscope*, by Joseph Goodavage) and never looked back.

In college, I started out studying psychology and philosophy because they seemed to be as close to astrology as you could get in those days. Then I discovered the Department of Religion, and that was a natural home for me. I graduated from the University of North Carolina at Chapel Hill, with a B.A. in Religion in 1971. My intent was to go on and get my doctorate after taking a year or so off.

That was thirty years ago. Sometimes I'm wistful about not having continued my education, but after knocking around Europe a bit and working briefly for the National Institute of Mental Health, my astrological practice just took off. By 1976, I was ready to "quit my day job." By 1979, I was booking clients ten months ahead.

In 1981, with Uranus transiting my Ascendant, a literary agent in New York asked me if I would consider writing an astrology book "on spec" which she would represent. She'd heard about my work through a local novelist who was a client and a friend of mine. One thing led to the next very rapidly, and within six weeks I had a deal with Bantam Books to write what would become *The Inner Sky*. That book came out in the summer of 1984. It sold well and got good reviews, at least outside the technical astrological community, which at first basically ignored it—I think there was a lot of prejudice in those days against the mainstream publishers. Bantam gave me a contract for a follow-up: *The Changing Sky*. Then my wife Jodie and I tempted Fate by writing a third book for Bantam, about the astrology of relationships: *Skymates*. Our then-new marriage survived our hubris (we were married in 1984 and *Skymates* came out in 1989). We've just published a new, completely revised version of that book, by the way, reflecting what twenty years together have taught us.

The good side of going to print with one of the major publishers is the instant fame they provide. You pay the piper with the short shelf-life of such books—they generally go out of print rapidly. There is also a lot of pressure on you to keep them simple, aimed at the lowest common denominators of the market. I parted ways with Bantam, and brought out new editions of the first three books with ACS Publications in San Diego, and quickly followed up with *The Night Speaks* (ACS; 1993) and *The Book of Pluto* (ACS; 1994). Meanwhile, the astrological world had discovered my work and I'd begun to speak at conferences. I remember my first one, in what must have been about 1986. It was an NCGR event in New York City. I think I'd met maybe one other astrologer whom I hadn't trained myself at that time. I got off the plane from North Carolina, cabbed into the city, and sat down on a panel next to Rob Hand. Like everyone else in the astrological world, I'd been reverently reading his work for years. I must have been bug-eyed. He was kind to me that day—I'll always be grateful to him for that.

I grew up in churches and always felt Christianity deeply throughout my childhood. My study of religion in college was not motivated fundamentally by intellectual curiosity—I was a "seeker" in the mode of the 1960s. Quickly enough I went down the usual cultural routes of that period: I got into Eastern religion and mixed in a dose of Carlos Castaneda. With my first wife, Michele, I got into a bad storm in small sailboat about eight miles off the coast of New Jersey one dark night in summer 1977, out among all the shipping heading for New York Harbor. It was definitely the hour of prayer—and I found myself praying to Jesus!

That was kind of sobering, and it took me a while to admit it. I was also involved with a group called the Brigade of Light at the time, which was basically like the Theosophical Society in terms of its belief-system, but with some crypto-Christian references thrown in too. Just to further confuse my metaphysical smorgasbord, I've also been blessed with many opportunities to sit with Tibetan Buddhist teachers. My point here is that at heart I am a religious type. That sense of the Great Journey has always informed my astrological thinking, practice, and writing. It never crossed my mind to see the chart from any perspective except a metaphysical, evolutionary one. Right from the earliest stages, all my work has revolved around those values. Reincarnation is something I've taken for granted since my childhood—like a sense of the presence of God, it's just something I feel I "know," even though I can't prove it.

My early Christian roots have led me to link spiritual evolution with the exercise of free will. That emphasis is absolutely central to my approach to astrology, and has gotten me into all sorts of interesting trouble with traditionalists who seem hell-bent on "delineating" people and telling them "what's going to happen to them." I see I'll have a chance to address all that more deeply in some later questions. I mention it now because it leads smoothly into my relationship with the most brilliant of the modern metaphysical astrologers, Jeffrey Wolf Green. From speaking at the same conferences, I'd known him superficially for a few years. An ethical crisis came up that had to be handled with some delicacy. Circumstances were such that the situation fell to Jeff and me. In the process we became fast friends, and realized that we were both doing kinds of astrology that, while technically very different, came out of the same set of spiritual beliefs and values. We were even both calling it the same thing: *evolutionary astrology*. We decided to teach some seminars together, in 1998. We did three of them—two in California and one in Arizona. They were transcribed. Meanwhile, Jodie had started our Seven Paws Press to bring out a wonderful trilogy of historical fantasy novels she'd written—and with an eye on the possibility of publishing some astrological work free of the usual dumbing-down pressures and financial disincentives.

She and I took the transcripts up to a borrowed cabin in the North Carolina mountains, hoping we could turn them into a book. After a few days up there we realized we had two books, not one. Seven Paws Press published Volume One of *Measuring the Night: Evolutionary Astrology and the Keys to the Soul* in February 2000. Volume Two came out a year later. Both have sold very well, establishing our Seven Paws Press with distributors, reviewers, and so on. Right now, we're not looking at other astrological authors, but we're definitely committed to Seven Paws's growing.

Around the same time that I was getting involved with Jeff Green, I also started an Astrological Apprenticeship Program. Now that I'm getting older, I was beginning to feel the need to do some serious teaching. The ninety-minute "workshop" format of astrological conferences is a catastrophe, in my opinion. It compels a heady, atomized view of the symbolism, rewarding hair-splitting techniques and systematically undercutting the wholism that underlies any effective approach to astrological counsel. Rather than swim upstream, I simply instituted my Apprenticeship Program. Each group meets for four days, twice a year, and we maintain email contact in the intervening time. It's proven profoundly rewarding to me, and I expect I'll continue it some form for the rest of my life.

Meanwhile, I continue to maintain a busy astrological practice. We're very focused on writing and publishing. Our web site (www.stevenforrest.com) is currently getting about 18,000 visitors a month. My books are available in many languages. I've made a lot of good and interesting friends around the world, and I am very happy to have come down this strange, seemingly anachronistic, existential avenue we call being a professional astrologer.

Wendy Z. Ashley: What I wanted to grow up to be was an actress, in theater, not film. I spent summers hanging around the summer stock houses of Ogunquit, Maine, hoping for any part in the productions. I got to paint the flats for the sets instead. In high school I was cast as Madame Arcati in Noel Coward's *Blythe Spirit*, a British comedy in which a newly married couple have to contend with the persistent spirit of his dead wife. Madame Arcati is a psychic come to rid them of the pesky ghost. She is brisk, batty, and sure of her vision into the spirit world. You can believe it was no problem for me to know that part. She was my mother! But this was the last play I was to be in. Instead

22

I married at 19 and had three babies in the first five years, so there went the acting career. Early in my married life I was able to study figure drawing in life classes in Ogunquit, where many fine artists were in residence. But art was not a compelling passion, at least not enough to aspire to a career in art. Today I have a career as an astrologer. I see clients, I have students, I lecture and I write. Since 1985, I have devoted myself entirely to my astrological practice.

2. WHAT ASTROLOGICAL SYSTEM DO YOU PRACTICE? DESCRIBE THE SYMBOL SET, ZODIAC, HOUSE SYSTEM AND ASPECTS YOU USE.

Demetra George: The easy answer to this question is that over the course of my career I have looked at the ten traditional planets; anywhere from four to 9,000 asteroids; used the tropical zodiac; the Placidus, Koch, Alchabitius, Porphyry, and whole sign house systems; only the classical Ptolemaic aspects; many other minor aspects; distinguished and not distinguished between the different kinds of aspects, orbs of aspects, orbs of planets, no orbs at all. But the authentic answer is more disturbing.

In 1994, I turned to my friend Kim Rogers-Gallagher and said, "I don't think that I am a real astrologer." What I meant by that statement was that while I erected the birth chart, and used it as a framework onto which to place the asteroids, that was the extent of how I used the majority of astrological techniques that were common to the discipline. Not that I didn't know the principles of modern astrology; I had written a definitive primer on the subject with Douglas Bloch, *Astrology For Yourself.* However, approaching astrology from a mythic perspective, it was the story of the gods or goddesses that were prominent in the chart from an archetypal mythological and psychological perspective that comprised the bulk of the interpretation. Their modification by sign, house and aspect seemed to be of minimal importance; and it didn't really make any difference which system was used. In fact, I saw how easy it was for both myself and other astrologers to keep adjusting the interpretations of a planet in a sign and house and aspect until "it fit," and that tended ultimately to render everything meaningless. To the extent that mythic deities are none other than the outer symbolic projections of the inner structures of the psyche that are common to humans of most cultures, there seemed to be nothing irrational in constructing a reading based purely upon which planetary deities were most outstanding at the nativity moment. But this was not "working the methods" of astrology.

Now my studies have taken me back to basics, back to the fountainhead, to try to unravel how all the methods were originally conceptualized and utilized, and to evaluate which of the modern methods are distortions, adaptations, or innovations of the original doctrines.

Evelyn Roberts: I use the Tropical Zodiac and Placidus House System. I find these cusps the most sensitive. I am a Psychological/Traditional astrologer and synthesize these systems in my work. Having experimented with asteroids and other points, I find that simplicity suits me best. I work with the ten planets, Sun through Pluto, plus Chiron and the True Lunar Nodes and the Angles. I use Sun/Moon and Ascendent/Midheaven midpoints, and if working with a person intensively I use more. Learning an array of techniques for me has meant more tools. A primary intention is to be realistic about what time allows and the requirements of the client. Aspects I generally use are the conjunction, opposition, square, trine, sextile, quincunx, semi-square, semi-sextile and sesquiquadrate. I have no hard and fast rules with aspects and sometimes use others, especially if they are exact. Experience has taught me to be flexible with orbs. I let the chart talk to me and if there are many close aspects I keep them tighter; if there are mainly wide aspects I allow them to be looser. I nearly always work with progressions, and frequently use other techniques like solar returns, astrocartography, electional and all methods of synastry work.

Gary Christen: I center my work around the Uranian System, although I am not limited to it. The symbol set is composed of the Cardinal Axis, ten known planets, Moon's Node, angles, and the eight hypotheticals of the System. The hypotheticals are Cupido, Hades, Zeus, Kronos, Apollon, Admetos, Vulcanus and Poseidon.

I work in the tropical zodiac. Since I have charts thrust under my nose all the time, I have to look at them through a quadrant system of houses. When I am in that position, I prefer Porphyry houses. When I do my work with my own tools and situations, I use the various house structures of the System. These are equal houses around the personal points and the planets themselves. All of these houses are ecliptic-based, except for the Midheaven houses (or as we Uranians call it, the "houses of the meridian") which is an equal house system drawn on the equatorial plane and projected to the ecliptic. The various house systems describe information from the point of view of the planet or factor they

24

are focused upon. The house cusps are used as points themselves and also form "reflexes" to other houses within a given framework.

The layout of these houses places the Ascendant and the Node as the first house cusp in their respective frameworks. The Midheaven and the Moon start the tenth house in their framework. The cardinal axis places 0 degrees Cancer as the cusp of the tenth house. The Sun and the rest of the planets are placed as the fourth house cusp with equal houses following.

I use the hard series of aspects down to the 11.25 degree opening for dynamic material and how the planets are working together (hard angles equals a blend of energies). If two planets are antithetical to one another (for example, Saturn and Uranus), then they don't blend well or form a difficult dynamic. If two planets like each other (for example, Moon and Venus), they blend into a happier dynamic.

Soft aspects in the 30 degree series (30, 60, 120, 150) are seen through the house structures. For example, if Saturn trines the Sun and is running ahead of the Sun, and the Sun is the cusp of the fourth house (of the Sun horoscope), then the trine to Saturn connects the fourth to the eighth house and isn't a lot of fun, but is focused on resources and "other people's money." If the Saturn trines the Sun and the Saturn is behind the Sun, then the connection is from the fourth (Sun) to the twelfth (Saturn) and causes personal difficulty for the native from unseen areas that need more attention.

So I don't really use aspects in any orthodox kind of way and in the System, we say that aspects and planetary placement (what sign is it in?) don't show the destiny of people; it is the symmetry between planetary factors that determines the individuality and destiny of the native. Which brings us to the central focus of my work, planetary pictures or symmetrical arrangements around a common axis. This concept includes the ideas of "what's so" in the horoscope and "what if" in the horoscope. An example of the "what's so" form would be hard aspects and completed midpoints, such as I relied upon in reading Joyce's chart. "What if" would be planetary pictures of three or more factors surrounding a common axis and includes antiscia, uncompleted symmetries and unoccupied midpoint structures. These structures are possibilities that can be triggered into action through transits, directions, progressions, synastries and other factors.

Hierarchy is determined by a ranking of planetary factors. The personal points consist of the cardinal axis, angles (Midheaven and Ascendant), Node, Sun and Moon. These personal points are neutral in action and are colored or influenced by rest of the factors in a horoscope or factors affecting the horoscope. Nothing happens (or is activated) unless one or more personal points are involved in a picture, the more personal points involved, the stronger the indication. Again, the rest of the horoscopic factors are treated as adjectives, describing the action and form that the personal points take.

I also look quite closely at planetary elevation. This is the planet closest to the top of the chart. The chart's shape and other dispositions also are taken into consideration. I particularly focus upon the paranatella (parans) present at the latitude of birth. Parans are the simultaneous crossing by two or more planets over the angles of the horoscope and are unique to the individual.

Of course there is more that I do than I can describe here, but many of the elements have been covered. It is the combination and application of these things that makes all the difference.

Hadley Fitzgerald: I use the tropical zodiac and the traditional symbols of the Sun, Moon, eight planets, and now Chiron. For the past twenty-five years I've used the Koch house system, not only because of my experience with its accuracy in natal interpretation, but also for its accuracy in timing progressions and transits through houses. I tend to use only the major Ptolemaic aspects with somewhat generous orbs.

John Marchesella: Modern Western astrology, for lack of a better title, is my system of astrology, but it's actually very simple and traditional: the twelve signs and houses, ten planets and the lunar Nodes, the tropical zodiac, Placidus house system and the major Ptolemaic aspects plus the inconjunct. I keep an eye on Chiron and the four major asteroids, but I don't work with them *per se*, and I dabble with the minor aspects in predictive work. My aim, however, is counseling, and that's the hallmark of my work—astrology as a counseling tool, but it is distinctly astrological. I distinguish this, by the way, from psychological astrology, which, in my opinion, imposes psychological theories on astrology, thereby diluting both and hampering the effectiveness of each. I am very decidedly an astrologer. The horoscope, as I use it, is the story of your life, and the predictive factors let us know where you are in that story. I do not make a distinction between natal and forecasting work. In brief, here is my definition of the components of the natal chart: the planets represent parts of character; signs represent how those parts operate; houses represent where in one's life they operate; and aspects let us know what happens on their way to succeeding (or not) in their operation.

26

Ken Bowser: I use the sidereal zodiac with the Fagan-Allen ayanamsa, e.g., essentially the Babylonian system with the addition of a horoscopos (Ascendant). I use the standard ten bodies from the Sun out to Pluto but none of the asteroids except Chiron, none of the Arabic parts and none of the hypothetical bodies. I use the Campanus house system, but I don't put a lot of emphasis on the houses or house rulers. The action is primarily with the planets, in my experience. I use the Ptolemaic aspects plus the semi-square and sesquiquadrate among the aspects in zodiaco, which is based on celestial latitude and longitude coordinates (the ecliptic system). I also put great store by aspects in mundo which are based on right ascension and declination coordinates (the equatorial system). From that it follows naturally that I use primary directions a lot both in mundo and interplanetary directions. I use midpoints. I also emphasize stars, especially those which are with the Lights and the angles, but only in mundo. In a nutshell I consider most important (1) the condition of the Lights; (2) the angles and any planets or stars they contain; (3) the closest, strongest aspects either in mundo or zodiaco.

Kim Rogers-Gallagher: Although I've played around with heliocentric astrology, I find that the geocentric system works better in my work with clients. (Helio does, however, seem to be quite telling when it comes to world events, and mundane astrology is one of my passions.) As for house systems, after experimenting with several (using my own chart, especially via transits) I've settled on Koch. Otherwise, I like to keep my astrology as simple as possible. I use the classical planets, Chiron, and the four major asteroids, Vesta, Juno, Pallas, and Ceres. Although I know lots of great astrologers who have, I don't much bother with minor aspects or hypotheticals, and I confess that I have never had the patience to work much with progressions. In my predictive work, I prefer transits, solar returns, lunar returns, and Venus and Mars returns—all of which "happen" quickly and dramatically enough to make my primarily Fire and Air sign personality happy.

Robert Hand: I use a modified medieval system, the main modifications being those needed to bring it into synchronization with modern needs and modern society. I describe the details of this at considerable length in the Strategy section of this article. I use the tropical zodiac, and whole-sign houses along with medieval aspects and orbs. I still also use midpoints and the 90 degree dial of the Hamburg school and Cosmobiology, although I do not use them in this article. I use the seven classical planets, plus Uranus, Neptune and Pluto. I do not use asteroids, comets, or any hypothetical bodies. I do not denigrate these. I just prefer not to use them.

Robert Schmidt: I practice Hellenistic astrology, which is the fountainhead of the Western tradition and the ultimate source for most of the astrological concepts and practices that are used to this day, although many of these had rather different meanings or interpretations in ancient times. In addition, it employed a number of concepts and techniques that were forgotten over the centuries.

Hellenistic astrology was not centered around the study of the personality, as much of modern astrology is. It is best characterized as event prediction and event description, insofar as it purported to predict and describe all the kinds of events that befall human beings. The human personality together with the inner events that human beings experience was simply a special topic to be investigated alongside many others concerned with outer events, such as parents, children, travel, wealth, eminence, etc.

Here I will give a brief and impressionistic synopsis of the Hellenistic system. There were three significators for the kind of event: a planet, a Lot (sometimes called an "Arabic Part"), and a house (whole-sign houses only). The signs had nothing to do with personality archetypes, but instead were used to describe the mode and manner in which events occur, according to sign gender, quadruplicity and triplicity, which same characteristics also imply a tropical zodiac. Much use was made of rulerships, and there were two other modes of rulership in addition to our rulership by sign and exaltation. Aspects were sign-based and did not depend on orbs. Many interpretations depend on sect, or the difference that a day or night birth makes. There were also numerous planetary concepts defined relative to the Sun, such as speed and horizontal visibility (orientality and occidentality), and a group of important conditions under which planets are said to "rejoice" (thereby becoming more benefic)—to name only the most commonly used concepts.

The Hellenistic system consists of three grand approaches to prediction. The Universal Techniques give information regarding the native's life as a whole, delineating the overall contours of the native's life and providing a kind of biographical profile. The Topical Methods address individual topics in the native's life, such as children, marriage, etc. The Time-Lord procedures constituted the central timing device and have a role analogous to the Dasa

Lords of Indian astrology; solar returns and transits are studied within the context of the current Time-Lords. These three approaches cross-reference each other in intricate and complex ways.

Ronnie Gale Dreyer: Jyotish (Sanskrit for "Science of Light"), or Vedic astrology, uses the sidereal zodiac, which is the actual position of the stars, as well as the 27 Nakshatras (Moon mansions) each consisting of 13 degrees 20 minutes. We use the whole sign house system, which means that the first house is comprised of the entire ascending sign (30 degrees), and each sign follows sequentially so that if, for instance, Leo, the fifth sign, was the ascending sign, the second house would consist of 30 degrees of the sixth sign of Virgo, the third sign would consist of 30 degrees of the seventh sign of Libra, etc. The planets we use are those that were used thousands of years ago when Jyotish originated, namely Sun through Saturn, as well as North Node (Rahu) and South Node (Ketu). All planets that are seven signs apart aspect each other and, in addition, Mars aspects planets four and eight signs away, Jupiter aspects signs that are five and nine signs away, and Saturn aspects planets three and ten signs away. We also use divisional charts based on harmonic divisions, and do not use Uranus, Neptune and Pluto. We also analyze planetary dispositors—the Lord of the sign that the planet occupies.

Steven Forrest: I'm quite open-minded in terms of technique. There are effective astrologers—and goofballs—in every tradition. That tells me that many systems are potentially effective, just like a dream can have more than one interpretation. Well, we astrologers are dreaming the universe!

Still, I think we benefit from focus—choosing a system and sticking with it. I use modern Western astrology, based on the Equinox and Solstice points, rather than the constellations. House systems are a vexatious question. Again, we find astrologers getting good results with all of the different systems. I personally find Placidus Houses to be most effective in answering the questions I ask. Where there are difference between Placidus and other systems in the birthcharts of people I know well and deeply, the Placidus system usually seems to reflect their realities more deeply.

My entire approach to astrology is very practical in that it's been shaped by the actualities of working with clients every day for nearly thirty years. Long ago, I learned that it's far better to spend twenty minutes talking about a truly elemental structure of the birthchart than to give one minute to twenty different structures. This reality has dictated a minimalist approach: I concentrate on going deeply into the basics. I recognize the power of many different techniques, but I use the five major aspects, and generally don't work with harmonics, asteroids, midpoints and so on.

Wendy Z. Ashley: I use either the Topocentric or Placidus house system and geocentric positions for the planets. Above 60 degrees of latitude I use an Equal House System since at those latitudes the Zodiac lies on, or close to, the Horizon. These far Northern charts would otherwise have four to eight intercepted houses! I use the Sun, Moon, Mercury, Venus, Mars, Jupiter, Saturn, Uranus, Neptune, Pluto, Chiron and the Nodes—no asteroids, black holes, Arabic Parts etc. This is because the mythic method is synthesis rather than analysis. I do however align every significant point in a chart to the closest Fixed Star by longitude (Zodiac Degree) even though I set the chart in the Tropical Zodiac.

In this way the chart contains both the Sidereal Locations and the Tropical Positions. In general I have found that the Tropical is superior to the star positions (Sidereal) for accuracy for locating the client's mythos, but this is not a hard and fast rule. It is justified, I think, because no new mythologies have been added to the sky in the last 2,000 years. Myths are older than the current age, and they are eternal. New myths are variations on old myths. There is the new mythology of space exploration but it parallels other older exploration myths, so it is really not new. It is true that the sky does have new constellations that were added in the sixteenth and seventeenth centuries. I refer to a collection of tools of various sorts that were tucked into small spaces betwixt the older constellations. Those additions that were other than tools were from those distant cultures visited by Europeans during the Age of Exploration. But even back in the older sky there are tools; for example, the Scales and the Sword of Perseus have been around for at least three thousand years. I include a list of the stars aligned to Joyce's chart to which I will refer in her interpretation.

I do not use the asteroids, primarily because there are at least 50,000 asteroids and while the famous ones (named for the Goddesses Juno, Pallas, Vesta and Ceres) may be more visible from Earth, they alone do not carry the archetypes of those Goddesses. The influence of these and any other Goddesses and Gods can be determined through the Signs, Houses, Constellations, Stars and Planets. My simple chart has 28 primary positions to consider in a reading—more than enough to do the job, and a big job for synthesis. The Stars themselves each have meaning, derived from its place in the constellation as well as from ancient star lore. I do *not* use the Ptolemaic system for star meaning wherein a star is likened to the planets—such as being of the nature of Saturn and Mars, for example.

In the mythic method, aspect orbs are very wide—indeed the earliest astrologers considered that all planets in the same sign were conjoined, all in opposite signs opposed, all in the quartered signs were in square and so forth. I might not go that far but certainly planets within 13 degrees of orb are in aspect. Mythic Astrology takes the visible sky as its base. After all, the chart on paper is not the horoscope. The chart is an approximate representation of the real horoscope: the sky at a particular moment and place. In this wise, planets are taken as "angular" when they are within one hour of crossing the angles. The consistent observer is well aware of the imminent arrival of a planet at an "angle." This means that a planet may be up to 20 degrees on either side of the Midheaven, Ascendant, Nadir or Descendant and still be considered angular. We also know that declination will affect visibility, and visibility counts in Mythic Astrology. Therefore a planet may be "angular" whether in a Cardinal or Cadent House. Thirteen degrees is the distance the Moon travels in a day. This is the orb of linking distances. It is a symbolic orb. But generally I do not substitute a set of schema for the thing experienced in nature, in actuality, the sky itself.

3. WHAT IS YOUR METAPHYSICAL VIEW OF REALITY? DO YOU DISTINGUISH BETWEEN THE BODY, THE SOUL AND THE SPIRIT? HOW IS EACH RELATED TO ASTROLOGY?

Demetra George: Philosophically, metaphysics is defined as a study of first principles. That we live in a cosmos that is alive, conscious, and pervaded by a creative intelligence, and that humans, as well as all sentient life, are not something other or separate from this universal being is about as primal as I can go. The body is the physical corporeal vehicle inhabited by a particular personality that provides a temporary domicile for the soul and spirit. The soul is the eternal part of our nature, and some would say therefore divine, that is the repository of all previous memories and holds the impressions of these experiences. The spirit is the spark that gives animation to the life force. In a very general sense, one might say that the Ascendant is related to the body, the Moon to the soul, and that the Sun signifies the spirit.

31

Evelyn Roberts: Separations between body, soul, and spirit exist only in our human senses and perceptions, and I believe our work is to align and integrate them on the journey towards wholeness. As an astrologer, massage therapist and yoga practitioner, this is affirmed for me through client interaction and personal experience. When an individual tries to deny, project or split off from elements of the self there is inevitably dysfunction close at hand. Astrology is a beautiful language and channel for describing and understanding the underlying unity of the earthly and the divine, the mundane and the mystical, the visible and the invisible. It shows us strengths and challenges and provides the map, which holds the key to aligning body, soul and spirit in a way that honors the individual and also acknowledges our vast oneness. Planets and elements powerfully describe how these energies manifest in an individual life. Earth planets and signs speak of the physical, Water the soul, Fire the spirit, and Air is the mental and connected to prana, the breath, and the unification of these energies. My personal image in astrology is of a woven tapestry, and as with the holographic model the whole is reflected in every part.

Gary Christen: This question and the next few that follow are sort of interrelated, at least in the way that I view this existence. These views are very subjective and are true to the way I perceive things. Others may hold similar beliefs and ideas, or not.

I am alive. I am not dead (not yet or I wouldn't be interested in writing this). Because I am alive, I am pro-life (not in the abortion debate sense, but in a larger, more pervasive sense). I simply divide impulses and energies into one of two camps. Things that promote, experience and assist life are good. Things that impair, limit or eliminate life are bad. Morality is a human invention and the universe doesn't care about such things. Morality and ethics should only flow from the criteria outlined above.

Life itself is the miracle. The combination of body, spirit and soul makes life. Break up any of those components and you have not-life, and the miracle is over. This existence is very tenuous and unique. It is not an objective existence, since our lens is ourselves and anything we interact with or experience is still an extension of our consciousness. Our reality is very personal and compares with others only through agreement on common matters. I see myself typing on the keyboard. Another's experience of the keyboard seems to be the same as mine, so the keyboard should exist in the world of agreement (a shifting level of reality), and I can consider the keyboard to be part of the objective reality (I hope).

Consciousness, however, is not dependent on this state of existence called life. Life as it is defined is the self-organization of carbon-based material. The self-organization of matter and energy creates consciousness. This is not necessarily carbon-based with a chemical construct creating thoughts and self-awareness. Any large-scale organization of the stuff of the universe has a form of consciousness. This makes the universe a very conscious place. Consciousnesses existing within other consciousnesses in larger and smaller states of organization characterize the universe. In this scheme of things, I like to refer to humans as "organized bacteria." We just cannot communicate with other organized bits of matter and energy yet, at least not in the way that we define human communication.

Time is a true illusion. It is a thing much like three-dimensional space. The way we experience time can only be understood through a metaphor. In the old book, *Flat World*, the inhabitants live in a two-dimensional world and the example is given of how the two-dimensional consciousness experiences a three-dimensional object. Imagine a flat plane containing only length and width and no depth. Now imagine a ball passing through this plane (time or a higher dimension is needed for this action to actually occur, so we just have to assume it is there). The two-dimensional consciousness would not perceive a whole ball, just a series of dots that grow larger and larger until the widest part of the circumference of the ball passes. The series of dots would then get smaller until they disappeared altogether. Now think of a three-dimensional consciousness experiencing time in the same manner. The three-dimensional consciousness would see events in a linear way, iteration after iteration following one another, seamlessly like a flow. And it would seem to be moving and this movement is in a single direction. We have a very limited view of these things, as humans are trapped between a three-dimensional form and its persistence in time. Time is a thing with some sort of dimensionality. The beginning of time and the end of time (if such a concept could be grasped) are a single thing, a cohesive whole.

There are other dimensions beyond time that time exists within and so on. This means that our conscious experience of time is a series of events glued together by the persistence of the past, rushing outward into some unknown future event sequence. However, time is a single unit of dimensionality and it is our perception of it that is limited. The beginning and end of this earthly existence is a whole thing like the example of the ball passing through "Flat

World." We experience the iterations of events as our life passes through our conscious lens. Our consciousness doesn't shift position. We are always in a timeless place in the deepest part of our perception. In Uranian astrology, the Midheaven, the seat of the soul, represents this deep part of our perception. The universal key that binds together the miracle of life, that specific point of perception, is a function of the earth. Only the Midheaven is derived by the plane of the earth, the equator. All other factors involved with life are a function of the interplay of the earth and the Sun, the ecliptic. The soul or divine spark of life is captured by the Earth for its mortal existence and organizes life and is then released upon death or the disorganization of the life form.

From an objective point of view (if such a thing exists), life as it exists within time is a single unit. It is a single thing from beginning to end. Think of a time-lapse movie of a flower blooming and dying and think of that sequence as a single event. The beginning of organization, the birth, the bloom of life and its eventual decay and disintegration are a single thing, and I can't even call it an event. It is a whole and part of a larger whole interacting with all the other wholes creating a larger single whole, until we have the entire universe as a single entity.

Now, if the perception of linear time is an illusion, then fate and free will have a strange place in this arrangement. It would seem as if the entire outer world is fated and we have no objective choices at all. Not the case, we do have free will, but it is a perceptual free will, not a proactive one. Free will exists in how we perceive fated events, how we view them. We are endowed with the illusion of free will. This illusion postulates that we actually have conscious control or influence over the events affecting our consciousness and being. This process is necessary for our survival. Read the stories of the people who have had a direct experience of god-like energy. They seem to be thrust into a state of being that cannot be persisted in. It can only be glimpsed and experienced in a temporal way, and that experience uniformly has a life-changing quality to it. The people that come through such an experience seem to be at ease about the mortal existence and untroubled by events the future may hold. They display an acceptance of things that they cannot change and seem to realize that the only real experience is in one's own perceptions, not the fiction of what we call real or consider tangible.

Hadley Fitzgerald: English language dictionaries give the Greek root of "metaphysical" as "after the physical," and its connotative use in our modern lexicon tends toward separating what is physical from what isn't. However, the Greek roots also mean "among" and "with" what is "natural, native, in the order of nature." So I turn toward the Aristotelian view that human knowledge originates in the physical world, and from that experience the soul sees through to the universal. I'm likewise in accord with von Bertalanffy's systemic view that we live "in a universe, not of things, but of symbolic stand-ins for things," that the *breakdown* of that symbolic universe "contributes to the growing feeling of life's meaninglessness," thus placing life on this planet in true jeopardy. My metaphysical view of reality is that everything in and around us is part of a greater whole and is "talking" to us all the time. We can pay attention or not, but our understanding of who we are and why we're here is directly related to the breadth, depth, and duration of our attention span.

The separation of body, soul and spirit in my childhood experience of Catholic (and scientific) orthodoxy was so counterintuitive that the seeds for my metaphysical view of reality (still a work in progress) began with my "retirement" from Catholicism at age seventeen. I subsequently wandered for seven years in a spiritual desert until astrology found me and put me solidly on my path.

I believe the birth chart maps the evolutionary work the soul has (chosen) to do. I believe the body is the vehicle the soul uses in order to go about that work in this life on this earth. I prefer to think of "spirit" as more akin to "heart," and I believe the heart/spirit is a bridge that connects body and soul in a unique way. Castaneda's Don Juan offers wise counsel: "Look at every path closely and deliberately. Try it as many times as you think necessary. Then ask yourself and yourself alone one question . . . *Does this path have heart?* . . . If it does, the path is good; if it doesn't, it is of no use."

John Marchesella: I don't have a metaphysical view of reality. Obviously, the physical body encases our human existence; the spirit provides the vision to steer us through this existence; the soul allows us see beyond the human experience; and the intellect gives word to all of the above. I don't think they have any relationship to astrology directly, except to say that they are represented by the four elements. We can say astrology is a language that gives expression to body, mind, soul and spirit; then again, astrology is one language I can use to give some expression to the concept of my apartment or my dog.

35

Ken Bowser: I don't have a metaphysical view of reality *per se.* I have some assumptions, beliefs, and things I consider likely. I don't know what reality is in an ultimate sense. To be able to answer that requires knowledge of the meaning of life, so for me it's a rhetorical question. It appears to be a mass of energy, some of which is highly orderly. One is in it and part of it, but I don't think reality can be grasped until it has been fully assimilated. My guess is that only people like Jesus Christ or the Buddha know what reality is. Reality is apparently too big to grasp except insofar as one can get confirmation of some pieces of it experientially, either in the laboratory or through conscious realization. I assume that physical reality is a manifestation of God, but venturing into the realm of the metaphysical begs the question, "How do you know?"

Unless somebody can demonstrate how they know ultimate truths or get the big picture, I tend not to be impressed. I assume, though, that some people express such a high level of awareness that one can be impressed of it without extraneous demonstration. The Dalai Lama and Yogananda Paramahansa come to mind. I assume that the difference between body, soul and spirit is a vibratory rate or energy frequency difference. But if somebody said, "Prove it," I wouldn't know how. Talk is cheap and sanctimonious flim-flam is rampant in the world of astrology. Since I think astrology ultimately is, in fact, a spiritual discipline, I don't strain to realize it. I assume I'll be shown when the desire to exceed my current state of modest development becomes an overwhelming need.

Kim Rogers-Gallagher: I see the difference between body, soul and spirit—and I'd like to add emotions to that list—as the magical duties assigned to the four elements. My metaphysical view of reality is this: I do believe in a higher power—I don't see how you can possibly look around this gorgeous planet and *not* believe in one—but I don't think you can label it "God," at least not in the traditional sense. When I'm grateful, hopeful, or in a fix, I usually talk to my Uncle Jupiter—Sagittarius's ruling planet—or The Goddess, since I feel more comfortable talking to a woman (after all, she'd be my girlfriend, right?) and I love the Druid/Pagan belief system. I wholeheartedly believe in reincarnation, and am delighted to see the emerging popularity of evolutionary astrology.

Robert Hand: My metaphysics are basically a modified Neo-Platonism. The main modification I have made in my Neo-Platonism is that I give the physical universe a much more important and positive role in the scheme of the universe than does the classical Neo-Platonist. In accordance with that, I consider the body to be the material aspect of the self, the soul to be both that which confirms life upon each living being, and that which makes each living person unique and in particular that special living person. Spirit I consider to be a word desperately in search of a definition. There is another term which I prefer, *Nous*, which is the Greek word for that which knows, one might say "consciousness," although that is another word that needs more precision in its definition. I believe that much of the conventional notion of spirit is derived from the philosophical conception of *Nous*, but the word "spirit" has become all mixed up with "soul."

I believe that astrology is a natural language which shows, through its symbols and methods, paths by which the soul realizes itself in matter and attempts to reach the most perfect and authentic definition of itself that can be done under the circumstances of the time and place of birth.

Robert Schmidt: From the study of Plato, I have become convinced that what we now call reality cannot be accounted for in terms of "the One" or any single principle alone, but another principle must be posited as well. Plato evidently called this other principle the "Indeterminate Dyad." In my view, the knee-jerk assumption of the primacy of the One has been detrimental to modern Western thought, and thereby to the foundations of astrology.

Whereas the One is the principle of all Self-Sameness, the Indeterminate Dyad is the principle of all Otherness, Difference, Contradiction, and Contrariety. Neither principle is prior to the other. In their interactions with one another, these two principles are together responsible for everything that is—consciousness, soul and materiality. In this view, soul may be regarded as the relating of One and Dyad, body and materiality the relatedness of One and Dyad; the soul touches the body and is touched or stirred in return. Although Plato would put consciousness (what I would call "spirit" for the purposes of this question) in a self-sufficient realm above the soul, I see it as the contact of soul with body, their relating and relatedness with one another.

In Plato's *Timaeus*, which seems to have provided the cosmological model for Hellenistic astrology, the two Platonic principles are correlated to the two primary celestial motions. The diurnal motion in its sameness is called the "motion of the Same;" the motion of the planets around the ecliptic in its inconstancy is called the motion of the "Other." The combination of these two motions constitutes the life of the cosmic soul, and this is the domain of astrological phenomena.

Ronnie Gale Dreyer: I am not sure how to answer this question, since I don't subscribe to any particular metaphysical view of reality. And if I do, it is not something I can easily articulate. I do believe that one's spirit, meaning how positive and at peace one is with oneself, has a lot to do with the physical body. Spiritual and emotional well-being usually leads to a healthier body. I say usually in that I do not believe that everything is related to our mind, and that everything in our body can be controlled. We also are genetically predisposed to things, including body shape and weaknesses, and our environment and upbringing have had a lot to do with our physical well-being. In terms of Jyotish, the mind and emotions are directly related to our physical well-being and this can be seen especially from the Moon, since this luminary rules our spiritual and emotional well-being as well as the body. Of course, the Ascendant and Sun also represent our stamina and our constitution.

Steven Forrest: My view is that we are all ancient streams of consciousness, evolving in mysterious ways towards goals we feel deeply but cannot even utter—or when we try to put them into words, we tie ourselves in silly knots of contradiction. This would follow logically if we assume that we attempting to describe an n-dimensional reality in three-dimensional terms, which I believe is a good way of saying it.

I accept the reality of reincarnation. I accept the purposeful, non-randomness of life, despite appearances. I do believe in the integration of body, mind, and spirit—in that sense I am really more a "pagan" than a representative of the Judeo-Christian-Buddhist-Hindu-Islamic tradition. I smile to write it that way, but there's a serious point here. Those traditions tend to look askance upon "this world." I don't. This world is just another plane of experience, another "astral plane," so to speak. Ask any physicist nowadays: we are made of dream-stuff. But being here, in these bodies, is a good thing. There are rich experiences available through our senses. They push us forward in the evolutionary journey.

The simple fact of our embodied presence here, in this benign, purposeful universe, suggests that we have reached a stage in our journeys where we *need* to be here. We benefit from immersing our senses in certain specific patterns of worldly experience, available only here, in this plane of reality. Those experiences are evolutionary rocket fuel—and their natures are described in detail in the astrological birthchart. That, to me, is very much the heart of astrology.

The chart describes two truths. The first is the pre-existing condition of the evolving soul—our *karmic predicament* at birth, in terms of strengths and weakness, sight and blindness. The second is our *evolutionary intentions* for this lifetime—what we are aiming to learn and what experiences will best support us in that evolution. The rest—all the usual astrological obsession about our personality traits—is nothing but the tools for the job.

Wendy Z. Ashley: I am not certain that I can express even for my own edification what my metaphysical view of reality is, certainly not in brief. I do believe that science gives us a good window on reality up to a point. I believe that what is called metaphysics is physics that has not yet been discovered. And there are limitations to what science is willing to address, to our impoverishment. The old debate between science and astrology is not yet dead—it still goes on to the detriment of both sides. Science is unwilling to address "meaning." This is where it falls short in function. Neither physics nor metaphysics gives the whole truth.

As to the body, mind, soul, and spirit differentiation derived from the four Elements used in Western Astrology, I would say that myth makes available a multilayered approach to the reading. Although I loosely subscribe to the Fire Earth Air Water schema that we inherited from Aristotle, primarily because it is rooted in a hoary tradition of a quartered cosmos that is itself a widely based metaphor, the usual use of the Elements is not as vital to my interpretation. Instead, in myth, body, mind, soul and spirit may be understood as four of the many layers or dimensions of the whole. For practical purposes these are indivisible when we live embodied on Earth. In other words, with myth one can do a reading about the physical-body world, or about the mental life, or about the emotions or about the spiritual life, using the same planets as attributes of any of these. I might add one could also do a reading about the family life, the social life, the philosophic structure and so on and so forth. What is harder for me to believe is that any of these are discrete or different. I believe the body-soul differentiation is perhaps a Christian notion, derived from Aristotelian thought. As such it is itself a belief structure. We are creatures who make sense of the world by classifications and systems of order. Astrology is just such a classification. We know its roots go back at least 17,000 years to the Paleolithic caves of southern France. I suspect it is 60,000 years old, actually.

4. HOW DOES ASTROLOGY WORK? IN WHAT WAY DO THE PLANETS, SIGNS AND HOUSES EXERT THEIR INFLUENCE? DOES THIS INFLUENCE "IMPEL" OR "COMPEL"? ON WHAT PART OF OUR BEING DOES IT OPERATE? CAN ASTROLOGY BE RECONCILED WITH ANY SCIENTIFIC MODELS OF REALITY?

Demetra George: I do not think that astrology can be reconciled with any current scientific model of reality. It is impossible to prove that the planets have any physical causal influences upon human behavior, and, in any case, I do not think that this is the way that astrology operates. Astrology can only work in a world view in which the cosmos is seen as a living, intelligent being, with a mind and a soul, as Plato suggested over 2,000 years ago. Planets, signs and houses do not exert any influence whatsoever; they neither impel nor compel. Rather, as the celestial handwriting of the cosmic mind, they simply describe what is. To the extent that individuals and events are not anything other than parts of this universal consciousness in manifested form, they will naturally conform to patterning implicit in this creative mind, which has been called by various philosophers the Form of the Good, the Prime Mover, the One, the Monad, and God, in the same way that the cells of the human body conform to the patterning of the DNA code.

Evelyn Roberts: I believe the heavens are the perfect mirror on a cosmic scale of our individual soul's condition. The natal chart is the seed that contains the potential for the unfolding of a life's journey. It is a map of the psyche, which the individual unconsciously projects onto the world, and through that mirroring is confronted with his or her soul's work. The heavens provide the bigger picture. It is again the holographic model of the whole being reflected in every part. Impel or compel? I think it our inescapable destiny to confront our own soul; the way we do this has more to do with individual nature, resistance or surrender than anything else. I don't believe the planets "do" anything to us; they reflect us and guide us as navigational tools on our earthly journey.

Through my eyes all of life is miraculous and mysterious; I don't believe there is a meaningless moment. I can't begin to analyze life through the eyes of a scientist, but if we only consider what is visible to the naked eye or technically measurable, then life is robbed of its divine essence and looks pretty bleak.

Many scientific thinkers are acknowledging astrology and some are deeply involved in it, and those numbers are rising. Perhaps it is just my nature to feel optimistic, but to me it feels positive. It is a modern idea to eliminate consideration for the divine from life; there was a time this was unthinkable. When we allow the soul its rightful place in the sciences, it can only add to its gifts.

Gary Christen: Astrology works through resonance. There will always be folks looking for mechanistic means to explain how astrology works. I learned very early that any closed system would reflect the conditions of the general universe. What causal mechanism creates this phenomenon is still a mystery, if there is one in the first place. The simple ideas of synchronicity do not postulate a mechanistic causal view of the machine of astrology. So from the current worldview, there must be some sort of mechanism. Yet, observation shows resonance at work with no word as to how, as far as I know.

I can only offer metaphors or analogies to describe this problem. The best analogy comes from the work of Dr. Rupert Sheldrake in his book entitled *Presence of the Past*. In it he describes how a primitive people with a mechanistic worldview would react to a television. In this story, the first question would be, "How do you get the people into the little box?"

The answer would be, "Invisible waves propagated into the sky and received by this little metal pole."

"No, we can't believe you, invisible waves, indeed," the primitives reply, "They must get in through this little string connecting the back of the box to the wall."

The primitives then proceed to take the box apart and notice that as they change settings inside the box that the picture is distorted. They come to the conclusion that the picture must originate from impulses contained in the wire and that the setting controls inside the box create the picture from this measurable hardware and energy coming into the box. So of course the wrong conclusion is reached as the primitives continue to distort the picture in a quest to ferret out the causes of this phenomenon.

Whatever the conditions that enable the analogy between planetary movement and corresponding human and natural phenomena, it works. This observation of the working of astrology came before any need to explain why it works. In our current world paradigm of reason and enlightenment, dating from the Renaissance, astrology has been put on the defensive. Never have the

41

mechanists taken astrology for its own worth and then attempted to find some explanatory model to describe why it works. They have only placed the field on the defensive by dismissing it without any investigation, on the logical grounds that since there is no rational explanation for astrology's workings, the astrological thesis cannot be plausible and must rely on belief and faith.

As seen by my statements in the previous questions, the idea of "impelling" or "compelling" living things from planetary "influences" is a little absurd. Earthquakes and other earthly events correlate with planetary alignments just like living things. Again it comes to the "fate versus freewill" question, and it is the invisible realms and our perceptions that determine choice, not the outer events that surround this process.

The current scientific models are relics of an uninformed age. There is a quiet but pervasive revolt going on in scientific and academic circles, and some elements of the astrological debate are greatly influencing the reasons for this slow change in thinking. We are winning this debate, slowly and surely. Our first allies were the early quantum physicists, and later the debate picked up speed when the movers in the fields of history of science and philosophy of science began to question the organized and systematic blackballing of astrology. There is a large vested interest in the scientific community based upon the rejection of the astrological hypothesi. Beliefs are at stake, and that translates into the competition for research money, educational funds and other perks that employ large numbers of people. This is not just a dry academic debate. Scientism in the mechanistic sense will eventually be realized as just another mystery religion requiring faith in a flawed doctrine based on an incomplete understanding of the basic premises of the working of the universe.

Hadley Fitzgerald: For all my years of using the valuable insights wrought via the astrological symbol system, I still have no idea how astrology "works"—at least in any sense that science or the "logical/rational" mind will, at this time, accept. Although the work of brilliant scientists like Victor Mansfield and Will Keepin is surely bringing us closer than we've ever been to a scientific rationale for astrology, Keepin is particularly careful to point out that astrology seeks to "map out the wisdom of the implicate order," and since meaning can't be quantified, astrology cannot ultimately be proved scientifically.

In any case, science evinces little interest in finding such meaning, let alone contemplating its ramifications. The scientific model describes reality by looking through a particular lens and requiring precise replications of the findings therein. Most of us who explore reality through a *meta*-physical lens don't discount science at all; we simply have a different focus. I'm often baffled by the stridency of those who seem desperate to prove astrology has no validity. I'm equally troubled by the formulaic misbeliefs these skeptics *continue* to hold—i.e., that contemporary astrologers purport a tangible, physical *influence* of the planets on the affairs of humans; that astrological tenets absolve people of responsibility for their life choices and decisions; that the primary purpose of modern astrology is to predict the future.

The idea of planets, signs and houses "exerting" an influence—as in "impelling" or "compelling" or both—has always struck me as rather odd. Astrology is a *language*, a *symbol* system. It signals, indicates, describes an interconnection, gives us access to and/or a representation of *some*thing that has its basis in the dimension of the numinous, the realm of the fundamentally indescribable. "Psyche" and "soul" are the still somewhat limited and synonymous terms for the part of us through which all of this operates. Michael Meade describes it as that place within us where "we long for the moments when the world behind the world enters the common life of things and we can feel the coincidence of eternity with time." Astrology provides a vast, superb bridge between our common life and the world behind the world; my experience tells me we've taken only our first few steps across it.

John Marchesella: Astrology works according to that part of the mind that is able to interpret symbols, and even more basic to that, it's that part of the mind that can endow something with symbolic content, be it chicken bones or stars. Astrology just happens to be one of the more complex and sophisticated systems of symbols. It works according to our quest for meaning. Other than that, I'd refer you to Jung's beautifully crafted mumbo-jumbo on the topic of *a priori*. (I do say that with respect and not irreverently.)

As for how the planets, signs and houses exert their influence, well, I think it's the other way around. We exert our influence on them! When the image in the mirror moves, the mirror isn't doing anything but reflecting; the object that is creating the image is actually doing the moving. So, I would say we project our inner states and knowledge (most of which is unconscious) onto the planets, signs and houses, in order to see ourselves.

Generally speaking, the parts of the psyche that are represented by the inner planets and have to answer to the Sun impel; the same goes for the softer aspects even if they involve outer planets. Whatever is antithetical to the ego, i.e. hard aspects and the planets beyond Saturn, compels. (Well, at least until a little psychotherapy or self-awareness, whichever comes first, enters the picture.)

Finally, when scientific models of reality acknowledge the dynamics of the model, then such a reconciliation will take place. However, let's not be childish about this. If astrology and science united, we must admit that there would then be another force created to maintain some sort of divide. Otherwise. we are simply magically thinking that the Great Father and Mother reunite and live happily ever after, or even more so, wishing that we could return to the womb. The split between science and soul fuels our quest for meaning.

Ken Bowser: I don't know the answer to this line of questioning and would be surprised if anybody does. If there is a way to demonstrate whether astrology is causal or symbolic, it has not been shown to date as far as I know. Short of such a demonstration, my view is that all such speculation about the matter is fruitless.

I suspect though that the answer to the question is consciousness-related, that is, those of us who are making do at a level of awareness that precludes knowing the answer to this question are forever shut out from the answer until our awareness is greater. In other words, the answer is probably a corollary of higher consciousness. You might as well pose the question, "What happens when we die?" Most people have a belief about the matter, and many think they know, but their positions are a far cry from knowing that can demonstrated. It's important to know that you know and not to confound knowledge with belief and assumption. All that can be said about the matter is that almost everybody feels a connection to a part of life which is beyond the here and now, or is a greater realization of the here and now than most of us enjoy, but that doesn't put people in a position to describe what is beyond their consciousness. Many claim high awareness, but if one puts oneself on another level, it has to be demonstrated or it's just talk.

I would only comment—and this comment is supposition based upon experience—that the stars tend to compel. I think fate is the operative agent in the world and that people have far less free will than they suspect. That statement begs the question, "What is the nature of fate versus free will?" I can't answer it. I think, though, that the position confidently embraced today with regard to people being autonomous free will agents is probably the ultimate absurdity. If that were true, the entire structure of astrology—which strikes me as clearly fatalistic—would collapse. Astrologers are assailed on this point constantly and have finally caved in since psychological astrology (the effect of Rudhyar's work) took over astrology in the West about forty years ago. Now that it is unpopular to say otherwise, astrologers have contended for the past several decades that their art is not really fatalistic; yet an astrologer has nothing to work with if people are not predisposed toward conditions, other people and circumstances in a predictable manner. That doesn't make us robots, rather actors reading scripts so that we can learn parts. Shakespeare was right: "All the world's a stage." The fashion of an era doesn't make astrology anything more or less than it really is. In the end what matters is to do it well, and all the talk about what astrology is or isn't strikes me as a distraction. I suspect that one doesn't come to understand the fate versus free will question by debating the issue but by practicing the art.

Kim Rogers-Gal lager: I believe astrology "works" for a very old-fashioned reason—one whose simplicity completely belies its genius: "As above, so below." After all, what could make more sense? In my opinion, our solar system is probably, in effect, a "cell" on a larger entity's "body," one of billions that work together, much like cells in our own bodies, to achieve a single goal. So of *course* cycles here on earth mirror and demonstrate the movements of the planets—we're *part* of the same "body" that they're part of, tied together in a "dance" of sorts, dictated by the rhythm of that body. Which leads very nicely to the subject of my humble opinion on through what process the planets, signs and houses exert their influence. I don't think they "exert" anything at all. They're all just part of a "living model" of what's going on in the entity we belong to—or "live on."

I also don't believe astrological factors either "impel" or "compel." I believe they simply provide us with a map—our own personal blueprint. Basically, I see the astrology chart as a very cut-and-dried assessment of what we're each made of, and what types of occurrences we can each expect to encounter throughout life. If we're clever enough to figure out just a tenth of what that "map" really means, we have an invaluable tool. If we were clever enough to understand all of it, I believe we'd be able to predict literally everything that will ever happen to us—and who it will happen with. But to say the chart either impels or compels is to imply, in a manner of speaking, that our knowledge of our chart is the reason it "works." It's not. Astrology doesn't need for us to believe in it to "work." It just does.

45

I don't believe these energies "operate" through a single or separate "part" of us. I think these energies simply describe us—everything about us.

I suppose that what I've just done is rewritten the macrocosm/microcosm theory. As a result, I guess my vote for the "scientific theory about reality that most accurately reflects what astrology really is," would go to the macrocosm/microcosm theory of life.

Robert Hand: I do not claim to know precisely how astrology works, but I am convinced that it does not work according to any model that would be acceptable to modern science. In fact I believe that what makes astrology far more important than it might otherwise be seen to be lies precisely in the fact that it *cannot* be explained by any modern scientific model of how the universe works. If astrology is in any meaningful sense real, then the modern scientific world view cannot be. This is not to say that science has no value. It obviously does have value. What I am saying is that if astrology has significant validity, then our view of reality cannot be limited to what science believes. It has to be much larger than that. Also, I do not mean to say that there are no measurable scientific phenomena behind astrology. There may very well be. And I believe that attempts to do research in astrology using conventional scientific means are well worth doing. I only object to limiting our view of reality to what such science can deal with.

I do not believe that whatever planetary influences there might be are determinative. That is to say, there is no necessary or inevitable outcome to any particular astrological combination. We may not be in total control of how any astrological combination in our charts may manifest. Such control, I believe, requires a degree of wisdom that most of us do not possess. But it is lack of wisdom, not planetary power, that deprives us of control. Fundamentally, I believe that astrology is the result of some kind of consciousness in the universe communicating with us by means of a symbolic language. This language has been created by it and by us. The details are obviously not clear, but I believe that this model is much closer to the reality behind astrology than any kind of model based on mechanical causation. I leave the identity of what that other consciousness may be to the theologians.

Robert Schmidt: According to my reconstruction of Hellenistic astrology, it was based on the following hypotheses: (1) that the cosmos is a living animal possessing both body and soul; (2) that the soul of the cosmic animal is infused with a rational consciousness, which is capable of knowing what may, can, and ought to happen in the human world; (3) that these cognitions have the structure of language, consistent with the classical presupposition that thinking is internalized speaking; (4) that the cosmic consciousness is creative or generative, using the cosmic soul as an instrument to realize the above-mentioned possibilities for human life, in much the same way that our own souls can move our own bodies once we have decided to take some action; (5) that this cosmic consciousness expresses its creative cognitions about human life through the observable celestial phenomena, in much the same way that we express our inner states by facial features or body language, which means that the celestial phenomena used by astrologers also have the structure of language; (6) that the role of the astrologer is to understand what the cosmic consciousness knows about his client through its creative activity.

I would describe this Hellenistic model of how astrology works as primarily epistemological, with a causal component. However, the planets do not cause anything directly at the material level as one body acting upon another; rather, they express the manner in which the cosmic soul is moving or bringing about changes in the cosmic body as directed by the cosmic consciousness. To the best of my knowledge, how the human soul moves the human body is still a mystery to modern science, so I don't see how modern science can be of much help in understanding how the cosmic soul moves the cosmic body. Finally, in this view, the planets do not work through the human being at all, but rather bring about events in the human world.

Ronnie Gale Dreyer: I don't know how to answer this question. I really do not know why the planets work, and I am not really acquainted with contemporary scientific models of reality. I take it on faith that indeed "as above, so below," and that the heavenly bodies exert influence on us. The horoscope and astrology simply proves that point over and over. I really cannot say more than that.

Steven Forrest: This is a fascinating and subversive question. I went into some detail about it in my 1993 book, *The Night Speaks.* There is actually a vast body of empirical evidence for the interaction of astronomical forces and cycles with physical and biological systems. In terms of a theoretical understanding of how astrology works, I've been particularly impressed with the work of Percy Seymour, who wrote *Astrology: The Evidence of Science.* His approach starts off with the notion of electromagnetic interactions between the Earth's magnetic field and those of the planets. As the planets shift position, the Earth's field is subjected to constantly shifting magnetic vectors, and it reflects those shifts—and also amplifies them through an arcane process of tidal resonance in the ionosphere. That is very "straight" science. Add another piece of straight science: the human body is an electromagnetic system, and its field is impacted by the larger fields around it. One more elegant touch: the amniotic fluid, with its high salt content, is a pretty good electromagnetic insulator. Thus, at birth, the child's body/brain system emerges from the insulation, and is imprinted "at the first breath" with the earth's electromagnetic field, which in turn reflects the positions of the planets. Seymour's work has many subtleties and refinements, but that is the bones of it. To me, it makes a lot of sense.

The trouble with it—and with any physical theory of astrological influence, for that matter—is that astrology does things that cannot be explained that way. Horary astrology is a prime example. One sets up the chart for the birth of a question, such as "Where did I leave my car keys?" One applies some technical procedures, and very often comes up with the correct answer. The problem here is that *the question has no body*. There is nothing here for the geomagnetic field to act upon. Yet horary works. We could make similar arguments for the charts of corporations. There are astrologers making lots of money by looking at the transits to the charts of businesses on the world's various stock exchanges. But a business has no physical body either.

Many of us nowadays think in terms of *synchronicity* as the mechanism behind astrology: Jung's famous "acausal connecting principle." That basically means the inherent meaningfulness of the universe "causes" things to occur, such as the way the Tarot cards tend to fall in meaningful patterns. I'm very comfortable with that notion, but I think Percy Seymour is onto something too.

None of this is really my field of expertise, but my gut feeling is that "astrology" is a word that embraces a lot of different dimensions, forces and realities, like the word "schizophrenia." In psychiatry, that word isn't used so much anymore. It's been replaced by more distinct and precise sub-categories. I wouldn't be surprised if something similar happens as astrology evolves: we will hear the word "astrology" less and less, as it is replaced by a variety of individual disciplines reflecting entirely different dimensions of the Earth-sky relationship.

As to the question of to what extent astrology can be reconciled with current scientific models of reality, we could make some interesting correlations between it and certain branches of the "new physics:" the uncertainty principle, ten-dimensional analysis, action-at-a-distance, superluminal processes. Maybe that will yield some harmony between science and astrology. But right now, I think there is a basic gulf between science and astrology, and that maybe we shouldn't be too urgent in our haste to bridge it. I think astrology has a long way to go. And true science is always "just beginning." My sense is that as the two disciplines evolve over the next hundred years, the trend will be increasingly toward their reconciliation. It will happen naturally, simply through each being true to its own course—because behind all our talk lies one single truth, and all roads lead there, eventually.

Wendy Z. Ashley: This question is easier to answer by acknowledging how it does *not* work. And scientists who oppose the study and practice of astrology oppose it on this basis: it does not work by any mechanistic physics that we now know, that is, not by any tidal or gravitational force. That is, not by Newton's first law of Physics. It is true that the Sun and Moon are near enough to have a gravitational effect upon Earth dwellers. But these effects most likely do not account in the main for why astrology should work. Nor does astrology work by any occult laws, if there are such things, although there have been writers to this effect, notably Emanuel Swedenborg. However, the lore of astrology is so old, and therefore its practices have so stood the tests of time, that its practitioners simply say, "It works."

To show a comparison: a painter need not know the physiology of the eye, the science of optics and the affects of symbol upon the psyche in order to produce an affecting painting. The painting "works" without the painter knowing what science lies behind his "art." So it is that the astrologer need not know what science lies behind her "art."

There were of course a great many discoveries in optics during the Renaissance, and those scientific discoveries did influence painting at the time. Certainly we know Leonardo was interested. Knowledge of the science behind seeing did not detract from Leonardo's art at all. In fact the techniques of perspective derived from that science soon began to be seen in the works of less scientifically inclined painters. Knowledge of the techniques improved paintings to the degree that the artist could better represent what the viewer saw in nature with his own eyes. Nowadays perspective is taught in every school with courses in drawing, in spite of the fact that representational painting does not now have the prestige it used to have.

Another example closer to the average individual's experience is that one need not know Newton's Three Laws of motion to drive an automobile down the road, even though those laws are very important to how an automobile can be driven. One needn't even know much at all about the workings of the automobile to drive one. We have mechanics to rely upon for that, although those who do know about the mechanisms are no doubt better drivers to some degree. But in spite of the fact that astrology "works" we have yet—in modern times—to be assured of what it is that makes it work. This is not so extraordinary when we know that there are other mysteries as great. We do not know for example what it is that makes an organism "alive." And we do not know what it is that causes us to "fall in love." (Of course astrologers would say it is Venus that causes love to happen.) And that is to the point. Venus is one of the planets, and at the same time Venus is a goddess. As a goddess she has a power. She rules over all things related to love. Without her, love cannot happen. Her planet then has her power.

Astrologers, scorned as they are by scientists, in reaction are tempted to find a scientific explanation for how and why astrology works. And when Newtonian physics fail to fit the bill, we look to some other explanation. We imagine if electromagnetic waves emanating from the planetary bodies or from their cyclical behaviors may not fit the bill as causative. I am not equipped to write with confidence about the laws of physics. I do believe we are getting closer to a time when physics will provide an understanding of how astrology works.

If astrology is a "woo-woo" topic for the scientist, it should be known that physics has been getting pretty "woo-woo" itself lately. What with Einstein's Special Theory of Relativity, Chaos Theory, Bell's Theorem, Unified Field Theory, and whatnot, we may be getting so far out we are getting to the core of it—the "it" being why astrology works.

We must consider this, that these new discoveries by sciences begin to remind us of the resonating metaphors of ancient cosmologies and mythologies. In fact, Chaos Theory with its fractals messes up what we've been using as geometry for a couple of thousand years. Euclidian geometry (circa 300 B.C.E.)—which astrologers use to plot aspects on the paper chart (and monitor screen chart, too)—does not hold up in hyperbolical and spherical systems, i.e. space. Which is where the real astrology happens. It's great for architecture and building, though, or local space.

There are two new geometries that can be used as a better model for what happens in location and time in space. They are called hyperbolic geometry and elliptical geometry. If the geometry of space is hyperbolic, then the universe will expand infinitely. If space geometry is elliptical, then the universe will expand up to a point, whereupon it will then shrink back to its Big Bang beginning, and maybe start all over again.

These compare to two cultural mythic cosmologies. The first is comparable to the Germanic myth where the world is eventually coming to a time when all life will end and even the gods will die. The second is comparable to Hindu myth that proposes that the universe breathes in and out over vast eons of time. When it breathes in, all of life is ended, when it breathes out, all of life returns again. Indeed, science now parallels myth as explanation. It almost asks, "which side do you favor?" The one you favor is the side you are on. The one you favor colors which you choose to do research on. Furthermore, Chaos Theory has replaced the clockwork universe notion developed at the same time that clocks were developed (and the clockwork notion ultimately developed out of the perfect forms notions of Plato and Euclid). In this way it is all a metaphor. It is not so much what it is we know, but how we need constructions by which we know.

One of the newest constructions (ideas) is Chaos Theory. It explores irregularities in form and movement. And it has demonstrated that we (in Western Science) have been laboring under a delusion. Chaos is not the antithesis of Cosmos. In fact Chaos is necessary to life. Chaos and Cosmos interact.

It turns out that the irregularities have dynamic regularities. The fractals of Chaos Theory have a geometry that is not static but is instead dynamic—in motion and flux. In fractal geometry a shape replicates itself regardless of scale. It can get—or be—larger and larger, or smaller and smaller. As each new "generation" of them is made they are just slightly "off" of regularity. A good visual example is the seed pattern on the face of a sunflower, in which mathematicians have seen a pattern described as "the Fibonacci series," a mathematical progression of numbers which seems to replicate—like fractals replicate—throughout nature. It is a fractal pattern of a dynamic of growth. There are only so many fractal patterns; perhaps these may be coalesced in the dynamics—movements—of the planets. These were once thought to move in regular Euclidian order.

Mercury is not so much an influence as a dynamic pattern which is replicated here and there fractally. Everything that lies close to the center and "jumps" quickly from spot A to spot D is astrologically "ruled" by Mercury.

That is because they are in the same order of fractal occurrences. Mercury behaves unpredictably because it lies within the effects of the Sun's enormous mass, so its position is altered by the way the Sun's mass makes space curve in its vicinity. Of course we have telescopes that enable us to plot Mercury's orbit, but it was once hard to predict.

So Mercury became the planet/god of the Trickster. Since it always is so near to the Sun, it became the Jester to the King. It became the sidekick to the Hero. It is Mercutio to Romeo. It is the advisor to the Caliph. Since it only makes its appearances at the hours of sunrise and sunset, it became the voices of the birds that herald those shifts between day and night, between the conscious and the unconscious times. Mercury is Hermes, guide of souls to and from the underworld. In "primitive" or animistic religions, Mercury took the form of animals which ventured at the borders of the cultivated and the wild worlds. The fox at the edge of the woods, the rabbit in the garden, and the squirrel in the seed bin are all small "Mercury" animals. Mercury is small, its orbit is small. The god Mercury was depicted as a beardless youth. He was a thief, like the fox, the rabbit and the squirrel. As the voice of the herald he was a singing or scolding bird. He was the cock who announced sunrise and the three cries of the cock that announced Saint Peter as a betrayer and a liar. He is that inner voice of dialogue with your warning half and is also the provocateur. We've seen this in old cartoons where the character has a little angel sitting on one shoulder and a little devil on the other. No one else can see these two characters but the hero of our story, and of course we the audience can see them. "Aw, go on" says the Devil. "What can it hurt?" "You'd better not," warns the angel. Mercury is twinned in this way because it is both Morning and Evening star. Since it appears before the Sun in the morning, it is "bright." Since it appears at Sunset it is "dark."

The Sign Gemini is Mercury's Sign. The twins are light and dark, good and bad. We have a choice. Being so near to the Sun, Mercury is the "observer of Ego," the witness to the self. Jiminy is another way of saying Gemini. You will recall Jiminy Cricket as the guide to Pinocchio, who sings " . . . and always let your conscience be your guide." So it is not that the planet Mercury influences the individual as a force, gravitational or electromagnetic or occult, but rather that it is a fractal form which all beings/forms/situations who have evolved to live in this solar system have within, a dynamic which happens then simultaneously way out there and also within—as well as everywhere else that is "between two worlds." As such Mercury is both a code, and a dynamic occurring at all scales and in all forms simultaneously.

It is not that Gemini is a sign that causes its natives to be talkative or to be shallow or to be intellectual. Rather it is that all of the signs and constellations make up a vast grid of interrelated forces in appropriate proximity to one another and in seasonal sequence, each of which has a fractal structure in relationship to all other fractal structures. The horoscope, which contains all of these, is like the DNA strand that contains only so many genetic elements such as everyone has, and such as every cell of every individual has each arranged in its own individual pattern. And whether the fractals are biological, psychological, sociological, spiritual, or genetic, each is responsive to that pattern, each of these being in its "primitive" cosmology but a layer of the same thing. Furthermore the planets', signs' and houses' operations are not only within as biological, spiritual, or psychological constructs and dynamics having their own schedule of formation and manifestation and eruption, etc., they are also external to us in the form of people, places, situations, objects, etc., that are also manifestations of the archetype existing in and of themselves. Our contact with these are not only projections, as the promoters of the archetype of the self as the creator of Maya or illusion would have us believe, but rather of the linkages on the great web of all of life. When I am under the "influence" of Mercury, I will then by "fate" encounter the thief, book, bird, or message. I will notice that someone has accidentally dropped an unmailed letter in the hall. It is addressed to Osama Bin Laden. Should I open it? Mail it? Read it? Leave it? I face a life's choice, dependent in part upon my values, strengths, and weaknesses. I have free will insofar as my character compels one behavior or another. But it is Fate or Mercury's time to address me. This was spoken of, in ancient times, as an appearance or manifestation of a god. This is metaphor, and metaphor is the best way to describe a fractal dynamic.

In this way, Mercury (as well as all of the other planets) cannot be said to compel, but to impel. That is because the very nature of the planet (dynamic fractal form) is always implicit, not explicit. And because its manifestation is only of a sort (all things having the property of that fractal pattern and dynamic), it is not possible to discern just which form it will take at its next appearance. When next Mercury shows up, will it be as a boy or a bird, as a letter or a phone call, as a thief or a joke, as a toy stuffed fox or a doorjamb? We cannot know for a certainty. Therefore astrology must use "omenclature," not "nomenclature." This drives people who study the prophecies of Nostradamus crazy! This is why some modern astrologers disdain all predictive astrology. This is what Jung tells us when he says:

> "The ground principles, the archai, of the unconscious are indescribable because of their wealth of reference . . . The discriminating intellect naturally keeps on trying to establish their singleness of meaning and thus misses the essential point; for what we can above all establish as the one thing consistent with their nature is their manifold meaning, their almost limitless wealth of reference, which makes any unilateral formulation impossible."
> —C.G. Jung (*Collected Works*, vol. 9, p. 80.)

In this regard Mercury is a ground principle—an archai. Jung means a primary archetype. The wealth of reference to which he refers are the multiplicities of possible manifestations. We could imagine that each of these has 1,474 possible manifestations. With Mercury they are bird, fox, rabbit, letter, joke, word, telegraph, telegram, piece of paper, small child, question, etc. etc. These for astrologers would be available in their books on keywords. What is amazing is that astrologers do as well as they do in descriptions and predictions.

It is not that astrology is inadequate to science, but rather that the application of the new physics is inadequate to an understanding of the process of life, and of course only then could it be used to demonstrate the "validity" of astrology. Quantum physics, Chaos Theory and Bell's Theorem have no application in psychological, biological or psychological models as yet. When they do, we will be closer to a rapprochement with astrology. In fact it may be that it is astrology that can demonstrate the functions of fractals in the psychic life of living beings. Of course astrologers too are way behind the times. The sky itself as dramatic imprint is not given credence. The piece of paper upon which the chart is drawn is NOT the horoscope. There is a vast lore of myth that lies behind astrology. Astrology lost sight of its mythic roots and truths long ago. After all, it was Socrates's crime that he debunked myth, and debunked the Gods as infantile images, over 2,300 years ago in Greece. It was shortly after that that astrology was transmogrified into a schema through a desire to regularize it. Surely something as perfect as the heavens was constructed in perfect, i.e. geometrically perfect form! From its geometric forms came its mechanistic mode. From its mechanistic mode came its regularity derived from a regularized order. Its regularized order came from its being derived from scientific laws.

With Chaos Theory we no longer have regularity. What a relief. It's like taking off a girdle. But it makes the learning of astrology more complex. In order for astrology to work even better it must be re-mythologized. Only then can its very useful codes restore MAGIC to our lives.

5. WHAT IS CONSCIOUSNESS? WHAT IS THE RELATIONSHIP BETWEEN ASTROLOGY AND CONSCIOUSNESS? CAN YOU DETERMINE SOMEONE'S LEVEL OF CONSCIOUSNESS FROM HIS OR HER BIRTHCHART?

Demetra George: Consciousness is awareness. Consciousness is not being passed out, bodily or mentally. Consciousness is being aware that your thoughts and actions affect yourself and others, and taking responsibility for the outcomes. If the astrological chart is used in such a way to understand one's motivations and behavior better, so as not to affect oneself or others adversely, it can be a tool to increase one's level of consciousness.

In general, I do not think that the level of a person's consciousness can be determined from their birth chart. The birth chart has the potential to describe the kinds of events that a person will experience, and to a certain extent their actions. However, the motivation behind the action is the real key to the level of consciousness, and that can change over a lifetime as awareness is increased in terms of how we actually do impact others. A person can still have the same action, but depending on the motivation, it will be with more or less consciousness. On the other hand, the more well-integrated the individual components of the chart are with one another, the more the potential exists for the individual to be conscious of his or her actions. But this is not a factor easily determined by contemporary astrological methods.

Evelyn Roberts: Consciousness means being awake in the broadest sense. It is honest self-reflection and examination on a path of acceptance, truth, integration, receptiveness, active participation and compassion. It includes admitting when we don't know and accepting that, and the ability to be wrong and to make amends. I strongly believe that consciousness involves knowing, accepting and working with our shadow material, or there are always demons in the basement. Transforming not transcending is key; it is easy in "New Age" thinking to believe we can rise above things. That is escapism; the way to create change is to move deeply into something, not rise above it, acknowledging that

55

life experiences are only reflections of the inner reality. The only way to change your world is to change yourself.

Astrology used with integrity allows for deeper self-knowledge, acceptance and reflection. I don't believe you can see the level of an individual's consciousness from the birth chart; this can only be discerned through interaction. I would never make that kind of presumption. In the birth chart we can see potential, and there are many levels on which that can manifest, from the lowest to the highest; the spectrum is limitless. The chart is not a concretized statement; it is a living dynamic, just like a human life, always carrying seeds for change and awareness. We play God when we become absolute in our judgments or assumptions.

Gary Christen: Consciousness must be differentiated from life. They are not the same, yet one contains the other and one can exist without the other. Life is an organized process moving in time. Consciousness is the organization of things and is a necessary part of life. I consider the world to be conscious, but not of necessity alive in the carbon-based living sense. The solar system is a complete consciousness, but cannot be regarded as a life form given our narrow view of what the prerequisites of life are.

Astrology cannot judge whether someone has a "higher" consciousness than another. This is a subjective and often-snobbish attitude held by many. What is a "higher" consciousness? We all live and die, passing through this miraculous mortal experience. Judging from the impartial view of the universe, does it matter that some humans or other living things have a certain quality of thought forms compared to others; does it make a difference? This is a personal question and a personal quest. The orthodox astrology shows some ability to make some distinctions, and the Uranian System has some very specific formulas to determine spiritual ability.

The real question is not spiritual, but is very basic. Are you happy and content? You could talk to God all day long and still be disturbed (many who do talk to higher beings on a daily basis don't have a good time in life). Destiny has everything for everybody. Some will have the realization of nirvana while others couldn't care less. Can we, as astrologers, make a good versus bad judgment about another's interests or actions? To me, it still comes down to looking at events as to whether they assist life or diminish it.

Hadley Fitzgerald: The closest I can come to a "definition" of this word-of-many-connotations is that consciousness is synonymous with awareness, understanding, perception, sensitivity, comprehension, mindfulness, an ability to observe internal and external phenomena, and to integrate what one observes with increasing degrees of complexity.

Since both the Buddha and a butterfly have a birth chart, there's obviously no absolute relationship between astrology and consciousness—i.e., the map is not the territory, and the MRI is not the body. Although your birth chart is the complete symbolic "road guide" for your journey, you're free to find one hotel and park yourself in it for fifty years, or you can explore every inch of terrain in—and beyond—sight.

The chart neither describes nor determines a person's "level of consciousness." Blessedly, this requires the astrological consultant to push ego aside and to stay present with the symbols and their possible range of meanings for the client. The astrologer must therefore bring all of his/her senses into the session *every time* with every client, so that the interpretation offered has value directly applicable to that person's life and *current* level of consciousness.

John Marchesella: Consciousness, in my definition, is simply the knowing of one thing by another. It is relationship, if you will. I don't think, however, that there is only consciousness and unconsciousness, knowing and not knowing. I think there is a broad spectrum to indicate degrees of knowing. And I don't think that there is a unique connection between consciousness and astrology, other than that there is a connection between consciousness and everything. Consciousness gives astrologers the ability to know astrology, but astrology is simply the language astrologers use to explain the world around us. Similarly, consciousness gives artists the ability to know their art, but the art is only a means with which they can express themselves. Also, consciousness gives my dog the ability to know me, but I am the tool he uses to survive in his world. And I certainly do not think there is any indication in the natal chart of the degree of consciousness about the Universe, *per se*. However, forecasting techniques, obviously, let us know when the native is entering a new degree of consciousness.

Ken Bowser: Consciousness is energy. That much is evident. I take for granted that interpretive skill is a function of consciousness, that the good mechanics, if they live their lives rightly, will be given access to higher levels of awareness. I think, until we get what may be called a state of grace, that astrologers are just mechanics who don't see things as they really are; rather they dance around the issue in interpretation. I assume it's possible to get an idea of the level of awareness of an individual from the horoscope, but I don't have confidence in my ability to see it clearly.

Kim Rogers-Gallagher: Consciousness, I believe, is awareness. The awareness of your life's mission, the effect of your actions on others, and the knowledge that we're all connected, part of a wonderfully detailed life force—a life-force that gives back what you put in. In other words, if you're kind to creatures that are smaller and less powerful than yourself (and yes, that includes insects), perhaps some day, when you need it, someone or something "above" you will do the same for you. Is that karma? If it is, well, then I guess I believe in karma. I don't believe that you can determine the "level of consciousness" of your client from a birth chart, which is why I always insist on talking to my clients, either in person or on the phone. I *do* believe that the birth chart shows patterns and unresolved issues, which I'm sure have a lot to do with not only this life, but past lives as well.

Robert Hand: "Consciousness" is another somewhat ill defined word but, unlike "spirit," it does not overlap with "soul." I identify consciousness with Nous, or that which knows, and one of its major functions is to provide the place in which there is language. (My wife, who is well-trained in semiotics and system theory, and I have been hammering away at the word "consciousness" for some time, and this seems to be a definition or characterization of consciousness that causes little stress to either of us.) Language is impossible without Nous, and the fact that astrology exists as a language of any kind indicates that there is some sort of consciousness within the universe independently of any individual consciousness.

As I state above, astrology is a language which describes paths by which the soul manifests itself in matter. The more nearly perfect the manifestation of soul in matter, the more powerfully present is Nous within an entity. The level of consciousness is a measure of the intensity of the manifestation of soul in matter. To the best of our ability, the function of the astrologer is assist the client in self-realization, i.e., in becoming an intense manifestation of Nous. For all of these reasons, the level of consciousness cannot be determined from the birth chart. It is our own task to achieve the highest possible level of consciousness, and as we become more enlightened, our will becomes more free and more able to raise our consciousness further. I do not dispute that sometimes external circumstances can assist and inhibit this process, and that among these is something like divine grace.

Robert Schmidt: With regard to the nature of consciousness, I have given my answer in question three—from a cosmic perspective. Hellenistic astrology certainly has means of making predictions about the body and the events befalling it, as well as evaluating the quality of soul of the native.

However, I am not sure I understand what people mean when they talk about someone's "level of consciousness." I am guessing that this means someone's level of self-awareness or self-consciousness. In the metaphysical view I favor, higher consciousness would not mean the soul's transcending the body any more than lower consciousness would mean remaining submerged in the body. Rather, higher consciousness would imply that the soul maintains a more perfect contact with the body. I do not at present know of any Hellenistic means of determining the level of consciousness of an individual so defined, although I would not rule out the possibility.

I have sometimes heard it said that the higher one's level of spiritual evolution, the freer that individual is from his or her chart, or at least the determinism of the chart. To this I would like to oppose the Hellenistic precept that the more the native yields to his chart and conforms to it in the realm of daily life, the freer the soul of that native becomes.

Ronnie Gale Dreyer: Consciousness implies to me that we are at a state where we feel and act upon everything that happens, and we do not make one move unless it has a very specific meaning. Nothing should be done blindly, and being "conscious" implies becoming fully aware and withholding judgment. I am not sure you can determine level of consciousness from the horoscope, but it is possible to show how easy or difficult it would be for the person to become aware of what his actions reap, and what he can do to improve or change them. You can also see how introspective someone might be, and if the ability to be honest and aware with oneself is a theme that this person might strive towards. It is also possible to see at which point in one's life the individual is most likely to become fully aware and thus "conscious" of himself or herself.

Steven Forrest: What is consciousness? That's one of those ultimate questions. I would stick to a simple, "chicken-soup" kind of answer. Consciousness is that feeling of spacious self-awareness you experience when you close your eyes.

I absolutely do not believe that you can determine the level of a person's consciousness from a birthchart. I feel very strongly about that, for a lot of reasons.

First, it is simply incorrect, and easily demonstrated as such. It's not difficult to find people with functionally identical birthcharts—they were born on the same day, with the places and times of birth arranged in such a fashion that their Ascendants and house cusps come out about the same. Their lives are usually uncannily parallel in terms of the *nature and timing of events*, but they are clearly operating on different levels of self-awareness. Not everyone with "Hitler's chart" turned out to be Hitler.

Second, to say to someone that he or she has an "unevolved chart" is obviously not a particularly supportive counseling technique. Even if it were true, what's the point? Related to that, many people with "spiritual charts" turn out to be drunks and escapists.

Consciousness is a vertical dimension. The astrological chart is a horizontal one. Any chart can be used in a way that is high up on that vertical axis—or way down near the bottom.

Wendy Z. Ashley: To me, simply, consciousness is "knowing." And "knowing" demands responsibility. Not knowing suggests either innocence, such as children have, or ignorance. Ignorance suggests, at worst, a decision to ignore what should be known, and at best, not having recourse to the information. Choosing "not to know" can be a spiritual crime or a psychological illness.

Generally one cannot determine a level of consciousness from a birth chart. Of course there are some charts that are *about* consciousness. But it seems to me that astrology can be a great tool for consciousness. Consciousness is the reward of the seeker. Yet no matter how much we know about anything, we never know all of it.

6. DO YOU BELIEVE IN THE DOCTRINE OF REINCARNATION AND THE LAW OF KARMA? IF YOU DO, THEN WHAT IS THE CONNECTION BETWEEN AN INDIVIDUAL'S BIRTH CHART AND HIS OR HER KARMA? DOES THE BIRTH CHART REFLECT THE KARMIC CIRCUMSTANCES OF THE PAST?

Demetra George: To the extent that many major religious traditions over the course of human history have believed in reincarnation and karma, their possibility must be considered. A Buddhist adage that my teacher Chagdud Tulku conveyed is, "If you want to know who you were in your previous lifetime, look to your present circumstances. If you want to know who you will be in your future lifetime, look to your present actions." From this perspective, the birth chart is a statement of the present conditions of an individual's life as result of his or her actions in a previous life.

Evelyn Roberts: I believe in reincarnation, and that life energy is a continuum changing in form, not essence. Karma is cause and effect; what we sow, we reap. I don't view the Universe as punitive; we suffer from getting stuck in patterns and repeating the same behaviors over and over, not because we have been "bad" in the past. I think the birth chart contains everything about us; it is as deep and complex as a human life and soul. I don't consider myself an esoteric astrologer and I rarely deliberately explore this realm with clients. There is usually enough going on in this lifetime to keep us busy. If a person is looking for this kind of work, I will refer them to someone more knowledgeable in this field. On occasion, a chart will speak to me in these terms, and I have had deep and meaningful openings occur that logical linear thinking can't explain. I believe they occur when the clients themselves are receptive, and in some way I am invited along for the ride!

I look to the lunar Nodes to indicate where on a soul level we have been and where we are going. The South Node can be inherent gifts we are born with or what we bring from past lives; the North Node is the direction that allows us to fulfill our life or soul purpose. It makes little difference whether I'm talking to a client who believes in past lives or not, only the language changes somewhat. I consider Saturn and Chiron the keys to deeply embedded issues that involve karmic material. I view the Ascendant/Descendant axis as unique and new to us, whereas the Midheaven/Nadir is what we have inherited, be it through ancestry or something less definable.

There are great astrologers who specialize in past life work; I respect what they do and acknowledge that their expertise is vast in this area and mine not. I am fortunate enough to have been educated in traditional astrology so my eyes have been opened to the richness, depth and history of the esoteric tradition.

61

Gary Christen: Funny thing about reincarnation, it has to do with someone else. That person that you were before is not you now. This is you and this is all you are going to get in life. (The Greeks called this "your lot in life," referring to destined conditions that contain the native's life.) Early on I became aware of my immediate previous life. I was able to read his biography and compare his chart to my own. Early on his issues and events paralleled both of our lives. Before I became aware of this person, I had already found myself moving away from the issues that my former self had confronted. I had evolved from the "karma" that he had engineered in his life. Did this knowledge matter to my life? Was it connected to my life? Who was this other guy, anyway?

This is the only life you will know and experience. The people who are your contemporaries ride this same life's wave as you do. You will not know anyone from the past, nor from the future. When you pass away from this plane, after all your peers pass away, so does your memory. Great beings are remembered for some time after they die, but they too will fade from collective memory. In the universal scheme of things, your life is forever. It exists within the forms of time, forever. If you have had a lousy life and were hassled by the outer conditions and miserable, that's all you get for eternity. If you have a lousy life and don't care and are still happy, that's all you get for eternity. Heaven and hell exist right here in this life. Eternity exists right here in this life. Better feel good about it.

Do we bring "karma" into this life? Yes. Does it matter? No. Life starts with a certain custom-made set of circumstances, and your attitudes towards them are all that matters. You cannot redo the past, and I'm not too sure you can influence the future. However, all these things and more can be seen in the chart just like a genetic bloodline.

Hadley Fitzgerald: Yes, I believe in reincarnation and karma, though I don't pretend to know *precisely* what either one means or how either one manifests in this life. Karma being defined as one's "work" and therefore one's "fate" in this lifetime has always made both intuitive and logical sense to me. The soul and the personality had best align to address that fate and undertake that work, but while our conversation with ourselves and others may not always make the distinction, life periodically reminds us that the soul doesn't give a damn what the personality wants.

In the Introduction to my forthcoming book, *Traveling Eternity Road*, I imagine a scene common to everyone who has ever lived on this planet:

Just before your scheduled departure for this incarnation, you're shown a detailed document that you understand is your map for the life journey ahead. There is much terrain to cover, one sort of continental mass here, a body of water, and perhaps an island, there. There are straight roads, bent roads, forked roads, rivers, valleys, mountains, forests, more than a couple of deserts. You will not be told *how* to navigate any of them, only that you must—even if that means avoiding some altogether. There are small squares and triangles and circles to mark lodging, weigh stations, rest stops, information centers, prisons and holy ground.

In all these places, there are symbols indicating people and situations you will encounter: some are clearly designated to ease your journey, some to make it excruciatingly difficult (I call them "dark teachers"); some to bring you gifts; some to wake you up; some will be there with painful obstructions they must throw onto your path; and some will wait with remarkable increments of grace.

Certain of these people will be quite recognizable; others will be well-disguised. All will have their own maps and contracts, their own life trajectories, too; but there are specific points at which their trajectories will cross yours, because life has its "necessary coincidences." The choices you make at these various points-of-encounter will write the broader narrative of your life.

Across millennia you've embarked on many of these journeys. You have your own unique evolutionary predicaments—an amalgam of old, unfinished business and new growing edges; thus, for every journey you've drawn a different map. The larger purpose and ultimate destination have never changed, but for now you are going to Earth to, in Kazantzakis's view, get conscious, to wake up, to find—and free—the endangered spirit of God. Every time you wake up a bit more, a piece of the God-in-you and the you-in-God becomes that much more available on the Earth, to the Earth. If you wish, you might even imagine yourself being "sent" there—and agreeing to go—as an integral part of the healing of the world's soul. Hence, this document—this birth chart—you're studying prior to departure is part map, part instruction manual, part contract.

John Marchesella: Reincarnation? Sure, what's not to believe? But I don't think it has a thing to do with astrology or vice versa, at least not in the way reincarnation is so trivialized in the West, and I mean by the Western New Agers, not by the naysayers. In fact, I would go so far as to say that using astrology to describe or explain past and future lives misses the whole point of astrology. It probably misses the whole point of reincarnation, too. Past lives, as they say, and astrology, I think, are mutually exclusive. As for karma, well, for the most part, if karma is the pattern of being, then I think karma *is* the natal chart; or perhaps it's more accurately said that the natal chart is a symbolic representation of one's karma.

Ken Bowser: I do believe in reincarnation and karma but because I don't have conscious awareness of it, that is, I don't know the law, I'm not competent to expound upon it. I suspect that one can see past life karma in the horoscope, but I wouldn't presume to expound upon it. Only those who know just what it is can do it. People without the awareness of the law have no business speaking on it. Belief is not enough. Knowledge is information corroborated by experience, and for the moment, I have only some information. The Hindus believe, for example, that the Moon's Nodes say a lot about one's past lives, but what the Nodes symbolize if anything in that regard is not obvious, and those who may know are not telling how they know it. It may be that knowledge is dispensed in trance or via dreams, which defies verification. People who do know—and know that they know—who have received information that way don't talk about it, because to do so invites ridicule. Spiritually developed people have nothing to prove.

Kim Rogers-Gallagher: I think that we are all souls with a mission to fulfill: to ascend one more evolutionary level with each lifetime. Our birth chart shows our current lesson, as well as the tools we packed to take along to help us "pass" our classes during this semester at Earth University. As for good or bad luck, I don't know that the Universe doles out either—at least, not under those labels. Bad things happen to good people all the time, and good things happen to bad people. It's all part of the lesson plan the Universe has decided we need to pursue to achieve the current piece of our soul's goal.

It's also true that even if we manage to do what we think of as a good job with our energies, through living a good and consciously positive life, we necessarily share our time on Earth with others—and many of them cross our paths, each with their own mission or agenda to fulfill. It's rather like we're all part of a huge dance, a wonderful cosmic choreography that seems to be what most folks consider destiny. Therefore, I see fate as the fulfillment of our studies here on Earth, occurring over the course of our lifetimes as we encounter whatever events and individuals the Universe sees fit to toss our way, either as tests or lessons.

Robert Hand: I remain somewhat agnostic about reincarnation. I do not know precisely what it may be that can be reincarnated. If the normal self or ego is an illusion, as many believe, then what can be reincarnated? This is a question which I have not answered, although I am aware that there are answers that have been given.

Karma is another matter. It is a clearer concept for me. But I hold to a much simpler and less metaphysical notion of karma than I commonly seem to see. The word simply means "action." I know that we are all limited in our freedom by both the internal and external consequences of things that have happened and that which we have done in the past. Some of this past action could come from previous incarnations, although the manner of the linkage is not very clear. But it is very clear that past actions in this life limit our freedom. The art of not creating karma is simply the art of living in such a way that we do not create consequences which prevent us from being free to become whom we are naturally supposed to become. We cannot become something other than what we are, but we can be what we are with a greater or lesser degree of self-realization.

Robert Schmidt: Although I consider it to be an interesting question, I have no personal experiences that would lead me either to accept or to reject the notions of reincarnation and karma. Nor I have I been able to answer this question on the basis of any metaphysical reasoning from the fundamental principles mentioned above, although I believe that the question is accessible to such reasoning. I would not, however, alter my metaphysical views simply in order to make room for these Eastern doctrines.

Furthermore, I do not consider this question to be essential for the theoretical grounding of astrology. I do think that it is ultimately inconsistent to reject the role of fate in human life and at the same time accept the possibility of karma.

Ronnie Gale Dreyer: To be immersed in Jyotish, one has to believe in this, since reincarnation is part of Hindu philosophy and part of a traditional Jyotish reading. The type of life that one has led will determine the issues that will face us in this life. Additionally, "karma" is simply the accumulation of all our deeds both good or bad, and the rewards and talents of our chart have been earned from past lives. For instance, in Vedic astrology the fifth and ninth houses provide what is called "past life credit." Difficulties in those houses will be things that were not utilized properly in a former life. At a certain point, we reach a state in which our karma is impeccable and we will never have to come back.

Steven Forrest: To me, reincarnation and karma are very much at the heart of psychological reality, and thus absolutely central to the deepest kinds of astrological interpretations. Such principles can probably never be fully "proven" in an objective, scientific sense, of course—even the most astonishing tales of verifiable facts from past-life memories can be explained away as psychic phenomena. Like a belief in God, these are profoundly personal matters. When I am sitting with a client, I always make a point of asking them if it is acceptable to them for me to use reincarnational language. I make it clear I am not pressuring them into accepting those beliefs, and that I can use different perspectives if they prefer—specifically genetic language, "family myth" language, or the simple language of "how God made you."

I also emphasize that something must have already existed in them before they were born—the straightforward proof being that even newborn babies have observable personalities. I find it interesting that after having done probably about 25,000 readings, only twice has anyone asked me not to speak of past lives.

If we assume that the universe is meaningful, purposeful, and non-random, then it would follow that every configuration in the birthchart is there for a reason. Astrology does not boil down to some gigantic roulette wheel. As soon as we start thinking that way, we recognize that we cannot describe the present birthchart deeply without looking into conditions that existed prior to the birth.

All I would add is that one can use astrology effectively to predict the stock market, to find lost objects, and to describe someone's character, at least in broad terms. None of those uses depend upon a belief in reincarnation. My aim though is to do the deepest kind of astrology of which I am capable, and that is inseparable from the notion of the evolution of consciousness through a succession of experiences over many lifetimes.

Wendy Z. Ashley: The issue of reincarnation may or may not come into a Mythic reading. Being trained in Astrology in the '60s certainly meant I was introduced to karmic astrology and the notion that we were put here on Earth to perfect ourselves over many lifetimes. And I certainly operated from that premise for a time. Every difficult aspect or transit was "a lesson to learn." Once

I began to see the life through the horoscope in a mythic approach, I began to see that karmic astrology was just another metaphor.

I have since come to prefer a different metaphor. What if we are, instead, tools of the gods? What if what we do here is an extension or embodiment of some archetypal forces at play? What if what we are and what we do is not self-created and self-reliant and self-directed, but is at once both humbler and more magnificent than that? What if the meaning of our lives could be discerned? What if Myth answered those great imponderable questions: Why was I born? What am I here for? Why did this happen to me? The mythic approach brings to light all of these matters and answers these very questions. And it integrates all of these into a guiding metaphor.

7. WHAT IS THE RELATIONSHIP BETWEEN FATE AND FREE WILL IN ASTROLOGY? WHAT IS DESTINY?

Demetra George: The relationship between fate and free will in astrology is a concern that has occupied the minds of philosophers, theologians, and astrologers from the inception of an astrological way of thinking at the beginning of the second millennium B.C.E. This question can be reformulated according to the ancient discussion, "Are the stars signs or causes?" The Babylonians believed that the movements of the planetary gods signified portents of coming events, but that the future was not fixed. Intercessions could be made by means of ritual and invocation to avert negative portents, and from this perspective, free will can be conceptualized as the possibility of entreating the gods to change their minds.

Claudius Ptolemy re-conceptualized astrology according to the doctrines of Aristotelian natural philosophy and Stoic fatalism. The planets, now stripped of their divine sentience, became the physical causes of all change on earth that had been absolutely predetermined by preceding causes, and astral fatalism was firmly set into place once the divinity had been removed from the planets. The Medieval compromise was that the planets had influence over the physical body, but not upon the soul which was incorporeal, and thus allowed for free will in the exercise of making moral choices in one's life.

In my thirty years of looking at charts, I used to think that people had much more free will than now seems apparent to me. Especially with the use of personal name asteroids, I see that the names of people with whom we have relationships have been patterned into our natal blueprint from the moment of

67

our birth, such as Prince Charles having the asteroids Camelia and Parks conjunct his natal Venus within fifteen minutes of arc. A certain amount of free will does exist to alter the conditions of one's nativity, but it does not seem likely to me that this can be accomplished by simply "making a choice to do otherwise," utilizing such means as therapy, visualization or affirmation. The possibility of genuine change is predicated upon a belief in the divinity and sentience pervading the celestial spheres, and the capacity to make direct contact with that consciousness through prayer and meditation and asking for an intercession.

Evelyn Roberts: I've always loved Jung's quote, "free will is the ability to do gladly that which I must do," which I read as free will being the ability, in a sense, to accept our fate. It is vital to understand and accept our own essence and the parameters that our life circumstances dictate we live within. I, for example, could not be a Sumo wrestler no matter how much I might want to be one; I'm the wrong race, not male and too small! Astrology mirrors who we truly are; it speaks of our physical, emotional and subtler bodies. When we are in a place of acceptance, we stop judging others and ourselves and become compassionate. As astrologers we have the tools to assist clients to "come home" to themselves. Call it fate or whatever, we all have a physical body, an individual nature, history, dreams, the crosses we bear, and they all belong to us and fit us. Usually discontent comes from the belief that we are unacceptable or not good enough. There is liberation in knowing that we are exactly who we should be. From that springboard we can be realistic about what we aspire to, meaning less disappointment and more success and fulfillment. Destiny to me is this life we are living; it's right here and right now, this is not the dress rehearsal. Being as fully alive and conscious as possible now is my personal goal, and what I aim to assist my clients in achieving.

Gary Christen: See the above as these questions have been dealt with previously.

Hadley Fitzgerald: Decades ago I heard Ram Dass say, in effect, "Absolutely everything is preordained, *and* you have complete free will. When you get that paradox worked out inside you, you're on a path to enlightenment." This remains the best explanation I've ever heard of the relationship between fate and free will.

"Moira" (pronounced "MEErah"), the Greek word for fate, is defined as the part, portion or share "which falls to one;" this is a good description of the birth chart and its progressions and transits over a lifetime. The chart symbolically describes only what "falls to us" to work with; from there we make choices commensurate with our level of consciousness. To the degree that those choices bind us to or free us from old patterns, we evolve and transform our fate—there are times in life to seize the moment, else the moment lets us go.

To me "destiny" is simultaneously more specific and more indefinable. In the words of screenwriter Dan Gurskis: "Some people, from the moment they're born, know what their destiny is. They live with it. It's as much a part of them as the color of their eyes. But it makes them a little old, too, because they understand. Everything."

Jung said something to the effect that while you're the protagonist in your own life and making consequential choices on a daily basis, you're simultaneously a spear-carrier, a bit player, in a much more elaborate drama. I believe that when we understand more about that drama, we'll understand more about the true nature of individual destiny. Most of us are not that evolved yet.

John Marchesella: I'll stick with Jung on this one because I've never heard any better correlation between the two. He said, "Free will is choosing to do what one must do." I certainly don't think it's any different in astrology than anywhere else. Astrology is just the language which we astrologers use to describe what one must do.

Destiny is a slightly different point. I think destiny is what our lives add up to. Destiny is the outcome of our choices plus our fate. For lack of more logical terms, destiny is the result of how we co-create our lives with the gods. Perhaps it's better to express it astrologically: destiny is the Midheaven.

If you're really asking if fate, free will and destiny are depicted in the horoscope, then I would say absolutely yes! Is the astrologer always able to read them in the chart? Absolutely not. But that's a problem with being the astrologer. It's not a weakness in the astrology.

Ken Bowser: I don't think there's nearly as much free will in play as most people, especially astrologers, are inclined to think. In any case, I'm sure I can't expound on the relationship between fate and free will, if there is one, because in the first instance, how could anybody know? My opinion is that such a relationship is entirely conjecture. Astrology is fatalistic but because that's an unpopular view in the West, astrologers declare their free will by fiat, as though the declaration could make it so. My opinion is that fate is the operative agent at work in the world, by and large, and that perhaps at a few—probably very few—moments in life, one can find oneself standing alone in the crossroads with fateful choices to make.

I think that before one incarnates into a body, certain choices are made at a spirit level—choices that relate to the sort of experience that will facilitate or accelerate growth. Once the mantle of the body is taken on, the life is acted out according to the script that was chosen at a higher level. I think astrology is a roadmap of the script, which is another way to describe destiny.

Kim Rogers-Gallagher: The more I study astrology—and event charts in particular—the more I believe that we really have little or nothing to say about what actually happens to us. Sure, we can make what we *think* are our own decisions, but how many of us have been thrust into circumstances we *know* we've tried our best to avoid? How many of us have consciously begun relationships we *knew* from the start weren't a good idea— yet, somehow, we felt compelled or obligated to "do the dance" with this person?

Free will, then, in my opinion, is simply attitude—the attitude we adopt when *reacting* to life events. And I believe that keeping our attitude positive, no matter what life brings, is the only thing we can ever *truly* have control over.

Robert Hand: What we see as Fate is two things. It is in part the consequence of being incarnate in the physical universe. Once one is born a human being, one is not free to be a cat or dog. One cannot fly without a plane, or walk through walls without a door. This is roughly equivalent to saying that natural law is a part of fate, and so it is. The second part of fate is a perceived necessity that is actually the result of not being able to see alternatives, or it is the result of attachments. Part of this kind of "fate" is also that which has become determined and made inevitable by consequences of previous actions (karma again). Once one has leapt off the cliff, one is not free to go back to the top of the cliff without hitting the bottom first.

But there is a third component of fate, that part of our destiny which is the result of our being particular individuals with particular paths of self-realization. As I have said already, we are not free to become something other than what we are, but we can become what we are at many different levels of being. While we are ignorant, and to the extent that we are ignorant, we cannot be free. We can

70

be free only when we can choose our paths consciously without attachment to things that are irrelevant, and without being driven by unconscious drives and emotional programs that we do not realize are operating.

Destiny is self-realization. One can fail to achieve it, but one cannot succeed in changing its course. And when one knows and understands that course, one does not want to change it.

Robert Schmidt: In modern astrological debate, the concepts of fate and free will are ill-defined. The modern rejection of any sort of fate concept seems to be based on resistance to the idea that our choices are in any way predetermined. It sometimes seems to me that modern astrology is more deterministic than ancient astrology, for to the extent that it assumes that the native's choices are restricted or limited by his or her "level of consciousness," it is positing some degree of determinism over choice, and thereby a limitation of free will.

To my knowledge, Hellenistic astrology never assumes that our choices are pre-determined, only certain events that befall the native or certain outcomes of his actions, and possibly only a limited number of these.

In any case, before entering into any debate on this issue, I would prefer it if all the participants had a basic understanding of the ancient fate concepts on their own terms. They are very numerous and very subtle and cannot even be cartooned as determinism or pre-destination in the modern sense. What saddens me is that when free will is opposed to an anachronistic caricature of the fate concept in such debates, the free will concept becomes equally debased and degraded.

Ronnie Gale Dreyer: There probably is not that large a difference between fate and free will. Fate, or destiny, does indicate the general direction that our lives will take us. If we believe in astrology, we have to believe that there is a divine plan that we must follow. Within that plan, however, there are many different roads to take. That means that we have been given certain qualities, parents, etc., that have given us the parameters in which we can apply our willpower or decision-making abilities. However complete free will is, in my opinion, erroneous, since whatever plan we attempt in life is always going to depend on the hand we are dealt (including innate skills and talents), parents, family, character, appearance etc. Whatever else we wish to make of our lives and for ourselves that is beyond the scope of simply our upbringing, is ALSO seen in the chart. For instance, the horoscope will show us if we have gifts from the family,

71

or we have to struggle to achieve greatness in life by developing our own talents. Sometimes we may think it is own free will that is allowing us to change our lives, but in fact it is set out in the chart itself.

Steven Forrest: My sense of it is that the fate versus free will question is precisely analogous to the central paradox of modern physics: you can prove that light is a wave—and that it couldn't possibly be a particle. And you can prove the opposite, too. Astrology's history seems to be mostly deterministic, with its Holy Grail being "precise delineation." And proving those astrologers wrong is like taking candy from a baby. People routinely do well under "adverse" influences, and crap out under "benefic" ones. On the other hand, anyone who looks at astrology with a truly open mind recognizes that it is accurate in its simple predictions way too often for us to dismiss those successes as lucky guessing or random chance. I believe that when we pontificate about fate and free will, we are like three-dimensional monkeys trying to speak authoritatively about the fourth dimension.

On a more down-to-earth level, the values that inform my actual practice of astrology are absolutely centered in the notion of human freedom. People who *believe in the possibility* of taking responsibility for the shapes of their own lives are the ones who most often prove traditional predictive astrology wrong. A belief in freedom seems to correlate with the reality of freedom, while a passive acceptance of Fate appears to be a central quality of people doomed to fit their "delineations."

In essence, I believe that consciousness itself is the prime variable in astrology. The more conscious we are, the more multi-dimensional the possibilities are for how the astrological symbolism will actually manifest. And the lazier and more inert we are, the more the older version of the craft seems to work. So I try in all my work to fan the flames of self-awareness and choice.

I use the word "destiny" idiosyncratically. It has a better feeling to it than "fate," so I think of destiny as the highest potential of the birthchart, and fate as what happens to us automatically if we fall short of destiny.

Wendy Z. Ashley: It is our *self* and *individual* oriented culture that gives us a belief in individual freedoms and choice, at least in theory. In actuality, fate and circumstances play a huge, if disregarded, even unseen, role in our lives. The entire studies of sociology, epidemiology, family systems, and genetics are all concerned with what is beyond our control or volition. We are all in the grip of

72

fate, whether through our collective identities, as sociology describes, or through our personal identities, which astrology and, to some degree, genetics and psychology describe. The fact is it is not a question of fate OR free will; rather it is fate AND free will.

Destiny is another matter and many are the attempts to discover our destiny. Jungians would say that discovering the Gods in operation in our lives is the discovery of the true Self, the God-in-Self. This involves both development of AND dissolution of the ego. This is what is called the Great Work, and in this work psychotherapy helps, and readings can help, too. To see one's self and one's life through a transcendent lens helps enormously, in fact.

Myth is one such transcendent lens. A mythic reading of one's horoscope is not however for everyone. It is not for those who have no capacity for metaphor. It is not for those who have as yet done no work in Self-realization. It is graduate work in this area. But it does provide an extraordinary lens through which the whole of a life, and the meaning of that life, might be seen. The myth can answer the questions: "Why was I born?" and "Why is this happening to me?" and "What is the meaning of my life?"

The mythic approach can be said to be Neptunian, in contrast to the more detailed mathematical approach that is Uranian. By Neptunian, I mean filled with a set of references that are a sub-text as inner script in symbolic imagery. This is not Neptune as illusion, but rather as "mystery." The myth is an imaginal structure underlying and uniting all of the elements of an individual's life.

These claims of mine are as yet without demonstration. There is little room here to give the entire basis for them; instead the proof will have to be seen in the reading.

8. HOW ARE ASTROLOGY AND PSYCHOLOGY RELATED? TO WHAT DEGREE CAN (SHOULD) THEY BE INTEGRATED IN PRACTICE?

Demetra George: The relationship between astrology and psychology actually may be quite tenuous. Astrology is predicated upon the belief that the birth chart, over the entire course of a person's lifetime, is an accurate description of a person's character, and that predictive techniques can accurately prognosticate the future. Psychology is predicated upon the belief that a change of a person's basic nature, and hence future actions, is possible through therapeutic techniques. There seems to be an essential contradiction here on the most fundamental level. The natal chart can be used quite effectively to help focus a counseling session and to help define the issues that are facing the client. But astrologers into psychology must decide if the veracity of astrology is subject to modification by talking therapy aimed at self-understanding, and psychologists into astrology must decide if the integrity of their discipline to produce behavior modification can co-exist with a system that prides itself on delineating behavior *a priori*. Both astrology and psychology each tend to become diluted when the attempt is made to merge them together.

Evelyn Roberts: For me personally, astrology mirrors our very existence; our psychology dictates how we function in life. As an astrologer I don't see any separation between the two. This is especially true in the work I do, so of course it is my bias! As individual studies I believe they enrich and complement one another. Psychology functions fine without astrology of course, and I wouldn't preach that you shouldn't have one without the other. My own psychotherapist knew no astrology and was powerfully instrumental in helping me completely change my life for the better.

At the same time astrology provides a map of the psyche, and in the hands of a proficient psychologist who has taken the time to study it thoroughly, this can only be positive. Astrology without psychology is harder for me to imagine, because of my background and my own personal make-up. My personal lens on life is a psychological one, and frankly my life was disastrous before I discovered that fact. However it is important not to make sweeping statements, and my reality is just mine. I have met many traditional astrologers doing really good work without the "conscious" use of psychology. I would however say that I feel it is almost impossible, and even dangerous, to journey with a client into territory that you yourself have not personally navigated.

Gary Christen: Psychology was a failed attempt to create the astrological premise without astrology. The concern with the inner state of the individual is a more modern notion, as ancient astrologers couldn't care less about your inner motivations and feelings. Yet, although they had the tools to examine these areas of life, the paradigms of ancient times didn't emphasize them. I think that the astrological terminology is superior to the language created through observation by the psychologists during this century. The traditional models of psychology have been largely discredited, and there is some struggle to create new ones. Unfortunately, behaviorist models based upon mechanistic physical manipulations and drug therapies are gaining momentum. This too shall pass.

The only way to integrate the two studies would be for all psychologists to learn astrology. The only advantage that psychology has over astrology is clinical training and exposure to crisis counseling. Astrologers need this sort of training, but that will only happen when we get research and teaching funds, which are in scarce supply for even the mechanist class. That is one of the modern reasons for the suppression of astrology; we threaten too many jobs and traditional social funding mechanisms.

Hadley Fitzgerald: I believe astrology is the ancient, soul-full progenitor of psychology. A thorough understanding of basic tenets of modern psychology is extremely valuable, yet from my earliest days as a psychotherapist, I've seen the best minds and most caring hearts in the profession put forth insightful interpretations of human experience that simultaneously and inevitably circumscribed it. Likewise, I see the patterns of meaning shown in astrological symbols as infinitely richer than either its proponents or opponents have allowed. Whatever our perspective, we need vast and adequate resources to take us more and more deeply into the human condition.

In everyday application, my first responsibility to the therapy client is to *refrain from* interjecting astrology into the work (there are also some clients for whom neither imaginal, symbolic, nor astrological work is appropriate). I keep the two perspectives overtly separate unless or until the therapy client specifically opens a door for discussion of his/her own spiritual concerns. However, something inside me is ever on the lookout for ways to build a sturdy bridge between psychology and astrology—between experience and meaning—because: (1) I know that's what I'm here to do; and (2) astrology continually makes me a better therapist.

In a broad sense, psychology focuses on helping people make a "better adjustment" in, and to, their lives. Astrology in its best form (thus far) holds a great reverence for people's uniqueness, their particular journey-like-no-other, and the specific ways they can best negotiate the open road that is their lifetime. As we become increasingly able to weave the two more seamlessly together, I believe we'll have more thought-full and heart-felt answers to the ongoing human question, "How, then, shall we live?"

James Hillman has written that we need a "psychological theory that grants primary psychological reality to the call of fate." I believe the sophisticated and mature practice of astrology will ultimately provide us with just that. The past decade in particular has shown me that my best therapy sessions include having free rein to work psycho-spiritually, astrologically, with the client. There's nothing like it—God's in the room.

John Marchesella: Astrology and psychology are two different languages to explain and express the same things. It is exactly like using the words "casa" and "house" to get across the idea of an abode. Since they are such simpatico languages, yes, they can be used a great deal in combination, but out of respect for each of them, I think we must be very careful of mixing them up with each other, too.

A third factor which should be included in the mix is counseling. I would describe it as the techniques to convey astrological and/or psychological information to the client. It is what we use to develop a relationship between the practitioner, client and the language of astrology. Many astrologers confuse counseling and psychology; they are actually two separate studies.

Ken Bowser: Astrology and psychology both describe patterns and modes of thought. They are allied in that sense but unless astrologers are trained as psychologists, they should not pretend to be psychologists. Astrologers should not set themselves up as therapists, although they often will be pressed into service as counselors, because people often unburden themselves to astrologers. If astrologers are trained as psychologists and have taken the classes, written the dissertations, earned the degrees and completed their internships, only then should they presume to venture into the realm of the psychologist.

Astrology is divination by the sky, and while it is sometimes explained in psychological terms, it is not psychology. Astrologers often want to ally themselves with something more respectable than their own art, but that's not a legitimate aim. My opinion is that it's better to let the psychologists do their job, and let the astrologer be one who learns to read the symbolism of the planets. Of course, one can be both an astrologer and a psychologist, but let one be a degreed, licensed and thoroughly trained psychologist before he or she brings discredit onto astrology due to psychological inadequacy, or harm to the client for the same reason.

Kim Rogers-Gallagher: Astrology and psychology—are they related? Well, as far as I can see, they have one thing in common: they're both languages—symbol sets—that attempt to explain the human condition, each with their own keywords and phrases. I also firmly believe that psychology benefits more from astrology than the reverse, however. Having a tool as powerful as ours can help psychological counselors to cut to the chase when dealing with a client's problems. And while having a knowledge of psychology certainly doesn't hurt an astrologer, our job as astrologers is not to have ongoing sessions to solve a person's problems. We're here to offer clients the knowledge of who they are, and what they are—what they're made of. We give them the ability to understand what they packed into their suitcase when they hopped on board the "evolution express." In other words, what your soul was expecting it might need for your stay on the planet.

Robert Hand: I think that it is a bad practice to try to alter astrology to conform to any modern psychological theory or system. I do not think that it is a bad practice to see how a modern psychological system and astrology may give each other information so long as the different modes of reasoning of the two systems are observed. Also, and most important, astrology, and the philosophies upon which it is based, has its own psychology which does no violence whatsoever to the foundations of astrology. Now of course one may say that if the ancients could make astrology conform to their philosophical-psychological system, why can't we?

The answer is that astrology and its related philosophies come from an ancient time and have a fundamentally different view of the world, the mind-body interface, and the relationship of subject to object. All systems of modern psychology, even the most radical, are too grounded in the contemporary world-view to be completely compatible with astrology. In the traditional view, there is a continuum between subject and object such that the distinction between them is much less defined than it is with us. With us it is more or less an absolute. We tend to make one or the other a cause, and the other an effect.

A scientist makes the objective, external realm causal to the inner world of the psyche. Then many radical New Age thinkers tend to make the inner subjective world the cause of the outer, objective one. To the traditional viewpoint they are both parts of the same formal matrix, and whatever happens in one will be reflected in the other. So we have Marsilio Ficino, a Neo-Platonist of the fifteenth century, advocating the use of the properties of objects (color, innate properties, etc.) in the environment to help with melancholia, while others of this tradition advocate meditational practices. There is no inconsistency here.

As long as these distinctions between modern and astrological psychology are observed, I have no problem with the use of astrology to analyze and illuminate psychological patterns within the native. At the same time, I don't think that astrology should be limited to that because it is equally proficient in illuminating the external world on its own terms, not merely as the result of someone's psychological make-up.

Robert Schmidt: Hellenistic astrology is based on the psychology of the cosmic soul, although it is not applied to the cosmic soul. It is not conceptualized in terms of the human personality, or reduced to it as its primary subject matter. However, to the extent that Hellenistic astrology describes events insofar as they are events, it can also be applied to the study of the individual human soul and its inner events, though as just one topic amongst many.

Ronnie Gale Dreyer: Astrology and psychology are related in that both studies are concerned with discovering aspects of the human psyche. Psychology presents a model by which a healthy individual functions, and if this model is applied to astrology, then those of us who are counselors can use the planets to achieve this model by viewing them as elements and aspects of the human psyche, and the transits and progressions as different life cycles that we all go through, including coming of age, midlife, retirement, etc.

Steven Forrest: In my view, there is really no fundamental difference at all between astrology and psychology. They are both the study of the manifestations of the human soul in the conscious mind and in the external circumstances it creates. Beyond that symmetrical core, there are some distinctions to be made. Some of them have to do with the present *cultures* of psychology and astrology. A few distinctions are actually basic to the two disciplines. In the latter category, I'd say that astrology is just plain bigger in its scope than psychology—and I am nowhere near slamming psychology with that point.

It's just that astrology can be used in predicting economic cycles, for example. That's not quite the natural domain of psychology, although there is some crossover. You would never go to your psychologist to help you figure out where you lost your wallet, but you might go to your horary astrologer. Your psychologist couldn't help you choose the optimal moment for your wedding, but your electional astrologer could do that. A psychologist might help you understand *why* you were sexually attracted to people who were inclined to abandon you, but he or she couldn't warn you about *when* to expect the arrival of one of them. An astrologer noting that Pluto was about to transit through an opposition to your natal Venus might be able to alert you very precisely about that.

I heard Rob Hand give a talk at a conference somewhere in which he made the distinction between healers and seers. I think that's useful here in contrasting astrologers and psychologists, although I look forward to a day when the distinction no longer makes sense. In the present cultural context, psychologists are generally far better healers than astrologers, while astrologers are far better seers. Most good astrologers have heard clients remark that they've "just learned in two hours what it took them six months to discover in therapy." But learning that we have a tendency to be attracted to abandoners, for example, is one thing. Working through it and changing is another—and psychotherapists are current better equipped to deal with that process.

Implicit in all this is my notion that each discipline can benefit enormously by learning from the other one. That's actually happening. Already we're seeing more "astro-psychologists," and more psychologists who are conversant with astrology. There are many symbiotic professional relationships between psychotherapists and astrologers, based on referrals. Eventually, the distinction between the two fields will become moot, I believe.

Wendy Z. Ashley: Of course astrology preceded psychology with its descriptions of individuality. Once psychology was accepted as the primary way to understand individuals, it followed that astrology would use its ideas in astrological practice. Before psychology was used in astrological practice, physiology was used. Reading astrological texts from the nineteenth and eighteenth centuries is quite an eye-opener. A noble brow signified a noble heart, a pure complexion, purity of soul, and so on. The chart delineated physical types, or physiogamy, including the very old use of the four types or humours: choleric, melancholic, sanguine, and phlegmatic, equivalent to Aristotle's Fire, Earth, Air, and Water. The discovery of psychology was, for me, a Western recovery of the "unconscious," the archetype of which had been repressed during the Enlightenment, which had debunked the hidden or mystery realms. The unconscious in psychology is personal, which suits the Protestant form of a Christian archetype of the individual. Jungian psychology recovers the pre-Christian unconscious through his concept of the collective unconscious. Anyway, the four humours have been recovered in Jung's psychological types in our era: intuitive, sensate, thinking and feeling. As you might expect, thinking is Air, feeling is Water, sensation is Earth and intuition is Fire.

This alone is useful in an attempt to do a psychoanalysis using the chart. Jungian and archetypal psychological ideas are the most useful for analyzing a chart. But in the multilayered structure of Myth, psychology is but one of the layers, so the reading is first of a mythology, and only one of its layers is of the psychology. This has consequences for psychology. If the Jungian analyst could use astrology to see the other layers as well, we would have a revolution in Western consciousness, a great "enlightenment." But for all practical purposes, because we Westerners have now been educated to a self-awareness that is entirely psychological, it is necessary that the approach of practitioner to client is that of a (psychological) counseling session. Therefore a basic education in counseling methods and ethics is a requirement if the astrologer would not do harm to the client.

9. ARE THE ASTROLOGICAL SYMBOLS UNIVERSAL AND ETERNAL, OR DO THEY REFLECT THE LOCAL CONDITIONS OF THE CULTURE AND THE SOCIETY IN WHICH THEY ARE FOUND? DOES THEIR MEANING EVOLVE OVER TIME AS SOCIOCULTURAL CONDITIONS CHANGE, OR DOES IT REMAIN FIXED?

Demetra George: Astrology's greatest strength is also her greatest weakness. Historically, the basic astrological symbols have had a remarkable capacity to adapt themselves to the norms and paradigms of the particular culture that is looking for meaning through the use of astrology. This has allowed for the survival and transmission of astrology through various cultures and time periods. On the other hand, contradictory belief systems can use the very same symbols to reflect back to themselves whatever precepts they hold to be true. And from this point of view, the astrological symbols can be interpreted to mean whatever a culture's needs and expectations are. Different cultures have assigned different meanings to the symbols, and the fact that the symbols can readily adapt to these variations and still reflect relevant meaning speaks to the universal and transcendental nature of the symbols themselves.

Evelyn Roberts: To a certain degree I think the astrological symbols are universal, but they also belong uniquely to each culture they are found in and evolve accordingly. Everyone has desires and personal values, and most people develop relationships; Venus is a universal image. However, if you told a woman in a remote Chinese village in an arranged marriage the myth of Aphrodite, she couldn't relate, at least not in the way a Westerner might. Her experience will be too different. Everything in life changes and evolves, likewise the astrological symbols. The discovery of the outer planets coincided with powerful shifts in the world and human consciousness in an uncanny way. The symbols are living reflections of our inner lives, so to me personally it would make no sense if they were static.

Gary Christen: Astrological symbols are universal and eternal for this solar system only. Go to another star system and you have to re-create astrology. This is not hard to do because the frameworks and derivation of symbology are the same anywhere you go in the universe. It is the number, period, speed and distance of bodies to the central Sun that need be taken into consideration. Also, the central Sun may be a binary or a black hole or a red giant or any number of primary starting conditions. In a talk I give on the great circles, I teach the class how to go about mechanically re-creating an astrological system on any physical body in space that orbits some sort of locally central star. This is a very straightforward exercise in spherical geometry.

What you are implying in the question has to do with the social conditions existing here in our local space in our cozy little solar system during human's existence through the ages. And the answer is yes.

The symbols are universal and unchanging in their core natures. It is in the application of them within a given cultural framework that the nuances of their meaning change. In Greek times, a strong Mars transit may have meant getting ripped apart by dogs. This was a strong possibility in those days. Early in the last century, the same Mars may mean being ripped apart by an explosion or a machine gun. This was a strong possibility in those days. You weren't likely to be cut down by a bomb or machine gun in Greek times, and you weren't likely to be ripped apart by dogs in the early part of the last century. Both events from different times still show the essential nature of Mars, its violence and energy discharge. Remember the above was for illustration only, and Mars usually isn't so extreme, except now we have great calamities that are just as violent as in the past. Car crashes, plane accidents and just plain dumb luck all are modern manifestations of certain planetary energies that operate today in their essential meanings as they have for time immemorial.

Hadley Fitzgerald: Our interpretation of the symbols has deepened and expanded—evolved—tremendously over the past several decades, let alone centuries. Just as we now interpret the same symbols on different levels for different people and contexts, I expect astrologers of the future will be working from frames of reference and dimensions of consciousness we can't yet imagine.

However, the absolute Truth behind the symbols will remain the same—and stay forever out of reach, thus compelling us to keep stretching toward it, yearning for it. In the words of Joseph Campbell: "We are the children of this planet . . . We are its eyes, its mind, its seeing and its thinking. And the earth, together with its sun—this light around which it flies like a moth—came forth from a nebula, and that nebula in turn from space. No wonder that its laws and ours are the same. Likewise our depths are the depths of space."

John Marchesella: Astrological symbols are universal AND a reflection of the cultural matrix from which they were developed. God, for instance, is a universal theme, but it varies in concept from culture to culture. Similarly, the meanings of astrological symbols evolve over time as a culture evolves, AND they transcend time and culture. However, no, they shouldn't remain fixed. They couldn't anyway, because symbols are living things.

Ken Bowser: The meaning of the symbols is universal and unchanging, but the values that people attribute to those things do change and are subject to a cultural matrix. Changing values can make universal symbols appear to change, but if the symbols themselves changed, that is, if their intrinsic nature were compromised, the entire context of astrological symbolism would collapse.

Kim Rogers-Gallagher: Astrological symbols are both universal and a reflection of culture. Take Neptune, for example, or Poseidon, depending on whether you prefer Greek or Roman mythology. This planet is known for spirituality and altered states, but it's also classically been a male god, which I just don't get. To me, Neptune is a Goddess in a pink gown, displaying distinctly "feminine" traits: sensitivity, receptivity, and compassion. So while the characteristics of this planet's energies are quite universal, I believe it's time for our culture to re-vamp her image, to allow her to evolve as our understanding of what she represents—our mass consciousness, that is—has evolved.

Robert Hand: I believe that both are elements in astrology. I believe that at the core there are symbol patterns that are common to all living things everywhere, regardless of culture, species, or even planet. These are like the archetypes of C.G. Jung, except that they are not limited to the human psyche. They inhere to some degree in the nature of existence itself. Again like Jung's archetypes, they have cultural expressions which are determined by the history and culture of different peoples. At this level the symbols change and evolve, although the greatest differences in the expression of the symbols are between cultures at the same points in time, rather than between different historical epochs within the same culture. Thus medieval Western astrology is closer to us in the expression of the symbolism than medieval or even modern Hindu astrology.

Robert Schmidt: I think that astrological concepts must take their meanings from the theoretical framework that motivates their introduction and regulates their employment. The modern meanings of basic astrological concepts are often considerably different than their original meanings in Hellenistic astrology, because modern astrology has a different theoretical foundation (and in some cases a different purpose). This is especially true of houses, aspects, and rulerships, which poses a problem since these concepts were introduced during the Hellenistic period as expressions of features of the Hellenistic theoretical framework that are no longer part of the foundations of modern astrology.

Within the context of a given theoretical framework, the basic meanings of concepts may remain constant, even though their concrete significations may adjust to a different cultural context. For instance, the original meaning of the tenth house in Hellenistic astrology was occupation or action in general; the ninth house signified everything that guides or directs one's actions, such as kingship and authority, religion, divination, etc. During the medieval Arabian period, kingship was shifted to the tenth, evidently as an expression of theocracy in which religion is understood to control and have primacy over governing. However, this change of the concrete significations of these two houses has not changed their fundamental meanings, only their interpretation within a given cultural context.

Thus, to answer this question we must distinguish between changes in astrology itself, and changes within a given tradition. The changes in astrology itself have been due to the different purposes that astrology is intended to serve within different cultures. Hellenistic astrology was developed for the purpose of event prediction and event description; if the native wanted personal or spiritual counseling, then he would consult a priest or study philosophy. The humanistic concerns of modern astrology, with its emphasis on the psychological or spiritual growth of the native, governed its reconceptualization of the tradition it inherited from the late Medieval period, although this may have been detrimental to its ability to make concrete predictions. I find it hard to see this change as an "evolution" of astrology, if by evolution one merely means advancement or improvement. If one means the adaptation of astrology to meet the needs and expectations of the modern therapeutic climate, then perhaps the term "evolution" has some value.

Ronnie Gale Dreyer: Astrological symbols are always both universal and relevant to the culture. The planet Venus, for instance, represents love in every culture. However the actual planet was used by the Babylonians to indicate cycles of war and peace. For whatever reason, much of that symbolism did not get handed down from culture to culture, and so it's quite important to trace what the planets meant in different cultures throughout the ages. In a country like India, the Sun, for instance, is malefic because it represents excessive heat and parching of the earth and destruction of crops. In our modern society, the Sun represents our self and our identity, which it represents in India as well. The distinction is that astrology is both symbolic as well as purely observational. Sometimes the physical reality of the planets does not mesh with modern symbolism that has little to do with observations of the sky. One difference between ancient and modern astrology is that in ancient societies, the planets were observed. Many modern astrologers cannot identify objects in the night sky at all!

Steven Forrest: Let me get at this one through a metaphor. When I was a little boy, I loved to look through telescopes. I'd focus on a tree through my apartment window, slowly turning the focusing rack-and-pinion. The effect was a journey "into" the tree, as first the closest leaves and branches would be in sharp focus, then ones slightly deeper into the tree, and so on.

I believe the astrological symbols work like that—they are very deep. What you see of them depends on the nature of your focus. From a close-focus perspective, the symbols are highly culturally-specific and also very mutable as human culture changes. From a deep-focus perspective, I believe they are eternal, immutable, and constant.

To illustrate the first perspective, simply consider the widespread references in the astrology of a century ago to gender-specific interpretations—the notion, for example, that a woman's tenth house would reflect the status and career of her husband. In those days, that was mostly a practical astrological truth. Women basically didn't have careers, and their status was in fact defined by their husband's place in the world. Try offering that kind of interpretation to a modern, independent female in New York City today and see if you get out of town alive!

The second perspective is clearly visible as we move deeper into the meanings of the symbols. A person born in the Olduvai Gorge at Mercury's rise in Gemini was as quick and communicative as someone born that way today. Twelfth house patterns in the chart will always correlate with the choice between conscious work in the life, or repeating existential patterns of loss and grief. I think a good astrologer learns to move fluidly from the contemporary to the eternal and back again, seeing each reflected in the other.

One passion of mine, relevant to these questions, is to point out the stranglehold that "classical" mythology has on modern astrological practice. Our planet names are Roman; our myths are basically Greek. My bumper sticker version of this complaint is that the Roman Empire *still* hasn't fallen! Those mythologies are profound. But, apart from some very cool Turkish blood I've gotten through my mother's people, those Mediterranean legends aren't in my genetic coding! My people were British and French and German—Celtic stock, in the broad, anthropological sense of the term. And we had a wonderfully vibrant mythic culture too. My wife Jodie, who is of Norwegian ancestry, got deeply into that mythos when she was writing her *The Rhymer and the Ravens* trilogy. She helped me see, for example, the way the Norse god Odin was connected with Mercury—and the way he brought in all sorts of divinatory and occult dimensions to the planet that are basically missing in the dry modern reading of the Graeco-Roman Mercury.

My point is that astrology really would benefit from including world mythology, and getting beyond this narrow Mediterranean tyranny. Where are the African stories? The Native American ones? The wisdom of the Taoist sages and Buddhist lamas?

Wendy Z. Ashley: The brief answer to both of these questions is "both." The long answer is fifty pages.

Demetra George: Astrology will change dramatically in the next century. Historically in the Western tradition of astrology, whenever a culture has discovered or rediscovered the ancient Greek doctrines, a renaissance in astrological thought has occurred. This happened when the Persians, Arabs, twelfth century Latins, and fifteenth century Italians each were exposed to the fountainhead of the original astrological teachings. This phenomenon is once again occurring with the translations of Hellenistic astrology now available in English for the first time. One major aspect of this renaissance is evident in a new generation of students attending educational institutions such as Kepler College and the Astrological Institute that are authorized and accredited. These students are learning the history of the astrological tradition with academic rigor and reading the primary sources of its origins. The results of this kind of education cannot help but to precipitate a new flowering of our timeless art and science, and restore its rightful role in the development of intellectual history.

Evelyn Roberts: I believe we are gaining ground in acceptance and respect by the general public; that is my personal experience. As the quality and integrity of astrologers improve, so will the approval rating. We are responsible for monitoring our own in a loving and supportive manner. Our full integration into society will reflect our ability to raise the educational standards for astrologers. We can only be successful *en masse* if we stand unified and accepting with all our differences. The nature of our work is one of honoring individuality; we need to really get it that our internal workings will be what is mirrored back to us. It is an immensely exciting time to be an astrologer. There will always be opposition; that's the nature of life. Instead of focusing on that, we need to keep our eyes on the huge vistas that are opening up to us. I see astrology in the present century moving out of the half shadows into full light.

Gary Christen: Every time astrologers get a good look at their past, it is in preparation for a revolutionary action. A new astrology is gnawing at the door. One of those "everything you know is wrong" types of discoveries is awaiting this field. Citing the above comparison with medicine, can you imagine what astrology will be if we have the resources of modern research at our fingertips? It isn't just the tools that will propel the field forward; it will be the first rate minds, the creative impulse that will burst forth in a new era of astrology. We will look back at folks like William Lilly and not see them as the giants in the field who have climbed mountains and set records that are still unbroken in astrology. We will look at them as quaint, misguided products of a pre-enlightened age that practiced astrology the way a witch doctor practices medicine. Not to say that the witch doctor doesn't have a lot to offer the modern world; he does, but more in the way of the spiritual approach and holistic attitudes that we find beautiful, not in his technique, which would disgust us. The same is true of astrology. Kepler told astrologers to clean up the baby, but to take care not to discard the baby with the dirty bathwater. We have yet to clean up astrology since Kepler made that statement and are still involved with methods and technique that are downright primitive.

We do, however, need to take care with our knowledge. In the wrong hands the world would be ill served by astrology. Ethics and adherence to strong moral and humane actions always need to be in the forefront of movement in our field. We could be in grave danger if astrology becomes central to human ideas in a perverted way. A super caste system could create more misery and inequality if it were based on astrology. Super elites could pervert the flow of whole societies in very negative ways. Astrology always needs to be on the side, as a commentator, as a guide for human existence, not as a deterministic medium to classify people and things according to planetary patterns. Also, there is the problem of people electing the birth of children under highly tuned planetary combinations and creating an unbalance in the general flow of things. The energies created by suffering are part of humanity and the rest of life, and are just as important for the furtherance of spirit as the energies that create happiness. Judgment is the problem. Saying that someone with a Moon-Saturn combination has a lousy life is a personal judgment, not a collective one. That Moon-Saturn combination brings energies into life that are very necessary for our existence. We need it all, the good, the bad and the ugly to make life interesting and beautiful.

One final word on the future. Kepler, in his music of the spheres, gave the Earth the sounds of "fa" and "me" from the musical scale. He said the world makes a "me . . . fa . . . me . . . fa . . ." sound as it orbits the Sun. He states further that he took it to stand for "misery . . . famine . . . misery . . . famine" into eternity. I believe in the human spirit, and I believe that humans are here for very specific purposes and are endowed with the ability for unlimited spiritual development. That will be our ultimate destiny.

Hadley Fitzgerald: Years ago Richard Tarnas commented that future generations will look back on the absence of astrology as a tool in psychological work "as being like medieval astronomers working without a telescope." That eventuality won't necessarily constitute a change in astrology, but it will mark a renaissance in our respect for and understanding of its intrinsic purpose and use. In turn we will integrate astrology—symbolic sight—more and more into our collective perception of what it means for a soul to be alive on this Earth.

To echo Kazantzakis in *The Saviors of God*: "I hope to say a word in time to my companions—a password—like conspirators. Let us make for the earth a heart and a brain."

John Marchesella: Simply put, astrology itself won't change. It will, of course, evolve to suit how the culture and the world change. I think it is more interesting how the practice of astrology will change, and change indeed it will! First and foremost, that it will be practiced to a much more widespread quantity is a major change. That, then, opens the door to the best and the worst of what certification has to offer. Hopefully, this will be handled in a responsible way by the astrological community, so that, let's say, Saturn and Uranus do not bring out the worst in each other.

Ken Bowser: I have no idea how astrology will change in the twenty-first century. I'm only confident that it will endure.

Astrology is one of the occult arts, and attempts to popularize it make me wonder about the wisdom of that. People have always wanted to break into the mysteries, usually for reasons that are profane, that is, for power, prestige, manipulation and profit. I think that motivation will keep the doors shut to all who take up the study for unworthy ends. I feel confident that the study of astrology is an individual consciousness quest which, if undertaken in the right spirit, can facilitate fast growth.

Kim Rogers-Gallagher: How will astrology change in the next hundred years? Well, with the discovery of new planets, solar systems, and even new galaxies, it had better change. If the planets are part of the language of astrology, new planets and bodies should necessarily broaden our vocabulary, allowing us to add new words—new adjectives and adverbs, specifically—to our astrological interpretations. I'd also like to think that folks will learn to accept astrology more confidently as our confidence, our knowledge, and our skills of interpretation broaden.

Those of us who have found astrology are unbelievably lucky to have it. Once you've really studied it, there's absolutely no way to argue against it. Astrology *works*—and unlike Tinkerbell, you don't have to believe in it for that to happen. Those of us who've been called to become astrologers are even more fortunate. We've been given more knowledge than the average bear, which allows us to become more wise, accepting, and understanding than others. In short, we're the new generation of "elders." Our challenge is always, always to represent astrology reputably and honestly, with the good of our clients and the wonderful gift we've been given in mind.

Robert Hand: I do not see astrology going away any time soon. If it could survive the eighteenth and nineteenth centuries, it can survive anything but total cultural annihilation. I also do not see it becoming part of the mainstream, at least not completely, any time soon. The reason is that the mainstream world-view and astrology are just too far apart. I do see astrology becoming more professional, and astrologers becoming more educated not only in astrology but in general.

I also think a great period of synthesis is coming upon us. At the moment, the various schools of modern Western astrology, traditional Western astrology, and traditional Hindu astrology are competing for people's attention. I think that ultimately creative individuals will begin to put these systems together, discard the weaker elements of each, and create something new. But unlike modern Western astrology, this new synthesis will have its roots firmly in an understanding of its tradition and will be a continuation of the past, neither ignoring it as modern Western astrology has done, nor idealizing it as some Hindu and traditional Western astrologers have done.

Robert Schmidt: I believe that astrology can make great strides in the coming century, provided that astrologers themselves undertake the rather daunting task of solving the "problem of astrology." Although it is not even clear at present just how this problem should be formulated, it would certainly involve examining and investigating the historical, metaphysical, scientific, and epistemological issues—at the very least—connected with the possibility of astrology as an exact discipline. I do not think it reasonable to expect that "they" (that is, academics or scientists) will do this work for astrology; nor do I think that it would even be desirable for astrologers to shirk the responsibility for solving this problem. Project Hindsight has shown that the astrological community itself can address the historical dimension of this problem. I see no reason why the astrological community cannot likewise deal with the other issues mentioned above, although it would take a major self-education campaign within the community to produce the persons capable of doing the remaining work. However, as the Greeks used to say: "Good things are difficult."

Ronnie Gale Dreyer: I think that, ironically, astrology will continue to go back to its roots, and the revival of interest in classical Western and Eastern systems will only continue. I believe that we will continue to interpret ancient systems in light of our modern world; classical systems will become more meaningful, and people will finally accept that we only have control over our lives to the extent that we make friends with the planets, and accept that their influence will always be there both helping and hindering us in our journey through life. I also think that Kepler College, the Sophia Project in England, and the various astrologers who are doing higher degrees that involve astrology will help legitimize its study and further our interest in its historical and classical roots.

I think astrology is an almost perfect system, and it works regardless of which technique we use, and whether or not we pinpoint how it works on a particular day. Thorough horoscope interpretation and forecasting, however, are only as good as the astrologer's proficiency in understanding his or her technique, communicating clearly, and listening to intuition. I believe that these three factors allow us to be good astrologers. However, if the astrologer misinterprets or misreads, that does not mean that astrology does not work. It simply means that the application of astrology is only as good as the astrologer doing your reading. Astrology itself, however, works perfectly.

Steven Forrest: Many of the changes coming to astrology will be driven by its wider acceptance by the general public. We're already seeing motion in that direction, and I suspect it will continue. We'll see astrology losing some of its zany image. We'll see it taken for granted in the mainstream—there will be more casual references to it in popular culture and entertainment media. We'll see astrology emerging as a somewhat conventional career choice. With that will come the inevitable need for standards, degrees, licensing, and so on. I'm accepting of this, and aware that in effect I've been pushing toward it in my work ever since I began. I'm also thinking I'm glad I am alive now in these

90

"outlaw" days in astrology's history. I enjoy the present edginess and the way that saying "I am an astrologer" presses the buttons of reactionary people. This is just mischief in me, and I don't want to make a religion of it. But I admit it's there.

More deeply, the bottom line is that truly effective astrological counsel helps people enormously. It needs to become more widespread, safer, and more accepted, for the greater good of everyone. As it becomes more conventionally acceptable, more conventionally-minded people will move in and take over with their rules, politics, and natty little shoes. Ob-la-di, ob-la-da; life goes on.

Modern psychotherapy is a powerful, effective system, and it's currently dying because of the HMOs. People just don't change deeply through the mandated six weeks of psychotherapy. It takes longer than that. Economic pressures are trying to speed up the psychotherapeutic process. The system is responding to that by becoming increasingly reliant on psychopharmacology—anti-depressants, mood-stabilizers, and so on. Soon enough, as word spreads about side-effects, there will be a public backlash against the over-prescription of those medications. Enter astrology. Our system is incredibly fast. We can do the analytic work of six months of psychotherapy in an hour. A psychotherapist who is also an astrologer will have a fat, natural niche in the coming environment. As the world gets crazier and more stressful, people will continue to need counsel. What I see here could take a variety of forms, but essentially it is the birth of true astro-psychology. That will be a dominant feature of the practical astrological landscape in the coming century.

Technology is always delightfully tough to predict. Certainly, computers have revolutionized astrology. That will undoubtedly continue. Artificial Intelligence will mature, and probably support the development of vastly improved "computerized readings." People will get online, pump in their birth data and a description of an issue they're facing. The machine will calculate the chart, and enter into dialog with them about it. It may even refer them to a local astrologer, who would be prepared by receiving a transcript of the dialog. It can be inexpensive, and it will be powerful.

A more important effect of technology is the way it will change the culture of astrologers themselves. Like all cultural change, this is a slow process. A generation ago, to be an astrologer you had to be able to do some picky arithmetic. That tended to select people as astrologers who were more left-brained than right—more linear, logical people, just because the arithmetic was daunting. But the important thing—the act of interpretation—is poetic and metaphorical, and thus better handled by people of an artistic temperament. So we have the phenomenon of astrologers being people who can get to first base (setting up the chart), but who tend to stumble on their way to second base (actually interpreting the thing in a lively, multi-dimensional way). The clearest evidence for this phenomenon lies in the tone of most of the astrological literature published in the past century—the writing is almost invariably dry, turgid, and boring. That baffled me for a while. It seemed that astrologers should be more like poets, since in the end a birthchart is more like a poem than an equation. With computers removing the hurdle of the arithmetic, I think a sea-change is happening in the culture of the astrological community. I think it will increasingly be populated by artists: poets, painters, and musicians. This change could have happened twenty years ago when hand-calculated charts started becoming the exception rather than the rule. *But cultural change always lags behind technological change.* It took the automobile a couple of generations to put an end to the cult of female virginity. It took television fifty years to destroy family and community. It might take computers half a century to bring the poets back into astrology, where they belong.

Wendy Z. Ashley: Uranus and Neptune in Pisces ought to help bring more mythic consciousness to astrologers.

Each of these questions is worth at least an eight-page essay!

PART TWO: JOYCE'S STORY

Born: January 16, 1943, 4:18 p.m., Pryor, OK.

Age 6 weeks: Moved from Oklahoma to Indiana to live with mother and maternal grandmother. My father joined the army.

Age 10 months (approx.): My father went to war in the South Pacific.

Age 3, March 1946: My father returned from the war.

Age 4, January 29, 1947: My sister was born.

Age 6, January 22, 1949: My brother was born.

Age 9, November 28, 1952: Very traumatic move to another state.

Age 11, March 1954: We moved again to a building with forty men.

Age 11, May 22, 1954: My beloved grandmother died suddenly.

Age 11, September 15, 1954: My youngest sister was born.

Age 15, July 1958: I had tonsillectomy surgery.

Age 16, March 1959: Systemic strept infection. Very ill for a year.

Age 17, May 1960: Graduated from high school.

Age 17, September 1960: I left home for college.

Age 19, June 15, 1962: I met my first love.

Age 20, Spring-late Summer 1963: Secret relationship with married school psychologist. In late August, I moved to a city to work.

Age 21, September 1964: Returned to college for last semester.

Age 22, February 1965: Moved to New York City and began new job.

Age 22, September 1965: Began graduate school in English.

Age 23, September 1966: Started being a teaching assistant.

Age 23, October 1966: Met Will, my future husband.

Age 24, Summer 1967: Traveled alone in Spain.

Age 24, October 7, 1967: Married Will.

Age 26, March 1969: We left to live in Peru.

Age 27, May 30, 1970, 8:20 p.m. (approx.): Arequippa, Peru, car accident.

Age 27, August 1970: Returned to U.S., began career change.

Age 28, August 1971: We moved to a Southern state.

Age 28, September 1971: Learned mother had advanced breast cancer.

Age 30, August 16, 1973: Mother died.

Age 31, December 1974: We moved out of our house and mini-farm.

Age 32, March 1975: To California en route to emigrate to New Zealand. June, to Hawaii. August, to New Zealand, stayed seven months.

Age 32, November 22, 1975, 8:15 p.m.: Auckland, NZ, spiritual initiation.

Age 33, March 1976-May 1976: In Australia, then returned to U.S. to start private practice in Polarity Therapy.

Age 35, July 4, 1978: Moved to New England to begin training.

Age 35, November 18, 1978: Separated from husband by my choice.

Age 36, September 1979: Began teaching classes and workshops.

Age 37, April 10, 1980: Changed name, reversing first and middle.

Age 37, May 14, 1980: Legal divorce decree issued, and became final November 15, 1980.

Age 38, February 14, 1981: To India to visit spiritual teacher for two months.

Age 38, October, 1981: Fell down stairs, broke thumb.

Age 39, February, 1982: First of many trips to the Caribbean.

Age 39, September 5, 1982: Ithaca, NY, made first flower essence.

Age 40, August 1983: Graduated from four-year professional training.

Age 40, August 19, 1983: Met Michael, my second husband.

Age 43, September 1986: Moved to New York City.

Age 43, December 1986: To India to see teacher, became engaged.

Age 44, August 23, 1987, 9:00 a.m.-10:00 a.m.: Grand Canyon. Spiritual wedding.

Age 44, January 12, 1988, 11:35 a.m.: Legal marriage in New York City.

Age 46, August 1989: Began protracted legal battle to protect father.

Age 47, January 31, 1990: My father died.

Age 47, May 31, 1990: My spiritual teacher left his body, a great grief.

Age 49, March, 1992: Trip to Egypt—initiatic and powerful.

Age 49, August 6, 1992, 2:25 p.m.: Sun River, Oregon, car accident.

Age 49, August 14, 1992, 11:00 a.m.: Bend, Oregon, spinal surgery.

Age 49, September 13, 1992: Moved to country north of New York City.

Age 49, November 19, 1993: My rabbit friend arrived.

Age 50, September 17, 1993, 8:00 a.m.: Great Neck, NY, spinal surgery.

Age 53, January 1, 1997: Began three-month trip to the South Pacific.

Age 54, September, 1997: Moved to country near a small Southern city.

Age 56, October 7, 1999: My first husband, still a good friend, died.

Age 57, April 9, 2000: My rabbit friend died.

Age 59, December, 2001: We bought our house.

Age 60, April 2, 2002: Smoke damage to our house.

Age 60, April 23, 2002: Ladder broke, I fell, shattered left upper arm.

Age 60, October, 2002: Travel in China, a life-changing experience.

Names have been changed to protect the identity of those involved.

AGE 0-9

Shortly after I was conceived, one of the deadliest tornadoes in Oklahoma history swept through Pryor. Although our family escaped harm, the tornado made a big impression on my mother and on me. Pictures of me as a newborn safe in my mother's arms were on the same pages in the family album as photos of the devastation wreaked by the tornado. The theme of change, often sudden and sometimes destructive, has run throughout my life.

I was wanted, eagerly awaited, and warmly welcomed to this world. My maternal grandmother came from Indiana for my birth. When I was six weeks old, my father drove my grandmother, my mother, and me back to my grandmother's small hometown. He left the three of us there while he went off to join the army. We saw him sporadically until I was ten months old. Then he went away to the war in the South Pacific, and I did not see him again until I was three.

During my first three years I was very happy, forming strong bonds with my mother and grandmother, who were both warm, affectionate, and loving. They were also fun-loving, and my grandmother had a great sense of humor and a wonderful laugh. As devout Roman Catholics, they nurtured my spirituality as well as my sense of wonder and my deep love for nature. In my earliest memory, in the autumn before I was three, *I am with my grandmother in the woods at the edge of town. We are standing beneath a large beautiful hickory tree, holding baskets in which we are gathering nuts. Everything is glowing. One vast unified web of life is filled with an inner radiance.* The essential unity experienced in that moment resonates throughout my whole life.

I was a sunny, gregarious and self-confident child. During the war, when my mother took me on the train to visit relatives in the city, I would walk up and down the aisle, talking to all the soldiers. I was also very precocious and could read, count and recite many nursery rhymes by the time I was three. I enjoyed helping with chores and being given responsibility. I loved sunlight, but when I was three I was kept in the darkness for what seemed to be weeks so that I would not become blind while I had German measles. The dance of light and darkness is also woven into my life tapestry.

I talked about my Daddy all the time although I only knew him from unconscious memories, photos, and what other people said about him. He was tall, handsome, intelligent, and charismatic. I was very proud of him. Life seemed perfect and would only become more perfect when he came home from the war. When he finally did come home, my whole life was suddenly changed in quite the opposite direction. He said I was too independent and self-assured, and he deliberately set out to break my will with stern discipline and physical punishment. He was from the mountains of Kentucky where a peach tree switch was preferred for its sharp sting, but a powerful hand would also do. I was terrified of him and began having nightmares. I was also terrified of a big ghost who would come down out of the high ceiling of my closet at night, but Daddy would say to me, "Don't be afraid of ghosts. I'm the only bogeyman. I'm the only one you have to be afraid of." He would not let my mother come to comfort me at night. I felt banished from paradise. My guardian angel was my only protector. In my big bed, I slept on the very edge so that she would have room for her wings.

One of my strongest early memories is from the summer when I was three and a half, when Daddy took me to Kentucky for the first time. Our first stop was the general store. Inside, in the dim light, I stood enthralled by all the exotic sights and smells. Strange people sat all around talking in a dialect I could barely understand. Just then someone handed me a piece of candy. I was just about to say "Thank you" when Daddy yelled, "Say thank you!" Startled, I hesitated. He yelled, "Say thank you, damnit."

Startled, scared, stubborn, I hesitated longer. He started violently spanking me, then yelling even louder when I started crying. Finally people pulled him away and made him stop. I felt ashamed, humiliated, and resentful. After that I was uncomfortable being the center of attention in large groups of people.

My sister was born shortly after my fourth birthday, and when I was six, my brother was born. There were more chores for me to do, but I enjoyed them. I loved my mother passionately, and I liked helping her. I always knew that I had a special place in her heart. She took good care of us and also made every occasion special. She extended every holiday deliciously. At Easter, she would let me dye eggs every day for weeks. Every Halloween she made me a magical costume. Mama also confided in me and asked my advice, which seems odd but actually felt quite natural. She sometimes said to me: "It is strange, but it seems as though you are the mother and I am the daughter." Even though I always felt cared for and nurtured by her, I understood what she meant.

My father was proud of me and would brag about me to others, but with me he alternated being warm and affectionate with being critical and demanding. If my brother and sister did anything wrong, it was I who was whipped with a stinging switch. My father seemed to enjoy dominating me, and yet he expected me to forgive him instantly and come sit on his lap. I loved, admired and feared him, but I was determined not to let him break my spirit.

I turned to my grandmother for support and comfort. Most days I would come home from school, do my chores, and then go to have dinner and spend the night at her house. We would stay up late, sitting at her kitchen table, laughing together, and talking about everything just like grownups. We were each other's favorite person in the whole world. She was like a strong old tree whose resilience and inner strength was transmitted silently and steadily to me. Although she had experienced adversity in her life, she exuded light-hearted joy and gave me gifts of spirit which have sustained me all my life.

Other than spending time with my grandmother, my favorite activities as a child involved nature, color, and movement. I was passionate about coloring and hunting Easter eggs, being thrown high in the air and caught by my uncle, planting flowers, swinging high for a long time, roller skating, riding my bicycle, doing somersaults down the grassy green slope, running barefoot in freshly-cut grass, picking plantain to feed my rabbits, lovingly caring for my bunnies and dolls, sitting under the grape arbor sharing secrets with my favorite cousin, running in the dark catching fireflies with my friends, visiting my city cousins, taking pictures with my Brownie camera, reading, simply drinking in color, painting with watercolors, listening to music, and dressing up at Halloween.

Our small town was evenly divided between Protestants and German Catholics, two distinct groups which did not mix. Our lives revolved in a relatively small orbit around the church. Every day for years the same boy carried my books on the walk to Catholic school. There the same three girls were my best friends. On weekends aunts, uncles, and cousins visited. My mother's two sisters together had five children, and my cousins were very important to me. Family, church and school were my whole world and I felt in place in it, grounded and connected. It was my mother's world. My father, who was an agnostic, lived in it but was not really of it.

He liked to think for himself, outside of conventional belief systems. He had wanted to go to college and law school on the G.I. bill, but decided that he should instead use his many construction skills to support his growing family. He worked very hard to provide for us, but he felt that in our small town his opportunities were limited. He talked of moving us to Peru. The idea of living in South America appealed to my own adventurous spirit. I longed to explore the world. Most of the year I traveled through reading, but in the summers from the time I was three years old until I was nine, I lived in what was to me a foreign land, the Appalachian mountains of Kentucky.

My father was born on a remote farm deep in the mountains and lived there until he left home at the age of fifteen. His mother had died when he was only two years old. She had worked herself to death, he said, caring for six young children while living a harsh pioneer life. His father and his second wife still lived on the old homeplace. Getting there was an arduous adventure, for after a certain point there were no more roads. From there on, we had to slowly maneuver a big truck down meandering creekbeds all day before finally arriving in the wide green valley cradled by mountains. To me it was the end of the world. Beyond was only wilderness: deep, dark, primal and awe-inspiring. I was welcomed as my father's child, as kin. I wore sundresses made out of flour sacks, ran barefoot, rode donkeys and horses, climbed mountains, listened to long-told stories, and learned to milk cows. Running wild over the mountains, exploring the creeks, I experienced many magical moments.

My desire to explore the outer world has always been balanced by my yearning to discover the inner. All of my life I have navigated by inner knowing and a deeply felt orientation to my source. As a young child my spontaneous nature was to be compassionate, generous and joyful. My father and my mother's relatives would often say, "She is naturally good, just like Grandma." After hearing that often enough, I became self-conscious and rather than being just naturally myself, I aspired to be good.

My natural spirituality was primarily shaped and conditioned by my Catholic upbringing. I delighted in the holy feeling of the Mass and the music, light, color, and fragrance that created a sacred atmosphere. As a child, when I would think about what I wanted to be when I grew up, I knew I wanted to be a saint, the lover and beloved of God. I especially wanted to be like St. Francis of Assisi, a blessing to humans and animals alike. As a Catholic, in addition to being good, I was supposed to avoid sin. Because there were so many sins, both mortal and venial, they were impossible to avoid. Guilt and shame began to cloud my natural joy. Nonetheless, I was a happy child, enchanted with life, seeing the bright side of everything.

AGE 9-17

When I was nine, several life-changing events occurred. At the end of the summer my step-grandmother in Kentucky died suddenly. My grandfather went to live with his daughter, and the wilderness began to overtake the gardens and pastures. Then suddenly on the night before Thanksgiving my father announced that a large nuclear facility was to be built in Ohio. He had bought a farm and other land, and we were moving the next day. He gave me a choice to stay with my grandmother whom I loved more than anyone on Earth or to go with my family. I wanted to stay with her, but I thought I should go with my family whom I also loved. I went, making a choice I greatly regretted later.

I never got to say goodbye to my friends. On the way to our new home, the truck carrying most of our things was in an accident right in front of us, and our belongings were scattered broken over the highway. When we arrived at the farmhouse, we found it had no running water, plumbing, insulation or heat except for one coal stove. It was also haunted by ghosts. I had to get up early to milk our cows, then wear high boots to wade through the knee-deep rushing waters of the creek to get to the road. I rode the bus to a country school with violent children who threw knives and threatened me. I was terrified. If I ventured outside the small schoolhouse, I was attacked and thrown to the ground by large gangs of boys. Academically, I was far ahead of the other students. Eventually I was skipped a grade ahead.

My mother, who had always been a vibrant presence at home, was gone until evening working in my father's new business. After the freedom of living in town, able to walk everywhere, we were suddenly dependent on my father for transportation. A source of pain for my mother and for me was that he would often say he was too tired to take us to church on Sundays. My life was narrowed down to home and school, and both seemed cold and bleak. I found my only comfort in nature.

In the Spring when I was eleven, we moved about fifteen miles away to my father's contracting business, lumberyard, and hardware store. He was still completing a boarding house for the nuclear plant construction workers. Soon after we moved, on May 22, my beloved grandmother died suddenly of a stroke. Although I had not been able to see her since we moved from Indiana a year and a half before, we wrote to each other, and I always felt her loving presence in my life. Her death was a great shock. I was devastated and felt there was no one left in the world who understood me. A few months later, on September 15, my youngest sister was born. I was thrilled to have someone new to love. I named my sister and took care of her as if I were her mother.

We lived in the boarding house, sleeping under the same roof with forty single men and three women housekeeper-cooks. Working there as a waitress, I enjoyed talking with the men and enjoyed their attention. I was also exposed to a dark side of life. Against my mother's wishes, I sometimes went with the housekeepers when they cleaned the men's rooms. I would see magazines lying around with titles like *True Crime* and *Sexology*. Their covers often had pictures of women tied up or lying murdered in a pool of blood. The vivid images evoked dreams in which I, night after night, hid or fled from a rough-looking man who wanted to torture and kill me.

At school, since I had skipped a grade, I was the youngest in my class surrounded by older girls and boys who were much tougher than me. I spent my time in class drawing and daydreaming, taking refuge in a fantasy world where I was a princess who had been sent, for some unknown reason, to live among strangers completely unlike her.

When I was twelve, I discovered a world where I felt blissfully and completely at home. My father built a large swimming pool, not for us children to enjoy, he insisted, but for the boarders and as a ready water supply in case of fire. I spent every spare moment in the water, swimming and diving hour after hour until I fell into bed at dusk exhausted. I was a water creature, in my element.

At night I dreamed in vivid color of swimming through subterranean rivers, sliding down vast snow-covered mountains, encountering wild animals, moving with a few companions through and on Earth as it was long long ago. At some point, I began to call these dreams, which I had had since I was four, my primeval Earth dreams. I also flew and glided between the trees in great forests, did aerial gymnastics and taught others how to fly.

Just before my thirteenth birthday, construction on the nuclear facility was completed ahead of schedule, the workers suddenly left, and our businesses collapsed. My father couldn't collect on money owed him, but he was determined to repay his debts rather than declare bankruptcy. It would take him many years to repay them, so during my high school years our family lived with intense financial and emotional stress. Although my father had always had a temper, his outbursts became unpredictable, violent rages. He would yell, criticize, and belittle us. My mother became worried, anxious, sometimes even distraught. Hypervigilant and full of turbulent emotion, I struggled to contain the chaos.

Daddy insisted that we children needed to work to earn our keep. He turned the empty lumberyard into a mini-farm with cows, pigs, chickens, and sheep. He expected us care for the livestock and work all day in the hot summer sun to grow a big garden. As the oldest, I was expected to work the hardest. My mother and I also had to can, pickle, and freeze the harvest. We had always enjoyed an abundance of good, nourishing, delicious food and that continued to be true, no matter how little money we had. In fact, we had so much that we were giving away much of the food we grew and canned. Both my parents were skilled gardeners, and my mother was a great cook. I was learning many skills that would serve me well later in life. I didn't mind working, but I resented Daddy for pushing me so hard and relentlessly.

The fear and paranoia of the Cold War era had seeped deeply into my consciousness. At night I dreamed of either North Korean soldiers or Nazi storm troopers invading our house, seeking us out to kill us. When I was thirteen, I acquired an extensive list of provisions for a bomb shelter and made one in a basement room. I also had a long-range plan to run away from home, taking my sisters and brother with me.

100

Under stress, my father became more controlling. All through high school he would only rarely allow me to participate in extracurricular activities or to spend the night at my friends' houses. He wouldn't allow me to date until I was sixteen, but he was sexually intrusive with me, speaking in a suggestive manner and trying to fondle me. I spent a lot of energy evading his advances. I was seething with rage which I could not express to him without provoking even more violence. I remember one day when I was fourteen, standing in my bedroom feeling my blood boiling and thinking that if I didn't control my anger I would actually burst a blood vessel and die. I made a conscious decision to suppress my anger. I unwittingly also subdued my vitality. I had always been very healthy, never ill except for croupe once as an infant and measles, mumps and chickenpox. Shortly after I decided to suppress my anger, I started getting sore throats; then my tonsils became inflamed and were surgically removed.

With the boarders gone, the building had forty empty rooms. When I was fifteen, I moved into one of them. Although we had many battles over the subject, my father refused to allow me to have a lock on my door. At night the door to my family's apartment was locked from the inside. I was on the other side with thirty-nine empty rooms and my very active imagination. I had nightmares of the devil coming up the stairs from the vast dark basement, slinking through the hallways, slipping into my room, and trying to get into my bed. I spent my nights struggling with him.

No matter how he treated me, I admired my father, the strong one. At thirteen and fourteen, I felt scornful of my mother for being weak and unable to protect me from him. I deeply loved and needed her, however, and by the time I was fifteen, we were close again. When my father hurt or disappointed me, she cried with me. With very few resources she did her best to help me feel confident. She taught me how to sew, and together we made all my clothes. I was pretty and bright and had many friends at school, but since my home was so unusual and I couldn't share in my friends' extracurricular activities, I always felt different, and somehow ashamed.

Spirituality remained important to me. Every night I officiated at bedtime prayers for my sisters and brother and also spent some time alone praying fervently. In a journal I made a list of all the virtues, and reflected daily on which ones I needed to live more fully. By the time I was fifteen, I was experiencing states of mystical union and bliss, but not all of my awakening sexual energy was transformed into spiritual experiences. I read all the "good parts" of sexy novels my friends passed around. All through high school, I had a crush on the same boy, entertaining fantasies of being with him in a swimming pool, kissing passionately underwater. Part of me wanted to be like the wild girls he dated.

Learning was always a joy and easy for me. I had an excellent memory and never needed to study so I spent all my spare time reading. My interests ranged from literature to history to science. I wanted to become a physicist, an archaeologist, or a doctor. My algebra teacher, who was always very supportive of me, encouraged me to participate in the state academic achievement tests. Every year in the Spring, the top two students in each subject from a school gathered in a regional school. Every year I took the tests in English, history and mathematics. I usually ranked first place in the region and fourth or fifth place in the state in each subject. Winning became extremely important to me. I liked confirmation of my ability, but it was not important to me to have others know.

In the Spring of my junior year, when I was sixteen, I woke up the morning of the first day of testing with a sore throat. I didn't tell my mother because I knew she would want me to stay home. Only after the tests were completed did I admit how sick I was. My mother wanted to take me to the doctor, but my father refused, saying we couldn't afford it. He simply ignored me as I got progressively worse for more than a week. My mother nursed me, but when my temperature spiked, my heartbeat accelerated, and specks of blood appeared in the pores of my skin, she called the doctor to come for a house call. I had a severe systemic strept infection. The doctor wanted to hospitalize me, but we couldn't afford it, so I stayed at home in bed on antibiotics, missing the last two months of the school year.

In the fall, very thin and weak, I started back to school but collapsed on the first day and had to be hospitalized. When I got out of the hospital, my doctor advised me to stay home the rest of the semester. It was a bleak time for me. Mostly I just lay with my face to the wall, picking off the plaster with my fingernails. Fluffy, my big red Persian cat, was my only comfort. By an act of will, I got myself together and returned to school for the Spring semester. I was still very thin, and I felt gangly and unattractive. Having been ill for almost a year, I had lost my momentum in terms of college plans. I was awarded a scholarship as the most outstanding female student in the county, but my father refused to allow me to accept it. He wanted me to wait another year. I felt I would surely die if I stayed at home, so I applied for and received a college scholarship, a board job and an NDEA loan. I didn't tell my father until that September, a few days before I left.

AGE 17-28

The day I left home I felt exultant, as if I had finally, with great will and effort, escaped from a whirling vortex of misery. I had not drowned or been broken. I had survived. I was free. I felt a deep sense of relief, expanding after long contraction,

102

gaining twenty pounds in the first month. I was optimistic, enthusiastic, passionately open to life. The outer world mirrored my new sense of ease. My board job involved checking meal tickets in my own dorm of several hundred girls. I enjoyed greeting them with a smile and soon knew each one. I loved my classes and was always the first one with my hand up to participate. Around campus I smiled at everyone, made many friends, and soon had a steady boyfriend.

My NDEA loan only covered bare necessities, and our family was still very poor. My mother sold milk and butter from our cows to make money for stamps so that we could write to each other. In the fall and spring I would spend about twenty-five dollars on fabric, and she would make me simple, elegant clothes. I learned to look great with very little money and very few clothes. It was important to me to feel that I had the bearing, manners and appearance to be at ease and confident anywhere.

The summer after my freshman year I got a job selling Bibles door to door. I didn't sell many, but I learned about human nature and became interested in psychology. My sophomore year I was counseled to narrow my interests so that I could choose a major. I was equally interested in natural sciences, social sciences, and humanities. I finally decided to focus on English, psychology, sociology and anthropology. Still a devout Catholic, I was developing a broader perspective through reading philosophy.

The summer after my sophomore year, three friends and I took the Greyhound bus to Cape Cod to find summer jobs. The first time I saw the ocean I felt I had truly found home. A few days after I arrived in Hyannis, I met my first love. Mike was seventeen days older than I was, but very mature. He was also intelligent, tall, handsome, and charming. Soon he got me a job in the same oceanfront restaurant where he worked. I was in heaven: being in love, being together, being on the water. The first four weeks I continued to attend Sunday Mass while struggling with the conflict between my religion and my desire for my beloved. Then I decided that a religion that made sex with a loved partner a sin was not in alignment with my own inner knowing. I left the church and began discovering my own way to meditate and connect with God.

Mike planned to go to medical school, and he was determined that we take absolutely no chances on my getting pregnant. I was equally determined not to lose my freedom, independence, and opportunity for an education. I also felt a deep longing to abandon myself to love, give up everything, live with him, and bear his child. At the end of the summer we each returned to our colleges, which were far apart. We both felt that our love was deep and eternal, much more than a summer romance.

My junior year was full with close friendships, being in love, and intense feeling. I had a new roommate, my best friend. Mike and I wrote frequent letters, but we could not afford to see each other again until Christmas. I missed him and thought about him all the time. A month after I was back in school, I was sure I was pregnant. Before I found out that I wasn't, I told him, and he became very upset. I became anxious and depressed and had a few sessions with one of the school psychologists. At Christmas, Mike and I met in a distant city and spent a passionate week together. My depression vanished instantly. We discussed our situation. Missing each other was distracting us from school. He suggested, and I reluctantly agreed, that our lives would be much less stressful if we trusted our love and focused on completing our educations. We would keep writing but not plan to see each other again for several years.

Back at school, I felt much more clear and balanced. After completing most of my courses for majors in English and anthropology, I still wanted enough hours for a major in psychology. As a way of getting more insight into the subject and into myself, I returned for sessions with Matt, the school psychologist I had seen a few times in the fall. Old pain from childhood soon resurfaced. Matt was very sensitive and a wonderful listener. One day rain was pouring outside, and I was crying when I said, "My real problem is that I am in love with you." I was shocked to hear him say, "I'm in love with you too." Although I was then, and still am, strongly opposed to getting involved with married men, I was thrilled to learn that my feelings were reciprocated. I was also very confused because I was still in love with Mike. Matt told me that he had never fallen in love with a student or a client before, and he had always been faithful to his wife. Just before the semester ended, he asked me if I would stay for summer school so that we could continue seeing each other. I agreed. He arranged for us to meet in his office for two to three hours every afternoon. We had long conversations, held each other and kissed, but restrained ourselves from going further.

Along with my summer courses, I also had a job with a great deal of responsibility. I was the assistant to the director of the largest dining hall on campus. We served twelve hundred students and conference attendees a day. I loved my job which required many different skills and gave me the opportunity to meet people. Being tall and blonde, I was used to getting attention from men, but for some reason that summer I was like nectar to bees. If I had accepted all the invitations, I would have had eight dates a day. There was no one I was interested in romantically, and I didn't even kiss most of them, but I was enjoying getting to know many different men.

At the end of the summer I only needed one more semester of school to graduate. Then suddenly the department chairman and Matt's wife discovered our relationship. Matt was in danger of losing his job. He asked me to leave school for the fall semester and return in the spring to graduate with my class. I reluctantly agreed, not foreseeing how that decision would complicate my life. I moved to a city chosen because Matt's friend was a psychologist practicing there. Matt himself entered therapy, and he wanted me to see his colleague. I had a few sessions with the colleague, but he seemed to regard me as a dangerous temptress from whom he needed to keep a cool and protective distance. I didn't find the sessions at all helpful, and I didn't have much money, so I discontinued them.

I soon found out that thinking I could sit out one semester had been a big mistake. As soon as I dropped out, I had to repay my NDEA loan at the same time that I was trying to support myself and save money to go back to school. In September 1963, I began working as an editorial assistant for a magazine. I also volunteered in a hospital and took classes at night to complete pre-med courses because I was again seriously considering becoming a doctor. By the time I completed the courses, however, I had decided that I didn't have the stamina to survive the sleep deprivation an intern endures.

In February, 1964, I met a painter who had shipped his trunk of jeans and Pendleton shirts and ridden his motorcycle across country to attend art school in my city. That winter and spring we rode his motorcycle around the city and countryside and had a very passionate sexual affair. He taught me to paint with oils, and we spent many happy hours painting together. After he left to go back out West, he asked me to marry him, but I declined. I cared for him, but I wasn't in love with him.

I went to my friends' graduation in June 1964, disappointed that I wasn't able to graduate with my class and feeling out of sync with my friends.

In September 1964, I returned to college for my last semester, again with a job as assistant manager of a cafeteria. After graduation, I left for New York City where I joined my best friend and college roommate in a Greenwich Village apartment. I found a job working as an editorial assistant for a magazine and began enjoying the adventure of life in New York. For the first time in my life, I was able to feast on art, music and theatre. I was planning to go to graduate school but felt torn between anthropology and English. I eventually decided upon English. I was accepted at one of the best university English departments in the country and began there in September 1965.

My first year I was a resident counselor in a dormitory, a role which challenged me to develop many new interpersonal skills. I was thrilled with my courses. Reading, discussing and writing about literature was a joy. In a highly competitive atmosphere, I was happy to be doing very well. I knew I could get a Ph.D. and go on to be a university professor, but I still was not certain what I wanted to do. I was in graduate school primarily to continue the great adventure of learning and growing as a human being.

My interest in literature was in many ways an expression of my passionate interest in human beings and my search for answers to the great questions. Since childhood I also had been enchanted with words, tones, rhythms, stories, images, symbols, metaphors, and myths. Through reading I expanded beyond my own personal identity and experience. Immersing myself in the imaginative world created by the writer, I participated in the inner lives of others, lived more lives than just my own, and in the process came to know myself and others better.

Over the Christmas holidays in 1965, I spent a week with Mike, my first love. Although we had a wonderful time together and still loved each other very much, we were no longer in love. Our lives were going in very different directions. He wanted to stay in his home state to practice medicine. After I finished my education, I wanted to travel. At the end of my first year of graduate school, I spent the summer on Martha's Vineyard, completely falling in love with the island and the sea. I had an evening job as a waitress in a very nice waterfront restaurant. I liked waitressing and enjoyed interacting with the customers. Except for when I was with people at work, I preferred solitude. In the mornings I bicycled to the beach to swim and to sit for hours meditating with the waves.

Beginning my second year of graduate school, in the fall of 1966, I was a teaching assistant in the English department. I liked teaching, found it was very natural for me, and realized I could be quite happy making it my life work. Living off campus with a woman friend, I soon met and began to fall in love with Will, an anthropology graduate student who lived downstairs. Bright, interesting, and passionate, he was five years older than me. He had a master's degree in political science and Latin-American studies and was well-traveled and fluent in several languages. He planned to return to Peru, where he had been a Peace Corp volunteer, to do fieldwork for his dissertation.

Will awakened my political and social consciousness. For the second semester advanced composition course, I could choose a research and writing topic for my students. Will suggested the Spanish civil war, a topic which could also bring awareness to current issues. Since I read and spoke Spanish and knew the literature inspired by the war, I agreed that it would be an interesting topic. By the end of the semester I had learned so much about Spain that I decided to spend the summer there. For two months I traveled alone by train and local buses, completely falling in love with the country and the people.

When Will and I met again at the end of the summer, his first words were: "Will you marry me?" I had been in no hurry to get married, but I spontaneously said, "Yes." We found a Unitarian minister who would let us write our own ceremony. At the rehearsal dinner, our families met for the first time. Will's parents had been divorced since he was twelve. In many ways his mother's strong personality was like my father's and his father's gentleness like my mother's. I liked both of his parents very much, but his father and I felt a special affinity for each other. With our families and many friends present, Will and I were married in the campus chapel at 6 p.m. on October 7, 1967.

We honeymooned at home, blissfully happy. That third year of graduate school I received an M.A. in English and completed most of the courses for a Ph.D. in English and American literature. I was also taking additional anthropology and history courses under the American Studies program. The summer of 1968 Will and I took our first trip together, driving across country to visit his brother in San Francisco, where we had a first-hand experience of Berkeley and Haight-Ashbury. Although we were not tempted to become hippies or revolutionaries, we were expressing our opposition to the war in Viet Nam. After California, we visited family, then accompanied my father to his Kentucky mountain birthplace. From the day I had left for college, my father had unceasingly criticized my choices. His inviting us to share what was most dear to him seemed to me to be a gesture of peace. I accepted his gift with an open heart, enjoying and appreciating him as I never had before.

From Kentucky we went to Martha's Vineyard, one of my favorite places, to spend the rest of the summer with Will's mother, aunt, and cousins. I enjoyed being with his extended family for long days at the beach and family dinners. Everything Will and I did together was fun, easy, and flowing. We rarely disagreed and never argued. As happy as we were, I was nonetheless becoming troubled by two major issues. One was that, although he was very warm and physically affectionate, Will had a much lower libido than I did. The other was tension in my relationship with his mother, in spite of both her and my best intentions and efforts.

When we returned to school for the 1968 fall semester, we learned that Will had received a grant to do his dissertation research in Peru. We would be living there for about a year and a half. We wanted to make a documentary film while we were there so we continued photography and filmmaking courses we had started in the spring. We also took our Ph.D. qualifying exams. At first I thought I would work on my dissertation while we were in Peru. I finally concluded that was unrealistic. I decided to immerse myself in the fieldwork experience, helping Will with his research and starting on my own dissertation when we returned. We both wanted children and felt the perfect time would be when we came back from Peru.

We had decided to drive there in our red VW bug, a daring proposition at the time. On a snowy March day in 1969, we loaded up everything we would need and drove south through Mexico and Central America. As we met people on our travels, I discovered a joy and talent in portrait photography. I found I could make connections with people in a way that helped them to open up and reveal their essence. In Panama, we put our car on a big Italian liner for the journey through the locks of the Panama Canal. After driving through Ecuador and northern Peru, we finally arrived in Lima. To get to the town that would be our home, we drove for six hours continuously uphill on spiraling switchback roads barely hugging the sides of the mountain. At almost 16,000 feet in altitude, we leveled off on a high plane, then dropped down to 12,500 feet and entered a high mountain valley. The town we had chosen was strung out for several miles on both sides of the road passing through the valley. A few miles past the town, the road climbed precipitously to higher mountains and then descended to the jungle. Behind the adobe houses that lined the road, the fields spread out and up the mountainsides in a tapestry of green and gold. The air was sparking clear, fragrant with eucalyptus. We were immediately entranced.

We arrived with a letter of introduction to a high school teacher. Don Moises was a true gentleman-scholar who welcomed us with open arms and introduced us to his extended family. They helped us find a simple adobe house. Our only furniture was a table and chairs and a bed. I washed laundry by hand and shopped in the local outdoor market. In the evenings Don Moises would visit, and the three of us would sit around the kitchen table, talking in the glow of the Coleman lantern. The nights were magical. In the velvety darkness, the stars seemed close enough to touch. Deep silence was shattered occasionally by choruses of barking dogs.

Our next-door neighbor was one of several shamanic healers in town. A medical doctor was available at the local clinic once a week. Señora Wally, the town pharmacist, seemed to bridge both worlds. Many people in town thought of her as their healer. From the first moment I met her, I felt inspired by her. I watched her hold a patient's hand, taking her pulse, in a sympathetic resonance. Very warm and perceptive, she knew what her patient believed would heal her and prescribed accordingly, from herbal teas and tinctures to aspirin to antibiotics. She touched me deeply and became a guiding light for me.

Señora Wally taught me a little about Andean medicinal herbs and from other women I learned about culinary herbs and foods. I decided to do a study of the local diet so I went to Lima to be trained by the UN Food and Agricultural Organization to do a nutrition survey. Returning to our town, I trained local women to assist me. Every day for many weeks, I was at someone's house for each meal, weighing and noting exactly what foods the family was eating. The nutritional value of the foods would later be determined from established nutrient composition charts, once we returned home and had access to the university computer. Later, in nearby Jauja, the first capitol of Peru and an important social and economic hub for the whole area, I discovered a treasure trove of newspapers dating back to the early 1800s. From them, I began putting together, like a puzzle, a history of the region. We also began making a documentary film of Jauja's colorful outdoor market.

We felt very peaceful living inside our house made of earth. As if they had just risen up from the great earth mother herself, the thick adobe walls sheltered us. Outside, walking on the mountains, I would sense places where a powerful energy emanated. Earth became more richly, resonantly alive for me. Sky, sun, moon, stars, planets, and the darkness of space became equally vivid. Night was vibrant with mystery, the veil between dimensions very thin.

For months we had been planning to leave on a trip in late May of 1970. First we would travel to the northern part of Peru, then go south. We set off down to Lima as planned, but when we arrived at the fork in the road where we could go north or south, we simultaneously turned to each other and said "Let's go south first." As the sun set on May 30, our second day of traveling south down the coast, I said, "I have never felt better in my entire life." I felt healthy, strong, vibrantly alive, and eager to get pregnant when we returned from our trip. As darkness fell, we headed inland to the beautiful colonial city of Arequippa.

We could see the city lights filling the broad valley below as we spiraled down the mountain. Suddenly we came around a curve to find a large truck with no lights parked right in the middle of our lane. With a mountain on one side, an abyss on the other, and someone coming in the other lane, we hit the truck. Sand on the road caused us to skid so that we were saved from going under the metal truckbed, but the front wheel on my side hit a truck tire, pushing the floor up into my feet, compressing my spine. I immediately knew that I was badly hurt. Will, who had been driving, was unhurt. At a very poorly-equipped hospital, I waited half the night before my spine was x-rayed and I learned that I had, along with other injuries, fractures of the T-12 and L-1 vertebrae.

The next day, Sunday, May 31, lying in my hospital bed, I felt earthquake shockwaves, distant ripples of a 7.7 magnitude earthquake in northern Peru. If we had not made the last minute decision to travel south, on this day we would have been in the city of Yungay. At 3:23 p.m., the entire city of Yungay and all who were there, almost twenty thousand people, were buried under eighty million cubic yards of snow, ice and earth. Our impulsive decision had saved our lives. We had eluded death but not completely escaped harm.

Later that day a doctor finally appeared, and I was put into a body cast. I felt like a flower whose stem was broken, but I was sure that I would heal very quickly and continue completely unaffected on my former trajectory. After our car was repaired, we returned to our town, completed our work, and in August said goodbye to friends, community and mountains, and left Peru. I had entered into the experience in Peru with the willingness to be totally changed, and I had been. On the flight home I grieved for the loss of our simple lives close to the Earth and the stars. I didn't see how modern conveniences could possibly be any compensation for all that we were leaving behind.

Along with Curry, our dog whom we had brought from Peru, we visited our families. My parents had been divorced while we were gone. Although my sympathies were with my mother, we also visited my father and his new girlfriend. When we returned to school, I took several courses but decided to put my dissertation on hold for a while. Profoundly changed by my experiences in Peru, I felt called in other directions. I was reflecting on my experiences with Señora Wally and pondering the subjects of health and healing. The computer analysis of the nutrition data I had gathered in Peru showed that the most well-nourished were the second from the bottom of the four groups economically. They were poor, and for the most part outside the cash economy, but they were eating an abundant diet of traditional unprocessed foods.

Intrigued by these findings, I began reading dozens of nutrition books and shifted my cooking style from gourmet to natural foods. Aside from thinking about health in general, I was interested for personal reasons. After years of taking my strong healthy body for granted, I was being forced to pay attention to it. My spine was still healing, and I was very focused on becoming healthy again before getting pregnant.

AGE 28-34

In August, 1971, we moved to the Southeast, where Will had a university teaching position. We wanted to create a simple, harmonious life in deep connection with nature and community. In the country about fifteen miles from town, we rented a small rundown tenant house with two acres of land so depleted that it was just white sand, too barren even to grow weeds. We spent countless hours refinishing floors, painting, and making fences. Because we could easily support our modest lifestyle on one salary, we decided Will would teach for several years and I would farm and do volunteer work. Then we would switch roles.

My mother came to visit us in September. I treasured every moment with her, appreciating her more than ever. A week after she returned home, she called to tell

110

us that she had been diagnosed with a rare form of inoperable breast cancer and had been given only a few months to live. In shock, I began researching alternative cancer treatments. In late November I traveled with her to a clinic in Mexico. She had a dramatic improvement. When she later had a relapse, she continued trying various therapies with some success.

Meanwhile I was taking a biochemistry course at the university, volunteering in a day-care center, and teaching low-income families about nutrition. Will and I were still planning to edit the documentary film of the Jauja market as soon as we had time. I also had from our trip to Peru thousands of my still photos, of which my favorites were the black and white portraits. I had been interested in photography ever since I saved to buy my first Brownie camera when I was eight, but when I read an article by Susan Sontag in the *New York Review of Books*, I changed my perspective completely and decided to give up photography. Her point, as I remember it now, was that the act of taking a photograph separates us from the present. We are not in the moment but outside it, a spectator. We ourselves lose our experience of the moment we capture on film. Had I not been in a time when I was radically recreating my life, perhaps the article would not have evoked such a deep response.

Shortly after moving to our country place, we had decided that if we were going to continue eating meat, we would take responsibility for raising and killing the animals ourselves. We started raising chickens. When the time came to kill them, we found it such a painful experience that we became lacto-ovo-vegetarians. We kept the egg-laying hens and decided to raise dairy goats for milk and cheese. Our dream was to create fertile soil which would nourish lush gardens and pastures. Thanks to my parents, I had a multitude of skills. Gardening, which had seemed drudgery when I was a teen, became a joyful pleasure. My spine had healed enough for me to do strenuous work, although I sometimes needed to spend several days lying flat to recover. Will, who had spent his childhood in New York City, was eager to learn and enthusiastic about all our projects.

Knowing that she might not live long, my mother decided to tell me family secrets. I learned that my father's mother, who had supposedly worked herself to death, had killed herself with rat poison (strychnine) when he was two years old. Probably manic-depressive, she had previously been sent twice from her remote mountain home to the state mental hospital. My father, who had threatened to kill me if I ran away from home, had himself run away from home at the age of fifteen and led quite an unconventional life before meeting my mother. I felt shocked and disillusioned that my father had not always lived according to the same values he had instilled in us, but I felt I understood him better. I also felt relieved to know consciously what had surely influenced me on an unconscious level.

With the war in Viet Nam continuing in spite of years of protest, the best hope for ending it seemed to be a new president. We pinned our hopes on George McGovern. I was elected a delegate to the county Democratic convention, and then to the state convention where we elected McGovern delegates to the national. After McGovern won the nomination, I began spending every spare moment registering people to vote. On election day, I drove people back and forth to the polls. When we heard that McGovern had lost to Nixon in a landslide, I was devastated and became disillusioned with politics. I concluded that if I wanted to change the world, perhaps I should start closer to home.

I turned my attention to our mini-farm which we hoped to make ecologically balanced and self-sustaining. We traveled all over the state and, one by one, brought home the goats who captured our hearts. Each one had a unique personality and became a dearly loved friend. Vicariously, I delighted in their heel-kicking glee as they ran though the pastures, making music with their bells. The goats, chickens and garden were providing most of our food and a deep sense of joy and satisfaction. As I read books on nutrition, herbology, and biodynamic agriculture, I condensed what I was learning into a newsletter. I was also helping Will teach his anthropology classes, and together we taught a course called "Alternative Lifestyles." Reading the complete works of Wilhelm Reich, we experimented with breathing and orgone energy. We practiced yoga, ran, and bicycled. Our friends were a diverse group, and we were woven into a lively community with many people, each of whom shared some aspect of our interests and ideals. Being the more gregarious, I usually discovered new friendships and activities that Will later shared.

Although this was one of the happiest times of my life, I did not always feel happily married. Will and I agreed on most things or adapted easily to each other, but we still had differences about sex. He also had a fiery temper. Most of the time he was mild-mannered and easygoing, but if something at work upset him, he would come home like a dark storm cloud. He could go on brooding for days before finally erupting into a rage which I found too reminiscent of my father for comfort. I was most disturbed by the tension between Will's mother and me. She had many wonderful qualities, but I experienced her as a third person in our marriage.

Since our tax dollars were financing the continuation of the Viet Nam war, we felt morally responsible, and Will wanted to leave the country. I was very reluctant to leave family and friends. I refused to leave as long as my mother was alive, but it did not look as though she would live long. We began the process of emigrating to New Zealand. I wanted to get pregnant and have a baby before moving again, but Will thought we should wait until we were settled there. I could see the logic of his position, but it ran counter to my feeling and instinct.

By March, 1973, Will had decided not to write his dissertation. I felt it would be a waste not to share what we had learned in Peru so I offered to co-write it. We began a process that, given other events in our lives, would take about a year to complete. He wrote two chapters, and I wrote two on the parts of the research I had done: the history and the nutrition survey. We co-wrote the introduction and conclusion. When we finished, we sent a summary in Spanish to the people of our town in Peru.

All of the Spring of 1973 I felt painfully torn between my desire to be with my mother and my feeling of responsibility to Will. He insisted that my primary responsibility was to him and that he couldn't teach and at the same time milk goats, feed chickens, and tend the garden. By March, Mother was so ill from pain medication that, at a cancer clinic, she went through an extremely difficult and painful withdrawal process. She called me and pleaded with me to come to upstate New York to be with her. As I write this almost thirty years later, I am sobbing. I regret more than anything in my entire life that I did not go to her when she needed me.

In July, 1973, I went to stay with my mother to care for her. On the morning of August 16, I left the room briefly and returned to find her dead. In the minutes after I found her, I alternated from moment to moment between profound grief and sublime exultation as I shared in her spirit's liberation. After a few hours the experience diminished in intensity but stayed with me for months. I thought of the Kalahari Bushmen, who believe that when any being dies, a hole is created in the web of the universe, and through that opening those left behind may get a glimpse of the Infinite. I knew that was true for I was standing in that opening.

When I returned home, I lay in bed for a week, exhausted and grieving, but also immersed in a profound spiritual experience. I decided the time had come to meditate in earnest. I began looking for a spiritual path. I didn't want a guru or a belief system, but simply a way to meditate. After being turned primarily outward for years, my attention was being drawn inward. The year before we had been initiated into a simple meditation technique by members of Ananda Marga, but I didn't resonate with my mantra. Will and I decided to try Transcendental Meditation. We were soon meditating twice a day. My sisters and brother also started practicing TM, and our meditation practice became a bonding force. I was the executor of my mother's estate. Because she had been so ill and some of her papers had been lost in a fire, my responsibilities took up a lot of my time.

In the months after my mother died, I dreamed about her every night and felt her spirit near, but life without her physical presence seemed incomprehensible to me. She had loved me unconditionally, accepting me and everyone else without judgment. She was consistently kind, compassionate and generous. Her worst faults were that she was sometimes shy, nervous, and unsure of herself. She was prone to worry. When she was grieving her own mother's death, she had lamented that she had not written to her mother more. She felt guilty that she had not done more for her. I never wanted to feel that way. As a child of twelve, I had vowed always to be good to my mother, and I had, but after her death I also was beset by regrets and guilt. She would have done anything for me, yet the one time she truly needed me, I had let her down.

In December, Will's father, a beautiful man whom I dearly loved, suddenly died. Will's mother was deeply affected even though she had been divorced from him for years. Although she had been unhappy about our moving to New Zealand, she became even more upset. As usual when we did anything she didn't like, she blamed me for it. Our relationship deteriorated, and Will's and my marriage also suffered.

Even as we made preparations for moving to New Zealand, we continued lavishing love and attention upon our animals and gardens. We had made and dug into our soil tons of compost. Minerals, seaweed and biodynamic preparations had enlivened it. The garden vibrated with energy and consciousness. Presences, intelligent forces in nature were communicating with me and I with them. I was having amazing experiences unlike anything I had ever heard of. Then in the summer of 1974, I read in *The Secret Life of Plants* about Findhorn in northern Scotland. There Dorothy Maclean communicated with the devas and nature spirits. After I wrote the community an eleven page letter describing my own experiences, they invited us to visit. We went to stay for a month in December just before leaving for New Zealand. While there I discovered flower essences and ordered a set of Bach Flower Remedies. We were very impressed with Findhorn and hoped to create a community like it in New Zealand.

Although leaving our gardens, animals, home, friends, family, and community was very difficult, I was excited about the new possibilities before us. I still had a number of years to write my dissertation, but I burned my bridges in a very dramatic letter to the chairman of the English department. Since our time in Peru, I had completely altered course. My new work was still unfolding, but it clearly involved enhancing awareness and health on all levels. I also began to understand and to articulate something that I had always known: that my purpose in this life is to integrate the full spectrum of experience: Heaven and Earth, Spirit and Matter, the sublime and the mundane.

In March, 1975, we began our journey to New Zealand, stopping for several months in California where we studied Polarity Therapy, a hands-on energy balancing work for which I immediately felt a deep affinity. I intuitively understood the principles and had an already well-developed natural ability to perceive and work with energy. In the Esalen Bookstore in San Francisco I bought books to take to New Zealand. Among them were books on the Feldenkrais Method and the Alexander Technique, two forms of movement awareness. While I was standing in the store, a woman walked in and put up a large poster advertising a three-year training in the Feldenkrais Method. I knew instantly that that was what I wanted to do, but it was out of the question since we were about to permanently leave the country.

We had plane tickets which allowed us to stop in Hawaii, Tahiti and the Cook Islands. Our first stop was the Big Island of Hawaii. We were so captivated by it that we decided to bypass the other islands and spend all our time there. All of June and July we camped in state parks. Wherever we were on the island, I felt the powerful energies of the volcanoes moving in me. I felt I was being initiated into my own deep transformational nature. Meditating several hours a day and having very intense experiences, I began to think that I could use some guidance. By a series of synchronicities, we learned about a spiritual path led by a teacher who lived in northern India. We both felt a deep inner knowing that it was right for us.

In mid-August, 1975, we left Hawaiian summer to arrive in New Zealand in late winter. We first stayed near Auckland with friends, then bought a small van and outfitted it to travel around the North Island. Wherever we travelled, we offered free Polarity Therapy sessions. Our van had no shock absorbers, and the impact reactivated the spinal injuries from the accident in Peru. I was soon in constant pain. We decided to stay near Auckland, becoming friends with several older people who helped deepen our understanding of vibrational healing. From England I received my first set of Bach Flower Essences, began learning how to use them, and offered them to everyone I knew.

When we had first arrived in New Zealand, we had applied to the teacher in India for initiation and been accepted. Our initiation, by proxy, was the evening of November 21, 1975 in Auckland. All the events of our whole lives seemed to lead up to that moment. At our initiation we vowed to meditate two and a half hours a day. The meditation began with focusing attention at the third eye with a mantra. From there the soul could move up through other dimensions, following the light and especially the inner sound to its Source. We were soon so enraptured with our inner journey home to God that we were often meditating six hours a day.

In March we learned that, because of new regulations, we could not do the work we wanted to do in New Zealand. We decided to return to the U.S. The day before we were to depart, we learned that our spiritual teacher would be visiting

Australia in May. We decided to fly to Australia to wait for him. As soon as I saw him, I fell deeply in love. He was the most beautiful, loving being I had ever encountered.

At the beginning of June, we returned home. By a series of synchronicities, we were soon practicing Polarity Therapy in a small city in North Carolina. I began studying astrology, reading scores of books, doing charts for all my clients, and paying attention to my own transits and progressions. Astrology was giving me more understanding of myself and others, but I didn't see myself becoming a professional astrologer. I still wanted to study the Feldenkrais and Alexander methods. That same year, 1976, the philosopher Thomas Hanna created the word "somatics" to identify these and other disciplines of mind/body integration. He defined the new word as " . . . the field of study dealing with somatic phenomena, i.e.,the human being as experienced by himself (or herself) from the inside." The inner current I had been following was converging with the gathering outer stream of somatics. It would be my good fortune to study with many of the pioneers, to benefit from their distinct insights and approaches and to creatively integrate them into my own work.

One of the books that I had carried to New Zealand and back was *Awareness through Movement* by Moshe Feldenkrais. It contained ten movement lessons which I recorded in my own voice so that I could lie on the floor and follow the directions without needing to look at the book. I immediately noticed an effect. After doing a movement with awareness on one side of my body, I would notice that I would feel larger, longer and lighter on that side. After doing a sequence of simple movements with minimal effort and maximal awareness, I would stand up lighter and taller, and move more easily.

In May, 1977, we studied for two weeks with someone who was still a student in the Feldenkrais training I had heard about in San Francisco two years before. Every day we had one group Awareness Through Movement lesson, and we each had one private Functional Integration lesson in which the trainee practitioner supported and guided our movements with his hands. Every day I felt more changes in the way I moved and the way I experienced myself and the world around me. On the tenth day, as I was walking down the street, suddenly I was vividly aware simultaneously of the whole environment and of my whole body, including every little bone. To experience myself so fully embodied was to me a revelation. As I continued doing a lesson every day at home, I found the results to be cumulative. Although there were many tangible benefits, the real purpose of the work is to develop awareness, clear intention, freedom, and integrity of the whole self. I experienced the movements, as they were intended to do, freeing up many old, conditioned patterns and habits of sensing, feeling, thinking, and acting. I was becoming more aware and integrated. I also began moving spontaneously in response to very subtle inner impulses, a phenomenon I had never heard described.

Will and I were very dedicated to our spiritual practice, which was the major focus of our lives. Every morning we arose to meditate at what mystics have called the elixir hour, the silent pre-dawn hours. We began at 3:30 a.m. and meditated until around 6:30 when we greeted the day with the birds as the sun rose. Being in tune with the rhythm of the day was very satisfying to me. We cultivated a serene atmosphere in our home and were very supportive of each other, but we lacked skill in communicating and resolving our conflicts. When Will told me that he no longer wanted children, I began to have serious doubts about our marriage. I asked him to go for marriage counseling with me, but he refused, saying he was perfectly happy. I began to think about leaving him, but I felt great inner conflict. I deeply loved him and appreciated his many wonderful qualities, but I wanted to be a mother.

In the fall of 1977, I had a very powerful dream: *I am standing at the foot of a vast mountain of light. When I step forward, I find myself spiraled up easily and effortlessly. I am one with it, absorbed in bliss until suddenly I remember that I had been with some friends and realize they must have fallen behind. I realize I have a choice: to go on without them or to go back for them. I realize it will be harder for me if I choose to go back, but, moved by a feeling of love, I decide to do it anyway.*

Instantly, I am back at the foot of the light mountain, separate from it, facing downhill. I walk down a short distance and on my left see a fence surrounding a vast savannah. Climbing over the fence, I begin to walk, encountering lions, giraffes, and wildebeests. Every kind of wild animal, all the wildness of the Earth, is present. Eventually I come to a farmyard full of domestic animals, and finally I enter a small building where there are people. My friends are among them. As soon as I go in, the door springs shut, and I am just as trapped as they are. The whole inside surface of the room is smooth with no apparent windows or doors. I know there is a way out, but the key is inside me. It is a particular state of consciousness that I know and must find again. I close my eyes. I make a few very subtle shifts in consciousness and finally I find it. In that instant the ceiling and all the walls disappear.

We find ourselves standing outside in a clearing by a forest, just at dusk. I know the way back to the mountain of light, but it is far and there are many obstacles ahead. Resolutely, I set off with my friends following. We walk through dark woods, climb over large boulders, go over waterfalls, and swim through underground rivers. Finally we arrive back at the foot of the light mountain. We are able to ascend, but it is more difficult for me than before, more climbing than gliding. I realize fully what I have given up by choosing as I did.

I awoke to a vivid awareness of the whole dream and the knowledge that I had already chosen to go back for the parts of myself I had left behind. I felt called to wholeness, as a sacred imperative.

AGE 34-40

Shortly after I had the dream, I heard about Giovanni, a psychologist and somatic educator in New England. I flew there in November to attend a workshop with a Feldenkrais teacher from abroad. There I met Giovanni, the teacher Ruth Alon, who would become an important role model for me, and Marilyn, my soul sister who would become my lifelong friend. Giovanni was going to be starting a two year training program in body-centered process in the summer of 1978. I knew it was my next step. I returned home to tell Will that I was moving to New England to do the training. He decided that he wanted to come along to do it also.

In mid-April of 1978, my body completely collapsed. I felt as if my life were hanging by a thread. There were perhaps many factors involved, including the prolonged painful conflict about separating from Will. In some way, however, my condition was mysterious. I found a local chiropractor, one of the first practitioners of Applied Kinesiology, who helped me slowly regain my balance. On July 4, we moved to New England.

In August, all twelve members of our group gathered to begin our training with a ten-day intensive taught by Giovanni, Ruth Alon, and Ron Kurtz, a brilliant therapist who was in the early stages of developing Hakomi work. All three were excellent, very creative, inspiring teachers. Those ten days were a turning point in my life, evocative of my first days in college when I entered a nourishing environment and began to flourish. When we began I was still thin and weak, but on the threshold of a new life. As we explored a form of rebirthing, I re-experienced my birth for the first time:

My mother is drugged with ether, unconscious, no longer present with me, unable to help me be born. I also am falling into unconsciousness, unable to move myself out into life. I know that I will surely die unless I mobilize all my consciousness and will. I do and I begin to move. Hard cold metal reaches in and grasps my head, hurting me, and pulls me out. The room is cold and I am lain on cold metal to be weighed and measured.

Our training integrated aspects of Feldenkrais movement awareness, Al Pesso's Psychomotor work, Ericksonian hypnotherapy, Rebirthing, and Bioenergetics. We were not only learning a whole new orientation and skills for working with other people but also going through profound transformational processes ourselves. By the end of our first ten days together, we had supported, nurtured and challenged

118

each other. We had danced and played together and become a community of close friends. We would become central to one another's lives, meeting one weekend a month and several times for ten day intensives over the next two years. By the end of that first ten days, I felt reborn, renewed, and eager to explore life. Will and I were stunned to find ourselves back alone together needing to decide where to go next.

Giovanni proposed that he, Will, and I live together, and we agreed. We found a lovely, large old house several miles from town. Built in 1830, its foundation walls were massive stones from the land itself. Circling the house were five sheltering presences, ancient maples too big for me to fully embrace. Seven acres of wildflower meadows merged into forest on three sides. Miraculously Sarah, our landlady, gave it to us for a very modest monthly rent, a fraction of its true value.

Finally willing to acknowledge that our marriage was in serious trouble, Will agreed to marriage counseling. After our first session, the therapists suggested we have a trial separation. Although I had been thinking about leaving for some time, the actual separation seemed sudden and literally happened overnight. The day after our counseling session, on November 18, 1978, Will left to stay in the city with a friend from our training group. As we said goodbye, we gazed into each other's eyes, acknowledging our deep spiritual connection and the eternal nature of our love.

We spoke on the phone often. As best friends who had shared everything, we naturally shared the pain of our separation. Even though I wanted it, I felt grief-stricken to lose him. He felt he was being rejected by me and was hurt and angry. I felt hurt and angry that he had been unwilling to address our issues and accept counseling earlier when it might have made a difference. I also was exhilarated, appreciating my freedom to discover myself and to follow my own rhythm without adapting to another person. Will and I saw each other one weekend a month at our training group sessions, where we had loving support from the others. Over time we used our new skills to heal our wounds and transform our relationship.

Meanwhile, I found myself in an unusual situation with Giovanni. He and I had found the house together and neither of us wanted to leave it. We also enjoyed living together. He was charismatic, creative, intelligent, warm, and playful. We were attracted to each other, but he was involved with someone, although he did not believe in monogamy and also saw other women. I liked our living arrangement because he was away half the week, working in the city, and I had the whole house to myself. I had no intention of getting involved with him. Nonetheless, by the end of the year, I found myself beginning to fall in love. In the beginning of January, 1979, I sublet my part of the house and flew to San

Francisco to spend several months studying Ericksonian hypnosis and neurolinguistic programming.

When I arrived in San Francisco, I had been a vegetarian for seven years. I was beginning to realize that my diet had something to do with my illness in the spring and the depleted state in which I still found myself. I could feel my cells hungering for something. When I had been initiated by my spiritual teacher, I had vowed to not eat meat, fish or eggs, drink alcohol or use drugs. I had also vowed to live a clean moral life, which meant, among other things, not having sex outside marriage. I was still meditating two and a half hours every day, and I took my vows very seriously, but I was also feeling more and more that I needed to listen to all of myself.

Aside from my vows, my feelings for animals made even the thought of causing them pain or taking their lives extremely painful for me. Out of compassion, though, for my own body, I was thinking of giving it some fish. Every day for a week, I visited the market and looked at the fish. Finally I bought a small piece, took it home, cooked and ate it. As I swallowed the first bite, my whole body sighed. The conflict about eating animals is something I have, so far, never resolved. Over the years I have alternated long periods as a vegetarian with periods of giving my body the animal protein it craves.

At the end of March I returned to New England and began offering private sessions in Polarity Therapy and body-centered process. I also studied Bodymind Centering intensively with Bonnie Cohen. Studying developmental movement and experiential anatomy with her deepened and amplified the awareness I had developed from the Feldenkrais work. I learned to be present and aware inside my organs, glands, bones, muscles, and fluids and to become familiar with the different states of consciousness each embodies. The summer of 1979, I spent a month in San Francisco and six weeks in Boulder participating in intensive Feldenkrais courses. By the end of the summer, the back pain I had been experiencing since the accident in Peru was almost gone. In the fall, I continued studying with Bonnie, and I began teaching classes and weekend workshops that I called Explorations in Awareness. I integrated what I had been learning from others for the last several years but created original lessons of my own.

For four more years Giovanni and I would share a home. Always we were friends and companions. In many ways we became family. We celebrated holidays and went on vacations together. We were lovers for periods of months or sometimes a year or more at a time. Only for short intervals was I ever the only woman in his life. Since I wanted to be the only one, I caused myself a lot of pain. During the periods when we were not lovers, I dated other men. As challenging as the situation was for me, I kept feeling that what I most needed to do for my own growth was to stay and to learn to love and accept him just as he was. I touched the depths of ancient grief, meditated and journaled, worked with my dreams, read books on relationships, went to counseling with Giovanni, consulted astrologers and the I Ching, and continued to stay. Later I would look back and think I must have been temporarily insane. Eros, karmic connections, self-delusion, and other factors were all, no doubt, mysteriously intertwined.

Although challenging, the five years I lived with Giovanni were for me full of great joy. Surrounded by close friends and a community of kindred spirits, I was learning, growing, and doing work I loved. I was still meditating at least two hours a day and spending another two hours outside every day going for long walks in the woods, bicycling, swimming or cross-country skiing. I danced exuberantly with friends, ran through the rain, and exulted in fragrant lilacs and the wild roses climbing the trees.

In the Spring of 1980 I filed for divorce from Will. At the same time I changed my name legally, reversing my first and middle names and resuming my original last name. In June, I began a four-year professional training with Moshe Feldenkrais himself. On Feb. 14, 1981, Will and I flew together to India to spend two months with our spiritual teacher. The time with my teacher was extraordinary for me. When I returned from India, I felt very clear, very complete in myself.

During the year of 1982, Giovanni and I met one weekend a month with a group of friends. We were planning an intentional community which never manifested. In the summer of 1982, one of those friends introduced me to a comprehensive system of Taoist meditation and chi kung. Since 1979, I had been receiving regular acupuncture treatments and studying the meridian system as well as tai chi. I was thrilled to discover that I could, through chi kung and Taoist internal alchemy, transform and evolve my own energies. At the same time that I began literally working from the ground up with Taoist practices, I continued with my other, more transcendent meditation.

At the end of the summer, on September 5, 1982, I made my first flower essence from a splendid mass of North American bamboo I found near Ithaca, New York. It called to me and I responded. After I made the essence, I took it, and I was amazed. My whole body became a hollow bamboo with a clear fountain of light energy in the center. Over the next four years I made almost a hundred essences, mostly from wildflowers that grew on or near our land.

By the Spring of 1983, I was finally able to accept Giovanni just as he was, discriminate clearly, and see that the time had come to move on. That summer I completed the Feldenkrais professional training. Although we were still living together, Giovanni and I were clear that our relationship was at an end. One chapter of my life was ending and another about to begin. I knew I wanted an outer marriage to mirror an inner mystical marriage. To clarify my intention, I wrote out a description of my ideal mate so that I could draw him to me.

AGE 40-49

In August, I attended a weeklong Taoist meditation and chi kung retreat. At the retreat I met Michael, but I thought of him only as a friend. I did not see him again until October when I visited him in New York City. The more I got to know Michael, the more attractive I found him. He could be tender, soft-spoken and romantic as well as very fiery and dynamic. A free-lance travel writer and photographer who also led groups of people to exotic destinations, he was even more adventurous and ardent about the inner spiritual journey. He had recently opened an ethnic restaurant so that he could spend more time at home in New York. He was nine years younger than I was, but that was not a problem for either of us. Shortly afterward, Giovanni moved out of our house, and a woman friend moved in.

I started a pattern of spending ten days at home, then five days with Michael in New York. When I was at home, I spent all my time working with clients. I stopped teaching weekly classes and taught only weekend workshops in New England and in North Carolina. In New York with Michael, I lived in a timeless state of love, ecstasy, and bliss as we explored the wonders of Taoist sexual alchemy. We felt we were united in a mystical marriage.

In the Spring of 1984, Michael took his parents and me on a trip to the high mountain kingdom of Hunza in Northern Pakistan. His parents were light-hearted and adventurous, and we got along together easily. That summer I took a training course to become a teacher of chi kung and Taoist meditation. After that I began teaching them in addition to the Feldenkrais classes and workshops I was already teaching. In the fall of 1984, I traveled to Lincoln, Nebraska for the first time to study with Marjorie Barstow, one of the first teachers trained in the Alexander Technique by F. M. Alexander. I realized immediately that the Alexander Technique, with its emphasis on vertical orientation, is a perfect complement to the Feldenkrais Method. I also realized that I could use it in my own way to communicate subtle experiences of core, essence, and spirit. Although she didn't seem to have any spiritual beliefs, Marj was a natural Taoist who embodied the principle of *wuwei*, effortless movement. I was inspired and delighted to see her, in her eighties, moving gracefully and easily. I wanted to move with that same light and effortless quality. After that first trip, I returned again and again to learn from Marj. For more than seven years, I spent at least a month every year with her. She was a great inspiration to me. I could see myself, like her, doing my best teaching in my nineties.

In the fall of 1985 Michael was abroad on an expedition for four months. I luxuriated in staying home in New England, devoting myself to work, and spending time with friends. I looked forward to his return and to the next stage of our relationship. Two years before, I had told him that being a mother was very important to me and that I wasn't going to get involved again with any man unless he was willing to get married and have children. He agreed to have children in two years.

While Michael was away, I was very aware that two years had passed. When he returned, we had a wonderful reunion, but when I brought up the subject of children, he said he had changed his mind. He wanted to put all his energy into creating an inner, immortal child. He refused to negociate or waver from his new position, nor would he go with me to a counselor even to discuss it. He said that if I decided having a child was more important to me than being with him, that he would accept my leaving. I felt misled, angry, and frustrated. I did not want to give up being a mother, but I was so deeply bonded with him that I did not see how I could possibly separate. I decided to continue.

About that time, in addition to my private practice and teaching, I started another business. My roommate had introduced me to some nutritional products made in Sweden from flower pollen. I loved the products and felt completely in resonance with them, especially since they were made from flowers. They were distributed through network marketing, so I became a distributor and began developing a large downline of distributors I sponsored. The work required presentation, leadership and coaching skills. I enjoyed the work and seemed to have a natural talent for it, but I wanted to improve my skills so I began taking seminars in leadership, relationships, coaching, commitment, time management, excellence, and many other topics.

After several years, the company shifted to a direct marketing approach and all the downlines disappeared. There were no lasting financial rewards for my efforts as I had hoped, but I learned a great deal in the process. While the business was in the active phase, I began spending more time in New York. In September, 1986, I moved there, but I still kept my part of the house in New England for a while and went there occasionally to work.

Michael and I were married on August 23, 1987 at 9:00 a.m. Eighty-five of our friends and family gathered to witness our marriage in a majestic setting on the edge of the Grand Canyon. We invoked the presence of God, honored the Tao, and read mystical poetry from Rumi, Hafiz and Shams-i-Tabriz. We called the spirits of all the directions, the Canyon, all the saints and sages, and our spiritual

123

teachers. By our own authority, under Heaven and Earth, we married ourselves. The ceremony was very powerful and afterward we felt profoundly changed. After our civil marriage in New York on January 12, 1988 at 11:35 a.m., we went to Hawaii for our honeymoon.

Back home in New York I continued establishing my private practice and began teaching weekly movement classes. I also taught classes in meditation, chi kung, sexual alchemy and tai chi, some of them alone and some with Michael. I continued participating in advanced trainings and exploring other practices. Generally I had spent several years training in a new approach and thoroughly integrating it before pursuing another.

For four years, beginning in 1988, I simultaneously studied in depth a number of practices that were very powerful for me personally as well as professionally. These included work with sound, breathing, and voice, as well as Authentic Movement. I also studied two innovative forms of work developed by Jungian psychologists: Roger Woolger's Soul Dramas and Arnold Mindell's Process Oriented Psychology, sometimes called Process Work. During those years my outer work and relationships continued evolving and flourishing. At the same time I was engaged in a deep inner process of embracing and integrating many conflicting and polarized aspects of myself. With an affinity for metaphor, myth and archetype, and a perception always tuned to pattern and synchronicity, I had long felt a kinship with Jung and Jungians.

In previous years I had moved through many developmental issues from my childhood, but after my marriage more rage toward my father surfaced. I also had more difficulty than I could ever have imagined moving through the grief I felt over not having a child and the anger I felt toward Michael. I could see clearly that I was choosing men who would decide they didn't want children while I identified myself with wanting them. There seemed to be more to it than a projection of my own inner conflict between freedom and commitment. In the first training with Roger, I vividly experienced three apparently past lifetimes in which I died in childbirth and several others in which I died at birth. I began to understand my experience of childlessness in this life. It was very healing for me also to experience lives in which I was a happy and fulfilled mother.

I had never been interested in ancestors or genealogy but had, on the contrary, tried to live unbound by my family's patterns. I was surprised when Rhoda, my father's long dead mother, began to communicate with me, asking for my help. She still seemed to be a tormented soul. Over the years I would have many amazing experiences with her as I embraced the grandmother I had never known.

As the rage I felt toward the father of my childhood bubbled to the surface and was transformed, I became able simply to be with my father in the present.

124

Acceptance, appreciation, and love slowly grew. In 1989, at the age of seventy-nine, he was still in excellent health with a clear mind when his wife, JoAnn, began making threats. By August my siblings and I had ample reason to believe that she was poisoning him. Before we could do anything to stop her, he was in intensive care, near death. Feeling I had to protect him, I called the local authorities. Perhaps because it was not so easy for JoAnn to continue whatever she was doing under scrutiny, my father improved in the hospital, and she took him home again. Once, when we arrived for a surprise visit, he was not drugged and completely conscious and lucid. He said, "She is poisoning me" and begged us to get him away from her. As the oldest, I spearheaded a legal campaign to get him out of her clutches, flying there repeatedly for court dates and meetings with lawyers but never succeeding. He died on January 31, 1990. I felt deep compassion for him, but I did not grieve.

After my father's death, JoAnn claimed there was no will and there were no assets except real estate. After much sleuthing, my brother and I discovered that while our father was unconscious in the hospital, JoAnn had taken his hand and marked an X on a Power of Attorney notarized by her friend, then used the document to liquidate all of his assets before his death. I wasn't going to give up without a fight. Over the next year, with a great deal of effort, my brother and I were able to locate and return to the estate about a third of the assets. We worked hard to get the money for ourselves and our sisters. For me it was virtually a full-time job. Although I had to work for it, I saw the money from my father as a healing balm, a way of balancing the pain and deprivation of my childhood.

Meanwhile, on May 31, 1990, four months after my father's death, my spiritual teacher in India left his body. Profoundly grief-stricken, I began to have powerful dreams. I understood them to mean that the time had come for me to completely internalize the guru and the father. In the summer, I spent two weeks with my brother on our family's land in Kentucky. There I felt very strongly the presence of my ancestors and began to appreciate and honor them. In August, Michael and I spent two weeks in California camping and communing with the redwood trees. That whole autumn I experienced a deep encounter with the inner masculine. In December I received the first part of the inheritance from my father.

At about the same time, I began a long, transformational descent. It began with a series of powerful and beautiful dreams of dark goddess figures, but when I saw the film "Jacob's Ladder," I plunged down into the sub-cellar of consciousness. Perhaps the image from the film that disturbed me the most was that of the ghoulish hospital attendants pushing the main character on a stretcher through endless sub-basement corridors. On my journey into the depths, I was

125

grateful for Sylvia Brinton Perera's wise *Descent to the Goddess* which I read again and again.

In the Summer of 1991, renting a room on a quiet Caribbean island beach, I created for myself a six-week silent retreat. I meditated, walked on the beach, swam and snorkled, but did not read. I spent hours every day alternating between painting, writing, sounding and moving, my process going deeper as I moved from one mode of expression to another. After such a deeply satisfying experience, I wanted to plan similar retreats for others to access their own inner knowing. Over the years my clients and students had included more and more singers, musicians and actors. In September, 1991, I began teaching Feldenkrais and Alexander in a training program for actors. I felt exhilarated and inspired working with them and was thinking of studying acting myself.

On February 14, 1992, with my husband and a group of people, many of whom were old friends, I traveled to Egypt. Since childhood I had felt a strong connection to Egypt but never before had an opportunity to go. From somewhere deep inside, I felt called to sing and dance in each of the temples. We landed in Cairo at night, traveling in the dark to our hotel in Giza. As soon as I lay down on the bed, I began having visions of past events in Egypt. The whole journey was for me one of revisiting places I knew, remembering other lives, and passing again through an experience of initiation.

In May, I had a very intense experience of a lifetime in Egypt: *I am lying on a stone table in the center of a room. Around me people are standing in ritual positions. They cut me open, take out my organs and place them in canopic jars on ledges around the room. Presumably I am dead, but I have complete awareness and even feel intense pain.*

The experience was so intense and overwhelming that I could not resolve it. The next evening, while dancing exuberantly, I strained my left psoas muscle. Gradually the pain increased.

At the end of May, I painted something that was at the time inexplicable to me, but which would prove to be quite prophetic. At the bottom of the painting, a blonde woman is upside down, bleeding. Beside her, her twin spirals up twined in growing green leaves. In the middle of the painting, a green man smiles out. At the top an invisible Sun radiates clear golden light. From the light, many eyes look out, clearly seeing all. The painting reminded me of a great goddess I had painted the previous December. A Kali-like figure, she holds the ocean and all life inside her and around her. In her mouth she holds a woman between her teeth. I knew that deep and powerful forces were active in my life. In June I went to the Caribbean island of Anguilla to housesit for friends. The pain I had been

126

experiencing reached its fullest intensity just before the new moon the end of June. When I went fully and deeply into it, the pain ended.

The next day I witnessed a turtle hatching. As she emerged from her shell, she ran, as fast as a turtle can run, straight to me where I stood about thirty feet away. To protect her from predators when she was still so small, I took her to my room and spent hours every day lying with her on my belly communing with her. At night I slept outside, under the stars, enveloped in mystery and contemplating infinity.

I had plans to fly home, then on to Oregon with Michael to spend a week vacationing with his parents. One morning a few days before I was to leave the island, I awoke with a strong intuition that it was not safe for me to travel. I knew that I needed to stay where I was for another week and then return to New York, cancelling the trip out West. I was torn. My mother-in-law had made our reservations a year before, and I knew that she would be very upset if I didn't come. Finally, overriding my intuition, I decided to make the trip. In Oregon, we had a lovely time. On the night before the next leg of my journey, the evening of August 5, 1992, in Sunriver, Oregon, I looked through a telescope and saw Saturn for the first time. I was mesmerized and deeply touched.

AGE 49-61

The next day, on August 6 at 2:25 p.m., Michael was driving me to the airport. Gazing out the car window at a perfectly clear blue sky, I was contemplating infinity. At that moment, as Michael sped through a red light he didn't see, our car was struck broadside by a big recreational vehicle. As I felt the impact on the car and on my body, I instantly knew that the shape of my life had been forever changed. When the car, after spinning around and going down an embankment, finally stopped, I found myself trapped, upside down, and barely able to breathe. As the intense pain threatened to overwhelm me, I prayed for the grace to endure. Michael was only slightly injured, but he couldn't help me. I saw many people surrounding the car, but they were also powerless to help. After some time, rescuers came. A woman paramedic came to the window and touched my arm. She said in a confident voice, "I know you are going to be all right." She spoke with such conviction that I believed her. After the firemen cut the car apart and peeled it open, they put me on a helicopter to the hospital.

Along with various cuts, I had nine rib fractures, a crushed and punctured right lung, injuries to my hip, knee, shoulders and head, and seven fractured vertebrae. The bad news was that my first lumbar vertebra was completely shattered, and a sharp fragment of bone like a spear was pushing my spinal cord

127

to the other side of the canal. Miraculously it had not severed it. The doctors were concerned that, with the slightest movement, the cord could be severed and I would be paralyzed. Before that happened they wanted to remove bone surgically from my pelvis, fuse all seven fractured vertebrae together, and stabilize them with long titanium rods. I couldn't imagine losing the beautiful undulating wave of spinal movement, one of my great pleasures in life. Finally the surgeons decided they would fuse only three vertebrae. They also agreed that I could have a second surgery in a year to remove the metal rods.

Although I was in great physical pain, I was not suffering. I was in a state of grace, simply present, saying to myself, "It is what it is." Through shock, I had been catapulted into the eternal present. Love and light filled me and emanated out from me. From the very beginning, I felt the experience was transpersonal and also that it was related to the spiritual evolution of the Earth. I was profoundly aware of all my friends and family praying for me. Dependent upon the nurses for everything, I deeply appreciated the quality of mercy they embodied. I did Authentic Movement with my arms, the only part I could move, and sang the pain. Michael was my witness, helping me form a cauldron vast enough to contain the immensity and depth of the experience.

As the day of the surgery neared, the memory of being cut apart in Egypt became very real to me. I was apprehensive, but keeping my balance, until I had one of the most intense experiences of my life. I was being given two pain pills every six hours. After three hours the effect would begin to wear off, so I had experimented and found it worked better if I took only one and saved the other to take in three hours. I told my doctor, and he said that was fine with him. Unfortunately one of my nurses decided that was contrary to drug control regulations, so she made me wait six whole hours after the last single pill I took before she would give me any more. Waiting so long for the medication, I lost and could not regain control of the pain. My nervous system felt on fire. I wanted to jump out of my skin and run out of the room, but if I moved at all I could sever my spinal cord and become paralyzed. I asked Michael to call Arnold Mindell and request that he do a process work session with me by phone.

Arnie asked me, "What is the pain like?"

I said, "It is like an ax hacking me apart."

He asked me to look for an image. I saw a cosmic egg cracking open, a whole universe being born. In that moment everything shifted, and I became centered and calm. Arnie asked me if I had a power animal. I told him about my turtle friend, and he suggested I go on a journey with her sometime. The surgery was the next morning, Friday, August 14, 1992, at 11:00 a.m. in Bend, Oregon. All of my friends and family were tuning in, meditating and praying for me. Bone was removed from the left side of my pelvis and used to fuse three vertebrae. Metal rods were inserted along my spine from L3 to T7. After the surgery, I was in pain more intense than anything I could ever have imagined. My whole consciousness, my whole reality, was pain. I didn't resist, but just merged with it.

I was fitted for a hard plastic brace just like a turtle shell. On September 3, we flew home. On September 13 we moved into a house in the country where I was alone most of the week. Deeply grateful for the ability to walk, a freedom I had come so close to losing, I took to heart turtle wisdom to go very slowly and to stay close to the heartbeat of Mother Earth. My work became simply to heal and, as Rumi advises, to "stay in one place and scatter the love." Like the cosmic egg, broken wide open, I was living in an ever-present awareness of the whole multidimensional field.

I went on a journey with my turtle friend: *A large sea turtle carries me on her back out into the ocean and then down into the very center of the Earth, where we merge first into each other and then into the whole Earth. After being Earth for a long time, we rise as turtle back to the surface of the sea and swim to shore on the island of Anguilla. In the sand high on the beach we lay a single large egg. In that moment we are separate again. I am inside the egg, a woman curled up dreaming, as the turtle covers me, walks back to sea, and swims away. After a long, long time, I, as dreaming woman, awaken, stretch and break out of my shell. I emerge into a dark, starry night, and walk to the edge of the sea to wash. When I turn around to face land again, a large group of Arawak Indians are standing there. Forming a large circle we dance together under the stars.*

Curled up, dreaming still, I healed and played with subtle micromovements to help my spine remember how to move. I had spent almost twenty years developing a very refined awareness of sensation and movement. In my current state, it was both a curse and a blessing. While I was often overwhelmed by acute awareness of painful sensation and restricted movement, I also felt the healing process as a deep cellular exhilaration. On November 19, a wonderful blessing arrived. I brought home Loplani, an extraordinary being in the form of a small brown lop-eared rabbit. He became my best friend, comforter, teacher, healer, co-worker, and much-loved child.

I also began what would become a time-consuming and stressful legal process. I had to sue my husband who was driving his father's car and was defended by his father's insurance company. On September 17, 1993, at 8:00 a.m. in Great Neck, NY, I had a second surgery to remove the metal rods. Afterward, I was extremely discouraged. I had worked diligently for a year, using all my skills and resources, hoping to regain most spinal mobililty. After the second surgery it was clear that because of the long immobility enforced by the rods, all seven vertebrae had fused.

I began to learn the delicate balancing act of accepting my limitations and at the same time doing everything in my power to move beyond them.

In 1994, when I began working again individually with people, I found that my work had become both more subtle and more powerful. I had always seen my work as both a form of creative self-expression and, through serving individual others, a way of serving the greater whole. After the accident, when I could do so little, I began to see that my most important service occurs silently and invisibly, as awareness and subtle communication between various dimensions of being. That summer of 1994, one aspect of that subtle communication began to take tangible form. With a helper to do the heavy work, I slowly began gardening again in a spirit of co-creation with the intelligence in nature. I started from the ground up, tending the soil, nurturing microbes and earthworms. Then I planted the flowers that called to me, including many roses. In their prime I made flower essences from them. Each essence was the fruit of meditation and multidimensional communication. I felt I was on a mission, but I didn't know what it was. I simply followed one intuitive step with the next.

Just before the autumnal equinox in 1995, I suddenly knew that I needed to combine seventy-two of the separate essences and alchemically fuse them into one. On September 21, 1995, Divine Love Elixir was created. Its purpose was to help heal the split we humans have created between ourselves and nature. Just after the winter solstice, I took it to the ocean to offer to all the waters of the Earth. The sea was perfectly still, but the moment I dropped it into the water, a big wave came up in response. Students and friends began taking a few drops before meditating. The next summer I continued making more individual essences for a purpose that was not yet clear to me.

In the Fall of 1996, I felt inspired to fulfill a lifelong dream to spend some time in the South Pacific. At first it seemed impossible. Although I had money from the insurance settlement, the trip seemed far beyond my physical ability. That was part of its appeal. I wanted to do something to stretch myself. Finally, with Michael's help, I worked out a way I thought I could do it. Michael would go with me on his way to Asia. I would pay for a friend to meet me there and do bodywork with me for several weeks to help me recover from the long journey. Then I would stay there on my own and fly home alone later.

On January 1, 1997, Michael and I flew to California to spend a few days with a friend who was about to leave his body. Then we flew on to Tahiti. Arriving in the middle of the night, we were welcomed with warm smiles, music, and fragrant garlands of flowers. The next day we took the ferry to Moorea, where a few days later we were remarried in a traditional Polynesian ceremony. From Moorea we flew to Bora Bora. In the lagoon we swam with sharks and stingrays, feeding them delicately from our fingertips. Just as we arrived on the island of Huahine, we both came down with dengue fever, also called bonebreak fever, because one's bones hurt as if they are breaking. After the fever passed, I felt as fresh and clear as a newborn.

It was as if I had been prepared for what happened next. On the site of an ancient temple by the sea, walking through a tangle of vegetation, I stepped suddenly onto a spot that seemed to be a portal. I was standing in a powerful, clear beam of light that passed from the center of Earth to a distant star. In that moment I entered into a healing and transformational experience that continued and deepened throughout the next several months in the Cook Islands. The deep, deep, dark blue sea and the luminous stars were both essential to that experience. At night I would lie on the beach, receiving streams of communication from the spirits of the stars. They spoke to me, and I listened.

I returned from the South Pacific in April, and Michael returned from Asia about a month later. In the South Pacific, for the first time I had seen very clearly certain energy patterns in our relationship. I felt I couldn't live with them any longer. Never having been successful at changing my partners, I began working on transforming my own part in those patterns.

For several years we had been looking for a new home. Finally we decided to move to the Southeast, to a small city in the Blue Ridge mountains. In August, 1997, we made a quick trip there and rented a beautiful house on a wild, forested mountain only twenty-five minutes from town. In September 1997, we moved. I was sad to leave behind the gardens I had created, but took along almost a hundred large pots full of roses, perennials and herbs. Loplani quickly adapted to his new home, bounding out the door the first day to explore the woods and mark his territory.

The day after we arrived, I saw an advertisement in the local alternative paper for a class in Playback Theatre, an improvisational form in which performers act out the stories of audience members. Michael joined me in a new class starting that week. In a fun, creative atmosphere, we made new friends and through them were woven very quickly into a community network of kindred spirits. When the class ended, some of us continued meeting once a week. Six years later we are still together, performing publicly from time to time.

That fall I began a three year training program with Gisela Rohmert, the founder of the Institute for Functional Voice Training in Germany. Although I had never had any musical training, sound and singing had always felt essential to my soul expression. In the training, which included professional singers, I was definitely extending myself far beyond my known abilities.

131

In the Spring of 1998, I began training in Holographic Repatterning, a process of identifying and transforming non-coherent patterns so that we can move to a higher level of coherence, order and awareness. The trainings, the sessions I was doing for myself and the sessions I began doing with my clients were all profound transformational experiences. In the summer I began teaching classes and workshops for the first time in six years. I felt very rusty. I taught Feldenkrais Awareness through Movement and led an Authentic Movement group. I also started teaching what I called "Moving from the Source," a subtle moving meditation I had been developing over the years.

On the Summer Solstice in 1998, I alchemically prepared a liquid essence of a stone a friend had brought me from Rumi's rose garden in Konya, Turkey. Then I combined that essence with seventy-two flower essences I had made in 1996 and 1997 to make the second octave of Divine Love Elixir. I put it in cobalt blue bottles with beautiful labels and began sending it as gifts to all the people who had touched my life. Its purpose is to support us in embodying all the Divine qualities that are our true nature. I thought that if I were to write a book, I would want it to say exactly what the elixir communicates non-verbally.

In September 1998, I spent a week at sea in the Bahamas swimming with wild spotted dolphins. It was an extraordinary experience which I would repeat the two following years. I had long felt a deep resonance with dolphins and whales, but especially dolphins. Swimming with them in the wild strengthened that connection and brought me into contact with individual dolphins. They became friends, living presences in my life. Even when I am far away from the sea, I am aware of them, and they often appear when I work with other people.

Our landlord wanted to sell the house we were in, so we needed to find a new home. On December 1, 1998, we moved our household and my portable garden once again. After a year in the country, we were ready to move into town. We could drive much less, be more spontaneous in our activities, and be more accessible to clients and students. Our house was encircled by big beautiful oak trees. Beyond our grassy back lawn was a woods for Loplani to explore, but because of the steep steps, he could no longer go bounding outside on his own. We had to carry him up and down. Shortly after we moved, I found a lump on his head. The veterinarian diagnosed it as an abscess and recommended surgery. I nursed him back to health, but the abscess began coming back. Concern for Loplani's health, researching healing possibilities, and caring for him became a part of my daily life.

In 1999, I began teaching creative process retreats as well as workshops blending Alexander, Feldenkrais, and Chi Kung. Since I found distance was not a factor in much of my work, I began doing more long distance sessions, usually by phone. I also began doing transformational work long distance with groups of people in the U.S. and Europe, communicating by email.

Over the years, I had stayed in touch with Will, my first husband, and his wife. Will had developed a serious illness and by the summer of 1999, he was in and out of hospitals and not sure how much longer he would live. Since we still followed the same spiritual path, we discussed how I could support him if and when he left his body. In the first week of October, he was hovering at the threshold, often unconscious. Although I was far away physically, I stayed present with him until he made his transition on October 7, 1999. Although we were both married to others and had spent very little time together for the last fourteen years, I felt I had lost one of the most important people in my life. I had known him longer than anyone except my siblings and cousins. With him I shared some of my best memories, my deepest happiness, and my spiritual journey.

Around the time of Will's passing, Loplani's health was deteriorating. I held him like a baby to feed him antibiotics, homeopathic remedies, and vitamins. Just when his health seemed to be improving, he died quite suddenly in my arms on April 9, 2000. He had always communicated to me, "Don't think I'm just a cute little rabbit. I'm really a great spirit in the form of a rabbit." That was never more apparent than after he left his body. His many friends came for a meditation vigil to honor him and to bask in his great spirit. Though in a tiny form, he was one of the great loves of my life, and he still lives in my heart.

In August, 2000, Rafi Nasser asked me to be the subject for *Under One Sky*. It felt right, and I spontaneously agreed. At first the proposal was that Rafi would simply interview me and ask me a series of questions organized around the twelve houses. Eventually I proposed writing a brief autobiography which I began in late February, 2001, in Puerto Morelos, Mexico.

In November, 2000, our landlord suddenly asked us to leave because he wanted to live in the house himself. We didn't want to move again, but we had no choice. In December, we moved again back to the country. I had always felt that when we found the right place, the nature spirits would sing. The land itself would sing to me. The night we moved into our small log home, we stood outside under the stars. I felt all the nature spirits come and embrace us. I loved our new home and, weary from four moves in five years, never wanted to move again. It seemed that moving, getting settled into, and maintaining houses was consuming a large proportion of my energy.

Maintaining my body had also required more energy since the accident in 1992. Although I had been growing and evolving, I could not seem to completely regain my momentum in life. I felt as though I had been on a cresting wave at the time of the accident, had fallen under, and been caught in an undertow. I would get back on my feet for a number of months or maybe a whole year, and then suddenly have some experience of being reinjured. My body was much more fragile than before the accident and surgeries. It required more attention and awareness of my limits.

I had enough awareness to take good care of myself. The accidental reinjury would usually come through someone else doing something impulsive, sudden, and too forceful or from some bump or jolt while riding in a vehicle. Each new episode of pain and limitation challenged me to find deeper reserves of patience, courage, and hope. Since I tend to suffer in silence and retreat to solitude when I am in pain, most people in my life do not have any sense of what I have experienced. After many years, I am still in the process of becoming fully conscious of this pattern of being accidentally injured.

In late December 2001, we bought the house we had been renting for a year and immediately began a series of home improvement projects. In April, 2002, in the chaos of a kitchen renovation, I forgot a pot of soup on the stove and caused smoke damage in the upper level of our house. After a very stressful clean-up, we moved ahead not only with the kitchen renovation but with several other projects. I was already feeling overwhelmed when, on April 23 around 6:00 p.m. a ladder, on which I was standing, broke. I fell to the concrete basement floor, shattering my left upper arm and shoulder.

I didn't want to rush off to the emergency room and get caught up in the chaotic energy there, so as soon as Michael helped me up from the floor, I walked into my office, sat down and took Rescue Remedy and homeopathic arnica. Then I simply sat there, and Michael sat with me, as I let the experience, the pain, and all the impressions just wash through me. When I felt I was completely settled, present, breathing, and embodied, I stood up, and we went to the emergency room. The many complex fractures took months to heal, with several setbacks along the way.

Although I had bounced back from both severe and minor trauma many times before, I felt shattered more deeply this time. I felt overwhelmed not only by residues of previous trauma but also by ancestral patterns. One night in excruciating pain, my experience was that of my grandmother Rhoda as she died an agonizing death after she poisoned herself with strychnine. As I had after the accident ten years before, I felt acutely the pain and struggles of others all over the planet and felt my heart being opened into greater compassion. I also felt opened into a much greater awareness. Having my boundaries broken was, once again, both devastating and liberating. Coincidentally, I had recently begun training in Somatic Experiencing, Peter Levine's approach to healing trauma. I have many

134

resources for healing completely, becoming even more resourceful and resilient, and helping others heal. As I write this, I am still in the midst of that process.

In October 2002, I had an opportunity to travel with my husband and a group of meditators to China. A brilliant and articulate teacher of Taoist internal alchemy and an inspiration to many, including me, Michael had led groups to China a number of times before. Each time, I had stayed at home on retreat, tuning in and meditating with him on the opposite side of the world. As he meditated in sacred sites, I also received transmissions from the Tao immortals and the spirits of the mountains. I wanted to be in those places myself, to have at least once an embodied experience of the living land of China.

Such long and arduous travel was a huge stretch for me, but a friend agreed to come along to give me massages. Flying over the ocean, I did a long meditative process to balance within myself the polarities of East and West, two very different modes of being. In China, I had many profound and sublime experiences. One high point was climbing to the top of Huashan, which means Flower Mountain. Its petals are five sheer granite peaks that can only be climbed by the precipitous steps carved into the rock over the last twenty-five hundred years by a succession of Taoist practitioners. On the central peak, I met a kindred spirit, an elderly Taoist nun tending a little garden in pots. She generously invited Michael and me into her tiny shrine, fed us noodles and tea, wrapped my cold, rain-soaked body in her warm Chinese army coat, and let us meditate blissfully for hours. I often remember her and smile to her up there on Flower Mountain.

When I returned from China, I turned my attention to completing this condensed autobiography. The process has been both challenging and rewarding. I have felt a conflict between keeping my privacy and revealing myself publicly, but I have been committed to being as honest as I can about myself while protecting the privacy of others. As I reflect on the first sixty years of this life, I am deeply grateful for being alive and for all the gifts and blessings I have been given. I live in appreciation of the One, immanent and transcendent, source and substance of all I that I might call myself or other. I give thanks to all those apparent others who have played with me the great game of dancing polarities. I am grateful for living in a time when the esoteric teachings of great mystical traditions, as well as the discoveries of modern science, have been revealed. I realize how blessed I am that my ancestors, from stardust to amoeba to my human family, have brought me to this moment. May I be a wise steward of their gifts and use them well. From my luminous core, I smile waves of love to all.

As I have encountered challenges in life, a helpful image for me has been this: one hand of God is inside a pot, supporting the integrity of its unfolding nature from within while the other hand is outside, exerting strong forces to shape it. In

Japan, where the art of pottery has reached sublime heights, the pot that is most prized is not the flawless, symmetrical one, but the one in which blemishes, unusual shapes and even cracks somehow come together in a unique beauty. Perhaps that pot is treasured because in its own way, it unites two great opposites: chaos and harmony. This is beauty of a great magnitude, a deep mysterious beauty. Such a vessel can hold the one Great Mystery, from which flows both the bitter and the sweet:

Shock, shattering bones, sharp searing pain, nausea, terror, torn flesh, cold sharp metal, violence, loss, anguished tears, being cast down and laid low . . .

And smiling eyes, laughter, music, light, sunshine, hugging, teaching, learning, playing, talking with friends, snuggling, solitude, babies, trees, river otters, ocean, tropics, warm seas, swimming with dolphins, islands, white sand, clear bright colors, aquamarine, kissing, being on the sea, in the sea, near the sea, snorkeling, succulent fruits, gardening, cooking, flowers, flutes, fertile soil, rocks, roses, lilies, daylilies, summer, singing cicadas, spring, emerald green grass, rabbits, soft fur, dark chocolate, goats, fragrances of rose, jasmine, plumeria, vanilla and coconut, waterfalls, making love, moving, meditating, butterflies, hawks, hummingbirds, turtles, seabirds, new snow falling, dark starry nights, evening star, new moon, full moon on water, reading, a clean house, long walks in the country, dancing, singing, acting, painting, telling stories, swimming in oceans, ponds, lakes, rivers and pools, whale song, chi kung, long warm baths, volcanoes, lightning, thunder, tropical rains, crowns and garlands of flowers, Polynesian dancing, massages, silk, velvet, high mountains, pandas, the call of loons, redwood trees, subtle energy, inner sound, following the mysterious unfolding of the Tao, running freely, jumping for joy, Rumi, Hafiz, ancient stones, the company of mystics, breathing, being alive now . . . .

PART THREE:
THE INTERPRETATIONS

THUMBNAIL SKETCHES

Demetra George: Here is a portrait of an early, unexpected tragedy that resulted in a lonely and isolated childhood, with the possibility of the inheritance of substantial wealth. Joyce may have found comfort by retreating into nature and books. In that inner world, her latent prophetic capacities are activated as well as the formation of an active intellect searching for spiritual truth. The Camelot legend mirrors a pattern around relationships as marriage to a charismatic dynastic figure to whom she feels unconnected, and love for another who meets her mind and heart. The healing of a primal wound regarding the communication of Joyce's beliefs is a path of salvation that leads towards her destiny.

Evelyn Roberts: On the one hand Joyce appears practical, intellectual, inquisitive and serious. Although probably less obviously so to outsiders, it feels as though she is at the same time complex, intuitive, imaginative and somewhat unfathomable. Weaving these diverse qualities together in creative as well as practical ways that bring her fulfillment in life may not always be easy. However, with such a rich and powerful combination of mental acuity, pragmatism and deep sensitivity, this challenge is probably one she is very capable of rising to.

Gary Christen: Joyce is governed by competing behavior patterns. One is an inner reality that is based on strong inner convictions and is fearful of the world. The other is an uneasy connection with others that leads to interactions that call into question her moral underpinnings. This reading calls attention to the various forces that influence these behaviors. Some show Joyce's strength while others show her weakness. It is the reconciliation of these forces that Joyce must take on as a lifelong task. By doing so, she becomes a bridge between people, connecting them to the outer world.

Hadley Fitzgerald: Joyce's soul is challenged to establish productive new synergies between commitment and freedom, instinct and intellect, tradition and taboo, order and chaos; to break through an old resistance to deep, alchemical connections with a few other humans; to redefine what constitutes true "wealth" for her and thus develop faith in her own intrinsic resources; to have the transformation of early wounds serve as a beacon of inspiration to others; to make it possible for dark truths beyond the culture's comfort zone to be heard from a fresh, creative perspective; to feel and to heal with integrity and style.

John Marchesella: In twenty-five words or less, how would I describe Joyce's inner character and outer life? Education, information, communication. She's the kind of person you want around when you're doing the New York Times Sunday crossword puzzle, even though you know she wouldn't need you to complete it.

Ken Bowser: This woman's horoscope is a testimony to how a difficult beginning in life can be overcome and resolved into success. The symbolism that shows distinct writing, speaking and organizational ability is clearly laid out. Excellent administrative ability, a propensity toward instruction and research as well as artistic creativity and a predilection toward the occult arts and spiritual disciplines is also indicated. In short, this extremely versatile and enlightened woman is a gift to both those whom she serves in a social context and those with whom she interacts personally.

Kim Rogers-Gallagher: I believe that Joyce is clearly someone who, like most of us, has a number of different sides to her personality. The initial impression you'd likely have of her is that she is outgoing and open, very friendly, chatty, and open-minded. But I also see her as someone who's really quite private, and very cautious in relationships—that is, someone who waits, watches, and bides her time before allowing someone to get too close. I'm also convinced that she has a career that is "secret" in some way, such as forensics, funeral home work, surgery, or that she may even follow a religious vocation.

Robert Hand: Joyce is an extraverted, sociable, talkative and generally agreeable person not given to quarrels and conflicts. She should be of above average intelligence, and somewhat serious and reserved. She is interested in ideas which are challenging and difficult, or abstruse, also in offbeat or even eccentric subjects. Physically, Joyce is graceful in appearance and looks younger than her years. She is of average to slender build. Her appearance should have a quality of tension combined with the appearance of energy. The overall structure of the chart suggests that she may have personal relationships that can be combative, but for the most part her life should be on an even keel and one which avoids extremes.

Robert Schmidt: Joyce's life is one that is not especially responsive to the state of the cosmic soul at the time of her birth, which some might call her "higher soul." This means that the cosmic soul is only imperfectly incarnated into her person, and as a result her life takes its course without its guidance and without regard for its concerns; more often than not, her life is subject to the vagaries and constraints of necessity. In fact, necessity is the central principle of her life. On the other hand, her life belongs almost entirely to beauty and is governed by it. Yet, however much she strives for this beauty, she often fails to take note of what must be provided in order to attain it.

Ronnie Gale Dreyer: In a nutshell, Joyce's chart consists of two extremes. There is a preponderance of planets in the eighth and twelfth "hidden" houses, which provide obstacles, indulgences and an inability to meet life head on in a way that combines the emotional, intellectual and spiritual. Her life is spent looking for love in all the wrong places. She also has Jupiter, planet of abundance, in the strong first house position which indicates vast opportunities as she matures for partnership, professional fulfillment, and, most of all, spiritual awakening.

Steven Forrest: In Joyce we see deep, subjective psychological intensity in a curious and paradoxical mixture with a penchant for the cold, clear eye of logical analysis. There is a fundamental privacy and self-sufficiency in her nature, and an evolutionary intention that pivots on a willingness to face life's more daunting dimensions squarely: loss, emotional woundedness, and bare-knuckled psychological honesty. To the extent that she succeeds in realizing these intentions, she emerges into her community in the roles of Elder and Teacher. A weaker response leads to emotional isolation, high levels of nervous tension, and possible depression.

139

Wendy Z. Ashley: Using Joyce's birth chart, I attempt to locate a mythology through the planets as vehicles for archetypes and the stars, signs and constellations as locations of mythologies that are the myth that she is living. The roots of astrology lie in an older mythologized sky, and the recovery of this material is the identification of those fractals as mythic themes and motifs that stand behind the source of astrological symbol and meaning.

Because I was not permitted any contact with Joyce as I would ordinarily have with a client, I used only those astrological factors in her chart as indicators of a possible myth which stands as a template behind the manifold experiences, drives, psychology and persons in her life. There were five possible myths that I described and related to her chart and described the most probable forms in her life. It will be only through her responses to these that we will be able to see which is the appropriate myth, or indeed if it is another myth altogether.

DEMETRA GEORGE: ASTEROID CENTERED

The strategy that I am about to outline is one that I have used for about twenty-five years. However, my work is currently in the process of great transition, but has not yet metamorphosed into its new form. But let me say that of all the methods of modern astrology that I am evaluating and reconsidering, the mythic use of the multiplicity of the asteroids is the only one that still remains stable. I have elaborated upon my rationale in the forum question number two.

When I receive the client's birth data, the first thing that I usually do is to ask for the source of the birth time. If it is a hospital birth certificate, I am generally confident that the time is accurate, at least within ten to fifteen minutes. However, if the response is, "my mother or father's memory," I am more suspicious, knowing from experience that the time may be off by as much as several hours or more. I am especially suspicious of birth times that have been rectified by pendulums, Sabian symbols, psychics, or speculations based on appearance and personality characteristics. In these cases, I tend not to make definitive statements about the Ascendant, planets in houses, rulers of houses, and transits over angles and through houses; instead I look primarily at factors that are true of the date of birth independent of the exact time.

Then I cast the chart using CCRS software with the extra asteroid module, CCRS ASTEPH created by Mark Pottenger. This is the only astrological software program that integrates the asteroids into all the other reports and techniques. I have a basic list of about 500 hand-chosen asteroids that I utilize for most readings. However, if I am doing in-depth research on a particular person or event, I may choose to run the 9000-asteroid list. These asteroid lists can be arranged either alphabetically or in a zodiacal sort from 0 Aries to 29 Pisces. It is the zodiacal sort that is most useful in the preparation of the reading.

The chart is cast using both Porphyry and whole sign houses, after having experimented with Placidus and Koch during the course of my career. The Lot of Fortune (or Part of Fortune) is included with the different formulas programmed into the computer for day and night births. I print out a biwheel chart with the natal chart in the inner wheel and the secondary progressions on the outer wheel, and a report of the dates of the progressed lunation phases. I place the outer planet transits around the outside, noting their aspects to natal planets for the duration of a year or so. I will also prepare a solar return chart.

Now I am ready to incorporate many of the asteroids into the natal chart, in addition to Ceres, Pallas, Juno, Vesta, and Chiron that are automatically included in the printout. Asteroids have been named after mythological deities from a variety of cultural traditions, as well as names of geographical places, concepts, and common personal names. Having worked with the asteroids since 1973, I have repeatedly seen that when a planetary body is significantly placed in the skies at the moment a person is born, the mythic biography of the god or goddess that shares the same name as the celestial body becomes a major theme in that person's life. The asteroid names of particular geographical cities, states, and countries, as well as those of people, when also prominently placed in the nativity, often manifest as important locations and relationships in the person's life.

The most significant positions are those conjunct the four angles and those conjunct or opposite the Sun and Moon. Then for the second level of significance, I also might look at asteroids conjunct the inner planets, or those completing major aspect patterns. The orbs for Ceres, Pallas, Juno and Vesta are the same as the orbs used for the traditional planets: generally six degrees for the sextile, eight degrees for the trine and square, and up to ten degrees for the conjunction and opposition. These four asteroids represent four of the most important goddesses in the classical Greek pantheon, and embody a wide variety of themes. However, for most of the remaining asteroids that have more limited and specified significations, I use a three-degree orb.

I scan the list of asteroids arranged in zodiacal order, beginning with 0 Aries in the list, against the positions of planets and points in the chart, and add from about twenty to forty asteroids that seem to be relevant or significant. There are certain ones that I automatically add to every chart, because they represent major mythic deities or refer to the most commonly inquired about issues, such as relationships and health. If the name of the person appears on the list, I will include that as well as the names of important other people in his or her life. Then whatever asteroids appear on the angles or other significant places mentioned above will be written in. In some cases, an asteroid is not prominent natally, but occupies the degree of a current outer planet transit, or at the degree of a progressed new Moon or progressed Ascendant, and these I might include as well.

142

I do not have any absolute fixed method of determining which asteroids to use. There is an element of intuition that arises when I assemble the chart. Below, I have listed many of the asteroids that I will scan and judge whether or not to include them. If I see a theme emerging, then I will go back and pull out the other asteroids that are in that family. For example, in Joyce's chart, I noticed that Arthur was on her Descendant, and then Merlin appeared conjunct her Sun and Lancelot with her Venus/Mercury; I knew a theme was unfolding and scanned for the other asteroids in that group.

Important in general: Dionysus, Urania, Artemis, Proserpina, Demeter, Persephone, Moira, Karma, Apollo, Hera, Zeus, Athene, Bacchus.
Health: Koronis, Hygeia, Isis, Podalirus, Aesculapia, Panacea, Asclepius, Makhaon.
Relationship: Sappho, Aphrodite, Psyche, Amor, Eros, Lust, Cupido, Pecker, Ariadne.
Prophetic: Kassandra, Pythia, Sibylla, Manto, Delphine, Dodona.
Concepts: Beer, Academia, Universitas, Wisdom, Astronomia, Philosophia.
Other: Hekate, Circe, Medea, Amazone, Penthesilea, Antiope, Hidalgo, Icarus, Daedalus, Poseidon, Medusa, Orpheus, Nymphe.
Celtic: Gawain, Arthur, Merlin, Lancelot, Guinevere, Excalibur, Camelot, Galahad.
Egyptian: Isis, Osiris, Horus, Hathor, Ptah, Amun, Nepthys, Sekmet, Kleopatra, Sphinx, Imhotep, Hatsheput, Neith.
Indian: Parvati, Siva.
Alcohol: Beer, Ninkasi, Bacchus, Dionysus, Soma.
Mesopotamian: Ur, Chaldea, Gilgamesh, Lilith, Ishtar, Innanen, Astarte.

Once the asteroids are set into place, I note the natal lunation phase. This was the topic of my first formal astrology class in 1973, and I have been using this factor since that time, setting forth my understanding of this topic in *Finding Our Way Though the Dark.* The lunation phase depicts the relationship between the two Lights, regardless of whether there is a classical aspect between them, and is as important as the placements of the Sun, Moon, and Ascendant.

In order to time the chart, I take note of the progressed lunation phase, secondary progressions, outer planet transits, profections, and the solar return. The progressed lunation phase reveals at what stage of the development of the soul purpose within a thirty-year cycle the person currently is. The dates of the

soul purpose within a thirty-year cycle the person currently is. The dates of the previous progressed new Moon are noted as the beginning point of the current cycle. The secondary progressed chart is then compared to the natal chart. Are progressed planets or angles conjunct or opposed to natal or progressed planets or angles? Have any planets or angles just changed signs, or have progressed planets gone retrograde or direct? Where is the progressed Moon by sign and house? The movements of the outer planet transits, e.g. Jupiter, Saturn, Uranus, Neptune, and Pluto, are noted for the duration of a year, checking which house they are passing through and what aspects are being made to natal planets. I may also see if the major asteroids are making returns to their own natal places.

Finally, I will profect the chart to the current year to determine which house is emphasized and which planet is the time lord for one year, from birthday to birthday. Looking at the zodiacal position of the time lord planet in the current solar return (non-precessed, birth place) and seeing what house it occupies in the natal chart as the area of life that will be lit up is the last step of the preparatory process.

The chart is then put away until about one-half hour before the session. Then I light a candle, look over the chart, taking note of where the natal planets are, which asteroids are significant, and what current transits stand out. I try to refrain from attempting to "figure out" what the chart means until I make contact with the client. My preliminary interview with the client involves asking what is their previous level of astrological background. If this is a first time reading, I will give a much more basic overview than if the client has had many readings (with me or anyone else) or is a student or practitioner of astrology. It is also important to inquire if there are any particular questions or issues that he or she wants me to be sure to address in the session.

The final act of preparation is a prayer that some kind of positive vision can be imparted to the client that will enable him or her to make sense of his or her life experiences and leave with a sense of purposeful existence.

Once the reading begins, there are certain points that I cover: for a first time session, a discussion of the lunation phase, natal and progressed, information about the Ascendant and its ruler, the placements of the Sun and Moon and their rulers, and any other outstanding patterns, plus some comments on current timing. I integrate the relevant asteroids that are significantly placed in the nativity, and try to uncover mythic themes that emerge. If the client has indicated particular issues, I focus on those. I periodically pause and ask for feedback from the client, making sure that what

144

is being said is relevant to his or her life experiences, and allowing the person to steer the direction of the session if wanted. Much of my interactive procedure is Socratic—asking pointed questions that facilitate the client's own process of realization.

My position ultimately is that the client knows his or her chart better than I do, because the chart is a blueprint of the life that person is actually experiencing. The client is my most reliable source of information as to how an astrological configuration manifests. I try to remain respectful of the client's religion, politics, moral values, and sexual preferences, and not make value judgments or disparaging remarks in these areas. Barring incorrect birth times and psychological denial, I try to have respect for the authenticity of the client's responses.

Some clients want to know what is going to happen, and others do not want this information. Instead, they want a focused structure that helps them to understand the issues at hand and the possible paths of action. Many clients just want somebody who will really listen to them talk, and provide feedback that helps them to clarify their situation. Regardless of whether the outcome is already pre-determined, we must act as if free will exists. I try not to take that away from my clients, even if it is an illusion. In the end, if the client has obtained clarity and feels as if he or she can leave the session with a purposeful sense of direction, even if the prognostication is for a challenging future, then something of benefit has transpired.

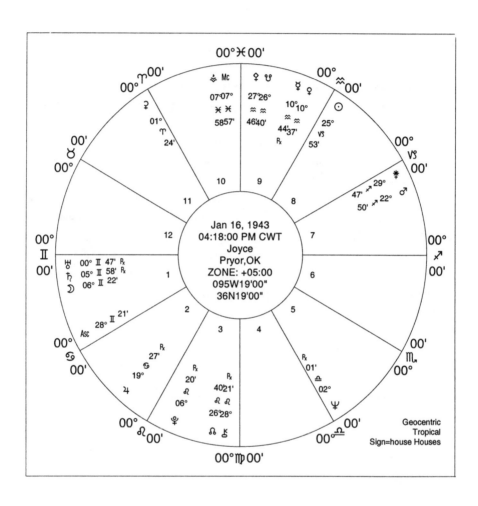

Significant Asteroid and Degree Placements for Joyce:

Kassandra 1 Taurus
Dionysus 11 Taurus
Beer 3 Gemini
Hephaistos 5 Gemini retrograde
Abundantia 5 Gemini retrograde
Hestia 7 Gemini retrograde
Erda 7 Gemini
Oklahoma 7 Gemini
Urania 9 Gemini retrograde
Artemis 16 Gemini retrograde
Dodona 27 Gemini retrograde
Metis 19 Cancer retrograde
Proserpina 20 Cancer retrograde
Daphne 25 Cancer retrograde
Hygeia 10 Leo retrograde
Demeter 19 Leo retrograde
Galahad 23 Leo retrograde
Sappho 1 Virgo retrograde
Poesia 6 Virgo retrograde
Aphrodite 10 Virgo retrograde
Persephone 18 Virgo retrograde
Moira 23 Libra
Lot of the Mother 23 Libra
Karma 24 Libra
Lot of Fortune 8 Scorpio
Pythia 9 Scorpio
Psyche 13 Scorpio
Gawain 26 Scorpio
Aesculapia 28 Scorpio

Apollo 6 Sagittarius
Amazone 7 Sagittarius
Penthisilea 7 Sagittarius
Philosophia 7 Sagittarius
Delphine 8 Sagittarius
Hera 21 Sagittarius
Hidalgo 22 Sagittarius
Arthur 27 Sagittarius
Gaea 27 Sagittarius
Camelot 1 Capricorn
Werdandi 9 Capricorn
Guinevere 12 Capricorn
Pre-natal lunation 15 Capricorn
Bacchus 20 Capricorn
Icarus 22 Capricorn
Medea 23 Capricorn
Rafinetti 25 Capricorn
Merlin 27 Capricorn
Panacea 4 Aquarius
Lancelot 10 Aquarius
Zeus 10 Aquarius
Lilith 19 Aquarius
Asclepius 23 Aquarius
Excalibur 24 Aquarius
Medusa 3 Pisces
Chaldea 7 Pisces
Skuld 7 Pisces
Nymphe 14 Pisces
Manto 16 Pisces
Eros 23 Pisces

READING

This reading of Joyce's chart will integrate the meanings of the asteroids with the more customary ten planet system. In the sessions that I normally do, I probably would not devote as much emphasis on the variety of asteroids that I have here. However, for the purpose of *Under One Sky*, this monograph is meant to be an exposition of the kinds of very specific information that the asteroids can provide, information that would not be readily available, if at all, with the more conventional approach. The comments on the basic structure of the chart serve as a framework on which to hang the asteroid interpretations.

The procedures used for this reading, for the most part, conform to the modern guidelines for the interpretations of the basic components of the astrological language. However from a mythic approach that I use with the asteroids, as stated in the Strategy section, signs, houses and aspects all become of secondary importance compared to the archetypal patterns revealed by the mythic biographies of the planetary deities themselves.

In some cases, two different asteroids will symbolize the same mythic deity; one is named after the Greek god or goddess and the other carries the name of its Roman equivalent, such as the Greek Hera and the Roman Juno. In a general way, they can be interpreted identically. If one wants to differentiate, one might say that the Greek deity represents the pre-Hellenic nature of the archetype, while the Roman-named equivalent embodies the later Classical adaptations made to that deity's character.

With the exception of the progressed lunation phase, that in Joyce's case relates to several asteroids in a very specific way, I am not including any prognostications about the future in this transcript.

I will begin this "asteroid" reading with a discussion of the lunation phase, which describes the natal relationship between the Sun and the Moon, the primary significators of the archetypal masculine and feminine principles. The Moon represents the wholeness of all the manifestations of the feminine energy prior to differentiation. As such, the Moon is the foundation for Venus, as well as for the four major asteroid goddesses, Ceres, Pallas, Juno, and Vesta. Hence, looking more carefully at the deeper symbolism of the Moon provides a larger context in which to understand the expressions of the multiplicity of the goddess-named asteroids.

Utilizing an eight-fold division of the monthly soli-lunar cycle, Joyce was born during the First-Quarter phase. Rudhyar called this phase "crisis in action," and Joyce may encounter many external crises over the course of her life that challenge the status quo of her life circumstances. The meaning of her lunation phase calls upon her to activate her will, and to take direct action in order to clear away obstacles from the past that prevent her from moving forward. She needs to anchor her growing sense of self-identity into the physical world by building structures that function as a foundation to support and contain her life purpose. These structures can be professional such as an office, physical such as a health regime, personal such as a home for security, or creative such as a specific art form that acts as a vehicle for self-expression. The kind of energy that the Sun and Moon utilize in the expression and actualization of Joyce's life purpose is predicated upon the need to take charge of her life, to act and to build, and this is precipitated by crises that break down old ways of being.

By progression, the lunation cycle describes the growth and development of some aspect of the life purpose over a thirty-year period of time. The beginning of Joyce's current cycle occurred in August 1991 when the progressed Sun and progressed Moon were conjunct at 15 Pisces, falling in her tenth house of profession and career. The natal asteroids close to that degree were Manto and Nymphe. Manto was a daughter of the blind seer Tiresias, and she became a prophetess of Delphi and then founded Apollo's oracle at Didyma in Asia Minor. The nymphs in Greek mythology were personified as nature spirits in the forms of nubile young women, the animating life forces dwelling in trees, rivers, caves, grottos and other natural formations. As we shall see shortly, a fundamental aspect of Joyce's personality that has to do with prophecy and nature was activated in 1991, and unfolds through its entire developmental cycle over the succeeding thirty years.

At this time, in March of 2002, Joyce is a little more than one-quarter of the way around this cycle. As she approaches 60 years of age, she returns to her natal First-Quarter phase, which spans from December of 1998 until February of 2003. During this period, Joyce is called upon to make definite decisions and take forceful direct actions to build and establish some kind of life structure that facilitates the actualization of whatever new aspirations were released at the progressed new Moon in 1991. If, for example, the progressed new Moon activated a previously latent psychic ability that was stimulated by contact with powerful forces of nature, this might be a time to establish herself professionally in this field, supported by an office or promotional materials, or to create a meditation environment in an outdoor setting that allows her to access the vibrant energies of nature.

Having discussed the lunation phase, natally and by progression, we can now turn to the main body of Joyce's natal chart. In Joyce's chart the sign Gemini was rising over the eastern horizon at the moment of her birth. On the outer level, the rising sign, also called the Ascendant, gives information concerning the personality and physical characteristics. Gemini rising denotes an active intellect, one that is full of curiosity with a need to make mental contacts with others and engage in verbal communication. On an inner level, the rising sign describes the core need of the soul, which, as Gemini is an air sign, speaks to the primal need for freedom of thought, and to express one's ideas and be heard and acknowledged. The asteroid that was ascending over the horizon at her birth, perhaps the most powerful point in the chart, where sky meets earth, was Dodona at 27 Gemini conjunct the Ascendant at 27 Gemini. Dodona is the name of one of the two most important oracle centers in ancient Greece (the other being Delphi), where priestesses would receive divine communications from gods, as responses to inquiries made by suppliants who made arduous journeys in order to receive advice from the deities. Dodona was a site that was sacred to Zeus, the supreme Olympian god, and the priestesses would listen to the rustling of the leaves of the sacred oak trees of Zeus as the medium of communication from the god. The priestesses would then relay the god's message to the pilgrims.

This theme of prophetic insights received though contact with the varied manifestations of nature is further emphasized. The planet that rules the rising sign gives further information about how and where the basic soul need will manifest. Mercury, the archetypal messenger of the gods who was able to travel to the underworld, is the ruler of Gemini, and in Joyce's chart, it is retrograde, indicating a mind inwardly turned or attuned to the inner world. More important is Mercury's conjunction with the asteroid Zeus (both at 10 Aquarius), who was the very god worshipped at Dodona and the one who inspired the minds of his priestesses with his wisdom.

As Dodona was the oracle of Zeus, the placement of the asteroid Dodona conjunct the Ascendant (the most powerful point in the chart), and of the asteroid Zeus conjunct Mercury, the ruler of the Ascendant (and thus one of the most important planets in the chart), locks in this theme, so to speak, connoting a prophetic capacity to look at the manifestations of nature as symbolic communications from the divine realm concerning portents of coming events or explanations of present or past events.

This emerging theme of prophetic insight is also signified by the placement of the asteroid Skuld exactly on the Midheaven at 7 Pisces, the second most powerful point in the nativity, one that signifies vocation and actions in the world. Skuld was one of the three Norns, or Fates, of Germanic mythology who sat under the great cosmic tree and decided the destinies of gods and mortals.

150

Skuld was the Norn of the Future, and her sister Erda, the Norn of the past, is conjunct Joyce's Moon (at 7 and 6 Gemini), one of the "givers of one's all" (along with the Sun), according to the Hellenistic astrologers. Thus the reception and communication of knowledge of the future and of the past that is gained through contact with nature as an emissary of the gods is one of the main features of Joyce's character and destiny.

Most ancient cultures had some sort of divination as a means to ascertain divine will and intention. Linguistically, the term divination was derived from the words which meant both "divine," as related to spirit, and "to foretell the future." It was also believed that the gods sent their messages through the signs in nature, such as the flight of birds, or rustlings of the leaves from sacred trees, or manifestations of lightning, thunder, and rainbows as communications from the divine realm. The voices of the deities were believed to be most pronounced at powerful places in nature, such as at waterfalls, springs, caves, grottos, and groves of sacred trees. Birds, because they flew high in sky and were closest to the heavens, were considered to be special emissaries of the gods.

In a live consulting session, these are the kinds of questions that I would ask Joyce in order to attempt to arrive at how this super-sensory ability operates. "If you are grappling with a decision that you need to make, and suddenly a certain kind of bird appears before you, can you derive some sort of symbolic meaning from this event that helps to clarify your dilemma? If you are distressed, does a walk in the woods or a sitting beneath a special tree calm and focus you? Does the sudden appearance of a rainbow or butterfly or shooting star at a critical moment in your thinking process trigger an intuitive flash of insight? Do others seek your advice, and a stream of words ensue from within some non-linear part of your being that gives them counsel? Do you have a sense of the fairy world or of nature spirits which imbue a kind of sentience to the plant or mineral kingdoms?" These are some of the ways in which the prophetic qualities associated with the forces of nature may come about in Joyce's life.

On a more mundane level, Mercury, the ruler of the Ascendant, is placed in the eighth house of the chart, which pertains to death and inheritances. It occupies the sign of Aquarius, which is the ninth whole sign house, pertaining to religion, philosophy, and higher education. This combination can indicate the use of her financial resources received through inheritance, trusts, settlements, or investments for the purpose of higher learning. We will further elaborate upon Mercury in our discussion of the Moon.

The Moon, a general significator of the mother and early childhood, is also in Gemini, and it is conjunct Saturn, a general significator of the father. Both the

151

Moon and Saturn occupy the twelfth house of sorrows and suffering. The modern planet Uranus is placed there as well, an indicator of sudden, disruptive and unexpected occurrences. The Moon is the ruler of the second house of material resources, which contains the benefic Jupiter in Cancer, in the sign of its exaltation, and Saturn which is the ruler of the eighth house of money gained through inheritances. The dispositor of both the Moon and Saturn in Gemini is Mercury, placed in the eighth house of death. Mercury is also the ruler of the fourth house (Virgo) of parents. The asteroids Beer (3 Gemini), Hephaistos (5 Gemini)—the lame smith god, Abunduntia (5 Gemini)—the Roman goddess of abundance, Hestia (7 Gemini)—-the Greek goddess of the hearth, and Oklahoma (7 Gemini)—the birth state, are all part of this configuration.

One can speculate that there may have been an unexpected accidental death or maiming of one or both of the parents at an early age, with the resultant inheritance of substantial wealth, either from the family estate or an insurance settlement. The presence of the asteroid Beer can indicate either an alcohol-related tragedy or some kind of alcoholic business as the source of the wealth. The Moon and Saturn in the twelfth house point to a lonely and isolated childhood, deficient in emotional nurturing and intellectual stimulation from others. As a result, a child might turn to the world of books for essential companionship. As an adult, feelings of being loved are interpreted as unconditional communication. Joyce may have an insatiable appetite for the accumulation of knowledge, and, for her, genuine nurturing is experienced as having somebody in her life who enjoys talking about and listening to the range of Joyce's intellectual interests. Emotional nourishment is equated to mental companionship. The presence in the twelfth house of Hestia, who was the predecessor of the Roman goddess Vesta (on her Midheaven) as temple priestess, makes me wonder if she was raised in a convent and surrounded by silence, or raised by a maiden aunt.

From an Eastern spiritual perspective, the twelfth house can also be read as the house of the *Bodhisattva*. This refers to the Buddhist concept of an enlightened being who consciously chooses to continue incarnating for the purpose of relieving the suffering of others and aiding them in their quest for liberation. The pattern that emerges is often that of the wounded healer, someone who has experienced some kind of suffering in the earlier part of life, which has the effect of deepening the compassion for the pervasive suffering of the human condition. As one becomes sensitized to this level of being, one can better recognize this malaise in others and reach out to help in selfless acts of service. Joyce's twelfth house planets can also point to such a role.

One more asteroid that is conjunct the Moon is Urania at 9 Gemini, one of the nine muses of Greek mythology who presided over the various arts and inspired poets and artists. Urania, the "celestial one" was the muse of *astronomia* and music, and is one of the signatures of astrologers. This theme is further signified by the presence of the asteroid Chaldea at 7 Pisces exactly on the Midheaven. Chaldea was first of all a geographical location of the area surrounding ancient Babylon and a designation of the Babylonian priesthood who were astrologer/diviners. Later it became an appellation for someone who had studied in the Babylonian mystery schools, and finally by the Roman period, anyone who practiced astrology was called a Chaldean. I suspect that Joyce is either an astrologer herself, or a student and patron of astrology.

Asteroids that are opposite either of the Lights are also significant in the person's life. The cluster that opposes Joyce's Moon are Apollo at 6 Sagittarius, the god of prophecy at Delphi, who is conjoined to the asteroid Delphine at 8 Sagittarius, the geographical place name of Delphi, the most famous oracle of the ancient world for over 1000 years. The linking of these two asteroids, similar to that of Zeus and Dodona, further emphasizes and amplifies the oracular potential of Joyce's nature. Oracles were given always as responses to questions, and for Joyce, this faculty becomes primarily activated when someone asks for her advice or counsel.

At 7 Sagittarius we find the asteroids Amazone and the Amazon queen Penthesilea who dueled with Achilles, the Greek hero of the Trojan War. The Amazons were tribes of female warriors that inhabited the area of the Caucasian mountains and the steppes northeast of the Black Sea. According to the legends, they created all-women communities, and fiercely defended their lands against invaders. With these warrior queens configured to her Moon by an opposition, Joyce, likewise, may have sought support and protection from women in her life, or perhaps developed her own martial skills in order to defend herself or other women. The archetype of the strong, independent, and self-sufficient woman is connected to the lunar theme of care and concern in Joyce's psyche.

The final asteroid that is opposite Joyce's Moon is Philosophia, the goddess of philosophy as a lover of wisdom, which further supports her Ascendant themes related to the quest for knowledge. Joyce is interested not so much in the random accumulation of information, but rather in a search for meaning that involves the big questions that have occupied the minds of great thinkers. What kinds of wisdom can be gained through an intuitive opening to spiritual forces is the question that connects the asteroid Philosophia to Apollo and Delphine.

The asteroids Skuld and Chaldea are exactly conjunct the asteroid Vesta at 7 Pisces, all right on the Midheaven, the point of professional, social, or spiritual vocation. These three asteroids are also in a very close one-degree square aspect to the Moon and Saturn, creating a conflictual inner tension between a public life and a private life. As the Roman goddess presiding over the Vestal Virgins, Vesta, one of the four major asteroids, holds the most elevated position in the nativity. The Roman vestals were chosen from among the most nobly born daughters and taken into Vesta's temple at an early age to be trained as priestesses who kept the eternal flame burning, symbolizing the protection of the Roman state. They were oath bound to chastity upon punishment of death by live burial in a tomb.

Preliminary speculations on the meaning of this asteroid pointed to a life marked by a fear of sexual intimacy or denial of personal relationship, with the sexual/relational energy being sublimated into one's spiritual practice or work. Further investigation revealed that the prototype for the Roman vestals were the temple priestesses of the ancient Near East, such as those of Ishtar. One class of priestesses, as living embodiments of the goddess, engaged in sexual relations with the members of the community seeking a healing or blessing. Virgin meant, not chaste, but rather unmarried. When sexual practice within a sacred ritual became tabooed, the priestesses sublimated the sexual energy, turning it inward to achieve union with god within. The Pythian prophetesses of Delphi became the brides of the god Apollo, as the Christian nuns became the brides of Jesus Christ. Modern day vestals may express either one of these extremes—a life of outer sexual abstinence or a life of so-called promiscuity, harkening to the call to offer healing to the suppliant calling at the temple. They might experience alternating periods of extended chastity or intense sexual activity.

For Joyce, I would think that Vesta on her Midheaven portends the social role of a modern day priestess. Placed in Pisces, a sign of psychic sensitivity and awareness of the connectedness of all life, Vesta has a calling to tend to the spiritual needs of others, and, at times, this vocation may seem as if it requires the placing of personal, marital or other types of committed relationships at an arm's length so that she may dedicate herself to her ministry. Combined with Chaldea, the astrologer's signature, and Skuld, Norn of the Future, astrology may be the vehicle through which intimations of a person's destiny are revealed.

154

Let us now turn to the Sun, the animating spark that gives expression to the life force. The Sun is in Capricorn, a conservative and reticent sign that has aspirations for social advancement and recognition. It is placed in the eighth house, which we have already mentioned is associated with death and resources accruing from death. As the underworld of death is a metaphor for the dark unconscious, modern astrologers have also associated the eighth house with depth psychology and the occult, both as investigations into the unseen forces behind visible appearances. The Sun is the ruler of the third house, which pertains to siblings, familiar travel, and writing. There may exist some connection between siblings or relatives and death and inheritances. Joyce may also have a need to understand and communicate about the unseen forces that appear to govern our waking lives. A number of asteroids are conjunct Joyce's Sun.

The first asteroid that is noteworthy for the purposes of this book, *Under One Sky*, is Raffinetti at the same degree as Joyce's Sun, 25 Capricorn. Personal name asteroids are often as significant in a person's birth chart as are the mythic named ones. Rafi (Rafael) Nasser is the project concept originator of this book, and his connection to Joyce is signified by this placement. As the Sun is the ruler of the third house of siblings, relatives, and writing, I wonder if there is a familial connection here, and if Joyce is using her eighth house resources to fund this book project through Rafi.

The asteroid Daphne at 25 Cancer is located opposite Joyce's Sun. Daphne, when pursued by the god Apollo, called upon Gaia for assistance (which is conjunct Joyce's Descendent and Juno, both relating to marriage). Daphne was transformed into a laurel tree to prevent her ravishment, and thereafter Apollo used the laurel as a primary symbol for his oracular Delphic priestesses, and he awarded a laurel wreath to the victors of annual games held at Delphi. Here we have another symbol of prophetic potential. In addition, this is the third time the symbolism of a tree has appeared in connection with prophecy; the other two being the oak tree of Zeus at Dodona and the world tree of the Norns. Joyce may have some kind of special relationship with trees, and they may provide a source of comfort for her, which allows her to tune into her intuitive insights.

The asteroid Medea at 23 Capricorn is also with the Sun. In Greek mythology, Medea was a princess of Colchis on the Black Sea who assisted Jason in his capture of the Golden Fleece in return for marriage. She was an herbalist who was demonized by the Greeks as a sorceress. After some years, Jason abandoned her and their two sons, in order to marry a princess of Corinth for increased status and power. The Greek playwright Euripides fashioned a drama in which Medea killed her two children as an act of revenge against her husband.

I might speculate upon the themes of working with herbs in a magical way, as in the preparations of amulets or potions, or of having had experiences in marriage of being abandoned for another woman, or issues around the loss or separation of children in some way related to death or custodial disputes. As the planet Venus, ruler of the fifth house of children and the twelfth house of sorrow, is also in the eighth, there may be some difficulty here. There may have been some problems bearing children which was a cause of great sorrow, or she may have lost children of her own to death or illness, or had them taken away or turned against her.

Another way in which this theme is indicated is in the grouping of the asteroids Moira at 23 Libra, Karma at 24 Libra, and the Lot of the Mother at 23 Libra, all in the fifth house of children and in a close square to the Sun at 25 Capricorn. Moira is the Greek triple goddess of Fate that represented the allotted portion that the gods dealt out to mortals. The significations of Moira were unavoidable and unalterable. Karma, from an Eastern perspective, is the circumstances of our life that are the results reaped from previous actions. These placements seem to indicate some kind of inevitable and fated occurrences, over which she has no control, in connection to her mother or as a mother to her own children.

The asteroid Icarus at 22 Capricorn is linked with the Sun as well. Mythically, Icarus is known as the winged youth who, in his attempt to escape imprisonment in the labyrinth of the Minotaur on Crete, ignored his father's warning not to fly too close to the Sun. He was filled with the intoxicating exhilaration of freedom and of ever-upward soaring. As his wings were held together with wax, the heat of the sun melted them and he crashed into what is now called the Icarian Sea. Icarus represents a desire for liberation, but the challenge that this asteroid presents is for the maintenance of self-discipline and control over one's free flight in order to prevent a crash landing. Icarus tends to be more stabilized in the earth sign of Capricorn, but as this symbol is connected to mountains, I would inquire if Joyce skis—flying through the air at fast speeds and, in the process, enjoying the element of risk and thereby flirting with death. As the eighth house is also the house of financial investments and Capricorn is a sign that relates to the business of the practical world, she may takes risks in high venture returns.

The fourth asteroid conjoined with the Sun is Merlin at 27 Capricorn, and this legendary figure leads us into another major theme in Joyce's chart. Merlin is one of a family of Celtic-named asteroids, and a number of these fall out in significant places in her chart. This indicates that the Camelot legend is one of the

156

primary mythic dramas in Joyce's life. Merlin was the famous wizard of Arthurian mythology, an inspired seer, magician, and shape-shifter who was a counselor and friend to three kings. Here we see repetition of the theme of prophetic insight that was discussed earlier in connection with the oracle of Zeus at Dodona, and of magical proclivities in connection to Medea.

Following this Celtic thread, we see that the asteroid Arthur at 1 Capricorn, King of Camelot, is conjunct Joyce's Juno at 29 Sagittarius, goddess of marriage and the seventh house cusp, the angle associated with marriage and the spouse. The asteroid Guinevere, Queen of Camelot, at 12 Capricorn is widely connected to Arthur in the seventh house of marriage, as well as conjunct her pre-natal lunation point, which in Hellenistic astrology is an indicator of debts being paid to you from the past. The asteroid Lancelot, Guinevere's secret lover, at 10 Aquarius is exact with Venus, significator of love and ruler of the fifth house of romance. The asteroid Excalibur at 24 Aquarius opposes Galahad at 23 Leo, and they are both aligned to the nodal axis. Let us see what kind of story these asteroids tell, beginning with the topic of relationship.

The four angles of the chart designate the most active and dynamic points. We have looked at the Ascendant and the Midheaven and now turn our attention to the Descendant, also known as the seventh house cusp. This point is related to marriage, and in Joyce's chart, Sagittarius occupies the seventh place. Gemini on the Ascendant speaks to her need for mental communication as an expression of her basic character, and Sagittarius on the seventh describes a need for a partner who can communicate with her on an intellectual, philosophical, and spiritual level. As Jupiter, which is the ruler of the marriage house, is in an averse (inconjunct) aspect to Mercury, ruler of the self, this lack of configuration between self and other points to the lack of interactive communication with the marital partner in regards to matters of higher knowledge. However, Jupiter occupies the second house, a place associated with money and material well-being, and this planet that signifies marriage is exalted in the sign of Cancer. Thus, the marriage will most likely produce financial affluence. Because Jupiter is retrograde, this may signify that at some point, the abundant money provided by the partner will be lost, taken away or taken back.

Jupiter is flanked by two asteroids—Metis and Proserpina. Metis, at 19 Cancer in this chart, gave Jupiter the potion that caused his father Saturn to regurgitate Jupiter's swallowed siblings, and thus enabled him to win the war that inaugurated his reign of supremacy as an Olympian god. Pursued by Zeus, Metis became pregnant with Athena. When prophesied that she would bear him a second child that would supercede him, he swallowed her whole and birthed

157

Athena himself from the crown of his head. This story might suggest that the spouse, signified by Jupiter, takes the knowledge of his partner for his own use, and then denies her expression. At 20 Cancer, Proserpina, the maiden daughter of Ceres, the goddess of agriculture, was abducted by Pluto, the god of the underworld, who made her captive as his bride and queen. Ceres eventually bargained for the release of Proserpina for part of each year. For Joyce, marriage could seem as a kind of abduction by a regal and powerful individual who attempts to control her as child-bride.

The Proserpina (Greek Persephone) archetype often suggests an early childhood tragedy, such as separation from the parents, physical or emotional abuse, sexual violation or some other kind of family crisis, and as a result the child is plunged into some kind of underworld reality where life becomes frightening and insecure. The psyche can become frozen at the age of the tragedy. The body matures, but inside resides a terrified child who develops great anxiety over being unable to cope with the responsibilities of the adult. With Proserpina connected to Jupiter, the significator of marriage, Joyce may gravitate to a partner who holds the promise of being a protector who will relieve her of the stress of dealing with the demands of the physical world. To the extent that she maintains the role of the dependent child, these kinds of unions generally proceed smoothly. However, if the woman begins to individuate and mature, the relationship can become quite stressful as the husband's role is predicated upon his wife's dependency, and often he is unwilling to relinquish his control and authority over her.

The asteroid Bacchus at 20 Capricorn is opposite Jupiter at 19 Cancer, and also in a wide conjunction to the Sun at 25 Capricorn. Bacchus was the god of wine, ecstasy, intoxication, and perceived madness. Again, we might ask if there is any kind of connection between alcohol, the spouse, and inheritance or investments.

Juno at 29 Sagittarius, the goddess of marriage, is another of the four most important asteroids. She anchors the seventh cusp at 27 Sagittarius, place of marriage. Juno, as the wife of the supreme god Jupiter, figures prominently in the charts of women who are wives of powerful and successful men. In the mythical biography of Jupiter and Juno (the Greek Zeus and Hera), Juno raged against Jupiter's numerous infidelities, but nevertheless remained sexually faithful herself and honored her commitment to preserving and enduring her marriage. With Juno in the sign of Sagittarius, Joyce has a need for shared ideals and aspirations in partnership. As Juno (and also her Greek cognate Hera at 21 Sagittarius) are conjunct Mars, god of war, she may encounter conflict, power struggles, and possible intellectual abuse as she struggles to express and honor her own belief

158

system, which may not be compatible with that of her partner. Joyce may experience inner tension as one part of her wants to honor her vows and benefit from the status and security that her marriage affords, yet the other part feels lonely and disillusioned with the lack of respect and genuine communication that she is given. This alignment between Juno and Mars may also describe a spouse who displays a militant or warrior nature.

The asteroid Arthur at 27 Sagittarius is exactly conjunct the seventh cusp and quite close to Juno. Arthur might be the actual name of her partner, or he might embody the heroic qualities of legendary King Arthur. As the asteroid Arthur is also conjunct with the asteroid Camelot, we see a situation in which a woman who is a royal princess in her own right, as was the Scottish Guinevere, is given in marriage in order to merge two dynastic families. This likewise may have been the underlying reason for Joyce's marriage.

Joyce has the asteroid Guinevere in the seventh house of marriage, and its alignment with the pre-natal lunation point indicates that some debt from the past is being repaid to her. The co-presence of Arthur, Camelot, and Guinevere in the seventh house allude to a dynastic marriage based upon previous familial obligations.

Arthur was the illegitimate son of the reigning king Uther Pendragon, raised in secret by Merlin. He proved his right to rule when he came of age by fulfilling the prophecy of being able to pull the magic sword Excalibur from out of the stone. Joyce has the asteroid Excalibur conjunct the South Node of the Moon, which in modern astrology is associated with past life karma. The nodal axis will be discussed more fully below, but for now let us point out that the conjunction of the South Node with Excalibur is another indicator of the significance of the Camelot theme in Joyce's life as unresolved circumstances from the past shaping the present life.

Merlin initially objected to the marriage union because he knew that Guinevere was secretly in love with Lancelot, the greatest and noblest knight of the Round Table. The passion was reciprocated, and they eventually became lovers. When the affair was discovered, Lancelot fled, but returned several days later to save Guinevere from being burnt to death. His actions split the Round Table and weakened King Arthur's realm. In the subsequent battles that followed, Arthur was mortally wounded and taken by a magic boat to Avalon. Lancelot retreated to become a hermit, and Guinevere became a nun at Amesbury, where she died.

Joyce has the asteroid Lancelot exact with Venus, the goddess of desire and attraction. Venus is conjoined with Mercury, the ruler of Joyce's Ascendant as

159

significator of the self and her need for communication. Venus rules the fifth house of romantic affairs and the twelfth house of secrets. We might wonder if in the aftermath of disillusionment due to the frustrated mental compatibility in the marriage, Joyce has been vulnerable to a secret affair with someone who embodies the magnetism of Lancelot and who has met her deepest needs for a genuine meeting of the mind. Venus is also opposite Pluto, and this combination can point to a powerful and compulsive sexual energy that has the potential to destroy the social structures that define Joyce's reality. Once again, the second and eighth houses that contain this opposition are the money houses, and one might ask whether the financial foundation of Joyce's life, especially that part provided by the marriage, was compromised or placed into jeopardy due to such a union.

One should also note the strong priestess/nun indicators that were discussed with Vesta on the Midheaven and Hestia conjunct the Moon and Saturn in the twelfth house. As Guinevere ended her days as a nun, Joyce may likewise recollect a strong affinity with that identity, which can have related to both her childhood feeling of confinement and her vocational destiny in some kind of spiritual service.

Let us now turn to the Nodal axis where, in modern astrology, the nodes of the Moon are believed to represent karmic issues. The South Node is a symbol of the past, and represents material carried over from other lifetimes in the form of deeply ingrained negative habit patterns or irrational fears that often act as obstacles to future growth. By contrast, the North Node represents the future path of spiritual integration and represents how new experiences can lead to personal growth. The South Node placed in the ninth house can indicate that the search for wisdom leads to endless travels, multiple teachers, inexhaustible supplies of books, and ongoing classes, with the truth becoming ever more elusive. The North Node in the third house indicates that the answers are to be found within one's own intuitive and meditative processes rather than in external authorities.

In Joyce's chart the South Node is conjunct to the asteroid Excalibur, Arthur's magical sword, and to the third of the four major asteroids, Pallas Athena, the Greek virgin goddess of Wisdom and War. The North Node is conjunct another Arthurian asteroid, Galahad, who saw the Holy Grail in a vision, and to the wounded healer Chiron.

Excalibur was an enchanted sword that prevented the loss of blood in battle. It is placed in the ninth house of long-distance travel, and as a past life symbol, I would ask Joyce if she has visited or feels a pull to visit the locale of Glastonbury in England, where Excalibur was purportedly forged. I would also query her as to whether she has ever had any kinds of traumatic real or imagined experiences concerning swords, knives, or other sharp-pointed weapons. Or perhaps has Joyce engaged in the art of fencing?

Pallas Athena was the goddess of wisdom, sprung from the head of Jupiter as his favorite daughter. Placed in the ninth house of higher learning, it is exactly trine Joyce's Ascendant. It reflects the theme we find running through this chart of a questing intellect that is ever exploring the horizons of her mind and the larger world of travel and cross-cultural belief systems. Honored as Parthenos, the virgin goddess who was the tutelary deity of the city of Athens, Pallas Athena was also an embodiment of the Warrior Queen, and her glyph represents a spear that was one of her emblems. She also had fashioned the Palladium after accidentally killing her foster sister in a jousting contest. The Palladium was a magical wooden statue that granted invulnerability in battle to whoever possessed it, which became conflated in later occult lore with the spear of destiny. The head of the Gorgon Medusa, serpent-hailed queen of wisdom, was affixed to Pallas Athena's breast armor, which functioned as an apotropaic device, repelling attacks.

Here with Excalibur and Pallas Athena, we see several magical weapons—the sword, the Palladium, the Gorgon's head—that all granted invulnerability in battle. As Pallas Athena disowned her femininity in order to embody the attributes of wisdom and military valor in the classical world, this asteroid can sometimes point to themes where women are put into predicaments where a vibrant intellectual life or strong physical talents threaten the more traditional subservient role expected in marriage and relationships. Keeping in mind the warrior energy of the Amazon asteroids that are opposed to Joyce's Moon, we might postulate that Joyce has used her intellect as a weapon in order to protect her vulnerability and defend her autonomy, especially when her beliefs and values are being challenged. The conjunction of Excalibur and Pallas Athena with the South Node suggest that this intellectual armor and relentless quest for higher knowledge, while a familiar and comfortable pattern, has not always served Joyce's best interests in the long run.

This South Node, one which is carried over from the past, is polarized by the asteroid Galahad and by Chiron, both conjunct the North Node which points the way for resolution and future growth. Galahad at 23 Leo is conjoined to Joyce's North Node of the Moon at 25 Leo. Sir Galahad, the pure and peerless knight, was the son of Lancelot. Legend has it that he alone saw the Holy Grail, which was an important quest for the Knights of the Round Table. After seeing the Grail in a vision and receiving a promise that his soul would live in the next life with Christ, many miracles took place around him. Upon his death it was said that a great multitude of angels bore his soul up to heaven. In modern astrology, the North Node points to one's future direction of spiritual growth. The search for salvation and redemption that is symbolized by the Holy Grail, which was believed to contain the blood of Christ that flowed from the spear thrust at the Crucifixion, is the journey that has been set before Joyce. The Grail quest is the search for truth and spiritual regeneration, and, according to the lore, the Grail may be seen only by those who have achieved a certain level of consciousness. Galahad's placement in the third house suggests the importance of looking inward for an illumination of inner wisdom rather than outward in the innumerable journeys signified by the ninth house. I might also inquire if Joyce has had a relationship with a Lancelot type of figure, if this person had a son who might embody the role of Galahad, and if such a son has a role in her spiritual salvation indicated by this asteroid.

Note that this is the third time that the symbol of the spear appears with the nodal axis, the previous two being the Excalibur sword and Athena's spear. The mythic biography of Chiron, the fourth planetary body in this configuration, also involves a pointed weapon.

Chiron, now classified as a comet orbiting not inside the asteroid belt, but between Saturn and Uranus, occupies Joyce's third house, associated with siblings, relatives, familiar travel, writing and communication. Chiron, as the mythical centaur who was teacher and foster parent to many of the Greek heroes, was wounded with a poisoned arrow either in the knee, thigh or ankle. I would call your attention to the asteroid Hephaistos which is conjunct Joyce's Moon. He was born with a lame foot, and I wonder if there is some kind of physical handicap from a pointed weapon that has befallen Joyce or someone in her family, and that has impacted the circumstances of her life. Chiron's wounds, however, are not only physical, but more often address the emotional and mental levels of being.

Chiron represents a place in our lives where we have received an essential wounding, which becomes our central life challenge and eventually leads us towards our destiny. Symbolizing both the victim and the wounded healer, Chiron in the third conjoined with the North Node points to some kind of difficulties in communication in early childhood that may have contributed to a sense of inadequacy. As a result, Joyce may have embarked upon a relentless search for knowledge discovered outside of her self. However the placement of North Node with Chiron in the third indicates the value of going inward to connect with truth, and through intuition accessing an inner wellspring of understanding that can be used to inform her decisions. Chiron symbolizes the quintessential shamanic healer. The wound, which entails a journey to the underworld and back, is the initiation. Chiron's credentials as teacher and healer arise from the school of real life experiences, and it is in the understanding and integration of Joyce's own experiences that her capacity for conveying meaningful knowledge to others will be realized. Third house avenues of expression include writing, speaking, and teaching.

We have seen four instruments for wounding connected with the nodal axis: the enchanted sword Excalibur, Athena's spear, the spear that pierced Christ, and Chiron's poisoned arrow. Yet, each of these weapons is mythically associated with a kind of divine protection. Excalibur prevented the loss of blood; Athena's Palladium and breastplate granted invulnerability, Galahad's vision of the Holy Grail which contained Christ's blood offered salvation and spiritual regeneration, and the arrow that pierced Chiron set him on the path towards the fulfillment of his destiny. These asteroids all point to the theme of the sacred dimension of wounding, where the wound becomes the agent that can lead one into a transfigured dimension of life. For Joyce, confronting and attempting to heal the wounds associated with her intellect, and perhaps with her siblings/relatives as well, is part of a story whose antecedent causes reside in the karmic past and whose resolution is part of her spiritual destiny in the present incarnation.

This asteroid reading cannot be concluded without a mention of Ceres, the fourth of the major asteroids. The mythological Ceres was the goddess who gave the gift of agriculture to the Greek people as well as the Eleusinian mystery rites. The story of her daughter Persephone/Proserpina's abduction by Pluto into the underworld and Ceres's efforts to recover her child was perhaps the best known of the ancient tales, as it became the basis for her initiation rites which were offered annually in Greece for over 1000 years. Astrologically, Ceres themes can point to a strong identification with being a parent, but also the loss and separation from parents and children as one enters into her pathos. Ceres also took on the role of a nursemaid, or foster mother to another child. It may also indicate a calling for working with the dead and dying in connection with her death/rebirth mysteries.

Joyce has the asteroid Ceres in the tenth house, a very dynamic place in the chart, associated with the profession and one's actions in the world. Ceres is in the sign of Aries, which can indicate that she had to be her own mother. Ceres is also opposite the planet Neptune in the fourth house of the parents, and Neptune can signify loss, dissolution, as well as idealism. Joyce may have emotional yearnings for an idealized kind of unconditional love and nurturing. The placement of Ceres in the tenth house and eleventh sign (from the Ascendant) may indicate her

163

actions to create or support institutions that provide for the needs of children who have suffered some kind of loss. Alternatively, it may point to some kind of hospice work. The Ceres/Neptune opposition at 1 Aries/2 Libra is making a tight T-square to the asteroid Camelot at 1 Capricorn, and I would ask if the marriage estate in any way contributed to this alignment, or if the responsibilities of the marriage estate created a conflict with the philanthropic gestures denoted by Ceres and Neptune.

In summation, several themes have emerged from the considerations of the mythic dimensions of the asteroid-named deities. One theme relates to a talent for oracular or prophetic talents linked with nature and combined with astrology as part of Joyce's spiritual vocation. We also see the possibility of sudden loss of parents in early life, accompanied by the inheritance of great wealth, and a certain kind of confinement or isolation that marked her childhood. Encounters with death, money, magic, and the world behind manifested reality are major and formative aspects of Joyce's life experiences. The Camelot drama involving Arthur, Guinevere, and Lancelot forms the patterning around relationships. Running through the entire nativity is an active inquiring intellect questing the world over for higher knowledge, and the fruits of this search ultimately are found through inner reflection. It is the telling of Joyce's story that for her will be both the healing and the offering.

EVELYN ROBERTS: ARCHETYPAL

STRATEGY

I use Solar Fire software; it is the first and only astrology program I have ever used. I've never found anything to complain about so I'm perfectly happy with it. Generally when seeing a client I have a swath of information from natal to transits, solar returns and progressions. With Joyce I used only her natal chart, and briefly referred to her transits. I looked at the progressions for my own information. Integrating them into the reading was restricted by the space allowed, and I felt that additional technical data could have made reading the text overly confusing.

It is rare for me to read a chart without that person sitting in front of me, or at least on the other end of a telephone. I had an immediate sense of the responsibility involved in analyzing the body, mind and soul of someone represented by symbols on a piece of paper. Without a familiarizing tangible point of connection to her, my deepest intention towards Joyce was not to be harmful in any way.

As I do before seeing any client, I carried Joyce around with me for a time, both in my head and on paper. I have charts strewn around my house, even in my car. I find it incredibly helpful to just "be" with a chart, for example sitting at a traffic light I'll absorb myself in it for a couple of minutes. So far there have been no resultant accidents or traffic violations.

In my experience there is no such thing as a simple chart or life, regardless of how things might appear; if there are they don't gravitate into my life or consulting room. I make note of contacts between my chart and the chart of the client. With Joyce my Sun closely conjuncts her Mercury/Venus conjunction, and my Mercury conjoins her Sun. I find it helpful to be aware of these contacts. Even more helpful is being aware of where there are no contacts of any kind, because this is where one needs to be particularly vigilant against making unfounded assumptions based on theory rather than experience. I use inception charts, and when seeing a client I draw up a chart for the appointment time, although this is often strictly for my own information. With this project I drew up a chart for the first time I started writing, and it was at a random uncalculated time. Sun, Moon, Mars and Jupiter were in the sixth, with Uranus rising. All very apropos, since I found myself from that moment on chained to my computer compulsively buried in this chart for several weeks.

I approach the chart believing that the range between the negative and positive manifestations of every aspect and possibility in astrology, as a reflection of life, is vast and possibly limitless. Most of us slide up and down that spectrum on our personal journey towards some semblance of wholeness.

When doing a chart in person I find I am able to allow the chart to unfold organically. I usually make one page of notes, starting with elemental and modal balance. I note angular planets, dignities and detriments, mutual receptions, etc., paying particular attention to the chart ruler. Then I make a note of the major configurations. I keep this to one side during a reading and use it as a cheat sheet should I get a brain cramp.

With Joyce I made it a more formal exercise and journeyed through the chart planet by planet, familiarizing myself with her. First I did this in a structured way, isolating each planet and analyzing its sign, placement and aspects, and making a page or two of notes on each planet or significant point. This way I could get a firm grip on the technicalities and, so to speak, facts of the chart.

Then I took time just to "feel" the chart. This felt important because there was no information about this woman, except for her willingness to participate in this study, which said a lot to me. I realize many astrologers work primarily in this way and with outstanding results, but it isn't familiar to me so I had to put new "eyes" on.

I start with the elemental balance and there is generally a wealth of information right there. This was particularly so in Joyce's case, especially when taking into consideration the houses. Among other things she has an overwhelming predominance of Air, very little Water, yet heavy tenanting of the Water houses. I have a personalized system for weighting the elements; as with everything in astrology it's what "feels" right and has proven so for me. I could have adopted it from someone else way back, but I honestly can't remember if I did. I count the Sun and Moon as two each, all the planets and the Ascendant and Midheaven as one each. I do not include the lunar nodes in my elemental weighting system, although they are important in my work.

At the same time I look at the Sun's element as indicative of the superior function in Jungian terms (re Karen Hamaker-Zondag's work). Even though the Sun is Joyce's only Earth planet, it is the primary planet of consciousness, and therefore I would assume her primary function to be sensory. Joyce

166

probably orients herself through her senses and is likely to manifest a degree of sophistication through this functioning. Fire being indicative of the intuitive would therefore be the inferior function, and where she could have more primal responses. This is also where the Muse resides, and is an important gateway into her own unconscious functioning.

Briefly, since she is a sensory type with an extreme amount of Air, I imagine her as intellectual with a strong need to feel grounded in reality. With low Water but the Water houses strongly tenanted, she might perpetually find herself confronted with the unconscious undercurrents of her own psyche, and that of others. She only has one personal Fire planet and with this element being somewhat unconscious, whatever inspires her and connects her to her own creativity and sense of inspiration and joy will be particularly vital. None of us actually "lack" anything; the question is how accessible or how unconscious is the functioning of these attributes. The means of accessing these aspects of our being needs to be congruent with where they reside. For Joyce this undoubtedly means she needs to look beyond her intellect and logic in order to connect with her creative, instinctual nature.

The modes are somewhat balanced with Joyce, so I paid note to which planets were placed in which mode and kept that in mind. I treat the elements and modes as the backdrop and then start layering and weaving everything over and through this.

Moving into the chart itself, I generally begin with the Sun, because it represents the life force center of existence. Many of us don't fully manifest what our Sun represents until the second half of life, because the Sun is where we are truly unique and individual. A strong sense of self is needed to muster up the courage to stand alone and unshielded by our "tribe." None of us do this all the time and some of us don't have, or sadly ever will have, a clear idea of who we truly are as individuals. When we can't rise with our Sun, we fall into its shadow elements and manifest the negative meaning of its symbolism.

The Sun is Joyce's only Earth planet. With the heavy weighting towards Air and a Capricorn Sun, I suspect Joyce has a serious, thoughtful, paradoxically diverse yet concentrated edge to her. It is not that one planet is any more important than another; as with the organs of the human body, all parts make up the whole. However existence without the Sun would be like life without a heart; it cannot sustain because it literally is the life force, just as there would be no life here on Earth without the physical Sun.

I started looking at this chart through the Ascendant and before the Sun, partially because of the quincunx relationship they share, and because it spoke to me that way. I view the Ascendant as the quest of our lives. If the Sun represents the hero, then I see the Ascendant as the path taken on that journey towards the true self. It is the light on the horizon that we aim for, which represents the moment we awaken to in this incarnation. It is also how we appear to others, our doorway into life, and can be the mask we wear.

The triad that I focus on as an entryway into the chart also includes the Moon. As the other luminary, the Moon is reflective, having no light of its own. This indicates our receptivity and relationship to the rest of humanity. Its function also has to do with our needs, emotional responses, roots and related experiences. Joyce's Moon is in the same sign as her Ascendant, Gemini, strengthening the significance of its symbolism. In a sense I consider the primary triad of Sun/Moon/Ascendant as the springboard from which I move into everything else. From here on out the tapestry began to weave itself through rulerships, dispositorships, sign and house placements, aspects and so forth. No planet lives in isolation, and even if unaspected or singular in its sign, element or mode, this will add just another unique flavor to the whole.

The obvious way to approach this exercise was through exploring particular character facets and life areas in an organized, categorized fashion. It isn't my way to be very methodical around this. So with the intention of being organized I just let it unfold, which may only make sense to another Neptune/Mercury soul. The categories I used evolved as I worked my way through the chart, and they mirror what felt like significant and emphasized life focuses for Joyce. I was aware of not being too absolute about anything, so language was important in this project. It felt inappropriate and presumptuous to say anything in a way other than emphasizing it as a possibility and not as a statement of fact. I also found myself being somewhat neutral and conservative in how I presented the information. Without prior knowledge of her beliefs, religious or otherwise, marital/family status, or accomplishments, it felt to me the most potentially constructive approach.

Some factors were more challenging for me than others, in particular the fact that Joyce's Mercury/Venus conjunction is so tightly conjunct the eighth/ninth house cusp in Placidus, my house system of choice. However I am Faculty of Astrological Studies trained, where Equal House is the preferred system, and I did note that if using this system, these two planets would be firmly in the eighth house. This could make me appear slutty with my house systems, but astrology is a fluid system, is it not? This dilemma would have been a key issue I would have explored in a verbal consultation, so I was very aware of being perhaps somewhat waffly around the fact they could have functioned as either eighth or ninth house planets, this being especially so with Mercury, as it is natally retrograde and technically moving back into the eighth.

I also found myself not wanting to key in too closely on Chiron without feedback, which speaks more about my own personal vulnerability with this planet than anything else. My experience is that it is highly personalized in its functioning and my instincts told me to be particularly cautious. I'm sure this would manifest differently if I had more experience with blind readings.

After the basic foundation was laid, my tenth house Saturn kicked in and I began to fill in any gaps, and revise, revise, revise. I have a newfound respect and awe for people who write for a living, and I have no idea how they ever actually complete anything. It was difficult to let Joyce go, and even now I keep mentally wandering into different areas with her and feeling that perhaps I didn't say or qualify this or that. The truth is that it isn't probably even remotely possible to feel complete in the analysis of a human life in 10,000 words or less.

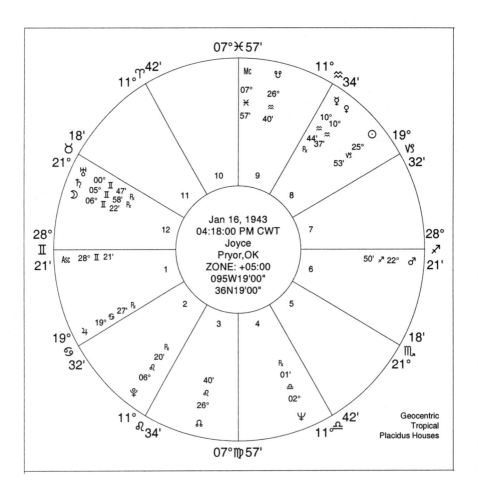

07° ✈ 57'

11° ♈ 42'

11° ♒ 34'

Mc   ☋
07°   26°
✈   ♒
57'   40'

☿
♀
10°
10°
♒
44' ♒
37'
Rx   53' ♑ 25'   ☉

18'
21° ♉

19°
♑
32'

♅
♄   00° ♊
05° ♊ 47' Rx
☽   06° ♊ 58' Rx
22'

10   9

11

12   8

Jan 16, 1943
04:18:00 PM CWT
Joyce
Pryor,OK
ZONE: +05:00
095W19'00"
36N19'00"

7

28°
♊
21'

Asc   28° ♊ 21'

1

2

6

50' ✈ 22' ♂

28°
✈
21'

19° ♋ 27' Rx
♃

3   4   5

20° Rx
06°
♇

40'
♌
26°

Rx
01'
♎
02'
♆

18'
♏
21°

19°
♋
32'

11°
♌ 34'

☊

11° ♎ 42'

07° ♍ 57'

Geocentric
Tropical
Placidus Houses

Personality and how she appears to the world

I envision Joyce as profoundly deep and complex, yet I doubt the first impression she makes will come close to disclosing this. With Gemini Ascending, and the chart ruler Mercury in Aquarius, she could appear gregarious and friendly with a very real, although detached, interest in anything and everyone. In truth her approach to life, ego intention, and sense of self are likely to be intense, serious, and focused behind this deceptively open facade.

With her strong emphasis on the Air element and Mercury ruling the chart, the left-brain, analytical-logical side of Joyce's nature may both appear and in truth be quite dominant and sophisticated. She has all the transpersonal planets, plus Saturn, Jupiter and Mercury retrograde, indicating a somewhat introspective aspect to her nature. Mercury was one day into its retrograde cycle at her birth and moving particularly slowly, probably intensifying her capacity for mental concentration and reflectivity.

She may be highly idealistic because her mind seeks perfection and at the same time sees endless possibilities (Gemini rising and the chart ruler Mercury in Aquarius). Obviously life itself does not conform to these principles, so for souls like Joyce, this can mean frequent disappointments. With her strong emphasis on Water houses, and her twelfth house Moon conjunct Saturn, more often than not how she may feel let down will be emotionally. This could cast a melancholic hue on her personality, perhaps even manifesting as a tendency towards depression. She could try to avoid showing this, with her eighth house private persona and intellectualizing Mercurial nature. Fortunately, the strong emphasis on Air probably gives her the ability to step back from situations to gain perspective. A point of relief can be that when she is centered and comfortable with herself, her boundaries will be clear and well defined.

Gemini rising indicates that her life's path is strongly tied to communications, the world of language and the sharing of ideas. She may be restless, inquisitive and have a persistent craving for stimulation and new experiences. Her agile Aquarian mind can give her the ability to engage almost anyone in a verbal or intellectual exchange. The Gemini Ascendant suggests her personal path and the information highway are on parallel tracks. However, with Mercury retrograding back into the eighth whilst on the cusp of the ninth, her mind will not be superficial, and even when seeming to engage in small talk there will be serious and intense undertones at play. I doubt she finds much merit in chitchatting.

With Mercury disposited by Uranus, I'd guess she gets "ants in her pants" when her boredom threshold is triggered, and she may try and move on quickly to the next thing or escape into her own mental terrain. Even with her open demeanor, broad-mindedness and interest in external factors, there could be a tendency for her to be subtly (and sometimes not so subtly) guarded and cool. Her retrograde chart ruler Mercury is on the eighth/ninth cusp and in the sign of Aquarius. Although it could be seen technically as a ninth house planet, by progression it retrograded back into the eighth house and did not actually progress out of that house until she was forty-one years old. The fact that she is probably a deeply private, acutely sensitive person will require acknowledgment, protection and honoring, and she may need to be the first person to do this.

Other, no less authentic facets of her personality will possibly include abilities to engage, charm and adapt; the chart ruler Mercury is conjunct Venus and trine the Moon. And at the same time, with the Aquarius overtones and Mercury/Venus opposing Pluto, there may be an ever-present subtle aloofness and simmering intensity about her. With the Mercury-Venus conjunction in Aquarius and Uranus-ruled, her social skills can be refined, although not necessarily in a conventional way. There could well be a delightful intriguing quirkiness about her, despite a potentially cool demeanor. However, if this combination of energies is operating unconsciously, with Venus trine the Moon in the twelfth and opposite Pluto, she could sometimes be like Pollyanna with a switchblade in her purse. She could then have a rather spooky unpredictable edge to her, and be congenial yet secretively defended.

I also see her as someone highly responsible with profound depth and steely determination (Capricorn Sun in the eighth, plus Saturn conjunct her Moon and trine her chart ruler and Venus). Despite her engaging demeanor, she's unlikely to be ostentatious. I'd be surprised if she were someone who liked to hold the limelight. If she ever takes the stage it will probably be to make a point and present her viewpoint, not to dazzle or impress. Air is stronger than Fire in this chart. Also, the emphasis on the Water houses indicates that she could feel particularly vulnerable when overexposed. Only when the importance of the subject overrides all else might she be willing to put herself center stage.

Even with her inherent charm, she could possibly on occasion turn disconcertingly icy if in a situation she dislikes, considers tedious, or where she

172

feels defensive. Saturn is co-dispositor of Aquarius and therefore of her chart ruler Mercury and of Venus, and conjoins her Uranus/Moon. With this triple conjunction in the twelfth house and sometimes operating unconsciously, it is possible she is often unaware of coming across coldly, or of causing others discomfort.

Original or controversial ideas may be particularly appealing to Joyce with her Airy Aquarian mind, and she could be capable of quantum leaps into radical and innovative realms. This may be accentuated by her Sun trine Uranus, plus Mercury and Uranus in mutual reception. She is probably acutely aware of life's dualities with her Gemini emphasis and Mercurial outlook on life. Her restlessness may be related to the fact that she knows that there's no such thing as a simple question or answer. Knowing there are so many possibilities could make it hard for her to slow her antsy Uranus-ruled mind down.

I see her mind as possibly having a cutting, comedic edge to it, with Pluto opposing her eighth/ninth Mercury, implying that her insights are razor-sharp, witty and insightful. This could sometimes come across as cynicism. Her radar will be finely tuned to any phoniness, with the combination of Air planets in Water houses, and she might at times be rather blunt with her observations, as well as uncannily accurate. When she is stirred, I imagine her to be potentially combative, with her voice and intellect being the weapons of choice (Mercury's co-rulers Uranus/Saturn conjunct in Gemini). She could possibly become Ms. Saber-tongue on occasion, with her fixed Mercury opposing Pluto. And she has the potential to be a formidable opponent with the staying power of a crocodile.

On the other hand, she might sometimes find herself emotionally and verbally paralyzed with so many Air planets in Water houses, and the Mercury/Pluto opposition. So we have the potential for a mixed bag of responses. She might gravitate between being an emotional introvert and a verbal warrior, which could be confusing for her and others.

Joyce is likely to be idealistic and deeply humanitarian with her Aquarian chart ruler. At the same time she can find individuals trying one on one, unless they interest her or have something compelling to offer. The classic Aquarian quote is after all, "I love humanity, but people I can't stand." Despite the fact that in theory with the Aquarian "socially correct" approach, she may feel she should be unbiased and nondiscriminatory in whom she associates with. The paradox of this Uranus/Saturn ruled sign is its theoretical liberalness combined with some pretty rigid standards. With Mercury/Venus on the cusp of the ninth house, idealism and high-mindedness is even more likely to be accentuated, especially around her values and approach to life.

With Mercury ruling her chart, I imagine her looking younger than her years, and she may be able to retain a youthful, energetic air all through her life. Also, with her eighth house Capricorn Sun there could be an inherent maturity about Joyce, an air of deep, even ancient sagacity, and a sense of profound knowing. If enough of her life's goals have been fulfilled, her reward can be an old age blessed with wisdom and peace, and a spirit that will get younger with the years. Rather than feeling heavier with time, there could be a lightening and brightening of both her and her view of life.

Achieving and knowing what she wants

Joyce would appear to have a certain eccentricity and a progressive mind set; yet contrary to this she may have surprisingly traditional and conservative views on life. Her Sun is in Capricorn and Saturn conjuncts the Moon. She could firmly believe in and adhere to the principle of "you have to earn what you get from life." She is likely to be responsible, ambitious and goal-oriented, and probably strives towards success in a controlled and disciplined manner. This could be challenged by the eighth house Sun's dispositor Saturn in Gemini conjunct both Uranus and the Moon in the twelfth house, emphasizing the mix of a logical approach playing out in an emotionally unpredictable, often unconscious way. This might complicate her quest to have an unimpeded aim at what she has her sights on. It might feel as though someone keeps moving the target on her at the last minute. There may always seem to be other, unwelcome guests at her party vying for attention and disturbing her concentration, namely unresolved or unconscious emotional issues and too many divergent possibilities and ideas. She could become frustrated by her own complex nature and consequently find herself judging these facets of herself and feeling guilty.

Gemini rising and an Airy Mercury indicate an endless quest for knowledge. She may frequently be too mentally restless to focus her attention on singular matters in the way her Capricorn Sun demands. Despite occasionally swirling in an emotional/mental web, I imagine Joyce ultimately has enough willpower and sheer determination to be the victor in these internal battles. Her eighth house Sun's dispositor Saturn sextiles Pluto, plus Uranus trines the Sun and conjuncts Saturn, which can ultimately help her hold her own ground in unexpected ways.

174

Her Cardinal Earth Sun resides in the Fixed Water house, and I would guess life has demanded that she build a steely core for survival's sake. At the same time an inner discordance could persistently pull her in different directions with Sun quincunx the Ascendant. Mars also sesquiquadrates Pluto, so her attempts to direct her energy effectively can stir up obsessive/compulsive complexes. It is as though who she is and the path she needs to take to achieve her goals never feel quite aligned. These same tensions can keep her alert, although perhaps edgy at times. Ultimately they may serve to heighten her awareness of the fact that life isn't tidy and cannot be boxed into neat little packages, so she can hopefully lighten up on herself.

She may have a tendency to overdo things, and ignore or be unaware of her limitations. Saturn, the Sun's dispositor, is in the twelfth conjunct Uranus and the Moon, Jupiter opposes her Sun and also widely opposes her chart ruler, Mercury. Joyce's only Fire sign planets, besides Chiron, are connected to the sixth house, Pluto ruling the sixth and Mars the co-ruler and in the sixth. Since they are also in a sesquiquadrate aspect, this could add to her potential to burn herself out physically. Mars itself is somewhat unintegrated with the rest of the chart, except for a trine to Chiron and a stressful aspect to Pluto. This could indicate a challenge when it comes to asserting herself or appropriately tapping into her own energy. These aspects describe how she could become victim to unconscious pressures while feeling driven, even compulsive, about achieving what she feels is expected of her. The resulting drain on her energy may cause her to become overly depleted, elevating stress and exhaustion levels, both physically and emotionally. Learning to conserve and regulate her energy might be, I imagine, essential to her health and well-being.

With Cancer on the second house cusp, ruled by the Moon conjunct Saturn, her emotional security and sense of self worth could be tied up with what she has in her bank account. This same planetary combination may mean that at times she won't feel deserving of what she has. It will undoubtedly be vital that for a true sense of self worth she lives a life congruent with her highest principles and ideals. Jupiter is in Cancer in the second house and is her only Water sign planet, and undoubtedly strongly connected to her emotional well-being. Her strong need for physical and material security may not always be apparent; the second house ruler is in the twelfth house and conjunct Saturn. Venus in Aquarius might compound conflicts around her material needs; her core personal value system could tend towards fairness for all rather than accumulativeness and self-interest. With the Moon in Gemini conjunct Saturn,

175

it may not be only material things that bring her security, but also an understanding of the mechanics and reasoning behind whatever she is faced with.

If her personal or financial security is threatened, she could plunge into confusion and dark and old fears, shown by the twelfth house emphasis, and Pluto in the second opposing Mercury the chart ruler. It isn't likely that she is particularly hedonistic or acquisitive (second house ruler conjunct Saturn, and Venus in Aquarius). She could just require her material stability to be solid enough so as not to cause her undue stress. When it comes to taking risks around her own security, Joyce will almost certainly hesitate and analyze before looking and leaping. This feature of her character is likely to be exacerbated by Fire's being the inferior function and more unconscious in its expression; she may need far more than blind faith to see her through lean times. However, with the Moon as ruler of the second house and trine the natural second house ruler Venus, and with Jupiter in the second disposited by the Moon, any potential crisis based on these insecurities probably has a built-in release valve. Her worst fears are probably rarely realized, and due to her own commitment and determination she could be more than capable of keeping any wolves at bay. With Jupiter and Pluto tenanting the second house it is also quite possible that she has wealth; if so, with Jupiter as ruler of the seventh it may have come to her through marriage.

Financial involvement with siblings or other family members is also possible, and could involve investments, inheritances or business arrangements. The Sun as ruler of the third is in the eighth house, and Jupiter the ruler of the seventh in the second opposes it. There may be tension around how much control she herself holds, and how much she needs to relinquish or share, also indicated by Venus opposing Pluto. These issues could hit a much deeper cord than may be outwardly apparent, and concern deep-seated fears she has around feeling repressed or manipulated. Chiron is in the third house conjunct the North Node and disposited by her eighth house Sun, emphasizing vulnerability and the need to understand and be in control of her own destiny. She probably has the psychological insight and savvy available to understand and negotiate these issues (the Moon ruling the second and Saturn ruling the eighth, both sextile Pluto in the fourth and trine Venus in the eighth/ninth). This appears to be a recurrent life theme due a concentrated focus around finances and values: what is hers and what is shared. Traversing this precipitous terrain will require honesty and clarity on Joyce's part. She is likely to have these qualities in spades, integrity probably being one of her strongest points, providing her with the ability to create some semblance of balance between healthy vigilance and rigid control.

It might be difficult for Joyce to extricate her own will from what others expect of her, or more to the point, what she thinks they expect of her (Sun in Capricorn opposing Jupiter, its dispositor Saturn conjunct the Moon, and Mars disposited by Jupiter and on the cusp of the seventh). I think she'll need to be wary of creating opposition in her own head, which will then of course incarnate itself somewhere and walk right into her life. She is probably a determined soul who feels supported when she has tangible stability and order in her life, having such strong Saturn related influences. Despite this, with so many outer planet aspects to her personal planets and the Water house emphasis, she is possibly living a life that constantly requires surrender to outside forces which mirror buried aspects of her own psyche. Although she may frequently feel that life gets turned upside down and that she is not in charge, with her strong Air she can hopefully gain the perspective from which to monitor her responses. I believe she will understand more through honest introspection and self-analysis rather than looking for the answers outside of herself. The tightrope she often walks could be between control and surrender, and she may need to be cautious because control could hold the upper hand, sometimes to her detriment.

When Joyce is taken into unconscious realms where she feels she has little or no power, it will probably be disconcerting for her. Emotional issues may be so threatening because she could feel as though she is free-falling into a black hole. The gift and the curse is that she has the potential for acute awareness and insight into the darker, more shadowy aspects of life, both within herself and in the world. The closest aspect in her chart, with only one minute of separation, is a sextile between the Moon and Pluto, and her Sun is in the eighth. She has every capability for incisive intuitive understanding of the deeper implications around emotional responses. Joyce could be a natural psychologist, but may feel much safer if she is probing into the emotional recesses of others whilst maintaining and guarding her own private self. Saturn the eighth house ruler is in the twelfth, and the Aquarian planets, inching their way from the eighth to the ninth, also have their co-dispositors in the twelfth.

I have a feeling she is someone you would want by your side during a crisis; this could be when she excels and leaves everyone else in the dust, with her Saturn/Moon conjunction and eighth house Capricorn Sun. Her dogged determination and depth of feeling would indicate that psychological investigation could be part of every aspect of her life, and may need to be for her own sanity. She could be involved in the therapeutic field, and if not, psychology may surreptitiously be a component of whatever she does. Pluto rules the sixth and sextiles her Moon in the twelfth. Neptune as ruler of her Midheaven trines the Sun in the eighth and the Moon/Uranus/Saturn conjunction in the twelfth. Saturn operating from the twelfth house of the collective unconscious is also the dispositor of her Sun and the ruler of the eighth. The feeling is that behind her analytical outlook, her personal radar is ever scanning the environment for hidden agendas or less-than-obvious factors. This will almost surely have to do with the environment she was born in and the tools she fashioned for survival. This is an energy that demands to be utilized, or it could be draining and overwhelming. The mechanism she might have crafted at a time when she needed to protect her developing psyche could at times come across as overly defensive, or intense, in a fully formed functioning adult. She will probably be less likely to be operating out of her unconscious, and consequently find life more fulfilling, if she has done her own psychological work.

I imagine it is vital that Joyce allow, and consciously bring into her life, whatever brings her joy and inspiration. She may need to warm and nurture her soul because life might often steer her through emotional land mines. Her creative, imaginative gifts and visions could provide her with an antidote to life's trials and at the same time with a sense of a higher, transcendent purpose. This might be achieved by opening herself up to the more mysterious, less reality-based facets of existence, the fantastical, the creative, the mystical and the beautiful. It might be that she experiences these elements of life as strong, although possibly unacknowledged, inner yearnings. Venus conjoins Mercury the chart ruler on the cusp of the ninth house, and rules both the fifth and the twelfth. Neptune, ruler of the Midheaven, trines Venus, although widely. They are also connected through Venus's dispositorship of Neptune in Libra. Plus her planets in the twelfth include Saturn and Uranus, giving a defined and highly original edge to how she could translate the imaginative into credible form. Moon/Neptune, two of the planets most connected with creativity and receptivity, operate from Water houses. Also the rulers of the fourth and twelfth, Mercury and Venus, are powerfully connected because they are tightly conjunct on the cusp of the eighth/ninth, giving a sense of intense sensitivity emerging and opening up to the higher realms of consciousness. Even if she displays no tangible evidence of creativity, it may simply reside in her way of functioning, ideas and day-to-day existence. Life itself is a creative endeavor; all our choices and interactions create who we are and where we are going. If that isn't art, then what is? Still it looks as though anything creative she embarks upon will involve the theme that pervades Joyce's life, the world of the mind: Moon, Venus and Neptune in Air signs and drawn together into a Grand Trine. It feels as though it could not help but involve the sharing and transmitting of ideas sourced from both the personal and the collective unconscious.

Parental influences and their effects on the psyche

I am cautious about approaching family issues without actually talking to the individual concerned. What the astrologer is looking at was in place before one even technically meets one's parents, and my work is not definitively predictive. In my experience there are a myriad of possible scenarios. Having said that, it would be hard to ignore the implications in Joyce's astrology, and therefore her existence, related to her family and heritage. I would say that a great deal of her life's work involves resolving deep-seated family issues, and placating or slaying the attendant demons.

Her Sun, Moon and Saturn are in Water houses, as is Neptune the ruler of the Midheaven. Mercury as ruler of the fourth house is retrograding back into the eighth, and Jupiter the co-ruler of her Pisces Midheaven, although not in a Water house, is in the sign of Cancer. Consequently these parental significators, and what they represent for Joyce, may be experienced and expressed through unconscious motivations that require more sensitive and intuitive understanding than anything else. If she does not acknowledge and pay attention to her own feelings, they may overwhelm her to a degree that could negatively impact her life. This degree of sensitivity probably has its deepest roots in personal, family and ancestral issues that might be almost impossible to access through purely intellectual, logical assessment. Mercury, her chart ruler, is also the Nadir ruler, tying together her personal identity with family roots, perhaps especially around the father. She may be required to go ever deeper into the psychological realms to understand this tie and the complex web it creates. The core issues may be deeply buried in the family's collective unconscious, and the memories of the actual events that precipitated the emotional complexes could have been lost irretrievably over time.

Mercury trines her Moon/Saturn conjunction, both planets conjunct Uranus in the twelfth. This flowing aspect hopefully facilitates sympathy and understanding of the deeper meaning of the family milieu. Uranus is an intriguing ingredient and could indicate sudden realizations or abrupt upsets, and probably all of the above. There is the possibility of adoption or abandonment being a part of her history, which could bring in a whole other "mystery" family matrix that her psyche might be dealing with simultaneously. This is of course only a possibility, and I certainly wouldn't stake my life on its inevitability. I nonetheless get a strong feeling of something unconscious at play in her life that reminds me of the saying, "always keep your eye on what you cannot see." Neptune in the fourth opposes her Sun/Moon midpoint and also quincunxes her Ascendant/Midheaven midpoint, adding possibly more uncertainty and sensitivity to the picture of her family and the potential for this to continue playing out in every area of her life. Her Moon/Saturn/Uranus conjunction is also square to the Midheaven/Nadir parental axis. Neptune in the fourth house of the father and ruling the Midheaven, which I find to generally indicate the mother, further convolutes the picture. A fourth house Neptune may mean not only confusing messages around her parents or her perceptions of them, but also possible idealization of them, perhaps particularly so if there has been some experience of loss. Home itself could have been an environment that harbored elements of illusion, uncertainty and possibly deception. With Jupiter as co-ruler of the Midheaven and ruler of the Descendant opposing her Sun, Joyce might have developed a pattern of feeling overwhelmed by forces that appear to be outside of her control. Hopefully she has surrendered enough to her own unconscious, so that through relinquishing control she has acquired some control, such being the irony of the "watery" realms.

The conjunction of Moon/Saturn/Uranus in Gemini could indicate emotional disturbances involving psychological or energetic splits, whether pathological or circumstantial would be the question. Were there conditions triggered by some emotional climate or a particular event, possibly playing out as externally obvious turmoil or as a persistent underlying, possibly unacknowledged, chaos? It feels as though there could be a multitude of questions and elusive answers behind this powerful grouping. This triple conjunction also squares the Midheaven/Nadir. The twelfth house placement of these planets makes me suspect that this could be something involving the collective psyche of the family, which of course might then manifest experientially in one or more individuals. The result could be, or might have been, shame, denial, tragic loss or possibly an incidence of confinement at some point in time. With the Mercury dispositorship of and trine to this grouping, plus Venus as ruler of the twelfth also in trine, she may well be the one who holds the key to freeing this questionable genie from the family bottle, i.e. unconscious.

Although there is the feeling that she is ultimately a survivor, the indications are that this is despite intrusions impinging on the free flow of nurturance at a formative period. I get the image of a cradle sitting on the San Andreas Fault. And there was undoubtedly no deliberate intention for this kind of turmoil on anyone's part, if it was the case. Her acknowledgment does not require casting blame; it may however be important so that she can break out of any outworn, self-defeating patterns of behavior. Her parents were quite likely loving, well-meaning people perhaps involved in circumstances beyond their control, rendering them unable to protect their daughter adequately. The implications remain the same, and chances are she was required to learn emotional self-sufficiency quite early in life. The defenses and muscles she developed will act as both her strengths and her armoring, sometimes serving her and other times hindering her.

I would say it is fortunate that Joyce was probably born with the potential to be emotionally insightful and intuitive. She appears to have the ability to arise out of emotional abysses (Moon/Saturn conjunction sextile Pluto). She has in effect two grand trines, one with Neptune, Mercury/Venus and the Moon/Saturn/Uranus conjunction. Another, although out of quality, brings in the Sun in Capricorn. With these configurations predominantly in Air signs and Water houses, and including the ninth house, Joyce probably has the sensitivity, insight and foresight needed for her to be the champion of her own life through the investigation and articulation of her instinctual nature. As always with inherent gifts, they can be taken for granted, and she may need to acknowledge and foster her own talents in order for them to be utilized. She could have more of a chance at success if she doesn't slip into playing the role of victim or being overly defensive, a potential tendency with the twelfth/eighth house emphasis around family significators.

Father or dominant "masculine" influence

The father or a paternal equivalent appears to have had a particularly powerful impact on Joyce. Due to this relationship, her life's path may take her deeply and intensely into the underlying meaning behind everything. Her relationship to her own animus may be layered with strata of emotional complexity, related not only to her life, but also to that of her family and back through generations.

It feels as though her journey towards wholeness will involve metaphorically mining that information and bringing it to the light of consciousness. The gems she extracts can be insights that shed light on the inner working of her own psyche and her emotional and spiritual inheritance. Her mind would appear to be the most incisive tool at her disposal for this task, and it will serve her well as long as she is master rather than servant. Early in life, her psyche probably registered that for the sake of survival it was not prudent to take anything at face value. Both her Sun and Mercury, the fourth house ruler, are in the eighth house, plus Saturn resides in the twelfth. Mercury does straddle the cusp of the ninth, although retrograding back into the eighth, and there is a sense of an emerging consciousness pulling her towards seeking the higher meaning. There is a push/pull dynamic that through its tension can create a kind of buoy, preventing her from sinking inwards.

In the absence of an actual father figure, there may have been some outside influence, possibly society itself or an authoritarian figure, that left a strong imprint on her life. It could have been family circumstances that felt overwhelming, with Mercury the ruler of the fourth opposite Pluto, and Jupiter in Cancer opposing her Sun. Neptune is in the fourth, and Saturn is conjunct Moon/Uranus in the twelfth. There was possibly the mentality of "that is how you raise a child; I was raised that way," etc., especially noting when and where she was born. Throw in her gender and the chips might have been stacked against her being given an equal-opportunity upbringing.

A dilemma around the father appears have been a split between authoritativeness and nurturance, possibly playing out through an inability to integrate those two things in an effective manner (Sun in Capricorn opposite Jupiter in Cancer, and Saturn conjunct the Moon, with this conjunction in the twelfth and square the Midheaven/Nadir). This could have resulted in both modes of expression becoming stymied or confused. It could have been a case of one parent having to assume both roles, as mother and father, possibly in a time or situation that wasn't supportive of this. She may also have been a serious, intense, perhaps confrontational little person, Sun in Capricorn trine

Uranus and opposing Jupiter. She might have had the mouth and mind to match her will (Mercury her chart ruler opposing Pluto and trine Saturn).

There is the feeling that the intentions behind whatever Joyce experienced with her father, or paternal equivalent, were laced with love. The situation was potentially softened by adoration as a component of a complex relationship; Mercury the ruler of the Nadir is conjunct Venus and trine the Moon and Neptune. This could also indicate a blurring of boundaries in a way that might have been mystifying. Neptune in the fourth house trines both the Sun in the eighth and Venus, and Venus disposits Neptune and rules the twelfth house. The sense is that in the face of possible confusion and challenges to her self-confidence and assertiveness, she maintained or developed a concurrent heightened sensitivity. Joyce's intuitive, receptive faculties appear to have come through any trials somewhat enhanced. Her Sun is trine Neptune, although out of quality. How she integrates and manifests this appears far from clear or simple, since we also have Saturn conjunct the Moon and Pluto opposing Venus.

This mixed bag of emotional messages could cause confusion in how Joyce feels and deals with the repercussions of this earliest masculine role model. Where this is likely to play out in her own life could be through her relationships to men, possibly authority figures, and her ability to effectively assert herself. With her Sun rather alone as the solo Earth planet with only one in quality aspect, the opposition to Jupiter, and Mars conjoining the Descendant, there could be issues around Joyce's owning her own animus. Men in her life, possibly starting with the father, could tend to embody and live out the parts of her that express creativity and affirm individuality, robbing her somewhat of these qualities herself should she allow it. If this has ever been the case, it may have been at huge expense to her resourcefulness, drive and self-expression, and if so hopefully it is well into the past tense.

There is the feeling of an early loss of innocence, Mercury as ruler of the Nadir and the ruler of the Ascendant opposing Pluto, and Jupiter as co-ruler of the Midheaven opposite her eighth house Sun. With her eighth/twelfth house focus she could have been overly aware of things beyond her capacity to process, through unconsciously motivated circumstances. She could have felt at the same time invisible to those around her (the Moon plus Saturn in the twelfth house as parental indicators, and Saturn is also the Sun and Mercury's dispositor). With her strong Air she may have learned as a child that the safest way to deal with emotions was to avoid or reason them away, and old habits die hard, even

183

when they no longer serve. On the plus side, she has the ability to utilize her mental capacities towards understanding the deeper workings of her own psyche and those layers of life invisible to the naked eye. However with the dominant focus on the Water houses, it will serve her to learn to surrender emotionally when appropriate, without over-intellectualizing feelings or situations.

With the Sun in the Fixed Scorpio house, plus Mercury also in a Fixed sign and opposite Pluto, too much resistance, rigidity or calculated manipulation may create tension. Loosening her grip, "letting go and letting God," could release a lot of this pressure. And I'm sure she can do it; she appears to be a judicious and empathetic being: Jupiter is exalted in Cancer and disposits Mars. Her chart ruler Mercury and Venus are on the cusp of the ninth, trine to Moon/Saturn, and her Sun trines Neptune. These qualities need to be directed homeward, which might be the challenge. With her Capricorn Sun and its dispositor Saturn conjunct the Moon, she may be overly proficient at self-denial, guilt and self-punishment.

Since her early years could have been spent navigating unpredictable emotional terrain, caution may be an almost cellular component of her make-up. Life may mirror those earliest experiences, and be forever requiring her to change and transform (eighth house Sun, and Pluto opposing her chart ruler). She can run but she can't hide, and she could be her own worst enemy if she tries to repress her emotions. On the positive side, Joyce's life appears to be like an initiatory process. If she has allowed herself to surrender to this, she could become remarkably insightful, astute and wise. There is a feeling of the Shaman around her, someone who has had to take a journey into the "dark night of the soul," on her way back into the light. With her understanding, intuitiveness, and quick questioning mind, it could well have been a journey that ultimately brings her to a place of richness and deep mystery.

"Mother" or primary nurturing influence

Joyce may feel the most nurtured when she understands and can somehow articulate the emotional terrain she finds herself in. It may also help if she can create a safe distance from which to observe the territory (Moon in Gemini conjunct Saturn/Uranus). This sounds oxymoronic, but it is her nature and needs to be honored. Emotional nurturance could feel like a limited commodity (Moon conjunct Saturn). Consequently she may sometimes seem overly cautious or inhibited in how she expresses herself emotionally. There were probably issues early in life that taught her not to expect unconditional love but instead to armor herself against feeling vulnerable and disappointed. Her Moon in its six- degree separating aspect from Uranus could indicate some disruption or sudden upset prior to her birth, possibly right around the time her mother might have realized she was pregnant. So in fact the emotional stage could have been set prenatally for her, making her core issues all the more elusive to understand and deeply rooted at a cellular level.

Joyce could at times appear to be emotionally calculating and cool, and on the other hand rather changeable and erratic in the way she expresses emotions (Uranus joins Moon/Saturn in this conjunction). This could also be an accurate summation of how she experienced nurturing in her precognizant environment. There is a sense of the maternal figure being over-burdened, possibly disturbed or having to deal with a great deal of uncertainty or upheaval in life. She could have actually been, or imagined herself, as the victim of circumstances beyond her control. At the same time, around the mother there is the sense of someone potentially highly sensitive, gentle and loving (Moon in the twelfth, in a Grand Trine configuration with Venus and Neptune, and Neptune rules the Midheaven). How these different messages translate into Joyce's ability to express emotions is not likely to be simple. She may be someone deeply aware on the emotional level (Moon/Saturn trines both Mercury on the eighth/ninth cusp and Neptune in the fourth). But as far as desiring emotional nurturance goes, it might be less painful to expect nothing.

Her mother may also have faced psychological challenges (the Moon's dispositor retrograde and opposing Pluto). I get an image of a powder keg sitting in the corner ready to go off at any moment, with Uranus being actively involved with her Moon, its aspects, and also in the twelfth. Some unacknowledged emotional chaos may have been churning in her early life, when ideally she would have been basking in the downy cradle of absolute safety and unconditional love. With a twelfth house Air Moon, a lack of mirroring and a sense of not being seen could create a theme in Joyce's life. This can make for loneliness and isolation. She might need to recognize this part of herself and somehow give herself the nurturing that others can't.

Abrupt and harsh losses may not be unfamiliar to Joyce, with both Saturn and Uranus conjunct the Moon and square to the Midheaven/Nadir axis. The presence of Uranus indicates that she is possibly always waiting for the other shoe to drop. Depression may not be unknown to her, with the twelfth house Saturnian emphasis and Mercury the chart ruler opposite Pluto the ruler of the sixth, and Pluto and Mars (co-ruler of the sixth) in a sesquiquadrate relationship. In a way, depression itself may hold the key to her dealing with anything that is blocking her personal happiness and the need to feel connected to and cared for by others. When one feels invisible, especially as a child, a sense of hollowness can ensue and it is easy to collapse inward with hopelessness. Reaching out brings with it the fear of rejection, which only exacerbates the pain. Depression is sometimes described as "unexpressed anger;" the psyche is literally raging and screaming out for help but is at the same time muffled.

Issues around independence versus dependence may be forever swimming around in her unconscious: the Uranian/Saturnian influences around the Moon. The safest route could feel as if it would be through becoming emotionally self sufficient, which of course will not ultimately resolve but instead compound the loneliness. There is at the same time a great deal of potential within these aspects of Joyce's psyche, and she has the gift of insight available with her strong twelfth house, and with the ruler of the twelfth, Venus, conjunct Mercury in the ninth and trining the Moon in the twelfth. Wherever we are wounded is generally where we have the potential to find the deepest well of compassion.

Joyce is possibly highly capable of channeling suffering into understanding, and from far more than just an intellectual angle. Over and over again, the razor's edge she probably walks is between over-intellectualizing the emotions, or prying open the emotional lockbox with her sensitivity, verbal insights and progressive ideas. The emotional complexity she inherited could run so deeply and unconsciously through her and her history that it might be quite buried in the collective psyche of the entire family, indicated by the heavily tenanted Water houses. Joyce and her gift for being emotionally astute could be the person with the gift (or curse, as the case may be) of actually having the ability to break open and cut through to the deeper implications. Out of this, deep and sustaining transformation is always possible. This could however put her in a vulnerable position, especially if there are others who find solace in keeping their heads in the sand.

With her twelfth house emphasis there is the theme of "serve or suffer," and a capacity for compassion and to give selflessly of herself could be among her great assets. These might be very real parts of who she is, and she may also be trying to vicariously self-heal through assisting others, although this obviously can't substitute for doing her personal work. She might be well advised not to get lost in self-sacrificial behavior. If she blocks or denies her own emotional

186

needs, she may be plagued with fatigue, depression and unsatisfying relationships.

Once Joyce has bonded emotionally, her staying power could be formidable (Moon conjunct Saturn). Although how she expresses herself emotionally may not be particularly "warm and fuzzy," it will probably be deep and enduring and able to stand the tests of time. With Venus trine her Moon there might be tenderness, kindness and genuine openness in how she relates, but without cloying sentimentality or excessive exuberance (low Water and challenged personal Fire, plus the Moon/Saturn conjunction). She will probably find it easiest to be committed and loyal when she feels she is being told the truth and accepted. She might possibly crave structure and permanence but even when she finds it, there could be the sense that any minute it will be blown to smithereens, with Uranus ever present. She may nurture others through giving advice, due to the Air influence and her strong Mercury, and through helping them in tangible ways (Capricorn Sun and Moon/Saturn conjunction). Whatever she offers of herself emotionally is likely to have enduring depth and substance.

How she ticks

As well as Joyce's intellect holding dominance in her life, her mind appears unique and fascinating: Air is her strongest element and Mercury in Aquarius is the chart ruler. She has the propensity to be insightful, original, deep, intense, idiosyncratic, and endlessly creative in her thinking. Allowing this full expression may not have always been easy; at times it could have felt threatening to express herself openly, with Mercury opposing Pluto. Her confidence in her own mental ability is possibly not that solid (Saturn in Gemini and in the twelfth). A possible irony may be that where she is particularly gifted, she may never feel quite good enough. This can also be the part of her inheritance that, through defining and restricting her, can ultimately challenge her into constructive resourcefulness, hopefully without crushing her in the process. In the same way that muscles are strengthened through resistance, so could her resolve be enhanced through putting her back into her deepest fears.

Joyce's chart ruler Mercury is only one day into its retrograde cycle at her birth and moving very slowly. This I believe could indicate the capacity for enhanced insightfulness as well as introspectiveness. She might also be determined and regimented in her mental faculties (Saturn trines Mercury), and an inherent insecurity possibly enhances her willpower through dogged discipline and the resolution not to be defeated. By nature she could be scathingly honest, objective and at times shocking (Mercury opposing Pluto and trine to Saturn, co-dispositor of and conjunct to Mercury's dispositor Uranus). This degree of honesty was possibly unacceptable in her home; perhaps she had laser insight into the underbelly of the family (both Luminaries operating in houses connected to the unconscious). There might have been rather unnerving stuff coming from the mouth of this babe.

If through expressing herself she is challenged or belittled, old survival complexes could get stirred up (Mercury opposing Pluto). Something antagonistic may become activated when she gets into unsettling verbal exchanges. Joyce needs to be careful not to get embroiled in inappropriate power struggles (Mars on the seventh house cusp sesquiquadrates Pluto). Other people could frequently appear to project their anger onto her. Should she become combative around defending her ideas or points of view she might activate strong, often unconscious, reactions (Saturn and Uranus as co-dispositors of Mercury in Gemini and in the twelfth). Worse still, the validity of what she has to say could be lost in the uproar, reopening old wounds around not being heard.

Nonetheless there is probably a constant stream of information flowing through Joyce that is creative and transformational, with her Mercury's being Uranus ruled and on the eighth/ninth cusp, plus these planets are in mutual reception. It could be the loss of a precious gift if her voice has been silenced, a possibility indicated by Pluto's opposing Mercury. Defensiveness and caution are probably part of her more conservative nature (Capricorn Sun, and Moon conjunct Saturn), and possibly at odds with everything she just "knows." Despite this she may have gracefulness and a gift with language and its application (Mercury conjunct Venus and trine the Moon). Language could be her emotional conduit (Air signs in Water houses) and possibly vital to her well-being. She could write either as part of her profession or for her own pleasure (the Sun rules the third; Venus the ruler of the fifth conjuncts Mercury the chart ruler). Research could be a way of utilizing her mind and her psychological propensity in a constructive and rewarding way, with Pluto opposing Mercury/Venus. What springs to mind are historical or psychological projects requiring sleuth work (her eighth house influences and Mercury ruling the fourth and retrograde). Mercury is technically a ninth house planet emerging from the eighth, and therefore will probably be best served through expressing higher mind truths sourced from the more shadowy, unconscious realms. Joyce might be a lover of, or involved in, the world of film or theater (Neptune as the ruler of the Midheaven trining the Sun and Moon and opposing their midpoint, plus Venus conjuncts Mercury and rules the fifth).

She may be a born comedienne with a combination of quick wit (Uranus dispositing Mercury and being in mutual reception), command of language (Mercury dispositing and trining Saturn), and probing incisive insights (Mercury opposing Pluto). Comedy requires diving into the recesses of human experience, extracting what we don't or would rather not see, and presenting it a way that surprises, shocks and titillates. Simultaneously, with Mercury conjunct Venus she is likely to have an inherent diplomacy and pleasant manner in how she presents ideas. It is fascinating that she might have a range of expression spanning from gentle graciousness to searing intensity. Any actress or writer would envy such a repertoire. Although scathing at times, she might be conveying thoughts rooted in her deepest values (Venus tightly conjunct Mercury). They might be thought-provoking, unique, original and against the norm, as both of these planets are Uranus-ruled and in the ninth. When she presents herself without defenses, she will probably be heard and appreciated, and any edges might naturally soften.

Boredom is probably not in her vocabulary: with the Aquarian, Uranian emphasis, the world could be her smorgasbord of information. Joyce is likely to have a love of learning and, with her potential command of language and wealth of information, as a teacher could be gifted and engaging. Her Sun rules the third, her Uranus/Saturn conjunction co-rules the ninth, and Mercury/Venus can be considered inhabitants of the ninth. She may have natural eloquence and a talent for diplomacy when presenting what is important to her in a receptive, encouraging environment.

Her mind could at times be a steel trap holding onto ideas or concepts, and at others could dart hither and thither cleverly objectifying and justifying. She may be open to flashes of insight and uncanny knowing (Uranus and Mercury in mutual reception, Saturn and Uranus, the co-dispositors of the twelfth house ruler Venus, being in the twelfth and in the sign of Gemini, and Neptune in a Water house trining both Luminaries). It could be as though she has radar connecting her with some higher intelligence or cosmic hotline. She may take this for granted and consequently dismiss it; nonetheless it could be like a background buzz. Flashes of brilliance might emanate from this woman, whether she is aware of it or not (Uranus trine the Sun and in mutual reception

189

with her retrograde chart ruler). She could have the ability to communicate emotions lucidly when the wiring between her instincts and intellect are synapsing (the Air planets in Water houses with several flowing aspects, and a Uranian influence). It is probable that language and communication are her skills, emotions her nemesis. If she can yoke them together positively she will be remarkably astute and insightful. When in sync, she could be scathingly honest and able to educate, entertain and enrich others with her rare, penetrating shrewdness.

Joyce may also be deeply intuitive and sensitive behind a congenial, intellectualizing, yet guarded veneer. She could be especially gifted, although in that "the fish doesn't know it's wet," she may not give it much credence. She could be a natural channel for the unconscious, although her natural inclination might be to control and analyze it away. Her acute awareness can have roots in having to scan the emotional environment for potential dangers as a child (Mercury the chart ruler and ruler of the fourth, and Venus the ruler of the twelfth opposite Pluto, plus the Moon/Saturn conjunction square the Midheaven/Nadir). Her propensity for being grounded will bring authenticity and integrity to this (Saturn dispositing the Sun and conjunct the Moon).

Unless her mind is productively occupied it could be like the proverbial "hamster in a wheel," spinning perpetually, using a lot of energy and going nowhere. I'd guess that with her strong Saturnian influences this won't be too much of an issue, and she certainly has what it takes to discipline her mind in a way that will make others sit up and listen.

Unconscious issues may be active for her and there could be a natural flow in how she expresses them. She could be a voice of reason arising out of a complex emotional arena.

Relationship rewards and trials

With Joyce's eighth house influences, and Venus in Aquarius opposing Pluto, relationships may be complex, intense and maze-like. They also potentially provide rich, fertile soil for self-realization. Choosing partners, lovers, friends or business associates who understand her complexity and walk the same path will be vital. Joyce will cherish her freedom and believe that relationships are the healthiest when they provide space and liberty. Yet the darker territories of intimacy are probably not unknown to her. She appears deep and enigmatic and could be lonely if she doesn't find her own tribe

(Jupiter the ruler of the seventh in Cancer, and Saturn the ruler of the eighth conjunct the Moon). Although she may appear cool with her Uranus-ruled Venus and Air Moon, her emotions probably run deep. There could be an air of aloneness around her with her Sun as a solo Earth planet with only one in-quality aspect to another personal planet, the opposition to Jupiter. Yet with her Sun in the eighth house and only personal Fire planet Mars conjunct the cusp of the seventh, she may be constantly compelled to move into intimate situations despite a contrary inclination to shy away.

Once she has made a commitment she is likely to be devoted and loyal (the Moon conjunct Saturn, and Capricorn on the eighth house cusp). Possibly to a fault at times, I imagine her tenaciously holding on when it might actually be time to let go. With Venus in Aquarius, Uranus conjunct her Moon and trine her Sun, she may simultaneously espouse the concept of non-attachment. She might give out mixed messages. If she blocks her need for intimacy, her sense of isolation could be deeply painful. With Jupiter ruling her seventh, Mars on its cusp and Venus in Aquarius on the eighth/ninth cusp, she probably needs others unafraid to plumb the depths of the psyche and willing to allow change through emotional honesty, without clingyness.

She could be appalled at her own capacity for that green-eyed monster, jealousy, having Venus opposing Pluto. This might be something she is vehemently opposed to in principle, having both her chart ruler, Mercury, and Venus in Aquarius. Behind this dilemma probably exists the delicate balance between her needs for deep intimacy and personal freedom (Aquarian planets straddling the eighth/ninth and Sagittarius on the seventh). With her second/eighth polarity involving the Sun, Pluto and Jupiter, relationships could be further complicated through power struggles, financial ties and commitments.

Joyce's desire nature is probably, like everything else, aligned with her mental functioning. Venus conjuncts her Mercury and their co-dispositors, Saturn and Uranus, are conjunct in Gemini. Passionate in her way, when it comes to intimacy she might initially be more comfortable thinking or talking about it than getting too deeply involved (Air outweighs Fire or Water). Her independent nature thrives perhaps more easily in friendships, although the underlying scenario could be quite different. Venus in Aquarius and Mars in Sagittarius ruling the eleventh are quite contrary to her more intense influences. Regardless of her conservative approach to life (Capricorn Sun and other

Saturnian influences), it might be a different matter when it comes to relating and matters of the heart.

Her relationships could be "different," with her being drawn to a variety of types, with her Uranian-ruled Venus, and Jupiter-ruled Mars on the cusp of the seventh ruling the eleventh. In true Venus-in-Aquarius fashion she may have friends who are completely dissimilar and not even acquainted with one another. Her values are likely to be firmly rooted in humanitarian principles and a sense of "fairness for all," with ideas such as ownership or preferential treatment going against her grain. However despite a desire for safe, non-consuming relationships, with Venus moving into the ninth yet still opposing Pluto, she may be prone to finding herself drawn into intense encounters. She might war with herself about the "right" way to be in a relationship, and the undeniable truth of her own feelings. Such battles cannot be contained, and are bound to rear their heads in real life. I guess that she is far too intelligent to consider herself a passive observer in her own life, and it might serve her best to keep a close watch on the undercurrents that keep stirring up these waters.

What she considers to be of beauty and value may be unusual. Her tastes, like her ideas, can be eclectic and highly personal. With Venus in Aquarius ruling the fifth, Joyce could be romantic, although possibly in a somewhat cool and detached manner. If a mother she is likely to be unique in her approach to parenting, possibly being very liberal and allowing her children a lot of freedom. However, with Venus opposing Pluto, she is probably acutely aware of the dangers in life. She might swing between being a free and easy parent, and her hidden fears playing out covertly through subliminal controlling. If she has not had children, then her creative projects and ideas will be her babies, and she may have had it both ways.

Joyce probably needs to test her ideas in the arena of life, and how better than through debate and dialogue? In this regard relationships could be stimulating and inspiring for her, with Sagittarius on the seventh house cusp and Mars conjunct it and ruling the eleventh. Spending time with energetic and broad-minded others might bring much needed joy into her life (Venus in Aquarius, Mars in Sagittarius ruling the eleventh house).

Her only personal Fire planet, Mars, is conjunct the Descendant, so if she ever allows others the power behind her throne, there could be trouble. Despite how things may appear with her Gemini Ascendant and Venus conjunct the chart ruler Mercury, social interactions could often be tense for Joyce, and she might never feel totally at ease. Mars the ruler of the eleventh is somewhat unintegrated with the rest of her chart, except through Chiron and Pluto, not the cuddliest of planets, and this exacerbates the feeling of her being a loner. This certainly doesn't mean she can't have satisfying relationships, she just might be more than typically aware of the inexorable fact that this is in truth a solo journey for all of us.

Inspiration, spontaneity and exuberance may not always be available on demand for Joyce, and her personal fires may tend to smolder rather than blaze. They are stoked by the understanding and security acquired through effort and logic. She has of course, I imagine, the ability for deep contentment and happiness, but if she isn't self-aware she could find herself attracted to puer-like, jovial or blindly optimistic characters as a way of attempting to fulfill this. With Sagittarius on the Descendant and the dispositor Jupiter opposing her Sun, these types may attract, disappoint, appall, and ultimately repel her. With Mars conjunct the Descendant, problems may ensue if others are the ones taking initiative or having all the fun. It is more important for her to keep her own enthusiasms alive rather than spending time observing or subduing someone else's (Moon conjunct Saturn in the twelfth, and Venus opposing Pluto).

She probably has her own adventurous, even at times outrageous side (Sun trine Uranus, Mars in Sagittarius, and Mercury/Venus conjoined in Aquarius). She could be an inspirational, motivating influence in her interactions with partners, friends, and any political or organized affiliations she is involved with (Mars ruling the eleventh house Aries cusp). She is probably the happiest in relationships that mirror her own principles, with the Sagittarian influence, and Mercury/Venus in Aquarius straddling the ninth house cusp. Feeling included could serve to soften her and enhance her receptivity; Jupiter is exalted in Cancer, in contrast to her more detached, inhibited side. Her generosity and kindness of spirit will probably be activated through creating and sharing joy, and nurturing others. When she can relax and be receptive, this energy may flow freely and act like a balm for her psyche. Her benevolence probably finds its purest expression when she feels secure.

Good stuff

I believe happiness and fulfillment come through the integration and acceptance of all facets of our being. It is through our strengths and propensities that we tend to excel and be the most sophisticated, and in the primitive nether regions of the psyche where we find the missing pieces. With the North Node in Leo, Sun in the eighth and Mars on the cusp of the Descendant, there is imperativeness around Joyce accessing her Fire, symbolizing optimism, faith and creativity. Mercury/Venus are very tightly conjunct the cusp of the ninth, closely enough to be actually considered tenants of that house. Chiron in Leo conjuncts the North Node in the third house, and life ideally leads her towards understanding where she is most wounded and healing her "divine child." In keeping with the rest of her chart, this conjunction in the third house indicates that this goal will be reached through her mental faculties. This and Gemini rising could indicate events or experiences involving siblings or her earliest learning environment as significant.

I would imagine it is vital that she foster whatever brings home a sense of her own creativity and uniqueness, simply for the joy of it. The Sun disposits the North Node and Chiron is in Leo. Fire is the inferior function, since the Sun is in an Earth sign. It could serve her to lighten up, be playful, and give full rein to her imagination. The potential importance of levity and joy in her life, in my estimation, probably can't be overstated. Creativity, intuition, and the fantastical realms may represent the more primal, least conscious parts of Joyce's psyche, and therefore could be a goldmine. Since this is likely to take her into her unconscious there may be resistance and fear at times, but a propensity for great satisfaction and pleasure probably exists when she allows that grace.

There may be a dreamy quality to her, and she could be imaginative and gifted in giving this form and expression, with Venus, the ruler of the fifth and twelfth, trine the Moon in the twelfth. A capacity for fantasy might have developed as a refuge from confusion and loss around home and family. She could hold a dream of the ideal home, in every sense, with Neptune being in the fourth and trine the Moon in the twelfth. This might motivate her to build on those dreams; Neptune rules the Midheaven and the co-ruler Jupiter is also in Cancer. Joyce's Moon is conjunct Saturn, and they both trine Neptune. This could be particularly evident in her personal values (Jupiter in Cancer in the second house, disposited by the Moon). This is where healing can take place. Despite her intellectualism and detached nature, with her strong Air and Mercury ruling the chart, Joyce's connection to something deeper and more ethereal may be what gives her enough inspiration to pursue her dreams (Mercury's co-dispositors Uranus and Saturn are conjunct in the twelfth, and the ruler of the twelfth, Venus, conjoins Mercury).

I believe she probably needs creativity and beauty, and to utilize her compassion and sensitivity positively in order to achieve a sense of fulfillment in her life. It feels as though somewhere in her life there might have been a muse or mentor who held and shared with her the key to her own treasure chest of mysteries, gifting her with a vision of possibilities and magical vistas. Venus is conjunct the chart ruler Mercury, is ruler of the fifth and twelfth, is on the cusp of the eighth/ninth and makes positive trines to the twelfth house planets. Mars, ruler of the eleventh, is in Sagittarius and conjunct the Descendant. Awareness of, and openness to, the mystical realms of existence might help transform the energy created by the conflicts she experiences between needing control and her emotional depths.

With Joyce, I get a vision of the heart residing between heaven and Earth, and crying out for attention. Her strong Air takes her into the "ethers" of heaven. Although her Capricorn Sun is the only Earth planet, she has strong Saturnian influences (Moon conjunct Saturn and her chart ruler being Aquarian). The urge towards grounding and control dominates and pulls her towards earthly concerns, while the Water houses emphasize emotionally charged experiences. She needs a center and refuge from her heady intellectualism, the need for control, and her emotional intensity. This may be a possibility when she connects with her own heart and its vitality. Compassion, joy and creativity could be the junction of these energies, offering her a sense of unity.

To keep her heart open, Joyce may need to shine and be adored. She will not suddenly be Isadora Duncan, but she might need to learn self-appreciation and to stop deflecting praise. Her Saturn-Moon and Capricorn Sun may feel that if they don't earn respect or praise through strife, it is not deserved. She might need to rewrite the earliest script of her life; she is worthwhile and valuable and deserves to be loved, simply because she is alive and special.

She probably has a gift for making logical sense out of broad fleeting concepts, both creatively and with illuminating insights. Beyond this she may have the ability to heal herself and others; she has Chiron in Leo conjunct the North Node, and a strong twelfth house: Pluto as ruler of the sixth, and Mars, the ruler of the eleventh and co-ruler of the sixth, in the sixth conjoining the Descendant. This might seem grandiose to Joyce, but I doubt it is. When she finds compassion for herself, it could become a beacon in her life. We don't suddenly become different people, but there is less stumbling in the dark and more acceptance and tolerance for others and ourselves, and the possibility of far more joy.

The sense is that Joyce is restructuring and reaffirming herself, possibly as a result of many upheavals in recent times. It is as though something deep and powerful is waking up inside her, with twelfth and eighth/ninth house planets having been particularly activated. It is as though a sleeping dragon is stirring, bringing with it the potential for new energy and creativity into her life.

As this is written, in the late summer of 2002, Joyce may have gone through a long period of shedding and surrendering any illusions or old baggage she might have been holding onto, possibly precipitating many metaphorical deaths and rebirths. Saturn has been making its way through her twelfth house, having its second return within the last couple of years, as well as impacting her Uranus and Moon. There have probably been sobering reality checks around her world view, relationships, self-worth and possibly her economic situation also. Anything repressed in her unconscious may have come under relentless scrutiny.

As Uranus transits her ninth house and slowly but surely approaches the Midheaven, her vision of the future and her ideologies could be shaken to the core, leading towards new and unexpected twists in her life direction. She might be opened up to possibilities she hasn't conceived of yet, even with her inherent Uranian world view.

Over the past year and through 2003, she will be gliding through foggy uncharted waters, as Neptune conjoins Mercury, her chart ruler, and Venus the ruler of her fifth and twelfth. This conjures up images of the mists between realities, a heavily shrouded region between the earthly and the mystical, where everything is hazy and uncertain but pregnant with potential. This could be a place where outcomes are completely out of mortal hands and not controlled by the desires of human hearts. What this signifies may not yet be clear to her, and in my thinking simply isn't predictable. The healthiest thing could be for her to open up and relinquish any control she "thought" she had. At the same time this is not a time to be delusional, and she may need to be wary of any addictive tendencies raising their heads. The spiritual realms will be more accessible to her, heralding a creative time. She would be wise to open the portals fully to the mystical, magical realms. Almost anything is possible, as long as her impulse to over-analyze or control does not dominate or stifle what is asking to be born.

Pluto has been sojourning through her sixth house for several years, and in the mid-nineties started opposing her twelfth house planets and connecting to her chart ruler. There may have been many reality checks and possibly harsh painful occurrences; she possibly faced health challenges and/or other losses. It is interesting that she has volunteered for this project at such a time. It shows courage and a relinquishing of control, quite perfect in view of her astrological landscape, but nonetheless awe-inspiring. She may be preparing to reassess her life and personal goals, and at the same time she has chosen to lay out a sacrificial altar, so to speak, and allow a group of strangers to analyze and dissect her very soul and being. This is a great leap of faith, and shows willingness to take whatever the Universe is dishing out. And she is doing this at a time when she can hardly be anything but acutely sensitive and vulnerable. It speaks highly of the fact that this woman truly lives all the courage in her chart, which is simply the mirror of her earthly and spiritual life.

Gary Christen: Uranian

This reading is an example of the methods of the *Uranian System of Astrology*. The Uranian System, developed early in the twentieth century by Alfred Witte and his associates, is a noted reformation of astrology based on ancient Greek roots and notable work from Kepler and Morinus. It is one of the first systems of astrological thought developed since antiquity to have a theoretical basis upon which all the elements of astrology are based. The tools employed are thoroughly modern, but the ideas are based upon a solid observational background.

However, I initially strayed from the Uranian method, because my first approach to reading this chart was my overall impression of the single most important feature of the chart, Joyce's Moon-Saturn conjunction standing on her East Point and square to her Midheaven. Completely subjectively and perhaps irrationally so, this is the thing about this chart that caused me the most thought and my largest stumbling block. Normally, I methodically investigate a series of items and try to discern patterns. Yet, my focus on this interior combination came before anything else was considered.

After my Moon-Saturn considerations, my method moved towards the delineation of the *Personal Points* in Joyce's chart. The Personal Points are the Uranian System's method of establishing a hierarchy among the myriad factors a horoscope presents. They are the Sun, Moon, and Midheaven for the inner group. These inner factors tell us about the inner state and motivations of the individual. We also have the Cardinal Axis, Ascendant and Moon's Node comprising the outer group. The outer group shows us how the horoscope integrates into the outer world and creates the various interfaces between the self and others.

When we interconnect the Personal Points by pairs, various important departments in life can be delineated. If I combine the Midheaven and the Sun, I am looking at the personal sense of direction the native is taking in life. Combining the Moon and the Node gives information about intimate emotional connections or about the mother's bloodline. I consider the interconnection of the Personal Points to be a framework of core life experiences, and the addition of the other factors of the horoscope describes the qualities of these experiences.

Uranian astrologers generally start with the *Cardinal Axis,* since this relates the native to the outer world. When I say outer world, I do not mean connections the native makes in day to day interactions. The outer world has to do with larger connections the native makes in the world, and the lasting conditions that the impact of the native brings to the world that all of us participate in. When I investigate the Cardinal Axis, I am looking at how the Cardinal points are connected with other factors in the chart. These connections can be expressed as graphic pictures, lists or formulas.

Many of the formulas you see in my text are the shorthand for symmetrical relationships between the *factors* listed (factors can be any element of the horoscope such as planets, house cusps, sign boundaries, etc.). We call these symmetrical relationships *planetary pictures*, and they are really quite simple to understand if one can visualize them. When you see a "/" (slash) between factors, it means the *midpoint* between those factors. For example, if Mars is at 10 degrees of Aries and Jupiter is at 20 degrees of Aries, then the midpoint between them is 15 degrees Aries and can be written as Mars/Jupiter, or (Mars+Jupiter)/2. Midpoints are sometimes referred to as *half-sums.* When you see an "=" (equal sign) between factors, the formula is referring to a connection between the factors that is based on some division by the hard series of aspects. The hard series of aspects are the conjunction, square, opposition, half-square or semisquare (45 degrees) and sesquiquadrate (135 degrees), as well as smaller harmonics dividing the circle by successive divisions by 2. These smaller openings such as 22.5 degrees (sixteenth harmonic), 11.25 degrees (thirty-second harmonic) and 5.625 (sixty-fourth harmonic) are very precise, and orbs are measured in minutes. These smaller harmonics are usually used in determining the subtle influences in a major planetary picture. Rarely are the smaller harmonic connections between factors used by themselves.

From these simple formula connections, larger ones evolve as we connect them together until unique signatures begin to resolve themselves in the chart. In addition, specific open points, such as an unoccupied midpoint, the degree that would make a T-square into a grand cross, a fixed star, another person's factors, etc. are called *sensitive points*. Sensitive points are latent places in the chart that are activated by transits, directions, progressions and positions from other charts. When we investigate the horoscope, we look to see what completes sensitive points to determine how they are going to manifest. Often during investigation we will look at a midpoint, and then look to see how another factor completes the *axis* (the actual place where the midpoint falls).

One method that clearly demonstrates axis, midpoint and symmetry would be the use of *antiscia*. Antiscia are reflections off of the Cancer-Capricorn axis in the horoscope. The Cancer-Capricorn axis is 0 degrees Cancer and 0 degrees Capricorn. An example of antiscia and a sensitive point using Joyce's chart is the picture of Neptune and the Ascendant. Joyce's Neptune is 2 degrees 1 minute Libra, and the antiscion of that position is 27 degrees 59 minutes Pisces. Her Ascendant is 27 degrees 53 minutes Gemini and squares the antiscion of Neptune by 6 minutes of arc. This is a completed planetary picture and can also be expressed as Ascendant/Neptune = (here the hard angle is a semisquare) *Aries* (shorthand for 0 degrees of any of the cardinal signs). This completed form carries an interpretation that is a natural expression of Joyce's being, and illustrates a picture where the sensitive point is occupied.

Often what isn't there gives us more information than the completed combinations. An incomplete sensitive point in Joyce's horoscope is the antiscion of the Sun. Her natal Sun lies at 25 degrees 53 minutes of Capricorn, and the antiscion is 4 degrees 7 minutes Sagittarius. This point is unoccupied by any natal factors. We can express this formula as Sun/X (where X is a sensitive point that is unoccupied) = Aries, or as Aries + Aries − Sun (literally adding and subtracting longitudes of the factors involved, here with 270 degrees + 270 degrees − 295 degrees 53 minutes = 244 degrees 7 minutes, or 4 degrees 7 minutes Sagittarius). What we are physically doing is looking at 0 degrees Cancer or Capricorn and finding the reflection of the Sun. Since it is unoccupied, it is sensitive to dynamic factors such as transits or a position in someone else's horoscope. For example, when Saturn transits the antiscion of Joyce's Sun, she experiences delays and obstacles in general. Or, if someone's Venus is at 4 degrees 7 minutes Sagittarius, she has an attraction to him or her and enjoys his or her company. We can extrapolate this method to include any of the factors contained in the horoscope (or other horoscopes) and look for sensitive points wherever we are investigating. Therefore, if I want to look at Joyce's attitude towards love, I would begin by investigating Venus to find out how her Venus operates. Then I would investigate the Midheaven to understand her general point of view. Her attitude towards love is the combination of the Midheaven and Venus, and several sensitive points resolve from the interplay of these two factors. It is really a visual thing, which is why we use calculation aids such as dials or tables.

Elements of the Uranian System are sometimes alien to those who have learned astrology with an emphasis on symbolic placement in the horoscope. This is because the system places more weight on the symmetrical relationship of the factors in the horoscope than on how they are placed. The system has specific tools for analyzing symmetry such as dials, graphs, lists of sensitive points, arc openings and presentation that can be daunting to a newcomer. However, this seemingly complex structure is built with simple to understand elements. One of the more alien and controversial elements of the system is the use of hypothetical planets, commonly called the *TNPs* (Trans-Neptunian Planets). These factors are early observational elements discovered by the very use of the system in timing, and via historical research.

The system doesn't rely on the use of the TNPs, but they are uncanny in the deeper description they bring to the interpretation of the horoscope and have often been the most significant factor in many charts cast for major events in the world. Still, the use of unseen and scientifically unverified factors in the horoscope is a heresy to many astrologers, and the Uranian System's reputation has suffered because of their inclusion.

The meanings and names of the TNPs are:

Cupido: United efforts, marriage, collections, groups, elitism, clubs, tradition, corporations and the family.

Hades: Old things, the past, history, defective, service and serving, decay, secrets, occult and hidden matters.

Zeus: Directed energy, discipline, structured, procreative, creativity, fiery, militaristic, passionate and leadership.

Kronos: Authority, high places, above average, bureaucracy, haughtiness and government.

Apollon :   Peaceful, technical, trade, advancement, expansion, far and wide, training and flow of knowledge.

Admetos: Standstill, death, beginnings, endings, origins, compression, rocks, stillness and profundity.

Vulcanus: Coercion, power, force, compulsion, fate, pushy, and rules the offer you can't refuse.
Poseidon: Light, spirit, culture, idea, high class, Neptune without the tricks.

I include them in the reading because they work so well and give information that otherwise couldn't be seen. Apparently, it is their uncanny accuracy that underlies the popularity of their use, especially among the people who are studying mundane material such as world events, sports or the stock market.

The reading progressed through the various personal point interconnections and naturally defined various areas of focus in Joyce's chart. The Sun and the Moon describe her parents, friends and various emotional factors as well as the interplay of her will and the men in her life. House placements and various points of view afforded by the *auxiliary houses* of the Uranian System gave me the basic building blocks upon which to lay the various planetary pictures. The auxiliary houses are frameworks constructed around any factor in the horoscope, and present information about the factor's condition in regard to everything else in the chart. An example of an auxiliary chart would be equal houses drawn from the Ascendant. Since the Ascendant rules local connections, the Ascendant horoscope describes how others see us and how we see others. In this example, the Midheaven is allowed to reside in any number of houses. In Joyce's chart, the Midheaven is in the ninth house of the Ascendant and Mars is in the sixth. If we look from the point of view of the Midheaven (Meridian houses, equal on the equator), the Ascendant is in the first house of the Midheaven and Mars is in the seventh. Others see her work as part of her occupation, and she sees work as part of her partnerships.

One of the tools I normally employ in my readings is entirely absent here. This is intended to be a natal reading pure and simple. As I read for my clients, I can't help but ask them questions about how they responded to important transits, progressions, directions and the interplay of the important people around them. I should note that the major partners in our lives have synastries with our horoscopes, bringing out combinations that we normally do not experience in our lives by completing latent sensitive points. These influences are like long-term transits for as long as the person affects the native's life. Since this is a blind reading and without such information, how Joyce has responded and grown through the blows and caresses of the astrological weather cannot be determined. When reading, I center the native in the now and wind the astro-clock forward and backward to determine how this person is the way they are. This is a reading of the potentials and probable outcomes of the impact of Joyce in the world. In many ways it is two dimensional, because it lacks the dynamism of time's passage in the development of Joyce's horoscope. It is best likened to a photograph of the possibilities that Joyce's life development holds. Use this photograph to see how the Uranian System operates. Often the Uranian System is considered more of a fatalistic tool than other forms of astrology, since it seems to rely so much on dynamic elements and seems fatalistic. This is a misconception arising from the strange tools, funny planets and precision employed by Uranian astrologers. The tools contained within the system are rich in their psychological depth, with clear definitions for the manifestation of all forms of behavior. The timing elements make the astrological reading of a life a seamless whole.

Joyce

January 16, 1943, 4:16 pm CWT
Pryor, OK

360° Dial

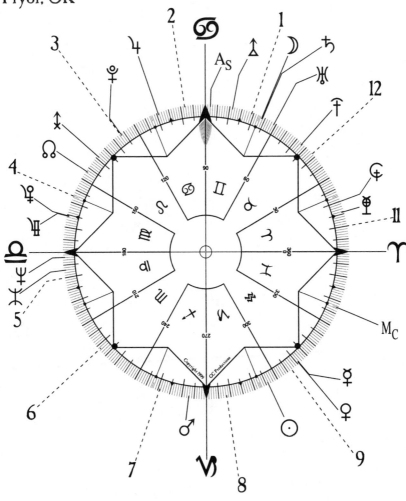

☉	Sun	25° ♑ 53'	ᴹ𝒸 Midheaven 7° ♓ 25'	Meridian House Cusps:
☽	Moon	6° ♊ 21'	ᴬs Ascendent 27° ♊ 53'	10th House 7° ♓ 25'
☿	Mercury	10° ♒ 44'ʀ	♀ Cupido 15° ♍ 19'ʀ	11th House 9° ♈ 55'
♀	Venus	10° ♒ 37'	⚷ Hades 19° ♈ 53'	12th House 11° ♉ 33'
♂	Mars	22° ♐ 50'	⚡ Zeus 19° ♌ 6'ʀ	1st House 10° ♊ 43'
♃	Jupiter	19° ♋ 27'ʀ	♄ Kronos 17° ♉ 16'ʀ	2nd House 8° ♋ 23'
♄	Saturn	5° ♊ 59'ʀ	♆ Apollon 15° ♍ 33'ʀ	3rd House 6° ♌ 43'
♅	Uranus	0° ♊ 47'ʀ	♇ Admetos 15° ♈ 42'	
♆	Neptune	2° ♎ 1'ʀ	⚶ Vulcanus 18° ♊ 53'ʀ	
♇	Pluto	6° ♌ 20'ʀ	♆ Poseidon 7° ♎ 0'ʀ	
☊	Node	26° ♌ 40'ʀ		

Joyce

January 16, 1943, 4:16 pm CWT
Pryor, OK

90° Dial

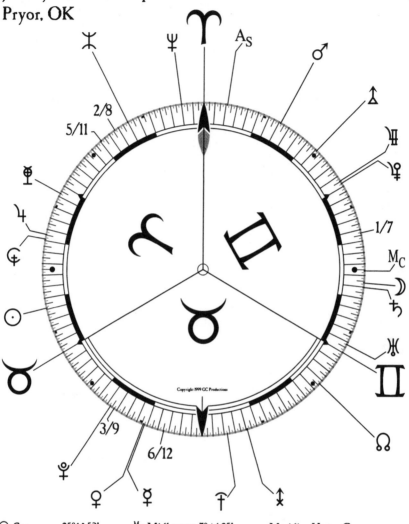

☉ Sun	25° ♑ 53'	ᴹ꜀ Midheaven 7° ♓ 25'	Meridian House Cusps:
☽ Moon	6° ♊ 21'	ᴬₛ Ascendent 27° ♊ 53'	10th House 7° ♓ 25'
☿ Mercury	10° ♒ 44'ʀ	⚷ Cupido 15° ♍ 19'ʀ	11th House 9° ♈ 55'
♀ Venus	10° ♒ 37'	⚸ Hades 19° ♈ 53'	12th House 11° ♉ 33'
♂ Mars	22° ♐ 50'	⚷ Zeus 19° ♌ 6'ʀ	1st House 10° ♊ 43'
♃ Jupiter	19° ♋ 27'ʀ	⚷ Kronos 17° ♉ 16'ʀ	2nd House 8° ♋ 23'
♄ Saturn	5° ♊ 59'ʀ	♅ Apollon 15° ♍ 33'ʀ	3rd House 6° ♌ 43'
♅ Uranus	0° ♊ 47'ʀ	⚷ Admetos 15° ♈ 42'	
♆ Neptune	2° ♎ 1'ʀ	⚷ Vulcanus 18° ♊ 53'ʀ	
♇ Pluto	6° ♌ 20'ʀ	♆ Poseidon 7° ♎ 0'ʀ	
☊ Node	26° ♌ 40'ʀ		

Bites on dried lean meat.
Receives yellow gold.
Perseveringly aware of danger.
No blame.

The case to be decided is indeed not easy but perfectly clear. Since we naturally incline to leniency, we must make every effort to be like yellow gold—that is, as true as gold and as impartial as yellow, the color of the middle (the mean). It is only by remaining conscious of the dangers growing out of the responsibility we have assumed that we can avoid making mistakes.

—*The I Ching*, translator Richard Wilhelm, editor Cary F. Baynes, Bollingen Series XIX, Third Edition, Princeton University Press.

First Impressions

I glanced at this horoscope several times before I began to write about it. I found myself continually thinking about the Moon conjunct Saturn square the Midheaven. Joyce takes life very seriously and creates worries for herself by internalizing the obligations she takes on in life. This dynamic is hidden from general view and operates subconsciously, coloring her self-perception and making itself apparent through her external actions. I continually have come back to this very combination, even though it does not dominate other people's perception of her, nor is it the strongest influence in her interaction with the world. The crux of this analysis really hinges on two things: her true internal sense of self-worth, and her moral standpoint. Joyce's self-worth issues stem from her Moon, Saturn and Midheaven combinations. Her morality and its operation come into question due to the placement of Neptune and its interaction with her personal points (Sun, Moon, Nodes, Ascendant, Midheaven and the Cardinal Axis, commonly referred to as the *Aries Axis*). These two sets of combinations and issues will be considered later.

My first views of this horoscope were scattered, and I spent a lot of time thinking and writing about her inner experiences. Getting the expression of

Joyce's inner experiences into the context of the rest of her life experience will be the theme of this reading.

Joyce's standing in the world as seen through the Cardinal Axis

How we relate to the world at large is a central part of any reading. One of the great tools of astrology is the use of the Cardinal Axis (Cardinal refers to the 0 degree point of Aries, Cancer, Libra and Capricorn; Axis refers to a line that all hard aspects, sensitive points, midpoints and symmetrical planetary pictures fall on). It is the one astrological factor that we all have in common and is the plane of all of life's interactions. Neptune is central to Joyce's world view and makes a square to the Ascendant, causing the mask that she presents to the world to be colored by the environmental conditions and the social circles that she moves in. In addition, the midpoint of Neptune and Ascendant stands within minutes of the Aries Axis. Others interpret her presence through their own projections because she acts like a mirror, reflecting what people perceive in her. In addition, Mars is setting, making her interactions with others somewhat aggressive. So she has a dual life: an internal one that worries and is quite pragmatic from the Moon-Saturn effect; and a flexible, yet aggressive, outer interface with her world that reflects and changes in the eyes of others, because of the interplay of Neptune.

The striking thing about Joyce's destiny in the world is the placement of and combinations to her Midheaven. Her Midheaven is 5 minutes from a 22.5 degree (sixteenth harmonic) aspect to the Aries Axis. Whenever we find a connection between the Aries Axis and the Midheaven, we know that we are dealing with a horoscope that will make a mark in this world. The events surrounding people with the Midheaven connected to the Aries Axis eventually find their way into the mainstream, and this in turn affects us all in some way. The combination of Joyce's strong lunar and Saturn aspects with the Midheaven and Aries Axis makes this placement quite strong. This planetary picture and placement bring her destiny out into the world. They bring her forward into this larger arena through work and responsibilities that connect her to the public. Since the Midheaven and Aries Axis are connected, anything that concerns her interaction with the world concerns her in very personal ways as well. Joyce's world view is also her personal view.

Joyce has *Sun/Jupiter* (the use of a slash between factors indicates a midpoint between them) standing on the *Midheaven* axis, which in turn connects to the *Cardinal Axis*. This is a combination that promises great opportunity and outlook. But we have to remember that this combination operates externally, and beneath it lie that hard lunar sensitivity and fear. Still, the combination brings her freedom and the ability to act in an expansive and grand way. She has her Sun contra-antiscion the Moon-Saturn conjunction, and this emphasizes the importance and seriousness of her relationships as well as elevating them to the public level. On the same Axis, Mercury conjunct Venus is contra-antiscion Kronos, giving her a high and noble expression in both her communications and her willingness to get assistance from authorities. In other words, she has a willingness to seize opportunities containing lofty ideals, while being involved with difficult public relationships.

Her Achilles heel is her attempt to rely on others. As seen above, *Neptune/ASC* stands on the *Aries Axis* and combines with many other Neptune-influenced planetary pictures. Her clarity communicating with others in her immediate surroundings will always be called into question. These relationships can bring her scandal or at the very least mistrust. Such strong influence in the world is always undermined by insecurities and confusion in her interactions with others. Yet, because of her Moon-Saturn, she has learned to rely on herself. People she depends on often break commitments at the last minute or just disappear from her life. If this were an extreme horoscope, then her associates would be getting her into big trouble and causing her great moral consternation.

Her Moon-Saturn is in the Ascendant-twelfth house square the Midheaven, making Joyce a multifaceted personality, involved in public affairs of one sort or another and managing things and handling the details from behind the scenes. She'd rather remain in the background, but her sense of duty and responsibility push her into the public arena. She comes across to others as pleasant, sophisticated and grounded due to her Mercury-Venus reflecting Kronos square Zeus on the Aries Axis. Sometimes she can display a great sense of humor due to the placement of Moon with Saturn. Saturn rules humor and many great comics have strong Saturn pictures.

The lunar effect

Joyce's Moon dominates her horoscope in a subtle way because it comes through the twelfth house of the Ascendant. From her personal point of view, the Moon overrides everything else in her horoscope and is her most personal influence, because it is conjunct the first house of the Midheaven. To put it another way, others see the indirect effects of her emotional and public life and consider it part of her career, while Joyce sees her emotional and public life as the dominant responsibility in her life.

Joyce has Moon-Saturn square Midheaven with the Moon-Saturn on the equatorial ascendant, making the impact of that combination very personal. Although the Moon- Saturn is in the twelfth house of the Ascendant, this is still a very public placement and professional aspirations are always important for Joyce. Joyce has experienced many professional setbacks and several delays in the advancement of her career, but she never quits and has achieved recognition for her skills. The *Midheaven* part of the combination equals *Vulcanus*, *Ascendant/Kronos*, *Sun/Hades Jupiter* and the *Node,* giving her a serving orientation, but the people she serves are leaders in their field.

Emotionally, Joyce defines herself through career and achievement. Here she has a clear detached view given by Poseidon on the second house cusp of the Moon horoscope (put another way, the Moon trines Poseidon), and powerful connections with *Midheaven=Node/Vulcanus.*

With *Mercury-Venus/Zeus Kronos=Aries* she can always back up her information with certification and proof, and Joyce presents her ideas and convictions in a strong but pleasant way. Combined with Moon-Saturn square Midheaven, Joyce can utilize her detached emotional abilities in a very positive way. She has to struggle with ethical and moral choices brought about through her professional associates. Joyce deals with powerful people whose moral instinct is not entirely sound, shown through the planetary picture *Midheaven=Aries=Venus-Mercury/Zeus=Mars/Poseidon=Ascendant/Neptune, Kronos=Sun/Jupiter Hades,* with the Midheaven square Moon-Saturn. Career situations provide Joyce with a great deal of stress, with a wide conjunction of Moon-Saturn and Uranus, and she has an underlying pull between the tried and true and the new and different regarding what she does. Upsetting the apple cart and starting new projects is always a choice for her, but it is in the background and she generally sticks with tradition and overcomes things by doggedly sticking to it.

Joyce's internal weak spot is her sense of romance attributed to the *Moon-Saturn=Venus-Mercury/Neptune*. She is a both a sucker for and a skeptic of romantic ideals. Early in life she wanted to believe all the fairy tales, yet her sense of reality discounted them. However, she must have allowed herself to believe in a love ideal at some point and was rudely awakened from the dream by the harshness of the world. For protection, Joyce does not allow herself the luxury of entertaining romantic notions. She tests ideals. For her to surrender to her romantic sensitivities, she must be convinced that the ideal is sincere. Joyce cannot bear the pain of disappointment. It amplifies her isolation and she then feels detached and angry.

Mom was a responsibility in Joyce's life and she is described by the planetary picture *Node/Cupido Apollon=Moon-Saturn* and *Node* near the first house of the Moon horoscope. Either Joyce's mother wasn't there (physically or emotionally) or she was omnipresent. All the steadfastness and internal centering as well as worries and depression came in response to her maternal influences. The connection to Joyce's maternal lineage is very strong, and her mother's side of the family has been the major familial influence upon her. By contrast, the influence of her father's side of the family is not nearly as strong as the mother's side. It is quite unclear whether Joyce's paternal roots were even revealed, as the closest factor to the first house of the Sun horoscope is Neptune and Poseidon, and they are a good distance into the twelfth house. In addition, she has *Mercury-Venus/Hades=Cupido-Apollon=Midheaven/Admetos*, and this picture only adds to the secrets and mystery surrounding her family. She lost connection to her mother's ancestral roots during her life or disconnected from an important piece of property or origin indicated by *Sun/Admetos=Moon-Saturn*. One way or another, her maternal lineage is dominated by the males on the mother's side of the family or a strong male bloodline.

Joyce's mother was a steadfast woman, highly focused and strong on family tradition brought on by Joyce's Moon-Saturn conjunction. She was not a lot of fun to grow up with, because that conjunction does not make her mother the most nurturing person in the world, particularly from Joyce's point of view. She was a worldly and wounded person and gave Joyce a strong sense of personal discipline. The possibility exists that Joyce either had a dominant mother or that her mother was absent from an early age. I am assuming that Joyce's mother was a powerful guiding influence on Joyce's development. On the one hand, Joyce's

Venus-Mercury conjunction reflects *Neptune* on the *Moon-Saturn axis*, so she has *Venus/Neptune* (to the minute) equaling the *Moon*, and her mother instilled in her a real emotional sense of romance and sensitivity. On the other hand, the same combination brings *Mercury/Neptune* equaling the *Moon-Saturn*, and her mother demanded the truth but never really gave it back in return. The possibility exists that the discipline demanded by her mother gave her a formal structure in which to play out her romantic and artistic ideals. Either way, these combinations create a bit of the love-hate attitude regarding her mother. She woefully feels the lack of warmth from her mother and has spent a good deal of time trying to fill that emptiness. Needless to say, emotional nurturing is not one of Joyce's strong points; however, Joyce, herself, may not see it that way. Her own point of view towards nurture is one of responsibility and self-discipline.

The Moon has a wide range of meanings in the horoscope and although dominated by the tight conjunction to Saturn, Joyce's lunar qualities do find expression through a brighter side. She has *Moon/Jupiter* standing on the *Ascendant* and expresses herself openly and graciously in the company of others. The fact that this same combination runs with Saturn means it is expressed through business and higher social dealings and doesn't really diminish her camaraderie with others. The happiness around others is amplified with *Venus-Mercury/Aries* equaling the *Moon*, giving her a vivacious chatty wit and charm. Joyce has Jupiter in the eleventh house of the Moon, and Jupiter is in a loose half-square to the Moon, making her friends a great emotional boost. Add to this *Node/Cupido-Apollon* sharing the axis with *Venus-Mercury/Aries*, and the social pecking order she is involved with reveals itself. Joyce takes her social interactions very seriously and has built her networking and business ventures around her social abilities. The Saturn is the key between someone who can act socially flamboyant and someone who is flamboyant. Joyce puts on a good show and enjoys herself doing it, but she doesn't act out lightly. She is quite calculating and never misses the small stuff. The big stuff is another matter and she can and does get the wool pulled over her eyes with *Mercury/Neptune* standing with the *Moon*. Even with the negative connotations of *Mercury/Neptune=Moon*, she enjoys a good story and can tell a few whoppers herself.

212

Turning the page to the expression of her will and the influence of males in her life, I have to focus on the lack of hard aspects to the Sun. When we encounter charts with many hard combinations, a lot of action is forthcoming and is quite dynamic. Joyce has very dynamic Moon, Ascendant, Midheaven, etc. combinations everywhere in her horoscope, except with her Sun. This does not diminish her strength of character or will but actually turns it out towards others. She sublimates her own will and aims to assist others in carrying out their goals. Joyce has a wide trine from her Sun to Uranus on the cusp of the eighth house of the Sun horoscope, making her independent-minded. This mild unorthodox streak makes her actions seem abrupt when she is dealing with other people's resources. She gets uneasy when she has to depend on others for the material support she needs to carry her life aims and objectives forward. The Node and Ascendant are both widely inconjunct the Sun, creating a loose yod type configuration on the Sun axis. This continues a trend developing in this chart that shows how much Joyce is dependent on her connections to function in life. Joyce is an important link between her close associates and the larger world. She connects people. This feature is very important and is one of her core reasons for being.

The Sun makes a wide opposition to Jupiter and is square to Hades, generally this means gain from old things. The striking thing is the Jupiter square Hades because it is quite close. Here we see the tendency for grandeur in her actions, held back only by lack of resources and deficiencies. Her Sun is in the eighth house of the Midheaven and also of the Ascendant, making the Ascendant influence deep and self-protective. She is earthy and pragmatic and has an inner sense of the mysteries in life. She can be quite occult, keeping the secrets of life with a serene acceptance of the transitory nature of existence.

She knows how to manipulate resources, both her own and those of others. Still, her will is weakened and her spirit and enthusiasm don't have the passionate depths that this placement calls for. This is due to the lack of dynamic and strong combinations to the Sun. The Jupiter influence through the opposition coupled with the square to Hades creates many occasions for possible gain and success but always at a price. There is always a problem with the flow of that energy, because it amplifies and pulls more energy out of her than it gives back in return. She sees men opportunistically: happy-go-lucky creatures to connect to and with whom to take a chance. With Hades in the picture, they always wind up being fixer-uppers with lots of problems. Her partnership with males is always a problematic experience. With the Hades square to the Sun, partnerships contain defects that are always connected to the past or because of actions in the origins of the relation. Sun and Hades combinations usually lead to health issues with males, and Joyce has Hades conjunct the seventh house of the Sun as well as Sun square Hades. Yet, even with the Sun's trine of Uranus in the eighth house of the Sun, Joyce is deeply tied to the resources of the males with whom she associates. Having Moon-Saturn in the eighth house of the Sun, these male ties go deeply into her sexual and emotional makeup. She has a deep-seated need for male influence in this life, no matter what the cost. The cost can be emotional, physical or financial and probably has been all three at various times.

Yet the male influence has been beneficial for her. She does find a measure of freedom through her pursuit of goals and opportunities, and others see this as a sign of her vitality. At times she can radiate optimism through her actions. She doesn't really see this effect. She sees it as coming from a position of responsibility when she knows what she is doing. Others just see it as optimism. Joyce, on the inside (remember Moon-Saturn), is not an optimistic person. When she looks to the past, she sees the gains she has made. When Joyce looks to the future she gets nervous, unsure of herself. She has to allow others to guide her to her future and, both rightly and wrongly, she follows.

Joyce's *Moon-Saturn* reflects *Cupido-Apollon* on the *Sun axis*. This is the mark of a methodical person and one who organizes carefully. It is also the mark of a teacher who imparts knowledge via theory or technique. She is not a hands-on teacher, showing physically how to do something. Instead, she explains how to do something or illustrates the underlying principle to a teaching. She can process large numbers of people, and separations in these circumstances are a joyous thing. When a group comes together for a specific purpose and then accomplishes that purpose, the separation generally is not a negative thing. It can be quite beneficial because the people Joyce influences can go on to better things. With Jupiter opposing the Sun she has high aims. The Jupiter is on the ninth house side of the solar opposition, leaning towards the law, publishing, advocacy and academics as areas of gain in her professional journey.

Joyce's father seemed like the happy-go-lucky kind of guy until one looks a little deeper and finds Sun opposing Jupiter square Hades, and Mercury conjunct Venus in the fourth house of the Sun. He has problems and defects that have been glossed over in Joyce's view and memory of him. He may have had health problems or money problems, but he still brought hope and some joy into her life. He was a teacher to Joyce and was her primary mental connection shown by *Sun=Moon-Saturn/Apollon-Cupido=Node/Mercury-Venus.* This combination describes how Joyce learned about love and art through her father's influence as well as the management of household affairs. While Joyce's mother brought discipline (or emotional repression) into her life, her father brought a structure into which to fit the discipline. While she has a great emotional and karmic tie to her mother, she enjoyed her father. This energy carries over to her view of men in general. She lacks the strong Sun vitality and the purposeful will that a powerful Sun placement would give. All of her strength and discipline comes through her powerful Moon. Her will and drive are sublimated through her emotional state and responses. It is here that she overcompensates for her weak Sun and creates a strong sense of purpose in her life. She has a strong need for male influence and will overlook or live with the flaws that the men bring with them. The condition described above also underlies the type of male energies she gathers around herself. She sees the good and overlooks the flaws. She knows the flaws are there, but she minimizes them.

Is the male influence predominant in Joyce's life? In her outer life, yes, by all means but in her inner life, not really. Her mother taught her the importance of setting boundaries and made her pay the price for letting down her guard. Joyce's father's influence gave her the ability to individuate and to create a unique path in her life as indicated by *Sun/Uranus=Aries Midheaven/Jupiter.* He contributed to her spiritual outlook and his presence laid the groundwork for higher spiritual ideals. *Sun=Mars/Uranus=Zeus/Neptune* can be a violent combination, and Joyce's father could demonstrate a violent temper (although this isn't a major part of his makeup), but ultimately he had his own sense of discipline that kept such tendencies in check. Joyce has Sun in both the Midheaven and Ascendant's eighth house, and *Sun=Pluto/Admetos=Moon-Saturn/Cupido-Apollon,* intensifying the impact of death and separation, and because of this heightened sensitivity Joyce will experience a profound sense of loss when her father passes away. It would be as if a transformation or change stopped dead in its tracks. For Joyce, change only occurs while life is present, and death brings an absolute standstill to this process and thereby a deep sense of loss. The effect of the death of the mother would be profound for Joyce, but would be seen as the normal passage of time, unless of course the mother was absent from an early age. With Joyce's Moon-Saturn and Midheaven combinations, the events creating her maternal influence could go either way—a strong maternal impression dominating all feminine activity, or little maternal influence due to death, absence or disinterest. Either way, the behavioral results from the lunar combinations will manifest the same way: a constant struggle with the forces of emotional responsibility.

Her connections to males seem to be marked by a sense of fate. Making connections in the world is part and parcel of Joyce's expression. Remember, she has Sun at the midpoint of Ascendant and Node, and that quickly makes intimates out of acquaintances. She meets compelling men who display their power and authority. From Joyce's perspective with *Aries/Sun=Pluto/Vulcanus=Midheaven/Zeus Kronos*, such meetings seem ordained and represent powerful influences. Communication in these circumstances is very pleasurable, happy and wide-ranging when her *Aries/Sun=Mercury-Venus/Cupido-Apollon* axis is activated. Although powerfully drawn to such influences, Joyce displays great common sense regarding her actions—*Aries/Sun=Jupiter Hades/Poseidon=Midheaven/Kronos*. As seen from the influence of her father, she is attracted to that which she lacks and has finely tuned male power and energy radar that is very sensitive to the energies that complete her.

Bringing the immediate environmental connections to males into focus, a different kind of picture emerges. Once Joyce filters specific males from the general impression, she gets very close, very quickly. The more she hangs around a particular male, the stronger her projection of him becomes, and she slides into a very intimate connection as indicated by her *Node* equaling *Sun/Ascendant*. When we look at her *Sun/Ascendant=Node*, and *Sun+Node-Neptune=Pluto, Sun+Ascendant-Neptune=Moon-Saturn*, we are describing her most intimate type of male connection. In this area of connection, she brings her power to the table and feeds it to the male, giving him authority over her life in many subtle ways.

Delving deeper into her intimate connections themselves the picture shifts once again. Joyce expresses love in many ways, as seen through her *Sun/Node=Mercury-Venus,* and her *Mercury-Venus/Jupiter=Cupido-Apollon,* from enjoyment of social activities to intimate conversations on any subject. She has the will to marry with *Sun=Moon-Saturn/Cupido- Apollon, Sun/Moon Saturn = Aries,* and feels comfortable with a legal commitment. Matters of faith help guide her intimate connections with *Sun/Node=Cupido-Apollon/Poseidon.*

Separation Issues

There is a dark cloud concerning Joyce's intimate male connections, and it revolves around separation, either through divorce or widowhood. When we see a string of combinations such as Joyce's *Sun+Node-Midheaven=Uranus Admetos,* her *Sun+Node-Moon-Saturn=Admetos,* her *Sun/Ascendant=Node,* and her *Sun+Ascendant-Moon-Saturn=Kronos=Neptune=Zeus,* with the Sun in the eighth house of the Ascendant and the Midheaven, the magnitude of the impact of separation takes many forms, pervades many areas of her life, ignites strong underlying emotional issues, and creates situations she doesn't enter into lightly. Remember, she will have or has had a very hard time with major separation from her father, and this energy carries over to any male intimate that she takes into her life. In response to these combinations, Joyce has built walls against letting passing affections affect her. She minimizes her emotional investment for fear of loss and only opens up when she has assured herself that she won't be abandoned. Joyce has a wide Node square Uranus, which makes connections and intimates come and go in her life with great regularity and with little attachment on her part. But this pattern breaks down when she has let a special connection into her life. The closer the connection, the more of herself is invested in it. While Joyce has no trouble with breaks in any type of connection, it is clear that a permanent break with someone to whom she is emotionally invested is devastating for her. Of course, with the Uranus energy, permanent separations occur suddenly and are seemingly out of her control.

Joyce's interface with others

217

Joyce's Ascendant is quite close to 0 degrees Cancer and stands at 27 Gemini 53, and this brings her connections into the public eye. She really cannot separate her environmental connections with her more worldly connections. This is wonderful for connecting people and places and makes the whole world one's home. Placing the midpoint of the *Moon* and *Jupiter* on the *Ascendant* inflates the impact of places and people on her, but the Saturn influence on the Moon gives her a calculating edge. Some youthful error should have served to sharpen this critical saturnine quality in her interaction with others.

Mars is just below the horizon, having just set in her chart, and when combined with Neptune creates the picture *Mars/Neptune = Ascendant*. When her frustrations build, she will lash out at others in her environment, blindly, often attacking the wrong person or situation. This placement also means Joyce puts out a very clear and refined personality signal, and everybody around her picks up on this signal colored by their own projections of her. To some folks she is entertaining and hilarious, to others a dead note with a reactive temper. This part of her interaction is not Joyce's fault or caused by her. She is always very clear and detached on an internal level. But others see her as they want to see her, and that creates a fuzzy interface with her environment. This clear internal outlook and fuzzy external interface can be likened to a soft-covered hard object, enveloped in fog, moving rapidly.

Mercury conjunct Venus is sesquiquadrate the Ascendant, heightening the importance of Joyce's social abilities and giving her charm and grace. This combination characterizes all of her dealings with her friends, associates and business partners in her immediate environment. When we look at the reflection of the Node on the Ascendant axis, it equals Cupido and Apollon (and furthermore, *Ascendant/Moon-Saturn=Cupido-Apollon and Vulcanus*) reaffirming the view of her involvement with a social hierarchy. These combinations bring along a strong sense of custom and tradition, yet also show an interested and liberal view of cultures and traditions alien to her own. Combined with the primary planetary picture on the *Ascendant, Jupiter/Moon-Saturn*, we see this structure channeling into business dealings, movement of real estate and interaction with the basic social foundations of society. This does not mean that she is wielding this power, but that she is surrounded by it. This is the immediate world she is immersed in, a world of tradition, social function and the conduct of business. Joyce in many ways floats through this world, sometimes seen, often times misunderstood, always social and interactive. The Neptune square her Ascendant gives her a light and mysterious touch and makes for the interactions to be a good show and very entertaining. However, she is sharp and misses nothing (again *Midheaven=Moon-Saturn* connected to the *Ascendant* through *Jupiter*).

A strong planetary picture in Joyce's horoscope is *Ascendant+Ascendant-Hades Jupiter=Moon-Saturn=Midheaven*, while her Moon is running in a loose semi-square to Hades and another one to Jupiter. Through a sixteenth harmonic (22.5 degree aspect), this Hades Jupiter is connected through the Midheaven to the Moon-Saturn. She gains through service work, serving others and organizations. These dealings with the public are essential to her. She feels that she needs to serve others and this motivation, when it finds proper outlets, solves some internal dilemmas for her. Her internal systems and viewpoints are conditioned by a sense of disconnection or loneliness. No matter how strongly she bonds, her sense of feeling connected is lacking. When she sees the effect of her efforts in service to others, she feels as if a soothing salve has been applied to her wound of isolation. Understand that she can feel isolated in a crowded room with close connections, as well as within the world of her closest intimates. It is through service and doing things for others that she has the sense of escape from the more isolated parts of her inner makeup. She gains through this combination, although compensation is not her only motivation. Simple acknowledgment of her contributions will go a long way with Joyce. With her Neptune square the Ascendant, she feels uncomfortable when too much praise is thrown at her. She recognizes her talents and capabilities and wants no more and no less than simple appreciation and proper compensation. Too little and she gets mad and feels taken advantage of; too much and she discounts it as flattery.

Love, Desire and Intellect

Joyce's approach to love with her Mercury-Venus is sunny on the outside and, with her Moon-Saturn Midheaven combination, obsessive on the inside. A wonderfully developed social demeanor rides in front of Joyce's love interactions. She is eloquent and attends to the social niceties but has no trouble expressing her desires and no shame in pursuing them. Her wants and needs run deep, and she is much clearer about them while in pursuit of a desired goal than when she actually attains it. All of this is seen not only by her Mercury-Venus conjunction, since Pluto opposes it along with trines by Moon-Saturn and Poseidon. However, when we talk about Joyce's approach to affection and desire, we are also talking about her mind and mental abilities. This is primarily because of the closeness of Joyce's Mercury-Venus conjunction; it has an orb of only 7 minutes of arc and consequently the planets are interchangeable. She loves to think, and thinks about love. The Pluto influence on her mental perception is quite clear. She scrutinizes information and its sources. It is quite difficult for others to lie to her without her perceiving it. The Saturn-Moon trine steadies the mind and heart, while the trine to Poseidon gives her mental clarity and spiritual desires. Joyce's interest in books, publishing and presentation of ideas is shown by her Mercury-Venus conjunction in the ninth house of the Meridian horoscope. She has Mercury conjunct Venus in the eighth house of the Ascendant, and this suggests that her interests and ideas are much deeper than normal and her projected desires more deeply mysterious or sexual than apparent.

Looking deeper into the Venus-Mercury combination, there is an exact thirty-second harmonic opening to Poseidon. Ideally, she would like to have mentally challenging Platonic connections. Her thoughts are very clear and pure when operating at their highest level. Joyce's *Mercury-Venus* also equals *Jupiter-Hades=Sun/Node=Uranus Admetos/Moon-Saturn=Aries/Pluto=Ascendant/Mars*, making all this clarity wither away when she is obsessing over an inescapable desire. Then Joyce turns these mental powers to probe and question herself in mental circles.

Joyce cannot love just anyone, only someone special. Once she perceives the special qualities that drive her obsessions and clarify her focus, this special person becomes the center of her desire and thoughts. She then pursues this person and has a quirky kind of luck in attaining the idealized desire as shown by *Mercury-Venus=Jupiter Hades/Uranus*. Even with her mental clarity and focused desires, Joyce is often greatly mistaken about her own perceptions. She can fine-tune into perceptions and intuitions that pass us mere mortals by, but this very finely crafted ability is not reliable when her mental focus is clouded by love. Joyce's refined style of perception is shown by *Mercury-Venus=Neptune*

Kronos/Vulcanus. She can perceive spirits and other unseen phenomena and feels comfortable with these kinds of connections; they don't scare her, not with *Mercury-Venus=Neptune Kronos/Vulcanus=Poseidon*. But once she connects physically to another person, separation is very difficult for her. Her love object may fall off the pedestal or be mean and reject her, but she can only separate through death or dissolution. It really has to be bad for her to voluntarily separate from a physical bond.

Joyce experiences her own perceptions vicariously through her intimates through the strength of her Midheaven and Node connections. She is a confirmed romantic as seen through *Moon-Saturn=Mercury-Venus/Neptune* (one of the tightest planetary pictures in her horoscope) and always has to learn to keep her expectations low (not too much of a problem with the Moon-Saturn conjunction square the Midheaven and Neptune square the Ascendant). She is flirtatious and sexy over a base of caution and reason. She doesn't surrender her heart lightly.

Work and Profession

Of course one cannot really talk about love and desire without bringing sex and work into the picture, particularly since Joyce has a strong Mars axis. Here we will look at the work side of Mars and other indicators of her professional activities. First of all, Mars is setting and opposed Vulcanus. She has a loose but powerful combination of *Mars=Ascendant/Vulcanus* that leads to a "tough guy" image or projection. She is direct and feisty, bold and brash; yet, she wears velvet gloves (due to the Mercury-Venus conjunction and its verbal and social charm). Joyce's Mars has a trine to Hades and another to the Node, and they form the picture *Mars=Node/Hades Jupiter*. She is no stranger to messy, dirty work and connects with people for the purpose of "cleaning up the mess." With *Mars=Ascendant/Vulcanus*, Joyce is just bowled over by a good display of confidence and power.

Joyce is quite clear about the operation of her energies and either works with propaganda, publishing or some other writing-related activity. This is shown by *Mars= Midheaven/Poseidon=Pluto Vulcanus/Mercury-Venus=Aries/Cupido-Apollon=Uranus=Admetos*, Mars on third house cusp of the Sun houses and Venus-Mercury on the ninth house cusp of the Midheaven houses. Of course, these same combinations show the importance of communication in all her energy exchanges. She has an overriding fear of sudden and complete breaks in her working relations. This is less so in regard to her expression of sexuality, because in that context the combination expresses itself in a different manner. *Midheaven/Poseidon=Mars* is mental in its operation and brings issues of morality into focus. When we look at *Mars/Poseidon*, it equals the *Aries Axis,* amplifying her issues of morality and giving it a political focus. Add to the same axis *Mercury-Venus/Zeus,* and we have a staunch defender of her truths with the proof to back it up. Her convictions are further backed by *Mars=Pluto Vulcanus/Mercury-Venus,* giving her a fine ability to dig for knowledge through research management of information. *Cupido-Apollon/Aries* brings to the axis the ability to handle both technical and traditional information. All of the above points to someone who is very good at taking a position and backing it up with solid and organized information.

Because of the interplay of the Ascendant square Neptune and opposing Mars, Joyce is always identifying herself through her professional mask. This mask is much more important than the transformations she experiences through her sexuality. Although the impact of her relationships is profound, and it can be devastating when they go awry, she feels extremely insecure when she is unemployed. As long as she has focus in her outer activities and professional status, she can cope externally with all her personal crises. Take away her professional focus and life becomes overwhelming. Due to her Mars in a sixteenth harmonic to both Uranus and Admetos, these events occur with great suddenness.

Joyce is a specialist in her activities. Mars in connection to Admetos brings enormous energy to her work. With Mars sesquiquadrate Pluto, and Mars opposing Vulcanus, she knows how to deal with people of power. Cunning and charming when she has clear directives, she can be indomitable. Yet, as we have seen elsewhere, so much depends upon the direction and influence of others, primarily authority figures. She is a subordinate and falters when she has to lead. Given outlines to follow, she produces a stellar performance. Joyce has great opportunities for her work, and it is this limitless professional boundary that makes me believe that this horoscope operates on a high level and overcomes any blockages that come to her in this life.

Sexually, she has great strength and stamina as seen through her *Mars=Pluto=Vulcanus*. Joyce is drawn to people who project their sexuality through their strength. She is attracted to the more seamy side that others can project. In other words, Joyce has a vulgar side in her energies and sexuality and can become involved in coarse acts led by her co-workers and intimates.

The analysis of the planetary pictures that form around Joyce's Mars shows a relentless energy. This energetic compulsion is seen primarily through a Pluto sesquiquadrate Mars. Since the Pluto is also tied up with her Mercury-Venus conjunction (*Mercury-Venus/Pluto=Mars*), things can get a little intense. Power issues plague her intimate relationships and to focus on these issues, we have to look at the planetary pictures that combine the *Mars* and *Mercury-Venus* axis that connects with *Admetos, Node/Moon-Saturn* and *Ascendant/Pluto*. When we look at the reflections of the *Aries Axis* off of the *Mars/Venus-Mercury* midpoint, it equals *Vulcanus*. When we reflect the *Sun* off the same axis, we get *Poseidon*. Earlier indications show that Joyce goes through a screening process until she finds herself in tune with one person, and an analysis of her Venus-Mars axis confirms this observation. When the *Venus-Mars* midpoint runs with *Admetos*, it means that only a very "special person" can create true sexual intimacy. Otherwise, she feels the need to suppress the sexual urge, and this combination makes her truly intimate circle very small and also limits the family circle. When she is focused on the "special person" who allows the Admetos energies to open up, then all of Joyce's sexual aggression takes over and drives her actions (the *Venus/Pluto* does equal *Mars*, after all). If she doesn't find reciprocity from the "special person," she becomes increasingly frustrated. Combine this *Admetos* limiting function with *Ascendant/Pluto* and *Node/Moon-Saturn,* and we get a person with a tight focus in matters of intimacy. Previously we talked about Joyce's separation issues in general terms, but now we can be more specific. The Moon's Node axis controls how a person bonds emotionally. When Saturn enters the picture, there is a deeper ability to bond, but it is a dependent bonding based on fears of separation.

Deeper Exploration

Joyce's thinking permeates everything she desires, and mental stimulation drives her on. Did I mention that she is obsessive? Joyce is on the hunt for very special things in life, very specific things with the way her Mars combines with Admetos and Pluto. She really cannot define these things, as they shift and change slowly with her Neptune and Mars combinations to her Ascendant. She displays one state of being when she is in pursuit, another when she is pursued, and another when the chase is over and time begins to wear on the situation.

Bear in mind that Joyce is not a flighty lover, pursuing one chase after another; these things are very serious for her (remember, she has Moon conjunct Saturn square the Midheaven). Oh, she can flirt and be quite seductive with her Mercury-Venus conjunction, but it is all fluff until something catches her interest. With Mars connected to Pluto it is as if Joyce—when she becomes interested in something or someone—shifts into an obsessive mode and becomes a predator. She starts thinking, scheming, and doing all sorts of conscious and unconscious things to advance her cause.

Now if I were her employer or a lover who was being pursued, I would harness this energy. It operates like the carrot held out in front of the donkey. Joyce will just keep going towards the goal, continually, relentlessly, even if it keeps receding into the horizon. Once she catches the object of her obsession, a change in Joyce occurs and her relentless energy atrophies. Mars with Pluto always needs to be in pursuit, otherwise complacency sets in. She doesn't gloat over her prize catch, but does revel in it for a while. Slowly, however, she starts to drift and get restless. She needs a new goal, a new obsession and will start doing things until some new desire forms in her consciousness. As the new goal forms, she moves towards it. If the former pursuit doesn't adjust or transform to fit this new paradigm, then the previous object of her desire is forgotten or discarded. She has an itch, and when she finally finds and scratches it, a new one appears elsewhere. The new itch makes her forget about the old itch. If the old itch becomes irritating and demands attention while she is concentrating on the new itch, uh oh, the old itch is in trouble.

However, if Joyce is pursued, the pursuer only has a chance with her if she is interested as well. Then she will encourage the pursuer in subtle ways. Like the maiden of yore, Joyce drops her handkerchief at an opportune time to signal to her pursuer her acceptance of the pursuit. Make no mistake about it; however, Joyce is passively controlling the entire situation. Remember, she supports the strength displayed by others. Once all this activity is over, she settles in and has to have the relationship develop, because she is always growing and changing her affections within the relationship construct. She needs the confrontation that this growth demands and if it isn't forthcoming, she creates conflict so that the resolution, again, creates growth. Without growth and evolution, she becomes obsessive about the lack of growth. Managing this energy is a Herculean task that requires great attention and care from her partner. One can see why Joyce needs a "special person." But once this "special person" is found, she expects it to be forever due to her *Node/Moon-Saturn* squaring *Admetos*.

Although Joyce seems happy, cheerfully serving and approachable, she has very specialized desires about whom she is intimate with. In another time people would call this "high standards," but Joyce doesn't have high standards, just specific tastes. Cognizant of her frailties and sense of responsibility, Joyce is wary about to whom she will become devoted. The style of partner she is drawn to is witty and intelligent, demonstrating power, confidence and sexuality. Joyce has *Moon-Saturn/Hades=Ascendant,* and she automatically takes on a subservient role and is uncomfortable leading. Once committed, she is fully engaged. She has a will to marry and although she gains in marriage, dissolution is inevitable as seen by *Sun+Node-Neptune=Pluto.* Much as she tries to hold things together, they drift. Sometimes the effect of this is sudden, with things going on without her acknowledging them until a disruptive shift (usually mean) occurs, and she is literally crushed by the loss. Yet, she has some great Jupiter combinations and gains from these crashes overall, although she will probably disagree with me on this. You see, with Moon-Saturn square the Midheaven, Joyce ultimately trades in emotional currency. Managing her emotions is the inner work that she finds most challenging, and she doesn't like to waste her time dealing with negative feelings. Money and possessions would seem important for her in the eye of the casual observer, but that aspect of her is tied to her professional self-worth and doesn't count for much when an emotional investment is at stake. So if Joyce's finances and net worth gain during a time of emotional loss, she isn't focused on these gains on an inner level. The material gain is not the issue; it is always the emotional loss that she processes internally.

Inner Focus

Joyce's inner orientation, her "point of view," is colored by the Moon-Saturn conjunction square the Midheaven, giving her a somber, realistic, practical outlook. Emotions swirl in her internally before they are communicated. Joyce has a strong and powerful sense of self and a fatalistic acceptance of things out of her control indicated by *Midheaven=Moon-Saturn=Vulcanus.* Joyce's *Midheaven=Vulcanus=Node,* and her outlook is greatly colored by her connections and intimates. She is always taking orders from someone, shown by *Midheaven=Ascendant/Kronos=Vulcanus=Mercury-Venus/Zeus,* usually someone in a position of authority. Being prone to influence doesn't get her down, it is the delays and obstacles that make her worry. One of the overriding items I mentioned earlier is her confrontation with morality issues. As she is following the influences of her connections, she is led down a dubious moral path. She has good blocking combinations that can be used to prevent her from becoming involved in situations that are morally suspect. Whether she utilizes this defensive energy or not, her connections have a hard time refraining from dubious actions of consequence. So, of course, Joyce is drawn into situations that she knows, quite clearly, she should not be involved in.

Luck and Money

Joyce has Jupiter in the first house of the Ascendant and it opposes her Sun, which is in the eighth house of both the Ascendant and Midheaven horoscopes, indicating involvement with lots of money, especially other's money or resources. Joyce's *Kronos=Jupiter Hades/Apollon-Cupido=Neptune,* and that shows capital involvement, particularly with inherited old money or money from criminal organizations. Money losses are also indicated through speculation or fraud. Never underestimate the power of *Mercury/Neptune=Moon-Saturn* and *Midheaven,* along with Neptune square the Ascendant for creating unclear or deceitful conditions. In other words, Joyce has to deal with major money issues, and her management abilities aren't the greatest. Joyce is terrific at organizational and data collection matters; it is her leadership decisions that are faulty, particularly shown by Neptune sesquiquadrate Kronos. She isn't really bothered by financial gain or loss with the Sun Jupiter opposition. Her professional standing is another matter, and this is very important to her. Understand that Joyce worries about everything and in particular about her finances, but those are not her highest priority.

She has a protective shield looking over her with the Sun Jupiter combination, but it is not airtight. Since her Jupiter runs with Hades by square, no matter how good an event is, there are problems. When it comes to relying on the past or her ability to produce proof (in the intellectual sense), she shines and things move very smoothly. When she has to rely on others for good things to happen, they are excellent in inspiring her spiritual life and lousy in assisting her with mundane affairs. Her interface with others is very mutable and although she can read others well, she ignores her better judgment and is too trusting. With Neptune square the Ascendant, others can never read her correctly either. Joyce finds herself surrounded by con men and mystics and shouldn't trust her mundane affairs to others. Yet she is not good at arranging her own affairs, as seen by the Neptune Kronos combination. This is problematic for her. She is much better suited to manage the affairs of others, since she has to discuss and consult with her superiors before executing critical decisions. With her clear sense of professionalism and good trine of Uranus to the Sun, when Joyce is self reliant, she has a good earning potential.

Home and Foundations

Joyce has Cupido conjunct Apollon in the fourth house of the Meridian horoscope. She has Neptune conjunct Poseidon in the fourth house of the Ascendant horoscope. In the Sun horoscope, Joyce has Mercury conjunct Venus in the fourth house. Her Mars stands in the fourth house of the Moon horoscope (while Mars falls in the tenth house and the Moon is conjunct the fourth house of the Saturn horoscope). The Meridian horoscope indicates that her personal view of her home life and basic origins is traditional and expansive. She sees the core of her family as an established unit, with history, chronologies and secrets. With the conjunction of Apollon, she sees her family connections spread far and wide and glamorizes the achievements of her ancestors. Her father was a welcome presence in the home, bringing love, art, culture and a strong sense of communication as seen through the Sun horoscope. Connections with her mother's presence in the home were marked by devotion, battles, passionate emotional displays and work. It is this part of her emotional makeup that translates into the need for professional achievement. Very little of these origins are seen by others, and her true home experience is not clearly observable by the people she is acquainted with in her daily and professional life. It is through her experiences with others that she has developed and shaped her spiritual outlook. Joyce's interactions with others have taught her the value of faith. Ironically, through both positive and negative interactions and influences with her environment, she has built a strong sense of spirituality. Joyce has to experience the inconsistencies and moral breakdown of others to avoid spiritual and karmic errors.

Odds and Ends

Her emotional outlook determines Joyce's sense of responsibility. This is seen time and time again in this horoscope via different combinations involving Moon and Saturn. She has seen the prestige of her family status fall during her life, particularly due to her father, her father's death or the actions of a mate as seen by *Sun/Neptune=Node=Uranus=Admetos*. She works extremely hard and has to handle much stress and situations that only resolve into black and white choices due to the conjunction of Saturn, the Moon and Uranus. With *Hades+Vulcanus-Node=Ascendant=Mercury-Venus*, Joyce has experienced mean deeds from others that have literally crushed her. Through it all, her spirituality continually becomes deeper and more focused indicated by *Midheaven/Poseidon=Pluto*. Although Joyce is not very good at managerial choices, she is an excellent diplomat and a very good negotiator. She has Neptune Kronos sesquiquadrate, developing inventive approaches towards her diplomacy. Joyce is quite creative in these matters.

Node+Moon-Saturn-Pluto=Ascendant shows that separation is marked in Joyce's life, and that difficult separations change her life's direction. Separation anxiety follows her throughout her life and continually brings material gain in its wake. That Moon-Saturn square Midheaven, and Neptune square Ascendant, again indicate that she goes from sad circumstances caused by dissolution and parting to much better ones with brighter hopes for the future.

Joyce repeats this cycle over and over, building her status in the world. It is the earliest partings that have had so much influence in her worldview and spirituality. Her dreams are marked by her connections with others. Powerful dreams and powerful connections with highly placed individuals lead her through life's odyssey. She so dearly loves her acquaintances and friends, and they bring joy, beauty, love and intellect into the foreground of her life. She needs their novelty, their intrusion. She carries many secrets. They must be a burden to her emotional state. Many are about her family origins and many are about events far away in both time and space. Joyce loves truth and hates falsehood. She loves movies and has powerful connections in media. Above all looms her innocent and platonic outlook. No matter how hard or realistic she can be, she has culture, faith and a certain softness underneath.

Final Words

A chart reading is a temporal experience, a snapshot of someone's life as seen through the limitations of the astrologer's own horoscope. As much as Joyce is mysterious to her acquaintances, she can be opaque to readers and astrologers. Her connection to astrology is well marked. *Uranus/Apollon* (the Apollon running in a tight conjunction to Cupido) stands close to semisquare to her *Midheaven,* indicating a personal connection to astrology. It runs with *Sun/Hades Jupiter,* showing fame and fortune through the service aspect of this book and other works she is involved in. The *Cardinal Axis* connects to *Neptune* through *Uranus/Apollon* and tells of a powerful need and desire to know the future and the difficulty of getting good guidance. She has *Node+Vulcanus=Uranus+Apollon,* showing the powerful astrologers and magicians gathered in her honor, and the power of these connections in the destiny of her life. In short, publishing and astrology are clearly shown here and in various other areas of her life. Joyce's life experiences are energetic, emotionally difficult and richly rewarding. She will leave her mark on her friends, family and the mundane condition of the world. Through her life, her soul continually deepens and develops, no matter what obstacles she has had to face. In the end, it will be her inner spiritual outlook that will be most important to her and to the people with whom she shares her faith.

HADLEY FITZGERALD: PSYCHOLOGICAL

> *There is a world beyond ours, a world that is far away, nearby,*
> *and invisible...a world where everything has already happened*
> *and everything is known. That world talks. It has a language of its*
> *own. I report what it says.*
> —María Sabina, Mazatec Shaman

Dear Joyce,

Before we proceed with an exploration of your chart, let me tell you something of how I approach this work . . .

In his travels over the course of a remarkable life, the Greek writer and spiritual seeker Nikos Kazantzakis developed a wise and challenging perspective on our human existence. He saw every person as a one-of-a-kind, unrepeatable piece of the whole spirit of God. Therefore, he concluded, we should each think of ourselves as solely responsible for the salvation of the world, since, when one of us dies, the particular play of our unique being, of our particular heart-mind—and what it could do for humanity—is lost to the world forever.

Our sacred task in this life, then, as Kazantzakis saw it, is to plunge far enough into our own souls to find and free what he saw as "the endangered spirit of God" inside ourselves—i.e., to reflect on and become increasingly conscious of our purpose, our life path, in the world. Otherwise, the contributions we came here to make remain undeveloped, and the world is ever the less for that. In its best form, astrology is dedicated to exploring the soul and freeing the spirit.

I take the birth data you've supplied, type it into an astrological software program called Kepler 6.0; the computer does all the computations for me and prints out the chart—or a series of charts—from which I derive all the material in our discussion. Whether I have a client in my office or on the phone, I'm always aware that I'm looking at several squiggles inside a wheel on a piece of paper. The challenge is to sift through the many possible layers of information available there until I can translate those symbols—and their patterns—in a way that has meaning and relevance for the person's life. Before I begin a consultation, I sit with that chart for a while and jot notes about it, but I pretty

231

much put them aside once I feel in sync with the client's physical or auditory presence. At a certain point, the soul seems to engage us both, and my goal is to honor its agenda.

Each planetary symbol can connote a seeming variety of characteristics and experiences, but there will be a theme running through all of them. Your psyche registers the theme, and over the course of your lifetime "magnetizes" people and situations in the world in order to participate fully in "earthing" the archetypal energies that support that theme. These are *profound,* bigger-than-life principles that get squeezed down through our earth-tube/body and into this third-dimensional reality. The symbolic patterns on that piece of paper detail the ways in which we can decipher what James Hillman calls "the soul's code"—or free what Kazantzakis believes is the "endangered spirit of God" in ourselves. Whatever metaphor works best for you, I take very seriously the privilege I have in helping you translate it into real-life terms.

In my professional practice, our personal contact and dialogue is essential to helping me best describe and understand how these archetypes speak through you—and about you. I don't need anything I say to be "true," so as we move through the session, I'd encourage you to speak your mind if you don't understand or agree with what I'm offering, or if an image I use doesn't resonate internally with you. Finding the words and images that *do* resonate is an integral part of our work together. It's virtually impossible that all of the options I present in the following written analysis could show up in your experience, just as it's possible that I'd fail to call forth *the* one—the linchpin—that most succinctly describes how a set of symbols is actually weaving its way your life. In a written format, there's a benign mandate to present too much material in order to demonstrate possible avenues for discussion and exploration. If we were speaking with one another directly, my language would be much more conversational, and the number of words here would be reduced by half.

I'd begin by taking a few moments to find out why you've wanted a natal consultation at this time—e.g., "What would you like to accomplish in our time together today?" Since you're in your fifties, you're likely to have at least *slightly* different concerns than you would have had in your twenties. Also, if you've been in therapy and/or some other self-searching process that you found productive, we would start off on a somewhat different track than if you were turning to these concerns for the first time. It would likewise be impossible in one actual session to address all of what follows on these pages, and even if we could, it would not necessarily be wise to do so, lest it quite overwhelm your psyche. During the course of the reading, I'd continue to listen for clues to what you've done thus far with the configurations I see in the chart, so that I could adjust the depth and complexity of my interpretation accordingly. My primary concern is that together we focus on the areas that have the most meaning for you, so that you can go away from this session and apply the content of the consultation to your life.

I wear two professional hats: one as a psychotherapist and the other as an astrologer, though for the past ten years or so, parts of those hats have been more and more seamlessly woven together. Time and again in both types of consultations, however, dialogue will occasion a serendipity wherein the client says a word or a sentence that triggers an image in my psyche—or pulls several images together. That often enables a deeper investigation of one or more links between the chart and the client's life experience. Depending on what happens next, the session *can* turn into something quite different than either of us had "expected" at the outset. On many occasions I've felt as if the archetypes almost literally popped into the room and helped us move the work along. Since that can't take place in print, I want to make my limitations in this format clear at the outset. Even more, I want to make clear that they are *mine alone* and should not serve to describe the limitations of astrology.

I try to resist language that suggests I know, and can now proceed to tell you, who you are and how you operate in the world. Such "telling" may exhibit a certain mastery, but it shows no reverence for the mystery of what we can discover together—neither does it honor the reflective capacity of the psyche. Therefore, I ask for your understanding as I attempt to approximate my in-person procedure of interpretation / question / surmise / integration—and various permutations of same—on these pages. Also, absent a dialogue with you, I can't *develop* an understanding of what you've done with what I see in some areas of the chart as opposed to others. "Sometimes," notes the poet David Whyte, "everything has to be inscribed across the heavens so you can find the one line already written inside you." As I've read back over the entire analysis here, the words have looked so very concrete, so unqualifiedly certain. You might find it frustrating at times when I circle around—or even miss the mark entirely—but I trust you'll still find it provocative and enlightening.

For my own frame of reference, I do think of you as "a soul dressed up as 'Joyce,'" and I tend to use language that distinguishes soul from ego. My therapist's brain imagines that by this time in your life, you have a considerable range of experience, so the manifestations of what I see may be much richer than my words here can suggest—and/or you may still be defending against (or struggling to integrate) certain more problematic parts of yourself. In working from a psycho-spiritual perspective, I'm attentive to the psychological blocks that stand in the way of both earthly progress and spiritual evolution, and I trust that whatever sounds didactic on my end doesn't insult you and the progress you've made heretofore. In any case, when "it" all comes together in my head, in my notes, in my dialogue with a client, I'm mindful of what Quincy Jones says about the process of producing a work of musical art: that once all the best music has been written and all the best musicians have gathered to play it, "we still depend on God walkin' through the room..." My experience of the astrological art is no different.

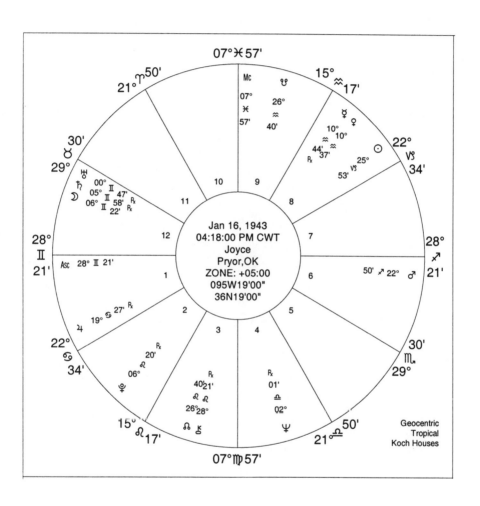

The core of our reality lives in unbounded time,
but our destiny is anchored and unfolds in linear time.
This sense of direction gives meaning to human life.
With a little work, we then discover in the unfolding of
our biography the traces of a marvelous, cosmic patterning...
—William Bryant, *The Veiled Pulse of Time*

Dear Joyce,

A birth chart cannot tell us whether a person is male or female; short or tall; gorgeous, homely, average, or "interesting-looking;" straight or gay; black, white, yellow, red, or a multi-cultural mix of all the foregoing. This lack of physical specificity not only makes astrology remarkably suited for our post-modern world of shifting boundaries and thinning veils between the worlds, it also frees the astrologer to advocate on behalf of the soul. One of astrology's many gifts is that it literally proscribes linear thinking: there is no objectively consistent this or that, right or wrong. Thus we humans can come to understand ourselves as neither angel nor demon, but as moving along an evolutionary continuum between both—being, if you will, angelic demons and demonic angels in a multitude of combinations and permutations. So, when my colleagues and I undertake an astrological interpretation, we enter into a dialogue with the sacred and profane, the conscious as well as disowned and unacknowledged attributes of that human being; we go in search of the unique power as well as the special music contained within him or her, and we do so in service to the highest good of that soul and our own.

When I first hold someone's chart in my hands, I make note of what draws my attention most immediately. Why did my eyes go there, I wonder, then I note where they go after that. I never lose sight of the central organizing principles in the chart, but neither does that first "pull" ever fail to tell me something. And so it was in your case that my attention was drawn right away to one of the most transrational areas of the chart[1]. Straightaway this tells me there is much more to you than meets the eye (including, possibly, your own eye for some portion of your life), and that life has pulled you into deeper and wider waters than others might imagine. I wouldn't be surprised if you've had various friends who would tell me—and in some detail—about the Joyce they're quite certain they know. But I wonder if there are many who really do know your deepest heart of hearts, know how much your need for control speaks to your desire to surrender it and merge with something greater than yourself, how surprisingly much you've looked to others to give meaning to your life[2], how much you yearn for love but resist opening fully to it (though you might tell yourself you fear getting trapped by it). This heart is a lonely hunter, so to speak, negotiating the vicissitudes of trust.

Your soul entered this life with an observant, investigative mind, a powerful imagination, a gift for vivid, clever, interesting, creative use of language—part of your lineage in this and prior incarnations. Along with this, there's an ability to tap into the realm of myth, mysticism and metaphysics, and an ingenious capacity for weaving together ideas from myriad sources, ancient and contemporary. You are also here to delve into some of the darker corners of the human psyche[3] *and* have conversations with your fellow humans regarding your discoveries—in other words, to listen and be listened to beyond the level of pure social interchange. All of this is meant to serve you extremely well in making your way in the material world, though you have to deal with your own emotional unpredictability as well as with the consequences of thinking/seeing outside the tribal-think box. "The normal" and "the usual" are not meant to be, as you have surely noticed, huge parts of your life's vocabulary.[4] Thus, you're challenged in that the stimulation, communication, and exchanges you need most in order to feed your soul can also turn into exquisitely refined defense mechanisms. The shadow side of your considerable gifts is that there are so many interesting experiential mountains to climb that you could end up getting to the top of none of them. You're learning that you do best to pick one (or two) at a time, climb it and, pretty sight or not, tell the rest of us what you learned on the way up and what you saw when you got there.[5]

Since the chart indicates considerable initial difficulty grounding and validating to yourself what you actually do have to offer, rather early in the session I'd ask you what *you* think about the degree of congruence/incongruence between your gifts-as-potential and what you've actually done with them thus far. I'd also want to know if you teach, write, have some specific spiritual practice, do creative healing and/or communications work in any capacity (even as an investment banker!), and/or have some place in the world by means of which both your imagination and that talent for speaking some darker truths can be used to support your own and others' visions of what is possible.

Paradoxical to the communicative presentation of self, your soul is discovering the value of both solitude and relationship as essential *parts* of your spiritual base.[6] In some ways you're an introvert who's learned to be an extravert, and emerging from your particular childhood, I would think you've needed to develop a healthy set of personal boundaries so that you can eventually thrive emotionally in relationships rather than simply becoming more clever and sophisticated in the ways of survival. Conscious solitude in this life is meant to become a soul-full experience—one that will eventually make a very rich inner life congruent with your outer, everyday movement through the world. This solitude is not to be confused with isolation, nor with masterful intellectual repression of your need for the few deep human relationships that are meant to catalyze your transformation over the years.

Such relationships carry themes of power and powerlessness, control and surrender. At times they may well involve your feeling "abducted" into realms of physical and psychological experience where ultimately (or repeatedly) an alchemical change takes place—i.e., something in you gets "cooked back," and you know you're different after the encounter. In the course of all this you may well "lose" and "find" people, possessions, ideas, emotional connections—again and again—so that you can ground your instinctual knowledge of when/how to hold on and when/how to surrender in this life.[7] The more that instinctual knowledge grows, the more your capacity to trust yourself in relationship to others expands.

While this may sound rather abstract to someone not living your life, I see your soul having agreed to go more deeply into certain layers of affective human experience than you have in prior incarnations[8], and/or wanting to go in a different direction in order to avoid the interruption of some work related to a past-life calling. In any case, you've known for a long time how to use knowledge to gain control of your environment, but the need is to get your emotions and gut instincts working in sync with your brain this time around, so that your creativity and range of experience can serve you and connect you with others in practical, productive, and at times profound ways.[9]

One part of you is hard at work on the process of internal integration and is likely to feel a particular loneliness in the process. "Where *do* I fit, really? What's my niche? Where do/can I belong?" are implicit questions of great import. Yet, since you have an innately ambivalent relationship with "the rules," and since your experience of your tribe and/or culture is that it has a hard time recognizing and valuing your gifts (and vice versa), another part of you has little

238

interest in belonging and carries a distinct preference for connection with the realm of fantasy, myth, and unlimited possibilities. Thus, we could say that in very specific, concrete, material ways[10], your soul has taken on the assignment to live into the deepest levels of the Serenity Prayer: "God, grant me the serenity to accept the things I cannot change, the courage to change the things I can, and the wisdom to know the difference."

For more than one incarnation, the relentless romantic and the diehard pragmatist in you have been at war, one alternately killing off the other so to speak, and the evolving soul now wants a truce.[11] If your creative, transrational, mystical leanings and your capacity to question/probe/report can be *productively* distilled in life's alembic, you emerge with an excellent blend of intuition, logic, and practical resourcefulness. Combined with your first-hand experience of human suffering and your ability to find the beautiful in the dark and unusual, the traditional and contemporary—*and* if you don't defensively calcify your eccentricities—you're well-equipped to enter a number of creative arenas with tools essential to being an excellent therapist, researcher, healer, hospice worker, social worker, mentor, counseling astrologer, teacher, writer, etc.—in some obvious or disguised capacity.[12] In any of these callings you could effectively and successfully apply hard-won understanding to the affairs of the real world.[13]

The blending of Darkness and Light, depth and breadth, stability and freedom, taboo and traditional is a central challenge in this incarnation.[14] Thus, encounters with the Shadow in self and others are essential to your soul's earthly experience—and those encounters begin early. Your soul set itself the task of cultivating a powerful individual integrity amidst the intense gravitational pull of a personal and collective tribe that seems to inform against what you're here to do—sometimes at nearly every turn. The wounding around your creative expression of feelings and ideas was constellated in your environment by age three.[15]

Throughout your life you hear the siren call of endlessly fascinating stimuli, drawing you toward a dissipation of your fine mental energy—i.e., using your creative mental gifts to avoid the deeps rather than to shine a light into them. As you learn to resist that temptation, and to do so in ways that focus instead of repressing your feelings, you can discover ingenious methods for pulling all your experiences and understanding into a center. When you begin to do that persistently, you not only hear your own words coming from your heart at last, you also find them going directly and dramatically into the hearts of others who need to hear them.[16] Ideally, this sets up a feedback loop that nourishes your soul in the process.

However, that combination of refocusing your feelings and resisting energy dissipation is an evolutionary *goal* in this lifetime, hence there are roads to clear on the way to it. Early on you developed a survival mechanism that enabled you to engage others without being truly engaged yourself. But at some crucial junctures in life, your ability to function this way doesn't suffice; you need to *feel* what experiences mean to you, lest you turn cynical in the face of repeatedly deflated fantasies and expectations. Life structures periodically get broken and reset so you can discover that what initially seems to be pulling you *away* from your center is ultimately pushing you toward a new level of honesty, integrity, and truth-telling both inside and around you. Hence, the soul experiences various types of "death" while trying to form the intense and transformative relationships that won't enable your defensive armoring. If all goes well, by the time you unzip your body suit and exit this life, you'll understand in your bones what Sam Keen meant when he said, "The ego must die a thousand times before the Self is born, and each little death is a rite of passage to a larger life."[18]

Absent these rites of passage in some form, your capacity to "live behind your eyes" and far from the world, observing, gathering perceptions, playing with possibilities, and assessing your environment could keep you somewhat adrift for extended periods of time—as in separated from yourself, not trusting your own power, torn between really wanting experience, accomplishment, and actually setting about the grunt work to make that possible. Your observational skills *can* function as a very useful talent once you've marshaled your capacity for self-discipline,[19] and I'd want to know if you feel you've learned to marshal it effectively.[20]

The astrological symbols that suggest an ability to talk yourself out of your feelings before you've had a chance to feel them *can* also signal a tendency toward agitated depression—or, at least, emotional repression. Without therapeutic intervention, this could have the effect of "flattening" your energy rather than driving you to direct it into productive channels—such productivity being essential to your evolution in this lifetime.[21] Again the question: have you by now, in some way, transformed this enormous amount of mental and imaginal activity from its use as a defensive shield (albeit a disarmingly attractive one) into being an instrument that gives you a place in the world? My hearing a couple of sentences from you at this point would go a long way toward directing a substantial part of this consultation. It would help me to know if early abandonment and/or lack of nurturing[22] galvanized your ambition[23]—e.g., "As God is my witness, I'll never feel powerless—or be penniless—again…" Or did it instead seem to dissipate your personal incentive to the point where you sought partners from whom you could garner an identity and sense of self-worth because *they* lived out, or "carried," your ambition for you?[24]

Acute sensitivity to your environment[25] makes you a natural "reporter." You can pick up pieces of information that, on the surface, seem disconnected/unrelated, yet when your multi-layered perceptions take those pieces down through various levels of consciousness and get them integrated, you come back up with a gestalt that can shift the perspective of those around you.[26] You can engage a variety of people at various levels, depending on circumstances, and your words carry more emotional impact—and ability to sell and seduce—than even you may realize at the time. Like a magician, you are charged in this life with learning how to use that power, and one of your first challenges in this regard was constellated around age 4½.[27]

When you want to, you can get straight to the point (and not suffer fools), but do it in a way that invites people to go there with you and invest in what you see and what you're saying about it. You can be persuasive, clever, very witty, ingenious, dramatic, and people around you are surely not bored. You don't do this superficially—there's a deep seriousness, even profundity, in you along with an inborn willingness to explore the darker recesses of human experience. But, again—and again—you may finesse your presentation and responses so well that your intellect, while appearing to be a bridge, actually becomes a shield in your encounters. Your chart is relationship-oriented, which tells me that you depend on connections with other souls to do much of your karmic work. You might feel that your mate(s) can best take care of your needs by never being boring himself, but if he's too successful at feeding your intellectual defenses, you could cheat yourself out of some vital karmic experiences regarding intimacy (in-to-me-see), stability, and trust.[28] Partners in sundry guises will be enlisted in this lifetime to help you awaken to a deeper level of compassion, so that you come to identify with human beings more than with ideas and can teach from heart-won *experience* this time around rather than from theory and idealistic abstractions.

My astrologer-self pictures you very early in life (perhaps even in the womb!) listening, soaking up all the verbal and non-verbal cues around you, and concluding that the world of feelings and emotions is perilous territory from which no traveler returns—so why go there? As you matured, some part of you may have intuited—and feared—that if you did "go there," you'd not only become deeply vulnerable to and dependent on another(s), you'd also become vulnerable to the suffering "soul of the world," which seemed equally overwhelming.[30] My therapist-self sees this an "early decision" (one that can govern your life for quite a long time because it made complete sense when you were young) and wants to know what you've come to understand about your feeling nature across the span of years. Even a brief response to this query would help me weave together various elements of your chart into a better understanding of how your soul is living out certain patterns. If depression (agitated or otherwise) didn't get hold of you early on, you quite possibly used your intellect and imagination to escape, to become emotionally invisible, though you might have thought of this as gaining control by soaring above the fray of emotional entanglements.[31] My therapist-self would want to know if you've experienced a kind of shame when some of your more primitive needs come up on your blind side—e.g., are you internally programmed to label such needs "selfish," "childish," "self-indulgent"? And/or have you drawn into your life others who exhibit their needs quite obviously and depend on you to rescue and take care of them? If so, what have you done about that as you've matured? Have you developed/expanded your compassion beyond a position of "rescuing"? Have you learned by now the critical difference between humility and humiliation? What has that meant to you? How has it affected your relationships, your ability to sustain accomplishments?

In my mind your chart triggers an interesting combination of archetypes: Cinderella and the Whistleblower. One is the abandoned child who had to disappear amidst the tribal family; the other is the child who saw—and shouted—to the whole town that the emperor was naked. One is redeemed from darkness; the other is the redeemer. One struggles to adjust to convention; the other defies it.[32] Both must take a gamble. As soon as you learned that speaking dark truths would earn you exile from the tribe, you also found ways to simultaneously engage and resist engaging the world. (This theme seems so pervasive.) Perhaps, then, the early assumption of responsibility seemed a valuable, even comfortable[33] armor against your highly-sensitized response-ability. I'd venture that your childhood was over by the time you were barely five months old.[34] "Emotional self-sufficiency" seems something of an oxymoron—and is not to be confused with emotional maturity—but I suspect you gave the appearance of it so early[35] that the idea of your having any particular needs would have been foreign to those around you—not that anyone

242

was checking. The chart tells me over and over that this soul wrestles mightily with the fear of being vulnerable (which you might also associate with being dependent) and therefore with the issue of your own needs versus others' expectations. "Fear" and "lack" are early, powerful themes here.[36]   I ' m n o t exactly sure which parent played which role, as they're quite woven together in your psyche, but your relationship with both of them, present or absent, provided considerable "training" in being distanced from what you're personally feeling. I'm inclined to lean on mother (or mother figure) a bit—if she was alive in your childhood—as I suspect you had to attend to her needs in order to keep her connected to you, perhaps also "offering" your creative gifts to her to try and make her happy. This, coupled with your own need to feel useful,[37] got you sensitized to others' implicit/explicit demands early on—and may even have given you a kind of pseudo-power. But it likely threw further and further into shadow the dependent part of you, thus increasing the certainty of the latter erupting into your adult relationships in rather intense ways.

Whatever the real-life circumstances (and our dialogue would illuminate a great deal here), your relationship with your mother/mother figure is quite complex. It seems to deliver—actually or by default—much that's positive in the sense of intellectual development, "support" of your yearning for a different kind of life than she had; but, again, it also supports/maps your old defenses and a certain kind of risk-aversion on a deeper emotional level.[38]

Since the ability to identify and "own" your own needs and feelings was obviated so soon after you were born, I would want to understand whether: you were pulled into acting out the family pain; and/or suffered bouts of depression because you had to hide your light under a bushel; developed a sophisticated counterdependent persona; and/or "escaped" into the world of dreams, fantasy and your own mind as a defense against dealing with any of this. I'm inclined toward the latter because of certain chart indicators[39]—and because in your early years there were still more sociological mandates for young women to fold into family dysfunction than there were opportunities to act it out.

Over years of doing this work I've observed there are nearly always some experiences, events, relationships in the early childhood environment that recapitulate unfinished business or unresolved trauma from a previous incarnation(s). So I'd want to explore with you whatever you remember or have been told about your life from 1946 to 1948, when much of the "soul's code" was activated/triggered.[40] Whatever the manifestations, however, they carry the theme of your soul having agreed in this lifetime eventually to transform the intellect from being an ego-oriented (however subtly), perhaps restrictive/dogmatic "weapon"[41] into a vehicle for healing, understanding, creativity and compassion. Again, relationships in sundry forms, beginning with your family, are central to this transformation as well as to the ongoing refinement and clarification of your perceptions.[42] So, during the first twenty years of your life the soul is observing, consciously and unconsciously and perhaps in complex circumstances, how people create and develop (or fail to create and develop) relationships with other people.[43]

Also, the adroit, strategic use of mental energy is imported from one or more lifetimes wherein your visions of and for the future, or your idealistic dedication to a radical (as in "non-tribal") philosophical/religious or ideological "cause" or community may have necessitated your closing yourself off to personal needs, feelings, relationships—perhaps martyring yourself, figuratively or even literally, in the process. This could have taken form in obvious or subtle ways; in the latter case, the image of the courtesan who wrests secrets from powerful men—and then smuggles them to compatriots—comes to mind. Your soul is familiar with the wounded idealism in Cervantes's lament: "Oh for the world as it is, traversed by men as they ought to be."[44] At this point in our consultation I'd ask if what I'm inferring here resonates in you at all, though I'm much more interested in locating and pinpointing a *kind* of energy you're trying to transform than I am in describing some actual past life which neither of us can reify.

Whatever came of our exchange, I'd want to weave it into the more pressing concerns of this life, wherein it's vital from an evolutionary perspective for you to experience intense, intimate emotional, sexual, and mental relatedness. While your mind probably became an excellent traveling companion and lover to your young self, it was a poor mother for the deepest yearnings of your heart. When we can't weep, we can't love. When intellect and emotion, mind and heart, are divorced, the soul sustains, suffers, a tremendous loss of grace. When they're reunited, the cage door is opened and the spirit soars. In this lifetime I perceive your soul as determined to get out of the cage of guilt, fear, blame, and hold the door open for others as well.[45] As you become more integrated and grounded in the world of feelings and relatedness—increasingly worthy of love in your own mind and heart—you incorporate into your consciousness and experience more of the "artist" and less of the "scientist" as a core motivator for, and component of, achievement.[46] Certain emotional entanglements come to meet you and demand your attention one way or another in order to set all this in motion.

Therapists usually begin work with someone by addressing family dynamics. In my astrological sessions, I pay a certain amount of attention to the archetypal parental symbols and significators[47] in the chart, because our initial human contact and conditioning in this life involve those who carry some essential energy the soul must deal with in order to evolve. These symbols have tended to have traditional gender assignments, but such attributions are less and less specific in the past few decades. So I wrestle with the thinking and language that imply equivalents (e.g., Moon = mother) and focus more on a type of *energy* that one or both parents carry. These symbols need not represent biological parents and could refer to any manifestation of a mother or father figure. In any case, the physical absence or presence of those who embody these energies points us somehow in the direction of our destiny by helping to constellate certain themes early on. Wherever one finds oneself on the continuum between love and cruelty in those formative years, eventually the soul wants to find ways not to take it personally. We have business here with these other embodied souls; they carry some kinds of energies that initiate our honing process. The better we can understand this, the more conscious of our karmic tasks/agreements—and their purpose—we can become.

I have some key questions for you at this point, Joyce, the response to any one of which could stop further inquiry and allow me to develop the themes around your answer(s).

For example, I want to know about your father's actual physical presence or absence in your childhood.[48] I *believe* that's who I'm looking at—though, again, your parents' roles aren't completely clear to me; so if the following should apply to your mother instead, some minor adjustments would be made in our discussion. If your father didn't physically die when you were about two years old, something about him and/or his life shifted in the early months of 1945 in a way that seems to have taken the "reality" of him from you—i.e., he "died" or became "unreal" to you in some other way. Mother's sadness or emotional unavailability and/or powerful sacrificial or martyr-type energy seems tied into this.[49] As I survey the patterns here, I'm reminded of Jung's observation that "Nothing affects a child so much as the unlived life of the parent."

Whatever the situation, I think it's been difficult for you to see your dad clearly for who he actually was—i.e., he's "there but not there"—which is what the soul had in mind as it set out to establish some deeper, more compassionate, more differentiated spiritual roots (a different type of "family") in this lifetime.[50] But my knowing whether your difficulty is generated from some near-mythic, idealized image of a physically absent father *or* from the presence of a father unavailable in myriad possible ways would allow me to direct my focus in our exploration of these parental significators in your life. There's a mystery here, a story that has enormous impact on your ability to differentiate an individual creative self vis-à-vis the larger tribe later in life.

If your father *was* around during your childhood (or if there was a stepfather, sibling, or father figure who took on his role), I'd ask for clarification regarding his energy in the "family" part of your psyche. Was he:

* dedicated to some higher purpose/service that "gave" him to the world and took him away from you (e.g., doctor, policeman, fireman, minister, soldier, etc.)?

* a "survivor" of some kind of illness or experience (e.g., bipolar, confined by polio, a war veteran with PTSD—formerly called "shell-shock")?

* an alcoholic—or otherwise addicted to some substance, process, or religion?

* a talented, poetic, sensitive, and/or frustrated artist whose creativity got buried (perhaps even turning destructive) in mundane necessities—thus sensitizing you to the shadow side of the Artist archetype?

* someone who used his mind and verbal skill to criticize, charm and manipulate at the same time?

* not your real father and/or not who everyone else thought he was—e.g., a philanderer, batterer, sexually inappropriate with you?[51] There are complex issues around sexual energy and sexual expression in your chart, so *one* possibility is that molestation is part of an early wound to your identity (this may have existed in your mother's background, too), a wound that could lead you eventually toward some deep kind of creative healing work in the world.

Another possibility[52] is that your father literally or figuratively "traveled away" from you and the family *in order* to provide for you, thus reinforcing the difficulty of being able to define him and his place in your life. In a discussion of your relationship patterns, I'd want to know if men (assuming you're heterosexual) who are unavailable in sundry ways have been part of your experience, and/or if you find yourself drawn to men who are interesting and adventuresome but have a needy and dependent shadow from which you find yourself eventually wanting to escape. Or, if there's a tragic dimension to the image of your father, you may have had fantasies that "if only I could've saved him, he would have…"—and thus you find yourself involved in relationships where "rescuing" in some form is a component.

Into your feedback regarding the above, I'd weave this further inquiry:

* Did your mother or a mother figure take your father's place on some level(s)—i.e., cover for him in his absence?

* Did she have her own set of mental/emotional/physical ailments with which you had to cope?

* Do you wish one parent had stood up to the other in terms of protecting you?

* Did one align with you "against" the other and then seem to abandon you to that parent in baffling ways?[53]

Answers to any of the foregoing questions would give me some real-life correlation to an archetypal signature—the *how* around the "missing" earthly father (and mother, in some way).[54] I'm focusing on this issue in some detail so that we can clarify the purpose it serves in the long course of your life—i.e., how it has influenced your sense of your own effectiveness in the world. Again, the internal dynamics of someone whose father was present but unavailable are subtly and significantly different from those of someone whose father was literally invisible, and I'm not able to address those differences theoretically here. But the uncertainty/mystery around your father and the family lineage is present, if for no other reason, than the soul's initial need to be pitched onto a learning curve. A "divine homesickness" is necessary to propel you into working creatively, via your own unique feminine perspective, and from your own deeply-felt experience. As an ideal consequence, you eventually find a place on the earth where you feel connected in a way that can never be taken from you.

In line with the above, I'd ask if *you* know about anything your mother's experiences while you were *in utero*.[55] You were picking up some specific fear and upset from her, but I can't know the nature of it. Were you wanted? Were you born at a time when your parents were ill-prepared for a child? Did you feel disliked and/or envied by your mom? In what I perceive as some abandonment or rejection by her (by default, neglect, or deliberately), it takes time fully to recognize and honor yourself as a woman. The easiest "slide," then, would be into using your intellect to make your way in this fundamentally left-brained society that prizes what we *do* rather than who we *are*. Your perception, imagination, quick wit, and shrewd ability to "work the system" would certainly make you an achiever—can even bring you a certain independence, prestige, authority. But the rewards also have a paradoxical limit: the identification with the masculine *could* be so strong and apparently "validating" that, in striving to live up to a left-brain, heretofore "masculine" image of success (and perhaps succeeding), your feminine, deep, sexual, vulnerable self is desiccated and doesn't get fully integrated into your life; so no matter what you do, you suffer from being overworked and undervalued. That's one possible scenario among many.

One of several possible astrological signatures of addiction is present here, too,[56] and I'd want to know if that's been an issue in your life. In the psychological context of your particular chart, addiction could come out of your feeling at times quite lost and/or empty,[57] without solid roots to hold onto on this earth.[58] From another perspective, addiction could come out of a relentless curiosity coupled with an intense shadow yearning to surrender and be taken over by something or someone.[59] Also, since the place of money and possessions and their relationship to your sense of your own value in the world is a subject warranting considerable discussion, the possibility of money being "the drug of choice" to soothe all ills could be factored in here. For a time in your life, money and possessions can look like love and seem like the answer to sundry problems hung on the trellis of loneliness and/or shaky self-esteem.[60]

If addiction in some form *has* been an issue, what have you come to understand about this? Has recovery expanded your spiritual perspective?[61] Has it helped you embrace your creativity more concretely and use it more consciously in your life?[62]

In all of this, however, I stay mindful of Hillman's observation: "I am not caused by my history—my parents, my childhood and development. These are mirrors in which I may catch glimpses of my image." And so it is with you, Joyce. In the various ways in which your parents were uniquely present and absent and your background proscribed, we get some early inkling of what the soul is trying to integrate in this lifetime. We see its powerful need to be recognized and loved for itself; to be deeply related; to emerge from exile and claim both your voice and the wound in it with style and authority; to redefine what real "wealth" is to you and thus have faith in your intrinsic resources; to have head and heart permeate what you know so that your unique perspective on what's considered taboo invites others to speak of it, too.[63]

I'd also ask you what you do with your anger. Since there's such a focus on independent self-expression and your ability to intellectualize your feelings, I'd want to know if your anger shows the straightforward courage of your convictions; or if it registers in your body in the form of chronic complaints or conditions because you "philosophize" it away in order to take care of your partner(s)—only to have it flare up eventually when you can't "reason" it away any longer. In the best of all worlds, you've come to understand that anticipating consequences, learning new skills, and mastering challenging tasks in your day-to-day life is an excellent way to direct and give meaning to your aggressive energies.[64] Your response here would guide discussion on how successful you are in meeting goals.[65]

And finally, if we had time and it seemed appropriate, I would ask you a couple of questions about an intense and critical time in your life between approximately January 1962 and March 1965.[66] A confluence of cosmic "gearshifts" during that period was intended to get you moving out of your head and your old defense mechanisms into a different relationship with your body and emotions, and into some very specific reality checks in terms of your soul's work in this lifetime. In other words, ego and instinct were trying to make a more soulful and integrated relationship with one another during this period. It's always possible to plug our ears to what Hillman terms "the call of Fate" and the "unacknowledged daimon's urgings."[67] So it's conceivable that with that fine mind of yours you managed to bypass Fate's call throughout the entire three-year stretch, but I'd hope that wasn't the case. If you did hear the call, I'd want to know whether you did so in the form of stellar and ingenious early achievement or monumental acting out of a lot of repressed emotions—or both! In any case, some old identity/persona/value system was beginning to be shredded, and there are strong indications that unacknowledged shadow material in the unconscious began to erupt and present itself in various areas of your life.

Given the tremendous convergence of astrological signatures during this period, *one* possibility is that whatever you did prompted people (including you) to think you were "out of your mind." The soul (again, since it doesn't really give a damn what the ego or the personality wants) would see this as encouraging—*any*thing that got you out of your head and into your body and feelings and needs in the world would initiate the process of turning your base metal into gold. What had been buried/hidden was struggling to find its way to freedom, to the light—a karmic logjam trying to break open at last.

I can't know what came together and/or fell apart here, as travel (cross-cultural experiences), illness, death, inheritance, sex, marriage and birth, education issues, drug involvement and its aftermath, challenges to your belief system could all have been experienced literally or metaphorically in so many ways—and somehow been interwoven on various levels. A classic way one *might* act out at least some of this energy would involve sexuality, to wit: a ("scandalous"?) love affair involving very intense emotions; alliance with someone who embodied your own ambitions; sex with serious repercussions such as a pregnancy—which could lead to the dilemma of a sudden marriage and/or abortion and/or giving a child up for adoption.

In any case, if you hadn't yet owned your ambition or didn't feel entitled to it, or if your identification with material possessions—and the extent to which their accrual or loss could or did define you—hadn't yet been brought into consciousness (from the soul's perspective), this could also have been a time for opportunities to act all that out via projection onto some significant other(s). The soul's purpose for doing so would be to have you begin to "die" to your old identity in the family/tribe, to begin to redefine "success" for yourself, to be freed of the limiting ways in which life in your family had "described" you and what you had to offer. There is a need to get—and *feel*—connected to someone/something larger than life, so you can find your own place in the larger universe rather than have someone else define it for you. There are points in this incarnation, as you've no doubt seen by now, where the faith you project onto others is betrayed so that you must develop a deep faith in yourself and the clarity of your own perceptions. That faith is meant to be a resource that's as good as—better than!—gold.[68]

Psychology offers many explanations for acting out, but I believe we do it—sometimes over and over again—so that, ultimately, we can *see* what we're trying to integrate. Ideally, during those two-plus years there were opportunities to begin to bring vulnerability and strength more into balance inside yourself. The ultimate effects might not have been understood for a long time, but in retrospect they could prove the obverse of the dictum of Socrates—i.e., the unlived life is not worth examining.

The exploration and analysis of a birthchart is, for both parties involved, a sacred trust, and not a day goes by without my knowing how blessed and privileged I am to be a guardian of it, Joyce. From my heart I thank you for granting me the opportunity to spend this time with you on your journey.

May grace surround you the rest of the way,
Hadley Fitzgerald, MA, MFT

NOTES

1. Twelfth house cluster: Air planets in Water houses.
2. Sun in eighth opposite Jupiter ruler of seventh; Moon, Uranus and Saturn square Midheaven.
3. Mercury and Venus in Aquarius at end of eighth opposite Pluto.
4. Gemini planets in twelfth trine Aquarius planets at end of eighth; Uranus, Neptune and Pluto strong in the chart.
5. Sun in Capricorn in eighth, dispositing to Saturn conjunct Uranus and Moon in Gemini, in turn linked to three other planets in Air.
6. Gemini Ascendant and Moon with Mercury ruler conjunct Venus in Aquarius, Taurus on twelfth cusp, and Sun in Capricorn in eighth opposite Jupiter, ruler of the seventh.
7. Sun in eighth opposite Jupiter ruler of seventh, plus ruler of Sun and eighth in twelfth conjunct Moon.
8. South Node in Aquarius in ninth, with rulers Uranus and Saturn, co-rulers of Aquarius, conjunct Moon in twelfth.
9. North Node in Leo in third, with Sun ruler in Capricorn in eighth.
10. Sun as singleton in Earth, Jupiter as singleton in Water.
11. Neptune in Libra trine Venus in Aquarius in eighth, opposite Pluto in second, the latter dispositing to Capricorn Sun in eighth.
12. Gemini twelfth planets trine Aquarius eighth planets trine Midheaven ruler Neptune Libra; Mars in Sagittarius in sixth.
13. Sun in Capricorn in eighth opposite Jupiter in Cancer on cusp of the second.
14. Sun in Capricorn in eighth with ruler Saturn conjunct Moon and Uranus in Gemini, in final dispositing mutual reception with Mercury in Aquarius.
15. Chiron conjunct North Node in third.
16. Leo North Node in third ruled by Sun in Capricorn in eighth; Gemini cluster in twelfth; Mercury and Venus in Aquarius opposite sixth ruler Pluto in Leo. Also, Sun in Capricorn in eighth would need to galvanize *some*thing through Saturn, Moon, Uranus in twelfth.
17. Sun in eighth, Venus and Mercury at end of eighth opposite Pluto in second.
18. Capricorn Sun in eighth opposite Jupiter ruler of the seventh, with Jupiter dispositing to the lunar matrix which includes the rulers of the Sun, Venus and Mercury in the twelfth.

19. Saturn, ruler of Sun, conjunct Moon.

20. Saturn conjunct Uranus, and both trine Neptune.

21. Uranus, Saturn, Moon in twelfth, Capricorn Sun in eighth as dispositor of Pluto in the second.

22. Uranus, Saturn, Moon in twelfth.

23. Sun in Capricorn in eighth, Saturn ruler conjunct Moon.

24. Jupiter ruler of seventh on second cusp opposite Sun in eighth.

25. Moon, Saturn, Uranus in Gemini in twelfth, trine Neptune in the fourth, trine Mercury, ruler of Ascendant and fourth, and Venus in eighth—Air trine in Water houses.

26. Mercury retrograde in eighth, Sun ruler of third in eighth.

27. Mercury opposite Pluto's verbal power, set off by solar arc around age four-and-a-half, and Mercury's dispositor Uranus in Gemini carrying the archetype of the magician-with-words; Chiron in third has some early wounding around speaking/mental abilities/ideas—and Chiron is ruled by Sun in eighth.

28. Sagittarius on seventh and ruler Jupiter in Cancer dispositing to the lunar conjunctions in Gemini in twelfth; Sun in Capricorn in eighth opposite Jupiter.

29. Only one planet in Fire dispositing to the one planet in Water, and converse progressions at six months show progressed Moon conjunct Venus.

30. Twelfth, fourth, eighth house connections.

31. Six Air planets, including Moon, Mercury, Venus—and in archetypal Water houses.

32. Gemini in twelfth trine Aquarius in eighth/ninth, and both trine Neptune in Libra.

33. Sun in Capricorn, Saturn ruler conjunct Moon.

34. Solar arc Saturn conjunct natal Moon, transiting Uranus conjunct Saturn and Moon.

35. Ascendant ruler Mercury retrograde conjunct Venus in Aquarius in eighth, trine the Gemini planets in twelfth.

36. Six planets in Air, the final dispositors being Mercury stationary retrograde in mutual reception with Uranus, only Jupiter in Water; Moon, Saturn, Uranus in twelfth square Midheaven; Pluto in second.

37. Sun in Capricorn/Earth, Virgo on Nadir.

38. Twelfth house matrix as part of Air grand trine in Water houses.

39. Sun in Capricorn, and all the Air in this chart.

40. Aspects between several personal planets became exact by solar arc during this period, and there were significant secondary progressions.

41. South Node in Aquarius, ruler Uranus conjunct Saturn and Moon.

42. North Node in Leo conjunct Chiron and trine Mars in Sagittarius, Jupiter ruler of Sagittarius opposite Sun ruling third.

43. Natal Mercury in Air retrograde at end of eighth, trine and ruling Gemini twelfth planets.

44. South Node in Aquarius in ninth, disposited by Uranus conjunct Moon and Saturn in twelfth, trine Neptune; South Node opposite Chiron in third; Pluto in second opposite Venus and Mercury, Sun in eighth.

45. Moon conjunct Uranus and Saturn square the Midheaven. Moon conjunct Uranus and Saturn can also take risks needed to get to the higher end of Pluto in the second. I ask the reader to be ever mindful that Saturn and Uranus are dispositors of the Sun, Mercury, and Venus.

46. North Node in Leo, South Node in Aquarius.

47. Moon, Sun, Saturn, Midheaven/Nadir axis.

48. Natal Sun in eighth inconjunct the Ascendant at exactly Joyce's age two, plus her progressed Moon square fourth house Neptune two months later, and Mercury ruler of the Ascendant and fourth conjunct Venus, ruler of the fourth house Neptune, both in the eighth; Venus also ruling the twelfth.

49. Moon's twelfth house configuration trine the fourth house Neptune, which rules the Pisces Midheaven. Saturn, ruler of the eighth (death, transition, transformation) is conjunct the Moon.

50. Neptune in fourth as cardinal point of Grand Trine Air.

51. Pluto second, Sun in Capricorn in eighth opposite Jupiter ruler of seventh, Moon ruler of second conjunct Saturn ruler of eighth in twelfth and square Midheaven.

52. Sun in eighth opposite seventh ruler Jupiter on cusp of second.

53. Moon conjunct Saturn and Uranus in twelfth, and trine Neptune, ruler of the Midheaven, in fourth.

54. Midheaven ruler Neptune in fourth aspecting six other planets, three of which are in the archetypal Neptune (twelfth) house.

55. Twelfth house planets and converse progressions at six months—early August 1942—show progressed Moon conjunct Uranus.

56. Neptune in fourth aspecting six other planets.

57. Moon conjunct Saturn and Uranus in twelfth.

58. Moon in twelfth trine Neptune in fourth.

59. Mercury and Venus in eighth opposite Pluto in second; Sun in eighth opposite Jupiter ruler of the seventh.

60. Sun in eighth opposite Jupiter ruler of seventh on cusp of second.

61. This would facilitate discussion of Neptune and the twelfth house on another level.

62. The Neptune archetype has a hard time manifesting at the high end on this earth plane, and thus needs much conscious attention and direction.

63. Sun in Capricorn in eighth opposite Jupiter ruler of seventh, North Node conjunct Chiron in Leo in third, South Node in Aquarius in ninth, Aquarius planets in eighth/ninth opposite Pluto in second and trine Gemini planets in twelfth.

64. Mars in Sagittarius in sixth, only planet in Fire. Except for a very wide applying square to Neptune, which will take effect by progression, Mars is unaspected with ruler Jupiter in Cancer.

65. Mars ruler of Aries on eleventh.

66. In 1962
* Progressed New Moon eclipse 15 Aquarius 17—20 Feb. 1962.
* Progressed Mercury, ruler of the Ascendant, SD (stationary direct) at 24 Capricorn 55—12 Oct. 1962, within one degree of natal Sun.
* Progressed Moon conjunct natal South Node—15 Oct 1962, and progressed Venus square natal Saturn (which is stationary direct).
* Progressed Mars was just past conjunction to progressed Juno.
* Transiting Jupiter (ruler of seventh) conjunct Midheaven and square Moon last two weeks in December 1962, while transiting Uranus was square Saturn (ruler of the eighth) and transiting Saturn conjunct Venus and Mercury.

In 1963
* Progressed Saturn stationary direct (ruler of eighth) by 1 July 1963.
* Progressed Moon square stationary direct Saturn—1 July 1963.
* Transiting Uranus (ruler of Midheaven) square Moon and enters fourth—Aug.- Oct. 1963 and Feb.-Apr. 1964.

In 1965
* Transiting Saturn (ruler of eighth) square Moon and natal Saturn (ruler of the eighth) and conjunct Midheaven—24 Feb. 1965.
* Progressed Uranus stationary direct (ruler of Midheaven)—12 Mar. 1965.
* Progressed Moon enters Aries—15 Mar. 1965.

67. James Hillman, *The Soul's Code: In Search of Character and Calling*, Random House, New York, 1996, p.8: "The soul of each of us is given a unique daimon before we are born, and it has selected an image or pattern that we live on earth. This soul-companion, the daimon, guides us here; in the process of arrival,

however, we forget all that took place and believe we come empty into this world. The daimon remembers what is in your image and belongs to your pattern, and therefore your daimon is the carrier of your destiny."

68. Pluto in second, Sun opposite Jupiter ruler of seventh on cusp of second, and Jupiter in Cancer dispositing to Gemini Moon. Jupiter is also co-ruler of Pisces Midheaven.

JOHN MARCHESELLA: MODERN WESTERN

The first glimpse of a natal horoscope has all the excitement of the sight of an unwrapped gift waiting under the tree on Christmas morning.

In this case, just as Joyce's chart is coming up on the computer screen, my eye jumps to her eighth house Sun, and hmm, it's in Capricorn; that's an interesting combination. And in a split second, those twelfth house planets in Gemini catch my eye. Plus Gemini is rising; how will that affect the reading? And the opposition to Mars in Sagittarius!

Before I let myself jump to any conclusions, the hard copy comes out of the printer and I can start my hands-on interpretation of the chart. I have some hard and fast rules of delineation to apply to the chart, but I also try to keep my mind operating like the shutter of a camera so that I can receive an impression of the chart's information as well.

More importantly, I keep these four points swirling in the semi-conscious state in the back of my mind:

1. Why is she coming for a reading at this time? (This implies some immediate connection to the current transits and progressions).
2. Who is she? (This, of course, is the natal chart, itself).
3. How will I deal with her? (Is this likely to be more of a straightforward astrological consultation? Or will she need more of a counseling session?)
4. What are my own initial reactions? (For instance, if I feel anxious while working on the chart, is it my own anxiety about something in my own life? Or might it be saying something about the client? What might be the projections and the counterprojections even before she gets here?)

In fact, these points are sure to become more conscious as I enter the reading with the client, but they might not be satisfactorily answered for me until after the actual appointment (and sometimes much, much later after the initial appointment in a follow-up).

257

Although it might be another hour of study on the chart before I understand the forecast, I never separate the natal chart from the predictive work, and vice versa. It is the transits and progressions (and other forecasting techniques) that determine which parts of character are in operation at any given time, what we are experiencing about our outer selves, and what we are becoming aware of. Yes, there is always an overriding theme in the nativity, and the astrologer may see it straightaway; but whether the client is ready to see such a "big picture" of his or her life depends on the transits and progressions of the moment. In other words, the current stage of the client's life affects the content of the reading and, therefore, my preparation for and expectation of the reading.

As for that overriding theme, by the way, experience has taught me that *either* there is one single theme that is formed by at least three major factors of the horoscope, *or* there are dual themes that rival each other and that duality, then, becomes the overriding theme in the life. All charts, however, like any great drama, are based on conflict; so I expect the horoscope to signify that too.

Now, as for those hard and fast rules of interpretation:

1. The Chart Pattern—This is the most obvious place to start since it is the first thing that we actually see of the horoscope. These patterns, e.g. bucket, bowl, seesaw, etc., were first described by Marc Edmund Jones, and I do find that they give a broad stroke description of the shape of the client's life. They also help to emphasize particular planets. For instance, the singleton in a bucket chart has great importance, serving as a threshold into life experience for the client.

2. Elements and Modes—I use these very much as the basic personality type, but again, at this beginning stage of interpretation, they only provide a broad stroke description. They will let us know some bottom-line character traits, some likes and dislikes of the personality, relationship issues and career indications. For instance, with lots of Air in a chart, but little Water, I would not expect this client to be a psychotherapist, unless perhaps there's a specialty in behavior modification. (In a few pages, you'll see how astrologers can contradict themselves). With lots of Water, however, I would recommend a career in the helping professions. Every astrologer has a different way of counting the elements and modes. I give two points each to the Sun, Moon, Midheaven and Ascendant, plus one point for Mercury through Pluto. (I do not include the Nodes or any other sensitive points). I think this is a good system to start with, but yes, it can be varied by giving extra points to the planets that seem more significant during the process of interpretation. This is particularly

258

helpful if the original count seems a little tied. Furthermore, the highest element and mode put together create the signature of the chart, which for the sake of simplicity associates the personality with a particular sign, i.e., with mostly Air and Mutable, Joyce would be called a Gemini type.

3. Modes of the Angles—I pay closer attention to these particular modes, especially for predictive purposes. They represent the speed of actual changes and events in the client's life, and not the inner development or character. For instance, it doesn't take too much of a big transit for those with mutable angles, no matter what's in the inner self, to go through a big change outwardly. Conversely, those with fixed angles, despite what's on the inside, can go through a similar transit and merely change the dust around the apartment. (Obviously, if there are different modes on the Midheaven and Ascendant, then this step won't tell us too much.)

4. Hemisphere and Quadrant Emphasis—This lets us know where the individual will spend his or her energy. It says something about character as well as the outer life. In other words, this reveals the degree of extroversion and introversion, the degree of contact with the inner world versus the need for outer accomplishment, etc. It will also clue us into the reading itself. For example, all else being equal, Quadrant I people might not say very much at all in the reading. Quadrant II individuals might want to discuss their plans, ideas, and lives. Quadrant III types are more likely to have concerns involving everyone else in their lives. And Quadrant IV clients might need to talk about their lives in the larger world.

5. The Ruler of the Chart—This is the ruling planet of the ascending sign, and if any one planet can be singled out as the most important one in the chart, this would be it! It is the god to whom one lives his or her life in service. It is the god one emulates. Another good expression to define the sign and house placement of the ruler is "this is where you find yourself." By that, we mean two things: (a) it is the area and style of life where, in fact, you will find yourself spending the most time; and (b) it is the where and how of your self-discovery and actualization.

6. The Sun-Moon Relationship—The importance of this might be obvious. It certainly describes the basic self, but it will also clarify what the individual most needs for self-esteem and well-being. The Moon must be satisfied in Her needs in order for the Sun to rise and shine, so to speak.

7. Lunar Nodes—I have no great insights to offer about the Nodes and I don't think they carry the mystery that so many astrologers assign to them. I just use them in a traditional, meat-and-potatoes way.

8. The Highest Elevated Planet—On a practical level, sometimes this planet can be used as an adjunct to the Midheaven for career direction; but more psychologically, it can be blended into the interpretation of what the individual is trying to achieve in life.

9. Anything Unusual—At this point, having a look at anything unusual in the chart helps us round out its theme. By "unusual," we mean unaspected planets, dignities or debilities, the most aspected planet, the tightest orb in an aspect, stationary planets, and anything else that might strike us as being a little odd or outstanding in meaning. In Joyce's chart, it will be that stellium in Gemini.

By now, there should be a good familiarity with the entire layout of the chart, specifically, the psychodynamics of the signs, the planets' placements as house rulers, and the aspects and configurations. Let me say that in another way: RULERSHIPS, RULERSHIPS, RULERSHIPS AND ASPECTS, ASPECTS, ASPECTS! Get what I consider to be really important in the interpretation of a natal horoscope?

That should make, then, for enough confidence to proceed with an astrological interpretation of the inner dynamics of character and how they play out in real life; or one can start reading the general areas of life, such as career, relationship potential, health, finances, etc., and how they interact with the inner world. The choice, I think, just comes out of the moment with the chart, and we're off.

Now, all of this prepares me for the reading, but what actually is said and how it is said has everything to do with another moment—the one that brings together the client and me. Then, we're really off!

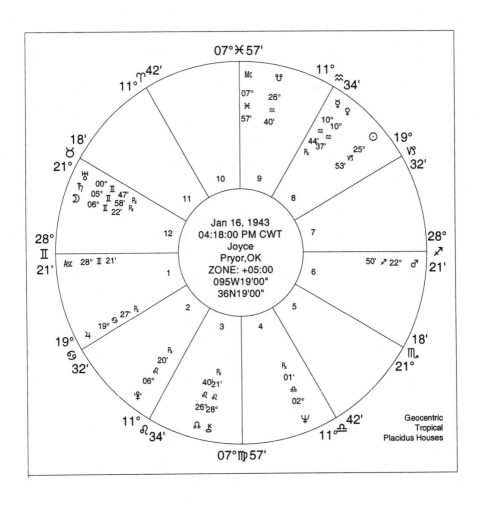

07°♓57'

11°♈42'

18'
21° ♉

28°
♊
21'

Asc 28° ♊ 21'

19°
♋
32'

11°
♌ 34'

07°♍57'

Mc ☊
07° 26°
♓ ≈
57' 40'

11°
≈ 34'

☿ ♀
10° 10°
≈ ≈
44' 37'
Rx

⊙ 19°
25° ♑ 32'
♑
53'

28°
♐
21'

50' ♐ 22° ♂

18'
♏
21°

01'
♎
02'
♈
Rx
Ψ

11° ♎ 42'

♅
00' ♊
05° ♊ 47' Rx
06° ♊ 58' Rx
☽ 22'

♃ 19° ♋ 27' Rx

♀
20'
♌
06°
♇

40' 21'
♌ ♌
26° 28'
☊ ⚷
Rx

Jan 16, 1943
04:18:00 PM CWT
Joyce
Pryor, OK
ZONE: +05:00
095W19'00"
36N19'00"

Geocentric
Tropical
Placidus Houses

First and most obvious, I see the chart pattern of Joyce's horoscope most closely suits the locomotive type with Uranus as the leading planet. That lets me know right away that I am dealing with a woman of vision, a vision that is a little on the unconventional side. So, that wipes out the staunch and stodgy kind of Capricorn. Well, I guess that's why she is willing to come for an astrological reading, which is not exactly a conventional thing to try. (I can't ignore, too, that she has volunteered to be the subject of this astrological project, an even more unusual thing. As objective as we must try to be, we can't pretend not to know what we know about the client before the appointment.)

Incidentally, some students may argue that technically Joyce's chart formation should be a splay. There are some liberties I take in Marc Edmund Jones' chart patterns. However, even in a splay chart, there is a strong Uranus-like tendency, which would give a similar interpretation.

I'll make a mental note, too, to see if the "Airy" qualities of Uranus are backed up by other factors. However, for the moment, let me point out that Capricorn's natural leadership skill will probably be enhanced by the locomotive formation. I'll have to consider that in Uranus's conjunction to Saturn (not to mention the Moon as well), and let's not forget Mercury, ruler of the chart, as the highest elevated planet. (We'll say more about that later too). Is leadership, especially in very individualistic activities, shaping up to be that overriding theme?

Perhaps she'll relate more personally to the word "authority." It's always imperative that the astrologer speaks in the client's language and not the other way around; and my initial work on the chart includes deciphering what that language might be.

Second, let's check the elements and modes. In my point system, then, we have nine points of Air, three in Water and two each for Fire and Earth. Obviously, this is an intellectual and communication-oriented personality type; the weight of Air does, in fact, back up Uranus's power.

If there had been more of a tie between two or more elements (i.e., six Air, six Earth, four Water and one Fire), we could give weight to more significant planets, such as the ruler of the chart. In this case, it's Mercury. He is also the highest elevated planet, often another heavily-weighted planet. We could give weight to the major configuration of the Grand Trine, which here is in Air, too. However, in Joyce's case, all of this is redundant. Clearly, we're dealing with a woman who enjoys her intellectual pursuits, will wind up sharing them with her community (which is yet to be revealed from the chart), and will share them through the means of writing, teaching or public speaking (which also is yet to be revealed). All of this will come into play with every area of life as well—career, romantic relationships, friendships, etc.—because the elements represent the basic personality type, which enters into everything one does.

By the way, astrology students may question how there can be such emphasis on the intellect when so many of the Water houses are occupied. Is she really that mental, objective and detached? What about the sensitivity and subjectivity of those Water placements? Easy. She is probably intellectual about matters of sensitivity. Perhaps she is objective about subjective subjects. Maybe she is mentally curious about matters of the soul. Don't be misled by the contradiction of Air signs in Water houses. This combination exists in many a good writer or student of psychology or the psychic arts, as well as in private detectives, interviewers and researchers, and even in those who can put high finance into clear words. We'll see if some of these abilities might even apply to Joyce specifically.

The prominent mode is Mutable with nine points. When combined with Air, that emphasizes her quick and facile mind. It's the ability to absorb and process information easily, and a way of talking to kings and paupers alike.

With the high Air and Mutability, the signature of the chart adds up as Gemini; so that's the particular kind of Airiness she exhibits. Multi-tasking, let's say, is an understatement! We'll assume all the split personality traits prototypical of Gemini apply very strongly to her, and that by lifestyle, she'll need two of everything—two homes, two names, two callings in life, often being of two minds, reading two books at a time and getting too distracted to finish either of them. As for the idea of that community, too, there might be two of them, each with its own method of communication. Of course, the planets in Gemini carry the same message; no pun intended. So perhaps, in addition to leadership, these Gemini qualities color the overriding theme.

Her intellectuality is most likely to be expressed as curiosity, THE most Gemini trait of all. (And again, she may have volunteered for this project with not a little curiosity about its results, or just for the experience).

Another important Gemini factor is that of peer groups, starting with siblings and cousins right on up to classmates and neighbors. So, we'll be sure to expect something interesting in those relationships. Oh, and by the way, let's not forget the Sun rules the third house of peers, and the North Node of the Moon is there too, giving more validation to the theme of authority in groups.

The ease of Mutability is most evident through her angles, which applies to her movement through life, so to speak. For instance, she is likely to have made (or desired) a number of actual geographic moves in her life. Perhaps she even looked forward to them. She can adjust easily from one job description to another. Basically, she is open to change. She might even seek it as a way of life.

However, let's not get too carried away. We have to keep in mind that the ruler of the chart, Mercury, is in Aquarius, a very fixed sign indeed! Yes, by lifestyle and personality, she may be easy, breezy and likeable. Surely, she appears open-minded to all. ("Appears" is the keyword in that sentence). In actuality, though, Joyce must be a woman of her own mind and making, not one to be easily influenced by others, or to take direction unless it is of her own will to do so. Here we see a major difference between outer personality and inner character. Her open-minded quality is not false. No, it is as real and functional as the skin on her body; but it is only skin-deep. Get just beneath the surface of Joyce, and we'll see a woman of stubborn-mindedness (bordering on the prejudiced), and of undefeatable will (especially in pursuit of the truth). That Mercury sits on the cusp of the ninth house, you see. If it's not too Gemini-like of us to mix metaphors, we might also say she controls her open mind with an iron fist. Case in point is this astrological experiment. She can emotionally afford to hear us astrologers say whatever we might about her chart, because she's so certain, first and foremost, that she knows herself best of all!

Don't think for a second that Mercury's retrograde position weakens this quality in the least. On the contrary, it might even strengthen it. From an early age, these Mercury-retrograde types learn their thinking is very individualistic indeed, neither better nor worse than the norm, just very different from it. Ah, here's another Uranus-like factor in our emerging theme.

To say more about Mercury as Joyce's chart ruler, we have a very bright and witty, personable kind of Gemini Rising person, with a mind like a steel rod (and we have yet to get to Mercury's intuitive qualities à l'Aquarius), in pursuit of the truth, so to speak, and other ninth house activities. Perhaps her pursuit brought her to foreign countries many times; maybe she even lived there for a while. Perhaps they led her to places of higher mind, such as university, academics and philosophy. Perhaps they carried her to a literary world. Cultural anthropology, art history and the humanities are all forms of the ninth house too. With Aquarius on the cusp, a slant toward social sciences may have been emphasized. In the course of her lifetime so far, it may have been all of the above, and still more ways to come in the future. (The ninth house activities are even more amplified by the South Node of the Moon there).

Our theme is certainly shaping up to be an idealistic one: to thine own self be true; just be articulate about it and make sure there's a point to your message! Well, let's think about it some more.

To round out the ninth house activities, we should include religion and spirituality on the list. However, with a lack of Fire and Water, she might have felt, at least in her youth, religion to be a little too rigid and spirituality to be too lofty. We'll leave some question marks on those pursuits, but even if that's the fact from her past, let's see if it remains so for the future.

A very important consideration of astrological consulting is the age and generation of the client. Obviously, what one thinks earlier on in life is often unthinkable at a later date, and vice versa. As for generational thinking, well, clearly, what is unfathomable for one generation often becomes a way of life for another. These are important points when choosing our words to convey astrological interpretations as well as when giving advice based on the chart.

There are two more important points to make about Mercury as the ruler of this chart. First, it sits on the eighth house side of the ninth house cusp. That adds a twist. For instance, if her life has been very much about philosophy, then it is more likely to be a psychological kind of philosophy. If she has studied the social sciences, then social psychology would be high on the list. As a more practical example, if her life has been in the world of letters, then she'd be equally interested in the profits and losses of the written works as in their literary merit. There can be a host of other interpretations, but the point is: when a planet sits on a cusp, let it blend the houses together, instead of jumping from one side to the other.

Secondly, Mercury's aspects are imperative! The aspects to the ruler of the chart let us know what we encounter on the path to self-actualization. In this example, these aspects are likely to catapult Joyce down her path. The conjunction to Venus provides talent, grace and a touch of divine intervention; it also assures her of genuinely being favored by the outside world and gets her invited into inner circles, so to speak. Luckily, I think, it sweetens up or softens a personality with a little too much Air, quite honestly. And let's face it—a little charm and some good looks never hurt anybody, especially in this culture!

Put that Mercury into a Grand Trine with Neptune, Moon, Saturn and Uranus (albeit wide-ish orbs) and now you're talkin' downright serendipity.

265

Joyce finds herself in the right place at the right time with the right thing to say and the right people to say it to! That's a Grand Trine in Air.

On the other hand, anyone with a Grand Trine can tell you it's not always as grand as what the old books say it is. Luck? A little. But it's more like built-in insurance, some protection from the gods, particularly in the form of its element. Also, without a hard aspect involved, a Grand Trine is like youth wasted on the young. However, Joyce does have a very potent opposition from Mercury to Pluto. Among other things, this provides:

1. enough interpersonal challenges to make life interesting, but not overwhelming.
2. the application of her inventive thoughts and brilliant insights to her personal and professional relationships.
3. a deep and penetrating mind (which we already established is also facile and intuitive).
4. the ability to hold her own (and probably even triumph) in intellectual power struggles, spirited debates and mind-twisting discussions.

This opposition aspect also adds a new dimension to our theme. Perhaps Joyce *expects* the outside world to disagree with her way of thinking, try to dominate her mind, and influence her thoughts; and therefore she is prepared with the willful attitude of a libertarian. I wonder what she thinks about Henry David Thoreau? Hmm, probably too romantic in a Watery way. Maybe I should ask about Thomas Jefferson?

Since Pluto rules the sixth house and sits in the second, I wonder if the outside world equates with service to money. I don't expect to nail this point down before the reading; nor do I want to, because it might be too touchy. It's better to approach it gingerly and with an open heart. Maybe she has to reveal it to me. (Remember: she controls her open-mindedness, so it'll be a good chance to give her some space). I know it represents a core issue of self-worth, and perhaps one of the few personal weaknesses in an otherwise very strong character.

I do, however, expect to listen for any sensitivity about money, the haves and have-nots in her estimation, for instance, or matters of bookkeeping, servants or feelings of servility, her co-workers and office environment, issues of the body versus the mind, and even her attitude toward pets. Ah, here is where my own dogs come in handy. Even before the reading begins, while she is

266

getting comfortable in the space, I'll see her interaction with my dogs and it might open up this all-important topic in the chart.

Sometimes we have to enter a reading knowing that we don't know all. Not only does it keep us humble, but it allows for spontaneity and it gives the client more opportunity to participate.

One final note about Mercury's significance in this chart: placed in the dignified sign of Aquarius, Mercury offers heightened intuition, a lightning-like mind and a keen wit, often biting, but never bitter. Its way of thinking is always creative, albeit a little chaotic, and particularly productive in problem-solving because it has an unusual perspective on things.

My next hard and fast rule of delineation is hemisphere emphasis. This makes for the introverts and the extraverts of the world. In Joyce's case, though, it is not easy to tell which she is with just a quick glimpse of the chart. The planets are positioned fairly equally north and south, and east and west. What will slant the emphasis, however, is that most of the personal planets are on the western side of the chart, making her more extraverted. That is NOT to say that is necessarily self-disclosing; that is an entirely other kind of dynamic and one that does not easily apply to Joyce at all!

By "extraverted," we mean the flow of her energy moves outside of herself and into the lives of other people. We might say that so much of her life is about the lives other people, that being with others and working with others will bring out the best in Joyce, and that for better or for worse, she is likely to find herself involved or even enmeshed (eighth house) in the lives of other people. Traditionally, this is said to be a life more geared by fate and outside events, rather than by free will and self-initiation.

For clarification, let us also state that a person can be extraverted in this way, and a person can even be gregarious, bubbly and well-liked as depicted by all of her "Airiness," but that same person can also be private, introspective and closed-mouthed about her feelings and innermost thoughts.

Ah, once again, we meet up with a challenge to being, and the insistence on being, a woman of her own mind and making. A theme is taking shape here.

Yes, it is very possible, even likely, to be popular, public and other-oriented, yet still keep one's own counsel. Just ask any good poker player! You can also ask someone who has her Lights in Watery houses, namely Joyce. This is the next step in my method of interpretation. The Ascendant and its ruler have everything to do with our existence in this world, but the Sun and Moon have so much more to do with the inner experience while we're here in human form.

Respectively, they are the spirit and the soul, so we must have a good understanding of them in the chart.

It is said that the Moon feeds, fuels or nurtures the Sun, and the Sun in turn brings awareness and light to the Moon. Of course, there are a myriad of interpretations for any Sun-Moon combination, but most simply put in Joyce's case, collecting information in intuitive ways (Moon in the twelfth house in Gemini) will enable her to become the teacher or authority figure that she needs to be in order to change the lives of other people in the most intimate and drastic of ways and win a valuable place in their lives (Sun in the eighth house in Capricorn). She will do this by making others aware of their potential and being sure they manifest it, often at the expense of something she herself values highly. Ultimately, and ironically, this results in a great personal loss for Joyce, and it is she who is changed by her participation with others. (Students will recognize we are doubly emphasizing the connotation of the Watery houses).

This is a very complex idea, so it's best to present it very simply, and then provide the many possible examples of it in her life, e.g., from the loss of loved ones to financial inheritances, from healing friends and lovers to being deserted by them and beginning anew, even from missing buses to being offered a free ride to her destination by a kindly stranger who just happens to be a millionaire, from being the free-flying bird to becoming the phoenix rising from its ashes, and on and on. Sometimes the silliest interpretations have great significance in the reading, especially in so intense a chart as this actually is.

Losing Joyce's love is the price that others pay in order to become who they were meant to be; and losing their love is Joyce's price to pay in return for the riches of her soul. This could not have been a very easy life, but instead one that knows great sorrow and loss. However, it has become a very deep one. And certainly it is a vastly different life than the very Airy one we first approached.

Joyce's is the kind of life that is well spent in service to other people. Although the twelfth house planets indicate a worldly awareness and the Aquarian tendency is humanitarian, let's remember that Mercury will insist that whatever she does, even if it's saving masses of people, she does it one by one, individual by individual. Perhaps this is the secret of her popularity too. She can attain leadership over groups of people with a sense of personal connection to each one in the group.

At this point, I would expect to be about halfway through my reading with Joyce. If a client has not been interactive with me by now, I use this mark as a chance to open a dialogue. I ask them if there are any questions at this point, if there is a need to clarify anything I've said so far, or if can I make anything more specific. Not only does this ensure that the client is getting what he or she came for, but it also provides an opportunity for the client to open up a little more personally if he or she feels comfortable doing so. (Actually, this moment even provides something for the client who has been interactive.)

Let us return for a moment to that Moon. Since it is placed in the twelfth house and conjunct Saturn and Uranus, Joyce's needs (especially the emotional ones) are not easily met. Whether it was due to a premature loss of her mother, through actual absence or figuratively, via depression, for instance, or whether it is just her own fierce independent spirit, reluctant to turn to others for help, Joyce has not experienced easy satisfaction in her lifetime. Others do not volunteer to come to her rescue, let's say, nor would she let them even if they tried; furthermore, she wouldn't be caught in a situation that required rescuing.

Luckily, an instinct turned her to those Airy wits and with the grace of the gods in her Grand Trine, she undoubtedly rose to the occasion (and continues to do so since Saturn promises some reward in later life). In other words, she is blessed with the quality and quantity of people in her life, and she naturally recognized how to use them as opportunity and growth. An opportunist? No, not at all; just one smart cookie! She's a street-wise kid in the guise of a sophisticated woman with a good education.

Before we leave the topic of the parental figures, there are these other points. Everything seems to indicate the father is as elusive a character as the mother. Saturn is in the twelfth house with the Moon; the Midheaven (symbolizing the father) is in the sign of Pisces, ruled by Neptune in a Watery house (the fourth), and the Sun (another paternal symbol) is in the eighth house in opposition to Jupiter in Cancer, which further denotes something slipping through her fingers like water! A premature death of the father? Alcoholism? Or just emotionally absent because he feels like a misunderstood genius or a soul too sensitive for the real world?

To further complicate the family picture, the contemporary ruler of the tenth is in the fourth, its other ruler is in the sign of the mother; mother and father are merged in a conjunction in the twelfth, and the ruler of the fourth is conjoined with the ruler of the twelfth! Did Joyce have any parenting at all? Was one parent playing both roles? Is there a saint-sinner complex split between the parents?

These questions have to remain unanswered until the reading, but I should certainly be prepared for an interesting tale of the family background, IF she

269

decides to share such information with me. After all, we have a very private person, not one for much self-disclosure, and from a generation which does not over-psychoanalyze; plus the history is so elusive that words might just be moot. In fact, that might be what I have to impart about her roots—one picture is worth a thousand words when a thousand words cannot do justice in describing an experience. Imagine how confounding that is to so Geminian a personality, verbal and articulate!

With such a family history, no wonder Air is the predominant element, and now I suspect the Water is repressed. This is what Carl Jung would call her superior and inferior functions, respectively. I will also be prepared to tell her that with so fuzzy a family picture, somebody had to wind up with enough Air to be detached and have perspective.

In the reading, this might be a good place to inject something about the siblings. Was Joyce the eldest who had to compensate for the absent parents? Even if she isn't actually the eldest, she might still have wound up with the responsibility of caring for the siblings. (And if she is an only child, then we assume the burden of childhood is loneliness). The rising sign, Mercury and the North Node, etc., suggest a positive relationship with them; the influence of Saturn in Gemini and Pluto in the third house indicate otherwise. But whether these ties are positive or negative, the significant point is: who is Joyce as a result of the sibling experience, and how does it affect her behavior and expectations in adult relationships in love, at work, with friends, etc.?

At this point, my mind is curious enough to leap into a detailed interpretation of these areas, i.e., the seventh house and its ruler. However, before we get into that, there's one more hard and fast rule of delineation. Have a glance at anything that is a little unusual. In this case, take a look at that stellium in Gemini!

I consider a stellium to be four or more planets (including the Ascendant and Midheaven) in a sign or house, and when it occurs, it is as though there is so much energy, too much energy, in that sign or house, that it shoots through its opposite, creating an overcompensation to balance the stellium. So, whatever might be said about all those Gemini dynamics, there is an equal degree of Sagittarius influence in Joyce. This, of course, reiterates what was already said about the ninth house pursuits, such as international travel, cultural interests, and her quest for truth and meaning in all things. Because this is even more emphasized now, we have to weave it into our theme and we will probably see

270

more of it in action in her life, such as an attraction to foreign men, social circles in the academic world or an identification with a philosophical outlook.

At this point, being sure not to lose or diminish anything that's been established so far, it is time to find in the chart the areas of life that everyone is always interested in—love, work, money and health. For these, we turn to the appropriate houses and what's in them, but most importantly, what rules them. This will describe what more often than not actualizes in a person's life. Planets and aspects, however, represent the dynamics of behavior. There is only a fine line between them, a line that most clients are not even aware of, but a line that is helpful to the astrologer.

For example, with so Airy a personality, and more specifically, with Venus in Aquarius, Joyce is likely to be very independent, keeping herself distinct from her love partner, protecting her individuality, a little free-spirited by behavior, and expressing her affection to her lover as friendship more than anything too sentimental, let's say. She might also have an appreciation for the unusual and unconventional, and not really in essence approving of the marriage institution.

One would think, then, she would wind up with a man who is a little detached himself, with a life of his own too. Not so! The gods deliver to her, instead, a man who is a little more traditional by values, certainly sentimental, even clingy, a man who is dependent by nature, and family-oriented. She's more likely to wind up with a man who is more Watery by astrological definition. Why? Largely because the ruler of the seventh house is Jupiter in Cancer! (Additionally, we attract people of the inferior function or repressed element; in this case, Water). That defines the guy in her life more than anything else.

The second house placement of Jupiter further indicates the partner's financial influence, probably a positive one since Jupiter is exalted in Cancer and the aspects made to it are not very adverse. More specifically, the second house is ruled by the Moon, and despite its conjunction to Saturn and Uranus, it is in a Grand Trine, indicating a steady flow of finances, especially through partnerships (business as well as romantic).

Yes, that opposition from Jupiter to the Sun needs to be woven into our interpretation too. So, we'll have to say something to her about overexpectations, be they of the man about his own goals in life, or her own high hopes about the man, or both. Since the Sun rules the third house, she might experience split loyalties between her siblings and her man. Another interpretation of that opposition is a noticeable, but not threatening, difference in philosophies and opinions between her and the partner. Then again, what can you expect from a Gemini rising with Mercury in Aquarius? If you want to play devil's advocate, then you have to expect to get burned once in a while!

Romantic relationships are likely to improve and ease for Joyce with age. She should see time as her friend. First of all, whoever said, "Life begins at forty," must have been a Capricorn. Moreover, all of us, with maturity, tend to grow out of Venus and Mars as the indicators of love, and move into our Sun and Moon as the relationship planets. Since the Sun in Capricorn and the conjunction of Moon-Saturn are better indications for the steadfastness and durability of love, instead of Venus in Aquarius (flighty, but fun) and Mars in Sagittarius (adventurous, but not to be owned). So, is one better than another? No, but the former is in better accord with whom she actually pulls in, namely, Jupiter in Cancer.

By the way, in an ironic twist of fate, that Jupiter influence also indicates the man is likely to bring to the relationship a very secure and stable family, perhaps something that Joyce secretly craves to compensate her own background. In this way, marriage might be more like getting adopted than getting hitched!

In her youth, I would have expected to offer a word of advice on love—behaving yourself does not necessarily mean having to live in the prison of your twelfth house. There is a way to be true to yourself and still be in relation to another person without having to live in repression, suffering, or in a double life. I assume such a smart woman already discovered that way.

For the career indicators, we look to the tenth house and its ruler. Quite honestly, with Pisces on the Midheaven, ruled by Neptune in a Grand Trine, Joyce will probably always wind up a very disappointed success. An oxymoron? Not really.

Generally speaking, the Pisces Midheaven is seeking a transcendental experience on the job. Similarly, these people need their authority figures, namely the boss, to play God. That's a tall order, and one that is bound to lead to disillusionment, which is part and parcel of transcendence too. Can she change her lofty expectations? Maybe, but not likely. And why should she? Isn't it better to be aware of the ecstasy one is really seeking in the mundane areas of life, rather than to live in fear of the resulting agony? What might ease the inevitable disappointment, however, is a sense of humor. Now that's where the objectivity of Air comes in handy!

So, where is the success promised in the chart? Primarily, there is Neptune as ruler of the Midheaven in a Grand Trine, more specifically, with Venus and the Moon, her planets of money and appreciation. Venus, also an indication of creative fulfillment as ruler of the fifth, is particularly well-placed on the aforementioned splendid Mercury. Lastly, a Capricorn is certainly willing at least to strive for success, and there is nothing to indicate a lazy bone in this particular Capricorn's being.

Another piece of advice to her is: with Pluto ruling the sixth house cusp of office routines, remember that no one is curing cancer there. This placement often takes the petty matters of the daily grind a little too seriously. Lighten up! And I'm not sure maturity will be too much of a balm for that one because Pluto is bigger than age.

As for the most probable choices of the actual profession, we must combine her personality type with the dynamics of the stellium and that Pisces Midheaven. However, bear in mind that with the Pisces Midheaven, in and of itself, as well as the overall Mutability of the chart, Joyce might have a number of professions, jobs and titles. That might be all well and good with the eternal student that Gemini rising tends to be, but nevertheless, every Capricorn would prefer to retire from a corporation with a gold watch and a healthy pension.

The Air of the chart is prone to communications and media, particularly with a slant towards education and research. Internationality must come into play with it too, but that's easy enough to satisfy in today's global mentality. And whatever media specialist came up with the expression "global village" must have had a stellium in Gemini with a prominent ninth house!

In a more practical example, however, and if the Pisces savior enters the picture, we might even suggest speech pathology as a possibility; that would satisfy the ability for one-on-one interaction. Similarly, psychology might be on the list of possibilities, but not strictly in a psychotherapist way—too boring and monotonous. Perhaps what can work, though, is psychology applied to the corporate world (even though she is not very corporate by nature) in the form of career counseling or human resources.

Whatever career she chooses, and more likely the career will choose her (the western side of the chart), remember her individualistic streak, her visionary quality, a touch of altruism, and the leadership skill in a community setting. These are really the ingredients to her profession.

Even more important than career is vocation, which is used to imply a calling. Joyce just won't get off the face of the Earth without teaching. We'd encourage her, too, to expand the definition of teaching to include writing. This is somewhat due to her Airy nature, and eventually, every eternal student must

273

share the information; but moreover, it's the typical Capricorn trait. A Capricorn is just not done until he or she achieves authority, and that manifests through the role of instructor.

I always prepare to be as well-rounded as possible, so that I can move freely around the chart in the reading when the client asks specific questions about real-life matters. I also work heavily with derived houses, which are useful when clients ask about the other people in their lives. For instance, we already established the great significance of Joyce's ninth house. On a practical level, that also represents her mother's health, siblings-in-law, and grandchildren, among other things. I'll take that into consideration so I can ask a question about those topics, which would not be unlikely in a full reading.

I also take into account any other houses which are significant in the chart as obviously being significant in the client's life, although perhaps off the beaten path of love, work, money and health. Rarely does one think of friends, for instance, as a big reason to have a reading, but those clients who have interesting eleventh houses do have such a need.

In Joyce's case, the eighth and twelfth houses are remarkable. So, yes, I would be prepared to discuss the "sex, death and taxes" of the former, and the "house of self-undoing" of the latter. More realistically, though, I'd try to find a productive activity for the planets in those houses, i.e., the aforementioned psychological studies or participating in a psychological community. We must add to the mix, too, the Earthy cusps. So perhaps the kind of psychology should slant towards bioenergetics, for instance, because it considers the body-psyche relationship. If it is a community involvement, then it must be in one that is able to make a difference.

"Making a difference" is a very important ingredient in Joyce's character. Perhaps it is better expressed as "actualizing change." After all, let's not forget the Capricorn part of the nature. In any or all activities, minor or substantial, her heart wants to see results at the end of the day, but her high count of cadent placements (plus so much Air) runs the risk of her living her life in her head. That's all well and good for intellectual projects and community participation; they are certainly virtuous. However, when all is said and done, in order to feel whole, Capricorn needs to manifest ideas in a purposeful way.

By this time in my preparation of the natal interpretation, my mind will have snapped an entire photo album, so to speak, of the current and ongoing transit of Saturn through Gemini, including the second Saturn return and Saturn crossing the Ascendant. (The time of this writing is January 2002).

Because predictive astrology *per se* is not the subject of this chapter, I will omit the many interpretations having to do with the passages of such transits and the other significant forecasting factors. However, be it an initial reading or just one of many, I cannot underestimate the importance of knowing the current astrological weather.

Also, what should be considered in the blend of natal and forecasting interpretations are the past transits and progressions. These can clarify the current trends, i.e., drawing parallels between the first Saturn return and the second one, and the first time Saturn crossed the Ascendant in childhood with the second time in adulthood and the current transit. In fact, it might be interesting to check back on the transits of Saturn on all of the angles in the past.

Just as helpfully, these past transits and progressions can clarify some points in the natal interpretation. For example, to emphasize the point that Mercury is the outstanding planet in her chart, I might be prepared to discuss with her the years that Mercury: (1) turned direct by progression and stationed on the natal Sun; (2) entered Capricorn and re-entered Aquarius; (3) crossed over its natal position and quickly thereafter moved into the natal ninth house.

To better understand the natal opposition aspect between Mercury and Pluto, I might bring up the years that transiting Pluto came into a square aspect with them.

For the especially curious student who looks beyond transits and progressions, we might also mention the recent solar eclipse of December 14, 2001, conjunct Joyce's natal Mars in the sixth house. We might be prepared to discuss developments in health, skills and the work environment (and other forms of the sixth house), but we'd also be ready to question what was happening with the eclipse at the same degree in December, 1982.

These techniques really help us to see the cyclical development in a person's life.

As I put my homework aside, I often bring to mind an anecdote of an actor client of mine. He's a Gemini rising man with a Scorpio Sun in the sixth house. I remarked to him that rehearsal must be a great joy for him, almost better than opening night. He agreed, but stipulated, "As soon as I'm cast in a role, I memorize every line in the play. I take the script with me wherever I go until every word of the play is ingrained in my head. Then, on opening night, I make myself forget every word, so that the performance is vital, spontaneous and real!"

275

I was so impressed with this preparation technique that I decided to apply it to my own work as an astrologer. Before the client's arrival, I try to know as many of the ins and outs of the chart as can be known, but I also have to admit that as soon as the client takes a seat in my living room, and I slip a cassette in the tape recorder, it's like looking at the chart for the first time.

Last but not least, my secret ingredient of every astrology reading is the Tarot. For the first ten years of my work, I drew a hard line: astrologers should do astrology and Tarot readers should read the Tarot, and any combination of the two will only confuse the client and lead to a misunderstanding of your role as astrologer! However, upon discovering *The Mythic Tarot* by Liz Greene and Juliet Sharman-Burke, and with a friend's encouragement, I gave the mix a try, and I'm very glad I did. First of all, it appeals to clients who are more visually-oriented rather than oriented to information or discussion. Secondly, the cards can uniquely provide a twist of phrase or a detail that can engage the client. And most importantly, the cards help me to know how to approach the client with astrological information.

I can almost predict ahead of time some of the cards that are likely to appear in a spread. For instance, in Joyce's case, with her Saturn return technically complete, but the transit heading straight for her Ascendant, we undoubtedly will see in her reading the Fool card, or the World card. Each of these indicates life-altering changes, ending an era in one's life and opening up an entirely new period. However, if the Fool appears, I'll know to emphasize the enthusiasm toward the new; but if it's the World, then we might have to discuss the need to wrap things up from the past before beginning with a clean slate. Another likelihood for this astrological combination is the appearance of the Death card, emphasizing the limbo that she would be experiencing instead.

At the close of the reading, I'd reiterate for Joyce the irony of this time. In a nutshell, she is a woman of great communicativeness, but she is in a period of learning the worth of silence. She's also smart enough to understand that. However, I would also have her look forward to that time when Saturn is finally over the Ascendant, and she can again share her experience with us.

KEN BOWSER: WESTERN SIDEREAL

STRATEGY

Joyce's horoscope is calculated in the sidereal zodiac using the Fagan-Allen ayanamsa. An ayanamsa refers to the difference between tropical and sidereal zodiac reckoning. Most readers will be familiar with tropical zodiac positions, but the positions in this interpretation are reckoned from a starting point that closely conforms to the frame of reference that was used in first millennium B.C. Babylon. That reference puts Aldebaran, the brightest star in Taurus, in 15 Taurus, and Antares, the brightest star in Scorpio, in 15 Scorpio. For the current era, five out of six people who have a celestial body in a tropical sign will find that it is placed in the preceding sidereal sign. But if a placement is in the last five or six degrees of a tropical sign, for those born since World War II, that placement will be in the early degrees of the same sidereal sign. For example, Joyce has 27 Gemini 53 rising in terms of the tropical zodiac. She has 3 Gemini 56 rising in terms of the sidereal zodiac using the Fagan-Allen ayanamsa. Likewise, her Sun in 25 Capricorn 53 in the tropical zodiac is in 1 Capricorn 57 in the sidereal. The north node of the Moon also stays in Leo in both forms of reckoning, but the other bodies change. Accordingly, she has Uranus, Saturn, the Moon and the east point in Taurus; Jupiter is in Gemini; Pluto is in Cancer; Neptune is in Virgo; the vertex is in Libra; Mars is in Scorpio, and Mercury and Venus are in Capricorn.

Campanus houses are used. No asteroids are considered, nor hypothetical bodies, Arabic parts, Greek lots or the nodes of any bodies except the Moon. The orientation is geocentric not heliocentric; the horizon under consideration is the rational not the sensible horizon; the parallel of the birthplace is geographic not geocentric, and parallax is not used for the Moon. Stars are used but only their mundo positions in right ascension.

What is most important in western sidereal astrology are the planets and their aspects to each other. Houses are not disregarded, but they do not have pride of place such as they enjoy in Indian sidereal astrology. Western siderealists accord the greatest value to angularity, elevation, dignities and the closest, strongest aspects, both in zodiaco and in mundo; that is, both with regard to the celestial latitude and longitude coordinate system and the right ascension and declination coordinate system. An angular planet is one that is near the angles. Those are the horizon and the meridian, the zenith and the nadir, the east point and the west point and the vertex and antivertex. The most powerful of this group are the horizon and the meridian, especially the eastern horizon and southern meridian, which have been called the "superior angles" since the medieval period. A planet within five degrees of the horizon or meridian thrusts that planet into great prominence in terms of character and behavior qualities particular to the body. An elevated planet, especially those in the ninth and tenth houses, has more power than planets below it. Generally, the principles of planets above the horizon manifest more readily than planets below the horizon. Planets that are in their traditional dignities or exaltations are very powerful. The exaltations are derived from heliacal and calendar phenomena particular to the lunar year 785-784 B.C. at Babylon. Those positions are 19 Aries for the Sun, 3 Taurus for the Moon, 15 Virgo for Mercury, 27 Pisces for Venus, 28 Capricorn for Mars, 15 Cancer for Jupiter and 21 Libra for Saturn. While Uranus is a sixth magnitude object, and therefore capable of being observed with the naked eye, without optical aid it cannot be distinguished from a star. It does not have any historical exaltation degree, since it wasn't discovered until 1781. During the lunar year from which the exaltations were taken, Uranus was in Sagittarius, Neptune was in Aquarius and Pluto was in Cancer. A body is considered particularly well disposed when it is in the sidereal sign of its exaltation and strongest of all when in the very degree of its exaltation. The least desirable position of a body is the sign and degree opposite its exaltation, for example, when the Moon is in 3 degrees Scorpio. A planet is also dignified when it is in the sign it rules and poorly disposed when in the opposite sign, its detriment. For example, the Sun in its own sign or at home in Leo is a good thing, but not so when in the opposite sign, Aquarius. Close aspects have much more power than wide ones, and conjunctions, squares and oppositions have more power than trines and sextiles. Furthermore, the so-called good versus bad nature of aspects *per se* is mostly disregarded in Western Sidereal astrology. That means an opposition or square, for example, between benefic planets like Venus and Jupiter doesn't transform the intrinsic nature of the planets into something unfortunate; rather, the effect because of the strength of the hard aspects is to render the relationship noteworthy for its power. In the same way, a trine or sextile between malefic bodies doesn't become something good merely because of the trine; rather, the effects aren't as harsh as when the same bodies are square because trines and sextiles are not as strong as squares, oppositions, and the strongest relationship of all, the conjunction. The exception to this rule applies primarily to the Moon, which cannot tolerate squares and oppositions without some untoward effect. There is an exception to this exception however: the opposition of the Moon to Mercury is consistently positive. It generally inclines toward a strong mind and success in scholarship. Mercury and Venus are also somewhat less able to stand up to the power of squares and oppositions without undesirable effects, although if the bodies are dignified there is usually not a problem. The intrinsic natures of planets are generally more important than the kinds of relationships they have.

A Western Sidereal interpretation relies heavily on aspect interpretation and the nature of the sidereal signs, and less on houses than is the case among tropical astrologers or Indian astrologers. The major predictive techniques, with respect to time, used by Western Siderealists are transits, primary directions, secondary progressions and solar and lunar returns.

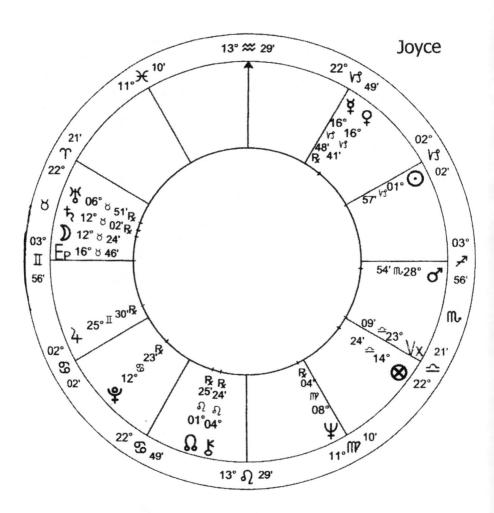

Joyce

I start with the Moon because it represents the gross physical body (whereas the Sun is the spirit that animates the body), the early life and family situation. Joyce's Moon is exalted in Taurus but very badly placed in a conjunction with Saturn, less than .5 degrees from exact; the Moon is also closely sextile Pluto, only 1 minute from exact. The conjunction is always overwhelming in effect for good or ill; here with Saturn, it speaks to the situation with the mother. Moon conjoined to Saturn, with both the Moon and Saturn sextile Pluto, suggests being abandoned at birth either by design or by the mother's death. Pluto in combination with the Moon points to distance between the native and the mother, that they could never bond and that the native received inadequate or no nurturing from the mother. The conjunction with Saturn exacerbates the matter and indicates that the circumstances of the birth mother were desperate, that she may herself have been in danger, and that the whole matter of Joyce's birth may have been shrouded in secrecy, since the Moon-Saturn conjunction is in the twelfth house. That Joyce may have been rejected by both parents, not merely her mother, is suggested by the direct midpoint Neptune= Sun/Moon, 53 minutes from exact and applying. That combination suggests confusion about parentage, or that obfuscation is thrown into the native's path with regard to the parents. This midpoint combination could also suggest "artificial" or stand-in parents, as would be the case if she was adopted.

There are five major indications that her life would be positive and productive notwithstanding a bad start. First the Moon is exalted in Taurus, which by itself indicates a good home, a good mother and that material needs would be met. Since this is contra-indicated by Saturn's conjunction with the Moon and Pluto's sextile to them both, I submit that both conditions are likely true, which would be so if she were adopted. Second, the ruler of the Ascendant, Mercury, is closely conjoined to Venus, the lesser benefic. The condition of the planet associated with the Ascendant sign says a lot about the luck and nature of an individual in broad terms. If Gemini rises and Mercury is with Venus, one can usually expect success and money, although Mercury with Venus and the Moon with Saturn tend to deny altogether or severely limit the number of children of the native. Next, the Moon is separating from the semi-square to Jupiter by 1 degree 54 minutes. Admittedly the aspect is weak but since the Sun is opposite Jupiter as well, both Lights are configured with Jupiter, the greater benefic. Such an augury is fortunate because Jupiter brings protection, aid, wealth, comfort, recognition, honor and fame. Joyce, who sorely needs as much Jupiter as she can get due to the serious afflictions to her Moon, would realize to some significant degree, both as a child and as an adult, the benefits of the greater benefic in the form of material well-being and considerable professional success. Finally, Joyce's natal Sun is only 3 minutes 32 seconds of right ascension beyond the first magnitude star Altair (*Alpha Aquilae*). Altair is renowned as symbolic of one whose ambition will bring the native into some degree of prominence.

As adults, people with Moon conjoined to Saturn are usually autocratic, efficient and cold. Their emotional life is compartmentalized, regimented and exceedingly orderly. Because the Moon is exalted, Joyce would nevertheless have considerable charm, but since she has Pluto sextile the Moon and Pluto opposite Venus, she would not handle intimacy very well. Moon-Pluto people are loners. They tend not to let other people into their lives very far. Joyce has other aspects to her Moon though, so she would appear to be more than merely a charming recluse. But because Saturn and Pluto make the closest strongest aspects to her Moon, she is at bottom very private, shrewd and a bit hard. The Moon is in a grand trine with Neptune and the elevated Mercury-Venus conjunction at the apex. Uranus is much too far removed from the trine to Mercury and Venus to be in relationship with them, but it is certainly well within a conjunction of the Moon (5 degrees 33 minutes), and Uranus is less than 1.25 degrees from the exact trine to Neptune. Some of the closest aspects in the chart, however, are mundane squares between Uranus and the Mercury-Venus conjunction, so that pair actually is in aspect to Uranus. Moon-Uranus conjunctions consistently produce unconventional people who are headstrong, independent, high-strung and without interest in the ordinary tasks in life. Lack of constancy with respect to residence frequently produces a sense of wanderlust as an adult, so I think Joyce has a peripatetic tendency and may have lived in many places during the course of her life.

The Moon is in a closer relationship by trine (4 degrees 20 minutes) to Neptune than she is in conjunction to Uranus, and Uranus is closely trine Neptune (1 degree 13 minutes) as well. Close relationships between the outer planets that last for weeks or even months are often hard to make out in terms of obvious manifestations unless they are connected to the Lights, or they are above the horizon, or they are in angular houses (1, 4, 7 and 10). The Uranus-Neptune trine is completely personalized here because the Moon configures both of them. Uranus involved with Neptune gives insight into the nature of

282

the unseen world. Because the Moon is involved in the matter, it would be completely natural for Joyce to understand—without having to work for it—the truth and the subtlety of higher levels of awareness. Saturn facilitates that tendency due to its trine to Neptune (3 degrees 58 minutes). Saturn in most aspects to Neptune tends to find the order in abstraction, if other factors support. Uranus and Neptune in combination frequently give rise to deep interest and ability in music and art. Joyce would therefore be capable of original works in that area, including literature since she has Gemini rising, which gives strong verbal skills. The downside of Saturn-Neptune is that it makes people feel insecure about the stability and continuity of their circumstances. Considering that, and that Saturn and Neptune are involved with the Moon, Joyce would likely feel, to a modest degree, generalized anxiety which afflicts many high-strung, creative people, particularly those with a mutable sign (Gemini, Virgo, Sagittarius and Pisces) on the Ascendant. It would not get out of hand because she has seven planets in Earth signs (both Lights, Mercury, Venus, Saturn, Uranus and Neptune), which keeps her grounded; in fact she may be known for an exceedingly dry wit. Moon trine Neptune by itself is materially fortunate. People with that combination tend to inherit and/or benefit considerably from the work of others that they didn't, strictly speaking, earn. The main effects are to magnify the imagination and the sensitivity to suffering, both that of the native and that of others. Also magnified are the so-called normal neuroses from which most people suffer—because her generation has Neptune in its detriment in Virgo. Moon trine Neptune is very receptive to and enthusiastic about the occult arts—surely Joyce is so disposed. Since Neptune is in the fourth house, that sphere of life—home and family—is one of the weak points in her life. Anxiety, misgiving, confusion and lack of stability surrounding that part of her life is a low level background condition which she handles with aplomb because Neptune is remote from the Nadir. However, Neptune is only slightly more than 4 degrees beyond the Nadir, which by turns should make her insightful, creative, careless and insecure. One could say that all people are like that occasionally, but I submit that Joyce experiences those qualities to a great degree; yet since Neptune is below the horizon and she has a Moon–Saturn conjunction, she controls her anxiety, dismay and tendency toward depression, such that others are unaware of how deeply she is affected by such things.

The very helpful trines between the Moon and Venus (4 degrees 17 minutes) and the Moon and Mercury (4 degrees 24 minutes) are the critical factors in her horoscope. Venus and Mercury are the most elevated bodies, and they give expression to all that is implicit in the other parts of the extended grand trine of which the Moon is an integral part. Moon trine Mercury confers kindness, understanding and a balanced view of life. These things are particularly underscored because the Moon is only 2 minutes (!) from the precise contra-parallel with Mercury. Moon-Mercury is also extremely good for one who works in writing, teaching, lecturing or publishing. Mercury has a lot to do with employment and, configured here with an exalted Moon, it suggests that one's job and art may be done at home or relate to houses, real estate and the things they contain. Occasionally people with Moon-Mercury combinations spend a lot of time on the road, living out of a suitcase. I think she has done that during some periods of her life because she has Gemini rising which inclines toward travel. The Moon trine Venus condition makes one the darling of the crowd, that is, in a general sense it inclines toward popularity. People with this combination are even-tempered, and have an uncanny ability to see what is required of them in order to keep the peace, avoid trouble and maintain a genial atmosphere. This quality is very important to Joyce because she has a strong tendency to blurt out the very things that will cause a commotion among less forthright and audacious persons than herself. That quality, symbolized by the mundane squares between Uranus and the Mercury-Venus conjunction, is distinctly off-putting and unpopular. The Moon-Venus trine allows her to get away with behavior that other people could not get away with, to the dismay of her opponents. Her Moon–Venus trine also suggests that she has what might be called "refined sensibilities." People with Moon-Venus like to be surrounded by quality, finery and art. It is often overlooked that the Moon has much to do not just with home, family and body but the prevailing condition of one's moment to moment world; in other words, ordinary conditions are lunar. Those conditions are overlooked in the search for the extraordinary. If somebody has an exalted Moon trine Venus they want, as a general condition of everyday life, to wear tailored clothes, drive fine cars and live in exclusive and luxurious residences, all the more so to confound the bitter memory of what is symbolized by Moon conjoined to Saturn.

Joyce has Gemini rising which makes her an intellectual, since the ruler of this intellectual sign is well disposed. Gemini is the most juvenile of the signs, and both men and women who have it rarely look their age. Other juvenile qualities attend Gemini rising, especially the tendency toward play, and fondness for children. The best elements of Gemini, from a practical point of view, are its cleverness, quickness, versatility and eagerness to learn. Joyce doubtless excelled in the classroom, learned to read and write early and fast, because Gemini rising gives strong verbal skills and surely has extended those gifts in adulthood. One who is hungry for information is characteristic of this sign.

Joyce is fortunate to have Mercury in a very close conjunction (7 minutes) with Venus. Mercury was stationary in right ascension the day before she was born, and it was only three hours away from perihelion at her birth. The Sun was applying to the inferior conjunction (on January 24) with Mercury. At inferior conjunction, Mercury is always retrograde; that is, Mercury is between the Earth and the Sun, instead of the far side of the Sun as at superior conjunction, so that Mercury is closer to the Earth at inferior conjunction than at any other time. Even if astrology is entirely symbolic and not the least causal, it follows even symbolically that a planet has a strong effect when it is near us. A planet in its station, retrograde or direct, is terrifically powerful. The old tradition about Mercury retrograde being unfortunate is totally without merit in my thirty-two years' experience. I know too many teachers and engineers with it to pay any heed to what it is supposed to portend. If anything, retrograde planets are *stronger* than direct ones and not the least impaired in their action. Mercury in Capricorn gives a sober and direct approach to the nuts and bolts of academia, but the conjunction with Venus suggests one who dispenses information so well, so effortlessly and so artfully that she could make other people want to know what she knows. Gemini rising with Mercury conjoined to Venus would make an excellent writer, teacher or speaker. She unquestionably has skills in those areas. The great virtue of the Mercury-Venus combination is grace and style, a fondness for arts and letters and an appreciation for the intellectual stature of civilization. People with this combination often literally dislike getting dirty and so won't have a garden. While people with this combination are not always sophisticated and rarely profound, they are smart, wily, crafty and adept at dealing with detractors. They are also not as nice as they appear to be from a distance. That condition is emphasized by the trines of the Mercury-Venus conjunction to Saturn, even though they are wide (more than 4.5 degrees). So Joyce would appear charming to an audience, but those who got to know her personally would see her hard and tough side personified by the Moon-Saturn conjunction, the Sun in Capricorn, and the underbelly of Mercury-Venus which is ostensibly delightful

285

but not a little sly and cynical. With this conjunction in Capricorn, that would be especially true.

Venus in Capricorn, while technically not a debilitation, is a position that is wanting in my experience. Only Mars and Saturn profit in Capricorn. Venus there suggests getting involved with people who are considerably older or younger—usually the former—than oneself, or one feels the distance of social or economic considerations in relationships or would-be relationships. In addition, people who are disagreeable, incompatible or distinctly odd frequently become the partners of Venus in Capricorn people. This quality is distinctly modified by the close mundane square between Venus and Uranus. Mercury was in the Midheaven when Uranus rose at Pryor, Oklahoma, within 1 degree on the day Joyce was born. It doesn't matter that they were off the angles at her time of birth. That the relationship existed at all on her birthday makes it very powerful inasmuch as it was so close. Venus in Capricorn mundane square Uranus, in the best of scenarios, suggests one who falls in love quickly, one who has early sexual experiences, one who is likely to be somewhat capricious and to do anything at least once, and one who becomes involved with someone of a different race, religion, creed, national origin or cultural matrix than one's own. But with the slightest concomitant affliction, and here there are two—Venus's trine to Saturn and her opposition to Pluto—one can experience unwanted as well as early sexual experiences. Furthermore, the opposition to Pluto often leaves people shut out from emotionally and sexually rewarding relationships, or they come in such profusion that one can feel desensitized to them. Pluto is an all or nothing switch. It acts vigorously or not at all. With Venus-Pluto combinations, relationships are never really over and can be rekindled instantly. In general though, Pluto to Venus puts emotional or actual distance between oneself and the love object. Prostitutes and celibates both have it. Pluto knows no middle ground. Joyce appears to have a fairly platic opposition, more than 4 degrees out and separating, but the opposition in mundo is only 3 minutes 6 seconds of right ascension which is .75 degrees. Because Pluto had more than 5 degrees of north celestial latitude at birth, it doesn't rise or set with its ecliptic degree. Because Venus herself had almost 1.5 degrees of south celestial latitude, she doesn't rise or set with her ecliptic degree either. The result in mundo, that is when Venus and Pluto were actually, not symbolically, on the horizon, is more than four times closer, in this case in mundo, than the opposition appears to be in zodiaco. That fact renders Joyce's Venus-Pluto opposition far more powerful than would first appear to be the case. It is an indication of a potent, sultry, smoldering desire nature, unrequited love and jealousy, all of which may very well be secret and unsuspected by those who think they know her well, because Pluto is below the horizon and remote from the angles. Actually, it gets more complicated because Pluto and Uranus are connected by mundane square themselves as well as with Venus; moreover, Uranus and Pluto are also configured with Mercury by mundane square, Uranus closely. Here is how that looks:

* Pluto sets in mundo when 15h 55m 40s of sidereal time is in the M.C.
* Uranus is in the Nadir when 15h 54m 41s of sidereal time is in the M.C.
* Venus rises when 15h 52m 34s of sidereal time is in the M.C.

In other words, there is a mundo T square between Venus, Uranus and Pluto. A similar but looser situation obtains between Mercury, Uranus and Pluto. It looks like this:

* Venus culminates when 20h 54m 02s of sidereal time is in the M.C.
* Uranus rises when 20h 52m 01s of sidereal time is in the M.C.
* Mercury culminates when 20h 51m 18s of sidereal time is in the M.C.
* Pluto is in the Nadir when 20h 40m 28s of sidereal time is in the M.C.

Even though the opposition between Mercury and Pluto looks wide at 13m 34s separation, that is less than 3.5 degrees in longitude; so actually the opposition between the two in mundo is a degree closer than in zodiaco, which renders it stronger than it appears to be. All the parameters of Joyce's grand trine, which these mundane squares plug into, have to be taken into account because it is the most important basic configuration in the chart. Mercury mundo square Uranus tends to make people outspoken, blunt, contrary and inclined to embrace non-standard points of view. They are frequently ahead of their time but equally often don't fit in well and evoke opposition. The best that can be said of this combination is that it is innovative, highly intelligent but not part of the mainstream. Mercury opposite Pluto is razor sharp intellectually, wants to get to the bottom of things and is frequently interested in uncovering the truth of a matter which is so old, half-forgotten or misunderstood that the true facts are unknown. People with this configuration are sometimes drawn to the study of dead languages. Mercury-Pluto investigates the way a detective would. People with this combination usually excel at school and do well in pure research or applied mathematics. Clearly then, Joyce is a highly intelligent, free-thinking individualist who lacks constancy in her relationships and has some difficulty with intimacy, although she is at once charming and engaging but private. She has the very close midpoint of Mercury=Sun/North Node, only 7 minutes from exact, which suggests much contact with children. She has all the earmarks of a teacher. Venus also makes the same relationship, that is Venus=Sun/North Node, but it is even closer to exact at only 1 minute from exact. That combination gives an avid interest in art. She could teach art or design.

The Node makes another important relationship with the Sun. The North Node makes the 150 degree or inconjunct relationship with the Sun, and the South Node makes the 30 degree or semisextile relationship with the Sun. A close relationship between the Sun and the Moon's nodes frequently points to someone whose work will have public impact, such as artists often enjoy. The Nodes in the third and ninth houses suggest a predisposition toward the affairs of those houses which relate, in the main, to education and the fruits of education.

The Sun in the seventh house in Capricorn, just short of the eighth Campanus house cusp, makes only one close aspect to a planet: a 49 minute parallel to Uranus. The Sun also applies to the trine to Uranus from 5 degrees out. The Sun in Capricorn is a perennial doubter, often lacking in confidence. It is also often subject to unusual physical or circumstantial limitations, which could be the case here with three bodies in Capricorn and a badly afflicted Moon. It is fashionable to downplay the negative element of Capricorn, as though the difficulties inherent in that sign could actually be overlooked. In fact, it is not a good place for the Sun because the solar qualities, which are active, creative, positive and generous, are thwarted in Capricorn. It is the sign of one who feels insecure no matter how much money is at hand, one who is practical, serious and not especially outgoing. There is an inclination to invest in land and only the best, most secure, conservative investments. Often poverty is the lot of the Capricornian but with the Sun opposite Jupiter, that is not likely here in adulthood. The opposition from the Sun to Jupiter, however is wide and separating, so wealth cannot be expected from it, moreover Jupiter is in its detriment and not angular. Still, the modest status of Sun opposite debilitated Jupiter is sufficient to lift Joyce into the middle class, which is out of reach for millions of people and a noteworthy achievement in view of her difficult beginning. The main effect of Sun opposite Jupiter is to make Joyce adventurous and to confound her conservatism and prudence with optimism and ill-considered indulgences, so that she vacillates between not being frivolous at all and too frivolous instead of a little. She is prone to take chances of a financial kind that don't turn out well, although her conservative approaches do succeed. Her common sense and prudence occasionally desert her and she is extravagant beyond her means. She entertains grand notions of religious cum spiritual realizations, only to find that they are sponsored by people who are not what they first seemed to be.

This issue is worsened by the fact that she has Sun trine Neptune, although since it is more than 6 degrees from exact, the effect is modest. Sun trine Neptune is an influence that deeply sensitizes the nature to a gossamer, ephemeral world that has as much subtle merit as misconception about it. The problem with this combination is telling one from the other. Sun trine Neptune knows that spirit is real but is likely to let fantasies have as much play as the subtle imagery that drifts into consciousness from the unconscious. She has an active imagination and sensitivity to subtle energy in approximately equal measure. Sun trine Neptune makes her somewhat more sensitive and emotional than she would be without it. Gemini rising is not sentimental but Sun trine Neptune is, so she is more prone to be upset, cry easily and to be too easily led than would otherwise be the case without the Neptune contact. Men may easily deceive her, drink too much and be more unreliable than she had bargained for. There is often a fondness for drama, fine arts and opera with this contact.

The best contact with Joyce's Sun is the trine to Uranus, because it is not debilitated in Taurus, and it is a closer aspect (5 degrees plus a parallel that is less than 1 degree) than either Jupiter or Neptune makes to the Sun. In addition, both of the latter are debilitated in Mercury's signs, which limit both their effectiveness and the quality of what they symbolize in her character. Neptune subtly weakens the Sun, but Uranus strengthens it with independence and the resolve to gain a measure of authority through original works and well-conceived and executed plans. Uranus is often seen in a troubled light but it is actually a first class benefic. People fortunate enough to have it often succeed in areas that are accounted prestigious. In the original exaltation scheme, Uranus was in Sagittarius, an aristocratic sign that stands for quality, legitimacy established via personal excellence, as opposed to the traditional sort, and the status and respect that attend money and power well earned. Uranus stands for all things excellent, outstanding, avant-garde, classically good, and in particular original compositions, works and solutions to long-standing and vexing problems. Sun trine Uranus addresses issues head on and sees them at another level than the one from which they heretofore have been viewed. It is casual, even "cool" in an unselfconscious manner. People who have this energy are perceived to stand for something solid, and certainly Joyce is seen in this way. It makes her a bit of an iconoclast, yet one who has won some authority. Sun trine Uranus tends to make one a boss, a manager, a partner (as in a law firm). It is somewhat unpredictable, as Joyce is, but has a vision which in the end is seen by less able or daring people as essentially correct well before anybody else knew it. Sun-Uranus has some bona fide charisma. Since Joyce has Uranus in the twelfth house, she could be expected to entertain some unusual and advanced positions with regard to the occult, which would exist alongside her bogus or misbegotten views. Notwithstanding these things, it should be remembered that neither the Sun nor Uranus are in, near or making an aspect to an angle, and the Sun-Uranus trine is not close, so the best that can be expected from the contact is modest. The qualities that attend the Sun–Uranus combination will not be known beyond her immediate circle of friends.

The most angular planet in Joyce's horoscope is Mars, powerfully placed in Scorpio, 5 degrees below the horizon in the sixth house. This placement injects an element of aggressiveness into her personality that invigorates it quite a lot in view of her seven planets in Earth signs. But since Mars is in the sixth house, health issues and accidents have probably plagued her through much of her life. The only aspect Mars makes of any significance is a sesquiquadrate to Pluto (1.5 degrees) fortified by a strong contra-parallel between the same planets (9 minutes). Mars-Pluto combinations are symbolic of an implacable will, perseverance, and the sort of steely resolve that can see Joyce through tasks and situations that most people would find daunting, if not impossible. Pluto makes extreme whatever it touches for good or ill. In this case, with both bodies well placed by sign, Joyce gets a surplus of energy and substantial physical reserves that make her a formidable figure and someone to be reckoned with. Mars makes four other relationships in zodiaco, which I consider of no account because they're too wide. Mars is semi-sextile the Sun but from 3 degrees out. Semi-sextiles are too weak for such an orb to be effective; likewise Mars inconjunct Jupiter from 3 degrees out. Mars makes 3 degree semi-squares to the Mercury-Venus conjunction, and while a semi-square is significantly stronger than a semi-sextile, 3 degrees is still too much to produce a noteworthy effect.

Jupiter in its detriment Gemini is in the first house. Jupiter is well placed in the first house because it confers protection and promotes growth, but it is so far below the horizon that its true value is somewhat limited. Jupiter has a lot to do with religion but placed in Gemini, the least religious of all the signs, its power to produce a strong faith in the conventional sense is circumscribed. Joyce is more at home in a cult than a church. The closest aspect that Jupiter makes is a mundane square to Neptune, 4 minutes 27 seconds (a bit more than 1 degree). Jupiter rose when Neptune was in the NADIR. Since both bodies are debilitated, this combination is likely to produce legal, financial and religious problems. There is also the distinct desire with this combination to say, "Stop the world. I want to get off." The urge to retire from the dusty hustle and hassle of the world is pronounced. A life devoted to service to others is another characteristic feature of this combination. Joyce is no doubt extremely hospitable, accommodating, idealistic and sensitive to the suffering of others. Like Moon-Neptune, Jupiter-Neptune is symbolic of receiving financial and material assistance that has not been, strictly speaking, earned. Since Jupiter and Neptune are in Mercury's signs, which points to an impersonal bureaucracy, she may receive money from the state. There is a great fondness for animals with the Neptune contacts. Joyce has Neptune with both Lights, Jupiter, Saturn and Uranus. With so much Neptune in her chart from various quarters, Joyce could become addicted to spiritualism in its various forms and inadvertently be tarnished by some scandal that she didn't really play any part in except through lack of discrimination.

Jupiter is semi-square Saturn (1 degree 32 minutes). That condition slows one's progress through life and makes material rewards come slowly too. It also is a depressing, dissatisfied influence, because people often feel that their efforts are not sufficiently rewarded or their responsibilities are too great. It is not, however, a sign of defeat, rather that what is to be gained in life that has lasting value only comes after a long and arduous struggle. Joyce is likely to feel with this semi-square that her life is a non-stop uphill battle. Since she also has the Neptune signs which suggest getting help in life, this Jupiter-Saturn combination obviously refers to what she gains by her own efforts, due to the position of Jupiter in her first house.

Saturn makes a close sextile (19 minutes) to Pluto, which is symbolic of a struggle against authority that most people don't undertake. This combination is doubly important because it involves the Moon. Saturn-Pluto as a combination symbolizes fighting against limitation; it is a mold breaker, or one who challenges authority and resists all attempts at confinement and containment. One tends strongly to want to find Saturn-Pluto combinations

291

away from the Lights because of the damage and difficulty they symbolize, particularly to the body and/or the family when they touch the Moon, as in this case. The sextile does not render the combination a good one, especially since it is so tight; it merely means that Joyce has had to fight hard against adversity and limitation in her life from the very beginning. She is probably stronger for it, yet would gladly give up her limitations if she could. Saturn-Pluto combinations impose harsh conditions on the native, particularly if they touch the Lights or the angles, that frequently impair mobility, block reproduction and circumscribe opportunity to some degree. Saturn makes two direct midpoint relationships that support this theme: Saturn=Venus/Neptune (21 minutes) and Saturn = Mercury/Neptune (24 minutes). The former limits her ability to find partners, and the latter requires her to fight despondency and gloom.

Saturn makes a conjunction with Uranus (5 degrees 11 minutes), which had been within orb of effectiveness for a year and a half when she was born. Too much should not be expected from long term configurations common to all horoscopes for extended periods, unless they touch the Lights or the angles, or the aspects are exact. Joyce personalizes the Saturn-Uranus conjunction because it is involved with her Moon. It makes her willful, tenacious, anxious to reform the conditions that confound her, a staunch advocate for the reversal of long standing policies which need overhaul and revision or to be discarded altogether. That makes her a thorn in some bureaucrats' sides, because the Saturn-Uranus conjunction will fight perceived abuses and not merely protest and walk away. Since the conjunction is in the twelfth house, Joyce is also likely to take issue with psychics and occultists who need to refine their craft.

Uranus also makes a very close mundane square to Pluto, only 59 seconds of right ascension from exact, which is less than 3 degrees. They are 65 degrees 32 minutes apart in longitude, which is much too wide to have any effect at all as a sextile, even a weak one. Sextiles are already weak when they reach a 3 degree orb. However, for the parallel through Pryor, Oklahoma, Uranus was in the NADIR when Pluto set in the west in mundo. That fact puts them very powerfully into a mundane square, whether they are angular at the time of birth or not. Uranus-Pluto in combination is a slow moving thing, even in mundo, but it makes three connections which keep it from being a dumb note and cause Joyce to personalize it to an extreme degree: both bodies configure the Moon; Pluto opposes the Mercury-Venus conjunction at the apex of her grand trine, and Pluto closely configures Mars, her only angular planet. First, Uranus and

Pluto together are a radical combination. The conjunction in the 1960s, the trine in the 1920s, and the opposition in the 1790s are demonstration of what a wild combination it is. Those were revolutionary times. Stability and adherence to the established order cannot be expected from people who have this combination as a natal condition if it plugs into the Lights or the angles. To some degree then, Joyce must be a fire-breathing hell-raiser. Saturn-Uranus wants to change things, but Uranus-Pluto wants either to destroy the old order or circumvent it completely. There is always present the attitude that manifests as rejection of the past and embraces freedom for its own sake, the end of restriction, the desire to go to extremes with regard to indulgences and self expression, and the very marked tendency to confuse freedom and license. This mundo square marks Joyce as a thoroughly modern woman who doesn't know the meaning of hidebound. She embraces change, sees the world as desperately in need of loosening up, and wants to implement those ideas in her little corner of the world. Three close midpoint combinations further this idea: Uranus=Moon/North Node (4 minutes), Uranus=Saturn/North Node (7 minutes), and Uranus=North Node/Midheaven (36 minutes direct). The first makes her instantly willing to lend her efforts toward a radical position; the second makes her essentially rebellious and unable to tolerate restriction in a generalized manner; the third inclines to make her impulsive and ready to adopt popular positions insofar as they address issues that bear on freedom versus restriction.

Finally, to test Joyce's rectified birth time, the following primary directions to the angles should work out pretty much on time if the birth time is right. Since I don't know where she lives now, and solar and lunar returns are very place-specific, this is the only quick test for the time. Primaries all take place during the first twenty-four hours of life, and except for transits they are the only predictive technique which is not place- specific. The primary directions here are those which direct the angles to the planets. There are so many interplanetary primaries that one could fill up several pages with them. Directions to angles in mundo are few in number, powerful and generally stand out in the life in bold relief.

The Nadir was directed to Neptune at age 23.27 years=April 1966. One suffers profound disillusionment, or goes down a road characterized by escapism. It signals a period when one is either trapped by circumstance, or in the embrace of spiritual rapture which could be bogus. The effect is strongest

293

for a period of about six months preceding the exact contact in April 1966, and for a period of about three months afterward.

The Ascendant was directed to Jupiter at age 24.38 years=May 1967. This is a time when you would experience a definite improvement in your life, more money, a good position, happiness and achievement. People often get the credentials or promotions they need to pursue their interests under this primary. The effect is strongest for a period of about six months preceding the exact contact in May 1967 and for a period of about three months afterward.

The Descendant was directed to the Sun at age 32.39 years=June 1975. This direction is very positive and corresponds to gaining power and responsibility, coming into one's own, getting success and acclaim. The effect is strongest for a period of about six months preceding the exact contact in June 1975 and for a period of about three months afterward.

The Ascendant was directed to Pluto at age 42.19 years=March 1985. This direction is usually symbolic of loss or a staggering blow that stops you in your tracks. Unless Pluto is configured with Jupiter, this direction is one of the hardest because it is often attended by the deaths of loved ones or sustaining injury oneself. The effect was strongest for a period of about six months preceding the exact contact in March 1985 and for a period of about three months afterward.

The Descendant was directed to Venus at age 49.75 years=October 1992. This is an excellent direction that often corresponds to meeting the love of one's life, getting one's heart's desire, finally achieving artistic success and the like. The effect was strongest for a period of about six months preceding the exact contact in October 1992 and for a period of about three months afterward.

The Descendant was directed to Mercury at age 51.3 years=April 1994. This direction is accompanied by fine works that relate to the best expression of one's skills in a technical or verbal manner. Problems which have been heretofore insurmountable are figured out; the book is finally written or published; one finds one's voice. The effect is strongest for a period of about six months preceding the exact contact and for a period of about three months afterward.

The remaining primary directions to the angles are far into the future. If the timing of these events is wrong, they should all be wrong by about the same amount if the birth time is close to being right. Primaries are a good rectification tool for that reason. That is, if all the events develop a year earlier than the stated birth time allows, the time should be advanced 4 minutes.

KIM ROGERS-GALLAGHER: LIGHT-HEARTED

STRATEGY

When I sit down to do a chart, I grab a yellow legal pad and my favorite pen, and ask the furry creatures who live with me for a volunteer to lap-sit. I believe that animals have far stronger intuitive faculties than humans—maybe because they don't let words get in the way of their observations. So, I love to have one of them with me when I'm doing a chart, whether it's on the phone, in person, or on paper. They seem to tune up my antennae simply by virtue of their presence, and I like to give my intuitive side first shot at any chart. At any rate, once my fuzzy partner and I are settled in at my desk, the first thing I do is what I've told my beginner students to do for years: I *look* at the chart. Not for aspects, planets in signs, or anything even remotely resembling methodology. What I'm after is a *feeling* for the entity—whether it's a person, an event, or a place—usually as a result of its shape. When my eye catches something striking—a pack of planets, an absence of planets, lots of angular planets, or lots of oppositions, for example—I stop, pick up my pen, and jot down my impressions. If I see a preponderance of planets across the top of the chart, for example, I picture a very public personality, one who considers career, reputation, and accomplishments to be primary—basically, someone who pays careful attention to his or her life's "bulletin board." A pack of planets below the horizon ordinarily tells me the opposite—that I'm dealing with someone who's less concerned with the "outer life" and more concerned with private matters, such as home, family, emotions, children, etc. It's funny, too—as much knowledge as I've accumulated from so many wonderful, knowledgeable astrologers over the years, it always seems that these "first impressions" are the ones that ring most accurate to my clients.

Once I've given my intuition time to kick in, I allow my Mercury to take over. I make an outline—basically, a breakdown of the tools this entity possesses, which will tell me what he or she expected to find when they arrived here on the planet. I start with the signs, aspects, and houses of the Sun and Moon, always noteworthy because they represent the "inner" and "outer" person, and then move on to the angles. I begin with the Sun, because I consider it to be the CEO or Executive Director of the corporation that's you. I think of the rest of the planets as directors of different departments of this corporation, but as the "head honcho," the Sun is indisputably in charge. He sends the other planets out to arrange and navigate life experiences that will allow you to learn your lesson during this incarnation.

Once that's done, I look at the Moon, the Head of Security and Comfort, to see what makes this person *feel*, how they cope with emotions in general, and what they do to make themselves feel safe and secure. The condition of the Moon also shows how this individual will go about showing their feelings—or not. A Fire-sign Moon in "exposed" houses such as the first or tenth, for example, will have far less trouble expressing his or her feelings in any circumstance, while an eighth or twelfth house Moon may stop at nothing to appear unaffected, preferring to show emotions only in private. The relationship between these two Luminaries is important, too, since it shows the "conversation" between the "inner" and "outer" person. So next, I look for an aspect between the Sun and Moon. If there's a connection, this usually points to a strong parenting experience—for better or worse. Even if they're not connected in any way, however, the condition of the Sun and Moon is a good way to get a thumbnail description of the individual's upbringing, the color of their parents' relationship, and therefore the types of relationships he or she may seek out in the future.

Next, I note whether the Sun and Mercury are in the same sign, since I've discovered that when Mercury is *not* in the same sign as the Sun, there seems to be a "two minute delay" when communicating. That is, the time it takes for the person to "translate" the Sun's experiences into Mercury's "language" often shows itself through caution, hesitancy, youthful shyness, or an amazing ability to "troubleshoot."

Next, I consider angular planets—that is, planets not only conjunct the angles, but also those who make aspects to the angles. I've discovered over time that these planets tend to "shout"—and I think it's for the following reason. Rather than holding twelve houses, think of the chart as really being *one* house, with twelve *rooms*. Each "room" shows a side of us, a slice of our personality that only comes out when a particular life situation presents itself, or when individuals who represent that life situation cross our paths. The angles, then, function as doorways that open up onto the outside world.

Continuing along that train of thought, then, it stands to reason that the Midheaven, which describes what we're "known" for, would function much like the "roof" of a house, allowing an "aerial view" of the individual's life, as would a home with the roof removed. The Nadir, the lowest point of the chart, correlates beautifully to the "cellar." In an actual, physical home, this is where we stash our dearest, most private possessions, and whether or not we take them out and look at them each day, what we store in our cellars says a great deal about what we need to be secure. This analogy takes us back to the meaning of the Nadir, basically our "emotional warehouse," where we keep not only the *memory* of how everything we've experienced *felt* the first time we tried it, but also the *results* of those first-time experiences. The Ascendant correlates to the "front door" of a home, which, although it may give little or no information about what's really inside that home, has everything to do with how comfortable and welcome visitors feel when they approach it. In that same fashion, an Ascendant that's "guarded"—say, with planets like Mars, Saturn, Pluto, or Uranus quite close to it—shows the possibility that it may be difficult for the individual to "open up" to others. The Descendant works well as an example of the "back door," because it shows how we act when we've left the "first impressions" of the Ascendant behind, and are operating with someone we've become comfortable with.

Planets in aspect to these angles, then, since they have "easy access" to the environment, have a lot to say about our relationships with others, and with the qualities that will show up powerfully in our lives. And aren't questions about relationships one of the first things any client brings to the table during a reading?

In short, I place heavy emphasis on a planet that is either connected to one of the Luminaries, or having an easy "out" to the environment via the angles. When I see a lot of angular planets, I know I've got what's usually a very strong personality, and the individual will usually identify quite strongly with the attributes of that planet or those planets.

The next thing I look for is a "theme"—say, several planets in Pisces, which is ruled by Neptune, several planets in the twelfth house, which is also ruled by Neptune, and Neptune on or aspecting an angle. If a strong "theme" exists in the chart, that "theme" will also inevitably show up in the individual's character.

When I'm done with all this and I actually sit down with my client, I try to explain the chart to them, rather than avoiding astrological lingo. Educating the person, as opposed to coming off like a soothsayer, to me, is primary. It grounds our astrology, and allows us to tell the individual *how* we arrived at our conclusions. I describe Venus and what she rules, for example, talk about the

297

qualities of the sign she's in, and explain, perhaps, that a square between Venus and Mars is much like an "argument" between these two planets, and between these two urges. I find that delivering the chart's information in this way legitimizes what I'm telling them and avoids the possibility of the individual wondering where exactly I'm getting my information. This also allows me to be more objective in my conclusions. Saying "this planet in this sign is often like this," for example, seems to work better than sitting down with someone and saying, "I believe *you* are... " It also gives me the ability to present problems without seeming to lay blame or criticize.

At any rate, that's the "how" of it. As far as software goes, although there are lots of wonderful programs out there, I prefer Solar Fire. I've found it to be fast, accurate, and varied in the techniques it allows me to use, such as Venus or Mars returns, which are quite helpful when the inevitable relationship questions arise.

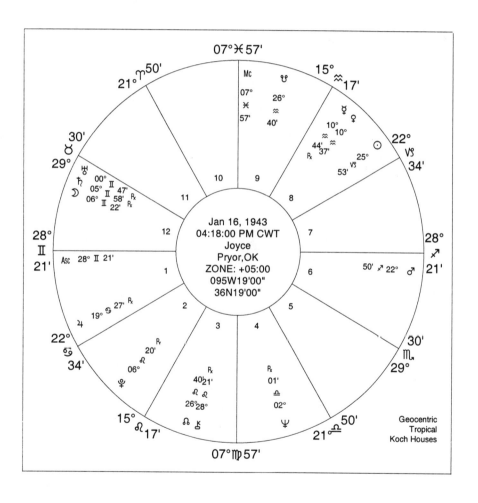

The first thing I noticed about Joyce's chart was that six of the ten traditional planets were banded together securely in tight, safe, little groups. This made me feel intuitively that she might be someone who thinks a lot about safety and security—and maybe even that she worries about it. The fact that these six planets are positioned above the horizon might ordinarily indicate that I was looking at the chart of a very public personality here, especially since the Sun and Moon are among them. But since they're all tucked into the eighth and twelfth houses, that doesn't seem to me to be the case. The eighth and twelfth houses, along with the fourth, are the Water houses. Since Water represents emotions, these are very private—and very secretive—places. And since the Sun and Moon are among the six planets in those tender spots, I immediately found myself wondering why she'd offer to be the subject of this project, a very public revelation of the deepest sides of her. I also want to mention how much I admire the courage it took for her to agree to do this.

First impressions done with, I grabbed a nearby cat, got out my yellow legal pad, and prepared to take some notes. I looked first to the Sun, the head of this "corporation" named Joyce. As I mentioned above, the Sun, the "CEO" of this chart, is in the eighth house, a dimly-lit place that's "owned" by Pluto, the most secretive and perceptive of all the planets. Planets that "live" in a house ruled by a planet necessarily take on some of that planet's qualities, much like people often exhibit some of the qualities of the surroundings where they live. Since Pluto is so good at operating "undercover," then, planets in his house always learn to operate that way, too. The Sun in this spot makes Joyce a combination analyst, detective, and observer—and a bit of an assassin, as well. In other words, when she's done with a relationship or situation, she's really and truly *done*—and there will be absolutely no more to say about it. No negotiating, no conversation, no explanations—and definitely no second chances. When she cuts something out and away from her life, it simply ceases to exist. It dies, in other words. In relationships, then, Joyce may have an "all or nothing" attitude. She probably either loves someone or really doesn't notice them much—there doesn't seem to be an in-between, with regard to relationships or anything else, for that matter.

In addition, thanks to what her Sun has inherited from Pluto's intense, calculating deftness at detective skills, over time, Joyce has likely learned a lot. Like not just how to meticulously and accurately *read* subtle clues, but also how

301

to send those subtle clues back out into the environment. Since she has two other planets in this shrewd place, including cerebral Mercury, I can also imagine that she would be quite masterful at typically "Plutonian" skills, such as using reflections in mirrors or windows to "watch," to assess a situation without seeming to. Mercury in this house can also be extremely "focused." In other words, when Joyce sets her thoughts on a project, it is likely impossible for her to think about anything else—or to change course—until that project is completely and totally finished, for better or worse. The high side of this intense, focused cerebral energy, then, is an ability to concentrate like many of us *wish* we could. Research and investigation, once again, and potent powers of analysis are also traits I believe she'd possess. The "down side"—or, at least, the more difficult side of Mercury's placement in the eighth house—is that, probably more so in youth, Joyce may have spent more than one long night tossing and turning. She's likely done more than one "instant replay" of a conversation or encounter, wondering what the individual(s) involved "really meant by that"—when, in fact, they "really meant" what they said, with no hidden agenda. As I said, however, this quality would likely have been far more difficult in youth.

I like to think of the way we get to know, and learn to operate, the astrological energies in our charts like this: imagine that you've just purchased a brand-new car. You love it, and it's great fun to drive, but it takes time to learn the thing—to learn how much pressure to put on the gas pedal and the brakes, or to locate the windshield wipers without taking your eyes off the road. At first, then, you may reach mistakenly for the radio in a rainstorm, hit the bright lights when you don't mean to, or stop and start too suddenly. But after you've had the vehicle for a while, operating it becomes second nature, as easy and natural as walking into your home at night and automatically flipping the light switch with your hand in the dark. In short, it seems that we all get better at learning how to operate our "vehicles" as time passes and we become more familiar with how they function. That analogy works well for all of our chart's energies, but it is perhaps even more true with the planets in the eighth and twelfth houses, since the "switches" in these houses are hidden—even to ourselves.

As Joyce grew older, then, she likely became less and less apt to use that Mercury to obsess, and instead learned to be quite good at using the "higher side" of it: understanding what was going on around her from tiny hints or clues she picked up from her environment, for example. In other words, after sixty years of "driving" this vehicle, Joyce probably knows instinctively how to use her Mercury to "read" a situation—through automatically reading body language for example, without even realizing she's doing it. In short, she likely now has a cerebral side much like a master chess-player, able to anticipate the next move someone will make or the next turn a situation will take.

Now, planets in the eighth house also like to be in control. They're excellent in crisis and emergency situations, since they don't often lose their heads or overreact, no matter what happens. In fact, the more urgent the circumstances are, the better and more skillfully eighth-house planets function. They seem to develop this element of control over events and relationships for a variety of reasons, but usually it's because there was a marked *lack* of control over their own life in their early years. That's also reinforced by the fact that this eighth-house Sun happens to be in Capricorn, and control is something the Sun in Capricorn absolutely must have. These folks often have control even when they *don't* want it, in fact. It's like they're automatically put in the position of being the "honorary principal" wherever they go, because others sense their competency and ability to organize.

The Sun in Capricorn also conjures up the image of a military general, however. The Sun is what we use to lead and take charge with, and Capricorn is nothing if not dutiful, above all else. Planets in Capricorn often mean that the people who own them quite literally wear a uniform, or that they have a need to carry on "official business." This is another indication that Joyce may have had a strict, severe, or highly-regulated upbringing, possibly because she was sent to a private or Catholic school (which would bring in the uniforms), to boarding schools, or even because someone in her family was literally in the military.

A military childhood ordinarily also involves a great deal of travel—of the long-distance variety. Although Mercury is technically in the eighth house, it's quite close to the ninth-house cusp. When I see a planet this close to any house cusp, I automatically consider it as having influence in both houses it straddles. After all, house cusps are imaginary lines—and there are no lines in the sky.

Long-distance travel, again, because of a "military" reason, is also indicated by Joyce's Mars in Sagittarius. Although we'll talk more about Mars later, I'd like to touch on it right now with regard to the possibility of a military childhood. Mars, after all, is the ancient God of War, and he's wearing the most travel-oriented of all the signs. Sagittarian planets are also quite curious, so if Joyce had been raised in a military environment, she would have had the opportunity to experience many different cultures while still being in possibly the safest, strongest, and most protection-oriented of all environments. This possible scenario would combine both needs of her Mars and of her protection-loving Capricorn Sun. Of course, on a deeper level, the Sun in Capricorn in the eighth house is also another "clue" that what we have here is someone who is an expert at handling crises. Keeping a calm, rational attitude intact in urgent situations necessitates a tremendous amount of self-control, and with the Sun both in Capricorn and in the eighth house, Joyce is undoubtedly great in times of emergency. In fact, it wouldn't surprise me to learn that she worked in an occupation that automatically made her the authority figure in situations that were both urgent and precariously balanced, delegating duties to others when those circumstances arose.

Regardless of what her early life was like, where she lived it, or of the nature of her career, however, and regardless of how much she may have tried at times to hide it, the qualities of Joyce's Sun are likely quite noticeable to others. Jupiter, the planet of expansion, is in an opposition to the Sun. Jupiter always has an entourage handy, and he naturally exaggerates the qualities of any planet he touches, first of all. But the opposition aspect also means that this aspect of her personality would primarily show up in her one-to-one dealings with others, especially in family situations, since it falls across the Cancer-Capricorn axis, which strongly relates to families. Jupiter is also the planet that owns Sagittarius, so he's where Sagittarian planets get their familiarity and fondness for long-distance travel. Putting Jupiter in aspect to the Sun in Capricorn links the two energies again, and provides yet another "clue" that leads me to believe that travel necessitated by professional duties is something Joyce has often experienced.

In addition to having the Sun in Capricorn, however, which is Saturn's sign, Joyce also has the Moon in a tight conjunction with Saturn—and I do mean tight. The two are separated by less than half a degree, in fact. With both of the "Lights" so tightly connected to this serious, dutiful planet, once again, the image of a strict, severe, or contained youth comes up. I also believe that Joyce was raised in an environment where showing "good manners," being civil and polite, and being respectful to authority figures were all highly emphasized. Along with what seems like a very genteel manner, however, Joyce's chart also seems to show a very strong "gut instinct."

With both the Sun and Moon in Water houses, which tend to turn up the volume on a planet's "antennae," Joyce's perception, intuition, and instinct are

304

all undoubtedly quite strong and quite accurate. If she was raised in a very rational, practical atmosphere, however, it may have taken her a bit of time actually to pay heed to that side of herself. That goes double since planets in these houses—especially planets as important as the Sun and Moon—often feel vague, mysterious and even untouchable, even to their owners, most especially during the younger years.

It's also interesting to return to the fact that it's not *just* the Sun and Moon who are focused on a need for privacy. In fact, of the ten traditional planets, Joyce has tucked seven of them protectively into Water houses. Again, these "rooms" give planets residing in them an innate love of privacy, caution, and perhaps even secrecy—not to mention mysteries, puzzles, and intrigue. The Sun in Capricorn adores working with "just the facts, ma'am." This combination likely means that Joyce is fascinated with forensics, investigations, etc.—in short, with anything that allows her to analyze facts perceptively and intuitively, yet be rational and practical at the same time.

But let's get back to the Moon, another well-guarded planet in this cosmic entourage. I think of the Moon as being the head of the Department of Security, Safety, and Comfort. In Gemini, it seems that "variety is the spice of life" is her motto. Change, then, is something that Joyce would likely feel comfortably familiar with, something that would make her feel as if all is well in the world. Since the Moon has a hand in describing the color of one's youth, as does Gemini, these are other indications of movement—and possibly a lot of it—during her early years. Joyce is also primarily "built" of Air and Fire. Her chart shows only one of the traditional planets in Water, and only one in Earth, which often means there wasn't much stability in the childhood home—geographically, at least. Since the Moon is snuggled up against Saturn—and remember, he's the "Military General" of the chart—when travel happened, again, it may have been necessitated by the duties or responsibilities of the structure of the childhood home and/or of the person who was in charge of that home. So again, this seems to indicate that moving was an ordinary, accepted part of life for Joyce as a child—and once again, a military upbringing comes to mind.

At any rate, since this Gemini Moon does live in the twelfth house, it's a given that expressing her emotions is something Joyce only does in private. In fact, the Moon in this house is famous for being absolutely horrified at the thought of letting *anyone* see how it's really feeling—especially when it comes to the "less popular" emotions: hurt, sadness, or anger, or other traditionally "difficult" emotions to express. The fact that Gemini is an Air sign, not an element that a planet as Watery and emotional as the Moon is classically very comfortable in, further reinforces a picture of someone who keeps control of her feelings in public situations, and intellectualizes them, rather than actually experiencing them, even in private.

Now, twelfth house Moons also point to someone who loves and needs privacy. In fact, they're known to often "hide out" or "hibernate" for days, preferring their own company (or the company of pets, perhaps, in the case of my own twelfth house Moon) above the strenuous, draining aspects of interacting with others. Although she may have a very successful career, then, as her Capricorn Sun would insist she did, Joyce undoubtedly likes to retreat to the safety and security—and privacy—of her own home, to "draw back and regroup" when being with others becomes emotionally tiring.

In addition to the strong theme of protection, privacy, and following the rules that's indicated by Saturn's touch, however, there is a bit of a rebel in this chart, too—but it's what I might call a "stealth" rebel. For starters, Joyce has two planets in Aquarius, Uranus's sign, in the eighth house, and Uranus, the owner of Aquarius and the King of Rebellion himself, is in the twelfth house. People who have Uranus in this house are often quite surprising to others—and sometimes even to themselves. This is an odd house for Uranus—in fact, since he's such a fast-moving, spontaneous, and radical kind of guy, it's hard to think of him in this house at all. When he is here, however, it may be an indication that something odd, offbeat, or unusual goes on in private—something that may even be considered "shocking," by society's standards, at least.

At any rate, with all that rebelliousness as well-hidden as it is, Joyce probably doesn't show this unpredictability easily, and when she does, it's likely a big surprise to those who know her—although I'd be willing to bet that very few people really "know" her. The funny part of all this is that with Gemini on the Ascendant, the "front door," again, of the chart, she would *seem*, outwardly, to be chatty, open, light-hearted, and carefree. As I've stated, however, the front door of any home has little or nothing to do with what really goes on in that home. In other words, the first impression someone makes is often quite different from what they're like when we get to know them—and that's most definitely the case with the owner of this chart.

But let's talk more about caution, and get back to rebelliousness later.

Joyce's Mercury, one of those planets in Aquarius, is, as I talked about earlier, not in the same sign as her Sun, so there is likely a bit of a "delay"

306

between the moment that she thinks of something and the moment she chooses to communicate it. And with the amount of caution this chart shows, she would already be liable to wait until she was absolutely, positively, completely sure of what she was saying before she'd actually say it. This, then, is a "double-dose" of caution that comes into play before Joyce opens her mouth, another indication of a someone who'd be absolutely terrific in crisis or urgent situations. As such, I see someone who'd make an excellent counselor, too—and someone who'd be able to work through emergency situations with others with skill and accuracy, managing to get everyone involved to perform their duties quickly and efficiently.

Joyce's Mercury is also exactly conjunct her Venus. By uniting Mercury, the planet of communication, with Venus, the planet of love, relationships, and who and what we hold dear, an astrological formula is produced. This formula is responsible for the concoction of sweet words and tender thoughts, from music to poetry to words of solace and comfort, such as a counselor would use.

Of course, Mercury is not just retrograde, it actually stationed to turn retrograde just a day before she was born. This is yet another indication, possibly the strongest we've seen so far, of a personality that would wait, think, and speak only when sure. Planets that are stationary seem to have stopped in their tracks, or "folded their arms" stubbornly—they have a point to make, and they won't be ignored. With Mercury in this condition, it's also another "clue" that points to a top-notch trouble-shooter. In Aquarius, a picture of someone who is quite comfortable in situations that others are not comfortable with is emerging. If we add in the fact that Mercury and Venus are also in a trine with her Moon-Saturn conjunction, we see that the side of her who loves and respects privacy—in fact, insists upon it—works easily with the side of her who knows exactly what to say to offer comfort in times of urgency.

Of course, since Venus is the goddess of love, harmony, beauty, and on a more surface level, money and possessions, this is also the chart of a very passionate, intense person. Those qualities would likely emerge only under what might seem like "odd" reasons, however, or under what others might think of as unusual circumstances. Still, this is someone who probably either loves with all of her heart, or not at all. Aquarius planets aren't famous for doing anything half-way. It's also interesting to note that Venus is in Aquarius, a sign that's not necessarily known for being especially "warm and fuzzy." Aquarius planets, in fact, are often viewed or experienced by others as being part of a personality that's often "cold" or "detached"—but I've found that that coldness is usually only displayed in a situation where emotional "self-defense" seems necessary to the owner. (I have the Moon in Aquarius, and I must admit, when I feel threatened or frightened, I "raise my warp-shields," so to speak. Although the Moon in this sign also supposedly makes me quite "chilly," any of my friends—most of whom have been in my life for at least one decade, all of whom will be in my life until the day I leave the planet—will tell you that I'm really quite the opposite.)

"Friends," however, is the operative word here. Aquarius is far better at relationships that are platonic than at anything even remotely resembling a restrictive emotional commitment—and "restrictive" is the operative word in this sentence. An Aquarius planet that feels "free" is a planet that can express love and affection without worrying that its precious independence might be revoked as a result. Trying to tie it down, however, impose rules on it, or tell it what to do, will cause an Aquarius planet—and its owner, of course—to head for the hills.

Adding a planet as objective and freedom-oriented as Venus in Aquarius to the intensity of the eighth house seems then to be a bit of a dilemma. It may be one of the astrological formulas for "Come Closer, Get Away Syndrome," as I like to call it. In other words, this may be someone who is completely and totally involved with a dear one when that dear one is present, yet quite able to function when they're not. The Aquarius costume that Venus is wearing, in other words, allows Joyce less chance of "obsessing" about the partner—which is something Venus in the eighth house could easily do.

Now, since the twelfth house is so jam-packed with planets, let's look at the condition of Neptune, the "owner" of that house. Neptune has also been tucked into a safe place, in the fourth house—indicating even more of the need for secrecy and even more compassion. At some point, I would have to say that there have been secret goings-on in Joyce's home, both her childhood home and her present home—but with Neptune in a trine to respectable Saturn, it's likely for entirely above-board reasons. Sounds like a paradox? Well, isn't that what we all are, when it comes down to it?

Neptune in the house that represents home also paints a picture of someone who "wanders," both physically and emotionally. This could, then, be someone who may wonder who and where they really "belong." If there was, as I believe, considerable movement in childhood, this would be yet another indication that Joyce really needs to set down roots of her very own to make herself feel safe and secure. I have also seen Neptune in this house indicate that there was something about the person's childhood that's a secret—in other words, that they may have been adopted, or not really know one or both parents. With the Moon in Neptune's house and Neptune in the Moon's house, a "theme" along these lines is established. That goes double even without the fact that the Moon and Neptune are also connected by a trine, which makes the flow of communication between them go off easily. And neither the Moon nor Neptune is involved in any traditionally "hard" aspects that would "interrupt" the flow or communication between them.

Literally speaking, of course, Neptune's placement in the house that rules home could also mean Joyce is most comfortable in a home by the water, or at a religious or extremely "well-protected" place. Perhaps she toyed with or actually took up a religious vocation. Since Neptune also loves "playing pretend," she may be a bit of an actress at times, too—or need to be, to do her type of work. Either way, she undoubtedly has a terrific imagination and a very strong belief system, and I'd advise her to give them both full rein.

Again, all this secrecy surrounding home, family, and early roots could indicate adoption, and if so, it would probably have been early on—during infancy, perhaps, when the progressed Moon would have come to a trine with Venus-Mercury, indicating a "written contract of sweet words and emotions," or around age two, when Pluto would have made an opposition to these two by transit.

Another paradox I found quite striking in Joyce's chart is the fact that while Neptune is well-hidden in the fourth house, she rules the Midheaven, indicating that she has a hand in what Joyce considers to be her life's work—her vocation. So again, rather than dealing with someone whose life is out in the open, there is another indication of secrecy here. Is she an agent? A detective? A forensic specialist? Or maybe, a nun?

But let's talk about the rebellious side of Joyce. In addition to the Mercury-Venus conjunction that's so very tight in Aquarius, a famously unpredictable and rebellious sign, she has Mars in Sagittarius, too. This is another planet-sign combination that's famous for having a strong love of freedom and giving the owner a highly restless personality, too. Mars is the ancient God of War, but he's also the planet who describes *how we take action*—and what motivates us to take that action. In Sagittarius, Mars is moved to act by several things. A love of travel and change is certainly on that list, along with the urge to pursue knowledge and a higher understanding of the big picture. Joyce is likely quite fond of all those things—and with Mars posited in her house of work, travel and instruction may play into her job duties.

Mars is also the planet that's most closely conjunct to an angle. He's sitting guard at the door of the seventh house, the place where one-to-one relationships are handled. And regardless of the fact that Mars is actually *in* the sixth house, being this close to the seventh house cusp, I don't see how his influence *couldn't* show up in relationships. Mars here could point to someone who looks for excitement, adrenaline, and adventure in relationships. Perhaps she had a fondness in youth for what we might think of as "bad boys," or perhaps there was a bit of drama in her early relationship experiments. At this point in her life, she has likely moved on to the "higher" side of Sagittarius with relation to others, searching out those who keep her mind amused and interested, and who stimulate her philosophical side. Either way, since Sagittarius is on the cusp of the relationship house, she absolutely can't tolerate being bored by a partner. In fact, that would be the quickest way to lose her attention—and her affection, too, adding the influence of Venus in equally restless Aquarius.

But what would incite this Mars to take action? Well, unfairness is at the top of the list of things that Sagittarius planets absolutely cannot tolerate—so with Mars in Sagittarius, injustice or intolerance would likely make Joyce lose her temper faster than just about anything else. Since Mars rules the eleventh house of friends and group affiliations, she may also be involved with people or organizations who share her ideals.

Well, now. We've peeked in at the planets in the twelfth house, and at the condition of Neptune. Let's take a look at Pluto, the natural planetary owner of the eighth house, the "room" where Joyce's Sun, Mercury, and Venus live. Pluto himself is in the second house, which has everything to do with who and what we hold dear, as well as with the traits and qualities, both in ourselves and in others, that we most highly value. Pluto here indicates someone who needs to be in total control of how the "daily bread" arrives. Like the Moon and Neptune, however, Pluto and Venus also share a very tight bond. In addition to the fact that they're in opposition, they're also in each other's natural houses. Connecting Pluto and Venus unites the principles of power, control, and manipulation with those of love, beauty, and money—and the opposition also occurs across the axis of resources, both personal and shared. This could mean that Joyce is often on the receiving end of gifts or inheritances, or that she deals with the finances of others. She may also be involved with death, literally or figuratively, through funeral home work, hospice care, medical procedures such as autopsies, or grief counseling. In fact, the more I look at what we've got here, including the extreme secrecy in this chart, and the fact that Mars, who rules cutting instruments, is in the house of work, the more I see the possibility of someone who may, indeed, work with the dead, or has lots of contracts with the goods of the dead. Then again, she may also be a veterinary surgeon, since Sagittarius loves animals, a twelfth-house Moon has incredible compassion for "little things," and, again, since Mars rules cutting tools.

Adding to this same theory is the fact that Pluto is also the "nose" of what I see as a rather loose, but still quite potent, "kite" formation in this chart. In other words, if we connect the Moon-Saturn conjunction by trine to Neptune and by trine to Mercury-Venus, an Air Grand Trine emerges—and, again, admittedly, it's a bit loose, but I think it's still notable. Add Pluto in an opposition to Mercury-Venus, and we have a "kite." What's a kite? Well, it's a grand trine with a "guiding force," in my opinion. So if the grand trine indicates ease—but, in some cases, laziness, too—Pluto's presence here would change all that by pushing those planets into action. Basically, he's a driving force, pointing to the *raison d'être* that these planets have conspired to produce. It's also a rather unusual set-up, and unusual set-ups indicate unusual lives.

So what is this kite aiming at? Complete and total independence of her finances, for starters. But also, since Pluto rules the sixth house and the Sun is in Pluto's house, it's another indication that the type of work Joyce prefers has to do with Pluto's topics, i.e., detective work, research, investigation, acting from "behind the scenes," etc.

The one planet we haven't really discussed at length yet is Jupiter—which is rather odd, considering he's in the first house, a very public place, and since he's a "larger than life" kind of guy. Jupiter is the King of the Gods, and as I said earlier, he never fails to enlarge the qualities of the planet(s) he touches. In Cancer, Jupiter's talent for putting others at ease emerges as a knack for nurturing, soothing and comforting—and since it's in the first house of personality and appearance, it's quite easy for Joyce to show this side of herself. Since Jupiter rules the seventh house of one-to-one relationships, this loving, sympathetic quality would necessarily come out in all her encounters. Her way of extending to others is through taking care of them—but with the Moon, the owner of Cancer, in the twelfth house, she likes to take care of them in private.

Joyce's nodal axis is quite interesting, as well. The South Node in Aquarius is particularly striking, simply because it's in Aquarius, first of all, but also because it (and, of course, the North Node, as well) is connected to Mars, and

311

because this axis is the only connection that Mars makes in this chart. When Mars touches the nodes, learning self-assertion, how to "just say no," and how to defend oneself are all huge issues, along with simply knowing when to act—and when not to act. In Sagittarius, acting with a "large" purpose—in other words, a mission of some kind—is primary. On another level, she may also be being asked by the Universe to learn to work precisely with iron, steel, or cutting tools.

The South Node in Aquarius and the house of higher understanding also indicates that there is a well of past-life memories that are quite unusual—and possibly, à l'Aquarius, quite striking as well. In Jupiter's natural house, long-distance travel is also once again shown as something Joyce is familiar with. In conjunction to the asteroid goddess, Pallas Athena, Joyce also seems to have arrived on the planet with a strong astrological history of strategy—perhaps, again, even military strategy. She's not only good at it and familiar with it from her experiences during this lifetime, then—she's been good at it for some time.

The North Node in Leo means it's time to shine—to take credit for what you're good at, and to show off a bit. Although it's totally unfamiliar territory to Joyce, she also needs to develop a strong sense of self-worth and pride. Putting the North Node in the house of communication means that learning to speak, write, and organize her thoughts is also of primary importance to Joyce's life-goal—and, because Mars is in the house of work, to her career, as well.

Learning the lessons of the North Node may not be all that easy for Joyce to accomplish, however. Chiron, the Wounded Healer, is attached to the North Node by conjunction. Now, I've worked a great deal with Chiron over the years, and I've found that, above all else, Chiron shows our "soft spot," our "Achilles's heel." In short, it's one of the most tender, easily wounded spots in the chart, so going after the lesson of the North Node with Chiron in the neighborhood could make that lesson a rather painful experience, at times. While Chiron is the place where we are at our most vulnerable, however, it's also where we're at our most compassionate. Ever hear the expression "you can't heal a hurt you haven't experienced?" That seems to have been penned exclusively for Chiron. In the third house, both the healing power of words and the ability of words to hurt are emphasized, which seems to work well with Joyce's Mercury-Venus conjunction in the eighth, and her Jupiter in Cancer in the first house. In short, the need for sympathetic and empathetic communications is indicated in several spots.

312

I've also found that wherever Chiron is posited in the chart is a place where we deal with what that which is "broken," "handicapped," or "wounded," but whether it ends up to be people, animals, or objects that bring us those experiences is hard to say. Folks with Chiron in the sixth house of work, for example, often find themselves in careers relating to health, worker's compensation, or literally, in the chiropractic field. Attached to the North Node, however, and in the cerebral third house, there is something about dealing intellectually with imperfection—and helping others to accepting it in themselves—that Joyce needs to learn this time out.

Since the nodal axis straddles the axis of long and short trips and higher and basic learning, it's also easy to see that Joyce may have traveled to get her education. Above all else, communication—learning to do it well, and appreciating the power of it—is definitely one of her quests on the planet this time out.

A look at the other asteroids also says quite a bit about Joyce's chart. First off, Juno, Jupiter's mythical wife, the goddess of marriage and commitment, is sitting right smack dab on the SEVENTH house cusp, a very potent spot for her, since it's the "door" to the house she most loves—the house of one-to-one partners and committed relationships. In Sagittarius, however, this ordinarily devoted goddess may be distracted or even a bit fickle when it comes to partners—unless, of course, she happens to find someone who's Sagittarian in nature: e.g., a world traveler, a teacher, a philosopher, or an activist, perhaps for women's rights or animal rights.

Vesta, the ancient priestess, is posited at the top of the chart, the most public spot there is. This is a further statement about Joyce's commitment to her career, as well as her absolute devotion to it. I just can't see her pursuing any career that didn't truly mean something to her—like a religious life, perhaps?

Vesta was also the goddess who was honored when a bride took fire from her mother's home to the home of her husband—so I see something in Vesta that carries a strong tone of family tradition in it. Perhaps Joyce is "following in someone's footsteps," career-wise? If we add in the influence of Ceres, the "mother-daughter" asteroid, posited in the house of career, this is stated twice.

I finished up my analysis of Joyce's chart by looking at the fact that six of her planets are retrograde, which traditionally indicates that these energies aren't fully developed until later in the lifetime. Since they're all attached to the planets in her "kite," I'd be willing to bet that she didn't discover her "true purpose" for quite some time, perhaps well into adulthood.

In all, the "wide-angle" picture I see here is of someone who is quite strong—stronger, in fact, than even she herself may know—quite compassionate, and extremely devoted to her causes, whatever those might be. And while she may express her emotions only in private, I would be willing to bet that those dear ones with whom she shares her life will never doubt for a second that she cares.

ROBERT HAND: MEDIEVAL

The analysis of this chart has been done from a modified medieval perspective. The "medieval" part of the method consists largely of the technical methods used, along with some of the medieval modes of analysis.

The "modified" part of the analysis consists of two things: first of all I have used the "modern" planets, Uranus, Neptune and Pluto. Obviously a medieval astrologer would not have used these planets because they had not been discovered. However, unlike most modern astrologers, I use these planets only insofar as they make aspects and occupy houses. I do not use them as house rulers or significators[1] of any kind derived from their relationship with the signs. Therefore, I use Saturn as the ruler of Aquarius, Jupiter as the ruler of Pisces, and Mars as the ruler of Scorpio. In fact in medieval and ancient astrology, Aquarius is Saturn's preferred sign, and Scorpio is Mars's preferred sign. I do not quarrel with there being a similarity between Pisces and Neptune, or between Scorpio and Pluto, but mere similarity is not the actual basis of rulerships.

But I do seriously dispute the modern association of Uranus with Aquarius on any basis, especially that of similarity. Aquarius is a fixed sign and Uranus is extremely changeable, if not itself the essence of change. Aquarius is a very social sign while Uranus often tends be either antisocial or to ignore issues as society generally sees them. Aquarius is of course a progressive sign, while Uranus can be either very radical (in the leftist sense of the word) or extremely conservative, as long as being conservative is sufficiently extreme, hence, radical. Uranus can be extreme in either direction. This is why one finds extreme conservatives with a strong Uranus. Of course Aquarians are also perfectly capable of being conservatives (although not so extremely). Two interesting examples are Franklin D. Roosevelt and our current vice-president, Richard Cheney, who are not only both Aquarians but who have nearly identical chart placements except for Uranus being more prominent in FDR's chart.[2]

Second, I do not "read" a chart in precisely the medieval manner, or more accurately, I do not limit myself to the kind of outer-world-oriented event prognostications that the medieval astrologers usually gave. There is very little characterological analysis in medieval astrology, and almost no effort was made

315

to understand the mechanics of any particular outcome. In fact the Greek word often used to designate astrology was *apotelesmatika*, or the study of outcomes.

In modern astrology there is a much greater emphasis on character, personality, and psychology. Some might say too much, but I feel that the use of astrology as a developmental tool for individual growth is a valid and important one. Thus my methods of analysis are different from the medieval in this respect. However, having said that, I also have to say that the methods of medieval astrology give me much more information concerning probable practical event manifestations than I get from any modern system. And there is nothing about the medieval techniques that prevents one from doing a modern personality and character-oriented type of reading. In this respect, combining modern delineations with medieval techniques is very fruitful.

Another of my modifications of the standard medieval practice involves houses. But here I go back to an earlier time rather than using a more modern method. The most common medieval house system was the one we call the Alchabitius system.³ The system I use is a house system which is normally associated more with Hindu and ancient Greek astrology than medieval, but was in fact also used by a number of early medieval Arab language astrologers such as Masha 'Allah, Abu Ali Al Khayyat, and Omar of Tiberius. We now call this system "Whole-Sign Houses." It is really is not a house system at all in the usual sense of the word.

In modern house division, there are two twelve-fold divisions of the chart, the signs of the zodiac, and the twelve "mundane" houses. In the Whole-Sign system, the signs also serve as houses in exactly the same manner as employed in modern Sun sign astrology. In the Sun sign method, one's Sun sign is used as the first house of the chart. In the ancient method, the rising sign (and sometimes other signs as well) is designated as the first house. This may sound like another system called "Equal Houses," but it is different. In Equal Houses, the houses start with the degree of the Ascendant, and then each subsequent house starts 30 degrees after the previous one. Each house cusp is the same degree of a sign as the other cusps, and the house commences with that degree.

For example, let us say that someone has an Ascendant of 12 Virgo. In Equal Houses, the second house would begin at 12 Libra, the third at 12 Scorpio, the fourth at 12 Sagittarius and so forth. Or in some versions of the system, the house might commence at 5 degrees prior to the cusp, say, at 7 Virgo for the first house, 7 Libra for the second, and so forth, the cusp's being the most intense part of the house rather than the beginning.

In Whole-Sign Houses with an Ascendant of 12 Virgo, the first house commences at the first degree of Virgo and ends at the 30th; the second house then is all of Libra, the third all of Scorpio, the fourth all of Sagittarius, etc. It is not clear whether 12 degrees of each sign is a cusp or not, in the sense of a cusp's being the most powerful point of the house, but it is clear that the houses commence at the beginning of the sign.[4]

In both Equal and Whole-Sign systems the Midheaven "floats," that is, it is not necessarily in the tenth house as measured from the Ascendant. Vettius Valens of the second century C.E. informs us that when this happens, the sign that the Midheaven is actually in does double duty, giving indications for both the "house" that it is in, as measured from the Ascendant, and for the usual indications of the tenth house.[5] Meanwhile in such a chart, the tenth sign from the Ascendant gives additional indications for normal tenth house matters. With Whole-Sign Houses I find that this works very well, with most people's careers being a combination of the significations of both signs.

The only other departures on my part from the medieval system are not really departures so much as the result of my selection of a set of a particular set of methods from late Classical and medieval authors. Every ancient and medieval writer also used his own peculiar subset of the available techniques. I do the same. It is just that my subset is not exactly the same as any one ancient or medieval author's. But I have taken some care that the methods I do use are theoretically and philosophically compatible with each other. Most of the techniques are medieval, and when I use any method that is earlier or later, I will mention it.

In this particular analysis I do something which I do not normally do explicitly in preparing for a client, although I do it implicitly and less systematically. In this article, I have shown the method explicitly in order to make the medieval method of analysis clearer to the reader. This consists of an analysis of the cosmic state of each of the seven classical planets,[6] noting what strengthens or inhibits the manifestation of each in the chart. I do the same for the houses. In medieval astrology, the purpose of this was to ascertain whether a particular planet or house was in "good" or "bad" condition. In the former case, this was supposed to mean that the planet or house would consistently manifest in the best possible or at least in a good way, in the latter case the reverse. In modern astrology, the categories of "good" and "bad" are usually judged to be too simplistic. We want to know what "good" is good for and in what way, and what "bad" is bad for and in what way. I support this, although

I think that the medieval methods do give us some sense of the probability of things working out well or badly in each area of life.

The interpretation follows a modified form of a standard medieval interpretation framework. The main modification will be that there are certain parts of this framework which modern astrology sees very differently, or which modern astrologers in general choose not to deal with. In the first category goes the discussion of "enemies." For a medieval nobleman, this was an important item for discussion. But while it is not completely irrelevant in modern analysis, most moderns, including myself, regard this area of life as having to do with personality patterns that get us into trouble more than with actual persons who are one's enemies. Also, in a blind analysis such as this, it is not a good idea to go too much into outer-world manifestations such as "enemies" without being able to talk to the subject whose chart is being analyzed.

In the second category, things that we choose not to talk about, is death. I am especially reluctant to discuss that area of the chart in a blind analysis. To do so would be in my opinion most irresponsible. I, therefore, list death as a category, but pass over it in silence. Other categories may not be completely analyzed, again because it is best to deal with them only when the client is present.

Here is a list of the standard Medieval categories for analysis:

1) Parents
2) Brothers and Sisters
3) Those Who Have Not Grown
4) Form, Figure and Constitution of the Body
5) Impediments and Infirmities of the Body of the Native
6) Qualities of the Soul of the Native
7) Impediments of the Soul
8) Fortune and Wealth of the Native
9) Honor and Dignity of the Native
10) Native's Magistery and his Work
11) Sexual Unions
12) Children and Their Relationship Toward the Parents
13) Native's Friends and Enemies
14) Native's Foreign Travels and Journeys
15) Religion and Faith
16) Qualities of the Native's Death

These categories as listed are taken from a sixteenth century textbook of natal astrology by Johannes Schoener,[7] but are derived from Ptolemy. In practice I do not usually take these topics in this order, nor do I usually cover all of them. However, for the purposes of this article I will do so, even if it is only to say that I am not going to cover a particular topic for the reasons that I have indicated previously.

Each of these categories are associated with a list of houses, planets and other points that are associated with them. These lists vary from source to source somewhat. The ones that I give will be a bit simplified from some of the medieval sources, but do include those factors that I have found to work.

The software used to prepare this reading is software for DOS written by myself for Astrolabe Software. Two packages are involved, Chartwheels II to compute the chart, and Printwheels for the printout. In the printout Koch house cusps are given, but also the signs of the zodiac around the outside. I used this format because I want to show the Ascendant and Descendant, and the Midheaven and Nadir as lines running through the center of the chart. I can only get this by printing out the other cusps as well. But for the houses I actually read the signs around the outside.

Table I – Dignities and Conditions of the Classical Planets.

Planet	Conditions	Judgment	Planet	Conditions	Judgment
Saturn	In first. Perfect Mutual Reception with Mercury. In its own Triplicity. In Hayz. In Trine of Venus. Retrograde. Essential Dignity=8	Fortunate except for being Retrograde	Venus	In the Ninth. Swift in Motion. Received by the Trine of Saturn. Trine of Moon. Essential Dignity=-5 but mitigated by the reception	Fortunate.
Jupiter	In a Succedent. In its Exaltation. In Opposition to Sun. Retrograde. In Sect. Essential Dignity=4	Fortunate but not perfectly so.	Mercury	Perfect Mutual Reception with Saturn. In first. Conjunct Venus. In its own bounds and Face. Retrograde. Essential Dignity=8	Fortunate except for being Retrograde.
Mars	In the Seventh. Peregrine. Swift in Motion. Out of Sect. In Bounds of Saturn. Essential Dignity=5.	Not fortunate.	Moon	In the First. Received by Trine of Mercury. Trine of Venus. Peregrine. Slow in Motion. Conjunct Saturn. Essential Dignity=-5.	Somewhat impeded.
Sun	In the Eighth. Swift in Motion. In its own Face. In sect. In Bounds of Saturn. Essential Dignity=1.	Somewhat impeded.		Other Conditions of the Moon. *With only Traditional Planets*: Moving from the conjunction of Saturn to the Trine of Venus. *With Modern Planets:* Moving from the Sextile of Pluto to the Trine of Venus.	

Table II – Conditions of Houses

House	Conditions	Judg-ment	House	Conditions	Judg-ment
1st—Gemini	Received by Trine of Mercury, its Ruler. Moon Present. Venus Present. Saturn Present. Mars Opposes.	Fair	7th —Sagittarius	Venus Sextiles it. Mars Present. Its Ruler, Jupiter, is Disjunct but Exalted. Saturn Opposes it. Moon Opposes it.	Poor.
2nd —Cancer	Jupiter Present in its Exaltation. The Moon, its Ruler, Disjunct Sign. Sun Opposes.	Fair.	8th —Capricorn	The Sun Present. Its Ruler, Saturn, is Disjunct.	Fair.
3rd —Leo	North Node Present. Sextiled by Moon. Pluto Present. The Sun, its Ruler, Disjunct.	Poor.	9th —Aquarius	Venus Present. Received by Trine of Saturn, its Ruler. Moon Trines it.	Good.
4rh —Virgo	Nadir Present. The Sun Trines it. No Planets. Mercury, its Ruler, Disjunct. Uranus Squares it. Saturn Squares it.	Poor.	10th —Pisces	Received by Trine of Jupiter, its Ruler, which is Exalted. Midheaven in it. Squared by Uranus and Saturn.	Fair
5th —Libra	Received by Trine of its Almuten, Saturn. Received by Trine of Venus, its Domicile Ruler. Moon Trines it. Sun Squares it. Neptune Present.	Good.	11th —Aries	Received by Trine of Mars, its Ruler. Received by Square of Sun, its Almuten. No Planets in it. Moon Sextiles it.	Good.

322

6th — Scorpio	Part of Fortune in it. Jupiter Trines it. The Sun Sextiles it. Mars, its Ruler, is Disjunct.	Fair.	12th — Taurus	Received by Square of Venus, its Ruler. Jupiter Sextiles it. Sun Trines it.	Good.

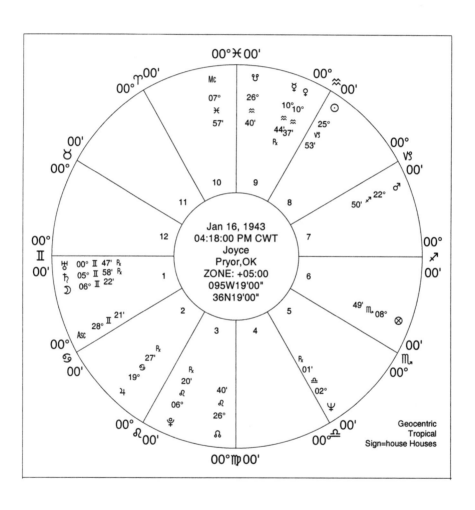

Before I proceed with the reading in the order of the topics listed in "The Strategy," I want to say a few things about Tables I and II. I want to remind the reader that the "Judgments" are only intended to give a rough idea as to how the planet or house is likely to work out if the native[8] does *absolutely nothing* to improve the outcome. Usually, good or favorable indications work reasonably well even if the native does nothing, where "impeded" or "poor" planets or houses need some conscious attention. One of the differences between most of the traditional works and modern works in astrology is that the moderns tend to place more emphasis on the native's ability to improve potentially negative manifestations of the combinations in the chart.

I. The Parents and Their State of Being.

The parents in the chart are indicated by the following:

The Father:
1) The fourth house, Virgo, and its ruler, Mercury. We would also use the sign of the Nadir separately if the Nadir were not in the fourth house. But in this case it is.
2) The sign and house of the Sun in a daytime birth, the sign and house of Saturn in a nighttime birth, and their rulers. This is a day birth, therefore we use the Sun sign, Capricorn, which is ruled by Saturn. As a result Saturn comes into play even though it is a day birth.
3) To a lesser extent we look at the Sun at all times of day. In this case this is redundant.
4) The sign, house and ruler of the Part of the Father. In this chart the Part is 7 Scorpio 59. Its ruler is Mars.[9]

The Mother:
1) The tenth house, Pisces, and its ruler, Jupiter. We would also use the sign of the Midheaven separately if the Midheaven were not in the tenth sign from the Ascendant. This is the same situation as with the Nadir sign for the father.
2) The sign and house of Venus in a daytime birth, the sign and house of the Moon in a nighttime birth. This is a day birth, so we use the sign of Venus,

325

Aquarius, and its ruler, Saturn. This tells us that Saturn is going to have something to say about both parents.

3) The sign, house and ruler of the Part of the Mother. In this chart the Part is 23 Libra 35. Its rulers are Saturn, which is the Almuten, and Venus, the sign ruler.[10]

As I have said, the medieval astrologers in particular added quite a few more indicators, but some of them are based on techniques which I do not feel comfortable using.

Now, when I refer to the sign of something such as the Sun, Moon, Venus, or Saturn, Part of the Father or Mother, I intend to use that sign as if it were the first house of a whole sign house chart. This is no different from the modern method called "turning the wheel" in which one uses the house of something as a first house and measures the other houses from it. In the modern method, for example, if we want to look at the relationship with paternal aunts and uncles, we would look at the third house from the fourth house, which is the sixth house. The method used here is the same, except that we use the sign containing a planet or Part as a first house, as well as using the fourth sign from the Ascendant for the father and the tenth sign for the mother.

We start with the fourth house. The fourth house actually to some extent stands for both the father and the mother, as it means parents in general. It is only when we want to make the distinction that we use tenth house for the mother. But we want to do that here.

General Observations in the Chart concerning the Father: The fourth house is Virgo, which is rated as in poor condition. This is because its ruler, Mercury, is in a sign, Aquarius, which makes no classical aspect[11] to the fourth house sign, Virgo. This is what it means to say that a sign's or house's ruler is disjunct. The ruler makes no aspect to the house. This weakens the significations of the house and makes it more difficult for affairs associated with the house to turn out well. And Mercury, the ruler, is retrograde which also does not help. The good news is that Mercury is conjunct Venus, and trine to Saturn. And that trine involves a mutual reception; that is, Mercury is in the sign of Saturn, and Saturn is in the sign of Mercury. This makes Mercury work much better than otherwise.

If we look at the relationship with the father from the point of view of the Sun sign and its ruler, Saturn, we get more information. The Sun is in the eighth sign from the Ascendant. This is not an especially fortunate placement because the eighth sign is disjunct the rising sign. Also Saturn, the ruler of the Sun sign, is in the first house, Gemini, which is of course again disjunct the Sun sign. But the Saturn is not especially unfortunate as Saturn goes. Saturn is in a daytime chart which it prefers, a masculine sign which it also prefers, and it is on the same side of the horizon as the Sun (both above) which means that Saturn is in its Hayz.[12]

Now if we look at the Part of the Father which is in Scorpio, we again have a ruler, Mars, which is disjunct the sign, and Mars is not in very good condition.

Judgments concerning the Father:

1) Joyce's experience of her father was not a bad one but it may have lacked closeness and warmth.

Reasons: None of the classic signs of a really bad father relationship are present. First, there are no afflictions in houses relating to the father. Second, there are no close hard aspects involving the Sun, Saturn, and Mars. Third, Neptune is not present in any of the relevant houses which might indicate that her father had an alcohol problem or something similar. However, the disjunctions between the houses and their rulers indicate a lack of closeness between herself and her father.

2) Her father was a fairly capable individual who may have had a high status in either his profession or his community or both.

Reasons: Saturn and Mercury are in good condition (aside from Mercury's being retrograde), being in strong Mutual Reception,

3) Her father may have had at least moderate wealth but with some serious ups and downs.

Reasons: This comes from the Part of Fortune being in the same sign and almost the degree of the Part of the Father. But the Part of the Father and the Part of Fortune are squared by Pluto, Mercury and Venus.

4) Her father may have existed in circumstances which he did not completely find supportive. These *may* have manifested in her father's having had bad health, or something else of the sort, but it is not really clear in which area of his life the difficulties manifested.

Reasons: Mercury, the ruler of the fourth, is retrograde.

5) Matters concerning her relationship with her father and his general state were more difficult early in Joyce's life than later on.

Reasons: The rulers of the relevant signs are in better shape than the planets occupying them. In general, rulers indicate later times of life than do the planets which occupy the houses.

General Observations in the Chart concerning the Mother: The tenth house is in better condition than the fourth. The main problem within this house is the squares from the first house planets, but this is not enough to undo completely the positive qualities that result from the ruler of the house being Jupiter exalted in Cancer and trining the house.[13] The tenth house itself is empty. The Midheaven degree itself has Venus as its Almuten. This is because Venus is the exaltation ruler of Pisces, as well as the ruler of the bounds or terms in which the Midheaven is located.[14] Venus is disjunct Pisces, but that is not a problem because Jupiter is in trine, and Jupiter is dignified.

If we go to the sign of Venus, we again come into the fact that Venus is trine to the Moon and to Saturn which is Venus's ruler. Thus Saturn receives Venus by trine. Venus is therefore in very good condition even though it is opposite Pluto.

The sign of the Part of the Mother is Libra which has Neptune in it, and whose sign ruler, Venus, is in trine to it (reception). And the Almuten of Libra, Saturn,[15] is also in trine to it (another reception.) The Moon also trines the sign, and the Moon is doing something else: it is going from the conjunction of Saturn and the sextile of Pluto to the trine of Venus. This is extremely positive for two reasons: the Moon is making a sextile to one end of an opposition (Pluto), and a trine to the other end which stabilizes the opposition (Mercury conjunct Venus). This means that the Venus-Pluto opposition is not likely to manifest in a strongly negative manner.

Judgments concerning the Mother:

1) The relationship between Joyce and her mother was very complex and held many opposing tendencies in balance. This would have give the relationship a fluctuating quality, sometimes going one way then the other.

Reasons: Every difficult indication that is present concerning Joyce's mother and Joyce's relationship with her is countered by something positive and also powerful. The Venus-Pluto opposition could have been a tendency toward jealousy or envy, emotional power struggles and guilt. In this chart, it is more likely to indicate a stronger than normal emotional involvement between them but sometimes a difficult one.

328

2) The mother-daughter bonding was stronger than average even with an outward appearance of reserve between them, and with strongly disciplined, sometimes restricted, communication between them.

Reasons: The Moon conjunct Saturn is often an indication of a problematic or difficult relationship with the mother. But the Moon is going from the conjunction of Saturn to the trine of Venus. This counteracts emotional alienation and distance.

3) Joyce's mother had a strong influence on Joyce's spiritual life, or she may have been foreign-born, possibly both.

Reasons: The ninth house is very strong and Jupiter connects with the indicators of her mother.

A final note: remember that while modern astrology would place the Moon-Saturn conjunction in the twelfth house, a difficult placement, whole-sign houses put the conjunction in the first house even though it is quite a bit above the horizon. Thus modern houses and whole-sign houses give a very different prognosis for the relationship between Joyce and her mother.

II. Brothers and Sisters.

Siblings in general do not usually have the same kind of impact upon a native as parents and, therefore, it is harder to say much that is reliable about them from a native's chart. In fact the whole effort of trying to derive information about persons other than the native from a birth chart (aside from the parents) is a very difficult procedure, especially because the houses that relate to these other persons often have many other significations as well. The third house is not only siblings, it is also other relatives (as long as they are of the same generation, cousins, for example), neighbors and other persons who are in the day-to-day environment, plus short journeys, writing, communication, etc. From this forest of possible significations, sorting out siblings is not an easy task. In traditional astrology there are things we can look at as well which help sort things out. We will see some of these below.

Siblings in the chart are indicated by the following:

1) The third house, Leo, and its ruler, the Sun.

2) Both medieval and Hindu astrology say that the planet which is the general significator of siblings is Mars. This will not be used much here. I just list it for the sake of completeness.

3) The sign, house and ruler of the Part of Siblings. In this chart the Part is 11 Leo 20. Its ruler is the Sun.[16] This means that Leo is the place of siblings both in terms of houses reckoned from the Ascendant and with regard to the Part of Siblings.

Judgments concerning Siblings:

1) There were probably not many, if any, siblings, or they had little impact on Joyce.

Reasons: Leo is one of the barren signs (along with Gemini and Virgo). [17] Also, the Sun, the ruler of the sign, is disjunct the sign. In addition, the ruler of the third house is in a house disjunct the rising sign and disjunct the ruler of the rising sign (Mercury).

2) If she has siblings, the relationship could have been difficult but not completely so. But something of a tragic or dramatic nature may have occurred in connection with siblings.

Reasons: The only planet in the third house is Pluto along with the North Node (a point, not a planet), but the sextile from the Moon and Saturn should have helped.

3) Siblings, if any, would have more likely been brothers rather than sisters. If there were several siblings (unlikely), there might have been one sister.

Reasons: A masculine sign in the third house indicates brothers rather than sisters. But the sextile from the Moon to Pluto would argue sisters.

4) There might have been a considerable age difference between Joyce and her siblings.

Reasons: This is indicated by the placement of the Sun ruling the third in Capricorn.

III. The Physical Form of the Native

We turn now to Joyce's physical form and appearance and to the general quality of her physical constitution. In medieval astrology this part of the analysis had two basic objectives. The first was to describe the observable physical form of the body, what the person looked like, etc. The second was to determine something much more technical, the type of the "complexion," a

330

term which originally referred to much more than the appearance of the face. It referred to the basic makeup of the body, as it is influenced by the four humors of traditional Western medicine taught by Hippocrates and Galen. The four humors are the blood, yellow bile, black bile, and phlegm. The physical-psychological types that correspond to the dominance of each of these four humors are the sanguine type, the choleric type, the melancholic type, and the phlegmatic type, respectively. These in turn correspond to the four elements respectively, Air, Fire, Earth, and Water.

Here are the main things looked at to determine both the appearance and the complexion type.

1. The Ascendant, its sign and its ruler or Almuten.
2. Any planets in the first house or which aspect the Ascendant within the orb of the aspecting planet. The effect is most powerful if the aspect is partile, that is, the aspecting planet is in the same degree of its sign as the Ascendant is in its sign.
3. The Moon by sign and phase.
4. Planets which aspect the Moon.
5. The season of the year.
6. The Ruler of the chart as a whole.
7. Any planet which is close to #6 in the power of its rulership over the chart as a whole.
8. Fixed stars which are near the Ascendant.

In this article I am going to simplify the list a bit, because some of the elements of the list are ones with which I am not sufficiently experienced, while others seem to be based on theoretically flimsy foundations. The ones that we are going to omit are the phase, but not the sign, of the Moon; the season of the year; the ruler of the chart as a whole (and other such ruling planets); and the fixed stars. There are serious theoretical problems with the Moon phase. The season seems to be too general a criterion and one which applies to too many people. If it is a factor, it must be a relatively minor one. The determination of the ruler of the chart as a whole and of those planets which share in that rulership has a serious problem. There is no standard method for their determination. Finally, there is too much disagreement about the use of fixed stars for us to apply them to this purpose at present. This leaves us with:

1. the rising sign and its rulers.
2. planets in the first house.
3. planets which aspect the Ascendant.
4. the Moon sign.
5. planets which closely aspect the Moon.

In our chart the rising sign is Gemini, and its ruler is Mercury in Aquarius which aspects the first house planets. The Moon is in the first house as well, along with Saturn and Uranus which conjoin the Moon and trine Mercury. Therefore, we would expect all of these factors to influence the physical type. Venus also trines the Moon, which should have an impact on the physical type. All of these planets are in Air signs, which seems to predispose Joyce to being a Sanguine type with a strong Mercurial influence.

Judgments concerning the Physical Type:

1) Joyce should be graceful in appearance and look younger than her years.

Reasons: This is due to Gemini rising and Mercury ruling the Ascendant. Also, the aspects of Venus both to the Ascendant ruler, Mercury, and to the Moon should make Joyce a fairly attractive woman.

2) Joyce is shorter and not as slender as she would have been with earlier degrees of Gemini rising. But she should not be stout.

Reasons: According to medieval astrology, the earlier part of Gemini tends to be more slender and taller, the later part less so. The presence of Uranus and Saturn conjunct in the first should further counter any tendency toward stoutness that might otherwise result from the late Gemini Ascendant and the first house Moon.

3) Her appearance should have a quality of tension combined with energy.

Reasons: This would be due to the Uranus-Saturn-Moon conjunction.

4) Her facial form should be a rounded rectangle, that is, a fairly regular face, neither narrow nor wide, in which the width of the face seems pretty much the same from the upper to the lower part narrowing only at the chin.

Reasons: This is due to Gemini rising with a prominently aspected Mercury. Hair color, facial coloring and such are impossible to determine without knowing anything about her ethnic background.

5) There may be some redness in her skin or hair coloring or freckles.

Reasons: Mars is in the seventh house not far from the Descendant. Any planet near an angle can affect the physical appearance. Mars indicates redness.

IV. Impediments and Infirmities of the Body.

Under this heading comes the entire corpus of traditional medical astrology. In modern terms, it is simply the method of finding out what kinds of illnesses or injuries a person is predisposed to. In modern astrology we usually just look to the sixth house, considering it to be the house of health. Actually in the tradition it was not the house of health; it was the house of illness. The house of health was the first house. Consequently, afflictions to the Ascendant, to its ruler, to the Sun and to the Moon were considered as well as the sixth house. Therefore, our list of things to consider in Joyce's chart is as follows:

1. The Ascendant and its ruler, Gemini and Mercury.
2. The sixth house and its ruler, Scorpio and Mars.
3. The seventh house, and planets in the seventh which aspect either the Ascendant or planets in the first. In Joyce's chart Mars is in the seventh, but it does not closely aspect either the Ascendant degree or any planet in the first, there being no planets in the first.
4. The Part of Azemene also known as the Part of Inseparable Infirmities, 14 Capricorn 47, and its ruler which is Saturn.[18] In Vettius Valens, this same Part was called the Part (or Lot) of Accusation and had a generally evil reputation. In medieval astrology it became more associated with illness, especially chronic illness.
5. Many sources add the twelfth and its ruler for chronic as opposed to acute illnesses. In Joyce's chart, this is the sign Taurus and its ruler Venus.

Judgments concerning Illnesses:
1) Joyce should have good health in general coming from a kind of wiry toughness (the Saturn involvement) and generally good energy.
Reasons: First of all we have the strong mutual reception between the first house ruler, Mercury (which is in the ninth), and Saturn in the first house, combined with Mercury conjoined with Venus, and both of these trine the Moon in the first along with Saturn.
2) There is a tendency toward illnesses of the generative organs and the excretory system.
Reasons: The sixth house is Scorpio. Also, the Azemene part is in Capricorn (Capricorn being the eighth house from the Ascendant).
3) Illnesses may also come from the lower back or kidneys.

333

Reasons: The ruler Mars is in the seventh house.[19]

4) There may be possible weakness or illnesses coming in the head region (physical not mental).

Reasons: The ruler of the Azemene Part is Saturn in the first house.

Judgments concerning Humor Type and General Complexion:

1) Joyce's health in general should be quite good.

Reasons: The sanguine physical type (see previous section) was traditionally considered to be the most balanced and well-tempered of all physical types. This is supported by the general conditions involving the first house and its ruler. So even though the sixth house and Azemene Part do give indications for various kinds of illness, these are not likely to be a major issue in her life, except possibly during periods when the transits indicate major stresses being placed on these parts of her body.

V. Qualities of the Soul of the Native.

Whatever the title of this section may sound like to modern ears, it does not refer to metaphysical or "spiritual" issues in reading the chart. To a traditional astrologer, an analysis of the native's soul is an analysis of the native's character. The word "soul" for a medieval thinker encompasses personality, character, psyche in the modern psychological sense (insofar as they thought of the soul that way), the general level of intelligence and, most importantly, behavior. In fact, the medieval delineations of the soul were extremely behavioral; that is, they spoke almost entirely in terms of what an individual was likely to do and how he or she was likely to behave. In my descriptions below, I will speak much more in modern psychological language than a medieval astrologer would have done. However, to illustrate the traditional style, here is an example from William Lilly, a description of the positive Saturnian temperament: *Grave persons, with a certain austerity, advised, excogitating profound matters, taciturn, solitary, laborious, patient, preservers of riches, sparing and thrifty, studious for the owne profit, zealous, mistrustfull.*[20]

Totally aside from the style of the character description, the method of deriving the description was completely different from the modern. Modern astrologers derive character somewhat non-rigorously from a mixture of Sun, Moon, and rising signs, along with a consideration of major aspects and combinations within the chart. Sometimes modern astrologers are so broad in their use of psychological interpretations that it seems that there is nothing in the chart in modern astrology that does not relate to personality and character.

The medieval method is derived from Ptolemy with some medieval additions based on Aristotle. It classifies character based on planetary types rather than sign types. In this it departs especially from modern astrology, which seems to think almost entirely in terms of signs. The medieval model of the soul consists of three levels:

Level I—The Vegetative Soul. This consists of the life energy of the body independently of any kind of consciousness that we can understand. The name for this level of the soul comes from the fact that it was considered to be the only level of soul found in plants. This level of soul is basically connected with the humoric type of the body and for the most part is derived from the same factors as described above. The ruler or Almuten of the Ascendant is also strongly involved here.

Level II—The Animal or Sensitive Soul. This is the level of soul responsible for sensation as in hearing and seeing, and for locomotion. This type of soul was considered characteristic of animals and roughly corresponds to the upper layers of the subconscious mind as understood in modern psychology. This is represented by the Moon and its ruler or Almuten.

Level III—The Intellective Soul. This is the conscious soul that reasons and is aware of its own existence. It is considered to be most characteristic of humans and other forms of sentient life. This is represented by Mercury and its ruler or Almuten.

It was common to evaluate an Almuten of the Soul by examining the rulerships of all three positions, the Ascendant degree, Moon degree, and Mercury degree, and finding a single planet that had the strongest rulership over all three positions taken at once. Such a planet along with any other planet that came close to its level of rulership, and also along with any planet that strongly aspected the first planet mentioned, determined the basic soul type. I have discovered that, making allowances for the extreme characterizations of the types given in the medieval literature, this is an effective technique. I should mention that sometimes the Almutens of each of the three points (the Ascendant, the Moon, and Mercury) were taken separately, but this does not lead to as clear a typing as one might like.

1) The Almuten of the Ascendant is Mercury.

2) The Almuten of the Moon is Mercury.

3) The Almuten of Mercury is Saturn.

4) The Almutens of all three taken together are Mercury and Saturn just about equally.

Judgments concerning Character Type:

1) Joyce is extraverted, sociable, talkative and generally agreeable, not given to quarrels and conflicts.

Reasons: Joyce is a sanguine temperament type.

2) She should be of above average intelligence, more serious and reserved than the usual sanguine temperament type. She should also be interested in ideas which are challenging and difficult, or abstruse.

Reasons: Her sanguine type is dominated by a mixture of Mercury and Saturn in mutual reception, in good houses, the first and the ninth. This indicates a positive Mercury-Saturn type. Such Mercury-Saturn types are good at organizing ideas and are good critics or judges of the ideas and thinking of others.

3) She should have considerably more originality and interest in offbeat or even eccentric subjects than one would normally find in the Mercury-Saturn or sanguine types.[21]

Reasons: Uranus is involved with the Moon and Saturn.

Judgments concerning Mental Illnesses or Problems:

Usually at this point in the medieval analysis there is a consideration of the "Impediments of the Soul." This would be a discussion of mental illnesses or other illnesses that might affect mental functioning or behavior. However, the consideration of personality problems in general is an area of astrology in which modern astrology is superior to traditional. Having said that, let us proceed.

1) There are very few indications of any serious emotional or mental difficulties.

Reasons: Joyce's chart is unusually free of all the medieval indications of serious mental difficulty. The three basic Almutens are Mercury, Mercury and Saturn. These two planets aspect each other in perfect mutual reception and there are no serious afflictions to either of them, aside from Mercury being retrograde. The only thing that might indicate something less than the ideal (aside from Mercury being retrograde) is that Pluto opposes the Venus-Mercury conjunction, and Uranus conjoins Saturn and the Moon. The latter has already been commented on, and the former does not represent any kind of serious mental or emotional problem. Again all the indications are of a person with a well-developed mind which functions quite well.

VI. Fortune and Wealth of the Native.

This is simply an analysis of how the native handles and gains money, and also her attitude and behavior towards possessions in general. The method I will use here is the medieval one, combined with one derived from the Greek astrologer Vettius Valens from the second century C.E. The usual method given by the medieval astrologers is derived entirely from Ptolemy, with some Arabic additions that I will not be using here. Here is what we will look for:

1) The second house and sign, and its ruler or Almuten, and any planets in it. In Joyce's chart we have Cancer as the second house sign, ruled by the Moon in the first, and with Jupiter exalted in it.

2) The house and sign of the Part of Fortune and any planets in that sign. The Part of Fortune is 8 Scorpio 20 in the sixth house from the Ascendant, ruled by Mars in Sagittarius in the seventh house, with no planets in the sign of the Part.

3) The eleventh house or sign counted from the Part of Fortune, also known by Valens as the "Place of Acquisition,"[22] and its ruler, as well as any planets in that sign. The Place of Acquisition is Virgo, the fourth Ascendant house, ruled by Mercury which is in the ninth.

4) The eleventh house or sign from the Ascendant, its ruler and any planets in that sign. This usage is implied in Valens, and explicit in Hindu sources. The eleventh house is Aries ruled by Mars in Sagittarius in the seventh. There are no planets in the eleventh.

Although I do not have any sources which explicitly state this, I believe that the eleventh houses from the Ascendant and Part of Fortune (the Place of Acquisition) are slightly different in signification from the second house counted from the Ascendant. I believe that the eleventh houses are more about how one gains money or wealth, while the second has more to do with one's manner of handling it. The house and sign of the Part of Fortune, I believe, has more to do with the general attitude toward wealth and therefore makes the most general statement concerning wealth. The modern method for evaluating wealth relies rather heavily on the second house. It just does not seem to give accurate or sufficient information. Modern astrologers do extensive mental gymnastics to account for this deficiency. Many modern astrologers say that the second house signifies "values" without defining what is meant by "values." The method shown here from traditional astrology which combines several portions of the chart has given me much better information on this subject. The Part of Fortune in particular, even though it has many more significations than wealth, is a very important point for this purpose.

Judgments concerning Wealth and Money:
1) She has a cautious attitude toward handling money.
Reasons: The second house ruler, the Moon, is part of the major complex of planets in this chart involving also Saturn, Uranus, Mercury and Venus. Saturn is generally a somewhat favorable planet in this chart and, therefore, does not impede the Moon as a significator of wealth.

2) Joyce should make her money directly by her own efforts (such as through self-employment) rather than from inheritance, family, or even a salary.
Reasons: The presence of the Moon ruling the second in the first indicates this. This is often an indication of self-employment.

3) She should be generally successful in handling money, although great wealth is not indicated.
Reasons: The presence of Jupiter in its exaltation in the second indicates this. The retrograde motion of Jupiter impedes the effect of the exaltation somewhat. Also, the ruler of the Place of Acquisition, Mercury, is well placed in the chart and is the Ascendant ruler as well as the ruler of the Place of Acquisition.

4) Her money comes from her action in the world, i.e., a career.
Reasons: Jupiter also indicates this (it rules the tenth). This may contradict #2.

5) Her income from a counseling or consulting profession, or from a profession that involves some kind of conflict or combat (attorneys, for example), income from a partnership, or income from a marriage. This last contradicts what we have seen previously and so may not be true.

Reasons: Jupiter ruling the tenth and the seventh can indicate this, as well as the location of Mars, which rules the Part of Fortune, in the seventh ruling the sixth house and the eleventh house.

6) She may have also made money from some kind of helping profession or service profession.

Reasons: The Part of Fortune in the sixth house, which is Scorpio, can indicate this.

7) Family or real estate could be a source of wealth.

Reasons: The Place of Acquisition in the fourth house indicates this. This is not consistent with other indications and may be of lesser importance.

8) The law, higher education, medicine, or occupations having to do with foreign persons or places, may be among the sources of income.

Reasons: Mercury in the ninth ruling the Ascendant and the Place of Acquisition shows this.

VII. Honor and Dignity of the Native and the Native's Magistery [23] and Work.

The medieval astrologers were much more likely to inquire into someone's social class and rank than we are, living as we do in a society where class is very fluid, and distinctions of rank (outside of the Republican Party) are not as important as they were in the Middle Ages. However, in this section I will concentrate on career and profession and not very much on social status, even though in traditional astrology the tenth house was used much more for the latter, which is not say that they did not also use it for profession. In this they followed Ptolemy, who primarily used that planet which last rose before sunrise as an indicator of profession, along with indications given by Mercury, Venus, and Mars.

This is an area where thus far I have found traditional astrology to be wanting. The main problem is that the traditional methods simply do not encompass the incredible array of possible professions that exists in the modern world. Therefore, I will be following the more conventional modern practice of relying on the tenth house from the Ascendant and its ruler, along with the sixth house and its ruler, which indicate the nature of the work. However, there are two major additions to the modern technique that I will be using, and they are from the Greeks, namely the Part of Fortune and its tenth and eleventh houses, and I also will use to a small degree the sign and house of the Part of Spirit. Therefore, here is our list for Joyce:

1) The tenth house and its ruler or Almuten. In Joyce's chart this is the sign Pisces whose sign ruler is Jupiter, but whose Almuten is Venus. This is because Venus is the exaltation ruler of Pisces, and also the ruler of the subdivision of Pisces known as terms or bounds, in which the Midheaven is located.

2) The sign of the Part of Fortune and its ruler, which are Scorpio and Mars in the seventh house from the Ascendant.

3) The tenth sign from the Part of Fortune and its ruler. This is Leo ruled by the Sun.

4) The eleventh sign from the Part of Fortune, which is Virgo ruled by Mercury.

5) The house of the Part of Spirit, not so much its ruler. The Part of Spirit is 17 Aquarius 25 ruled by Saturn. [24]

6) The sixth house from the Ascendant and its ruler. This is again Scorpio ruled by Mars.

This may seem like a rather large array of factors, but there is a structure here. These do not all contribute in the same way to the profession. Since most professions are not perfect expressions of the combinations within a chart, some may not contribute at all. We have no way of knowing that without having Joyce present to interview.

The Midheaven and its sign and ruler contribute the most important determinants of career simply because for us, social status is largely a matter of what we do for a living. The Part of Fortune and the tenth sign from it have to do with one's career, if that career is either (1) a family occupation or something derived from early life tendencies; or (2) more directed to making money than its being the means by which one defines oneself within society. The eleventh sign from the Part of Fortune, already previously introduced in connection with wealth, also tells us something about how that wealth is acquired, but again really has more to do with the task of making money than with the description of a career. Yet it can be useful in career determination as well.

The Part of Spirit does not always operate as a career determinant. In fact I am convinced that it really operates only in the charts of those people who live at a fairly high level of self-realization. According to various Greek sources, the Part of Spirit is a point that has to do with consciously chosen action, self-determined roles, and relates to a career only if that career is an accurate manifestation of who a person really is.

The sixth house is primarily a house of illness, but the ancients also called it a house of slavery and servitude. From this comes our notion of its being a house of "work." As you can see, our notion of work is somewhat watered down from the ancient notion. However, there is general agreement that it can relate to profession if there is some strong connection between it and the tenth house. Such connections include the following:

1) The ruler of the tenth house may be in the sixth or the other way round.

2) There may be aspects between tenth and sixth house planets.

3) There may be an aspect between sixth house planets and the Midheaven degree.

4) The tenth house, or the Midheaven, and the sixth house have the same ruler. In such cases the sixth house should tell us more about one's work than about illness.

Some of the comments below will be similar to those made in connection with wealth. See section VI.

Judgments concerning Profession and Career:

1) Her career may be a helping profession (nursing, medicine, healing in general, counselling).

Reasons: The sign Pisces on the Midheaven in Joyce's chart tells us this. These indications are consistent with what we found as possible sources of income in the previous section.

2) She should achieve notable success in her career, or make a considerable amount of money from it, or she should be in a profession concerned with money. This does not accord very well with #1.

Reasons: This is shown by the sign ruler, Jupiter, being exalted in the second house.

3) Her career may also involve the law or higher education.

Reasons: This is due to Jupiter. This is also supported by the fact that the Almuten of the Midheaven is Venus which is in the ninth house, conjunct Mercury, the Ascendant ruler, and trine first house planets. This is confirmed by Scorpio's being the sixth house, and the house of the Part of Fortune's being ruled by Mars in Sagittarius which has to do with these things. Also, the sixth and tenth are both ruled by Jupiter and therefore interact.[25]

4) She should be successful in the kind of career indicated in #3.

Reasons: This is indicated by the mutual reception of Mercury and Saturn.

5) We have other indications of counselling or other seventh house oriented professions.

Reasons: Scorpio and Mars figure in this regard because Scorpio is both the sixth house and the house of the Part of Fortune and its ruler, Mars, is in Sagittarius in the seventh house.

Supplementary Comments on Profession and Career from the Part of Fortune:

The tenth house from the Part of Fortune and its ruler, the Sun, are about the only element in this grouping which does not seem to support the general trend of the symbolism, except that Leo is the third sign which indicates writing and communication. This would be compatible with what has been said above.

The eleventh house from the Part of Fortune, also known as the "Place of Acquisition," is ruled by Mercury, which brings in all of the significations concerning the ninth house and the first house. We can say that with the first house ruler and the Almuten of the Midheaven in the ninth, and with the mutual reception between the ninth house and the first house, the ninth house and its themes are extremely important in this chart.

There are also some parts involved with career but I have not yet had enough experience with them to use them intelligently.

VIII. Sexual Unions.

Under this heading is encompassed marriage and all other forms of major sexual relationship. Here in the early twenty-first century, the issue of marriage is so deranged that I would not begin to try to answer the question of whether a person is, or should be, married. Nor would I attempt to guess a person's sexual orientation. Therefore, I will not do either here, and I will analyze the chart on the assumption that Joyce is heterosexual. For sexual relationships we consider the following:

1) In a woman's chart, the Sun, its aspects, and its ruler or Almuten. In Joyce's chart the Sun's ruler is Saturn.

2) Also in a woman's chart, Mars, its aspects, and its ruler or Almuten. In Joyce's chart Mars's ruler is Jupiter.

3) The seventh house and its ruler or Almuten. In this chart it is Jupiter.

4) In all charts, the general condition of Venus.

Judgments concerning Sexual Unions:

1) Joyce may attract partners who are somewhat overbearing and domineering although possibly quite successful in life (as many generally consider success), and may be persons of some substance and social significance.

Reasons: The Sun is in Capricorn. Its only aspect is the separating opposition with Jupiter. Also, Mars is in the seventh and its ruler is Jupiter. In addition Jupiter is in its exaltation.

2) Her partner or partners may be between seven and fifteen years older than she is, and should be well established in the world at the time of the beginning of the relationship. The partner or partners may have been married before and may have children by a previous marriage.

Reasons: This is a classic pattern with Jupiter ruling the seventh and being involved with the Sun in a woman's chart. However, the strong Jupiter symbolism can also be fulfilled by the partner's having strong Jupiter symbolism in his chart.

3) Joyce's partnerships may be or have been more than normally combative.

Reasons: Mars is in the seventh house. I often say with this placement that the native "is looking for a worthy opponent." The placement can indicate combative relationships, which may be due to either to the native or to her choice of partners. But it is actually a combination which can work out quite well in our culture if the following principles are observed. First, the partner must be a *worthy* opponent, that is, one the native can respect. Second, both the native and the partner must be capable of expressing grievances, having any necessary disagreements or disputes openly and getting them over with. Third, the native must be able to stand up for herself. Sometimes a seventh house Mars in a woman's chart indicates that she has handed all of her own aggressiveness and self-assertiveness over to the male or other partner and left none for herself. In such a case, Mars in the seventh can be truly unpleasant. But this is something that cannot be known from the birth chart by itself. This requires knowing the client.

4) Despite the previous, Joyce is quite able to express love.

Reasons: In Joyce's chart Venus is in excellent condition (see Table I), and it is connected to the Moon (which is not in quite such good condition by itself).

5) If she has problems in relationships, they are more likely to come about on account of the persons with whom she has relationships than because of her own actions.

Reasons: This is due to the combination of #3 and #4 above.

6) There is a strong disposition toward more than one marriage or equivalently important relationship.

Reasons: It is traditional that mutable signs rising and setting (Gemini and Sagittarius) indicate two or more marriages. Also, see #3.

IX. Children and Their Relationship Toward the Parents.

There are two traditions regarding children. Both of these are found in traditional astrology, only one in modern astrology. According to Ptolemy (and in this he is followed by many other classical and medieval sources), the houses for children are (and in this order of significance) the tenth, the eleventh, the fourth, and the fifth plus their rulers. The other tradition looks only at the fifth house. This second one is most common in modern use. The four-house system makes sense if we look at the meanings of the houses. Particularly in the charts of women, one can say that having children is something that one is supposed to do, part of one's social role. This is why we have the tenth house and its ruler. The eleventh house was called the house of the "Good Spirit" and was in some systems naturally associated with Jupiter, which in turn was considered to be the natural significator of children, hence the eleventh house. The fourth house is more often associated with ancestors than descendants, but it is always connected with the family, hence children. The fifth house was called the house of Good Fortune, and children were considered to be an essential element of general good fortune, hence the fifth and children. We can also see how these houses work once we accept the tenth and eleventh as being connected with children, because the fourth and fifth are the tenth and eleventh houses of one's spouse (tenth and eleventh from the seventh) and, therefore, presumably these houses signify one's own children as well as those of the spouse. The problem with this system is that it gives a rather large number of possible significators. The idea is to look at the signs, occupants, and rulers of these houses, their general condition, and the qualities of the signs involved.

344

Most important is the division of the signs into three categories, fruitful, semi-fruitful, and barren, with the planets also fitting into these categories. The fruitful signs are the three water signs, Cancer, Scorpio, and Pisces. The fruitful planets are the Moon, Venus, and Jupiter. The semi-fruitful signs are Aries, Taurus, Libra, Sagittarius, Capricorn, and Aquarius. (There are no semi-fruitful planets. All of the planets are fruitful or barren.) The barren signs are Gemini, Leo, and Virgo. The barren planets are the Sun, Saturn, and Mars. Mercury takes on the quality of whatever it aspects.

Now for our purposes here, I am going to use the fifth-house-only system because of its greater simplicity, along with the Part of Children. The Ptolemaic system definitely shows promise, but we have not yet sorted out its complexities. So we have the following indicators:

1) The fifth house, its occupants, and its ruler and Almuten. In Joyce's chart these are Libra with Neptune in the fifth house, and Venus as house ruler along with Saturn as Almuten.

2) The Part of Children, its sign and ruler and Almuten. In Joyce's chart this is 14 Taurus 26, [26] the ruler is Venus and so is the Almuten.

Judgments concerning Children:

1) Assuming Joyce was in a position to have and want children, the likely number would be one or two.

Reasons: We have Venus as a ruler twice, a planet favorable to child-bearing. But Libra, Taurus, and Aquarius (where Venus is located) are only semi-fruitful signs. Saturn, the Almuten of the fifth, is in a mutable sign which tends to double the number otherwise indicated. Therefore, I would have to regard Venus as the strongest indicator for children in Joyce's chart because of its double rulership over the fifth house and the Part of Children. Venus is well placed and well aspected, so if she has chosen to have children, she should be very fortunate with them especially given the conjunction of Venus with Mercury the ruler of the Ascendant.

2) But there may have been some difficulty in child-bearing that might have even prevented children altogether, or the oldest child could have had frail or sensitive health, or later a drug or alcohol problem.

Reasons: Neptune in the fifth is a negative indication for both having children and for the health of the oldest child.

345

X. Native's Friends and Enemies.

In medieval astrology the house of friends is the same as the modern, the eleventh. Enemies were placed into two categories, open and hidden. These are the same houses as in modern astrology, the seventh and the twelfth houses. However, in both Hindu and Greek astrology, the signification of open enemies is given to the sixth house rather than the seventh. There is clearly something to this idea, but it is also evident from experience that the seventh has much to say about open conflicts and the persons with whom one has them. We will use the medieval/modern system in this article.

So for friendship we have the following:

1) The eleventh house, its occupants, and its ruler or Almuten. In Joyce's chart this is the sign Aries, which has no planets in it. The sign ruler is Mars, the Almuten is the Sun.[27]

2) The Part of Friends at 2 Pisces 17[28] ruled by Jupiter.

3) Venus.

Judgments concerning Friends and Friendships:

1) There is a strong competitive or even antagonistic element in her friendships, or that she is attracted to rather strong and individualistic friends. The latter would favor male friends over female, but the requirement could equally well be met by strong women.

Reasons: This is due to the quality of Aries as the eleventh house combined with the Mars' sign rulership.

2) Friends may be the occasion or cause of her spending or having to borrow money.

Reasons: The Sun is the Almuten of the eleventh, and it is in the eighth house widely opposed by Jupiter in the second.

3) She has the ability to make people like her, but friends are neither unusually beneficial nor harmful in her life, nor is she likely to have a large circle of friends or to be one who joins a lot of groups.

Reasons: See #1 above. Also there are no planets in the eleventh, nor are its rulers especially prominent in the chart.

For enemies we have the following:

346

1) The twelfth house, its occupants and its ruler or Almuten. In Joyce's chart we have Taurus as the twelfth house. It has no occupants, and its ruler is the Venus in the ninth about which we have said much in other connections.

2) The seventh house, its occupants and its ruler or Almuten. In Joyce's chart the seventh house is Sagittarius with Mars in it, and Jupiter as the ruler.

I use no parts here because the only part devoted to enemies involves the cusp of the twelfth house and, as I have mentioned previously, cusps are not clearly defined things in whole-sign houses.

Judgments concerning Hidden Enemies:

1) Secret or hidden enemies are not likely to be much of a problem.

Reasons: Venus, the ruler of the twelfth, is the only indicator we have for secret enemies. It is a benefic. It is also in excellent condition. This is not an especially strong indication of having major problems with actual persons who might be secret enemies. But "secret enemies" is only one signification of the twelfth. It could indicate self-indulgent habits that cause her problems however.

2) There may be aspects of her love-life that she has preferred to keep hidden or secret, or those aspects of her life may have been somewhat difficult.

Reasons: Venus in the twelfth. Modern astrology uses "self-undoing" as a twelfth house phrase. This refers to the ways in which we unwittingly cause or attract trouble to ourselves. And it is also a house of secrets.

3) She may have strong sympathy for persons who are downtrodden or in difficulty.

Reasons: Again Venus in the twelfth can indicate persons who work with various kinds of institutions such as hospitals, mental institutions, or in more benign places where people go to withdraw from the world.

Judgments concerning Open Enemies:

1) Conflicts with open enemies or opponents may be severe although not totally destructive.

Reasons: Mars in the seventh and Jupiter, the ruler of the seventh, opposes the Sun.

2) These are not conflicts which Joyce seeks out actively.

Reasons: The strong and benevolent nature of her natal Venus prevents her from liking conflict.

3) These may be conflicts at law which involve money.

347

Reasons: The Sun-Jupiter opposition from the eighth to the second is a warning of this.

XI. Various Ninth House Matters: Natives's Foreign Travels and Journeys, Religion and Faith, Learning and Education.

I lump these subjects together because they are all ninth house, and it is often difficult to distinguish between the ninth house as signifying religious and spiritual matters, and being a place which signifies of long journeys. The same is also true with regard to the ninth house and education and learning. I have had little experience with the various Parts or Lots associated with this house, and will not use them here, although they may eventually serve to enable us to distinguish between these various significations of the ninth house.

So for all of these categories we have the following indicators:

1) The ninth house, its occupants and its ruler or Almuten. In Joyce's chart this is the sign Aquarius, ruled by Saturn and occupied by Venus conjunct Mercury.

2) The third house, its occupants and its ruler or Almuten. In Joyce's chart this is the sign Leo, which has Pluto in it and is ruled by the Sun.

Most modern astrologers would recognize the connection between the third house, and education and learning, and would also have no difficulty connecting the third house with travel, albeit of a more local and short distance variety than the ninth house. However, the connection between the third house and religion might be less known. But in fact the third house was traditionally as much a house of religion as the ninth. Originally the ninth house was called the "House of the Sun God," or simply "God," while the third house was the "House of the Moon Goddess," or simply "Goddess." And that was the original distinction; the ninth was the house of the masculine aspect of divinity, and the third house of the feminine. Later this became a distinction between religions in power, or religions that involved the whole of society (the ninth), versus those that were either out of power, or which did not involve society as a whole (the third), i.e., sects. In the Middle Ages, the third house was definitely connected with heresies.

Judgments concerning the Ninth House and its Concerns:

348

1) The result of all of this should be a strong interest in ideas, especially those ideas which appeal to both intellect and the emotions.

Reasons: The ninth house is very powerful in Joyce's chart. The Ascendant ruler, Mercury, is in the ninth house in mutual reception with the ninth house ruler, Saturn, in the first. Also Mercury is conjunct Venus, and trine the Moon.

2) She has a strong interest in ideas that are unconventional and "far out," even though they make sense and are logical when viewed dispassionately.

Reasons: Uranus in the first house trines Mercury and Venus in the ninth. But we also have Mercury trine Saturn.

3) She has strong convictions concerning her personal ideology and beliefs. and does not change her mind easily.

Reasons: The third house has Pluto in it which opposes the ninth house planets in fixed signs. The Sun, which rules the third, is in the eighth opposing Jupiter.

4) She is not likely to be a member of a conventional religious group.

Reasons: Any religious tradition that she would follow would have to satisfy the requirements of #3 and #4.

5) When she is interested in something, she gets into it very deeply. This would make her good in research, and in following any thought to a logical conclusion.

Reasons: Pluto is in the third house.

6) Her general intellectual ability is excellent, even though she sometimes approaches these matters with an intense and emotional attitude.

Reasons: None of the preceding should cause damage to the overall good quality of the Mercury-Venus conjunction in the ninth house. First, the opposition with Venus is separating. Second, while Mercury is retrograde and therefore applying to the opposition, it will be first aspected by the Moon and by Venus. These planets "cut off the light" of the Mercury-Pluto opposition. Third, the triple conjunction of Uranus, Saturn, and the Moon makes a trine to one end of this opposition and a sextile to the other end. This kind of combination stabilizes oppositions tremendously and makes them much more likely to be productive. Pluto's effect makes her intellect more intense and emotional as mentioned above. The ninth house combination with the planets in the first would indicate by themselves a rather detached and intellectual approach to both ideas and religion.

7) She is in some danger of being intellectually obsessive, getting into power struggles about ideas.

Reasons: Pluto is in the third, and the eighth house position of the Sun ruling the third supports the effects of Pluto.

XII. The Qualities of the Native's Death.

This will be brief. Modern astrologers as a whole believe that forecasting the time and nature of one's death from a chart is not a proper thing to do. I agree. I also believe that we could not do it very well even if we tried. And it would be extremely irresponsible to do anything of this kind with the chart of a person whom I have never met, and with whom I have had no contact. Therefore, I will not take up this subject.

Concluding Remarks

It is not possible to do a really good job of analyzing a chart where one has no contact with the native. Even when one gives delineations which are "accurate" or "correct," the "blind reading," as these are called, is of limited usefulness. The astrologer has no opportunity to penetrate to the deeper levels of chart understanding, nor does the astrologer have the opportunity to suggest ways in which the native may improve his or her lot or performance in some area of life, or to raise the level at which the chart symbolism operates. I have had many clients who have astounded me by the manner in which they intuitively moved to the course and to behavioral changes that made their difficult charts work at an astonishingly high level of creativity. I can truly say based on observation that difficult charts can have very fortunate outcomes.

Given the limitations of the blind reading, therefore, I have chosen to make this entire reading an exercise in how one goes about handling the main areas of life with the methods of medieval astrology, with some references to ancient techniques. I do not know how "accurate" I have been in this endeavor, because I have no way of knowing at what level Joyce is living her life. And this chart does not tell us this! I have no doubt that every manifestation of the symbolism of the chart that actually occurs and has occurred in Joyce's life is a reasonable and appropriate manifestation. I cannot say that I have picked the correct ones to describe in this reading. I have just been able to select what I consider the most likely in view of my knowledge of common human behavior. I hope that the reader has found this a useful demonstration.

NOTES:

1. The term "significator" referred to without qualification is planet whose signification is derived from the rulership of a house, or from having rulership over a degree or degrees occupied by some set of astrological points. This is opposed to a planet's "general signification," which is derived from the planet's own nature. Thus Pluto can signify underworld forces by its own nature, and can express it through a house that it may be located in, but has it no connection with a house or group of points located in Scorpio unless it aspects them, or is itself in Scorpio.

2. FDR's birth data are Jan. 30, 1882 at 8:45 p.m. LMT (01:40:56 UT, Jan. 31) in Springwood, near Hyde Park, NY (41N48, 73W56), while Cheney's are Jan. 30, 1941 at 7:30 p.m. in Lincoln, Nebraska (40N48, 96W40).

3. It actually precedes Alchabitius and the Arabs in general. It is a Greek method.

4. For further information see Robert Hand, *Whole Sign Houses* (Reston, VA: ARHAT, 2000).

5. Vettius Valens, *Anthology, Books V & VI*, trans. Robert Schmidt (Berkeley Springs, WV: Golden Hind Press, 1994), p. 30.

6. Moon, Mercury, Venus, Sun, Mars, Jupiter, Saturn.

7. Johannes Schoener, *Three Books on the Judgement of Nativities*, trans. Robert Hand (Reston, VA: ARHAT, 2001).

8. "Native" is the word traditionally used to indicate the person for whom the chart is being read. In this case the native is Joyce. It is easier than saying, "the person for whom the chart has been cast," or, "the person born at this time."

9. The method of computing the Part of the Father is as follows: In a daytime birth take the Ascendant, add its longitude to that of Saturn and subtract the longitude of the Sun. In a nighttime birth take the Ascendant, add its longitude to that of the Sun and subtract the longitude of Saturn.

10. The method of computing the Part of the Mother is as follows: In a daytime birth take the Ascendant, add its longitude to that of the Moon and subtract the longitude of the Venus. In a nighttime birth take the Ascendant, add its longitude to that of Venus and subtract the longitude of the Moon.

11. The classical or "Ptolemaic" aspects are the conjunction, sextile, square, trine and opposition. Minor aspects do not count in this case because we are taking the aspects from sign to sign.

12. Hayz requires that the diurnal planets, Sun, Jupiter, and Saturn, be above the horizon, in a masculine or diurnal sign, in a daytime birth, or that the nocturnal planets, Venus, Mars, and the Moon be in nocturnal signs, above the horizon, in a nighttime birth. There is some disagreement between the Greek sources and the medieval sources about Mars as to whether it prefers nocturnal signs, which are also feminine, or diurnal signs, which are also masculine. I go with the Greeks who said that Mars preferred nocturnal signs.

13. This is the meaning of "received." It occurs when a sign, planet, or other point makes a major aspect by sign or by degree to one of the planet's major rulers, those rulers being the sign ruler, the ruler of the sign by exaltation, or the Almuten which is a planet that rules by having the most dignities in the sign of the house, planet, or point in question.

14. The "bounds" or "terms" are irregular divisions of signs that are ruled by Mercury, Venus, Mars, Jupiter or Saturn, never the Sun or Moon (at least in the common systems). Tables of these are to be found in a variety of books or sources on traditional astrology.

15. Saturn is the Almuten of Libra in diurnal charts, because Saturn is the exaltation ruler of Libra, and it rules all Air signs in daytime births.

16. The method of computing the Part of the Siblings is as follows: In a daytime birth take the Ascendant, add its longitude to that of Jupiter and subtract the longitude of Saturn. Some sources in a nighttime birth take the Ascendant reverse the positions of Jupiter and Saturn. This is a daytime birth so we can ignore this issue.

17. See section IX on Children for a longer discussion of fruitful and barren signs.

18. The method of computing the Part of Azemene is as follows: In a daytime birth take the Ascendant, add its longitude to that of Mars and subtract the longitude of Saturn. In a nighttime birth take the Ascendant, add its longitude to that of the Saturn and subtract the longitude of Mars.

19. The only area where traditional astrology equates the signs and houses, that is, saying something like the first house = Aries, the second = Taurus, etc. is in the area of melosthesia, the relating of body parts to the chart. Thus Aries = First House = Head, Taurus = Second House = Throat and Neck, etc. The seventh house, therefore, is the same as Libra with regard to affected organs and limbs.

20. William Lilly, *Christian Astrology* (Original, London: 1746; reprint Regulus: Exeter, U.K., 1985), p. 539. Punctuation and spelling as in original.

21. See also section XII on the ninth house.

22. Vettius Valens, *Anthology, Book II*, trans. Robert Schmidt (Berkeley Springs, WV: Golden Hind Press, 1994), p. 31.

23. "Magistery" is an older form of the word "mastery" and was used especially in connection with one's work or craft. It is a direct anglicization of the Latin *magisterium*.

24. The Part of Spirit in a day chart has the same formula as the Part of Fortune in a night chart, and vice versa.

25. As an example of this, many of my clients who were born in a foreign country but who live in the U.S. have Leo rising. This causes the fourth house (home) which is Scorpio and the ninth house (foreign places) which is Aries to be ruled by the same ruler, Mars.

26. The method of computing the Part of Children is as follows: In a daytime birth take the Ascendant, add its longitude to that of Saturn and subtract the longitude of Jupiter. Some sources in a nighttime birth take the Ascendant, add its longitude to that Jupiter and subtract the longitude of Saturn.

27. This is because the Sun is the exaltation ruler of Aries and also rules all Fire signs in day births. This gives two rulerships to Mars's one, or, in the weighted medieval system, the Sun gets 8 points while Mars gets 5.

28. The method of computing the Part of Friends is as follows: In a daytime or nighttime birth take the Ascendant, add its longitude to that of Mercury and subtract the longitude of the Moon.

Robert Schmidt: Hellenistic

Strategy

Hellenistic astrology has not been practiced for nearly two thousand years. In my contribution to this book I am trying to develop a prototype for an initial reading of a client's chart that is based on Hellenistic techniques—one that ideally would also fulfill the needs and expectations of modern persons. In the surviving texts, Hellenistic astrology is most frequently presented as a system for predicting concrete events in the life of some native. But it is virtually impossible to do a fully responsible and completely detailed Hellenistic reading within the scope of a section of this book. The business of prediction is very challenging, even from the Hellenistic perspective.

As a system, Hellenistic astrology is elaborate and intricate, with complex internal cross-checks and cross-references that must be examined before we can be confident of any isolated concrete prediction. Events that are possible in certain areas of the native's life, as determined by the topical approach, cannot be realized unless the planetary lords of a given topic are activated as "time-lords" at appropriate times in the native's life. Conversely, events that seem likely during a certain period of time through the study of time-lords cannot occur unless these events have been determined to be possible through the topical approach. And any event that is possible according to the topical approach and likely through the study of time-lords must still be one that is allowed to fit into the overall context of the native's life as sketched out by the universal techniques.

Ideally, all the special topics of the native's life should be studied in detail before we can be sure of any one of them. For instance, certain kinds of illnesses or injuries make it impossible for the native to have children. Certain professions may make travel likely, others preclude it. A monastic life prohibits marriage. And so forth.

Similarly, all the individual time periods of the native's life should be studied in their sequence, since one does not get a divorce unless previously married, gain a promotion unless previously employed, or receive an inheritance unless someone has died.

Such a complete reading of a chart could take weeks, even with computer assistance (which in any case is not yet available for most of the tabulations and calculations that have to be done in a Hellenistic reading). But, as here, this is often impractical due to time constraints.

It is also a standard Hellenistic maxim to know as much as possible about the native's condition and circumstances: the sex, culture, ethnic background, social status, etc., for this must usually be known if a concrete prediction is to be exact.

Finally, it is also desirable to be able to check a few events that have already occurred in the native's life, since the determination of certain ruling or supporting planets in Hellenistic astrology is tricky in some charts, and it is helpful to have a means of rectifying their selection.

Since we cannot do a complete reading here, and we know little in advance about the native beyond her sex and the fact that she was born in this country in the Midwest, we must instead concentrate on the universal techniques of Hellenistic astrology, which can to some extent be studied in isolation from the rest of the system. These techniques dominate all the individual topical and time-lord inquiries anyway, and are presupposed by them, so they should reasonably be the focus of an initial reading for that reason alone.

However, these techniques are also designed to give a kind of biographical profile of the native in fairly broad sweeping strokes. Since the universal techniques involve metaphysical conceptualizations about the native's life as a whole, they can yield interesting insights about the essence and existence of the native. Though these insights may be somewhat different from what modern persons have come to expect from an astrological reading, I nevertheless believe they can be very satisfying for those who have a desire to know themselves.

Consequently, in preparation for an initial profile reading, and as the foundation for any more detailed chart interpretation, I apply the seven basic universal techniques to the chart. Hellenistic astrology is not "holistic" in the sense that every planet is of equal importance in the life as a whole. The universal techniques help me identify the central planets in the chart and the role they have in grounding and organizing the life.

These techniques may be grouped into two classes. The first class consists of four techniques. One of these studies the priority of the solar principle over the lunar, or vice versa, in a given chart, by determining which Light predominates over the other. A second technique studies the separation of the solar and lunar principles by focusing on the Lot of Fortune. A third studies the union of the solar and lunar principles in the Prenatal Lunation. The fourth studies the ascending sign, which represents the relation of the solar and lunar principles to each other. The appropriate rulers of these four significators are said to be the planets "having a relation to the nativity." They may be understood as the planets that support the nativity as a whole, or the ultimate subjects upon which the nativity as a whole is predicated. Of course, just a few or even a single planet may serve all four support roles. But if there are more than one, we may reasonably conduct an investigation as to which of them provides the ultimate substratum for the chart.

The second class consists of three techniques that determine the ruling planets in the nativity and consequently how the nativity as a whole is governed. We might call them the planets in which the nativity is inherent and to which it belongs. One of these techniques identifies the most autonomous planet in the nativity, a potential tyrant. Another establishes the planet that has the best connections. A third determines the planet that has the most legitimate authority to rule. All three of these planets may leave their own unique qualitative stamp on the life. Of course, one planet may hold two of these three offices, or even all of them. Under the latter scenario, we may have a powerful, legitimate governing principle that cares for and manages the life of the native as if that life were its own estate. If there is more than one ruling planet, then we may reasonably inquire about the ultimate lord of the nativity as a whole.

One of the advantages of Hellenistic astrology is that all the particular relationships that need to be examined in the full study of any one of these seven universal techniques are motivated by and find their coherence in an underlying paradigm specific to that technique. This explains why some planetary relationships are important in one technique but not in another. Underlying the first four techniques are four interconnected paradigms that have to do with the interplay of light and surface in different ways, invoking concepts such as color, reflection, luminosity, shadow and so forth. The second three techniques employ the underlying paradigm of the government of a household or kingdom, and the distribution of ruling functions in such a domain.

What is more, the interconnected underlying paradigms in each of the two classes have the advantage of helping me navigate through the techniques in a less mechanical fashion, one that is more specific to the nativity in question. It also helps me string the reading into a more continuous narrative and provides intelligible concrete language suitable for explaining the chart to the client.

The ultimate goal of my initial reading is to find the unique signature of the chart. This naturally would be recorded in relationships among the central planets of the nativity, and it is reasonable to suppose that it consists of the relationship between the ultimate supporting planet of the nativity and the lord of the nativity. So I try to steer my initial universal reading of the chart to the identification and interpretation of this relationship as a kind of concluding flourish.

If I were to continue the reading in a second session, I would begin to delineate the other combinations that the central planets enter into, first with each other, and then with the planets that do not have such a central role. I would leave the delineation of combinations of planets not central in the manner described (even if they appear to be highlighted by angularity or tight configuration) to the more specific examinations of different areas and times of life.

Only after these introductory sessions would I commence a study of individual topics and periods of time in the native's life, using the topical approach and the time-lords respectively. However, I would for the most part be applying the same kinds of logic and rationales that I employ in the universal techniques, except that now they would be focused on specific areas and time periods of life instead of the life as a whole.

Before leaving this outline of my approach to an initial Hellenistic reading, let me say just a few words about the kind of chart I prefer. I like the zodiac ring chart wheel, which has the sign divisions demarcated. This is useful for much Hellenistic work insofar as it places so much emphasis on sign-mediated planetary relationships. Within this ring I generally choose a Porphyry house system in order to assess regions of greatest planetary strength. I normally suppress the outer planets (and all the asteroids). Although I believe that the outer planets can be conceptually integrated into the Hellenistic framework, I think it is important to be able to read a chart from the classical planets alone, since I believe that the modern emphasis on the outer planets has caused us to lose contact with the classical planets. I have the Lot of Fortune printed in the chart, being careful to make sure that the software prints out the nocturnal Lot of Fortune correctly. It is fairly easy to enter the Lot of Spirit by hand (which is almost as important as the Lot of Fortune), since it is symmetrical to the Lot of Fortune across the Ascendant/Descendant axis. In a detailed reading, I use certain tables that I have prepared myself in order to organize the basic data of the chart, which is a bit time consuming. At the present time, some of the most interesting time-lord procedures must still be calculated by hand in lieu of adequate software.

358

Finally, I have developed a technical astrological language that more faithfully represents the meanings of the original Greek terminology, which I have been slowly introducing in my lectures and writings. However, because I would have had to explain so many unfamiliar terms in the course of this reading, I somewhat reluctantly elected to employ modern terminology so as not to distract from the logic of the exposition.

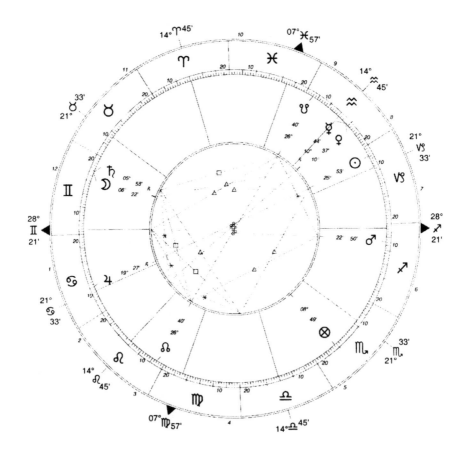

First I will discuss the planets that Joyce's life is all about, those upon which it hinges, those upon which it is ultimately predicated. Then I will turn to an examination of the planets to which her life belongs.

The Degree to which Joyce's Life Comes to Light

Joyce was born during the day. In technical terms, her nativity belongs to the diurnal rather than the nocturnal sect. This simple fact has astrological significance. It means that her life must come to appearance through its own luminosity, like the Sun; if she had been born at night, her life would be one that manifests by the reflection of light, like the Moon.

I am going to apply a technique that is intended to assess whether a given diurnal nativity may shine forth with the intensity of a star of the first or second magnitude, or one of lesser magnitude. For this purpose, we study the elemental triplicity in which the Sun is found; for nocturnal births, we would study the Moon in this way.

In Joyce's chart, the Sun is in Capricorn, an Earth-like sign. The position of the Sun in her chart is one of the places where the event of Joyce's birth can make an initial impression on the cosmic soul—namely, through something in that soul that is akin to the Earth element in the mundane world. Conversely, her own life tends to conform, with respect to its own initial luminosity, to the state of the cosmic soul at that moment—at least to the extent that it can. Thus, the initial luminosity in her life will be conditioned by the Earth element. By this I do not mean dirt and stones. Metaphysically speaking, Earth is a principle of self-definition and self-limitation which by this very nature does not conform well to boundaries imposed on it from the outside.

The Sun as a principle of luminosity, however, is not naturally suited to being in the Earth element. It wants to shine forth spontaneously out of itself. When it is in Earth, all it can do is make this element translucent after the fashion of crystals, rather than something self-luminous. It would have been better for the Sun to be in the Fire or Air element in order for Joyce's life to be truly luminous at birth. Nevertheless, a translucent life is better than one left altogether to darkness.

However, the Sun is in the eighth sign from the ascending sign. This sign is in aversion or unconnected to the ascending sign by configuration, which would ordinarily mean that it would be unlikely that Joyce's life from the outset could in reality participate in the solar principle, even to the limited extent of becoming crystalline and translucent.

Despite the poor prospects Joyce's life has for shining forth from the beginning, we can still inquire whether and to what extent the cosmic soul takes note of it. This is determined by studying any planets that can "see" or aspect the Sun by the classical configurations of the sextile, square, trine or opposition. Planets occupying these places would represent the eyes of the world upon Joyce's life at the time of her birth. Only Jupiter is in a position to look upon the Sun, but due to its retrogradation during opposition it tends retract its initial testimony, as if it were not sure it noticed anything at all. Consequently, the world at large takes little notice of her birth, and we should not expect any great initial celebrity for her, as we might find in the case of a child of royal or distinguished parents.

To what extent, then, can Joyce achieve visibility during the course of her life? First we have to locate her own life in the chart—not her lineage, but the life she herself will be leading. Now, it is up to the Sun to designate the planet that signifies Joyce's own life in the chart, which it does through the rationale underlying the triplicity lords. Triplicity lords gain their office by appointment from some other planet that occupies their triplicity. In the present nativity, the Sun designates the triplicity lords of Earth as representatives of Joyce's life: Venus for the first part of the life, then the Moon for the second part of the life, with Mars cooperating for both parts. It is worth noting that all three of these planets belong to the nocturnal sect, which means that they do not serve the function of bringing a life to light as well as the diurnal planets Sun, Jupiter, and Saturn. (Mercury is also a nocturnal planet in this chart since it sets after the Sun, so it is also somewhat dysfunctional.)

Let us first look at Venus as the first and principal significator of her own life, which concerns the period when her visibility is most naturally in the context of her family. As a nocturnal planet, Venus is better at representing the life by reflection than by inherent luminosity. But since this is a diurnal chart, reflection results in a reduced visibility, just as the Moon is much harder to see during the day. Venus is also in Aquarius, an Air-like sign. It would have been better if Venus were in the Earth or Water element, where reflection takes place more naturally.

Be this as it may, we now come to the really central issue in this analysis. Venus is in the ninth sign, which is cadent. Whereas angular signs are epicentric, meaning that they are centers around which something revolves, cadent signs are eccentric, meaning that they are off-center and not the center around which revolution takes place. This means that during the first part of her life, Joyce's life is not a natural center of attention around which other lives of her Earth-like tribe revolve, namely her extended family.

Mars, as a cooperating significator of the life, can come to the rescue of Venus somewhat, particularly since it is in an angular sign. Mars gives Venus the power to attract attention away from other lives that are the natural center of attention; since Mars is contrary to the sect, this is at the expense of these other lives.

There is still another, less negative prospect for redeeming this first part of Joyce's life. Venus itself can appoint another planet to represent the first part of Joyce's life. This appointment can be bestowed on the first triplicity lord of the element in which Venus is found, namely Air. This lord is retrograde Saturn in the ascending sign Gemini, which is its own element. Since Saturn is angular and a diurnal planet in a diurnal chart, it would thus naturally represent her as a center of attention in her immediate family, although this centrality is more restricted than that of being the center of one's tribe or extended family. However, since Saturn is retrograde, her life moves in a contrary direction to that of her family circle; thus, she may have been a center of attention for somewhat less than positive reasons.

We may reasonably ask how visible Joyce's life is during this first period beyond her family and to the world at large. Planets configured with the triplicity lords testify as to whether there is anyone looking on to see this life, whatever its intrinsic visibility. The Moon and Saturn each cast a ray by trine into the degrees preceding Venus, and thus they represent some spectators to her life during its first years. Saturn, however, generally fails to notice, particularly when retrograde as it is here. The Moon, on the other hand, suggests that she did come to some general attention.

So much for the first part of her life. Sometime in her twenty-third year, or perhaps in her thirtieth, after the ascensional time of Capricorn or Aquarius in which the Sun and Venus respectively are found, her life may well have begun to manifest much more visibly, because this is when the Moon takes over responsibility for representing Joyce's life from Venus, and the Moon is strongly angular in the ascending sign. This is also when Joyce's life comes into its own, and is more subject to notice by the world at large. Often such a change-over is heralded by some fairly dramatic event. (It is remotely possible that this change-over could have occurred as early as her eighth year, when the synodic period of Venus was completed.) Like Venus, however, the Moon is contrary to the sect and works better by reflection than by shining forth with its own light.

During the second part of her life, when the preconditions for visibility are so much better, there is still a problem. This is because there are no planets aspecting the Moon by casting their rays before it in Gemini. Thus, her life has become very reflective, but for the most part there is no one to look on. However, Mars continues to cooperate with the Moon, and again helps the Moon draw attention to the life.

Despite these difficulties, there may still be certain times during the course of her life that Joyce's life may come more into conformity with the life the cosmic soul has in mind for her, or during which she attains to some measure of visibility. These times can be determined by studying the time lords established by the procedure of decennials, which we cannot pursue within the scope of this reading.

The Form of Joyce's Life

Next I will examine the form that was fashioned for Joyce's life at the time of her Prenatal Lunation, a form that will act upon the raw material of her life.

The Prenatal Lunation is the New or Full Moon that most immediately preceded her birth, where the Sun and Moon are yoked together in a union of the masculine principle with the feminine. Here the Moon represents a receptacle or container, the Sun a principle that directs an essence to flow into this container. But a Prenatal Lunation is a lunar application, which means that the Moon now transmits this essence to some other planet as object, represented by the sign ruler of the Moon in the lunation. As material is acted upon by this form, we may liken this event to a form impressing itself on this material. The planet whose essence the Sun directs into this container is the first planet to which the Moon makes a bodily application after the Prenatal Lunation itself, and this is the form that is actually imposed on the matter represented by the sign ruler.

Joyce's Prenatal Conjunction (or New Moon) occurred in the sixteenth degree of Capricorn. We study this lunation in the natal chart itself. The Prenatal Conjunction is more solar and active in nature, while the Prenatal Full Moon is more lunar and passive. In a diurnal chart, it is better to have a

Prenatal Conjunction, as a consequence of which the Moon will be waxing in the natal chart, and this is the case with Joyce.

The sign ruler of Capricorn is Saturn. Because it is angular, Saturn turns toward the form ready to accept it, although because it is retrograde it backs away somewhat. The first planet to which the Moon bodily applies after the Prenatal lunation is Venus, so Venus represents the form that will first be directed into the lunar container by the Sun, and then transmitted to act upon Saturn. Saturn and Venus are trine to each other, and thus the matter is a suitable fit for the form. As we will see later, this combination is at the very heart of Joyce's life.

The Topic and Passage of Joyce's Biography

Next let me begin to examine what sort of topic Joyce's biography ought to have, the basic theme her soul would choose. For this purpose we will study her ascending sign, the most important house in the chart. As is the case with the preceding two techniques, this house likewise signifies the life as a whole—not according to the predomination of luminescence over reflection in this chart, not according to the union of masculine and feminine principles, but rather according to the union of soul and body that constitutes a life, although not yet a physical life, but the kind of life that is the true subject of a biography. Thus the soul we are referring to here is the soul of the life Joyce will lead, and the body is the body of such a life; it is not yet the soul that animates the body we would call Joyce.

The ascending sign is called the "helm," the handle of the rudder, the instrument by means of which the ship is steered. The ascending sign signifies the soul, which is what guides or steers the body. The sign ruler of the Ascendant is then the planet that has its hand on the helm, that which leads or guides the soul itself. This planet is also called Spirit, the guardian and director of the soul. In Joyce's life, it is Mercury that steers her soul. Interestingly enough, Mercury itself has the role of a leader of souls. Mercury is in the ninth sign, which is where we will find the basic topic of her life. In its most fundamental sense, the ninth is the place where we find the principles that guide the actions performed by the native. These principles may be authority, philosophy, religion, or even esoteric disciplines, which should be the underlying theme of her life. Mercury is also in the second decan of Aquarius, which belongs to it. This means that it regards the basic theme of Joyce's life as its own, and accordingly her story is told in the first person.

The relationship between the ascending sign and its ruler is different than the relationship between the predominating light and its ruler, or the Prenatal Lunation and its ruler. Whereas their respective rulers support the predominator or the Prenatal Lunation, the Ascendant and its ruler support each other, though in different ways. The sign ruler accepts the allotment of the ascending sign, and the ascending sign chooses or appropriates the ruler. Neither one is the ultimate subject or support for the other.

However, notice that Mercury is a nocturnal planet in this chart, and therefore contrary to the planetary party in favor. The ascending sign would naturally rather choose a planet belonging to the sect, but this is the planet allotted it, and it must make do, but it does indicate some reluctance on the part of the soul of Joyce's biography to listen to the advice of her personal guardian.

Conversely, Mercury is also severely retrograde in her chart, and just about to set under the beams of the Sun. Since it is in the ninth, the place that governs actions, we see that instead of applying these principles for their proper purpose, in this story Joyce is using them as an excuse for retreating from the burden of her actions. She retreats so much that Mercury, the narrator of her biography, is in imminent danger of going into concealment, which could mean that it has gone into hiding under a false persona or *nom de plume*, or else it has become so inconspicuous that we the readers lose sight of the central character in her story. It is interesting that Joyce, the person this reading is ultimately about, has agreed to subject herself to blind readings by a number of astrologers. Since astrology is a ninth house topic, and Mercury signifies astrology, the symbolism seems rather good.

Although neither the Ascendant nor its ruler can be said to be the ultimate support for the other, we can nevertheless identify a planet that supports them jointly. This is a planet in the ascending sign itself, provided that there is one, as in this case. If there were no such planet, things would be a little more complicated, but in principle we could still find such a supporting planet. Of the two planets in the ascending sign, we favor the one that has some rulership there. The Moon has none, but Saturn is in its own triplicity, so we favor Saturn.

Saturn will tell us something about the time underlying Joyce's story, not necessarily in terms of ordinary clock time (although this may still be the case), but rather in more subtle ways.

The temporal sequence of the signs is interesting in that it combines both the daily clockwise motion of the signs and the opposite ecliptic motion of the planets at the same time. For instance, the ascending sign represents childhood, the tenth sign maturity, the seventh seniority, and the fourth old age and death, reflecting the clockwise diurnal motion. However, the twelfth represents the period before birth, the second the period after birth; the ninth the period before maturity, the eleventh the period after maturity; etc. These subsystems around the angles represent the natural order of planetary motion.

Thus, in our seafaring metaphor, the Ascendant signifies embarking out of port, the tenth is reaching the halfway point, the seventh begins the voyage home, the fourth is the final leg of the journey and the voyage's end. However, the twelfth represents preparations prior to departure, the second events after departure up until midway; the ninth the period prior to midway up to midway, the eleventh the time from midway up to the halfway point of the voyage.

Since we have a planet in the ascending sign, we pick up Joyce's story just as she is just embarking on her life journey. The ship she will be sailing in represents the body that carries her biography along, and it is this ship that marks the time. This is why I said above that Saturn would tell us something about the time in the life.

If there had been no planet in the Ascendant, but one in the tenth sign instead, we could say that her story begins in mid-passage. However, since Saturn is retrograde, the story has to go back in time for a while before catching up with the present.

The condition of Mercury also tells us something important. Although the story begins as I described, the narration is from the point of view of some period of time immediately preceding mid-passage, which means we have a kind of double flashback.

Ideally, this passage from Joyce's biography would end at about age 55, which is the sum of the synodic periods of the two planets in the ascending sign: Saturn 30 years, and the Moon 25.

There is an additional curious feature worth noting here. Mercury and Saturn are in mutual reception, or in each other's signs. This indicates that the story being told by Mercury takes exactly the same amount of time as the voyage she has undertaken. The story teller does not run out of time with his narrative, nor try to belabor it long after it has reached its concluding flourish. Again, it is interesting that this passage in Joyce's life was completed just prior to her agreement to do this project.

Collaterally with the study of the essential properties of the human life, we must also investigate those properties that belong to it accidentally. For this we will make use of the Lot of Fortune, which is in the ninth degree of Scorpio in Joyce's chart, ruled by Mars in Sagittarius in the twenty-third degree. The Lot is calculated in a day chart by taking the ecliptic interval from the Sun forward in the order of signs to the Moon, and extending this same interval forward from the ascending degree in the order of signs; at night, we take the same interval and extend it backward in the order of signs from the Ascendant.

This algorithm for calculating the Lot of Fortune tells us two things immediately. First, that we are studying the separation of the solar and lunar principles, which here means the disjunction of the principle of purpose or design (the Sun) from the principle of forethought (the Moon) that tells how to achieve the purpose or execute the design.

Secondly, since the algorithm is an arithmetical proportion, it tells us that the cosmic soul can only see into the realm of chance or luck and grasp it by analogy, and not by declarative statement or predication.

Just as the predominating Light made the element in which it was found either fiery and luminous or reflective, and as the Prenatal Lunation made the sign in which it is found Water-like, so the Lot of Fortune makes the sign in which it falls more Earth-like and tangible. Luck has to do with what emerges spontaneously and impersonally within Joyce's life. Joyce's life so far is only an idea without instantiation in an actual physical being, and how can an idea be touched? Only if it has something resembling tangibility. This is provided for by the Lots generally, which makes the signs they occupy sensitive to impressions from real physical bodies and concrete events, just as our own souls are receptive to impressions deriving from the sense of touch. The Lot of Fortune is special in that it is the place where the cosmic soul can be touched by everything that has to do with the corporeal nature of the individual human life. However, since that which touches something else is stirred in return, it means that the corporeal nature of the individual is also moved to conform in its bodily nature to what the cosmic mind supposes it to be, to some extent at least.

The treatment of the Lot of Fortune is somewhat analogous to that of the Ascendant, although whereas that treatment concerns the higher soul and temporal body of Joyce, this treatment concerns the receptivity of the cosmic soul to the individual physical body of Joyce.

When the Lot of Fortune is in a cadent sign, as it is here, it means that the cosmic soul tends to shrink away from the touch of the individual, whereas it would bend inward invitingly if the sign were angular. Nevertheless, there are several planets in a position to feel this initial impression somewhat due to the configurations of their signs with Scorpio, namely, the Sun, Mercury, Venus, Jupiter. These planets also represent the extent to which Joyce's life touches the lives of others, and thus we see that though her life was not visible to many according to the analysis above, it nevertheless could have touched many other persons.

So the actual physical birth of Joyce made a kind of slight and remote impression on the cosmic mind. However, it is the sign ruler that must pick up this impression, however minimal, and spread a report of it throughout the cosmic mind generally.

The sign ruler in this case, Mars, is in a sign adjacent to the sign of the Lot, so it cannot feel the initial impression directly transmitted through one of the seven rays it emits, but only indirectly insofar as it is configured with planets that were impressed by the Lot, which can only be Mercury and Venus in this case. However, Mars is in an angular sign, which means that it is adept at turning this impression into a message that it broadcasts to the rest of the soul generally. But since it could not itself directly feel the impact due to its being in an adjacent sign, the report that it sends out is more in the nature of a rumor that it heard from elsewhere. Mars spreads its report through a medium that has a nature something like water; consequently, it distributes its report in a form resembling a taste. This is the pungent taste proper to Mars.

The content of this rumor concerns the topics that belong to the seventh whole-sign house that Mars occupies, and relate to issues of the body, such as marriage and death. The Moon is in a position to acknowledge this report because of its opposition to Mars, although somewhat antithetically and reluctantly, as if it did not quite like the report; but since it did not sense the impression represented by the Lot directly, it cannot corroborate it anyway. The Sun cannot acknowledge the report because it is unconnected to Mars, even though it had some weak secondary impression of the original impression represented by the Lot.

In view of this, it would seem that seventh house issues, which should be important accidents connected to the essence of the life, may not be reliably

369

read from this analysis alone. The cosmic soul knows this, knows that the life does not perfectly conform to what the cosmic soul has initially been thinking about the life in respect to matters concerning Joyce's corporeality. It knows that it must reexamine these issues in more detail to become fully informed about them. (And this applies to me as well, insofar as I am trying to interpret the thoughts of the cosmic mind as expressed in the observable celestial phenomena.) It even has a device for doing this further examination, which is the study of three other fundamental lots that are closely connected to the Lot of Fortune, but we cannot pursue this further within the confines of this reading.

The Lot of Spirit concerns the luck of an individual in a different way. It is through this Lot that we determine to what extent the individual soul of some native can be persuaded to act in conformity with the life laid out for it in the cosmic mind.

The Lot of Spirit is the inverse of the Lot of Fortune and is always found symmetrical to it along the Ascendant/Descendant axis. In Joyce's chart, the Lot of Spirit is located in the eighteenth degree of Aquarius. The sign occupied by this Lot is the place where the cosmic soul can make contact with the individual soul of Joyce, "eaves-dropping" on its thoughts and intentions and influencing it in return. This is because the Lot has the power to give the sign it occupies a nature akin to the Air element, which has a greater affinity for thought, so that the sign will be more receptive to the commands issuing from the Sun, these commands being carried through the Air element; conversely, the sign will be more receptive to the individual soul, enabling it to "hear" what the individual soul is thinking.

In Joyce's chart, this sign is also cadent, a place where the cosmic soul naturally tends to avert itself from individual souls in order to be more self-absorbed, which means that it can initially only hear the thoughts of Joyce's soul with difficulty. The sign ruler of this Lot is Saturn, and it is this planet that potentially has the power to persuade the individual soul to act in accordance with the life thought out for it by the cosmic mind. Saturn receives its own instructions in the form of commands issued from the Sun and Moon, but more from the Sun which is the commanding principle, and since this is a diurnal chart, the Sun can issue its commands unimpeded. But the planet that has to persuade an individual soul has to have more tact and guile and turn the commands into persuasive advice.

370

Saturn, however, is in a sign unconnected to the Sun, which means that it does not hear the Sun's commands, although due to the fact that Gemini and Capricorn are signs that ascend in the same amount of time, the advice that Saturn would offer is "accidentally" in agreement with what the Sun would command if it could only find Saturn. Saturn is conjunct the Moon, so there is another chance for Saturn to receive its instructions, but the Moon is contrary to the sect and thus not functioning in a properly regal manner.

However, this is all somewhat moot, because since Saturn is retrograde, it tends to withhold its instruction anyway. So we must conclude that Joyce's soul is not getting much advice from her higher soul to guide her actions.

There is one final point to consider before we leave the subject of Lots and the accidents in Joyce's life. As is the case with the Ascendant and its sign ruler, neither the Lot nor its ruler supports the other, but instead they are jointly supported by another planet. To find this planet, we look for planets angular relative to the Lot of Fortune in clockwise order. The first planets we find are Mercury and Venus making an inferior square to the place of the Lot. Venus is in its own bounds, and thus it becomes the planet ultimately supporting all the accidents in the life, in a manner similar to how a planet in the Ascendant (or other angle) supports the essential properties of the life. But whereas the planet supporting these essential properties does so by putting them in a temporal setting, a planet in one of the angles of the Lot of Fortune gives a kind of foundational place for these accidents. Thus it is Venus that ultimately makes room for accidental events in Joyce's life to the extent that they may conform to the chart and thereby become predictable.

Finally, I will only mention the Lot of Basis, which is a kind of analogue of the Ascendant. The Lot of Basis is determined by taking the shortest ecliptic arc between the Lot of Fortune and the Lot of Spirit and projecting this interval from the ascending degree. In Joyce's case, this Lot falls in Libra. Since this Lot signifies the separation of events that emerge spontaneously but may still conform to the nativity, from events that may be persuaded to so conform, the Lot of Basis is the ultimate foundation of all events that are subject to blind chance and are not predictable from the chart.

Summation and Conclusion to the Study of the First Four Techniques

In each of the four techniques above, a certain planet was singled out as providing support for Joyce's life in a certain respect. These planets may be understood as the planets upon which her life is ultimately predicated. We may reasonably ask whether one of these planets is qualified to represent the ultimate substratum of her life.

There are two considerations here. First, according to which of the four techniques is her life more in conformity with what the cosmic soul has in mind for her life? This could be called the most reliable technique of the four, and the support planet it produces is arguably the ultimate supporting planet of the nativity. Secondly, for techniques that are equally reliable and produce different supporting planets, which of these planets is more fundamental?

As for the first consideration, the Sun, the Prenatal Conjunction, and the Lot of Fortune are all in signs in aversion to the ascending sign and thus unconnected to the life. The sign ruler of the ascending sign itself is in the ninth and thus connected to the life. The planet supporting the Ascendant and its lord is Saturn.

As for the second consideration, Saturn is the ultimate support planet in the first technique, the final triplicity lord in the study of the Sun; Saturn is also the sign ruler of the Prenatal Lunation; it is also the planet that has original governance of the times by being present in the ascending sign and having a relation to that sign by triplicity rulership. Venus is the supporting planet for the treatment of the Lot of Fortune by being the most angular planet relative to this Lot. Thus, I would conclude that Saturn is the ultimate supporting planet in Joyce's nativity, and might be called the administrator of her nativity.

The Government and Ultimate Ownership of Joyce's Life

In what has preceded we have identified the planets that are central to Joyce's life, the ones around which her life revolves and those upon which everything in her life ultimately hinges. But even though these planets are instrumental in the manifestation and realization of her life and provide it with its defining qualities and properties, they do not yet tell us anything about the actual physical existence of such a life, whether it is in fact instantiated in one individual called Joyce. We gain insight into this issue (as does the cosmic mind itself) by studying the dominant planets in the life as a whole, which are potentially three, although in some nativities one or two. At the same time, these planets represent the government of the nativity. Out of these three emerge one that is entitled to be called the lord of the nativity, the planet to which the life as a whole belongs.

The most influential planets in the overall government of a life may be defined as: (1) the planet that is strongest and most autonomous in the nativity; (2) the one best connected to the four principal significators of the nativity; (3) the one possessing the most legitimate title to rule.

The Sun and Moon do not qualify as candidates for lord according to any of these three techniques for the simple reason that they are the planets that ultimately bestow this title on one of the remaining five.

Although there are some mechanical rules for determining these planets, they often have to be applied with some latitude and good judgment in particular cases.

First we need to find the planet that is most autonomous in the chart, which is naturally a candidate for lord of the nativity. Thus we look for planets that occupy the places they themselves rule. Jupiter is in its own exaltation, which means it is held in high esteem; it is also in its own bound, which means that it owns itself and is not indebted to another. Saturn and Mercury are in their own triplicity, which means they are their own subjects and subject to no other. Venus and Mars are in their own bounds, which means that they also are indebted only to themselves.

In this consideration, presence in its own bounds is more important than any other kind of rulership. Presence in its own sign comes second, because then a planet is identified with its own property. Presence in its own triplicity comes third, as then a planet is its own subject. I would award this contest to Venus, because even though Jupiter is also in its own exaltation, it is retrograde; Venus is also in a better place than Jupiter.

Next we will look for the planet that has the best connections to the five most authoritative significators. This is the planet that is most closely connected to the Sun, Moon, Lot of Fortune, Prenatal Lunation, and Ascendant by certain special relationships that have to do with the nature of these five significators of the life. This planet again turns out to be Venus. Venus is making a heliacal rising at almost exactly 15 degrees from the Sun (the standard Hellenistic interval for an ideal heliacal rising), and thus speaks with the authority of the Sun; Venus is also in a lunar application by figure with the Moon, which casts its ray by trine at 6 degrees Aquarius 22 minutes, just before Venus, so this planet also has the favor of the queen. As we said above, it is the first planet to receive a bodily application from the Moon after the Prenatal Syzygy, which means that this planet has a royal pedigree. Venus also possesses a fairly tight inferior square to the Lot of Fortune. Finally, Venus is in the ninth, well connected to the Ascendant by trine, and furthermore in the very place of kingship.

The rules for finding the planet with the most legitimate right to rule can often be somewhat complex. We consider the Sun, Moon, Lot of Fortune, Prenatal Syzygy, Ascending Degree in that order in day charts, but reversing the order of the Sun and Moon in night charts. We see which of these significators predominates in this hierarchy by being in one of the best places, most outstandingly the ascending sign, the tenth sign (the Hellenistic Midheaven), and the eleventh sign, usually defaulting to the Ascendant if none of the significators is in the places mentioned. Since only the Moon is in one of these places (the Sun and Prenatal Syzygy being in the eighth, the Lot in the sixth), the Moon is the predominating significator.

We next consider the dispositorship of the Moon in the following order: bound lord, domicile lord, exaltation lord, and trigon lord. The first of these to aspect the Moon or to be in the same sign as it, in such a manner that the Moon "sees" the dispositor by casting its partile ray earlier in the sign than the dispositor itself, qualifies as the planet with the most legitimate entitlement to rule the nativity. In Joyce's nativity, the bound lord does not qualify because the ray of the Moon falls in the bounds prior to those occupied by Mercury. However, Mercury is also the sign ruler, and the trine ray of the Moon does fall in Aquarius before Mercury. Thus Mercury is the planet with the most entitlement.

Summation and Determination of Lord of the Nativity

Venus is the planet that belongs more to itself than any other, and it is also the best connected planet in the chart. Mercury is the planet to whom the nativity as a whole belongs. But Mercury is in the bounds of Venus, so the entitlement of Mercury actually belongs to Venus. Thus, Venus is the lord of this nativity, the planet to whom it belongs. This strongly suggests that this nativity is about a single physically existent person, or we might say that it is a correct chart.

Conclusion and Signature of the Nativity

But I determined Saturn to be the planet ultimately supporting this life, the planet of which the life as a whole is predicated (which furthermore is its own

374

subject in that it is in its own triplicity). Even though the ultimate subject and the ultimate owner of this life are not the same planet, nevertheless they are closely connected. Venus, the planet to whom the nativity as a whole belongs, is in the sign of Saturn, the planet ultimately supporting the life as a whole. It is the function of Saturn to administer to the nativity as a whole, but because Venus is in a sign ruled by Saturn, it is the responsibility of Saturn to administer to Venus. Saturn can perform this function well because it trines Venus, although it is also retrograde. Thus, these two principal planets are in the proper relationship to one another with respect to their roles in the life as a whole, and this constitutes the unique signature of Joyce's life.

RONNIE GALE DREYER: VEDIC

STRATEGY

As a matter of course, my readings are consultations wherein my client sits across from me, or at the other end of a phone, and I can verify events from the past that can influence the present and future, as well as zero in on which choices the horoscope provides. For instance, Jupiter may mean teaching, but it could also mean publishing, the ministry, or law. Once the client can verify which choice he or she has made, then the reading can make sense at each step and proceed logically. Because astrology is not an exact science, the "blind" reading may present a range of roads that Joyce may have taken, or not taken. With no feedback, I have tried to present many possibilities. It would be presumptuous of me to assume to know exactly which path she has taken, when there are many options open to her. Some indications in the horoscope, however, seem to be corroborated in different ways, and in those instances I will probably be more precise and affirmative. I usually read the chart by beginning with the Ascendant, then the Moon, and then I describe the houses. By the time I reach the end, I may have discussed the issues pertaining to that house in other sections, so there will be repetition. This sounds different when the reading is oral than when the reading is in written form.

Before I even look at someone's horoscope and its accompanying planetary periods and transits, I close my eyes, center myself, and clear my mind of any thoughts. Once that has been achieved, I can study the horoscope objectively without any preconceived notions about it. The methodology is a combination of studying the material through proven formulas combined with a certain level of intuition in trying to assess exactly how different indications in the chart may actually manifest given the age of the client.

I interpreted Joyce's chart using Jyotish, the astrology of India that has been utilized for thousands of years. More commonly known as Vedic Astrology, there are some very distinct differences from the system used here in the West. The greatest difference lies in the fact that Vedic Astrology uses the sidereal zodiac (based on the actual, rather than symbolic, positions of the planets), which at the present time (2004) is approximately 23 degrees 50 minutes behind the tropical zodiac. (This ayanamsa is based on the work of K.S. Krishnamurti.) In 1943, Joyce's birth year, the ayanamsa (difference between zodiacs) was 22 degrees 58 minutes. Additionally I do not use Uranus, Neptune and Pluto, since they were not used in Classical Jyotish, and I utilize the whole sign house system, which is constructed so that the sign of the Ascendant comprises the entire first house, and each sign that follows comprises an entire house. In this particular chart, the Ascendant is Gemini. This means that the entire first house is in the sign of Gemini, the second house is Cancer, the third house is Leo, the fourth house is Virgo, the fifth house is Libra, the sixth house is Scorpio, the seventh house is Sagittarius, the eighth house is Capricorn, the ninth house is Aquarius, the tenth house is Pisces, the eleventh house is Aries, and the twelfth house is Taurus.

I use a second chart called the Moon Chart or Chandra (Moon) Lagna (Ascendant) that places the Moon as the first house, and all the planets are then calculated from the position of the Moon. This means that since the Moon is in sidereal Taurus, this sign would function as the first house, followed by Gemini in the second house, Cancer in the third house, Leo in the fourth house, etc., with all the planets placed in their respective signs. I also use the Navamsa chart which is based on the ninth harmonic chart, and serves as another way of looking at the person's life and, most importantly, their relationship life. There are also other harmonic charts and other variables that I use to make a final assessment of the chart. To forecast different phases in Joyce's life, the Dasa system is used, and that divides the life up into planetary periods and subperiods. I also use transits for the current period in order to get a better idea of what issues might be of concern at the present time.

To prepare for the actual reading, I look at the chart's patterns and shapes, and then I take note of planetary signatures and combinations that stand out. I mark all these down on a sheet of paper. While the first set of notes indicates certain outstanding features of the chart, the next phase is to analyze the chart by beginning with the Ascendant and going through the twelve houses. I mark down the planets that occupy and aspect each house. Then I note the planetary ruler of each house, where it is placed, how it is aspected, and general condition (i.e. whether it is involved in a Yoga, if it is in the house of a friend or an enemy, etc.). If, for instance, the same planet aspects a house and its ruler, the nature of that particular planet and what it represents could be the strongest influence. Finally, I look at the house position of the planet's dispositors (the lord of both the sign and nakshatra [Moon mansion] in which the planet is placed) in order to see what other subtleties are connected with that planet, and what areas of life it is influencing. After assessing the strengths and weaknesses

378

of the planets, and judging how I think they might function and which areas of life they will affect, I look at the Vimshottari Dasa System, in which the life is divided into planetary periods and sub-periods. Each Dasa (age), sub-period, and sub-sub period provides a window of planetary influences that pinpoint when the influences of the chart might manifest. Because I view the chart as being filled with many different choices and potentials, Vedic astrology provides a way to see when these potentials and difficulties are likely to manifest.

The software I use is Parashara's Light published by Geovision Software. I use the interpretations inserted into the software sparingly, since each software developer uses particular texts from which to take identifying planetary combinations. These interpretations are at times helpful, but because I may disagree with some of the textual interpretations, and since they are stock interpretations and not synthesized, it is most important for me to study these charts completely on my own without looking at the interpretations provided in the software. The software does contain the texts of some of the classics, and I often use that since it is easier to do this on the computer than search through the actual books.

Worksheet for general impressions of the chart

1. Mars is in its own sign of Scorpio in the very last degree. Mars is Atma Karaka. Mars is Ruchaka Yoga (in its own sign on an angle from the Moon) - strong survivor instincts.
2. Moon is exalted and is Vargottama (same sign in birth chart as in Navamsa). Moon is in its own Nakshatra - strong lunar characteristics though Moon is afflicted.
3. Sun is Vargottama.
4. Eighth and twelfth house emphasis - Moksha houses; six planets in the sixth, eighth and twelfth Dusthana houses - more hidden, restrained, spiritual, research oriented.
5. Capricorn and Taurus - Earth sign emphasis.
6. Parivartana Yoga - Venus and Saturn in mutual reception.
7. Tight conjunctions of Moon-Saturn and Venus-Mercury (Venus wins planetary war).
8. Mercury and Venus form Raj (royal) Yoga (ruler of first, fourth [Mercury] and fifth [Venus] houses); also Aristha (sorrow) Yoga (ruler of first [Mercury] and twelfth [Venus] house).

9. Vipareet Raj Yoga - ruler of sixth (Mars) in sixth, ruler of eighth (Saturn) in twelfth, ruler of twelfth (Venus) in eighth.
10. Sakata Yoga - Moon is twelfth from Jupiter.
11. Chandra Lagna has ninth house emphasis.
12. Jupiter in first house in Dig Bala position (directional strength).
13. Saturn falls in navamsa.
14. Sade Sati (Saturn transiting the sign before, of, and after the Moon).
15. Chandra Mangala Yoga (Moon and Mars mutually aspecting).
16. Dhana Yoga with Mars (eleventh house lord), Moon (second house lord) and Saturn (ninth house lord) in sixth and twelfth.
17. Budha Aditya Yoga - Sun and Mercury conjunct with no combustion.

Second Worksheet

First House: Gemini ascendant. Jupiter occupies. Mars aspects. Mercury is ruler, placed in Capricorn in the eighth house, closely conjunct Venus (wins planetary war), and conjoins Sun (Budha Aditya yoga).
Second House: Sun, Venus, Mercury, and Saturn aspects. Moon rules, placed in Taurus (exaltation) in twelfth (eleven places away) closely conjunct Saturn, aspected by Mars. Mars and Moon are Chandra Mangala Yoga.
Third House: Rahu, Ketu aspects. Ruler Sun is in the eighth house (six places away) in Capricorn, and conjunct Venus and Mercury.
Fourth House: No planets occupying or aspecting fourth house. Ruler Mercury placed in eighth (five places away) house with Sun (lord of third) and Venus (lord of fifth and twelfth) closely conjunct.
Fifth House: Aspected by Jupiter. Ruler Venus placed in the eighth (fourth from it) with Mercury (lord of first and fourth) and Sun (lord of third)
Sixth House: Mars occupying it with Ruchaka Yoga. Last Degree. Atma Karaka. Moon and Saturn aspecting it. Ruler is Mars in its own sign and own house.
Seventh House: Jupiter aspecting its own house. Rahu aspecting seventh house. Ruler Jupiter placed in the first house in an enemy's sign, aspected by Mars (lord of sixth and eleventh houses).
Eighth House: Mercury retrograde (lord of first and fourth), Venus (lord of fifth and twelfth) and Sun (lord of third) in Capricorn in the eighth house. Raj Yoga between Mercury and Venus. Ruler Saturn (eighth and ninth house ruler)

placed in twelfth (five places from it) with Moon (second house ruler) and in Parivartana Yoga with Venus.

Ninth House: Ketu occupies, Rahu, Mars, Saturn, and Jupiter aspects. Ruler Saturn aspects its own house. Ruler Saturn is in the twelfth (four places from it), aspected by Moon (ruler of second) and Mars (ruler of eighth and eleventh).

Tenth House: No aspects. Ruler Jupiter in the first house (four places from it) aspected by Mars (lord of sixth and eleventh).

Eleventh House: Rahu aspecting. Ruler Mars in the sixth house (eight places from it) in its own house, aspected by Saturn (lord of eighth and ninth) and Moon (lord of second).

Twelfth House: Moon and Saturn occupies. Mars aspects. Ruler Venus placed in eighth house (nine places from it) conjoined with Sun and Mercury.

Dasas:

January 16, 1943 - July 3, 1950 - Moon
July 4, 1950 - July 2, 1957 - Mars
July 3, 1957 - July 3, 1975 - Rahu (North Node)
July 4, 1975 - July 3, 1991 - Jupiter
July 4, 1991 - July 2, 2010 - Saturn
July 3, 2010 - July 2, 2027 - Mercury
July 3, 2027 - July 2, 2034 - Ketu (South Node)
July 3, 2034 - July 2, 2054 - Venus
July 3, 2054 - July 2, 2060 - Sun

Jyotish (Sanskrit for "Science of Light"), also known as Vedic, or Hindu, Astrology, is based on the sidereal zodiac. The difference between the sidereal and tropical zodiac lies in the ayanamsa (the difference in degrees and minutes between 0 Aries and the point at which the equinox actually occurs). To calculate sidereal placements (which are precession-corrected), subtract the appropriate ayanamsa for the birth date in question from the tropical positions. There are several different ayanamsas used in India, but the one employed here is the Krishnamurti ayanamsa, which at present is approximately 23 degrees 50 minutes. (This also varies from the Fagan-Bradley ayanamsa used among Western siderealists.) Vedic astrology employs a whole sign house system, whereby each house is comprised of an entire sign, beginning with the Ascendant. In Joyce's natal chart, sidereal Gemini is the Ascendant, which means the first house consists of the entire sign of Gemini (and any planets in that sign), the second house consists of Cancer, the third sign consists of Leo, etc.

To read the North Indian-style chart (top), follow the signs-houses of the Vedic chart by starting with the Ascendant (the top central box) and proceeding counterclockwise. The number 3 indicates that Gemini, the third sign, is the Ascendant. The houses are always in the same positions, but the signs contained therein vary depending on the rising sign. To read the South Indian-style chart (bottom), in which the signs are always in the same places, proceed clockwise from Aries which is always the second sign-house from the upper left. The Ascendant is marked with "As." Traditional rulerships are used in Vedic astrology so that Mars rules Scorpio, Jupiter rules Pisces and Saturn rules Aquarius; Uranus, Neptune and Pluto are not used. Aspects are different than in Western astrology, and Yogas, special planetary combinations, are an important feature. In a sidereal chart, exact timing of transits may differ slightly from a tropical chart.

Diagrams courtesy of Parashara Light Software,
published by Geovision Software.

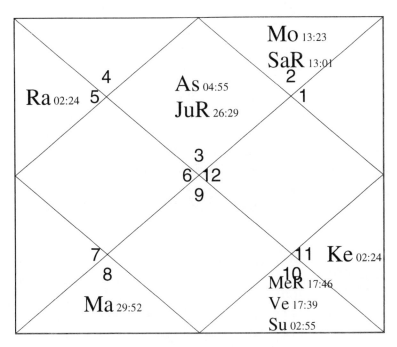

North Indian Chart

South Indian Chart

		SaR 13:01 Mo 13:23	As 04:55 JuR 26:29
Ke 02:24			
MeR 17:46 Ve 17:39 Su 02:55			Ra 02:24
	Ma 29:52		

Moon (10y)   0 yrs. to   7y5m

Antar	Beginning	Ending
Moon		
Mars		
Rahu	01-16-1943	06-04-1943
Jupiter	06-04-1943	10-03-1944
Saturn	10-03-1944	05-04-1946
Mercury	05-04-1946	10-03-1947
Ketu	10-03-1947	05-03-1948
Venus	05-03-1948	01-02-1950
Sun	01-02-1950	07-04-1950

Mars (7y)   7y5m to   14y5m

Antar	Beginning	Ending
Mars	07-04-1950	11-30-1950
Rahu	11-30-1950	12-18-1951
Jupiter	12-18-1951	11-23-1952
Saturn	11-23-1952	01-02-1954
Mercury	01-02-1954	12-30-1954
Ketu	12-30-1954	05-28-1955
Venus	05-28-1955	07-28-1956
Sun	07-28-1956	12-02-1956
Moon	12-02-1956	07-03-1957

Rahu (18y)   14y5m to   32y5m

Antar	Beginning	Ending
Rahu	07-03-1957	03-16-1960
Jupiter	03-16-1960	08-09-1962
Saturn	08-09-1962	06-15-1965
Mercury	06-15-1965	01-02-1968
Ketu	01-02-1968	01-20-1969
Venus	01-20-1969	01-21-1972
Sun	01-21-1972	12-14-1972
Moon	12-14-1972	06-15-1974
Mars	06-15-1974	07-04-1975

Jupiter (16y)   32y5m to   48y5m

Antar	Beginning	Ending
Jupiter	07-04-1975	08-21-1977
Saturn	08-21-1977	03-03-1980
Mercury	03-03-1980	06-09-1982
Ketu	06-09-1982	05-16-1983
Venus	05-16-1983	01-14-1986
Sun	01-14-1986	11-02-1986
Moon	11-02-1986	03-03-1988
Mars	03-03-1988	02-07-1989
Rahu	02-07-1989	07-04-1991

Saturn (19y)   48y5m to   67y5m

Antar	Beginning	Ending
Saturn	07-04-1991	07-06-1994
Mercury	07-06-1994	03-16-1997
Ketu	03-16-1997	04-24-1998
Venus	04-24-1998	06-24-2001
Sun	06-24-2001	06-06-2002
Moon	06-06-2002	01-05-2004
Mars	01-05-2004	02-13-2005
Rahu	02-13-2005	12-21-2007
Jupiter	12-21-2007	07-03-2010

Mercury (17y)   67y5m to   84y5m

Antar	Beginning	Ending
Mercury	07-03-2010	11-29-2012
Ketu	11-29-2012	11-26-2013
Venus	11-26-2013	09-26-2016
Sun	09-26-2016	08-02-2017
Moon	08-02-2017	01-02-2019
Mars	01-02-2019	12-30-2019
Rahu	12-30-2019	07-18-2022
Jupiter	07-18-2022	10-23-2024
Saturn	10-23-2024	07-03-2027

Ketu (7y)   84y5m to   91y5m

Antar	Beginning	Ending
Ketu	07-03-2027	11-30-2027
Venus	11-30-2027	01-29-2029
Sun	01-29-2029	06-05-2029
Moon	06-05-2029	01-05-2030
Mars	01-05-2030	06-03-2030
Rahu	06-03-2030	06-21-2031
Jupiter	06-21-2031	05-27-2032
Saturn	05-27-2032	07-06-2033
Mercury	07-06-2033	07-03-2034

Venus (20y)   91y5m to   111y5m

Antar	Beginning	Ending
Venus	07-03-2034	11-02-2037
Sun	11-02-2037	11-02-2038
Moon	11-02-2038	07-03-2040
Mars	07-03-2040	09-02-2041
Rahu	09-02-2041	09-01-2044
Jupiter	09-01-2044	05-03-2047
Saturn	05-03-2047	07-03-2050
Mercury	07-03-2050	05-03-2053
Ketu	05-03-2053	07-03-2054

Sun (6y)   111y5m to   117y5m

Antar	Beginning	Ending
Sun	07-03-2054	10-21-2054
Moon	10-21-2054	04-21-2055
Mars	04-21-2055	08-27-2055
Rahu	08-27-2055	07-21-2056
Jupiter	07-21-2056	05-09-2057
Saturn	05-09-2057	04-21-2058
Mercury	04-21-2058	02-25-2059
Ketu	02-25-2059	07-03-2059
Venus	07-03-2059	07-02-2060

General Tendencies

This chart presents two very different patterns and life circumstances that eventually come together in midlife, once Joyce has experienced some hard knocks, and lessons to learn throughout her life. On the one hand, there are planets in the sixth, eighth and twelfth houses, otherwise known as hidden houses. Many planets in this area of the chart present obstacles in the life, childhood difficulties, isolation, loneliness, and an inability to connect and express one's feelings honestly and easily in social situations. Instead, artistic, scholarly and spiritual pursuits would be a more accessible area for Joyce to express herself—since she will not have to be judged by others. The other part of her chart is a well placed Jupiter in Gemini in the first house, the Nodes in strong placements, and Mars in the sixth house which all provide strength of character, and the will to survive and overcome a difficult childhood, tendencies towards isolation, and health issues (physical or in the form of depression), which in someone else's chart could have left a lifetime scar. Because the Jupiter Dasa occurs between the ages of 32-48, and Jupiter returns to its own position at the approximate age of 36, this points to the fact that Joyce has a learning curve in which her greatest fortunes, achievements and happiness will come at a time when she has been able to resolve other areas of her life.

The water houses, also called Moksha (Sanskrit for "liberation") houses, are emphasized in this chart, as are the Earth and Water signs (a preponderance of planets are in Taurus, Scorpio and Capricorn). There are rises and falls and great dramatic changes in the life. There also should be accomplishment later in life, financial ups and downs, and ultimately some very difficult and yet some very good relationships. Moksha houses favor the quest towards a spiritual life and, as such, Joyce will be preoccupied with this throughout her life—despite all the trials and tribulations and successes and disappointments.

Now to the specifics.

The most important areas of the Rasi Chart are the Lagna, Sanskrit for Ascendant, and Chandra, Sanskrit for the Moon. The Ascendant determines your fate, your character, your direction, and your individual approach through life's journey. The first house rules destiny, appearance, general health, and fame. It is the condition of the first house (planets occupying and aspecting it, and placement of the ruling planet) that determines how strong the will is, and

385

how easy or difficult it may be to fulfill goals. The Moon, on the other hand, is the most important luminary in Vedic Astrology, mostly because it travels so fast, and the Moon's light overtakes the Sun, which burns too brightly and parches the land. It is the Moon's Nakshatra, or Moon Mansion, that determines the planetary period that starts the person's life. Whereas the Ascendant rules destiny, appearance, and one's outward direction in life, the Moon rules one's mother, emotions, memories, and ability to have been nurtured and to nurture. Most importantly, the Moon rules the mind and reflects the state of one's mind, and whether or not one can attain peace of mind and balance in one's inner life. The Moon indicates our level of stability, our ability to tolerate stress, and is a reflection of our inner hopes, dreams and fears. If the Moon is well-aspected, there will be peace of mind and an ability to focus and concentrate. If the Moon is afflicted, there will be depression, fear and an inability to create a balance between our thoughts and our feelings. The chart reading begins with an analysis of the Ascendant and the Moon. This will also incorporate many other aspects of the chart.

Ascendant

Joyce's ascendant is 4 Gemini (Mithuna) 55 minutes and falls in the Nakshatra (Moon Mansion) of Mrigsira, which spans 23 degrees Taurus 20 minutes to 6 degrees Gemini 40 minutes. Gemini is the sign of the twins and a mutable Air sign. This means that there is a lot of vacillation, versatility, and the need to always be juggling different things at one time. It will provide Joyce with a love of ideas, a passion for intellectual pursuits, and the need to communicate with people who think the way she does about the world around her. She is interested in everything around her—from politics to music, and from travel to art. She loves being stimulated through dialogue with others and can be talkative, even thinking out loud, humorous, youthful, and cheerful. The more thoughts and ideas that she can sink her teeth into, the better. She may be giddy, nervous, and a much better talker than she is a listener. As a Gemini Ascendant, Joyce loves to juggle many things at once, and though she is probably versatile with many interests, it is difficult for her to maintain focus in order to bring a project to completion. She is probably restless, with a need to move around; her motions are animated and her eyes often roam as they speak to you. Geminis love film, television and magazines, and are very good at sales and marketing, and may even be very good at writing, accounting, advertising and organizing. They love doing things with people and are not usually noted for their tendencies to stay in one place.

While these qualities apply generally to people with Gemini rising, Joyce would not have displayed all these traits early in life, since most of her planets are placed in the hidden houses. This means that she is very private, and much of her learning and self-expression may have been done in her own unique way. She may have learned more through traveling, reading, and developing her own unique style of self-expression. This may have been through flouting conventional attire, writing poetry, or keeping journals. Whatever creative form she may have chosen would have led towards a more introverted means of satisfying her great curiosity and desire to dialogue with others. While she seems to be very clever, glib, eloquent, and a master of words, she can, at the drop of a hat, be very private, close up, and not want to be around people at all. In fact, she is probably only close to very few people, though she may have many acquaintances. Because Gemini is known as a sign that is quite superficial, talking and communicating easily does not really mean that one is communicating from one's heart, or sharing emotionally. Indeed, you can talk to someone like Joyce for hours, and discuss politics, culture, art, and her political views on a variety of subjects, but you might never really know what she is thinking on a very deep level. She might love to talk to you from a distance, by email or by telephone, and love to write things down. In fact, she might have many notes in many notebooks and on different pieces of paper.

Although Gemini rising is most known to be social, it is also very superficial, and very often projects are discarded before they are completed, and too many things are attempted at one time. This could be simply because Joyce is restless and so used to movement that anything short of continual stimulation might pass itself off as boring. There is a love of travel, an active mind, mental vacillation, enthusiasm, talkativeness and clever qualities along with the ability to seduce others and attract people towards her. She is often fickle and can easily change her mind within a matter of seconds. Geminis may satisfy their need for constant mental stimulation through meaningful conversations and diversions such as lectures, museums, films, concerts and the theater. They are intelligent, witty, wonderful conversationalists but very poor listeners. Their greatest challenge is to complete what they have started since they are usually involved with two projects at once.

Geminis are often good with the hands and are quick in terms of writing, typing, or sports that require the arms. There is a love of diversity and moving around. There is not enough consistency however until later on in life. The early part of the life is spent in searching for happiness, and Joyce will probably go through several difficult relationships before she is able to have a more meaningful one. Later on, probably in her mid-thirties, there is much more ability to have a good partnership and to pursue some goals that could have to do with teaching, law, publishing and religion.

The Ascendant is located within the nakshatra (Moon Mansion) called Mrigsira, which spans 23 degrees Taurus to 6 degrees Gemini, and is ruled by Mars. Mrigsira literally means "antelope's head," or "face of a deer." (See *The Nakshatras*, by Dennis Harness, Lotus Press, 1999, p. 19.) Like the deer, those born with either the Ascendant or the Moon in this nakshatra are restless, aimless, and have the intense desire and need to feel free and independent. This points to the fact that Joyce probably changed residences a few times, traveled extensively, and may not have felt settled until her mid-thirties. In fact, as a young woman, she might have felt trapped by being in one place for too long, or simply found it difficult to feel grounded. Again, that feeling might subside later in life, although the love of travel will always be with her.

Just as the deer is restless, it is also scared and timid. In keeping with that imagery, Joyce probably started out life as a timid, shy and nervous child whose emotional needs were not always met. While they are very frightened animals, they are also very graceful, and she may have had a love and talent for dance, or some other physical activity where synchronized movements are important. In this particular chart, the instability that seems to be a theme in the first part of her life is not merely out of choice as a young adult, but a way of life that was thrust on her as a child. She may have had an early change of residence, or simply experiences between parents that caused a great deal of uprootedness. This may also have been caused by a change of residence, or change in the family structure, at a very early age, and this trend only continued to give her a restless feeling throughout her life, and a desire to search for something meaningful and spiritual. Since her childhood may have been spent alienated from others, either due to illness, which prevented her from participating in activities, or due to feeling separate from her environment, she must have learned early to create her own space and to communicate with the world in unique way. For whatever reason, there seems to be the need to sample different things in life. There should be many long journeys, both physical and spiritual, and because the Ascendant is in the sign of Gemini the twins, and the nakshatra of Mrigsira symbolized by the deer, searching becomes a way of life.

This also means that there is a lot of physical movement in the early years, and perhaps spiritual movement in her later years.

Because there is a lot of international travel noted here, or at least living in places different from her own cultural milieu, she also might be very good at languages, or she will work hard to create her own special language through the arts, especially poetry, music or dance. In fact, she is probably most comfortable on her own and, until she reached a period of maturity in life, was not very comfortable in her own skin. For that reason, and as we will see later in the reading, she is not always considered to be warm and compassionate, even though she might be witty and a good raconteur. One important lesson for Joyce to learn is how to express and show feelings, without thinking that they will overpower her.

Health

Gemini rules the lungs, the chest, and the arms, making her prone to colds, bronchitis, pneumonia and, at worst, emphysema. While Jupiter provides protection against many obstacles, good recovery and healing abilities, and general optimism and fortitude, its kapha (wet and phlegmatic) influence can contribute to respiratory ailments caused by too much mucous or water accumulation in the area of the body ruled by Gemini, in this case the lungs. The result may be water on the lungs, mucous accumulation, bronchitis, asthma, and general short-windedness. Good health and physical well-being can be easily maintained with sufficient rest, fresh air, correct eating habits, smoke-free environments, and plenty of exercise. However, if a condition like asthma was present as a child, this could be one reason that there was insecurity and alienation from others. She should avoid smoking and try to pace her life to allow time for relaxation. With Mercury in the eighth house of chronic illness, ailments like asthma, allergies, respiratory ailments and bronchitis might plague her throughout her life especially during times of great emotional stress.

Gemini rising will also give Joyce a high-strung, insecure and nervous nature. She may speak out of turn, and laugh at inappropriate times. The Ascendant rules general health, and she will probably have had mental and/or physical health issues from the time she was a child. There seems to have been something restricting her from playing with other children whether an ailment, or simply feeling alienated due to moves or family problems. In addition to the lungs, there may be afflictions to the eyes, and diabetes may also be prevalent (due to the influence of Jupiter on the Ascendant and Venus on the Ascendant ruler). In fact, the entire facial area, throat, neck and thyroid may be prone to illness and injury, and these may have been especially problematic during the last several years. Her legs and ankles may also be weak, and it would not be surprising if she had a bout with polio as a child.

Although there is a talkative, nervous nature, Joyce like most Geminis may be masking a tendency towards depression if she is alone and is confronted with herself. In Joyce's case, depression may be substituted with sexual liaisons or indulgences, at least in the early part of her life. At other times, she may simply get depressed, remain isolated, or use her poetry to express deep melancholy and depressed feelings. Although this is typical of Gemini Ascendants, who have an unusually strong need for activity to mask depression, the tendency towards melancholia and depression is strengthened by the ruling planet Mercury's placement in Saturn-ruled Capricorn in the eighth house of the occult, sexuality, research, and business. This combination will give her a love of psychology and other subjects that she may early in life have to do in secrecy. Because Mercury rules the way we communicate, and because the Moon is in the twelfth, her ability to speak to people and make jokes would probably have remained hidden until later in life when she can raise her self-esteem. She might be very witty, but known to just a few.

Ruling Planet Mercury

Because Mercury, Joyce's ruling planet, is in the "hidden" eighth house, she may spend time utilizing her intellectual interests in studying psychology, parapsychology, dreams, hypnosis, and other metaphysical and psychological areas in which one can delve into the mind's inner depths. The dispositor of Mercury is Saturn in the twelfth house, which makes one more introverted and hidden. Joyce might be drawn to professions that keep her by herself, such as research, or the arts with their rehearsing and practicing. Even though Gemini is usually talkative and social, Mercury's foray into the Moksha eighth house will subdue the self-expression, and cause the rather active mentality to be somewhat self-conscious and insecure. This placement, however, will also make Joyce's mind rather unique and interested in subjects that are not necessarily held in interest by the general public. Again, they could be metaphysical in nature, and they could also be extremely artistic and highly creative. Because Mercury is sitting in the sign Capricorn, Joyce's speech will be terse, rather than rambling,

390

and there could be sarcasm. There is a great deal of wit, and Joyce possesses an eloquent style and a talent for poetry and writing. Because of the proximity of Mercury to Venus, and because Venus is at the lower longitude, it is said to win the planetary war with Mercury, meaning that the qualities of Venus—the heart—will oftentimes overrule Mercury—the intellect. Her way of speaking will be sweet when she needs it to be, but it can also be harsh and cutting and sarcastic when that applies. There is at times a coldness in her tone, because she simply wants to cut loose and have control over her own time. However Venus's power over Mercury means that often she makes choices based on comfort, desire and love rather than thinking things through. In other words, the heart will sometimes overpower the head, and desire will overpower reason. Up until the age of thirty, these desires were probably harder to control, or they could have also have been repressed. In any event, she was not able to come to terms with her desire nature in a healthy, balanced way until after the age of thirty-two, most probably. The combination of Mercury, Venus and the Sun are going to be strong forces for the dissemination of ideas. Her mind is very eclectic and she probably has a strong desire to do something in the fine arts, possibly dance, poetry, music, or drama. There will be love of the arts and music and poetry, and she will have the ability to heal. With so many planets in Capricorn, she will have to take plenty of calcium to avoid osteoporosis, and arthritis may also plague her as she ages. Additionally with so many planets in the eighth house of business, she may become involved in an alternative business, especially one in which products that have to do with beauty or luxury—herbs, perfume, clothing—are sold. More than not, however, this chart will point to poetry, writing, music or some other branch of the creative or dramatic arts.

With Mercury in the nakshatra of Shravana, ruled by the Moon in the twelfth house, the love of poetry and teaching, which Shravana-influenced people excel at, is even more pronounced. With Mercury ruling teaching, writing, astrology, psychology, and Venus (which wins the planetary war with Mercury) ruling perfume, jewelry, clothing and the arts, she might be anything from a published poet to a psychologist to a spiritual minister to a manufacturer of herbal products. She might love jewelry and even do that as a sideline.

Some of these obstacles she must overcome are likely health-oriented, and either Joyce or her mother, most probably, had to battle illness and, at the very least, depression. There is a lot of parental strife, and the early loss or separation from one of them probably caused some of the isolation and hostility in the chart. There could have also been some kind of abuse in the family, or simply distancing from the parents. It is difficult in a "blind" reading to zero in on exactly what the dynamics were in the home, but it is safe to say that there was either a lot of changes of residence, or a mother who was not a very nurturing figure. The father may have been absent and he may also have been short-tempered, angry, or a military figure.

Venus, which rules artistic endeavors, luxury, partnership and the need to be loved, will overwhelm Mercury's ability to engage in practical mental pursuits. In other words, the heart overwhelms reason, and Joyce found it easy to satisfy her senses and the need to be loved, more than scholarly pursuits. She could have simply put her own needs and longings aside for the wants and needs of someone else due to the need to be loved and accepted. She may also have given things up for the artistic life, and the need for pleasure tends to overpower the desire to communicate. There will probably be some indulgence in matters of the heart, and Joyce will probably find that this part of her nature might get her into trouble. When this desire to be loved is channeled into self-love and creative productivity, or love of a higher ideal, her life will be much more harmonious. This will probably be more easily achieved later in life after learning from some hard knocks. Because Venus rules the twelfth, there is loss of security and perhaps the mother early in life. However, since Venus also rules the fifth house, her life may take on more meaning if and when she has children and must assume responsibility. She may spend her lifetime trying to heal the wounds wrought by her early childhood and especially the early loss of or separation from one parent.

The combination of the Sun with Mercury is called a Budha Aditya Yoga and gives great intelligence. Happiness becomes a lifelong quest, and it is possible that this person will never be fully content except when performing service or some selfless act either for the family or in the form of spiritual practice.

With Mars aspecting her Ascendant, Joyce could be argumentative, temperamental, and rebellious as a young person. Even as she ages and becomes mellower, this quality of becoming offensive and impatient at first will never be lost. Mars will also provide a sense of ambition and aggression, and Jupiter will provide optimism, though indulgence. She may be adventurous, temperamental, aggressive, independent, assertive, accident-prone, and have physical prowess. The Mars Dasa between the ages of seven and fourteen would have been very difficult and filled with possible illness, trouble with siblings and other circumstances that were difficult for Joyce to deal with. Family turmoil is at the top of this list. She will be lovely to look at since the ruling planet is so tightly connected to Venus. With Mars aspecting the ruler of the ninth house of the father and the father itself, this physical and angry planet seems to be the one that is directed at and most associated with the father. She may have acted out and tried to leave home, or she may also have simply developed a world of her own, and her own artistic world, to create a more harmonious universe and reality for herself.

Whatever endeavor she attempts, and whatever ups and downs might ensue, it is important to realize that Jupiter, the planet of abundance and optimism, occupies the first house. This position is known as Dig Bala, which means that Jupiter, the ruler of her seventh house of partnership and tenth house of career, provides its blessings and will save her life many times. Symbolically, this position will provide optimism, hope, sudden opportunities, and lucky meetings with other people, even when she thought that all around her was lost. Jupiter will also provide spiritual and physical healing properties so that even though her childhood may have been wrought with illness, there is a lucky star that will help overcome all obstacles. It also means she has the blessings of the Guru (Sanskrit for Jupiter), and a meeting with a mentor, spiritual teacher or partner (who either is her teacher or will lead to a teacher) will come to her during the course of her life. This position will elevate the partner and the career, and may also bring her fortunate children—but again this may have to wait until she has reached the age of thirty-five. Mostly, Jupiter acts like a lucky star, and provides protection and the ability to forge ahead. It also means that opportunities will happen when she least expects them, and especially during any Jupiter sub-period or major period. Because the Jupiter cycle is from thirty-two to forty-eight years old, these years should have brought many opportunities for career, partnership, and even children. It is very fortunate that Jupiter is in the first house because it provides the balance, optimism, and healing that she needs from time to time.

If we look at her Chandra Lagna (Moon Chart), we see that the planets that were in the eighth and twelfth hidden houses switch to the first, seventh, and ninth houses from the Moon. This means that her horoscope takes on a new role when we look at the subtleties of what has been occurring with Joyce internally, as opposed to many of the adventures and misadventures she has experienced on the external level. This reversal of chart influences shows that during the course of her life—most probably in the Jupiter cycle between the ages of thirty-two to forty-eight and the years 1975-1991—she will become

393

successful in areas of life represented by the ninth house: teaching, publishing, religion, law, higher studies, and travel. She may feel comfortable in an environment that is academic, spiritual, creative, or one in which she can be left alone.

The Moon

The Moon will show Joyce's state of mind and emotional perceptions that Joyce has throughout her life. It also represents her mother, the way she was nurtured, and her own capacity for nurturing others. The Moon is in Taurus, its sign of exaltation and the place where the qualities of that planet can shine and be brought to their highest level. These qualities that describe how she would like to be seen by others include patience, reliability, and the capacity to love, nurture, protect, and encourage others. Her need to be needed, as a mother figure, as well as the desire to be recognized for her sensuality also plays a large part here. Those Taurean attributes are emphasized because the Moon is also placed in the nakshatra of Rohini, ruled by the Moon. Also known as Moon Mansions, the twenty-seven Nakshatras are considered to be the resting places, or wives, of the Moon who as a male deity travels through the zodiac each month. Literally meaning "Red Cow," Rohini is said to be the Moon's favorite wife because she possesses the most wonderful traits of the Moon namely patience, the capacity to nurture, stateliness, beauty, sensuality, and charm. She is also the most sensual, jealous and possessive—qualities Joyce may be plagued by because the Moon, while exalted, is also afflicted. There are a lot of desires when the Moon is in Rohini Nakshatra, which, according to Dennis Harness, is a punishment for the Moon's being so infatuated with her. The difficulty with this Moon is that it is hidden in the twelfth house of isolation, debt, secrecy, addiction, and excess, and afflicted by Saturn and Mars, both natural malefics. This means that Joyce will experience the difficulties represented by the twelfth house, before she can begin to experience its strong points— spirituality, compassion, and liberation.

The biggest problem Joyce will face is dealing with her emotions, and learning how to heal the wounds of her past. Because the Moon is afflicted, the Mother herself was a difficult person, depressed, or physically disabled. She might have even separated from Joyce early in her life, leaving her either without the physical presence of her mother, or with someone who had many problems of her own. It seems that Joyce was not nurtured as she should have been, and therefore it would have been difficult for her to be able to express herself emotionally. She may have found that artistic expression was much easier for her since she did not have to relate to people, which did not come easily for her. She may have been very reticent, or did not speak from her heart. She would have gone through extremes from being very cold, controlled, and even repressed (aspect from Saturn) to being very angry and rebellious (aspect from Mars). The greatest lessons Joyce has had to learn in life are how to be compassionate, and not to ask others to prove their love by submitting to her desires and wishes. This is not intentional, but may have simply been Joyce's way of feeling that she was loved and needed. The difficulties however mean that it will have taken her many years before she was able to learn to love freely, and to be able to open herself up and express the warmth and love that the exalted Moon is capable of giving. Because the Moon will always be tested, the biggest challenges she will face throughout her life are balancing the need to be alone with emotional insecurity; learning how to give and accept love without controlling and masking her feelings, making it difficult to "let someone in;" and overcoming the tendency to have others "prove" their love and loyalty due to her mistrust of people who profess to care and then continue to disappoint. Once she learns to be compassionate without judging her own shortcomings as well as those of others, she will become a wonderful teacher to others. Until that time, she will probably be involved in difficult emotional relationships, but will be able to make great strides in her studies, or creativity, and eventually spiritual practice.

Mars, the natural indicator of sex, desire, and physical violence, will emphasize her passionate nature and even bring on recklessness and rebellion in the early years of her life. It is placed in the sixth house of health and enemies, and this will affect the health of the mother in the early years of Joyce's life and, with the Moon and Saturn so closely connected, may imply a separation from the mother in her early years, or the mother's physical or emotional health problems. This may also have indicated that during the Mars Dasa, there was a separation or illness of an older sibling. Because Mars rules the eleventh house of profits, and is placed in the sixth house of obstacles, litigation, competition, and enemies, it may also indicate that at one point in her life she had a financial windfall which was taken away from her due to litigation, or she may have started lawsuits to recoup earnings that she felt were due to her. Mars has the highest longitude and therefore is considered the Atma Karaka, the indicator of soul and spirituality. While Mars is aggressive and indicative of enemies, it will provide the spiritual path that she will follow as her life progresses.

Since the Moon is one of extremes (hidden in the twelfth house of secrets, imprisonment and excess, and aspected by Saturn and Mars, two malefics), wonderful qualities of giving, patience, and encouraging and protecting others will not be able to shine through as much as Joyce would like them to. Much of this probably stems from her own difficult childhood, and also because she is fearful of rejection and insecure. Saturn's influence on the Moon may indicate that she will turn to spirituality, renunciation, and solitude, especially in her later years. The Moon's position in the twelfth house in a very close conjunction with Saturn makes the elements of guilt, repression and punishment loom rather large, and Joyce may have felt that it was easier to repress and control her emotions, rather than deal with learning how to be even-handed about her desires. On a positive note, she probably used the more desirous nature earlier in life, and during the middle and latter part of her life, she has become more ascetic and creative. This position can give her periods of excess, followed by guilt and even self-destructive habits as "punishment." It may also mean that she indulged in sexual excess, spending, eating, or drinking to compensate for an emotional void. More than likely, though, it would simply describe the complex nature of her emotions and her emotional life that would run the gamut from being angry, fearful, repressive and excessive. These qualities have a good chance of finding balance after the age of thirty-five, when the spiritual nature of this placement will make itself felt.

Although people who do not know Joyce might think that she is very friendly, bright and cheerful, people close to her might experience the moodiness, need to be alone, and detachment that she expresses in her private life. Most important for Joyce is to have control over her life, and anyone close to her must learn to respect her need for privacy and secrecy. With an eighth and twelfth house emphasis, Joyce would always tend to feel the need for solitude and, at the same time, always feel misunderstood or that she has been dealt a bad hand. With the Moon in the twelfth house conjunct Saturn, she may have a difficult time maintaining friendships, and needs her own space in which to create, meditate and heal. She may have to learn to nurture and to express her emotions in a giving way without always expecting something in return. Eighth House emphasis provides interest in the occult and psychology. With Mars as one of the predominant forces in this chart, she may be described by some as having militant tendencies and strong ideas. In fact, she probably will fight for her beliefs, and some may find her quite argumentative and opinionated. There may be guilt after excess, and she may go through periods of excess early on in her life, and then denial and renunciation later in her life. She may also have simply given her money away to charitable causes, or to people who have taken advantage of her.

The Second House

The second house rules early childhood and learning, as well as money and assets. Parts of the body indicated by the second house are the face, neck and throat. This house receives aspects from Mercury, Venus and the Sun in the eighth house, and from Saturn in the twelfth. The Moon rules the second house, is exalted and in its own nakshatra, and yet is in the twelfth house receiving a very close aspect to Saturn, and an aspect from Mars in the sixth, which is lord of sixth and the eleventh, and the Atma Karaka. With so many planets affecting the second house, we can assume that Joyce's childhood was probably a mixed bag. With Saturn's close aspect to the Moon, there may be early death, separation, or emotional wounds by one or even both parents. There could be life abroad at one time or another in her life, maybe her childhood. But if she did not live abroad when she was young, it is most probable that she changed residences and lived somewhere that she felt alienated from. With the Moon afflicted by Saturn and Mars, her eyesight may suffer, and she could have had some kind of difficulty with her feet or even her circulation. She would be withdrawn as a child, something that was already discussed earlier. She might be very extravagant, and go to extremes between being excessive and being frugal. She may have had financial ups and downs throughout her life. There could be vanity, money spent foolishly, and many travels throughout her life. She may have been experiencing many difficulties with her finances in the last few years. She may also have given away money to charitable causes, or to someone whom she felt was a teacher, or even may have given a lot of money to her children, if she has any.

Between 1998 and 2004, when Saturn transits the sign before the Moon (sidereal Aries between April 1998-June 2000), the sign of the Moon (sidereal Taurus between June 2000-July 2002), and the sign after the Moon (sidereal Gemini between July 2002-September 2004)—a condition known as Sade Sati (Sanskrit for "7½")—she may have health difficulties either with herself or a loved one, and she may then be less able to be charitable to others. Any

397

financial, physical or emotional suffering she may face will be especially felt from July 2001 through July 2002. At the same time, she might have some remarkable spiritual breakthroughs, and any loss that she may experience should be parlayed into her spiritual practice. Another way of healing herself would be through volunteer and charity work, when possible. She might also tutor others in her area of expertise. In any event, her life has probably changed over the last couple years, and she will probably be living more sparsely—in a different manner and in a different place. On the health front, areas that could be affected during this six year period are the eyes, throat, and thyroid. She may also have to be careful of diabetes, especially the feet, the digestion, or female illnesses affecting the breasts and reproductive system.

Because the second house rules appetite and money, and the twelfth house rules debts, she may have had bouts with eating disorders, drinking problems or bad spending habits throughout her life. With Venus aspecting the second house, there will be great loss as well as great pleasure and gains through the creative arts. Money will probably be earned through twelfth house matters like spiritual practice, research, creativity, anything done in solitude, and contacts with foreign countries and other international business. There may also be spiritual pilgrimages to foreign places, and long journeys to find a teacher. She has to be cautious since she may be easily deceived by potential lucrative business deals, and may also be lured and enticed by spiritual teachers with false promises since she is very idealistic, and a spiritual seeker. It seems as if the early part of her life may have been spent rejecting any type of teacher, even being cynical and distrustful about taking advice from anyone. This attitude could very easily change later in her life by learning both humility and how to trust—something that is difficult for her to do. Her intellect is quite sharp, and for that reason, Joyce can also be quite cynical.

The aspect of Saturn to her second house, as well as to her Moon, the ruler of the second house, means that this planet of discipline, age, work and structure will be the strongest influence on the house of assets and speech. This will give her a harsh speaking quality, and often she has had to spend many hours learning how to be tactful, and how to make herself understood by others. For many years, she may bitterly complain about being misunderstood when, in reality, she may not be very clear or diplomatic, so that people either do not understand her, or do not want to listen to her. Work that involves study and therapy and psychology would be expected from this chart, as well as something highly creative. It seems as if she will be able to parlay her abilities into teaching or publishing or therapy. This may or may not include her creative gifts, which she will continue to pursue whether or not they are part of the way she earns a living. She would be a very good teacher, either for creative pursuits, research, or spiritual studies.

Ruled by the Moon, her mother would have to have been either physically or emotionally distant, leaving her with a hole of insecurity that needed to be filled. She may have a tendency to spend a lot of money as well as earning it. There seems to be money that comes in from research, or from inheritances, legacies, and insurance claims. With the exalted Moon in the twelfth house, there is beauty, strength and determination to hold the family together. As the result of an uprooted childhood, she may have put her needs aside and created her own world. There are dramatic ups and downs where childhood, education and finances are concerned. If she has children, she may have one child who will be problematic, and cost her money. She can be quite argumentative and needs to control her emotions to protect herself from being hurt. In addition to creating her own environment, she will learn and struggle to retain control of her finances and, ultimately, her life. In general, the issue of "control" is one that pervades her life.

Third House

The placement of the North Node in Leo in the third house provides willpower and courage that is developed and perfected as life goes along. There are difficulties early on in life, and since the third house rules the lungs, there is a great chance that Joyce was asthmatic, or ridden with some sort of chronic illness affecting that part of her body as a child. This reiterates the theme of a difficult childhood. In the Dasa of Rahu (North Node), during the ages of fourteen to thirty-two, there would have been great drama and upheaval in Joyce's life, ranging from a complete change of residence to a lot of mental exhaustion and depression. These difficulties would especially be highlighted at the beginning and at the end of that period, and she may have had a major move or change in her life when she was between thirteen and fifteen years old, and then again when she was thirty to thirty-two years old. This period could have been one of intense relationships or even a marriage—but one which was not easy and would not have lasted beyond the age of thirty-five at most. With the ruler of the third house placed in the eighth house, there would be a potential for depression and excess, as well as strong tendencies towards research, metaphysics, psychology or poetry. With highly compulsive, greedy north node in the third house, Joyce probably has a strong sensuality and many desires as this concurs with the rest of her chart. It also means that she is quite stubborn and does not take well to opposition. This is also why she is comfortable on her own. When you do not like opinions that are different than yours, it is easier simply to work on your own and not answer to anyone. With the third house ruling the mind, communications and siblings, there may be no siblings or there may be a sibling who has difficulties. Often the goals are not realized because of the ruler of the third house of courage being placed in the eighth house, meaning her longings may not be able to be fulfilled.

The Rahu period, which runs from the age of fourteen through thirty-two (1957-1975), would be the time in which the struggles of Rahu would create a lot of change, chaos and struggle in Joyce's life. She may be vying for a position, for artistic success, or may be working towards a degree. Her desire to find her own voice comes at a high price though, since her personal life is very problematic, and she may have to choose between career and home. The years between 1968-75 may have been the most tumultuous of her life with one activity after another. This may have been when she had a very volatile relationship—and may have had a child or at least have been pregnant. It would not have been a very happy period however, and she would have had a major loss during these years, especially between 1971-73. These years entailed a difficult Saturn transit, as well as the years of the Rahu period. These years bring loss, endings, aloneness, alienation, and at their extreme may have brought hospitalization or imprisonment. She could have, on the other hand, withdrawn voluntarily, and retreated to an ashram or to quiet country living. There should have been a trip to a foreign country, or self-imposed isolation in pursuing an academic degree or artistic endeavors. It is difficult to pinpoint, but it is a time when she would have started to realize that her life needed to take a different turn, and spiritual practice, discipline and structure would be needed. By the time she reached the age of thirty-two, her life was in the process of changing, since the Jupiter cycle spanned 1975-1991. Once she reaches the age of thirty-five to thirty-seven, her life will begin to be filled with the blessings of Jupiter, and everything that she has worked so hard to achieve might actually be hers. This change will most probably come about through the meeting of a teacher, or a relationship, and she will have many years of well-deserved success.

Rahu in the third house gives a spiritual way of thinking and the need to pursue metaphysical goals, often to the detriment of material goals. This will give her a sense of pride, an adventurous spirit, and might provide funds. If there is a sibling, this would cause some difficulty. With the Sun, ruler of the third house, placed in the eighth house, there will be depression—corroborated by the Gemini ascendant. With a malefic in the third house, the lungs are definitely weak, and one should really make sure that there is a smoke-free environment and that one lives where the air is clear and one can breathe. With the Sun as the ruler of this house, Joyce will be self-assured and strong-minded. Though intelligent, mentally disciplined, willful and highly creative, self-confidence is lacking due to the ruler placed in the eighth. Gemini rising people are extremely ambitious and will strive diligently to achieve their hopes and dreams. There may be a short temper and one may say things one did not mean to say. There will be a great desire in the Rahu period to achieve success, but for the most part Joyce will work against herself and might possibly self-destruct until her life takes another turn.

Fourth House

There are no planets aspecting the fourth house itself. Since changeable Mercury is the ruler of the fourth house of vehicles, the mother, fixed assets (homes and land) and happiness, all these attributes are subject to fluctuations with Mercury as their ruler. The placement of this planet in the eighth house means that the above-mentioned areas will be afflicted or troubled. Mostly, it indicates that the mother, who is also represented by the difficult Moon placement, was quite troubled, depressed, or prone to physical or emotional injury. Since the fourth house rules happiness, its ruler Mercury placed in the eighth house corroborates the fact that Joyce is not by nature a happy person, and is prone to many bouts of melancholy and depression. It is through therapy and spiritual renewal, as well as creative self-expression, that she may at some point in her life be more positive.

Fifth House

As for the house of children, intelligence, and good fortune from past lives, there are definitely mixed results, ranging from the very best to the most detrimental. With Jupiter aspecting the fifth house, there seems to be the possibility of children in the Jupiter period between the ages of thirty-two to forty-eight. While there may have been children in her Rahu period, there may have also been difficulties surrounding births, and possibly a child that was miscarried, terminated or even given up for adoption. The aspect of Jupiter to the fifth house provides for opportunities for children and higher learning during the Jupiter period. There should be great productivity in the Jupiter period, since this planet is clearly the strongest planet in the chart. She will be looked after and her children should also be looked after. Children born in the Jupiter period would have much more ease than those born during the period of Rahu. There should be much more interest in community service work as well. With Libra occupying this house, and Venus as its ruler in the eighth house of sexuality, there is definitely the need for flattery, admiration and respect. Joyce would have to be passionate, charming, sensual and artistic, and feel most productive when involved in a relationship or working in a creative partnership. Her children will be physically attractive and artistically gifted. The joy she could have with children will make up for the difficulties early in life. If she does not have children, she will take on the role of teacher or mentor, to satisfy maternal instincts. All in all, finances and investments are quite complicated. Both the ninth house of opportunities and the second house of assets have an array of planetary aspects that combine the most malevolent forces with the most beneficial. There will be wealth and strength, and crudeness of speech. Education could remain incomplete or finished later on.

Sixth House

Mars, the Atma Karaka or spiritual teacher of the chart, is in its own sign of Scorpio, which makes it very strong in its desire and willpower to overcome obstacles—also called open enemies. Health issues will be burdensome and there will be constant renewal and regeneration in her desire to be physically and spiritually sound. What may have started out early in life as a rebellious spirit will prove to be inspirational as her life progresses. Even with the current setbacks that she might be experiencing, she is a fighter, and has experienced so much adversity that she is almost used to it. Because Joyce has had to fight to be understood, the road has not been easy. This position of Mars means that there will be the ability to fight her enemies, and that she will have the survivor skills she may need to get through different life struggles ranging from a difficult childhood, unstable home life, residence changes, and excess. Mars in its own sign, though in the last and weakest degree, means that she has the ability to fight enemies, and at one point in her life she may have had a court battle or have had to fight to retain either money or position. With Mars aspecting the Ascendant, or personality, as well as the Moon, the second house ruler, her manner might not be the most warm and friendly. In fact, she can be very aggressive, even hostile, when she feels that she is not receiving what she is entitled to. She is also a much better speaker than she is a listener, and can easily interrupt others before they are finished speaking. She might fight for her ideals, and rationalize anything she does for the sake of the right cause or in order to be "right."

During the cycle of Mars, there could have been a loss or an illness that was quite devastating to the family—either a problem with the mother or with an older sibling, if there is one. This could have had repercussions for quite a few years. There will have been be a lot of anger, and it is in this period that she may have really decided that she needed to find her own form of expression. She might be accident-prone or have a tendency toward anemia or blood ailments, since Mars rules the blood and the muscles.

Mars in Scorpio will provide the indulgence and sensuality that seem to go along with the rest of the chart. Additionally there will be vitality and a highly competitive streak. Joyce must learn to channel her anger in a healthy way before she can use that competitive spirit to her advantage. Mars is placed in the nakshatra of Jyeshta, ruled by Mercury. Jyeshta bestows a strong sense of speech, love of poetry and interest in the sciences; however, she first needs to get past all the difficulties and obstacles that life has wrought. She will be a wonderful teacher as she matures. It is that strength that she will draw from during difficult times—especially between 1998 and 2004, when she might be caretaker to someone else or deal with health issues of her own. There may be legal disputes and difficulties with the people she works with, so that it helps to work for herself. She would like to be entrepreneurial, which could work for a while, but will go through many ups and downs. She must learn to work cooperatively with others or opt for self-employment. In the latter situation, there is a need to be less rigid with colleagues and/or employees. There is no doubt that she is passionate, has desires fulfilled through ambition and hard work, has good earning power, is wealthy and sensual, and will conquer the competition and overcome adversities. With Mars in its own sign, and the seventh sign from the Moon, she has what is called Ruchaka Yoga, which provides a sense of ambition, willpower and determination—sometimes to the detriment of everyone around her—in her quest to fulfill her goals and find a way of expressing herself.

There are no planets placed in the seventh house of partnership, but its ruler is placed in the first house and is aspected by Mars. Jupiter's planetary period ranges from the age of thirty-two to forty-eight. Because Jupiter is placed in the first house of destiny, and is in its position of directional strength ("Dig Bala"), she has always received the blessings of the teacher, and has managed to find hope and salvation even when it seemed she might not recover from her emotional, physical and spiritual losses. This position ensures that by the age of thirty-five, she will be in a new period where success, happiness and peace of mind might change the direction her life was taking before that time.

Her seventh house of partnership is influenced by both Mars and Jupiter, which means that she could have two marriages or at least two very meaningful relationships in her life. She may have two marriages and other short affairs. It is difficult to pinpoint, however. Since Rahu is aspecting her seventh house, there would probably be a difficult marriage or relationship during that period between the ages of fourteen to thirty-two. With Mars aspecting the ruler of the seventh house, this relationship could have been problematic. It could have been passionate and sexual, but at the same time volatile and potentially abusive. There may have been a court battle, and fights for money both during the marriage and after the marriage. However, it seems that the second marriage would be much better for her. Because of Jupiter, it could be with someone who is much older and wiser and someone who would bring her stability and even help her career. Jupiter's Dasa might bring her success in both marriage and career, and could bring her fame and recognition within her chosen field. It is most likely that this relationship was very important for her. She may also have had one marriage and many difficult affairs. Because Mars is the Atma Karaka of the chart, it is also possible that her second marriage or partnership would revolve around spirituality and spiritual teachings. Or, in the alternative, she may simply turn to spirituality during her Jupiter period, after having two difficult relationships. In any event, her life will have changed once she reaches the age of 35, and the spiritual and creative side will take over. She will probably come in contact with a very special teacher, or become one herself, and that will change the course of her life.

The benefic influence of Jupiter will begin to make itself felt during her mid-thirties. Because the influence of benevolent Jupiter in the first house is much different from that of Mars, the Moon and Saturn, in the houses of obstacles and loss, the planetary periods in her life will have dramatic effects in setting up times of struggle and times of comfort. Whereas the Moon, Mars and Saturn form a confluence of difficult forces, Jupiter bestows its blessings.

Jupiter will make her an optimist and will allow her to heal herself. With Jupiter in the seventh house of the Navamsa (ninth harmonic) chart, and ruler of the second house, there should be some financial opportunities that come as well as great opportunities for partnership. She may also live abroad in this period—a theme that runs throughout her life. This does not mean to say that Jupiter will be all good, because it is still excessive and wasteful. She should have really tried to have gotten this under control during her thirties and forties, because there is finally some happiness regarding children, relationships and opportunities. There may be loss and disappointment at the end of the Dasa, and she may spend these years having to adjust to a different way of life. This would be the period for career success, and she could meet her spiritual teacher, and finally also feel that her life is more controllable. Jupiter is in the nakshatra of Punarvasu, ruled by Jupiter, and because of that she will have every opportunity for happiness. It is during this time that she should be setting roots down.

Because Jupiter, the ruler of her seventh house of marriage and partnership, is placed in the first and aspects its own seventh house, there should be an attentive, loving partner who is also successful, good-natured and considerate. The partner could be someone whom she has come to respect as a teacher, or even someone younger who will be a student or an attorney, teacher, theosophist, journalist or linguist. The partner should be generous and well-educated, and someone whom she has learned from or who has led her in the direction of her spiritual teacher. There may be some ego and power issues that the couple would have to work out. In any event, even if the relationship ends, the Jupiter Dasa (from age thirty-two to forty-eight) will emphasize Jupiter's benevolent position in this chart. There may be a second, more successful, peaceable relationship in this time. In this period, she may do some public speaking, and be able to teach the lessons that she has learned in life. There should be more financial comforts as well. There may be an opportunity to own one's own business.

Eighth House

405

In addition to what has been already said about planets in the eighth house, there is a mutual reception (Parivartana Yoga) between Saturn (ruler of the eighth) occupying the twelfth, and Venus (ruler of the twelfth) placed in the eighth. This will add to the confluence of themes connecting the twelfth house of loss, excess, isolation, spirituality, research and meditation with the eighth house of metaphysics, psychology, sexuality, inheritances, and assets of the partner. There is a Raj (royal) Yoga in this house (Venus as ruler of the fifth with Mercury as ruler of first and fourth) that provides great affinity with singing, poetry, drama and dance, as well as an Arishta (sadness) Yoga (Mercury as ruler of the first with Venus as ruler of the twelfth). This means that this combination of Mercury and Venus will both bring her wonderful talents and also bring her a lot of sadness and solitude. She may not have been able to succeed in her chosen profession, or perhaps it was cut short due to an unseen set of circumstances. She may then have been depressed due to loss of her ability to create, or she may have also suffered due to a child, or due to a relationship. While these may have caused much suffering, she would have been able to transform sorrow into spiritual or creative happiness.

Even with love of the arts, music and poetry playing a strong part in her life, sensuality and the quest for pleasure, comfort and love often overpower many of the intentions that she has. The sensuality here is quite strong and may in fact need to be tempered at some point in her life. On the other hand, if this can be channeled into the creative arts and a spiritual practice, she will be blessed. While a preponderance of planets in the eighth house will give a love of psychology and the occult, chances are there are varying degrees of sustaining this. There are personal obstacles, relationships and mental health issues that take years to process and for Joyce to understand how to synthesize them all. With the Sun in the eighth house, there could be some damage to the eyes or, more likely, difficulty with the father who may have separated from the family early on and, if there was a stepfather, he might not have been a good influence. If the father did not physically separate from the family, then he would have been a difficult person to reach, and may even have been a military figure, which would have also made sense in terms of the restlessness that was part of her youth. The search for a father figure is a theme that is reiterated throughout her life and could lead to her finding a relationship with someone more established, and eventually meeting a spiritual teacher.

Many of her unique creative abilities will probably offset the depression already spoken of earlier in the reading. With Venus placed in the eighth house, there will be a period of sexual indulgences, and Joyce may have at one time in her life relied on her sexuality and charm to get her way with the opposite sex. There may be a desire to have one's own business and succeed in the arts, writing, or teaching fields, but only after she will attempt to succeed in the arts.

Since the eighth house is the second from the seventh, the house of partnership, it describes the assets of the partner. Because Saturn-ruled Capricorn, the sign occupying the eighth house, represents financial success and ambition, she may turn to a partner to satisfy her need for material security. But with Saturn symbolizing frugality and limitations, important business decisions should be made only after ample research and with great foresight. Because Saturn is in the twelfth house, there may be great limitations on finance. She would want to engage in business, but due to some excess there does not really seem to be the ability to have as much of a successful business without the help of others. She will have to learn how to handle finances, since she will go through periods of earning and spending, and then deal with periods of frugality and loss. Although she is charming with Venus in the eighth, the Sun and Mercury placed there will give her problems with friendships and the ability to trust others. This has already been discussed.

Ninth House

This area of the chart which represents the father, values, philosophy, religion, publishing, law, academics, finding a teacher, knowledge, travel and, most of all, opportunity, is influenced by all the malefics—Ketu, Rahu, Mars and Saturn—as well as Jupiter. Ketu, which occupies this house, means that the father, or father figures, are spiritual and influential teachers. There is an opportunity to successfully combine her philosophy with her lifestyle, especially after the age of thirty-two when the Jupiter Dasa begins. Because Jupiter aspects this house, it is during that period that the blessings of the Guru will make their presence felt. This can be in the form of a marriage as well as a teacher. This may be one and the same person, or it may be someone completely different. With Rahu in the third opposite the ninth, she will always have to struggle between fulfilling her spiritual goals and living comfortably in the material world. This struggle will continue throughout her life. Once she enters her Saturn period, she will be able to lessen her attachment to material things, and due to circumstances will also be spending much of her time alone. Saturn aspects the ninth house, which is ruled by Saturn, and this would present a positive disciplinary influence on the area that has to do with academic achievements. She may be a researcher, or have studied something very intently that pertains either to metaphysics, religion, philosophy or psychology. Her father may have even been her mentor, and he may have been a very serious person, a scholar, or even a minister. Mars aspecting Saturn and aspecting the ninth house would also mean that he could have been a military figure, and someone with a very bad temper. At the same time that she may have had a close relationship with her father or stepfather, there is also a difficult relationship. This also may mean that she has had a variety of male figures throughout her life who have been her mentors, each of whom has represented each of these qualities. Whatever the situation (and that is something that an in-person reading would verify) actually is, the father, or father figure, or even grandfather, would have been a very complex figure, and Joyce's complicated relationship with men would stem from this problematic relationship. Whoever may have served as a father figure would have had very strict values, and could have even been a spiritual figure. There may have been some physical abuse within the home, since the Moon (which rules the second house of early childhood), and Saturn (which rules the eighth house of sex and death, and the ninth house of the father) are placed in the twelfth house of secrecy, addiction, and loss. In addition to a strong mystical and spiritual side, reiterated with the influence of Ketu, Jupiter and Saturn on the ninth house, there is a powerful need to express her own ideas and simply to be her own individualistic, unique, and—to others—unusual self. Happiness will eventually come but not without some sacrifices along the way and a lot of compromising in terms of working for others, rather than only wanting to argue about ideas. There will be scholarly activities in this chart and there will be research done, perhaps even in foreign countries, or at least in places that are foreign to her native upbringing. Chances are that there were disruptions, separations, and possible violence in the home. With Jupiter aspecting that house, it seems likely that Jupiter would bring about the real opportunities for learning, and that eventually the writing and publishing promised in the early years might finally come to fruition. There should also be teaching appointments, and awards and honors. There may be disappointments once she passes the age of fifty, and these years may prove to be especially difficult for her. There may be the loss of a partner, or the loss of someone else close to her. She may be experiencing some health problems, which could have to do with the eyes, the throat, or the neck.

In addition to the transit of Saturn going through the house before, of, and after the Moon, Joyce's Saturn Dasa began in 1991. During the first few years of the Saturn Dasa, between 1991-1994, Joyce would have made a major life change. This could indicate that someone whom she valued either separated from her or might have passed away. The benefits and opportunities that were present in the previous sixteen years will take a different turn. There may be the loss of a position, cancellation of a contract, or the decision to change her environment or career. Saturn's influence will bring more isolation, time spent alone, or travel to foreign places for research purposes. There may also be emotional difficulties, depression, or a physical ailment for which she may have to spend money. There could be major problems or difficulties with the knees, bones, teeth or gums, all ruled by Saturn.

Tenth House

With Jupiter, the ruler of the tenth house of career and recognition, placed in the first house of fame and destiny, she has the promise to be very successful in life. This will not be easy, and her success will only be achieved after having fought many obstacles. There will be difficulties with teachers and mentors, and arguments with colleagues and others with whom she may have to work, such as directors, editors, professors, or simply chairpersons. The fact that the Jupiter is retrograde, as are Mercury and Saturn, simply means that she is even more willful than normal since retrograde planets are strengthened and intensified. This means that her stubborn qualities and need to control (Saturn retrograde) are made even stronger, as is her inquiring and curious mind (Mercury retrograde), and her need to do everything to excess (Jupiter retrograde). Her luck and ability to find opportunities throughout her life are also strengthened by Jupiter's retrograde position in the first house. As noted throughout the text, the Jupiter Dasa, from July 4, 1975-July 4, 1991, would have been a time when she would get things published, acquire teaching positions, or start to be recognized in the field of her choice. Since Jupiter is in Gemini, her career could have to do with writing, communication, or even some type of business. It is in the navamsa of Venus, and that would mean that Venus and Mercury and the Moon would bring success in anything to do with film, poetry, dancing, clothing, perfumes or anything having to do with art and beauty. She will strive to be recognized for her sensitivity, generosity and artistic talents. Often confused about which profession to choose, she may vacillate before finally deciding on a career. She will however be skilled in more than one area, and she may simply not be able to make her living at what she is most proficient at. Jupiterian professions, which may be pursued, include teaching, the law, religion, or publishing. There may also be litigation and struggles to achieve what she wishes to achieve in this period. She may try her hands at massage or healing or something that involves touch.

Eleventh House

There are no planets aspecting the eleventh house. The ruler of the eleventh is in the sixth house of obstacles, health and litigation. Because the eleventh house is the eighth from the house of the mother, it is possible that during the Mars Dasa between 1950 and 1957, there was a family loss that caused Joyce to become aggressive and begin a period of rebelliousness and self-determination. She should have spent time abroad and, as already stated, may have had financial gains that were either earned amidst difficulties, or colleagues and competitors with whom she constantly had to compete in order to succeed. There may have been fights over inheritances and alimony that were won at a high emotional price. She probably has always felt a little cheated when it comes to receiving recognition, either in the form of position or money for the work that she has done. It is possible that other people have stolen her ideas, or simply that she has to struggle to get along with others. Relationships do not come easy for Joyce because she is very attached to her own way of doing things. Compromise and cooperation are things that it has probably taken her many years to learn. Because Mars-ruled Aries colors this house, there may be a tendency to spend money as quickly as it is earned, often resulting in foolhardy investments. Because she may feel either underpaid or unappreciated, quarrels with colleagues are not uncommon. With the eleventh house symbolizing the older siblings, brothers or sisters may have more aggressive personalities resulting in a difficult relationship. Or there may have been no siblings at all. There should be financial gains and recognition in the Jupiter Dasa; however, there will also be challenges to the career from colleagues, directors, or people with whom she is competing. Since Mars is receiving an aspect from Saturn, ruler of the eighth and ninth houses, and from the Moon, which is the ruler of the second house, there will be financial gains in the life, though they will most definitely fluctuate. Money most probably can be earned through publishing or teaching.

410

The Moon and Saturn occupy the twelfth, and Mars aspects it. The ruler Venus is placed in the eighth house of life and death matters and is conjoining Mercury and the Sun. This combination brings a very complex twelfth house and will bring her debt, isolation, and excess as well as great creative, intellectual and spiritual achievements. I have already addressed the position of the Moon and Saturn in this house and will just reiterate that there should be a great battle between excess and solitude. Although she might seem to love to present her ideas and talents to a wider audience, she has a difficult time expressing what she truly thinks and feels. With Saturn and the Moon in her twelfth house, and Mercury in Saturn-ruled Capricorn in the eighth house and retrograde, Joyce is an intense thinker and is fascinated with the mysteries of life, and might search relentlessly for answers. Since the eighth house rules life and death issues, the theme of death might have occurred early in her life, and may also dominate her studies as well as her creative ideas. All of her eighth house planets—Sun, Venus and Mercury in Capricorn—are disposited by Saturn and, due to Saturn's placement in the twelfth house, the quest for peace and solitude governs her life. There is a tendency to spend a lot of time alone, so that any profession which requires that will be one that suits her. Spiritual practice is also embraced. Once she enters her Saturn period, which lasts from 1991 to 2010, this search for spiritual salvation will be the dominant factor. As already stated, the years between 1998 and 2004 may be especially difficult, and if she can transform feelings of loss by meditating, and giving selflessly to others, her life will be transformed. This will not necessarily change the financial and emotional losses of this period, but it may make it easier to have faith that things happen for a reason.

What Vedic Astrology has to offer that other astrological systems do not is a set of very definite remedial measures called "upayes" that one can utilize to ameliorate difficulties inherent in the natal chart, as well as during the current planetary period. I would recommend that Joyce do one or more of the following:

1. Ask the priest at a Hindu Temple to perform a ceremony known as a puja. He will either ask for the Moon's Nakshatra, which is Rohini, or simply do an all-encompassing ritual for all the planets. This ritual if done on a Monday, the day of the Moon, can help with both her health and her emotional stability.
2. Do a selfless act to forget about her own problems and have compassion for those in worse circumstances. Donate clothing to a woman's shelter, give some time to a friend in need, or volunteer to help people less fortunate. That could entail working in a soup kitchen, or tutoring someone who cannot read.
3. Repeat a mantra that can help afflicted planets or difficult periods. During this long Saturn dasa, and especially during Sade Sati (1998-2004), repeating the mantra for Saturn will employ the blessing and not the wrath of this most afflicted planet. This mantra is Om Sri Shanaishwaraya Swaha. Because Saturn provides hard lessons, she should also, while chanting the mantra, think about what Saturn represents—limitation, structure, wisdom and difficult karmic lessons to learn. Because the Moon is afflicted and is so closely conjunct Saturn in the twelfth house, this mantra should cleanse Joyce and help relieve both physical and emotional suffering. She should repeat the mantra for 40 days.
4. Gemstones are favored by people who like jewelry and can resonate with the power of natural minerals. It is usually recommended that one wear the gemstone representing the ruling planet. For her ruling planet, Mercury, Joyce should wear an emerald set in silver. If she cannot afford an emerald, then tourmaline is another beautiful green stone. Stones should be set so that they touch the skin either in the form of a ring or an amulet. For protection during Saturn's planetary period, she might want to wear a blue sapphire set in silver, or in the alternative, an amethyst or lapis lazuli. For Sade Sati, Saturn's transit over the Moon, a ring made from an iron horseshoe is appropriate.

STEVEN FORREST: EVOLUTIONARY

STRATEGY

Software is a minor concern for me. All the available astrological programs seem to do the job adequately. If I had to go back to setting up charts by hand, I'd sigh once and get out my Table of Houses and my ephemerides. Some programs have various bells and whistles that other ones lack; most do something unique. My everyday working astrological software happens to be Matrix's Winstar II Plus, Version 2, which is accurate, comprehensive, and fairly intuitive. I often use A.I.R.'s Star Trax programs too, which are fast and have some cool tricks up their cyber-sleeves. Occasionally I use the popular and excellent Solar Fire, mostly because it can list the planetary nodes. On my PDA, I'm using Delphi and AstroPocket. They're of necessity limited in scope, but even those modest programs would do ninety percent of what I need in my professional practice.

I set up Joyce's birthchart in Winstar. As usual, I enabled Placidus house cusps, the Mean lunar nodes, and "standard" aspects—which boil down to the common Ptolemaic aspects, plus the eighth harmonic spread, plus parallels. I concentrate primarily on the Ptolemaic aspects in my analysis, but I like to keep one eye on those other dimensions as well. Sometimes they flavor the words I am saying about the more important layers of the picture. For example, I noticed that the Saturn-Uranus conjunction was enhanced by the planets being in parallel as well. Also, Pluto's parallel to the Ascendant intensified the "Plutonian" qualities inherent in Joyce's eighth house Sun. But these are relatively minor factors to me; I'm a great advocate of trying to think as deeply as possible about "minimalist" astrological techniques.

With Joyce's chart before me, I began the real work: interpretation. My absolute first aim in that department is to get a sense of the big picture. Astrology provides endless detail; there is really no practical limit to the depth of the symbolism. I think it would take longer to provide a "total" astrological analysis of a life than it would take to live it.

So I focused initially on the basics.

My written presentation of Joyce's birthchart echoes the style and order I use with my clients: almost always, I begin with an analysis of the "primal triad" of Sun, Moon, and Ascendant in terms of sign and house, then go on to follow a logical trail through the planets, winding up with a look at the lunar nodes. That way, the reading begins with loud, clear, easily verifiable information, proceeds into more subtle territory—and saves the bulk of the more elusive karmic material for the end. Hopefully, by then I have won some right to the client's trust and openness to the deeper, less immediately verifiable, messages.

My actual *thinking* about a chart does not follow exactly the same outline. Right off the bat, I always concentrate hard on the lunar nodes, adding them to the basic Sun, Moon, and Ascendant mix. Experience has taught me that probably the single most pivotal astrological factor in terms of setting the tone of the personality is the Moon's South Node. As I've described elsewhere in these pages, I view the South Node as representative of the emotional tone of a person's karmic patterning. But even a very "practical" astrologer can verify my core point: whatever its ultimate meaning, the emotional signature of the South Node reflects the underlying emotional moods, assumptions and attitudes of the human personality. Thus, with Joyce's South Node in Aquarius in the ninth house, all that traumatized "Exile" feeling came through very strongly to me right from the beginning. It is the foundation upon which everything else is constructed.

Immediately upon seeing that nodal pattern, I knew for example that the more isolating dimensions of the eighth house Capricorn Sun and the twelfth house Moon-Saturn conjunction would be emphasized. I knew that the ninth house flavor of the Node would support the mentally-expansive dimensions of her powerful Gemini influences—but that it would not support the more frivolous, lighthearted and playful parts of that sign. And of course an Aquarian South Node adds quite a lot of vitality to her already-powerful natal Uranus.

The nodal axis also taught me that, in order to maximize the helpfulness of the reading, I would need to recognize that the ultimate evolutionary intention of Joyce's life lay in moving toward her Leo third house North Node. Thus, anything pertinent to a general "warming and opening" of her character and attitude would need extra emphasis.

The importance of the lunar nodes in general struck me early in my astrological explorations. I began to rely on them heavily almost from the beginning of my work. In the astrological literature, there is a pattern of vagueness about them—that, or a tendency basically to ignore them. Increasingly, I have come to view that lapse as a systematic, underlying error in modern astrological practice. At this point, if I could know "just one thing" about a person's chart, it wouldn't be his or her Sun sign; it would be the position of the Moon's South Node. That's how powerful it is.

Moving back to the strategy of my analysis of Joyce's chart, in presenting the blend of Sun, Moon, and Ascendant one naturally encounters Uranus and Saturn—they're linked with the Moon through the conjunctions. Furthermore, Saturn rules the Capricorn Sun. I'm not always rigid about this in practice, but most of the time I'll look at any planetary conjunctions to the primal triad in the course of analyzing the Sun, Moon, and Ascendant, just as I did here. I consider such planets effectively to be part of the primal triad itself.

The planetary ruler of the Ascendant always presses for attention. That is especially true with Joyce, as Mercury rules not only her Gemini Ascendant, but also her Moon. It was thus the next natural stop in the journey, after the primal triad and its conjunctions.

I am constantly on the lookout for *themes* in an analysis, for ways that the chart hangs together internally. In this case, as soon as my attention turned to Mercury, a clear path through much of the rest of the chart opened up before me. Mercury is conjunct Venus, which immediately led me into the all-important territory of human relationships. After introducing Venus, I used it as an opportunity to go back into the primal triad, re-interpreting and deepening my understanding of those elemental factors from a relationship perspective. That kind of thematic integration is, to me, the hallmark of skillful astrological analysis. I always strive for it.

After looking at the Venus-Mercury complex and tying it back into the primal triad, I continued to follow the thread of relationship symbolism. Venus and Mercury are opposed by a second house Pluto. Also in the second, we see Jupiter opposing the eighth house Sun. Thus, Jupiter and Pluto both became pertinent to the themes of intimacy in the chart. I used that perspective as a doorway into their symbolism—and then stretched out to embrace other, non-intimate dimensions of those two planets.

The second house themes of money and resources—and also of self-confidence—led naturally to my thinking about Neptune in the fourth house, with its familial associations. That left us with only Mars outstanding. Its close association with the seventh cusp allowed it too to be carried forward on the general tide of relationship symbolism, before bringing in its sixth house layers.

In Joyce's chart, this daisy-chained logical coherence of powerful relationship themes exists in interesting and sharp tension with the "exile"

415

patterns of her South Node and her primal triad—and of course that paradox then became the central "meta-theme" of the reading, as the chart itself dictates.

With the analysis of the planets completed, I moved into describing as explicitly as I could what had been implicit throughout the interpretation: the karmic story and the soul's intentions as revealed in the lunar nodes and their planetary aspects. There, the key lay in understanding the way Joyce's present personality reflected the unresolved issues from previous lifetimes—and more importantly, how her present personality could be used as a vehicle for getting on with her own evolution. Thus, I tried to weave my imagery of her soul's long history and larger purpose into the mundane psychological realities of one transitory life. That single goal, increasingly, is emerging for me as the single most powerful dimension of evolutionary astrology.

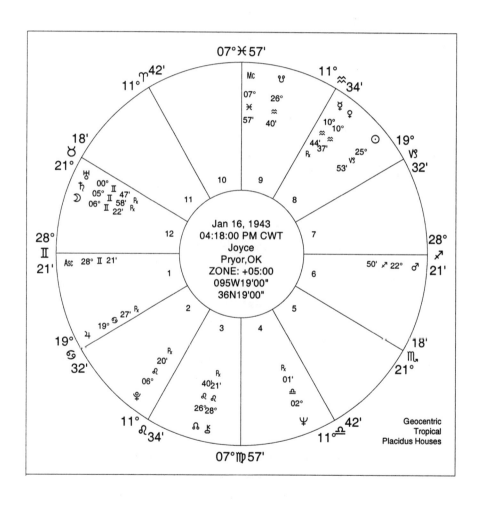

There are places we only go alone. The realm of death is one of them. Another one, much of the time, is the realm of truth—the desolate, uncomfortable kinds of truths we see, but would never utter: the beloved parent whom we sense won't live much longer; the friend's sweet, life-giving dream that will never come to pass.

This theme—*solitude in the face of fierce truth*—is absolutely central to our understanding of Joyce's natal chart. Her Sun (identity) lies in Capricorn, the Sign of the *Hermit*. Saturn, Lord of Solitude, lies in a close conjunction with her Moon (her heart and soul). Saturn and Capricorn are also the symbols of *winter*—and of the virtues which might allow one to survive that harsh season: self-discipline, resourcefulness, the adult ability to dry one's eyes and face reality squarely. Joyce possesses these qualities in unusual abundance.

Consistent with their wintry symbolism, Capricorn and Saturn both correspond to the archetype of the *Elder*—and anyone meeting Joyce when she was an eight year old child would have said, "She's going to make a great old lady." The ultimate truth of that intuitive prophecy would actually depend upon a series of wise choices she might make as she threaded the labyrinth of the life that lay before her. As we will see, the possibility that she would die bitter and broken also existed.

The sheer fierceness of the truths she faces in this lifetime are indicated by the Sun's presence in the eighth house. This is the traditional "house of death." Often people with the Sun in this position have their lives shaped by significant or untimely deaths, but the symbolism runs deeper. Death is *emblematic* of eighth house reality, which actually refers to anything which makes people uncomfortable, and which is thus rendered *taboo* by the culture: disease, aging, sexuality, or even our more trenchant psychological impressions of others. From an early age, Joyce felt drawn to a consideration of these deeper layers of life—and quickly discovered that she would be punished for speaking out loud about them. *Thus her natural solitude was exaggerated by social punishment and conditioning.* She became, archetypally, the Hermit in the house of death. And part of the deal she made with God was that if she didn't go after these deeper kinds of truths in herself through psychological self-scrutiny, they would *come after her* through traumatic and extreme events.

The theme of "unlucky" events being triggered by the slightest failure to adhere to her higher soul-intentions is repeated dramatically by her Moon,

418

which lies in the twelfth house. Often called the house of troubles, the deeper meaning of this house is connected to higher states of consciousness. Despite her grounded, street-smart qualities (Capricorn Sun and strong Saturn), Joyce has felt intuitively since her childhood the presence of *something larger than herself* in this universe. With authority-questioning Uranus in her twelfth house and aligned with her Moon, she may have rebelled against calling it "God." The words don't matter. The point is, there is an innate spiritual instinct here—grounded (Saturn) and iconoclastic (Uranus), but still vivid and personal.

The key to the evolutionary understanding of this twelfth house lunar configuration lies in recognizing that Joyce came into this world to learn to "practice the presence" of the Divine, independently and objectively, but also relentlessly. If she stayed with that intention and made space, ideally each day, for some inner time, there would be a profound opening of her spiritual, mystical, and psychic faculties in this incarnation. If, on the other hand, she became attached to the usual worries and attractions of this world, then she would trigger a numbing pattern of personal loss. Essentially, *anything which became more important to her than her spiritual life would be taken from her.* That was the deal she made with the Infinite when she embarked upon this life.

Clearly, Joyce came into this world playing for very high stakes. With her eighth house Sun, she would be asked to face psychologically extreme conditions and situations—the sort of which people generally find it "inappropriate" to speak. With her twelfth house Moon, she was asked actively to maintain a high level of spiritual sensitivity—the alternative being a triggering of even more loss in her life. On top of all that, she was asked to do this deep work in a fundamentally solitary, dry-eyed, and self-sufficient way.

If she got it right, she would become a Wise Woman, held precious by her community—more about that later on. If she got it wrong, she would become moody, bitter, and brooding, and likely seek patterns of escapism and self-numbing behavior, just to turn off the pain and loneliness. Alcoholism, for one example, is often "predicted" for people with this kind of chart. That's a possibility, but it is certainly not the higher ground, which is also fully available, nor is it the only dark path.

Joyce's Moon and her Ascendant both lie in Gemini, adding another very significant layer to the picture. Traditionally, Gemini is associated with language, alertness, and intelligence. The Ascendant itself represents how we "dawn" on people—the "mask" we wear. Thus, we can assume that Joyce's social self-presentation would be verbally fluent, quick, and mental in orientation. The deeper layers of the birthchart shine through the Ascendant in much the fashion of light inside a church shining out though stained glass windows. The logic, strength and self-possession of the Capricorn Sun and the Saturn-Moon conjunction, given a Geminian "spin" as they entered the world of self-expression, would produce an impressive, engaging and probably slightly intimidating *persona*. Joyce wouldn't "miss much." She would radiate a certain toughness and street-sense. She could "get in your face."

This toughness and street-sense, along with her quick skill with words, would be one of the masks her solitude wears in the world.

A veil of words could also mask her sensitivity, a quality people would tend to underestimate in her. The profundity of this sensitivity is incalculable—there's her Moon, Saturn, Uranus conjunction in the mystical twelfth house. To that we could add that when we "peel away the layers of her onion" and get down to her deepest center—which is to say, look into her fourth house—we find mystical, sensitive Neptune. But there's also the innate *reason* of the Capricorn/Saturn influences in the mix, allying naturally with the mental crispness of the Gemini Moon and Ascendant. And her natural solitude—she would very likely be content to keep her sensitivity to herself, and is profoundly well-equipped to do that.

Add our earlier references to the ease with which even relatively slight evolutionary failures trigger dramatically extreme existential consequences for her, and we can recognize that her innate sensitivity might very well have been "fried" at an early age. She did not come into this world to become shell-shocked, but she would have to play her evolutionary cards right to avoid that outcome, despite her considerable strength and resiliency.

A high Gemini archetype is the *Teacher*. With Joyce's Moon in that sign, we could say that she has the "Soul of a Teacher." With her Ascendant there, she also wears the "Mask of a Teacher"—she's got the outward skills, in other words, to live that teaching role. Not all teachers stand in front of classrooms, though: "Teacher" here basically means a conduit of information into the world. All the writers and journalists are potentially "teachers" in this sense, as are all the broadcasters and filmmakers and other "media" people. Gemini, in the purest sense, has more to do with open-minded receptivity toward surprising, disjunctive data than it has to do with any kind of authoritarian academic posturing as an "expert." Thus, Gemini, even though it is the sign of the Teacher, is also the sign of wonder, amazement, and a sense of the miraculous. It has more to do with *curiosity* than it has to do with "being right."

Thus, we observe a certain irrepressible fascination with life in Joyce, a quality which painful experiences could not fully extinguish. And this plucky drive to *keep on learning* underlies her high destiny as a Teacher. She is an acute observer of life. Out of those observations—often of life's extremities, as we've seen from the rest of her chart—she would emerge, not with answers, but with shocking questions and mind-stretching, paradigm-shifting (Uranian) perspectives. Those would be her "teachings"—and high on the list of qualities that could make her a precious "Elder" in her community.

To teach this way, she would have to learn that whatever she has figured out about life, the truth is bigger and wider. People carrying this much Geminian energy have signed up for a wild ride. Either they embrace the chaos of life, or the rug keeps getting pulled out from underneath them—yet another reminder of the high stakes for which Joyce is playing.

Let's add one more element to this part of the stew. Her Gemini Moon is in the twelfth house, so these teachings would have something "spiritual" about them. I put the word "spiritual" in quotes because I'm using it broadly—many novels, for example, never mention the word "God," but are full of spiritual teachings nonetheless. Most poets worth reading are spiritual teachers—and again that does not mean they write theologically.

The whole question of religion is a sensitive one here. Capricorn and Saturn are drawn to tradition and structure. Given half a chance, the strong Neptune and the twelfth house Moon are inherently mystical. They are even drawn to the quiet of a contemplative, cloistered life. On the other hand, operating in tension with her religious instincts, is that endless, almost scientific, questioning curiosity indicated by the Geminian influences and further aided and abetted by the "trouble with authority" inherent in the powerful Uranian theme. I would thus guess Joyce to be a lot more "spiritual" than "religious."

So far, we've been looking at Joyce's *primal triad* of Sun, Moon, and Ascendant, along with the two planets that happen to be aligned with her Moon. Let's summarize:

The Sun represents who she is at the level of *ego* and *self-identity*. She is thus the Hermit in the house of the taboo, or the Elder in the house of death.

The Moon is her *soul*. Thus, she has the soul of a Teacher or the soul of the Observer, in the house of spirituality—or the house of troubles, if she's off target.

The Ascendant is the *mask* she wears. Thus, she wears the mask of the Teacher, or the Observer, or the Storyteller—her outward persona is flavored with those mental, verbal archetypes.

Before we follow the planetary trails more deeply into the logic of Joyce's birthchart, let's switch gears into a truly evolutionary perspective. What we've seen so far is primarily descriptive astrological psychology, with a little spice of the deeper themes. To embrace them fully, we must go beyond thinking of this woman as a conglomeration of traits. Instead, we ask the following question: *why, in a meaningful, purposeful universe, would a soul be using such a set of tools?* Why would it take such a risk?

No soul comes into this world with an eighth house Sun unless it intends to make a visit to the Underworld. The intent here is a dive into the psyche's deep dark: a soul-retrieval, an act of self-healing, making *the unconscious mind conscious.*

When this soul steels itself by adding Capricorn energy to the eighth house stew, we learn that it has prepared for a journey that promises to be long and arduous, requiring *sustained self-discipline* and a cold eye for hard truth. Saturn's conjunction with the Moon amplifies those themes of endurance and objectivity even further.

The Gemini influences add another dimension: that this journey into darkness requires a radically open-minded intelligence, ready for shock and surprise, and armed with a capacity for coolly detached observation—the sort of attitude often reported by emergency medical technicians accustomed to working grotesque crash scenes. That the Moon is in the twelfth house suggests a pre-existing condition of spiritual receptivity—but one that must be pushed to its limits if Joyce's soul is going to endure the processes we are describing without shattering. For all her innate strength, she cannot do what she's set out to do without consciously employing God's help. She benefits from *seriously rigorous spiritual practice* (Saturn)—and if she doesn't undertake such practice, something darkly akin to it may very well be thrust upon her: illness, confinement, grievous loss. Furthermore, with Uranus in the twelfth house matrix, she is very much *on her own* with her spirituality. She is *individuating* there, learning to feel her own way forward into the Mysteries without external guidance. If she seeks outward guidance—religions, gurus, spiritual masters—it will fail her.

What could have caused these extreme and disconcerting conditions? Any answer capable of holding up to rudimentary logical scrutiny must accommodate one inescapable fact: this is Joyce's *birth*chart. Therefore anything that caused her to have these configurations had to *pre-date her birth.* When we get to the Nodes of the Moon, we'll consider that pre-birth material with some precision. For now, let's continue our journey around her birthchart.

Mercury takes on tremendous power in Joyce's chart through its rulership of her Ascendant. We find it placed on the cusp of her ninth house, in Aquarius, tightly conjunct Venus. (Some might quibble that Mercury is actually in the eighth house, but with only twenty-three minutes of arc separating it from the ninth cusp, its action is clearly thrown forward.) The planetary ruler of the Ascendant not only has its power boosted; it also partakes of the deeper meaning of the Ascendant, becoming part of how we "get our act together" in the outer world. Almost always, it figures very prominently in the obvious, outward shape of the biographical life. In Joyce's case, this directs our attention to three factors. First, the ninth house. Second, the sign Aquarius. And third, through its conjunction with Mercury, the planet Venus. Let's take these elements one at a time.

To a significant degree, her life is "happening" in the context of the ninth house. Any of the standard key words for that house may be relevant here: travel, higher education, religion, law and belief-systems. Any or all of them may have played pivotal roles in her biography. I would expect significant elements of *culture shock* to be present in her life too. I say "culture shock" rather than simply saying "travel" for one simple reason: under ninth house stimulus, sometimes the foreign elements *travel to us* rather than us to them. The key here is contact with that which is culturally, mythically or socially *alien*, of which I suspect there has been no shortage in Joyce's life.

Underlying these observations is a pervasive sense of Joyce's life feeling fundamentally like a *Quest*—there's a true key word for the ninth house. With the ruler of the Ascendant there, for her to feel sane and centered and engaged energetically with her life, she needs a steady diet of wonder and learning. Despite the stoic and enduring qualities of her birthchart, she has a distinct "don't-fence-me-in" attitude. That adventurous attitude exists in sharp tension with her existential vulnerabilities to the loss of what she most needs and cherishes in life.

With Mercury and Venus both in Aquarius, the logic of that rebellious sign is felt very prominently in Joyce's psyche, adding more fuel to the powerful Uranian influence upon her Moon. This is part of a more general observation

423

emerging from our exploration of her particular birthchart: a tendency for patterns of *redundancy* to build up in the symbolism:

* A Saturn-Moon conjunction joins forces with the Capricorn Sun.
* The Moon, The Ascendant, Saturn and Uranus all lie in a single sign, Gemini.
* Two Aquarian planets join forces with a prominent Uranus.

Thus, at the high end of the spectrum, we see the archetypes of the *Elder*, the *Teacher*, and the *Rebellious Genius*, respectively, all orchestrating the higher evolutionary logic of her life. At the low end, we again see the same three principles, but expressed darkly: arduous, lonely, endless struggle, linked to outward chaos and inward rationalization, punctuated with earthquakes, lightning bolts, and erratic choices.

Specifically, the Uranian/Aquarian themes emphasize that Joyce has simply reached a point in the evolutionary journey of her soul where the experiences that would feed her happen to lie outside the context of mainstream cultural expectations. A certain "existential trajectory" lay ahead predictably for a little girl born into a family of her ethnicity and demographics in Pryor, Oklahoma in 1943. Outwardly, there would have been nothing inherently wrong with such a life, but it would have left Joyce's spirit starved and withered.

Focusing more narrowly upon Mercury as the ruler of the Ascendent, we recognize that this Aquarian need for *rebellion against the social forces that would otherwise rob her of her real life* would have to manifest in vigorous, iconoclastic intellectual freedom (Mercury/Aquarius/Ninth House) and probably in the act of asserting her soul's autonomy by *leaving home*, literally. To get her "act together," she would have to pay the price of freedom.

The remaining dimension of Joyce's Ascendant-ruling Mercury is its tight alignment with the planet Venus. Only seven arc-minutes separate the two planets, effectively merging them into a single "meta-planet." In addition to further reinforcing the Aquarian and ninth house themes we've already explored, this also introduces a new—and very loud—note into the music of the chart. There is, incongruously, a powerful Venusian element to this otherwise distinctly self-sufficient woman. And it shows: anything linked to the Ascendant Ruler also becomes part of our outward social demeanor. There is almost always something endearing, even magnetic, about Venusian people. As we have seen, Joyce is a strong, formidable woman. Human nature, complicated by sexism, conspires to place such women in *pariah* roles—in this case, we would see a vulnerability to the "bitch" projection. The strength of the Venusian energy here is not sufficient to obviate all that, but it does mitigate it. Many strong people of both genders would find Joyce appealing and fascinating, if not exactly "charming" in the conventional sense. Insecure people, and some simply milder ones, would be more cautious and either intimidated or threatened by her.

Going more deeply, Venus is of course the proverbial "goddess of love." This brings us to the profoundly serious—and profoundly central—theme of human intimacy in Joyce's life. Two opposing forces are engaged in a titanic psychic tug-of-war here. On one hand, we have her marked self-sufficiency and independence. On the other hand, we have the actual intimacy-centered evolutionary intentions of her soul for this lifetime. These are supported by certain "Venusian" aspects of her nature.

Her self-sufficiency and independence we've already discussed. The former is symbolized by her prominent Saturnian, Capricornian and inwardly-directed twelfth house influences. The latter is indicated by the powerful Uranian and Aquarian themes.

As we have begun to see, the more intimate themes of Joyce's life are supported by the prominence of the planet Venus. But that fact is overshadowed by an even more basic force: the presence of the Sun in the eighth house. Earlier, we looked at her Sun's house position in the context of its connection with emotionally-charged "taboo" material. We used death as an illustration. Here's another illustration: sexual realities. Who has not been driven to their ragged edges by sexuality? Who is comfortable speaking of that aspect of life with complete honesty and candor? What sexual relationship that has lasted more than three consecutive weekends has ever failed to bring up unresolved psychological issues for both people? This is all eighth house territory.

Earlier, we observed that with her eighth house Sun, Joyce's intention for this lifetime involved a healing journey in the dark: a "soul-retrieval." To make a point as clearly as I can here, I am going to go ten percent too far: *There is no way Joyce can succeed at her soul-retrieval without the catalytic impact of a lover upon her.* The very issues she needs to resolve in this incarnation are brought directly to the surface in the process of bonding sexually—or in attempting to do so. I said I would go "ten percent too far." Here's what I meant: it is in fact possible to have an eighth house relationship that is not physical or erotic. Two nuns in a convent could do that and keep all their vows. The real key here is

425

stark naked honesty and self-revelation, to the point that it feels difficult. Close-up, no human is easy to know. Physical intimacy is a kind of "yoga" that stimulates all these unsavory, unresolved parts of ourselves into expression—and many a romantic ship goes down as soon as the dragons of the unconscious mind raise their heads. Typically, simple friendship involves considerable "artful dodging" around these sore places. We call that maneuvering "respect" or "good boundaries," and it is not to be despised. But in the eighth house, where Joyce's sanity-giving Sun lies, we must "go all the way" with another human being. We must directly reveal the actual, underlying condition of our soul, warts and all.

Correspondingly, Spirit gave Joyce an inwardly passionate nature, and a desire to connect deeply with a few other people. The strength of her Venus amplifies all that—she is basically a loving person, despite her hard edges. Also, with Venus linked to her outward vibration through its tight alignment with Ascendant-ruling Mercury, there is a good chance that her emotional appeal is augmented by physical grace, even beauty. That a strong and externally-visible Venus indicates physical attractiveness is not always a reliable astrological principle, but it often works. It's just the soul's way of saying, "Come help me do my relationship work—you can't resist."

With the Sun in the eighth house, little brings more sheer aliveness to Joyce than a deep, honest, psychological connection with another like-minded soul. She's wired for it—and yet, in her youth, she was repeatedly driven to take refuge in her formidable inner Capricorn fortress, as we have seen. The world is generally not welcoming to the kind of psychological intensity that, for Joyce, is the essence of real intimacy. *Thus, she has a dangerous capacity to adjust to solitude. She can survive without the very thing she needs if she is to thrive.*

I do not know Joyce's sexual orientation, and I know of no reliable astrological technique for determining it from a birthchart. If Joyce happens to be a gay woman, the heterosexual language I'm about to use can be easily adjusted to accommodate that reality.

The man who would be the ideal mate for Joyce would, above all, have to be strong enough to stay in the same ring with her. She is a powerful, trenchant woman, and probably does not always suffer a fool with good grace. Even when wrong, she can be persuasive. And when scared or threatened, she can close up as tight as a dungeon. She can also be controlling, moody, and slippery. None of these shadow-traits ultimately define her personality, but they are present—and the real-world challenges of intimacy will surely invoke them. Thus, the need for strength in a mate goes beyond the need for parity and

426

equality. It also includes the fact that anyone who is going to trigger the catalytic effect upon her which we've described will have to be capable of bashing through her walls from time to time.

Let's add that Joyce's ability to trust eroded early as a result of the world's rejections of her nature. Anyone who would be a suitable partner for her would help her address that issue in two ways. The first way we've already described: he would be *accepting of her intensity.* The second is very simple: he would have to be *trustworthy.*

Underlying these observations, by the way, is the synastric principle that planets in a person's eighth house describe his or her *natural mate.* Here, we see the mate described in solar and Capricornian terms: a strong person (Sun), with integrity and trustworthiness (Capricorn).

It bears repetition that the evolutionary intention behind Joyce's need for such a relationship is that it provide a crucible of healing for the deeper wounds of her soul. Whatever was hurt inside her would be brought to the surface by these kinds of relationships—ideally, to be faced and nurtured into health. Of course we must also recognize a pair of darker options. First, untrusting and self-isolating issues in Joyce could destroy such relationships, even with worthy people. And, as a reflection of these issues within herself, she might make unwise choices in the intimate arena, choosing partners who, in retrospect, were actually *symbols of her unresolved fears.*

We can apply similar synastric logic to Joyce's Venus.

Knowing that it lies in Aquarius tells us that the right kind of relationship for her would have to satisfy basic Aquarian requirements: freedom, space, and respect for each person's autonomy. An Aquarian Venus often correlates with relationship choices that lie outside the scope of conventional expectation—or even "propriety." Big age differences, racial differences, major cultural or economic differences, all are common with Venus in Aquarius. Thus, even to *recognize* the natural mate, individuation is a prerequisite. Since individuation almost always takes time to develop, early marriages often prove unstable for people with this configuration, mostly because they "chose" someone, not by their own lights, but rather by the mythology of their culture.

The association of Venus with Ascendant-ruling Mercury through the conjunction does more than elevate the centrality of Joyce's relationship concerns. It also defines them as "mercurial." The notion that she would therefore be "fickle in love" is often the standard interpretation. This is neither necessarily true, nor fair to Joyce, who is ultimately a loyal and stalwart

Capricorn. More accurately, Joyce is *easily bored* by most people. That may sound harsh, but Mercury always requires considerable stimulation. For Joyce, a natural mate is therefore someone capable of interesting conversation, a fascinated *listener,* someone open to endless learning. Adding the Aquarian element, this individual is interested in ideas and perspectives of an "odd or eccentric" nature—as perceived by conventional people.

That the Venus-Mercury conjunction occurs at the cusp of the ninth house furthers the same theme: the ninth house, like Mercury, is drawn to the exotic and the extreme, that which lies outside the pre-existent cultural perspective. With Venus there, Joyce's natural partners in life are inclined toward education, cross-cultural experience, philosophical speculation, and travel. A conventional prognostication here is that Joyce is destined to "marry a foreigner" or to "meet her husband in a foreign land." These statements are best understood as metaphors for the notion of the stimulation we associate with the exotic—but, because of that, it is not unusual for the predictions to "come true."

We've observed two fundamental relationship indicators in Joyce's birthchart: her eighth house Sun and her Venus-Mercury conjunction. *Each of them receives an opposition aspect from a second house planet.* The Sun is opposed by Jupiter in Cancer, while Mercury and Venus are opposed by Pluto in Leo. Let's begin unraveling this dimension of Joyce's chart by understanding the nature of the second house.

In conventional astrology, the second house correlates with money. Classically, it was defined a bit more broadly: "movable possessions." Generalizing, we can see it as symbolic of the *material basis of survival*—everything that enables us to live. Psychologically, material lack fills us with feelings of *insecurity,* while material security supports feelings of being able to cope with whatever might come up—thus: confidence, dignity, and a sense of legitimacy. It is these two inner states that figure centrally in a psycho-spiritual perspective on second house symbolism: on one hand, that sense of security, legitimacy, dignity and self-confidence; on the other hand, self-doubt and insecurity. Where there are planets in a chart, there are evolutionary lessons to be learned. Thus, it would emerge immediately that Joyce was born with a pervading sense of self-doubt—in a nutshell, she had come into the world to *prove herself to herself.*

Before we dive into all that, let me briefly say that in terms of material security, certainly the standard astrological interpretations here would center on predictions of Joyce's material affluence. Jupiter, the traditional "Greater

Benefic" would be expected to bring comfortable financial circumstances—perhaps through inheritance, due to its association with an eighth house Sun (legacies). Financially, Pluto is often seen as a benefic influence too, despite its scary reputation at more psychological levels. Its position in the second is consistent with the existence of a "family fortune"—and also a bit ominous of the sort of treachery, deception, and other unsavory behavior that serious money often breeds in family situations.

Be all that as it may, to me the central significance of these second house planets lies in their reference to underlying currents of psychological self-doubt in Joyce. These currents have four sources.

First, even though my faith in "fortune-telling" astrology is limited, if Joyce were in fact born into wealth, as a conventional reading of her chart might indicate, she would be a natural candidate for a common phenomenon among affluent, reflective people: feeling guilty and unworthy regarding their "good fortune."

Second, we turn our attention to Pluto. This planet, "The Lord of the Underworld," is the natural ruler of the eighth house, where Joyce's Sun lies. As we have seen, she has been systematically shamed for her "psychologicalness" and for her "suspicious" (read: *penetrating*) view of life. From an early age, the message that "there is something wrong with her" has been hammered home, driving her inward—and manifesting as internalized shame and self-doubt.

Third, looking at expansive, "lucky" Jupiter, we recognize that, in terms of "proving herself," Joyce actually sets a very idealistic standard for herself—and living up to such a standard is not easy. This is a delicate area. Joyce certainly came into this world "armed for bear." As we have seen all along, her chart suggests a high degree of industry, seriousness, and depth, as well as most probably a sharp mind—and a destiny that involves her having something to say to the larger populace. Most of us live average lives; that's what the word "average" means. Most of us don't do grand things in the obvious sense. We support our dignity by taking joy in our simple victories: raising our children well, living with some integrity, making our relationships work. Kids probably benefit from their dreams of being astronauts and movie stars. Adults, on the other hand, benefit from simpler kinds of self-acceptance. Against that common sense backdrop, we see Joyce, who in fact came into this world to do something bigger than all that. In her soul, she knows it. And if she falls markedly short of that grand Jupiter vision, she feels a corresponding sense of a kind of weird

429

failure in her life, even in her seeming victories. *Thus, her own high aspirations can constitute a third driver of self-doubt.*

Fourth, we must recognize that Pluto opposes Venus while Jupiter opposes her eighth house Sun. Both of these are relationship significators, as we saw earlier. In Joyce, any self-perception as a "failure in relationships" would quickly internalize as a pervasive theme of self-doubt and, through Pluto, perhaps self-sabotage or martyrdom. This is an insidious risk. Joyce is demanding and intense. She's alternately profoundly self-sufficient and private, then almost confrontively "present." Being close to her is not a task for the faint-hearted. But her natural soulmates are *not the faint-hearted either!* Nor are they the conventional people she was "programmed" to entertain as marital possibilities. Thus, we see something akin to a set-up for "failure" in terms of early intimacies, which then sequences into those second house issues of self-doubt. That in turn could sequence into her avoiding the whole painful issue of love by taking refuge in "Fortress Joyce," thereby cementing the mess into place.

Let's remember that, while self-doubt is distinctly a theme in Joyce's life, even if she were to succumb to it, her *appearance* would still emphatically be one of feisty aplomb.

Positively, then, what can she actually do to prove herself to herself?

First, on the chance Joyce was born into affluent circumstances, she would need to cultivate an attitude of simple acceptance toward that fact—essentially, a faith that Higher Intelligence had deemed those resources necessary to the fulfillment of her evolutionary intentions. She should use them to open doors for herself, make appropriate decisions about generosity, and benefit from the results.

Second, she would need to learn to honor her own depth and psychological curiosity, never allowing anyone to shame her for it—and recognizing that such shaming originates in the other person's fear, and not out of his or her superior "psychological adjustment" or "coolness quotient."

Third, very simply Joyce actually needs to do something "grand" with her life. High aspirations, *even if they were to lead to failure,* are vastly more appropriate for her than a safe life, lived "small."

Fourth, and hardest: Joyce's sense of the success of her own life depends upon the formation of a few profoundly revealing and profoundly transformative soul-friendships. To reach the highest pinnacle of her potential, at least one of those bonds would ideally have to involve the ancient, mammal-

mysteries of sexual bonding—and thus the full embracing of the mysteries of her own Womanhood.

Also relevant here is the presence of a Libran Neptune in Joyce's fourth house. Earlier, we referenced this configuration in terms of its reinforcement of her powerful twelfth house focus: Joyce carries the mark of the Mystic, with its attendant implications of reflectiveness, psychic sensitivity, need for quiet time alone, and spiritual inclinations. There's more to know about this placement, though. Always, the fourth house is pertinent to issues of *home and hearth*—family, physical abode, clan-issues, and the domestic side of marriage. With sensitive—and potentially deceptive—Neptune there, we need to ask some pressing questions about her origins. Before we actually pose them, let's affirm that the questions may or may not have answers. It's important for us not to slander anyone in Joyce's family without good cause. Here are the questions: What was the *mirage* in Joyce's family of origin? What lie had they agreed upon? Why was it necessary for Joyce to live like a ghost in her own home? What form of escapism took a toll on the sanity of the family?

Mystics are forever giving things up—sexuality, money, comfort. There are deep reasons for that ascetic behavior, but they also alert us to a less-conscious dimension of Neptune. Where it lies in the birthchart, a person is vulnerable to not claiming what he or she legitimately needs for the evolutionary journey. Under Neptune, we can observe a kind of *unconscious, unnecessary, and spiritually inappropriate self-sacrifice*. This theme is especially strong with Joyce because of the way Neptune's warning is backed up by her strong twelfth house emphasis. With Neptune in the fourth house, the risk in this regard is that she would *surrender her evolutionary need for a sense of home.* This is pertinent to issues of intimacy as well—as everyone knows, "a house is not a home;" a home requires loving relationships too.

Neptune is also connected to the larger issue of where she actually lives: her domicile. Positively, we recognize that Joyce's soul possesses a distinct "land sense." For her, living in a place with the "right vibrations" is profoundly significant. Here, we are out near the edges of what we can see astrologically, but the exploration of some symbiotic relationship between *soul* and *place* is central to her evolutionary intentions—something akin to a Native American feeling for a "sacred mountain." Going out even further on thin ice, let's add that Neptune is the "god of the sea." Joyce's natural home could possibly be by the sea, literally—but let's recognize that Neptune here really refers more to any

431

place that fills us with "oceanic" feelings. That generally refers to locations that are spacious: oceans certainly . . . but also mountains and deserts, even prairies.

That Joyce benefits spiritually from such magical rapport with her physical home is implicit in the deeper meaning of Neptune in the fourth house. So is the martyr-notion that she could surrender the fulfillment of that need unnecessarily and inappropriately.

The only planet we've not yet mentioned is Mars. It lies in the Fire sign, Sagittarius, where its passionate nature finds easy resonance. It's about five degrees below the western horizon, placing it in Joyce's sixth house, but also in a conjunction with her Descendant—and therefore making an opposition to her Ascendant. Other than a trine to her North Node, that is the only major aspect Mars makes in her chart; it contacts no other planet by Ptolemaic aspect. This lack of aspects, paradoxically, is quite empowering to a planet, lending it considerable *autonomy* in the psyche. The challenge is that its relative lack of integration into the rest of the chart can also lead the planet to operate as an *autonomous function*—with a mind of its own, so to speak. The resultant volatility is of course particularly dramatic when the unaspected planet is Mars, with all its passionate, "hot" implications—and doubly so when Mars lies in a Fire sign, as it does here.

Thus, we can imagine God offering Joyce a bit of advice at the end of the proverbial cosmic diving board: fasten your seatbelt.

Mars, the "war god," is in the sign of the Gypsy: right away, we recognize another wild force stoking the fires of adventure. It adds heft to the fact that Joyce's Ascendant-ruling Mercury lies in the house of the Quest. Furthermore, she can be fierce (Mars) in defense of her ideals and her freedom (Sagittarius). Let's add that this Mars placement also suggests that she can be profoundly, even exhaustingly, devoted to her sense of duty (sixth house). Together, all this implies that Joyce is a natural *crusader*. In keeping perspective, we must remember that Mars makes no planetary aspects: all these edgy functions, however noble, can easily get out of balance and become extreme, perhaps even to the point of impacting her health.

The sixth house pertains to our *mentors* as well, leading us to hope that someone came along in Joyce's relative youth who acted as a "hero" for her, modeling passion, adventure, idealism, and the general notion of life "lived large." Traditionally, this mentor role would be filled by an aunt, but clans are now fairly fractured nowadays. In general, we've also shattered our ancient mentoring traditions. The astro-counseling reality in the modern sixth house context often lies more in a consideration of the wounding impact of a *lack* of proper mentoring in early life. What trusted adult came along and *honored the fire* in this young girl? Who taught her the *way of passion?* Quite possibly, the answer is "no one." If that is the case, that absence would have added to the subjective sense of isolation and alienation we've been noting all along.

Mars lies close enough to the seventh cusp that we must relate its action to the house of Marriage as well. We've already emphasized the importance of intimacy to the fulfillment of Joyce's evolutionary intentions. Now we learn more. First, we see yet another indication that her natural partnerships are with strong individuals—"Mars people." Such men and women are honest, direct, rough-and-ready types, capable of profound loyalty. Critically, they are *not intimidated* by Joyce, which actually frees her to be spontaneous around them rather than "walking on eggshells."

Another dimension here is that Joyce is learning *the art of intimate conflict*—and that doesn't just mean fighting, but also implies conflict resolution. That interpretation is explicit in having the war god near the gateway to the house of intimacy. It is also implicit in much that we've already explored regarding the realities of her eighth house Sun, which always goes for the deeper waters in any human relationship.

It must be emphasized that with Mars both strong and unaspected here, Joyce's expression of anger in intimate situations could have a life of its own. It would take a lot of conscious effort on her part to avoid unseemly episodes of overreaction—using nuclear warheads when a whack with a nightstick would do. One underlying source for this potentially unfortunate dynamic lies in her Saturnian tendency to bottle things up for too long, then release them all at once. Let's add that any astrologer who conveyed to Joyce the notion that this issue was simply a part of her "character" which she must learn to accept would be doing her a disservice. As we indicated above, the true soul-intention here lies in learning the art of intimate conflict resolution. Part of success there lies in choosing the right people with whom to practice: people who are capable of holding up their end of the bargain. Another part lies in addressing her own issues: fear of intimacy, and unresolved hurts from the past, could manifest as self-defensive, isolating anger. Mere explosiveness on her part, while it might be a pressing force in her psyche, would ultimately be a sign of failing to learn the deeper lesson. Getting it right is fully within the scope of her power. We are living beings—we must be wary of any astrologer who tries to capture anyone in an inescapable, one-dimensional description.

We now move through the Looking Glass into the deepest, most underground, layers of Joyce's chart. We are ready to consider the Nodes of the Moon. These are mysterious and powerful symbols, giving us insight into Joyce's pre-history: the time before her birth. The South Node of the Moon, lying in Aquarius in her ninth house, represents her past, while the North Node, opposite the South in Leo and the third house, pertains to the evolutionary future she is trying to create.

The South Node can be understood in a variety of ways. My belief here is centered on the notion of reincarnation. In that view, the South Node represents *unresolved emotional issues left over from prior-lifetimes*—dynamics which pressingly haunt us in the present life until they are released and resolved. I will use reincarnational language from here on out. Before I get started, let me add that one can also view the South Node in other ways. One is simply to say it's "how God made Joyce." Another is to see it as representing the genetic coding underlying her present character—that is, ancestral "past lives" reincarnated in her quite concretely through the mechanisms of DNA. This genetic view also correlates with the idea of a "family mythos," since we share psychological as well as physical genetic coding with our families and our familial ancestors. Certain psychological traits therefore run down the hereditary, genealogical line.

Please translate out of the reincarnational model and into one of the other ones if you are uneasy with the idea of past lives.

Let's begin with the South Node—with Joyce's past, in other words. It lies in Aquarius. Right away, that tells us that she has been marked emotionally by unresolved issues linked to her playing an *outsider role* relative to a dominant culture. That's simply in the nature of Aquarius, the sign of the Exile or the Dissident. Since we are dealing specifically, by definition, with *unresolved* issues from the past, an effective strategy here lies in focusing on the darker or more wounding dimensions of any archetype linked to the South Node. Thus, we must immediately consider the scars of *repression* and *punishment* that are often visited upon civilization's outsiders. All this tells us that Joyce was born with a deep-seated sense of not fitting in—and of the imminent possibility of punishment or attack. These painful emotions survived her passage through death and rebirth, leaving her somewhat shell-shocked, but also with considerable independence and self-sufficiency. In fact, we now understand more deeply the actual origin of those themes in her present character.

The South Node lies in the ninth house, giving us more concrete clues as to the nature of the prior-life story. Any of the standard astrological associations with this house may prove relevant: journeys, education, religion, belief-systems, culture shock, ideals and values. Linking them integratively with the Aquarian pattern moves us dramatically closer to specificity. For example, we have words for people forced to take a journey (ninth house) as a result of rejection by a dominant society (Aquarius): *refugees, exiles*. When someone is an outsider in relation to the culturally-dominant religion or belief-system, he or she is called a *heretic*. In terms of education, one studying material that is outside the framework of a society's dominant paradigm is often called a *flake* or a *quack*—and given the close association of religious institutions with educational ones throughout much of history, thinking about education cycles us back to the word "heretic" again.

The planetary ruler of the South Node always carries us deeper into the karmic storyline. It typically offers insight either into a pivotal chapter of the prior life or simply another dimension of it. In this case, with the Node in Aquarius, astrologers might disagree on the identity of the planetary ruler. Some would use the modern ruler: Uranus. Others would use the classical ruler: Saturn. Personally, I try to pay attention to both, but I concentrate on the modern rulership—Uranus, in this case. With Joyce, the point is moot: Uranus and Saturn tell the same story: they are conjunct in Gemini and the twelfth house, and aligned with the Moon. The two possible rulers of South Node are thus in agreement, adding clarifying details.

Following the clues, we see that the twelfth house provides a concrete sense of a "scene" or "situation" in the past life scenario. One classic twelfth house scene is the *monastery* or *convent*. In the light of the fact that one of the possible elements in our reading of the placement of the Node itself was "religion," a possible pattern is emerging: that Joyce was a contemplative or mystic, but in the context of a "heretical" religion. The twelfth house also correlates with prisons, hospitals, dungeons, and places of confinement, and also with grievous loss. Considering the fates common to "heretics" historically, those associations don't strain the imagination very much either: perhaps she was martyred somehow, or imprisoned—or suffered terrible loss through being geographically exiled, as we considered earlier.

Uranus (and Saturn) both lie in Gemini, which resonates strongly with our previous ninth house South Node theme of education. We keep seeing this same pattern: clearly, Joyce's soul has emerged from some manner of *scholarly tradition*. The apparent contradiction with our earlier "religious heresy" themes dissolves as soon as we remember that historically, institutions of religion and institutions of education were functionally indistinguishable.

Gemini often references writing; it's easy to visualize Joyce copying holy handwritten manuscripts, for example. Remember that the words "clerk" and "cleric" come from the same root. Lest we are beguiled by images of a tranquil monastic life, let's recall that we are dealing with something that was named heresy by the dominant society, and probably punished somehow.

The Moon itself cannot be ignored, lying conjunct the South Node rulers. The Moon always has domestic associations, adding credence to the imagery of a "live-in" religious institution: the monastery or convent again. It is also linked to emotional states, providing an interesting counterpoint to the more intellectual themes (Gemini, ninth house) we've indicated so far. There was something heart-centered, something of a devotional nature happening here too. Once again, a little knowledge of history resolves the apparent contradiction: the present disconnection between scientific, academic scholarship on one hand, and concerns of a less rational nature on the other, is a modern invention. It could have no relevance to any prior life, except a very recent one.

Going out on thinner ice, there are another couple of lunar associations that might have relevance to our inquiry. First, the Moon is linked to the phenomenon of *memory*. Given the intellectual tone of the rest of Joyce's Nodal symbolism, the feeling of *prodigious feats of memorization* leaps out. This quickly associates in my mind with the notion of *oral traditions*, rather than written ones: the Druids and the Inca, for just two examples, were culturally and spiritually advanced, but had no written tradition. The same can be said for many "primitive" societies.

The second possible lunar association would be with the notion of the Great Goddess. The Moon can have a lot of meanings, and that's only one of them. Given the tone of everything else we're seeing, the idea that Joyce had some prior-life association with Goddess-worship emerges as a possibility, as does the possibility that she was involved with a scholarly but pre-literate culture. Please do note that, unlike her "pariah" status, neither of these ideas—that Joyce was involved with Goddess-worship or with pre-literate traditions of scholarly memorization—are *dictated* by the symbolism. They are merely *consistent* with it. Furthermore, given the unhappy fates of such religions at the hands of the currently-dominant patriarchal religions, these notions blend logically with the profuse imagery of persecution.

There are more past-life hints in the chart. Any planet lying in a square aspect to the Moon's South Node suggests something that blocked or vexed the person in the prior lifetime. It represents a hurtful or wounding reality, or a challenge that defeated him or her. Thus, it represents a set of issues left unresolved from the past—a "skipped step," as Jeffrey Wolf Green puts it. Even though the aspect is out of quality in terms of signs, Uranus is square to Joyce's South Node. Thus, this planet plays a dual role: it is both the Nodal ruler and it is square the Node. We've already considered this from the first viewpoint. Now, looking at Uranus from the second perspective, it emerges as the epitome of calamity. Inherently, Uranus embraces the imagery of "earthquakes and lightning bolts"—sudden, unexpected events that alter everything. With Uranus in the twelfth house, the traditional house of Troubles, these events ripped the foundation of Joyce's prior-life sense of reality out from under her, probably in the blink of an eye. In this, our earlier logic about the fates of "outsiders" seems to have reached its typical conclusion: intolerance and worldly power triumphed, leaving Joyce either dead or exiled. The presence of Saturn (chronic, long-term vexations) conjunct Uranus leads me toward the latter conclusion: *exile.* We've already seen powerful symbolism for that idea in the simple presence of her South Node in the ninth house. These present, more subtle, structures echo that elemental theme.

What might any of these speculations imply in terms of the practical realities of Joyce's present life?

Faced with incomprehensible trauma, people tend to "go away:" to *dissociate* psychologically. We see the phenomenon in the sensitive solider coming home from the nightmare of war, or in the woman who has experienced rape. This notion of psychological dissociation correlates powerfully and directly with the Uranian/Aquarian family of symbols. Wherever we see them, we can often find the mark of this kind of response—and thus the fingerprints of deep-seated, unresolved trauma. In considering Joyce's karmic pattern, we see a classic study in this patterning: her Aquarian South Node, ruled by (and squared by) a twelfth house Uranus. Long ago, in another time and another body, she lost everything for her beliefs. This is a soul that has known utter and total desolation. *And she carried that wound forward into the present life, unresolved.*

What have we accomplished in this Nodal analysis? Critics of this kind of astrology often complain that there is no way any of this could be verified, and so a tricky astrologer "could say anything." Certainly, I would be the first to admit that reconstructing karmic material from the present birthchart is slippery business. At best, I believe that we come up with a parable that *parallels* the actual prior-life narrative. I'd like to add that the techniques we have used are simply an extension into an uncustomary realm of fairly traditional methods of astrological analysis: putting together the messages of signs, planets, houses, aspects and rulerships.

It is not necessary to accept reincarnation to benefit from astrology, but if we assume that the universe is non-random, it follows that there are *reasons* Joyce has this particular birthchart. Logic then dictates that those reasons must pre-date her birth. Reincarnation is one way of making sense of that conundrum. The belief that we live in a random, meaningless universe is no more defensible logically than the belief in meaningful evolution through a succession of lifetimes. And if we accept the latter, it does not seem to me to be unreasonable that we could find traces of the prior-life story in the present birthchart, like footprints in the snow.

In any case, the proof of the pudding is the relevance of the karmic story that emerges through the South Node to Joyce's present life. Do the emotions, attitudes, self-imagery—and psychic scars—implicit in the tale we've spun resonate with her current reality? Do they help explain issues she faces? Do they add something beyond what a conventional psychological analysis of her childhood would provide?

I believe in reincarnation personally, but in my view there is no way we can justifiably claim literal, point-by-point, fact-by-fact, accuracy in the karmic stories we evolve from the South Node. I do believe that if we weave a tale that is consistent with the symbols and neither adds to nor violates anything we've learned from them, that we learn something profoundly relevant and helpful: what we have may not be a fact, but it is a truth. Any novel worth reading can make the same claim.

Based on what we've learned so far, and adding a single non-astrological ingredient—Joyce's Oklahoma birthplace—my fantasy is that she was a spiritual leader, a contemplative, and probably a storyteller, among the Cherokee who were brutally driven from their traditional home in the forests of the American southeast on the infamous "Trail of Tears." As "heathens," they were accorded no rights by the dominant white Christian invaders. Their way of life was "heresy;" they were "outsiders;" their land was stolen without hesitation. Decimated, shell-shocked, and confused, the few survivors among these woodland people were forced to eke out an existence on the unfamiliar prairie.

The desolation and sense of unreality these sad exiles must have felt resonates perfectly with the tone of Joyce's South Node.

Evolution continues. However bleak the prior life landscape, there is always a way forward. It is symbolized by the Moon's North Node. For Joyce, it lies in Leo in the Third House.

Leo is of course the sign of the Lion—the "King of the Beasts." It was not the lion's ferocity, but rather those qualities of grandeur and presence in the creature that led our astrological ancestors to name the sign after a lion. Leo carries "star quality." There is an aura of *aristocracy* and *natural authority* about it. We've all had the experience in group discussions of a mild-mannered person making a quiet suggestion, which is completely ignored. Then, after several minutes, a more commanding individual makes precisely the same suggestion—and everyone reacts as if they'd never heard such a brilliant idea in their lives. This is Leo energy.

Sometimes it's the singer, not the song.

In human discourse, one should never underestimate the importance of a degree of *theatricality*. "Personality factors" are hugely important in terms of determining the quality of the hearing a person receives. Leo represents that attribute of *effective style*.

Emphatically, we are *not* describing Joyce in these words. What we are describing is her lunar North Node: the evolutionary intention of her soul. To go forward with her journey, she needs to *develop* these qualities—qualities that will make her voice heard.

The word "voice" is particularly relevant here since the North Node lies in the third house, with its natural references to speech and writing. Joyce has come into the world with something important to say, and she is attempting to become someone whose voice (third house) is sufficiently commanding, authoritative, and impressive (Leo) that no one can ignore or dismiss her.

Let's add that Leo is also simply the sign of *joy*—a feeling that life is good, that people are supportive and accepting, and that we are comfortable being here in the world. The easy self-expression Leo represents is vigorously enhanced by such positive feelings of belonging. Pitted against Joyce's attainment of this kind of power and palpable well-being, we see her entrapment in the self-containment and caution of the martyred exile. We see the shell-shock of the survivor. We see the crippling sorrow and fatalism of one who has lost everything. Those attitudes are understandable. Joyce came by them honestly, through tragedy, and we must of course view their existence compassionately.

Still, the next step in her evolution is clear: she must recover. The universe is patient; she can take her time. But the eleventh grade follows the tenth grade. Joyce's evolutionary intention lies in getting past the hurt, shock, and silence her prior-life story engendered in her.

Given her soul-history, she has something powerful and useful to tell us. She is not here "finding something to say." She already *has* something to say, and did so from birth. She is recovering enough confidence in herself and trust in the goodness of other people to be *able* to say what she already knows and understands.

That Joyce has natural skill with language is a notion we encountered early in our analysis: her Gemini Moon and Ascendant suggest that she can be clear, verbal, and articulate. Mercury's conjunction with Venus probably even adds quirky eloquence: she has the voice of the artist—the poet, the storyteller, perhaps the novelist. Now, in considering her Nodal axis, we recognize that in the karmic past, she was in fact already operating as some kind of teacher or storyteller. That's plainly evident when we note that the ruler of the South Node—Uranus—is in Gemini, and conjunct a Gemini Saturn and Gemini Moon! *But bitter loss undercut her faith in life, in her voice, and in herself, driving her down into silence.*

With her North Node in the third house, her soul is clearly intending to "get back on the horse that threw it." She was robbed of her voice; the stillborn stories she was never able to tell haunt her today. They constitute a "skipped step," left over from the karmic past.

Joyce's power was taken from her then; in this lifetime, her intent is to *become too powerful a voice for that silencing ever to happen again.* With that goal accomplished, she has a message for us:

It is a tale of the triumph of hope over the hard face of reality, of forgiveness over hatred.

It is a tale of the frailty of death, told in the voice of the Elder and of the Lion.

440

WENDY Z. ASHLEY: MYTHOLOGICAL

I have Alphee Lavoie's Star Trax Millenium for computing charts, as well as Solar Fire. I can use either of these programs to compute a basic chart. To do a reading I calculate a chart in Tropical Placidus, or Topocentric, and then add the fixed stars outside the wheel. I fill the chart in with lines locating the primary aspects. Except for the fixed stars this is really a basic, simple, conventional chart.

I am indebted to Michael Munkasey of Seattle who generously provided me with his Star Lists that I use with every chart that I do. One astrologer whose work with the fixed stars and sky mythology I hold in great regard is Diana Rosenberg of New York. Her study course is exhaustive and well researched. She has kindly given me a copy and I will refer to it in my study of Joyce. Bernadette Brady has a calculation program that is an exciting resource when it comes to fixed stars. But it locates the significant stars by parans and not by longitude, which is the technique I believe is the more useful. The stars that are in alignment with the Sun, Moon, planets, Nodes, and angles of Joyce's chart are appended to this page on Strategy.

The chart before me is the map of a myth, and my task is to uncover which myth. The word "myth" is related to the word "mouth" and refers to the myth as a "story." The characters and motifs and elements in the story/myth are a metaphoric parallel to the experiences and elements in the life of the owner of that chart.

The myth/story is like a play and is a kind of script for the player/owner of the chart, and that script is played out in part through unconscious drives and complexes. In astrological terms the stage set for the play is a constellation. The curtain rises; on the stage before us is a scene, say a path through the deep woods at night. Already we have an inkling of what the story will be about. In human terms we arrive on the stage set that includes our family with its circumstances and capacities. The members of our family and the early characters in our lives carry the archetypes of the myth. Our mother will carry whichever archetype of the Great Mother is in our personal mythology as represented in our chart. Our father will carry the archetypal form of the Great

Father as he is indicated. And we will be formed by these archetypes and carry them within as the cores of our complexes.

R.D. Laing said, "We are all born into the second act."

The mythic associations are therefore not primarily psychological. They are of Fate—in this case Fate as the family and situation into which we are born. But the myth is also our life reenacted as the story of a particular god or goddess. That god's or goddess's story and function lives again in and through us. So again, which myth is Joyce living?

The method for uncovering a myth proceeds in stages. The evidence is in the gathered threads with which I will weave a tapestry about the life before me.

First I locate the angular planets, that is any planet within 20 degrees on either side of an angle (the first, fourth, seventh, or tenth house cusps). The importance of such a planet is from the belief, in mythic times, that it stood for a god or a goddess who was present at the birth. This is because the angles were conceived as doorways between this mortal world and the spirit worlds beyond. Of course the planets stand for types—or better put—archetypes. And I will base my reading upon which planet has the lead in the play. I also consider the traditional ruling planets.

Next I take note of the date of birth, and whether it is near to any time of the year that was likewise considered to be an interface between this world and that one. And I take note of any planets lying along those same Zodiac points. If someone has planets near 10 degrees Taurus, for example, his or her mythos may have to do with Beltane or May Day or the Floralia.

Then any dramatic positioning of the planets must be taken into account. The existence of a stellium in a sign or aligned to the stars of another constellation must be considered. The drama of certain aspects will also suggest a mythos, a conjunction or opposition of the Sun and Moon, for example. I note particularly the hour of the Sun in a daytime birth and the hour of the Moon in a nighttime birth. If the Sun is about to set in the west, and the Moon has already risen and is on the horizon in the east (in the twelfth house), it also carries an archetypal Sun/Moon polarity.

A great cross in a mode often helps me to locate the mythos in one of the Great Ages. Those Ages for which there are recorded myths do not extend far back in time, about 4,000 years, but since succeeding cultures were built upon and included the myths of previous cultures, we can see beneath the surface back at least some 8,000 years. We do also have some ideas of the mythologies from before then, because there are artifacts that can be reasonably supposed to

442

represent certain enduring mythic motifs, which, after all, are based in the world of nature.

A fixed cross for example, or an alignment of the significant elements in a chart with the stars of Taurus, Leo, Scorpio and Aquarius, is reminiscent of the Age of Taurus, from 4,000 to 2,000 +/- 400 years B.C.E. And that era has a consistency of myths, whether Egyptian, Greek, Mesopotamian, Indian, Chinese or Native North American. A cardinal cross suggests the Age of Aries, and a mutable cross, the Age of Pisces or of Gemini.

Lastly I consider the alignment of planets, Nodes, and angles with the fixed stars, generally within an orb of 1 degree, sometimes as much as 2 degrees or 3 degrees. In general, it is not possible to know ahead of time without corroborative material whether the influence of the myth will be found in the sign or among the stars. Joyce for example has three planets in Gemini, and while Uranus is aligned to one of the Pleiades, Saturn and the Moon are among the stars of the Hyades, which are on the face of the Bull constellation. This is a dramatic conjunction, and given that Saturn is one of her ruling planets, it may even hold the pattern for the archetypes of her myth. These stars belong to the sign and constellation Taurus, but because of precession are now in the sign Gemini. So which one is it? There is one myth, that of Phaeton, which may pertain because it has elements of both, and I will be outlining it as a potential myth for her.

I say POTENTIAL myth, because I can find no way after seventeen years of practice to determine which myth my client is living without some feedback from her or him, or, in the case of my writing about famous individuals, some anecdotes that help to locate the myth. Every chart is representative of a number of myths, if only because the myth belongs to a culture, and the mythic astrologer has no way of knowing in a "blind" reading whether the mythos of her client is Greek, Japanese or Lakota Sioux.

When I first began to find the mythology that an individual was living I asked—as is customary in astrological practice—for no personal information whatsoever before commencing the reading. There were, to my thinking, two advantages to this practice. One was to have no pre-judgments about my client or her circumstances, and the other was that if the reading were accurate, it would be all the more convincing or helpful to the client if I could have had no way to know beforehand of anything I was to tell her. It was a way of proving the validity of astrology over again with each client. That worked well enough with pure astrology but proved to be difficult with the mythology.

In my early practice in locating a myth for my client, I often had to relay all of the alternative possibilities (and there could be a dozen of these), and then I'd let my client decide which myth was the best fit for her. To give you an idea: suppose my client has an angular Venus, the Moon in Taurus and Libra rising. Then she, or he, would have a "Venus" mythology. The question now becomes which Venus mythology? In conventional astrological practice I would describe the effect of a powerful Venus in her psychology, and that influence would generally hearken back to the allegorical qualities of Aphrodite as love goddess and goddess of the aesthetic drive. And in traditional astrology that would be sufficient, but if she were living out the mythos of a different Venus divinity, it would be way off the mark.

As an astrological planet, Venus is the vehicle of an archetype, not of a psychological quality, which is how we have become accustomed to the astrological usage. The psychology can only come after the identification of which Venus.

Venus is representative not only of the goddess Venus/Aphrodite, but as the Evening Star it also represents all divinities who follow the Sun/Hero down into the underworld, just as Aphrodite followed Adonis below when he was killed by a boar in the hunt. Venus is also all those who are stolen into the underworld as well. As the Morning Star, Venus is all who ascend from the underworld returning themselves or bringing another back into life again. Venus is Snow White and Sleeping Beauty, both of whom fell into a deep sleep to eventually be awakened by the kiss of true love. She is also the lovely princess who by a kiss restored the humanity of the Frog Prince. Venus is Persephone or Proserpina, Kore, Flora, Pomona, Psyche, Ariadne, all of whom descend to the underworld. And she is all goddesses whose mythos is of a marriage, like Harmonia, Freya, Idun, Blodeuwedd, and Euridice. Venus is the "flower maiden." Venus is Circe as seductress who turned men to pigs, and she is also Miss Piggy who will stop at nothing to get her man, er, frog. In fact pigs and boars are her animals. Venus was the planetary vehicle for Ishtar, Anat, Ashera, Inanna and Astarte, all of the ancient Middle East and all of the Age of Taurus. As the Morning Star the Greeks identified Venus as Athena. Venus as the Morning Star is also Aurora, or Eos, as well as Dice. Venus is Galatia who was made by Pygmalion, as well as the famed Helen of Troy. As a male love figure, Venus is a component of Hermaphrodite, and is the flower youth, Hyacynthus. He is also Adonis. Venus is Erzuli, Butterfly Woman, Parvati, and Shakti. One "dark" Venus is Phaedra, wife of Theseus. Triple forms of Venus include the Horae and the Graces as

444

well as the Charities: Aglaia, Thalia, and Euphrosyne. In the central part of North America, the Morning Star is a great warrior, masculine and not feminine. In Central America, Venus is Quetzalcoatl, the Feathered Serpent, a god not a goddess. And this is not a complete list of variations. Of course what most of these have in common is the behavior of the planet Venus, which is comparable to the behavior of the divinities represented by it. So if my client has a "Venus mythos," which one will I choose to relate to her or him?

Other indicators in the chart will assist in narrowing down the field, leaving only a half dozen possible myths. But that is still a lot of material. Early on I would describe a number of these possible "Venuses." This method was too overwhelming for my clients. It is a big enough task to ask them to "think" mythically with one myth, let alone five or six. But as my clients began to relate to the myth that they felt was their own, they began to share with me experiences from their lives that were obvious parallels to the myth. In a counseling practice, I would then be able to draw for them other parallels from their lives as well. These parallel experiences to the myth are the myth rewritten in their own lives. The archetypes in their lives were symbolically the same as elements in the myth.

As my success with the mythic perspective grew, I began to solicit stories at an early point in the reading—actually remembered experiences from my client's youth (a time in our lives when we experience things most archetypally, and a time when we are becoming our adult selves.) I do not want the story of their childhood but just remembered events. James Hillman, the renowned writer on archetypal psychology, says we only recall archetypal moments unique to the inner archetypes of our complexes. As such these remembered stories are fractals of the myth we are living.

They say, "God is in the details." That is exactly true in those childhood stories.

But in this case these stories are not available to me. So I will have to approach Joyce's mythic astrology reading as I used to have to do, by telling more than one story and seeing which one is the closest to her life story in whatever biographical material she provides. I do hope she will relate one or two of those fractal archetypal memory stories, so that you may have an opportunity to see the myth in her life.

445

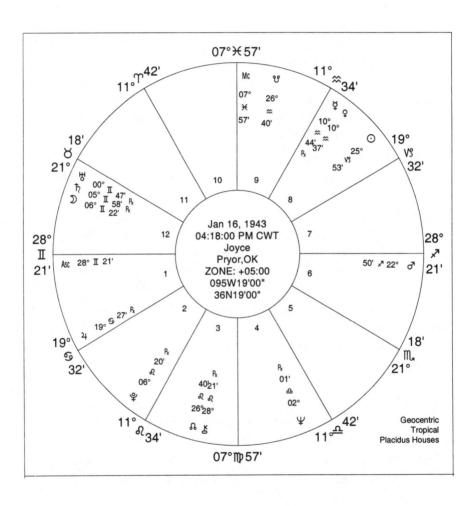

STAR ALIGNMENTS FOR JOYCE

Jan. 16, 1943, 4:16 PM CWT
Pryor OK 95 W 19; 36 N 19

Uranus is at 0 Gemini 47 aligned with Al Kalb al Rai *rho* CEP and Pleione 028 TAU.
Saturn is at 5 Gemini 49 aligned with Prima Hyadem *gamma* TAU.
The Moon is at 6 Gemini 21 aligned with Secunda Hyadem *delta* TAU.
The Ascendant is at 27 Gemini 53 aligned with Polaris *alpha* UMI.
Jupiter is at 19 Cancer 27 aligned with Mulipheins *gamma* CMA.
Pluto is at 6 Leo 20 aligned with Benetalnash *theta* UMA.
North Node is at 26 Leo 40 aligned with Alphard *alpha* HYA.
Chiron is at 28 Leo 20 aligned with *psi* UMA and Algetha *gamma* LEO.
The Nadir is at 7 Virgo 25 aligned with Thuban *alpha* DRA.
Neptune is at 2 Libra 01 aligned with the Ascelli *tau* and *theta* BOO.
Mars is at 22 Sagittarius 50 aligned with Ras Alhague *alpha* OPH.
The Descendant is at 27 Sagittarius 53 aligned with Eltanin *gamma* DRA.
The Sun is at 25 Capricorn 53 aligned with Terebellium *omega* SGR.
Venus is at 10 Aquarius 38 aligned with *theta* SGE.
Mercury is at 10 Aquarius 38 aligned with *theta* SGE and near Al Bali *epsilon* AQR.
South Node is at 26 Aquarius 40 aligned with *beta* PSA.
The Midheaven is at 7 Pisces 25 aligned with *nu* CYG and *pi* and *tau* AQR.

Joyce's chart consists of these signs and constellations:

AQR	Aquarius	LEO	Leo
BOO	Bootes	LIB	Libra
CNC	Cancer	OPH	Ophiuchus
CMA	Canis Major	PSA	Pisces Austrinus
CAP	Capricornus	PSC	Pisces
CEP	Cepheus	SGE	Sagitta
CYG	Cygnus	SGR	Sagittarius
DRA	Draco	TAU	Taurus
GEM	Gemini	UMA	Ursa Major
HYA	Hydra	UMI	Ursa Minor

"The ground principles, *the archai*, of the unconscious are indescribable because of their wealth of reference.... The discriminating intellect naturally keeps on trying to establish their singleness of meaning and thus misses the essential point; for what we can above all establish as the one thing consistent with their nature is their manifold meaning, their almost limitless wealth of reference, which makes any unilateral formulation impossible."
—C.G. Jung, *Collected Works*, vol 9, p. 80.

The horoscope is just that thing that Jung is describing. It is the "ground principles"—it is composed of *archai* or original forms. They are the signs, houses, Sun, Moon, planets, aspects and stars that comprise the map, the mythography, of the horoscope. And the reason there can be so many approaches to a reading is from just that. And even here, in my reading, I must relate more than one mythos for Joyce, since I do not have those reflections on her life that she would supply in an actual reading that would serve to affirm that one myth that is uniquely hers, so that I then might go on to further explore and amplify her mythos here. As I have explained in the Strategy portion of this contribution, I usually ask my client to bring three or four memories from youth that can be told as narratives. These will help me to locate one of the possible mythologies to be found in each chart. When two individuals have the same chart, they may be living different myths. I do not have Joyce's direct responses to the myths, and those responses are the most exciting and confirming part of any mythic reading. When we have them, we can then see divine intervention and wisdom in a life. Instead, this attempt at a mythic reading must merely function to show a methodology of how to relate a myth to a horoscope. It will also help for the reader to know mythology as well as astrology.

Joyce

Joyce was born with an angular Mars at the beginning of the second year of America's involvement in World War II. We must explore the effect of this Mars in the sixth house on her early life. Since the ruler of the sixth is on the cusp of the third, with a wide (12 degrees) applying opposition to the Sun in the eighth, we have the potential for a wartime family hero who either died in the war or was gravely injured. The most likely candidate for this role is either an older brother or a brother of one of her parents or grandparents, because of the stellium in Gemini, and because the Sun (hero), ruler of the third (house of siblings with Leo on the cusp), is in the eighth. The ruler of the third in Capricorn indicates that she will have had older siblings, and her Gemini rising indicates the importance of siblings. Or because she was born with the Sun in Capricorn, it may even be her father (Capricorn is the sign of fathers) who was wounded or killed in the war. In my Strategy section I refer to how when we arrive on the scene (are born), there is already a drama (mythos) in progress. This looks to be the drama in progress in Joyce's very early childhood.

An alternative interpretation would be that Mars stands for the wounder rather than the wounded. Contemporary astrologers are apt to use Chiron alone for the motif of wounding, but it was first and primarily Ares (Mars) who in mythology was a wounded god. He was also a god who inflicted wounds, and is depicted always with a sword or spear—the wounding weapons of the warrior. The wounding of Chiron on the other hand was accidental. The sort of wound taken or inflicted by Ares is more deliberate and more brutal. In fact the stars surrounding the area of her Mars and Descendent are all related to wounding, the crushing foot of Ophiuchus, the stinger of the Scorpion, the flames of Ara the Altar and the barb of the arrow aimed by the Archer.

The angular position of Chiron (within 9 degrees of the fourth house cusp) amplifies the archetype of "wounding," and Chiron would incline her to the "healing" of the wound. The motif of the wound itself, the inflictor of the wound, and the bearer of the wound are indicated when a person is born with an angular Mars. Whatever sign or house Mars occupies gives us the place of the wounding.

Since Mars is the planet of coming of age rites, it also carries the archetype of the Initiation, the Initiator, and the Initiate. Joyce's Mars is in Sagittarius. This can mean that the "wounding" is in the area of religion, especially since the ruler of her Ascendant—Mercury—is in the ninth house of religion. This wound initiated Joyce into a lifelong involvement with what astrologers used to call "higher thought." And it suggests that she is an "initiate." Of course Mars in the sixth can simply suggest being accident prone, as well.

The Astrological Factors Suggesting Her Myth

In general then, each of the following five attempts to identify the myth that Joyce is living is based upon the same archetypal factors—her angular Mars and its association to the archetype of wounding, her angular Chiron and its association to the archetype of healing, the emphasis upon Saturn with its conjunction to her Moon, her Sun in Capricorn and its opposition to her Jupiter in Cancer, and finally her Mercury/Venus conjunction in the ninth.

Possible Myth #1: The story of Phaeton

This is the myth that I brought up as a potential myth in my Strategy section. This myth contains some of the motifs in Joyce's chart, but probably not enough of them. The unusual conjunction that Joyce has of Uranus, Saturn and the Moon in earliest Gemini is aligned with an asterism of stars called the Hyades. They comprise the "face" of the constellation of the Bull—Taurus. Her Saturn is conjoined to the first of the Hyades and her Moon to the second. The name means "water bringers," and they are called the "weepers." In Greek archeo-astronomy, they are the sisters of Phaeton who stand weeping with grief on the banks of the river in which he was drowned. There is a river in the sky under Taurus. It is called Eridanus. But Joyce has none of the stars of that river in evidence.

Phaeton is that famous boy who went to find his father who was Helios, the Sun. Proud of what the boy he'd left behind as an infant had become, Helios offered him any gift he chose to have. Phaeton asked that he be allowed to drive his father's Sun chariot across the sky. His father sadly had no choice but to allow him to do so, but knew he had neither the strength nor the wisdom to hold the horses to their course. Morning came and the boy rose in the chariot from the sea. His strength waned as he drove the four chargers to the highest point. On the downward course he could not hold them to the path, and nearer and nearer they came to the earth below. The blazing Sun began to scorch the lands below. Seeing the endangered world, Zeus took a hand and dashed the boy and the chariot into a river, where the flames were quenched and the boy was killed. His sisters came to the bank to mourn his loss. The tears they shed fell into the river and became golden drops of amber, and they themselves were transformed into poplar trees that stand trembling on those banks to this day.

As mythic figures, the Hyades are really incidental to the mythology that is primarily about their brother. But since Joyce's chart has an indication of a lost brother because of her angular Mars and Chiron, and because the ruler of her

450

third is in her eighth opposed by Pluto and Jupiter, it just may be this myth which is fundamental to her destiny.

This is an apocryphal myth, one told as an explanation for something, and also has a moral to the tale, as fables often do and true myths do not. For example, the Hyades were metamorphosed into trees and their tears into the sap from those trees that hardened then into amber, a substance that was found at the bottom of flowing rivers. Nonetheless some of its elements carry the motifs of a probable older true myth, one whose history was long before classical Greece existed and which is now lost. It is also a very small myth, and I must work to extract all of its meaning.

Nonetheless, going with what we do have—if this is Joyce's mythos, then here are the motifs of Phaeton.

She will have lost her father or have been abandoned by him, because she has the Sun in Capricorn in the eighth and Saturn conjoined to Uranus in the twelfth. Her father will have been a mystery to her, Neptune ruling her tenth, and she may have made him heroic in her imagination, because her Sun is in Capricorn opposed to her Jupiter. The Sun and Jupiter in aspect may carry the archetype of the "big" man. She may have aspired to follow in the family footsteps, pursuing the same career or path in life as did her parent or grandparent, because her ruler of the tenth is in the fourth, or the ruler of the house of profession is in the house of family. She may have set out very young to achieve her ambitions because of her angular Mars and its implication of there having been an early quest for an education. Her Mars is in Sagittarius in the sixth. She may have lost a brother when young—she has the ruler of the third in the eighth—and may have taken on the archetype of the heroic in his stead, because her Mercury is in opposition from the eighth to Pluto in the second, and because she has Mars in the sixth in Sagittarius, sign of ethical obligation as sacrifice in the sixth. She may have lost him or a friend through a drowning accident because the just risen Moon is conjoined to the ruler of the eighth, an asphyxiation death. She will work at a center, perhaps a religious center, in service—this is a counter motif to the youthful narcissism of Phaeton. The center is indicated by the star Polaris at 28 degrees Gemini, conjunct her Ascendant by longitude as well as by the motif of the tree(s) in the myth.

In this myth and the two following there is the motif of the loss of a sibling.

Possible Myth #2: The Story of Iphegenia

There is a myth under the aegis of Artemis about a young woman named Iphegenia (if-eh-jen-I'-a). The Greeks associated Gemini with the mythologies of Artemis. Iphegenia is "Artemis-like." The graceful virgin Iphegenia is the second daughter of Agamemnon and Clytemnestra, who are the King and Queen of Mycenae. Their story is but a part of what may be described as a "great" myth, because it is very long and has many characters in it. The doings of the House of Atreus have to do with the start of the Trojan War.

It was Agamemnon's brother Menelaus whose wife, the beautiful Helen, was stolen away by Paris, son of Priam, King of Troy. And so Menelaus, King Agamemnon, the famous Odysseus, and other great kings and warriors of Greece decided that together they would avenge Menelaus's honor and go to Troy to bring Helen back to her husband. They were gathered on the shore at Naupolis with their fine long vessels drawn up on the beach waiting for a favorable wind to carry them across the Aegean Sea, when it happened that Menelaus was hunting for some stew meat for the pots set up at the shore. He slew a hare with young for their dinner, thereby offending the Goddess Artemis. She determined that as a punishment for this crime, no wind would come for them. Days and weeks went by and still no wind blew. The warriors were losing their patience. They grumbled about how they could be at home, looking after their own affairs, instead of hanging about on this beach.

In exasperation and fear that he would lose his fighting force, Agamemnon consulted his seer. "You must sacrifice your virgin daughter Iphegenia to the Goddess to appease Her wrath," he told the ruler.

And so Iphegenia was lured from her home on the hilltop castle. Her mother was told that the young woman was to be married to Achilles at the warriors' encampment. It was a lie of course, and there was a curse on the House of Atreus because the grandfather of Agamemnon and of his brother Menelaus had already eaten his own children in a stew. That curse was now about to descend upon Iphegenia.

When she arrived, she was taken instead to an altar, which had been set up on a hill. She was told that only by making this sacrifice would there be honor once again for the Atreus family. She was laid across the altar and held down by priests and Agamemnon, her father, raised the knife to plunge into her breast. Some say the story ends here. Some say that the Goddess Artemis herself intervened at this point and substituted a deer in Iphegenia's place and carried Iphegenia across the wine dark sea to Taurus or Turkey. There, acting as the priestess of Artemis, she would sacrifice sailors who were shipwrecked upon that far shore to the Goddess. At any rate, following the sacrifice of the daughter, the winds came, and the men set sail for the shores of Taurus (Turkey) and Troy.

After years had passed and the war was long since over, Iphegenia's own brother Orestes was shipwrecked not far from the temple of Artemis. He was brought to the High Priestess Iphegenia, and something about this "stranger's" appearance stayed the knife in her hand. Each noticed that the other had the same fine golden brown hair. They discovered the long-lost sibling-other and this reunion brought great joy to their hearts, and tears poured down their cheeks at this unforeseen reunion of brother and sister. They spent all the night sharing what had happened with them in the intervening years.

Orestes promised to take Iphigenia home to Greece, and he fulfilled his promise too. Both of their parents were now dead, Agamemnon at the hand of his wife, Clytemnestra, who was killed by her own son, Iphigenia's brother Orestes. It was their sister Electra who had urged him to do this murder of retribution. The story of Electra and Orestes' crime is told in an opera entitled "Electra." The story of the whole family drama is told in Aeschylus's triad of plays called "The Orestia," and these of course are another story. This is all part of the BIG myth, and here we are focused upon Iphegenia's part in the stories.

If this is Joyce's mythos, then here are the motifs of Iphegenia that she will have lived out in her life.

She may have had a father or an uncle who was in the military, most likely as an officer, because of her angular Mars in Sagittarius. She may have come from or married into a noble or wealthy family, because of Jupiter in Cancer in the second and the Sun in Capricorn in the eighth. Male honor in the family would have taken precedence over female functions and sensibilities, also because of Jupiter in the second in Cancer opposite Sun in Capricorn in the eighth. She may have been betrayed within the family for the purpose of family ends, this because of the emphasis in Gemini. She may have had to put her own life on hold, and may have difficulty accomplishing goals with Saturn conjunct the Moon in the twelfth. She may have been expected to sacrifice her own self for family pride because of her Pisces Midheaven and Virgo Nadir. She would have a great concern about the effects of war on women, with her Moon on the horizon in the opposite sign and house to her Mars. She would have a drive to make something of herself—to achieve fame and recognition. There would be much travel abroad because she has Mercury, ruler of her Ascendant, in the ninth house of travel. She would serve her religious community, to which she would be deeply committed because of Aquarius on the cusp of the ninth and because its ruler, Uranus, is conjoined to Saturn and the Moon in her twelfth. She would have a mother who struggles to have her own power because of Chiron in Leo on the cusp of the fourth square the Uranus/Moon/Saturn complex. She would have a brother who died or who lived through a catastrophic situation, because of the Sun, ruler of the third in the eighth house. She would be attracted to a man who is like a sibling (twin) to herself, because of her three planets in Gemini. He is likely to be a foreigner, or she will have met the "other" abroad, because she has Sagittarius on the seventh house cusp. She is not likely to marry. (Artemis is not a marrying goddess.)

As Joyce shares the story of her life for us, we should see these motifs of this myth if this is her mythos. But if it is not, we can try out the next possible myth which is also Greek but told of Crete, an older civilization.

Possible Myth #3:   *The Story of Callisto and Helice*

This is a story of two sisters who save a child from being devoured by his Father. The two sisters are Callisto and Helice (kal –ees'-toe and hell-eese').

The story of the Greek gods and goddesses began long ago in Crete. There lived there a pair of Titans, Chronus and Rhea Cronia, and unlike the other eleven pairs of Titans, it was their destiny to be the great-grandparents of the Greek pantheon of the classical age. They had between them six children, Hestia and Poseidon, Demeter and Hades, and Hera and Zeus. Now it had been foretold that one of these children would grow up to overthrow his father and replace him as the ruler of all of the gods. Chronus, their father, circumvented this fate by swallowing each child in its turn as it was born. Rhea grieved mightily for her lost children, and when the youngest was born and his father demanded to see him, she presented her husband with a stone wrapped in a baby blanket. He took what he thought was his youngest baby and swallowed it down.

But Rhea had taken the infant to be hidden deep within a cave. She left it in care of a troop of youthful warriors called the Curetes. They placed the baby on the floor and danced around it, banging their spears against their shields and making enough noise to prevent old Chronus from hearing the baby's cries. In the usual version of this tale, the infant is left to be nursed by a she-goat—Amalthia. But another version has the baby Zeus left in the care of two nursing mothers who are the bear sisters—Callisto and Helice. Nursed by his bear mothers, the baby grew strong and healthy. When he grew up he found an

454

emetic that his mother gave to old Chronus, so that he vomited back up the other five siblings. And Zeus did overthrow his father and sent him away under the world to live as a stone himself.

Callisto is one of the names the Greeks gave to the constellation Ursa Major, the Great Bear. Helice, which means "twisting about," is the Cretan name for Ursa Minor, the Little Bear. Since Joyce has the degree of the pole star, Polaris, the *alpha* star of Ursa Minor rising, she has a possible relationship to the two bears. She also has the Nadir aligned to another pole star, Thuban, *alpha* Draco. Thuban was the pole star 5,000 years ago. Her Pluto is aligned to *theta* Ursa Major and her Chiron is aligned to *psi* Ursa Major.

Given that the tradition of two Sky Bears exists from archaic times, and given that the bear carries the archetype of the protective mother (especially of protection from the destroying father, since male bears will frequently kill bear cubs in order to bring the mother into estrus), then this bear version is the more ancient, and the goat version is not older than the domestication of goats. To understand and amplify this myth, one would have to be able to relate the symbolism of bears to the client's life. This is another "Artemis" mythology, because bears are Artemis's animals, as are deer, hares, and hunting dogs.

This myth has been retold in a modern film, with therefore a more modern set of referents to its motifs. Joseph Campbell would say to his students, "The modern version of the myth is in the movies." For this myth I would refer my client to the film "Fried Green Tomatoes." The film opens with two women, a housewife played by Kathy Bates who visits with a nursing home resident played by Jessica Tandy. Ms. Tandy's character is relaying to Kathy Bates's character the life story of two women—who were friends from childhood on. One knows how to charm bees. Golden (Solar) Artemis has a bee form, as was depicted on Cretan intaglio seals. Joyce's Pluto is near to Preaseape the Beehive. Bees of course have an archetypal relationship to the honeycomb-robbing bear. The other woman has an abusive husband and is rescued from him by her friend. Together they open up a restaurant, "The Whistle Stop Café," where they serve their famous fried green tomatoes. When the husband comes to steal the baby he is stopped by the women.

If this is Joyce's mythos, then here are the motifs of Callisto and Helice. Since the ruler of Joyce's fifth house of children, Venus, is in her eighth house in opposition to Pluto, and since this could signify the loss or near loss of a child, and since her Venus is in Aquarius, the natural ruler of the eleventh house of other people's children, this could carry the archetype of an endangered child who might have been herself, a sibling or her own child. She would have had a "devouring" father with her Sun in Capricorn in the eighth with Pluto opposed to her Ascendant ruler, Mercury. She would be involved in rescuing endangered children, with her angular Mars widely trine Chiron in Leo, the sign of children. She might be a nurse or advocate for a child who is deaf or is catatonic, because of her Saturn conjoined to Uranus and the Moon in the twelfth, sextile her Pluto in Leo in the second, since Pluto is ruler of the sixth which concerns health matters. The Drum—including the eardrum—is under the rulership of Rhea Cronia, the savior mother. She will be very much an independent woman since she has the Sun in Capricorn and Moon conjunct Saturn. If she is a mother she will have six children, the youngest being her champion, and she will have to protect them from the domination of their father because the ruler of the fifth, Venus, is in opposition to Pluto. Because of this same aspect her children, or when Joyce was young, her sibling, will be endangered by illness. She will have a very special closeness with another woman because her North Node is in the third, and because it is conjunct Chiron ruler of the fourth, she may share her household with that woman. She may work as a teacher (which is a bear function) because of her Sun-Jupiter opposition, and because Mercury, her chart ruler, is on the cusp of the ninth. Bears are shamanic animals, and her Mars is conjunct the star Rasalhague, which is the *alpha* star of Ophiuchus at 22 degrees Sagittarius, and it is called "the head of the shaman." She may require a lot of solitude—going into her "cave," because bears are solitary animals and because she has her Sun in Capricorn in the eighth, and because her Moon is conjoined to Saturn in the twelfth, which like the eighth is a house of solitude. This is a much smaller and more obscure mythos, but if Joyce's life does not "bear" out this myth, then I would like to relate yet another.

456

The Mul-Apin Map

Diana Rosenberg writes about the use of the stars of Aquarius, seen here on this Syrian sky map (The Mul-Apin Map), where in place of the familiar "Water Bearer" we see a woman enthroned with a dog at her feet.

Diana Rosenberg writes alluding to this goddess in her Sidereal Aquarius/Tropical Pisces section of her great work on the fixed stars:

> "One of three surviving fragments of the Euphratean planisphere calls the 11th (equinoctial) month *Idu As-a-an*, 'The-Month-of-the-Curse-of-Rain' (or) Shabatu/Shevat—January/February). The Tablet of the 30 Stars from Birs-Nimroud, 'at least as old as 3,000 BC' (Brown), written in Babylonian cuneiform and copied from an older tablet, starts with the Urn of Aquarius and ends with the Sea-Goat, an order that dates it to the time when the winter solstice, then the start of the calendrical year, was in the stars of the Water-pourer (Al Bali, Epsilon Aquarii, the westernmost star in the figure, marked the winter solstice about 3,100 BC, about the time writing first developed in Sumer). Originally, this figure may have been a vessel only: Gu, 'Urn' (Akkadian *Qu-hasbu*, 'streams').

'I am a physician, I know how to heal,
I carry with me all the herbs...
texts for healing...cures for all.'
    —The Gula Hymn of Bullutsa-rabi

On very ancient *kudurru*—boundary stones carved with constellation figures—the area which we know as Aquarius shows instead a seated goddess with a dog: this was Earth-goddess Gula, 'The Great Doctoress,' daughter of Anu, God of Heaven, and consort of Ninib (Saturn). This is extremely interesting, as Anu is surely connected to Uranus (Greek Ouranos), and Saturn and Uranus are both considered rulers of Aquarius; however, they rule the *tropical* version of the sign. Tropical Aquarius still overlaps the original sky figure by about 19 degrees, from 11 Aquarius on. Invoked in incantations as the healer of disease, Gula could at will inflict illness or restore health; she was 'life-giver' and could preserve the health of the body and remove sickness and disease 'by the touch of her hand.' Her power could be used for evil as well as good, and appeals to her could bring on the very diseases she was able to heal, or strike an enemy with blindness. Sometimes referred to as 'lady of the netherworld' who restored the dead to life, Gula actually occupied a unique intermediate position between the gods of the living and the gods of the dead. According to Brown, the ancient asterism *Gu* 'Urn,' which included only part of the Ptolemaic Aquarius, supplies a punning reference to Gula ('The Great') who was associated with the goddess Ba-hu whose name implies 'wasteness' and 'the watery deep.' There have been suggestions that GU.LA meant 'Great Man' or 'Giant,' but there is little evidence to support this idea, and it does not fit the star-pattern. In India this constellation was *Kumbha*, 'Water-Pot', a name that may be derived from that of a storm-god. In many nations the Urn was a well-bucket. According to Grun's *Timetables of History*, between 3,000 and 2,500 BC, 'Sumerian medicine discover(ed) the healing qualities of mineral springs.'

This would connect the concept of healing (Gula) and water (Urn), at just the time in history when the stars of the Urn marked the Winter Solstice."

We do not have Gula's "story" or myth, and hence we must rely upon what scarce material evidence and what obscure references there are to her to understand who she is and thereby to flesh out the possible elements of this goddess in Joyce's life.

In other words what we have here is an *archetype* and not a myth. Joyce's Mercury, her ruling planet, is aligned to *epsilon* Aquarius, Al Bali, the star to which Ms. Rosenberg refers in her piece above as the star that marked the winter solstice at about 3,000 B.C.E.

As Joyce's own date of birth is near to the winter solstice, there is some evidence then for the principal goddess of this season to express herself in Joyce's life and purpose. Joyce has Mars in the sixth house, and this is a significator of the archetype of the wound as a health issue. This, coupled with her angular Chiron (at 28 Leo it is only 9 degrees from the Nadir) means that she is initiated through the archetype of "the Wound," or hurt into the healing of the wound as a life purpose.

As daughter of Anu-Uranus, and consort of Ninib-Saturn, Joyce has a Moon- Saturn- Uranus conjunction in her twelfth, indicating a life in service because of the influence of her father and of her partner. We do not know which planet was the vehicle for Gula, but as she holds urns it may be the Moon, which is in most cultures the planet of the waters.

It was said that Gula watered the tree that grew in the center of the garden at the center of the world. Such a tree can only be the *axis mundi*, and it is this very tree with its twining serpent that we meet with 2,000 years later in the Judeo Garden of Eden. The Middle Eastern traditions have it that there are four rivers that run out from Eden, which is the garden at the center of the world. This lore comes down to us in the more familiar Judeo-Christian tradition as a morality tale. And there has been a great deal written about what it means, its historical references, its symbolism, etc. Joyce has the star that crowns the current *axis mundi*, Polaris or *alpha* Ursa Minor, conjunct her Ascendant.

Suffice it to say that this tree and its four rivers are a *cosmology*, and the guardian of that tree is an archetype—a pre-Arien Age archetype from a time pre-dating heroic endeavor.[1] At this stage in pre-history, the blessings of the garden are available to all.

This archetype is one of the availability of the waters of life to all—that is to everyone who lives in one of the four quarters of the world, since the rivers of life flow to the four directions—and this means that Joyce would have a belief in the availability of a good and healthy life for each and every one. But because the rulers of her sixth house (Jupiter and Pluto) both oppose her Sun, she would be frustrated in her attempts as a healer to prove out this belief through her own powers and through limitations upon her opportunities to be effective. This reminds me of the suffering of Sophia, in a marked contrast between the earthiness of her sexuality and the idealization or rather spiritualization of her wisdom.

Since Gula is both a life giver and a death giver, she is clearly from the pre-heroic mythologies, a chthonic goddess whose opposite functions were not differentiated into good and evil. The dog who is her agent and familiar bears out in itself this duality that is undifferentiated. Dogs are associated both with predation and destruction, and are frequently associated with death since they are natural scavengers. They were anciently also associated with healing. The belief was that a dog, in its slavish devotion to a mistress, would absorb into itself any ills that threatened the vitality of its owner.

Modern understanding is beginning to see the affection of this animal as a healing and life-giving force in itself, as a loving companion.

Finally, other writers, attempting to make sense of the association of this animal with an "unclean" reputation with the goddess of healing, tell of how it is known that the saliva of the dog in licking wounds has an antiseptic quality. Furthermore, early Gemini as a constellation is associated with the familiar two dogs in the sky, Canis Major and Canis Minor. Her Jupiter is aligned with Mulipheins *gamma* Canis Major.

Gula-Bau, whose name connotes limitlessness, was married to Ninib or Saturn. He is a victor-king of the later style age of heroes. But the Judaic pair Binah and Chokma are reminiscent of this pairing in the Cabalistic Tree of Life. Binah is Saturn and has a dolphin form, and is particularly reminiscent therefore of Gula. There is possibly an evolution of a most ancient form, Gula, into a later form, Binah.

If the primary divinity of Joyce's mythos is Gula, then here are the motifs that manifest in her life.

We can be certain of a few of these archetypal situations in her life, even though we do not have here a fully fleshed-out goddess or the actual mythic story. She will have a drive to live her life as a healer because of her angular Chiron and because the planet that rules her Ascendant, Mercury, is conjoined to the star Al Bali, *epsilon* Aquarius, the hand of the healer. She will be involved with a healing institution or center, or with a gardening center because Polaris conjoins her Ascendant, and Thuban or *alpha* Draco conjoins her Nadir. She will suffer for her spiritual life, religion or beliefs with her ruling Mercury in her ninth opposite Pluto, and the ruler of the ninth, Uranus, conjunct her Saturn in the twelfth. She will have a husband who has a position of power or importance gained through intelligence and family influence, because she has Jupiter in Cancer and Mars in Sagittarius on the cusp of the seventh house. There will be a family history of healers because she has Neptune, the ruler of the tenth, in the fourth, and Virgo ruled by Chiron as ruler of the fourth, as well as the Moon conjunct Saturn in the twelfth in trine to Mercury at Gula's star, Al Bali. She will have a great appreciation of dogs and a belief in the dog as a life enhancer, because the stars of the two dogs are near her Ascendant.

Possible Myth #5 : *The story of Turtle Island*

A native North American myth may pertain to Joyce. I cannot relate any mythology of the people native to her birthplace in Oklahoma, but one widely extant story is native to New York State where I presume she now resides.

461

Sometimes the mythology of an area that we carry within somehow calls us to the place or to the people of that mythology. I have been doing this work now for over twenty-five years and have found it a mistake to conclude that one's truest mythos will be from the culture into which one is born. The power of myth is such that it may mold the life of an individual who has never seen or known of the people or place from which it came. So it is that I found that an African-American ex-convict had a perfect fit with Dionysus, a Greek god, while a German woman student's life was true to Amaterazu, the Japanese Sun goddess. "Go figure," as my kids used to say.

This is a story that is told over a very wide part of the United States by many Native Americans about how "Turtle Island," the world we know, came into being. It is a story told by the people of the Five Nations, as they were known, the Iroquois, the Seneca, the Huron, and the Mohawk, as well as by the neighboring Canadian Ojibwe.

I will paraphrase the story here for you for there are more than a few versions, and I am not giving the Native names of the story since they vary from tribe to tribe.

"Once there was a girl who lived in the land above the clouds. Down below where earth is now there was nothing but water as far as the eye could see. Now it happened that she became ill and as her father knew the ways of healing, he determined that he would heal her.

The thing that he needed for the medicine was to be found at the very end tip of the root of a great tree that grew in that land up there. Carrying his daughter to the tree, he lay her down at its base and he proceeded to dig.

Just when he reached the tip of that root, the tree, roots, trunk and leaves and the girl with it fell out of the hole he had made, down into the waters below. The girl clung to the tree as it floated upon the waters. All of the animals in the waters below gathered in great concern around her.

'How can we help her? She obviously is not made to live in the sea!' They exclaimed at her beauty and called a council among themselves to save her. Since she had been sent to them, it was up to them to provide a place for her. Beaver said that the bottom below was made of mud, and if it were brought up to the surface it would serve to make something solid for her to stand upon. Turtle volunteered her back for the mud to be placed upon.

First, Otter dove and was gone such a long time. He came up exhausted and empty-handed, and expired on the spot. The Beaver too failed in the same way. The Muskrat tried next and failed as well. The diving birds tried too. Finally an old Toad woman volunteered and the animals whispered among themselves. 'Surely she is too old and feeble!'

But after she had been gone a long while, she finally came up by Turtle's shell and coughed up a few grains of mud. The beautiful young woman spread the mud thinly in a circle on Turtle's back. The earth grew and grew and Turtle grew too, until it was the size of the world we know.

The Tree was planted in the center space and sheltered all who came to it. Then the young woman felt the life within her stir. She was to have two babies, twins, one good and helpful who did all to ease the way of others, and his name was Sapling, and the other was hard and cold and desired nothing more than to create trouble for one and all. His name was Flint.

Flint saw some light shining in through his Mother's armpit and he kicked his way out, but Sapling was born gently in the usual way. The birth of Flint killed their mother, but Sapling took her face and sent it into the sky, and it became the shining Sun. Then he took the Moon and stars from her breasts and sent them into the sky as well. From her body came all the plants and herbs that might be needed. Flint tried to undo his brother's good works. The boys were raised by their grandmother, and as they grew the good brother grew in goodness, and the bad brother grew in evil deeds. Whatever Sapling did, Flint tried to undo. Whatever Flint did, Sapling made better, even if he could not undo his brother's destruction. Eventually they fought, and although Flint was defeated, his evil helpers continue his work. And eventually from Sapling came the people that populate Turtle Island."

This is a very feminine mythology. It is a Great Mother mythology, and the archetype of the Great Mother is at its heart. People who carry this mythos as the archetypal structure of their destiny usually have to deal with a great illness in their life, either in themselves or in another. This myth cannot be seen in the same way that Greek myths are seen. Greek myths are highly psychological. This myth is, in a larger sense, instructional, even if its instructions do not seem explicit. It is also a much bigger and more sophisticated myth than I can tell here.

Nonetheless this myth is lived, as are other myths, through its motifs.

If Joyce's mythos is of Turtle Island and Sky Woman, then here are the motifs that manifest in her life.

She will have a very special connection to her father in her search for healing, because she has Chiron near her fourth house cusp and it is quincunx

463

her Sun in Capricorn. Because of these same indicators, her grandmother may have raised her. She will have a great love of the earth, because of her ruling Mercury conjoined to her Venus with both in trine to Neptune in the fourth. That her father will have loved her deeply is indicated by her Saturn and Moon in conjunction and in trine to Neptune in the fourth as ruler of the tenth. Her ruling planet in Aquarius may indicate the loss of her mother, being orphaned. Above Aquarius in the sky is the constellation Cygnus, the Swan. The mythology of geese and swans are connected to stories of being orphaned, or left behind. This also indicates that her mother's home is in the sky, and this makes the mother into a sacred being, which is also indicated by her Sun in the eighth opposite Jupiter in Cancer in the second. She may have two children, most likely sons, with her three planets and Ascendant in Gemini, and the ruler of her fifth conjoined to Mercury, god of twins. She may face the constant struggle between the forces of destruction and creation, with alternating outcomes in her endeavors, also due to the small stellium in Gemini in the twelfth house in opposition to Mars in Sagittarius in the sixth. She may over identify with the side of "good" and wish to deny shadow—a Geminian complex. It may be this is the form of the two opposite boys in the story.

The chart and mythos indicate that she would be willing to sacrifice herself for the well-being of others, with her Pluto ruler of the sixth opposite by house to the Sun in Capricorn in the eighth. She will search for a home where she can put down roots and will have been uprooted from her childhood home. This is indicated by Polaris, *alpha* Ursa Major, conjunct her Ascendant, and by the conjunction of Thuban, *alpha* Draco, to her Nadir, and also by her Moon-Saturn-Uranus conjunction. It is also indicated by her angular Chiron in square to the Moon in her twelfth. (In Native animal imagery this is indicative of Beaver, who builds a home in the waters.) She will have a great sense of play and joy in life because her ruler, Mercury, is in trine to the Moon in Gemini. (In Native imagery this is indicative of Otter, a playful animal of the waters.) She may be involved with the birthing experiences of others, because Saturn is ruler of her eighth house of sexuality and is conjoined to her Moon, the planet of gestation, and both are trine Mercury conjoined to Venus, the ruler of the fifth. (The Saturn-Moon conjunction is indicative of Toad or Frog, animals of the waters and of gestation and parturition in native imagery.) The Toad is an old lady, and the old lady in her chart is indicated by the Moon/Saturn conjunction as well as by the Sun in Capricorn. The old lady is Grandmother, a figure of wisdom and nurturance and caring in Native myth. Joyce will very much value being a Grandmother, an elder, and a counselor to those younger than she is. (The Turtle itself lives to a very old age and carries the archetype of Grandmother too.)

Now we will have to wait to see whether Joyce will tell of her life with attention to its circumstance in ways where we can see the mythos, and in ways that help us to see which of these five is the most likely mythos. Or I may have missed entirely, since we did not have an opportunity to confer before the reading, and instead I have read this "blind" in the old occult way.

We are all nowadays trained to describe our lives sociologically and psychologically and these do not always bring the myth to light. Instead, if we were to relate those incidents and persons which seem to have fixed themselves into our memories, and after all we do not remember everything, then we would see the myth shining through. I ask clients to bring with them to their appointment one to four memories of incidents from the first twenty-three years of their life that they can relate in a narrative. These incidents are fractals of the myth that they are living, and so help me to eliminate the other myths I might see. Perhaps someone else born at that same date and time lives out those other myths.

Knowing one's myth is not necessary, but once discovered it brings all of the elements which were otherwise disconnected into a relationship where each is necessary to the whole. The myth then becomes a mandala of instruction about what to do next. It becomes a realization that one has done well to have come this far. It allows a place from which to view one's life that is transcendent. And that is a wonderful gift to have.

NOTES:

[1] *Occidental Mythology: the Masks of God,* Joseph Campbell, Viking Penguin, New York, 1988, pp 13 and 14. In Chapter One, "The Serpent's Bride:" "...we recognize the usual symbols of the mythic garden of life, where the serpent, the tree, the world axis, sun eternal, and ever-living waters radiate grace to all quarters..."

Epilogue

Under One Sky was conceived by the light of a broad-minded philosophical question aimed at the heart of an ancient science: what is the essential nature of astrology? That question has arced across the diversiform astrological landscape featured in this book like an arrow, embracing in its sweep a grand array of perspectives qualified by nose to the grindstone interpretations. How has the material in this book transformed my understanding of astrology? What have I learned? What purpose has this experience served for me? These are the issues I dive into below.

WHAT IS ASTROLOGY?

Many fascinating questions can be asked about astrology, but reasonable answers can't be expected to follow unless the root question *What is astrology?* is first considered. Why? Because any question probing the inner workings of astrology, its development, or the limits of its explanatory competence will invariably make assumptions about its fundamental nature. Absent a well-defined metaphysical foundation, any account of astrology will stand up to rational scrutiny like a sand castle battling the rising tide. Without an understanding of its philosophical roots, astrology is likely to remain an impenetrable mystery in the mind of the advocate and an irrational superstition in the opinion of the skeptic.

The problem of placing astrology into a metaphysical framework is that it doesn't fit neatly into either one of the two most popular choices: materialism and idealism. The planets are physical objects and the astrological signs are idealized forms, and according to astrological theory these two realms interact constantly. Astrology has one foot grounded in the substantial world of solid matter and the other foot planted in the insubstantial world of abstract mental forms, and those two limbs supposedly walk in unison across the sky and reflect the daily unfolding of our lives. But how can astrology be constructed of material and mental stuff at the same time? This bold claim offends the philosophical sensibilities of both material science and idealistic religion. Astrology trespasses on both sides of the strained boundary line that separates those two spheres.

This breach is the source of the bond that unites these traditional foes in their common opposition to astrology. Astrologers have attempted to repair this metaphysical offense by retrofitting astrology into exclusively materialistic scientific or supernatural idealistic frameworks. In my opinion, neither school of thought has been successful because astrology doesn't belong to either category,

467

but instead calls for the creation of a new one. This is my assessment after having closely scrutinized all the material in this book.

Let's examine the evolution of the idealistic and materialistic astrological positions more carefully before considering a third possibility that throws new light on the essential nature of astrology.

RELIGION VERSUS SCIENCE

The pre-modern cosmological model was developed by Aristotle (384-322 B.C.E.) and made definitive by the great astronomer Ptolemy (c.100-170 C.E.). Subsequent philosophers and theologians overlaid various religious concepts onto this scheme. Until the Copernican Revolution which marked the dawn of the modern age, the universe was envisioned as an onion-like structure formed by a series of concentric shells with the earth lodged at its center. Each of the seven classical planets—Moon, Mercury, Venus, Sun, Mars, Jupiter and Saturn—was embedded in a crystalline sphere rotated by a team of angels led by God or, some would argue, by demons and other nefarious beings. Beyond the planetary spheres was the sphere of the fixed stars and the *Primum Mobile*, the boundary of creation beyond which lay the tenth and highest heaven—*the Empyrean*—where God sat on His throne bathing in supernal light, listening to the *music of the spheres* rising up to Him from the lower heavens as they danced around the still earth. Beyond this topmost level nothing existed.

The Aristotelian cosmos was geocentric, finite, closed, and bounded by God in all directions. In this scheme, *Divine Will* was encoded in the ticker-tape-like movement of the planets in their daily rotation around the vault of heaven. Spiritual beings of various grades were dutifully dispatched to fulfill the wishes latent in the Mind of God, which were reflected in the motion of the celestial bodies. Accordingly, astrology belonged to the realm of the *supernatural* and was tightly woven in with religion, divination and magic.

Fast forward to the sixteenth century: at the age of thirteen, Francis Bacon (1561-1626) entered Cambridge, where the official college charter stated "*that all students and undergraduates should lay aside their various authors and only follow Aristotle and those that defend him*" and forbade "*all sterile and inane questions departing or disagreeing from ancient and true philosophy.*" The presumptive authority of Aristotle's philosophy was uncontestable during the Middle Ages and the Renaissance. But a series of events that took place over the course of the next century shook and eventually shattered the infallible faith that learned men had in the *Philosopher's* inerrant wisdom. Bacon himself initiated the epochal assault on Aristotelianism. His *Nuovum Organum* laid out a new vision. European philosophy, he contended, had confused religion and science to the detriment of both. He wrote, "*One must give to faith those things that are faith's, but if the question is what is the nature of God's creation, then it is not human fancy that must be consulted. There is one place to learn the nature of God's creation and that is the study of nature itself.*" By the eighteenth century, the seed of Bacon's vision had fructified and natural philosophers—i.e. scientists—were applying the empirical method he championed to prove Aristotle repeatedly wrong.

Copernicus (1473-1543) had already demonstrated that a heliocentric model of the universe was a more accurate predictor of planetary motion than Aristotle's geocentric model. After Bacon, new discoveries were made that further undermined faith in the Aristotelian cosmological scheme. Aristotle believed the orbits of the planets were perfect circles, but Kepler (1571-1640) proved they were elliptical. Aristotle had taught that the surface of the Moon was perfectly smooth, but Galileo (1562-1642), using a telescope, saw with his own two eyes that the face of the moon was pockmarked. Aristotle claimed that more massive objects fell with greater speed, but Galileo proved him wrong again. Aristotle believed that the laws of motion in the heavens were different than the laws of motion on earth, but Isaac Newton (1642-1727) demonstrated that the same universal law described terrestrial and celestial motion. Newton's brilliant insight dealt the decisive blow that finally truncated the old cosmological model. The apple that fell on Newton's head was dragging along with it the Aristotelian sky.

The natural philosophers of the Enlightenment categorically rejected the presumptive authority of tradition. The Royal Society of England, founded in 1660, adopted as its slogan *Nullius in verba*—"*Don't take anybody's word for it!*" Empirical observation and experimentation became the new arbiters of knowledge displacing the writings of ancient philosophers. With revolutionary zeal, Europe liberated itself from the suffocating stranglehold of an erroneous religious worldview that had intellectually strait-jacketed the Western world for almost two thousand years.

Many of the early natural philosophers were *deists,* who believed in a non-interventionist God who had set the universe in motion, which was now ticking away like a giant clock. Later thinkers did away with the notion of God altogether, arguing that only objective, physical substances that could be measured and quantified should be granted ontological status; only those things you could detect with the five physical senses or their technological extensions qualified as real. The metaphysical tides were quickly turning, and waves of materialistic sediment were washing up on shore as rapidly as the undertow was pulling the old religious beliefs out to sea.

The consequences of this paradigm shift were radical. In pre-modern times, priests and philosophers always looked up towards God and the heavens for a revelation of *higher* knowledge. *Things happened on Earth because God had willed them in heaven.* The traditional chain of causation always pointed down from the more elevated spiritual heavens to the lower mundane world.

Modernity inverted that orientation. Since God and spiritual revelations were no longer considered a viable source of knowledge, scientists sought out answers about earthly events by reaching down towards the basic building blocks of matter. The view emerged that the veils separating mankind from Ultimate Truth were made up of matter and lay in the direction of the infinitesimally small. Instead of looking up to God and the spiritualized *macrocosm*, scientists began to look down at the material *nanocosm* for explanations about what was happening at the level of the human *microcosm*.

Materialists asserted that the behavior of any given object could only be understood by *reducing* it down into the particles that constitute it, and observing those elements operating at that lower level. To understand psychology, therefore, you had to go down a level and consider biology; to understand biology, you had to go down a level and consider chemistry; to understand chemistry, you had to go down a level and consider atomic physics and so on. The causal chain in the materialist paradigm runs up from the lower level particles to the higher level whole they constitute. *The lower levels cause the higher levels happen.* Following this logical train, Ultimate Truth about the nature of reality was to be found buried at the bottommost level of physical reality: at the core of matter.

Materialists disavowed religious beliefs and ideas which were intimately tied in with the Aristotelian worldview. Once the old cosmological scheme went bankrupt, astrology, which was heavily invested in it, lost its currency in the minds of the intelligentsia. The new materialistic paradigm could make no theoretical allowance for a *supernatural* account of astrology. Materialists argued that physical matter and energy alone formed reality, and denied the existence of immaterial entities like angels, demons, an invisible God and even the human soul.

Some astrologers and scientists, inspired by the intoxicating spirit of modernity and the undeniable genius of the age, tried to rehabilitate astrology within the context of the materialistic paradigm. They applied the reductive principle of materialistic science to astrology, which they treated as a natural science like physics or chemistry. They argued that astrology could be accounted for by some as of yet undiscovered cosmic force capable of interacting with and informing the physical body. They scoured the electromagnetic spectrum and the quantum world for these forces. Their theories presumed that waves or particles are emitted by the celestial bodies that precipitate physiological changes that were

470

observable at the higher human level. They imagined that these forces bombarded the body like a collision involving trillions of nanometric billiard balls whose consequences could be perceived coherently at the level of human behavior.

However, hard evidence in support of materialistic theories of astrology has not been forthcoming. No one has been able to account for the structure of the twelve-fold zodiac reductively, nor have cosmic energies been detected that can be directly correlated to astrological theory. This failure sounded the *crack* of the guillotine against the cutting block. Astrology, once the queen of sciences, was dethroned and eliminated from the realm of objective science.

Materialistic science has correctly concluded that so far, the basis for astrology has not yet been confirmed within the bounds of its analytical methods. But it has wrongly concluded that this is the end of the road for astrology. Our story is about to take an unexpected twist and become really interesting.

HOLISM

In recent years, materialism has sustained a devastating attack led by prominent scientists and philosophers who are proposing a new world view—*the holistic paradigm*—that threatens to displace it, just as it had previously displaced the old Aristotelian world view. Under this scheme, reality is conceived as a nested hierarchy—a *holarchy*—that extends from the subatomic level, through the atomic, molecular and cellular levels, to the animal and human levels and beyond.

Each level or *holon* is simultaneously both a *whole* made up of lower level particles, and a *part* of a higher level whole. For instance, the hydrogen atom in a water molecule is a both a whole made up of quarks and an electron, as well as a part of that water molecule. The holarchy can be pictured as a series of concentric circles. Each circle represents a holon which circumscribes the *subholons* that constitute it, and is circumscribed by the *superholons* that it constitutes. In our example, the elementary particles that make up the hydrogen atom are its subholons, and the water molecule of which it is a part is its superholon. Consequently, the universe is not made up of objects, it is made up of holons: wholes that are part of larger wholes, and parts that are wholes of smaller parts, all situated within a holarchy that embraces a single reality that extends indefinitely in the direction of the infinitely small and the infinitely large.[1]

The holistic paradigm subverts materialism by asserting that a holon cannot be reduced into its *subholons* without remainder. That is, the sum of the particles does not equal the whole they make up. At every level of the holarchy, a new layer of novelty and creativity is introduced that cannot be accounted for reductively by its subholons, any more than a group of isolated words can account for the joke they create when strung together in the proper order. A new wave of creativity emerges at every level of the holarchy; every holonic level cracks another cosmic joke.

At the level of the human holon, this concrescence of novelty assumes the form of *self-reflective consciousness*. The holarchy grants human consciousness ontological weight. This means that *your thoughts and feelings are real*, and that human subjectivity can't be fully accounted for in the reductive terms of biology and chemistry. The causal power of the subholonic levels of reality is not denied—a glass of wine will alter your experience of reality—but more to the point, certain aspects of human consciousness simply elude a reductive explanation. Holism argues that your consciousness, emotions, thoughts, intentions and mind are more than merely the shadow of the neuronal discharges firing off in your brain. But how can something immaterial like consciousness also be real?

Materialism equates the words *material, physical, sensible, objective* and *real* on the one hand, and *mental, abstract, idealized, subjective* and *unreal* on the other. On the basis of this equation, it concludes that the body is real; the mind is not. For materialism, the line drawn between material and ideal, real and unreal is fixed. Holism, however, considers material and ideal to be equally real. Holism argues that these two categories—material and ideal—are not fixed at all. They are relative and shift in meaning across holonic levels.

Every holon will experience its subholons as physical, material entities, and its superholons as idealized abstract forms. If we miraculously granted reflective self-consciousness to the hydrogen atom in our water molecule, it would recognize the quarks and electrons that constitute its body—its subholons—as material objects. It would not, however, *perceive* the water molecule to which it belonged as a material object. It might acknowledge its attraction to the other two oxygen atoms. But *water molecule* would remain an abstract idea that it could only grasp *conceptually*. Similarly, as human beings, we *perceive* the subholons that make up our bodies (organs, cells, molecules, atoms etc.) as material reality, and we *conceive* our superholons (Cosmic Soul, Cosmic Mind, the world of Ideas and Forms, God and other idealized abstractions). The key notion is that holism attributes reality status to idealized forms. *Your thoughts and feelings are immaterial but real.*

The holistic view rejects the materialistic claim that the causal chain moves exclusively upwards through the holarchy. Holism argues that causal traffic runs in both directions. If each level of the holarchy is real, then causality must be *bi-directional*. Material subholons and idealized superholons are capable of interacting causally with each other. Materialism only admits the possibility of the lower levels causing effects on the higher levels. A materialist would say that the real physical brain causes the unreal abstract mind. A holonic thinker would say that *the real physical brain and the equally real abstract mind cause each other*. By acknowledging bi-directional causality, holism recognizes the actuality of *psi* phenomena through which a mind can interact causally with animate and inanimate matter (psychokinesis), and a mind can interact causally with another mind (telepathy).

Holism erases the philosophical dividing line that marks the traditional boundary that separates religion and science, mind and matter, real and imagined, subjectivity and objectivity. It heals the psychological wound of modernity which denies human consciousness and the human spirit a place in the cosmos. Holism is a seductive alternative to materialism. But are the bold claims of holism backed up by science? Has science shown that consciousness is real? That mind can affect matter? Without empirical evidence, the holistic paradigm remains a pretty winged idea looking for place to roost.

The answer is an unequivocal *yes*. Scientists are stacking up incontrovertible evidence to support the claim that consciousness is real. Here are three examples of a list that grows longer daily.

William A. Tiller, Ph.D., was a professor at the Department of Materials Science at Stanford University for over thirty years. He begins the preface to his book, *Conscious Acts of Creation*, with the following words: "*This book marks a sharp dividing line between old ways of scientific thought and old experimental protocols, wherein, human qualities of consciousness, intention, emotion, mind, and spirit cannot significantly affect physical reality, and a new paradigm wherein they can robustly do so!*"[2] In the rest of the book, Tiller documents the results of numerous experiments that substantiate his claim. One set of experiments, for instance, showed that directed consciousness can move the pH level of water upwards or downwards (depending on the specific intention) by a large amount.

Dean Radin is a physicist who has studied a phenomenon dubbed "*field consciousness*," which suggests that focused bursts of human consciousness on a global scale, triggered by events like the opening ceremony of the Olympics games, the Academy Awards, and the terrorist attacks of September eleventh, affect the distribution of numbers produced by computerized random number generators. During periods of sustained global consciousness, the random number generators consistently produce statistically significant number sequences that exhibit order. This is like tossing coins during these peak periods and landing heads or tails 55% of the time instead of the anticipated 50%. Similar experiments conducted at Princeton University and the University of Amsterdam confirm these results.[3]

Rupert Sheldrake is a biologist who believes that holons at every level of the holarchy are organized by *morphia fields*, which are fields of information that order the activities of the particles contained within them. These fields, he speculates, are inherited by organisms in addition to their genetic material. Morphia fields develop and become grooved into nature through constant repetition. He writes: *"I prefer the idea of Nature as governed by habits... These habits are maintained by a process I call morphia resonance, the influence of like on like. For example... if children learn to play a video game in Japan, it should be easier for children to learn the same thing in other countries... This hypothesis is of course controversial and is still being tested. Most of the results so far point towards these effects being real."*[4] Sheldrake believes that human beings have created enduring morphia fields through the countless repetition of religious rituals over millenia.

The results of the experiments conducted by Tiller, Radin and Sheldrake are just three links in a long sturdy chain of empirical data that supports the philosophical position underscored by the holistic paradigm. The work of these three scientists implies that consciousness is real, can interact causally with matter and other minds, and that habitual patterns of subjective experience are remembered by the universe. This notion leads us back to astrology.

TOWARDS A THEORY OF ASTROLOGY

A theory of astrology that does not require the introduction of superhuman forces like angels, or subhuman quantum rays, can be built on the foundation established by the holistic paradigm. A model of reality that recognizes *psi* phenomena can account for the actuality of astrology purely in terms of human consciousness.

If projected consciousness is real, then the vault of heaven is sprinkled with the soul-print of every human being that ever stared in wonder at the numinous beauty of the resplendent sky. Over eons, numberless hearts directed their prayers and devotional supplications skyward at celestial objects they worshipped as divine beings. If intentionality is a reality-shaping force, then the particular forms of consciousness lofted up by our ancestors would have imprinted themselves into the fabric of the cosmos as patterns of *emotional* and *mental* information. And repeated bursts of focused intention beamed continually at specific celestial objects would have fed and animated *psycho-noetic fields* born of human consciousness. The Hermetic aphorism astrologers are fond of quoting—*as above so below; as within so without*—becomes a scientific conjecture from this side of the holistic paradigm.

If this idea holds any water, then the history of the evolution of the planetary gods should reflect the history of the evolution of human consciousness. And this common epic should be painted in the vivid colors of astrology on the body of heaven.

474

Perhaps the first delicate tendrils of consciousness were extended skyward twenty-five thousand years ago, when our Paleolithic ancestors first realized that the Moon and women participated in the same monthly ritual. The reassuring synchronicity of these cycles provided these Stone Age hunter-gatherers with a deep-seated sense of spiritual connectedness to the cosmos that counterbalanced the terror evoked by the harsh living conditions of their Ice Age environment. Instinctively, members of close-knit tribes would huddle together at night and direct their supplications for food, shelter and protection to the Moon, their heavenly mother who waxed and waned monthly like a milky white breast. They worshipped her as Mother Moon, the life-giving celestial queen, and the heart-felt emotions that fueled their veneration eventually created a stable morphia field which shamans, priestesses and initiates could tune into through prayer and dance, and from which they could draw down psychic guidance in times of need.

The significance of the astrological Moon corresponds precisely with the archetypes and qualities that were projected at Mother Moon. The astrological Moon signifies among other things: *mother, matriarchy, woman, tribe, family, shelter, home, milk, the womb, protection* and *food*. The astrological meaning of the Moon reflects the core psychological needs, desires, values, archetypes and social structure of the hunter-gatherer people that worshipped her. From the holistic perspective, the semantic equivalence between the Moon goddess and the astrological Moon suggests that the emotional forms and desires directed at Mother Moon were absorbed into her physical body and continue to emanate their psychic power through her.

The second celestial body to be supercharged by human consciousness was the Sun, which superceded the Moon as the preeminent deity sometime during the Bronze Age (3,200- 1,000 B.C.E.). In the Bronze Age, an unprecedented wave of confidence and optimism entered mass consciousness. A bright and sunny mood enveloped the collective psyche of humankind and displaced the dreary darkness and insecurity that characterized the more ancient worldview associated with lunar worship. This psychological shift was directly linked to a technological breakthrough: the invention of metallurgy. Forging agricultural tools and weapons in a fiery furnace required manly strength. The metal instruments born of fire roused in men an awesome sense of power and control over Mother Nature. By deploying archetypal male qualities like *willpower, physical prowess,* and *discipline,* superior metal farming tools like the heavy plow were crafted and *forced* the land to produce vastly larger harvests. Surplus food stocks instilled in humanity a sense of mastery and control over their lives. It was male power and fire that had finally tamed the wild and unyielding feminine Earth. In elemental terms, *male Fire* asserted its supremacy over *female Earth*. The fire in the metal was the source of

475

the brash self-assuredness of the solar age. This psychological shift was expressed religiously with the Sun King—*the fire in the sky*—eclipsing Mother Moon as the preeminent deity.

The astrological meaning of the Sun reflects central psychological needs, desires, values, archetypes and social structure that were exalted during the reign of the Sun King: *father, patriarchy, man, confidence, power, warmth, wealth, gold, radiance, generosity, vitality, victory, kingship, willpower, success, glory* and *ego*. These ideals, which were projected skyward throughout the age of solar worship, are equivalent to the astrological signification of the Sun, suggesting once more that the emotional forms and desires directed at the Sun King were psychically downloaded into the physical body of the Sun and continue to radiate beside its physical light.

Beginning in the seventh century B.C.E., a group of thinkers appeared in Ionia—the western coast of Turkey—who asserted for the first time in the history of Western thought that the universe behaved in a rational way, and that therefore it could be understood through the rational mind. These men, also known as the *pre-Socratic philosophers*, rejected the mythological view that natural events were caused by capricious gods meting out rewards or punishments. *Things happened for a reason.* They were convinced that cosmic phenomena were governed by rational laws that could be apprehended mentally. Some of them concluded that the material universe must have been created by a supremely rational but immaterial being, a Cosmic Mind. They embraced and began to worship *reason* as the supreme divine principle.

By this time the five visible planets—Mercury, Venus, Mars, Jupiter, and Saturn—had already joined the Sun and the Moon as objects of divine worship, but sometime during this period a new kind of *morphic field* was directed skyward—the twelve-fold symmetrical *Zodiac*. The Zodiac and the astrological planets are different kinds of morphic fields. The astrological planets are psychic fields that outpicture emotional qualities and desires. The Zodiac is a mental or *noetic* field that outpictures the structure of the rational mind. The Zodiac forms the Cosmic Mind which reflects the structure of the human mind, while the astrological planets form the Cosmic Soul which reflects the structure of the human soul. Macrocosmic consciousness mirrors microcosmic consciousness.

The Zodiac is made up of twelve astrological signs evenly distributed around a central point. The meanings of the twelve signs were not derived empirically. Each sign means what it does by *mathematical necessity*. But how can the astrological signs, which are symbols of abstract *qualities*, be related to mathematics which deals with symbols of abstract *quantities*? A clue to this elusive question lies in our common usage of the word *value*, which can be used to denote either

476

qualities or quantities. The zodiac translates angular values into corresponding human values. This is how it works:

In astrology, *all meaning is an angle*. The angular relationship between two signs endows them with their qualitative meaning. The clearest example of this principle is the relationship between two opposing signs which lie, by definition, 180 degrees apart on the wheel of the Zodiac. Opposing signs are mutually defined by keywords that mean opposite things, *antonyms*. For example, one of the positive qualities associated with the sign of Aries is *decisiveness*, and therefore one of the negative qualities associated with Libra, the sign that opposes Aries, is *indecisiveness*. Another example: one of the positive qualities associated with Libra is *patience*, and therefore one of the negative qualities associated with Aries is *impatience*.

This basic principle defines the relationship between the positive and negative qualities of all six opposition pairs that form the Zodiac. Here are some examples: Aries *(decisive/impatient)*, Libra *(patient/indecisive);* Taurus *(stable/dull)*, Scorpio *(fascinating/unstable);* Gemini *(open-minded/deceitful)*, Sagittarius *(truthful/dogmatic);* Cancer *(tender/hysterical)*, Capricorn *(controlled/callous);* Leo *(warm/egotistical)*, Aquarius *(altruistic/cold);* Virgo *(precise/doubting)*, Pisces *(empathic/believing)*. The antonym is the *semantic formula* that defines the relationship between signs that are 180 degrees apart. Other semantic formulas will define other angular relationships (i.e. 30 degrees, 60 degrees, 90 degrees, 120 degrees and so on). Astrology is a form of semantic geometry.

Since some ancient philosophers believed that God was a geometer who had designed the cosmos along rational lines, they naturally projected the twelve-fold rational Zodiac into the void of space where, in the guise of the Divine Mind, it instituted universal order by bringing all the planetary gods and their corresponding psychic fields into a meaningful angular relationship. Just as the God of the newly developing monotheistic religions was taming the woolly polytheistic gods on the religious front, the Zodiac was given dispositive power over the planetary gods. Both of these developments signal the major theme that marks this era—the power of reason to order the disunified psychic forces that move the human Soul.

Throughout the modern age (beginning in the seventeenth century), three additional planets were discovered in our solar system: Uranus, Neptune and Pluto. The astrological meaning assigned to each one reflects the spirit of the age in which it was discovered.

Uranus was discovered in 1781, a few years before the French Revolution, just as the Age of Reason was peaking. Some of the keywords that pervaded mass consciousness during that era include *progress, innovation, science, empiricism, experimentation, technology, industry, the future, advancement, humanism, liberalism, revolution, individuality, humanitarianism, secularism,* and *freedom.* Each of these ideas reflects the astrological meaning of the planet Uranus. *The spirit of the age is embodied by the astrological meaning of the planet.*

The bloodletting of the French Revolution (1789-1799) dampened the faith in human progress that had characterized the first part of modernity. During the *Reign of Terror* (1792-1794), thousands of aristocrats and members of the clergy were summarily executed. It was not the high-minded *Enlightenment* ideals that had sparked the revolution, but the *Reign of Terror* that came to symbolize it.

During the early part of the nineteenth century, new artistic and philosophical trends emerged that redefined modernity. Romanticism was an artistic movement that counterbalanced the heavy weight placed on science by Enlightenment thought. Romantics championed emotion over intellect, intuition over rationality and spiritual naturalism over natural science.

Another movement that sought to redefine modernity was German Idealism, which repudiated the empiricism of the previous age. Empiricists argued that knowledge and truth are arrived at objectively through the observation of the external world. The Idealists argued that knowledge and truth are arrived at subjectively through the contemplation of the mind and Spirit. Philosophers like Kant and Hegel believed that consciousness shapes the world, not the other way around.

The major themes of this era are summed up by the following keywords: *Romanticism, artistic expression, the imagination, intuition, subjectivity, sensitivity, inner experience, consciousness, mysticism, spirit, idealism, socialism, teleology, spiritual evolution* and *prophetic vision.* Each one of these keywords is also associated with the astrological meaning of the planet Neptune, which was discovered in 1846 as the spirit of this epoch was peaking. *The spirit of the age is embodied by the astrological meaning of the planet.*

At the dawn of the twentieth century, a dark and heavy mood had settled into mass consciousness in Europe. "God," Nietzsche (1844-1900) had proclaimed, "was dead." The belief in eternal salvation, heaven and a providential God that had encouraged the faithful to persevere through adversity had been quashed during the modern age. The soothing balm of a belief in a blissful afterlife had been removed, exposing a deep existential wound.

For most people the hope of personal advancement seemed bleak. Working conditions were dismal and only factory owners appeared to benefit from the broken backs of their impoverished workers. Some social critics began to question the cost of progress. The ascendancy of European culture was undeniable, as were the impressive achievements of science, and yet technological progress seemed to

478

be in an adversarial relationship with the psychological well-being of the modern individual. The sociologist Emile Durkheim (1858-1917) concluded that modern urban life had eroded the common values that traditional religion offered. He called the feeling of alienation, anxiety and nihilism brought on by this condition *anomie*. Life in the modern world had become utterly meaningless, and depressing.

The theories of Sigmund Freud (1856-1939) were a dominant theme that emerged in twentieth century thought. Depression and other psychological disorders characteristic of life in the modern world had never before been the object of scientific scrutiny. Freud described the dialectical tension operating unconsciously between the id and the superego—human instinct and internalized societal pressures. The conscious mind—*the rational ego*— was, according to Freud, a marionette pulled about helter-skelter by *irrational* forces originating in the unconscious mind.

Freud's ensuing theories of the psyche undermined the longstanding and dignified status that had been accorded to the rational ego by ancient Greek philosophy. The idea that "rational" behavior was shaped largely by *irrational* unconscious forces shook the modern world to its very core. Freud's psychological theories became increasingly popular following the Great War (1914-1917). After the war, people on both sides of the conflict were loath to explain what the fighting had been about. Once hostilities started, the war took on a life of its own and no one could stop it. Many post-war artistic and philosophical movements echoed Freud's views about the dispositive power of the irrational side of human nature and the meaninglessness of human existence.

The themes of this era are summed up by the following keywords: *darkness, heaviness, death, hell, sexuality, the unconscious, powerlessness, irrationality, impotence, subversion, anomie, fascism, totalitarianism, nihilism, psychology* and *despair*. Each one of these ideas is associated with the astrological meaning of the planet Pluto which was discovered in 1930. *The spirit of the age is embodied by the astrological meaning of the planet.*

Civilizations have come and gone. Prideful nations that once ruled the world have vanished, leaving behind a pitiful scattering of pottery shards and dilapidated stone ruins. Mighty rivers have dried up, lush valleys desiccated into arid desert plains, and where massive mountains once stood hills now roll. Nature is in a state of perpetual change. But from the human point of view the Sun, Moon, the planets and the stars invariably round their celestial circuits, seemingly forever. The sky is the enduring backdrop in the unfolding drama of human existence.

The Sun, the Moon and the planets—*which sometimes feel close enough to touch*—bless us daily with their shimmering presence. The stars our ancestors used as guides when they travelled the ancient Palaeolithic trails are the same ones that breathe a sense of wonder into your Soul when you look up on a clear summer night into a lucid sky that seems to open up forever. The Moon that casts a broken track of light over rippling water and ensnares the silent gaze of lovers is none other than Mother Moon. The glorious life-giving Sun King the ancient Egyptians celebrated is the same sempiternal orb that Socrates greeted daily and inspired Turner's exquisite paintings. The sky is the shared legacy of humankind. *We live under one sky.*

Abraham, Moses, Krishna, Mahavira, Buddha, Lao-Tzu, Zoroaster, Plato, Aristotle, Jesus, Mohammad, all the saints, sages, prophets and philosophers of all religions, all the great artists from Phidias to Rodin, Sophocles to Shakespeare, and Ovid to Wordsworth offered part of their soul to the sky when, in a breathless moment, they were caught off guard by the humbling beauty of Venus shying away from the rising Sun at dawn, the inspiring brightness of Jupiter conjoining a pale lunar crescent at midnight, or blood red Mars over the horizon proclaiming the sky for himself on a dark moonless night.

If consciousness is real, then a soul-print of every human being who ever lived exists in heaven. And if the sky is populated by whirls of human prayers, it carries within its body the legacy of our species. And perhaps this entity, this Cosmic Being, pours its essence into our formless being with the first breath of life, seeding patterns of consciousness that blossom into what we call the human soul. And maybe that soul continues to reverberate harmonically with the ever-shifting patterns of the living sky that engendered it. And as the members of succeeding generations of the human family mature, they perpetuate the ongoing cosmic dialogue by projecting their consciousness back into the womb of space, which will seed future generations. And thus unfold the chapters of a story that began when the first hominid pointed a finger at the stars and formed a word to describe the magical feeling that overcame her spirit.

Samuel Taylor Coleridge brushed elbows with this vision in his poem, *The Aeolian Harp*:

> *And what if all of animated nature*
> *Be but organic Harps diversly fram'd*
> *That tremble into thought, as o'er them sweeps*
> *Plastic and vast, one intellectual breeze,*
> *At once the Soul of each, and God of all?*

Ponder that question the next time you feel the watchful eye of the zoetic sky looking down at you.

480

I began this book because I wanted to know what the essential nature of astrology was. I realized this specific question wrapped itself around many others I couldn't answer either. I felt tormented by that darkness. But in the midst of that unlit space I heard a voice. I listened to it speak. I believed it when it said that these questions could be answered. I followed the instructions I was given as best as I could. The task that lay before me was Herculean but once I took that initial step, momentum overcame inertia and I had to go on. I would have never done it without knowledge of my birth chart. I would have shied away from the challenge. But the symbols nodded their assent and encouraged me to jump over my shadow.

Darkness has yielded to light. The twelve astrologers I was privileged to work with lifted up my understanding. Their work helped me dispel many myths about astrology, and brought into reach vague intuitions that hovered beyond the grasp of reason. I read many books and spent many hours thinking about astrology during the time this project was developing. I cried out to the sky several times to beg for help. The sky was kind. Gradually a coherent picture began to emerge, part of which I shared above. But that vision is limited and may even strike a dissonant chord with you. And that is the purpose in my telling it to you: to stir you up and get you to think about astrology in creative new ways.

The time is ripe to take a leap from faith to reason. Astrology has worn a dunce cap and stood in the corner for too long. It is mislabeled an irrational superstition. Every astrologer knows that astrology is the *soul of reason*, and yet most of us are clueless about what it is and how it works. *Knowledge empowers.* Astrology itself is on an evolutionary journey, and your hands are on the steering wheel. I hope this book inspires you to stretch the horizon of your understanding of this majestic science that carries within it the key to the mystery of destiny, which is locked away in the vault of heaven under the canopy of the starry sky.

NOTES

1. Ken Wilbur. *Sex, Ecology, Spirituality*. Shambhala, 2000, pgs. 40-85.
2. William A. Tiller, Ph.D. *Conscious Acts of Creation*. Pavior, 2001, p. xi.
3. Dean Radin, *The Conscious Universe*. Harper Edge, 1997, pgs. 157-174.
4. Rupert Sheldrake. *Natural Grace*. Doubleday Dell, 1997, p. 25

GLOSSARY

Besides the contributors to *Under One Sky*, glossary sources include:

Burnham, Robert Jr. *Burnham's Celestial Handbook*. Dover, 1978.
Devore, Nicholas. *Encyclopedia of Astrology*. Philosophical Library, 1947.
Hand, Rob. *Horoscope Symbols*. Para Research, Inc., 1981.
Louis, Anthony. *Horary Astrology*. Llewellyn, 1991.
Jeanette Girosky, 1011 West 8th St., Erie PA 16502, (814) 459-2819, jgirosky@localnet.com.

almuten: an Arabic term for the planet of major influence in a birthchart, derived by essential and accidental dignities.

antiscion: reflection of a planet's position off the Cancer-Capricorn axis. For example, the antiscion of 0 degrees Gemini is 0 degrees Leo, because both are 30 degrees off of 0 degrees Cancer, and both are 150 degrees off 0 degrees Capricorn.

antivertex: where the prime vertical intersects the ecliptic in the east.

asterism: a constellation; also the three signs of the same Element.

Atma Karaka: Vedic—planet with the highest longitude, considered the indicator of the soul and spirituality.

ayanamsa: the number of degrees of difference between the tropical zodiac and the sidereal zodiac.

bound lord: a planet which rules the degrees occupied by another planet.

bounds: irregular divisions of signs into five segments, ruled by Mercury, Venus, Mars, Jupiter or Saturn. Each segment is ruled by one of the five planets, called its "bound lord."

bounds, in its own: a planet is in its own bounds when it occupies the degrees of a zodiacal sign within which it has rulership.

cadent: houses that fall away from the angles: three, six, nine and twelve.

Cadent planets are those in cadent houses.

Cardinal Axis: the axis formed by 0 degrees of the Cardinal signs: Aries, Cancer, Libra and Capricorn.

contra-antiscion (also called **contrascion**): point opposite the antiscion. See antiscion.

dasa: Vedic—an age or ages in one's life, said to be governed by a particular planet.

decan: a 10-degree subdivision of a sign. Each 30-degree sign has three decans.

decennial: Hellenistic—a time-lord procedure in which each planet is assigned a period of 10 years, 9 months, in succession according to the zodiacal order of the planets in a given nativity, starting with the Sun in a daytime birth and with the Moon in a nighttime birth.

declination: way of indicating distance in degrees north or south of the ecliptic.

derived houses: a technique that renumbers the houses. For example, the seventh house is the house of the marriage partner, and if we call it the first house of the marriage partner, then the eighth house becomes the marriage partner's money, or the second house of the marriage partner.

detriment: a planet is said to be in its detriment, usually the sign opposite the one that planet rules.

dignity: a planet is in its dignity when it is in the sign it rules. also, the strength of a planet determined by its domicile, exaltation, trigon and bound (terms), and face.

dispositor: ruler of a sign on a cusp of a house, or ruler of a sign that a planet is in.

diurnal: during daylight hours. A diurnal chart is the chart of someone born during the day.

domicile: each sign is the domicile of a given planet, which is said to rule it.

When a planet is in one of the signs it rules, it is said to be "in its own domicile."

domicile lord: equivalent to, in modern astrology, the planet which rules a sign.

east point: the zodiacal degree that would be rising if the person were born on the equator.

elevation (by house position): any planet that's in a position above the horizon in a geocentric chart (a chart cast as if the person were standing on Earth).

exaltation: planets are said to be exalted, or very strong, in certain signs. The planet associated with a sign via exaltation is called the "exaltation lord."

geocentric: Earth-centered.

harmonic: fractional divisions of the 360 degrees of the zodiac. For example, 360 divided by 2 equals 180 degrees, the second harmonic or opposition aspect.

Hayz: a masculine diurnal planet above the horizon in a daytime chart, and a feminine nocturnal planet under the horizon in a nighttime chart.

heliacal rising: when a celestial body becomes visible again after being hidden by the Sun's light.

heliocentric: Sun-centered.

IC: the astrological Nadir.

inconjunct: a 150-degree aspect.

inferior square: a square from planet A to a planet in a sign which precedes planet A in the zodiacal order of the signs. A planet in Cancer makes an inferior square to a planet in Aries.

in mundo: reckoned on the equator and based on divisions of the Earth's rotational period in time, not in degrees along the ecliptic.

in zodiaco: based on degrees of longitudinal distance along the ecliptic.

Lot of Fortune: another term for the Part of Fortune, one of the many Arabic parts. In a daytime birth, it is derived by this formula: Ascendant + Moon - Sun. In a nighttime birth, it is derived like so: Ascendant + Sun - Moon.

Lot of Spirit: see Part of Spirit.

Luminaries: the Sun and the Moon.

lunar return: when the transiting Moon reaches the exact degree and minute of the natal Moon.

magnitude: brightness of a star.

MC: the Midheaven.

midpoint: the zodiacal degree at the shortest distance between two planets or degrees. The midpoint of 0 degrees Aries and 0 degrees Gemini is 0 degrees Taurus.

mundane: mundane astrology is the astrology of world events.

Nakshrata: Vedic—the Moon mansion. The are twenty-seven Nakshratas, considered to be the resting places of the Moon. In Vedic astrology the Moon is male, and travels through the zodiac every month.

Navamsa: Vedic—the Navamsa chart is based on the ninth harmonic chart.

out of quality: an aspect that is in effect by degrees but not signs.

parallax: a change in the apparent position of a star relative to a change in the position of an observer.

parallel—of declination: two planets the same number of degrees north or south of the Celestial equator.
—of latitude: two planets the same number of degrees north or south of the ecliptic. Both are said to have the nature of a conjunction.

Parivartana Yoga: mutual reception.

Part of Fortune: see Lot of Fortune.

Parivartana Yoga: mutual reception.

Part of Fortune: see Lot of Fortune.

Part of Spirit: one of the Arabic parts. Its formula is Ascendant + Sun - Moon.

partile: an exact aspect is said to be "partile."

perihelion: the closest point of a planet's orbit to the Sun.

platic: wide; said of an aspect that is in orb but whose orb is not exact.

prenatal lunation: the new or full Moon that occurred before birth.

prenatal syzygy: see prenatal lunation.

primary directions: a way of determining the influences of the altered relationship between the cuspal and the planets' places on successive days or years after birth, based on the diurnal rotation of the Earth on its axis. A common usage is to set one year of life equal to four minutes of arc.

puer: psychological term that means, roughly "Peter Pan syndrome," men who refuse to grow up. The feminine equivalent is **puella.**

quadruplicity: the four signs that are divided into the three groups of Cardinal, Fixed and Mutable.

Rahu: Vedic—North Node.

right ascension: distance on the celestial equator east from the spring equinox, or distance on the circle of declination.

Royal Yoga: Vedic—also Raj Yoga. Formed when one planet that rules the trikona (trinal) houses (one, five and nine) is associated with another planet that rules a Kendra (angular) house (one, four, seven and ten).

rulership: a planet is said to rule over a certain sign or signs.

secondary progressions: a type of progression in which the planets are progressed approximately one day for every year of the native's life.

sect: Hellenistic— the distinction between a day birth and a night birth. In a diurnal birth, the diurnal planets (the Sun, Jupiter and Saturn) are said to be "of the sect," and the nocturnal planets (the Moon, Venus and Mars) are said to be "contrary to the sect." When a planet is contrary to the sect, it signifies impasses.

semisextile: a 30-degree aspect.

semisquare: a 45-degree aspect.

sesquiquadrate: a 135-degree aspect.

sidereal time: a measurement of time based on the difference between two successive passages of a fixed celestial point over a point on the Earth. A part on the Earth's return to the same relationship with the Sun is 1 degree of arc or 4 minutes of time.

sidereal zodiac: zodiac based on the actual current positions of the planets, which are generally about 23 degrees earlier in the signs than the tropical zodiac.

solar return: when the transiting Sun reaches the degree and minute of the natal Sun.

stationary direct: when a planet's motion turns from retrograde (backward) to direct (forward).

stationary retrograde: when a planet's motion turns from direct (forward) to retrograde (backward).

synastry: the astrology of relationships.

synodic period: the time it takes a planet to return to the degree it occupied natally when the Sun has returned to its own natal degree.

time-lords: planets that rule during certain periods of the native's life.

topical approach: Hellenistic—a focus on individual areas of life (family, travel, work), where each topic has significators (a planet, house and Lot).

trigon lord: see triplicity lord.

triplicity: the signs in one of the astrological Elements: Fire, Earth, Air and Water, that form an equilateral triangle when the same degree of each of the signs is joined with a straight line.

triplicity lord: Planet that rules a triplicity. In Hellenistic astrology, this changes from day to night. The Moon rules the Earth triplicity (Capricorn, Taurus, Virgo) by night; Venus rules it by day.

tropical zodiac: the circle of the twelve signs divided according to the solstics and equinoxes, starting at 0 degrees Aries, the degree occupied by the Sun at the vernal equinox.

under the beams (also, **under the sunbeams**): within 8.5 to 17 degrees of the Sun, considered a weak accidental debility.

vertex: the point where the prime vertical intersects the ecliptic in the west.

west point: where the prime vertical intersects the local horizon in the west.

yod: three planets in aspect: two sextile each other, and the third quincunxes both of them.